Classroom Assessment
Supporting Teaching and Learning in Real Classrooms

Catherine S. Taylor
University of Washington

Susan Bobbitt Nolen
University of Washington

PEARSON

Merrill
Prentice Hall

Upper Saddle River, New Jersey
Columbus, Ohio

Library of Congress Cataloging in Publication Data

Taylor, Catherine S.
  Classroom assessment : supporting teaching and learning in real classrooms / Catherine S. Taylor, Susan Bobbitt Nolen.
      p. cm.
  Includes bibliographical references.
  ISBN 0-13-097427-7
  1. Educational tests and measurements. 2. Grading and marking (Students) 3 Effective teaching.
I. Nolen, Susan Bobbitt. II. Title
  LB3051.T2926 2005
  371.27—dc22   2003027803

Vice President and Executive Publisher: Jeffery W. Johnston
Publisher: Kevin M. Davis
Development Editor: Autumn Crisp Benson
Editorial Assistant: Amanda King
Production Editor: Mary Harlan
Production Coordinator: Cindy Miller, Carlisle Publishers Services
Design Coordinator: Diane C. Lorenzo
Photo Coordinator: Kathy Kirtland
Text Design and Illustrations: Carlisle Publishers Services
Cover Design: Thomas Borah
Cover Image: Getty One
Production Manager: Laura Messerly
Director of Marketing: Ann Castel Davis
Marketing Manager: Autumn Purdy
Marketing Coordinator: Tyra Poole

This book was set in Century by Carlisle Communications, Ltd. It was printed and bound by R. R. Donnelley & Sons Company. The cover was printed by Phoenix Color Corp.

Photo Credits: p. 1 by Silver Burdett Ginn; pp. 26, 151, 342, 369 by Anthony Magnacca/Merrill; p. 50 by Lynn Saville/Prentice Hall School Division; p. 70 by Laima Druskis/PH College; p. 131 by Anne Vega/Merrill; pp. 190, 261 by Scott Cunningham/Merrill; p. 230 by Karen Mancinelli/Pearson Learning; and p. 309 by Sheila Valencia

Pearson Education Ltd.
Pearson Education Singapore Pte. Ltd.
Pearson Education Canada, Ltd.
Pearson Education—Japan

Pearson Education Australia Pty. Limited
Pearson Education North Asia Ltd.
Pearson Educación de Mexico, S.A. de C.V.
Pearson Education Malaysia Pte. Ltd.

10 9 8 7 6 5 4 3 2
ISBN: 0-13-097427-7

Preface

This is a book about students and teachers: student learning and effective teaching. It is *not* a textbook about how to give tests and grades. Done well, assessment can help students learn complex and important ideas and develop the knowledge and skills they need to evaluate and improve their work long after they leave your classroom. Done poorly, assessment can inflict lifelong damage to students' curiosity, their images of themselves, and their opportunities in the future. In short, assessment has the power to do tremendous good or tremendous harm. Our goal in this book is to help teachers and other educators understand this power and use it wisely and ethically.

SUPPORTING TEACHING AND LEARNING IN REAL CLASSROOMS

In this book, we show how assessment plays a central role in the everyday lives of teachers. From planning instruction, to listening to students as they struggle and explore, to deciding the composition of small groups, to communicating the results of assessments to students, parents, and others, teachers use assessment every day of their professional lives. Throughout the book, we provide examples based on the assessment experiences of teachers with whom we have worked and students we have known. We show how teachers can effectively use assessment to support the learning of increasingly diverse groups of students, from kindergarten through high school (and beyond). We consider the impact of assessment decisions and practices on student learning and motivation and on the experiences of students with different abilities. This is a book about assessment with a heart.

We have organized the book around our philosophy as teachers and teacher educators. Many textbooks on assessment begin with information about how to create test items and tests, but we begin with a focus on *work worth doing*. Real work is at the center of this book—work that helps students understand why they learn what they learn. Just as a piano teacher teaches beginners to play songs at the same time they are learning chords and scales, we ask you to think about real applications of knowledge and skills before thinking about assessing the parts of the whole.

TEXT ORGANIZATION AND SPECIAL FEATURES

Section 1: The Role of Assessment in Supporting Teaching and Learning

In the first section of the book, we introduce you to a new way of thinking about assessment in your classroom. This section introduces you to some of the important concepts and content of this book, and it tells you about our philosophy of assessment. The text does not present a collection of separable skills to be memorized and forgotten. We hope to convince you that by learning this material you can be a more effective teacher—one who is more successful at helping students learn, and who is able to argue effectively for your own philosophy of assessment.

In Chapter 1, we orient you to a way of thinking about assessment that is grounded in the belief that all valid assessments can be used to support teaching and learning. We explain why educators must move beyond a view of assessment as something that happens only on tests to a position in which assessment is a natural, indeed inseparable, part of good teaching. In this chapter, we describe the book's organization, including concepts and themes that you will find throughout the book. We describe general considerations for assessing students with special needs, including those with disabilities and those who are still learning to speak and write in English.

In Chapter 2, we elaborate on the role of valid assessment in effective teaching. We begin at the beginning of a teacher's work: deciding what is most important for students to learn. Unless you have a clear sense of what is most important, you cannot effectively plan for instruction or assessment. We share resources for making these important decisions and show you how to construct learning goals and objectives that are powerful and flexible teaching tools. Finally, we give you examples of how teachers in real classrooms can use assessment throughout the instructional process.

Chapter 3, Effects of Classroom-Based Assessments on Students, lays out the motivational framework for this book. The connections among classroom instructional and assessment practices, student motivation and persistence, and student learning are described. If students are motivated to learn, assessment information and supportive feedback can be seen as personally useful. We provide general suggestions for supporting student motivation to learn, to which we return throughout the book. We also discuss the role assessment and feedback play in students' developing ideas about the subjects they are learning: Is math an exploration of patterns or a collection of memorized formulas? Is social studies the development of citizens in a democracy or the names of state capitals? To the extent that students see assessments as relevant to their own goals, they are more likely to use assessment results and teacher feedback for their own learning and growth.

Section 2: Performance Assessment

When students have learned deeply and thoroughly, they can use their knowledge in flexible and complex ways to do the real work of musicians, scientists, historians, artists, and writers. In this section we show you how to create both formal and informal performance assessments in a variety of subject areas for all of your students. Chapter 4 introduces the idea of assessment of valued performances. Chapter 5 presents information about how to use informal performance assessments to guide instruction and students' learning. The assessment techniques in this section can serve a broad range of purposes, from efficient ways of "sizing up" students at the beginning of the year, to diagnostic assessments of struggling readers, to creating graduation projects that require students to combine skills and understandings across subjects and from years of schooling. In both chapters we discuss the implications of performance assessment for student motivation. We provide models for giving feedback on student work that support both further learning and motivation. Here, as elsewhere, we give suggestions for adapting assessments for learners with special needs. We also examine issues of validity and reliability for performance-based assessments.

Section 3: Classroom Testing

The three chapters in this section focus on creating and evaluating tests. Chapter 6 describes how to plan for and build a test, including tips on how to make tests more "friendly" for students and how to use test results for your own feedback and planning. Chapter 7 presents guidelines for traditional test items (multiple-choice, short-answer, completion, matching, and true-false), and Chapter 8 presents guidelines for performance items (essay items, performance tasks, and standardized direct writing assessments). Together these chapters should help you evaluate the tests you find in textbooks and staff rooms, as well as help you create tests that truly fit with your instruction and complement your assessments of valued performances. As with other chapters, we also address issues of reliability and validity, students with special needs, and motivational issues in testing.

Section 4: Summarizing Student Achievement

In the final section of the book, we present a variety of ways to summarize and communicate about students' achievement. In Chapter 9 we present a variety of different ways to summarize grades, including comparative grading (not a favorite), criterion-referenced grading, and standards-based grading. In Chapter 10 we give guidelines for developing and using portfolios to communicate about students' learning. This chapter puts the students at the center of the summary process—making them agents in communicating about what they are learning. In Chapter 11, we describe a variety of ways to communicate about students' achievement to parents and other adults. Finally, in Chapter 12, we describe standardized tests, where they come from, and how to use them in your teaching without letting them dominate good teaching and good assessment practice. Throughout these chapters we discuss reliability and validity, children with special needs, and issues of motivation.

A FEW FINAL WORDS

We hope that this book can help you embrace assessment as a way to support yourself and your students. We wrote it because every day we see teachers who feel overwhelmed by the power of standardized tests and by their lack of knowledge and skill in creating assessments and interpreting assessment information. We know that a preface cannot adequately communicate how powerful and positive assessment can be in your classroom. If you have had positive assessment experiences, you may read this book to look for ways to create similar experiences for your students. If you see assessment as an inherently negative part of teaching, you may read this book with reserve.

We hope we can empower all of you to see the potential for assessment to help students be more successful in school. The stories we tell and the examples we give throughout the book come from our own experiences as teachers, as friends of teachers, as teachers of teachers, as mothers, and as former students. Let us know what you think.

ACKNOWLEDGMENTS

We would like to acknowledge all of the people who have contributed to the shaping of this book. Thanks to all of the teachers we have met who work to be fair assessors of their students and who have taught us so much about what it takes to bring theory into practice. Thanks to all of the students from the University of Washington Teacher Education Program who brought stories about assessment from their classrooms. Thanks also to the students from the program who piloted the book, showed us the gaps and errors, and told us they liked it! A special thanks to Min Li, our colleague and friend, who piloted the book in her class, read it cover to cover, and gave us detailed feedback. A special thanks also goes to Scott Stage, who helped us describe how to work with education specialists about students with disabilities. Thanks to Greg Daigle for his cheerful clerical support, to our colleagues within and outside the UW who remained excited and interested, and to all of the researchers and assessment specialists whose work has contributed to the ideas and strategies presented in this book. Every chapter of the book was drafted at the University of Washington's Whiteley Center. We could not have written this book without the opportunity to retreat to the Center, where we had the rare gift of a quiet place to work together and away from the demands of family, work, and daily life.

We would also like to thank the reviewers of this book: Jarene Fluckiger, University of Nebraska at Omaha; Susan Giancola, University of Delaware; Jay Graening, University of Arkansas; Diane H. Jackson, University of Central Oklahoma; Allen H. Seed, University of Memphis; and Ralph Woodward, Eastern Oregon University.

Finally, we are grateful to our families for their unwavering support and understanding throughout this project.

Catherine Taylor
ctaylor@u.washington.edu

Susan B. Nolen
sunolen@u.washington.edu

Discover the Companion Website Accompanying This Book

THE PRENTICE HALL COMPANION WEBSITE: A VIRTUAL LEARNING ENVIRONMENT

Technology is a constantly growing and changing aspect of our field that is creating a need for content and resources. To address this emerging need, Prentice Hall has developed an online learning environment for students and professors alike—Companion Websites—to support our textbooks.

In creating a Companion Website, our goal is to build on and enhance what the textbook already offers. For this reason, the content for each user-friendly website is organized by chapter and provides the professor and student with a variety of meaningful resources.

FOR THE PROFESSOR—

Every Companion Website integrates **Syllabus Manager**™, an online syllabus creation and management utility.

- **Syllabus Manager**™ provides you, the instructor, with an easy, step-by-step process to create and revise syllabi, with direct links into Companion Website and other on-line content without having to learn HTML.
- Students may log on to your syllabus during any study session. All they need to know is the web address for the Companion Website and the password you've assigned to your syllabus.
- After you have created a syllabus using **Syllabus Manager**™, students may enter the syllabus for their course section from any point in the Companion Website.
- Clicking on a date, the student is shown the list of activities for the assignment. The activities for each assignment are linked directly to actual content, saving time for students.

- Adding assignments consists of clicking on the desired due date, then filling in the details of the assignment—name of the assignment, instructions, and whether it is a one-time or repeating assignment.
- In addition, links to other activities can be created easily. If the activity is online, a URL can be entered in the space provided, and it will be linked automatically in the final syllabus.
- Your completed syllabus is hosted on our servers, allowing convenient updates from any computer on the Internet. Changes you make to your syllabus are immediately available to your students at their next logon.

FOR THE STUDENT—

Common Companion Website features for students include:

- **Chapter Objectives**—Outline key concepts from the text.
- **Self-Assessment Questions & Journal Activities**—Complete with sample responses for students to check their understanding and apply chapter content.
- **Web Destinations**—Links to www sites that relate to chapter content.
- **Message Board**—Virtual bulletin board to post or respond to questions or comments from a national audience.

To take advantage of the many available resources, please visit the *Classroom Assessment: Supporting Teaching and Learning in Real Classrooms* Companion Website at

www.prenhall.com/taylor

Educator Learning Center: An Invaluable Online Resource

Merrill Education and the Association for Supervision and Curriculum Development (ASCD) invite you to take advantage of a new online resource—one that provides access to the top research and proven strategies associated with ASCD and Merrill—the Educator Learning Center. At www.EducatorLearningCenter.com you will find resources that will enhance your students' understanding of course topics and of current educational issues, in addition to being invaluable for further research.

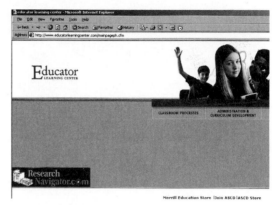

HOW THE EDUCATOR LEARNING CENTER WILL HELP YOUR STUDENTS BECOME BETTER TEACHERS

With the combined resources of Merrill Education and ASCD, you and your students will find a wealth of tools and materials to better prepare for the classroom.

Research

- More than 600 articles from the ASCD journal, *Educational Leadership,* discuss everyday issues faced by practicing teachers.
- A direct link on the site to Research Navigator™ gives students access to many of the leading education journals, as well as extensive content detailing the research process.
- Excerpts from Merrill Education texts give your students insights on important topics of instructional methods, diverse populations, assessment, classroom management, technology, and refining classroom practice.

Classroom Practice

- Hundreds of lesson plans and teaching strategies are categorized by content area and age range.
- Case studies and classroom video footage provide virtual field experience for student reflection.
- Computer simulations and other electronic tools keep your students abreast of today's classrooms and current technologies.

LOOK INTO THE VALUE OF EDUCATOR LEARNING CENTER YOURSELF

A four-month subscription to Educator Learning Center is $25 but is **FREE** when used in conjuction with this text. To obtain free passcodes for your students, simply contact your Merrill/Prentice Hall sales representative, and your representative will give you a special ISBN to give your bookstore when ordering your textbooks. To preview the value of this website to you and your students, please go to **www.EducatorLearningCenter.com** and click on "Demo."

Brief Contents

Contents

5   Informal Performance Assessment   131

SECTION 3   Classroom Testing

6   Introduction to Classroom Testing   151

12 Using Information From Standardized Tests 369

Section One The Role of Assessment in Supporting Teaching and Learning

INTRODUCTION TO ASSESSMENT

1

When most people think about assessment, images of tests come to mind—tests in all their diverse forms: essay exams, multiple-choice tests, standardized tests, physical fitness tests, and dozens of other types of tests. The way testing is done in education today comes from methods of scientific inquiry used to build theories. The method goes something like this: Randomly assign a group of objects (for example, pea plants) to two conditions. One is an experimental condition; objects in this condition get a treatment (for example, the treatment might be organic fertilizer). The other is a control condition; objects in this condition get no treatment. Apply the treatment to the experimental group; test to see what happens to the objects that do and don't have the treatment. There may be differences among the individual objects (some pea plants in the fertilizer condition may grow faster and produce more peas than others); however, the purpose of the study is to determine whether the treatment had a systematic effect on the treated objects. The tests are unbiased measures of plant growth. It is a simple idea, and simple ideas are compelling.

Translating this idea into the world of education requires making several assumptions. The first assumption is that students are randomly assigned to schools, teachers, and educational programs. The second assumption is that students are randomly different from one another—some will learn better than others. The fact that students benefit differently from an educational program is just part of the random differences inherent to the individual student. Third, tests are trustworthy and impartial judges of students' knowledge and skill at the end of an educational experience.

A simple and compelling idea.

This image of education has several major problems. First, students are not randomly assigned to districts, schools, or teachers. Poorer districts tend to pay teachers less than wealthier districts; wealthier districts tend to have more money for ongoing professional development of teachers. In some of the poorest districts, there are not enough certified teachers; therefore, teachers work with emergency certifications—teaching while they learn how to teach. Hence, the educational treatment isn't systematically applied to all learners.

The second problem with the model is that different children benefit from different forms of instruction. Children come to school with vastly different experiences—rich and diverse experiences. However, some children's background experiences are similar to the ways of thinking and types of knowledge that are valued and taught in schools, whereas others' background experiences represent different ways of thinking and types of knowledge (Heath, 1982). Children who come from cultures that value ways of thinking and types of knowledge taught in school generally "catch on" to what is being taught, whether or not instruction is effective. Children who come from cultures that value ways of thinking and types of knowledge quite different from what is taught in school need a more nuanced education—one that shows respect for the students' values and beliefs while still helping students to gain the knowledge, skills, and ways of thinking valued by schools.

The third flaw in the model lies in the notion that tests are impartial. In fact, there are many elements of tests that favor one student over another. Some students are good at memorization while others are better at creating networks of ideas. Some students already know how to discriminate between good and bad examples (i.e., in a multiple-choice item format) while others have only been taught to look for what is correct. Some students communicate effectively verbally while others are better at representing ideas through equations, diagrams, drawings, graphs, and charts. Hence, given the complexity of what students are to learn in school and the different skills students bring to the testing situation, a single test can never adequately address the diverse ways in which students learn and represent their knowledge and skills.[1] In addition, the very nature of what is tested can *mis*-educate students. For example, when students experience social studies as a collection of historical or geographic facts, they come to see historical or geographic thinking as memorization rather than examination of evidence to make sense of events, human movements, settlement patterns and the like.

Finally, in the era of standards, when the goal is for all students to achieve standards, the notion of a "test" at the end of a "treatment" must be replaced with a new meaning of assessment. Teachers must use tests and other assessments to determine whether their students are achieving the standards, to decide whether to revisit critical knowledge and skills, to enhance instruction when necessary, and to reassess as students develop the knowledge and skills stated in the standards. This means that one-size-fits-all instruction will not do. It also means that some students will move faster than others in one subject area and slower than others in another subject area. Teachers must create a flexible learning environment wherein students can continue to learn critical knowledge and skills beyond the timing of a test. Tests and other assessments become tools for intervention rather than impartial rulers to see which pea plants grew the most and produced the most peas.

With the push toward standards and standards-based assessments, some people appear to believe that state and national tests are magic bullets that will make schools better places, make teachers more accountable to children, and make schools more accountable to the public. At the same time, a large volume of evidence suggests that when teachers, school administrators, and policymakers focus *too much* on test scores, teacher professionalism and children's experiences in schools are diminished (Lomax, West, Harmon, Viator, & Madaus, 1995; Shepard, 1989; Smith, 1991). It seems that the more people focus on assessment, the more distressed teachers and students become. So how is a teacher to resolve the dilemmas of assessment?

As individuals who teach teachers how to create, evaluate, and use assessments in the teaching and learning processes, we find ourselves on both sides of arguments about assessment. From our own experiences and from the research on assessment, we know that by creating and using high-quality assessments, teachers become clearer about what they want students to learn—the goals of their teaching. The process of assigning scores to student work helps teachers clarify standards and expectations for that work. The process of developing systematic ways to assess valued performances, essay items, and performance tasks helps teachers better understand the meaning of national and state curriculum standards. Student performance on classroom assessments helps teachers plan better instruction, adjust instruction, and intervene so that students actually learn what is valued. If teachers do not assess students, or if classroom assessments are not aligned with instruction, children who are at risk may fall further behind and teachers will not know whether their instruction has been successful.

---

[1] In this book we use the term *knowledge* in its broadest sense: facts, principles, concepts, algorithms, formulae, etc. We use *skills* to refer to the thinking, behaviors, and strategies students use to process information or complete tasks (e.g., working in groups, conducting scientific investigations, interpreting authors' perspectives, painting a still life, playing a duet, participating in a debate). We use *concepts* to represent big ideas within each discipline or subject area (e.g., costs and benefits, democracy, independence, character development, elements of design, rational number).

On the other hand, we are aware of a growing body of research on how *high-stakes* standardized tests affect children, teachers, and schools. High-stakes tests are those that are used to make graduation and promotion decisions about students or to make decisions about the success of schools and school districts—some tests are used for both purposes. Research has shown that, when students, teachers, and schools are evaluated on the basis of standardized test scores, teachers tend to narrow the curriculum and teach only what is on the test (Shepard, 1989; Smith, 1991). In these circumstances, teachers also tend to narrow their own assessments to formats similar to those used on standardized tests (Lomax et al., 1995). In addition, the way knowledge and skills are tested on standardized tests affects the way teachers teach the knowledge and skills (Shepard, 1989; Yen, 1993). Finally, excess attention to tested content and item formats occurs more in schools that teach poor and urban children than in schools that teach suburban and middle-class children (Lomax et al., 1995).

In summary, positive effects happen when teachers are involved in the assessment development process and when they are engaged in using assessments to make decisions about students' level of knowledge and skill. Negative effects happen when standardized tests are used as the sole measure for evaluating students, teachers, schools, or districts and when teachers feel pressure to raise test scores (Smith, 1991). In the majority of cases, the negative effects of standardized tests have more to do with the *uses* of assessment information than with the tests themselves. However, that is not always the case.

If assessment tools and processes have both positive and negative effects, how can you get the positive effects and avoid the negative ones? We can't promise that standardized test scores won't be used badly in the school or district where you teach. However, we can promise that you can be empowered to take control of the assessment process—to know how to use assessments wisely, with compassion, and in ways that support your students and help you become a better and more successful teacher. It can be difficult for teachers to avoid compromising their own practices in the face of standardized tests when they lack knowledge and skills in assessment. If teachers don't know the subject area or don't understand the state and district curriculum standards, they may teach in ways similar to the way standardized tests assess these subjects (Shepard, 1989). Through this book, we hope to give you the tools you need so that you won't have to compromise effective practices and so that you can improve ineffective ones.

In this chapter we highlight some of the key ideas and issues that are woven through the remaining chapters of the book. First we clarify our definition of assessment and our assessment philosophy. Next we address assessment ethics, including the effects of poor assessments on teachers. In the third section, we discuss the different purposes of assessment. In the fourth section, we discuss assessment of children with special needs, including both students with disabilities and students who speak English as a second language. Finally, we discuss the reliability and validity issues of classroom-based assessments. We refer back to the ideas in each of these sections when we present and discuss different assessment tools and processes throughout the book.

WHAT IS ASSESSMENT?

Assessments are both *tools* and *processes*. When a science teacher creates a test that is used to determine whether students have learned what she wants them to learn in science, the test is an *assessment tool*. When a teacher writes directions for students to use as they engage in a performance (e.g., participate in a debate or write a poem), the student directions and the rules the teacher uses for evaluating students' performances are also assessment tools. In contrast to these tools, the *Cambridge Advanced Learner's Dictionary* (2002) defines assess as "to judge or decide the . . . value, quality, or importance of something." Hence, assessment also includes the *processes* teachers use to evaluate the quality of their students' work and the success of their instructional practices. Assessment includes the thinking and procedures teachers use make these evaluations. Finally, assessment helps teachers decide what to do next—change instruction, revisit an idea, give students an opportunity to revise their work, etc. Because assessments can be both tools and processes, we will use the term *assessment tools* to refer to the tools and *assessment processes* to refer to the processes of making decisions about the success of students and of instruction.

Assessment tools can support students' learning when the wording of test items and directions for performances give the students clear ideas about what is important to learn and the criteria or expectations for good work. Assessment tools can support students' learning when they match instruction and truly draw out students' knowledge and skills. *Assessment processes* can support students in several ways: (1) When teachers use students' responses, performances, and products to fairly and accurately assess what students have actually learned in school, students see teachers as allies in their education. (2) When teachers give students appropriate feedback so that they know what they have learned and what they still need to learn, students can focus their efforts on improvement. (3) When teachers use evaluations of student work to adjust instruction so that *all* students learn the valued knowledge and skills, students are more likely to be successful in school. (4) When teachers engage students in self-assessment and peer assessment, students can develop a better understanding of what knowledge, concepts, and skills they are to learn.

In this book, our intent is to help you learn the knowledge and skills needed to create high-quality assessment tools and to develop fair and accurate assessment processes. When you create good assessment tools and use fair and accurate assessment processes, you can more easily communicate your expectations to students, parents, and school administrators. In addition, your decisions will be well-informed. When students, parents, and administrators know your expectations and understand your assessment processes, they are less likely to depend on standardized test scores as the sole measure of students' accomplishments and as the sole measure of your effectiveness.

OUR PHILOSOPHY OF ASSESSMENT

Ms. Johnson[2] is an experienced and dedicated kindergarten teacher. She wants to give students fun literacy experiences to support and increase their motivation to read and write. A few years ago, she participated in a large collaborative research project with other teachers and university researchers. She, along with other teachers, learned about children's phonological awareness development and how it influenced learning to read and write. Ms. Johnson also learned how to use several fairly brief observations both to assess the phonological awareness of new kindergarten students and to plan instruction to help all her students develop these skills. Ms. Johnson found that the assessment processes helped her focus instruction for individual students and their reading skills improved.

[2]Throughout this book, although the vignettes are true, the actual names are changed to protect the identity of teachers and students.

Although the research project is over, Ms. Johnson still uses the assessment processes she learned during the project, keeping a file box with a card for each child to help her monitor their progress and plan for instruction. Using this assessment information, she develops engaging activities for the children in which they can practice, without drilling, the specific skills next on the developmental trajectory for each child. She reads rhyming books and books with patterns in the sounds. She leads students in singing fun songs such as "Apples & Bananas" that require children to substitute initial sounds of words; they play games where they sort small toys by initial sounds, and so forth. As the children work, Ms. Johnson monitors their ability to segment sounds, their understanding of letter-sound correspondence, their inventive spelling, and the like. Periodically she does individual assessments when she needs more information, noting the results on the child's card. At conference time, she can look at her note card for each child, pull out a file of the child's completed work, and have an informative conference with the parents or guardians. During conferences, she emphasizes growth and can provide examples of fun activities to do at home to provide children with additional practice while preserving their motivation to read and write.

In her day-to-day interactions with kindergartners, Ms. Johnson demonstrates our philosophy of the ideal relationship among learning targets (learning goals and objectives), instruction, assessment tools, assessment processes, and decision making. She has clear learning objectives identified for her students; she assesses to see where her students are when she first gets to know them; she uses instructional strategies to increase their knowledge and skills; she assesses to see if the instruction is successful; she communicates to others about the progress and success of students.

Fundamentally we believe that the purpose of schooling is to help students become smart, responsible, and conscientious adults in a democratic society. Every child should leave school able to read critically, write and speak effectively, express herself or himself creatively; and use the knowledge and skills of mathematics, the sciences, health, fitness, and the social sciences. Children who can use knowledge and skills to make their own decisions and to critically evaluate the proposals and decisions of others have a better chance of becoming responsible adults and are more likely to function as contributing citizens in a democratic society. Therefore, we see instruction and assessment as a set of tools and processes that should support all students' learning and that should help you make wise decisions in your classroom. In our view, any assessment tool or assessment process that detracts from or interferes with students' learning—that prevents them from learning all that they need to learn to be able to live and work in the 21st century—is not valid.

FIRST, DO NO HARM: ETHICS IN ASSESSMENT

Most teachers have very little time with students. Elementary teachers generally have one year; secondary teachers generally have an average of one hour a day for a trimester, a semester or a year. Yet as teachers, you are expected to teach critical knowledge and skills, to help all students meet standards, and to make accurate decisions about your students at the time you report grades to students and parents. Given this context, every assessment choice you make—whether tool or process—should help you in your work. When assessment tools and processes are effective, they can give you useful information, they are consistent with your purposes, and they help students make sense of schooling. When assessment tools and processes are ineffective, they provide little or no useful information and interfere with students' ability to make sense of schooling, which, in turn, makes teaching even harder. Worse, poor assessment tools and processes may cause students to leave school believing that they are not able to learn or be successful. As Darling-Hammond (2001) said, "The only financially viable way for school dropouts to participate in our economic system is through criminal behaviors." Given that poor assessment processes can so adversely affect students, the ethical responsibility of educators is "first, do no harm."

The Dangers of Mismatch Between School and the World Beyond School

Assessments have a very high valence for students. Students find out very quickly that the judgment of a teacher has implications for them—whether the judgment is a "happy face" stamp (☺) on their work or a score of 75% on a test. Parents and guardians respond to grade cards and marks on assignments. Teachers smile more often at students who are doing well and show exasperation with students who are not doing well. Older children tell younger children which teacher is harder (expects a lot of work for a grade) and which teacher is easier (gives higher grades for less work or easier work). Slowly students are educated into a mind-set that assessments and grades matter very much. Yet, for many students, assessment tools and processes are mysteries they cannot solve.

One reason for the mystery is that, too often, schooling seems unrelated to the real world beyond school. When teachers teach knowledge and skills without helping students understand where the knowledge and skills are needed in life within and beyond school, students may lose motivation for learning. For example, mathematical procedures can be taught along with familiar applications or as a set of algorithms to be memorized. When teachers teach algorithms and do not help students understand why the algorithms work, or where they apply, many students become confused by all of the discrete parts of mathematics. Too many begin to believe they are "no good in math" and cease to try to understand the concepts. Hence their performance in mathematics gets worse as the mathematics taught moves further away from the concrete world (Schoenfeld, 1988).

When teachers give assignments that are completely unrelated to the life experiences of students (for example, a writing prompt such as, "Write an essay about how your family celebrated Christmas," will be inappropriate students who come from non-Christian families), students find that they cannot please teachers without disowning a part of themselves. Standardized curriculum and standardized tests that are intended to be useful for students from any and all backgrounds, can, at times, seem bland and uninteresting to students—leading to poorer quality performances. Over time, a mismatch between school and the real world of students may lead to further detachment from school as more and more students fail to make sense of what is taught.

Meanwhile, life beyond school is full of interesting challenges and experiences. Teachers can take advantage of students' experiences and interests; they can take advantage of the high value placed on grades. Teachers can use this link to assign work that is authentic and connected to the lives of students—work that helps students make sense of the knowledge and skills they are learning in school. In various chapters of this book, we will describe ways to link assessments to the real world beyond school.

The Dangers of Mismatch Between Assessment Tools and Instruction

Almost everyone has had the experience of taking a test that seemed unrelated to the content of lectures or to the activities done in class. Although this is more common in secondary school than in elementary school, the lack of connection can also happen at the elementary level when students don't know the expectations for assignments, class participation, or citizenship. Too often teachers separate assessment and instruction so completely that they do not make certain what is assessed is the same as what was taught.

This separation and the subsequent mismatch occurs for several reasons. First, in the case of tests, some teachers believe that if students read the text and listen to their lectures, the content tested will be covered. They use the textbook test, or a test developed by the faculty at the school, without any review to make certain there is a good fit. Students, on the other hand, typically see the teacher's lectures as more important than the textbook— until they take the first test. Initially, students focus their studying on what the teacher says. If the teacher uses lecture time to elaborate and expand on the ideas in the textbook (e.g., adding enriching stories about a time in history or describing the history of a scientific idea), the textbook test will not reflect these elaborations and expansions. Once students see the tests, they realize that the classroom time is not important to their grades. They may even cease to participate in discussions or to listen to the teacher's lectures.

Another reason for mismatches between instruction and assessment tools is that some teachers believe students should "just know" expectations for good work. They have very detailed expectations for students' products and performances but do not provide those expectations to the students.[3] To be a fair assessor, you must give students all expectations for their work and take the time to teach students how to achieve those expectations. Similarly, students should not discover the expectations for class participation or citizenship *after* grades have been sent home to parents.[4] These should be a public part of the grading policy given to students from the beginning.

A third reason for the lack of connection between instruction and assessment occurs when teachers focus on teaching facts or algorithms during class time and then ask students to apply those skills in novel situations during the assessment. Although the best way to know whether someone understands a principle, skill, or concept may be to ask students to apply it in a new situation, if they have not had experience applying principles, skills, or concepts to new situations, they are unlikely to be prepared for the applications on the test. To make the assessment tools more consistent with instruction in this situation, the teacher would identify multiple situations in which knowledge and skills apply. Some situations would be explored in class and others given on a later test. Only then will assessment tools match instruction.

Another situation in which the mismatch between assessment tools and instruction occurs is when teachers hastily prepare a test the day (or night) before the test is administered.

---

[3]A teacher once told Catherine that all students should know how to title and label a graph—no instruction was needed. Yet, the examples students saw every day, in the newspaper and in textbooks, were much less informative than what the teacher expected from her students.

[4]A teenager once told Catherine that she was getting a D for class participation in her English class. When she asked the teacher about the grade, she was told that she never raised her hand in class. She told the teacher that she had raised her hand at the beginning of the year, but when the teacher never called on her, she stopped raising her hand.

This situation is more likely to occur when teachers dislike giving tests and delay the chore as long as possible. Hence, little attention is given to the quality of the test items or to whether they represent what was taught. When students see the test, they are likely to be frustrated by both the quality and the mismatch. Again, students may develop distrust for the teacher and/or detach from the classroom experience.

Assessment tools will not match instruction when teachers assign work (e.g., book reports, five-paragraph essays, lab reports, open-ended math problems) without teaching students *how* to do the work. Often complex assignments are given as homework. Students with well-educated parents may learn how to do the work at home. Other students might attempt the task and do a poor job. Finally, some students will not even attempt the work—afraid to make a mistake or uncertain where to begin.

Chapter 4 is focused on the integration of assessment tools, assessment processes, and instruction. When there is little distinction between assessment and instruction (i.e., when students are engaged in authentic work that becomes both a vehicle for instruction and results in products or performances that are assessed), many of the mismatches described above will not occur. However, well-developed tests can also be well integrated into the instructional process, helping to ensure that assessment does not have long- or short-term harmful effects on students. Chapter 6 shows how tests can be incorporated into a performance-based classroom.

The Dangers of Avoiding Assessments

Some teachers are so concerned about the potentially harmful effects of assessment tools and processes that they try to avoid using them at all. Yet avoidance can have negative consequences as well. For example, the following is a true story.

Sarah was in fourth grade when reading became so difficult that she stopped trying to learn how. She had received no reading instruction beyond second grade. By fourth grade, she had such ineffective strategies for reading multi-syllable words that reading nonfiction text became nearly impossible. Sarah was too embarrassed to tell the teacher or her parents that she couldn't read. Instead she developed several strategies for coping. When she did social studies or science homework, she would say things like, "Mom, I don't understand this. Could you explain it to me?" Wanting to help, her mother would read the material and explain it. At school, Sarah would stay in during recess and lunch times. She would spend the time asking her teacher about the material they were reading—gleaning whatever information she needed to get through the rest of the day. The teacher believed that Sarah was having social problems. She willingly spent time with her but recommended that the family get family counseling. When it was time for standardized tests, Sarah skimmed nonfiction passages and got the main idea. Because half of the passages were fiction, she did well enough that neither the teacher nor the parents suspected that she was having difficulty reading. In short, Sarah developed strategies that allowed her to get decent grades and to do well enough on standardized tests to go unnoticed. Between fourth and fifth grade, Sarah's family moved to another state. She arrived in the fifth grade well behind her peers in reading. Her fifth-grade teacher reviewed her records and found that her parents were educated. She decided that Sarah's poor performance in class was a result of a poor attitude. She began to punish Sarah for being slower than the other students. She put her in the hall to finish assignments that the other students had finished in class. She criticized Sarah about her poor performance and attitude in front of other students. By the middle of fifth grade, Sarah was doing so poorly in school that she wrote on a page in her note-book, "I'm too dumb for school." When her mother found the note, she talked with Sarah and immediately arranged for testing by a school psychologist. The psychologist unearthed the reading problem and arranged for intensive reading instruction. By the end of sixth grade, Sarah caught up with her peers in reading and went on to be successful in high school and beyond.

The behaviors of Sarah's fifth-grade teacher were clearly inappropriate. However, both the very supportive fourth-grade teacher and the very destructive fifth-grade teacher had failed to do classroom-based assessments to look at reading Sarah's skills and strategies. Imagine what could have happened if Sarah's mother had not intervened. Research suggests that Sarah's future would not have been very promising (Maughan, 1994; Self, 1985).

The failure of teachers to gather useful information about students can lead to student failure—failure that can be avoided. It is also important to note that standardized test scores were not good measures of reading for Sarah. Teachers must do their own assessments to verify what they find in school records. In this book, we will present ways to develop and select tools that can be used to assess students' strengths and needs. We will also introduce strategies for early assessment of students to find out whether any of your students are at risk. Finally, we will demonstrate and describe assessment processes that are more likely to provide support for students and less likely to do harm.

Developmental Issues in Assessment

One way that assessment tools can be harmful is when they are not developmentally appropriate for the students. When teachers ask students to complete tasks that are not within their developmental reach, the students are set up for failure. Throughout this book, we will be discussing the developmental appropriateness of various assessment techniques and providing examples from primary, intermediate, middle school, and high school classrooms.

Some general issues, however, merit a discussion up front. There has been a push over the last 20 to 25 years to expect greater academic achievements from younger and younger children (Elkind, 2001).[5] Some of these expectations arise from the use of standardized multiple-choice tests to assess students.

Research on testing has shown that children and adults find it easier to recognize a correct response than to create one (Martinez, 1990). This is particularly true at early stages of expertise. First-graders who cannot reliably produce a complete sentence with appropriate punctuation and capitalization can, nonetheless, choose the correct response from a forced-choice item like that shown in Figure 1–1.

Because many first-graders can recognize the correct response in items like this, educators have come to believe that they should expect first-graders to learn to *use* correct punctuation and capitalization (Lairon, personal communication, 1991). They may use prepared worksheets and other materials with exercises similar to the items on standardized tests. Using these materials, teachers teach the rules of capitalization and punctuation, and children

---

[5]For example, some of Susan's students once reported that the principal announced, on welcoming them to the site of their first field experience, "My elementary school is a college prep elementary school."

Look at each sentence. Mark the sentence that is correct.

A. John went to the store,

B. john went to the store.

C. John went to the store.

Figure 1–1
Example of a Multiple-Choice Item Measuring Knowledge of Capitalization and Punctuation

learn to apply them in the worksheet context. But have they learned to use them in their own writing? The same students may not be able to reliably produce complete sentences, much less use capitalization and punctuation correctly. Similarly, seventh- and eighth-grade students can be taught to apply the algorithms of algebra, and tests may show that they can do so proficiently. Does their performance on tests mean that students understand *why* the algorithms work? Do students' scores indicate that students can select the appropriate algorithm to solve a real-world problem? Probably not.

Some assessment tools or combinations of tools can help you decide whether students truly understand what you have taught. Limiting yourself to a few types of test items will provide you with very limited data on which to make important educational and curricular decisions. When classroom and school district standards are set, educators must make decisions about when students are capable of certain kinds of thinking and learning. These decisions will be made, in part, by using knowledge of children's typical performances on assessments. Throughout this book, as we describe various assessment issues, strategies, and processes, we will return to these developmental issues and consider the relationship among content taught, types of assessment used, and the setting of challenging but realistic standards for your students.

The Effects of Assessments on the Experiences of Teachers

Although the main focus of this book is on student assessment, we have not forgotten that teaching should be work that teachers want to do. We find that when we use good assessment practices in our own teaching, we are excited about teaching and about seeing our students' work. We are delighted when our students show through their work deep understanding of the skills and concepts we teach.

When teachers use poor or inadequate assessment tools and processes, they are just as unhappy and frustrated as their students. Unfortunately, many teachers do not know how to fix the problem. In addition, when assessment is used, intentionally or unintentionally, to control or punish students, students begin to see teachers as untrustworthy and mean. Students develop strategies to "get around" teachers. Cheating becomes more common and students learn to play the game of school—doing just enough to get the grades they want (Anderman, Griesinger, & Westerfield, 1998).

Teachers who advocate for students may find themselves disillusioned about teaching when they unwittingly use assessments that are inconsistent with instructional methods. In such cases, students may resist the innovative instructional methods that don't prepare them for the assessment tools. Students can become cynical about activities that are unrelated to the real objectives of the class—as shown through the assessment tools.

For example, Mr. Hanks and Mr. Johnson were seventh-grade teachers who used inductive methods of teaching mathematics.[6] Their assessments, however, were very different. Mr. Hanks, a first-year teacher, was teaching the first instructional unit of the year. The focus was on geometry—perimeters and areas of circles and polygons (shapes with three or more sides). He had the students work in groups using grid paper, rice, and other hands-on strategies to discover the relationship among the diameter of a circle, the circumference, the area, and pi (π). He had them use grid paper to explore the relationship between rectangles with the same perimeter but different areas, and between rectangles with the same area but different perimeters. He had them draw different polygons on grid paper and extract their own formulas for finding the areas of different polygons. At the end of the unit activities, Mr. Hanks gave the students the end-of-unit test from the textbook. The test was completely computational and asked students to find the areas and perimeters of circles with particular diameters and rectangles with particular dimensions. The students did poorly on the test. Mr. Hanks then moved on to a unit on the relationships among fractions, decimals and percents. He put students in groups and gave them the first exploratory task. The students balked at the work. They grumbled that the work was stupid. They asked whether the activity would be on the test. Some grudgingly did the activities; others became disruptive. Student resistance continued throughout the second unit and, once again, test performance was poor. Mr. Hanks decided that the methods he had learned in his teacher education program were not useful. He began lecturing on and demonstrating the algorithms presented in each subsequent chapter of the book. Test performance improved.

Mr. Johnson was also a seventh-grade mathematics teacher. Like Mr. Hanks, he used hands-on activities to help students explore mathematical ideas. He taught them how to use a set of criteria (steps and thinking processes) to evaluate their own problem-solving processes. He had students work in groups to solve their problems and then to present their solutions to the whole class. He had the students use problem-solving criteria to ask the presenters about the various strategies and decisions they used in the problem-solving process. After all groups had presented, he led a discussion of the differences in their solutions and solution processes. He showed them formulas for computing the areas of circles and polygons and for computing the perimeters of certain polygons. He asked them to explain how the algorithms related to their hands-on explorations. When the first unit test came around, Mr. Johnson selected a few items from the end-of-unit test in the textbook and added several of his own. He gave the students some new shapes and asked them to derive algorithms for finding the area of these new shapes. He gave them new problems to solve about the relationship between area and perimeter. He asked them to generate a formula for the circumference of a circle using grid paper, string, and circles of different sizes. He scored the computational items for accuracy and the problem-solving items for effective use of strategies. Students did well on the textbook items and used effective problem-solving strategies to tackle the unknowns. After reviewing their work, he returned the tests to the students and gave them an opportunity to revise their work, when they understood concepts and algorithms better. As students began the second unit, they tackled the small-group problems with enthusiasm. They began to look at the textbook to see how the algorithms and formulas in the text related to their small-group work. When they shared their solutions, they made the links to the textbook procedures themselves.

[6]This story is based on research conducted by Proulx (1994).

At the end of the unit, students were eager to take the test. They knew that the tests related to what they had learned, both in terms of content and in terms of problem-solving processes.

It is fairly easy to see how the relationship between the assessment tools and the instruction affected Mr. Hanks's and Mr. Johnson's teaching experiences. What may not be so evident are all the techniques Mr. Johnson used that were successful. First, Mr. Johnson helped the students make clear connections between what was in the textbook and what they were doing in their small groups. Second, he valued the problem-solving process as much as the mathematical procedures. He created criteria for a problem-solving process and taught students how to use them. On the test, he used some of the items from the textbook test but added problem-solving items similar to the ones students did in small groups. His scoring rules focused on both the accuracy of computation and the use of problem-solving processes. Mr. Johnson used many strategies to make clear connections between classroom actions and his assessment tools. He also communicated his expectations and his values through both the instruction and the assessment tools. By giving students the opportunity to revise their work, he set himself up as an advocate for students' success—holding them accountable for the knowledge and skills he was teaching.

PURPOSES OF ASSESSMENT AND ASSESSMENT PROCESSES

The strategies Mr. Johnson used are typical of those in a standards focused educational environment. When teachers are committed to the success of their students, they set up procedures in their classrooms that enhance the likelihood of that success. There are many purposes for assessment tools and processes—not all of them are for the purpose of helping all students to be successful.

There are three common purposes for assessment within and beyond the classroom. The first purpose is to assess students' understanding and skill so that teachers can choose or create the instructional methods necessary to help students improve in both understanding and skill. The second purpose is to assess students' expertise at a certain point in time—generally at the end of some period of time. End-of-unit tests, final performances and products, and grades are typically ways of assessing and reporting students' expertise. Some standardized tests are also intended to assess for expertise. The final purpose of assessment is to see how students' performances compare to the performance of other students. This purpose is called assessment for comparison or selection.

Students' understanding and skill can be assessed using *preassessments* and *formative assessments*. Preassessments are given *before* instruction to help teachers plan instruction. Formative assessments occur *during* instruction to determine whether instruction is successful and so that teachers can adjust instruction if necessary. When teachers want to assess students' *conceptual understanding,* they create tools that will allow students to show their understanding. Teachers are less interested in whether students get the right answer than how they come to an answer in the first place. Assessment tools are designed to find out whether students have misconceptions that interfere with understanding or whether they have naïve conceptions that need to be challenged so that students can move to the next level of understanding. For example, because Ms. Johnson was teaching students how to read, she assessed their knowledge of word sounds. She focused her instructional activities on giving her students experiences with the phonemes they needed to learn.

Similarly, if a science teacher finds that his students lack understanding of various root words, prefixes, and suffixes that are critical to science vocabulary, he can add instructional activities designed to develop students' vocabulary. If a teacher is teaching the concept of heat and finds that students think that blankets create heat (a naïve conception based on personal experience with blankets), through investigation the teacher can help them see how blankets trap body heat but do not generate heat.

Teachers who are focused on student learning of *skills* use assessments to find out what students can and cannot do—and then determine what to teach them next. If they want students to be skillful writers, teachers may look at students' use of writing *processes* to see where students can improve—in generating ideas, in the organization of ideas, and in the use of revision skills to elaborate on ideas, improve word choices, sentence variety, transitions between ideas, and so on. Alternately they might look at samples of students' writing to determine whether they know how to make effective word choices, logically organize ideas, select useful details to support ideas, and so on. They can then intervene by giving each student the tools she needs to further develop the skills.

Typically preassessment and formative assessment tools are used to make instructional decisions about whole groups of students. *Diagnostic* assessments provide detailed information about strengths and weaknesses that can be used to plan targeted interventions for individual students. Teachers can create their own diagnostic assessments to find out individual students' strengths and weaknesses in skills or prior knowledge needed for a unit of instruction. Specialized diagnostic assessments are also available in particular subject areas. For example, *Diagnoser* (Levidow, Hunt, & McKee, 1991; Minstrell, 2001) is an on-line assessment tool that identifies students' conceptions of physical phenomena, accompanied by suggestions for physics teachers to use in teaching scientific concepts.

Assessment for expertise is very different from assessments of students' developing understanding and skills. Tools and processes for assessment of expertise are used to find out what students know and are able to do at a given point in time. Assessments of expertise are sometimes called *summative* assessments. The role of the assessment information is to make summative statements about each student's level of knowledge and skills. These tools are also called *criterion-referenced* tests because they measure curriculum standards. When assessment tools are used to measure expertise, there is less interest in students' developing understanding and skills or in diagnosing individual students' strengths and needs. Tools used to assess for expertise must be developmentally appropriate for the age of the students. The knowledge, skills, and level of expertise expected for children at a certain age are often defined by state or national standards. In essence, assessment for expertise is typically intended for external accountability. When you give students grades, you will be accounting for their achievement to those beyond the classroom. When you give students state tests, you will be helping the schools to account for student achievement to parents and guardians, policymakers, legislators, and taxpayers.

Sometimes, assessment tools that are used to assess expertise are also used to determine whether students will be promoted to the next grade level or whether they will graduate. When promotion or graduation decisions are made based on assessment results, test makers have to gather evidence that the assessments truly reflect the knowledge and skills that are the targets for student achievement (validity) as well as whether, if the students are assessed again, they will get the same or about the same score (reliability). Hence, the validity and reliability of scores is a critical consideration for tests that are used for such critical decisions.

Because no single test can provide scores that are as stable as necessary for graduation or promotion decisions, the *Standards for Educational and Psychological Testing* (1999) indicate that such decisions require multiple forms of evidence. Classroom performances and grades are viable sources of evidence and, therefore, should be valid and reliable as well.

When assessment tools are used for selection and comparison (for example, *norm-referenced* tests), users are less interested in what students have learned than in how students compare with other students. Therefore, assessment tools used to rank or select examinees are designed to find *differences* between students. These assessment tools include items and tasks that are well above what is expected of students at a given grade level. They also include items and tasks that are much too easy for most students at the given grade level. Although makers of assessments used for comparison and selection purposes map the items to learning objectives, their main concern is whether the scores are reliable (i.e., whether the students would rank in the same way if the test were given again) rather than whether the assessments target the most important curriculum standards for a given grade level. The focus is on reliability of scores because the scores are used to make important decisions about students—whether they need special services, whether they should be admitted into the gifted and talented program, whether they will be admitted to a highly prestigious college, whether they will get a merit-based scholarship for college. Chapter 12 presents information about how standardized criterion-refernced and norm-referenced tests are developed and how to interpret standardized test scores.

Very few teachers are concerned about assessment for selection and comparison purposes. Teachers typically focus on assessment of developing understanding and skill and assessment of expertise. If you are clear about what you want students to learn, you can use many of the same tools for assessment of understanding and skill as you do to assess their expertise. Chapters 4 through 8 describe how to develop assessment tools that can be used to assess for understanding, skill level, and expertise. When you use effective assessment processes, you can use the results of assessments to further support your students in the development of their expertise. This book is intended to prepare you to create assessment tools and processes that give you the information you want and to evaluate published assessment tools to determine whether they are likely to give you the information you want.

ASSESSMENT OF STUDENTS WITH SPECIAL NEEDS

Some of the most common questions teachers ask have to do with how the concepts, skills, and strategies outlined in state and national standards apply to students with special needs. Throughout this book, we will highlight ways in which it is appropriate to adapt or modify assessment tools and processes to accommodate students' individual needs. The special groups we consider are students with limited English proficiency (LEP), students who need some assistance but do not qualify for special education services, and students who qualify for special education services. Assessment tools and assessment processes for these students carry with them some particular responsibilities. You must not only be fair and accurate, but also make certain that you do not place blocks in the way that limit students' successful learning and demonstration of that learning. One way that standardization of instruction and assessment hinders students with special needs is that they often have difficulty showing what they have learned if they are required to demonstrate their knowledge and skills in the same ways that other students do.

Students With Limited English Proficiency

Most students with limited English proficiency (LEP) are recent immigrants who speak fluently in a language other than English or are young children who have been reared in homes where English is not spoken. Students who are still learning English are called English language learners (ELL), but only those who do not meet the standard on a test of English proficiency are designated as LEP. Even those who have lived in English-speaking countries for many years, but have lived primarily in communities where their native language is spoken, may have difficulty learning and performing in English. On average, it takes between one and two years for ELL students in English-speaking schools to attain conversational fluency in English. (This depends somewhat on the age of the student and whether the parents speak English at home, as well as on the specific language programs available in the schools.) Academic fluency, on the other hand, can take many years to develop.

Students who are ELL generally have different kinds of experiences in their home communities and may not have the breadth of cultural knowledge of their new country that many teachers take for granted when they give assignments. ELL students may have great difficulty reading a text in English if they must translate word by word with the help of a dictionary. Even if they translate the words, the sentences may not be clearly comprehensible (because of the differences in the grammars and word meanings for different languages). The student may lose track of the meaning of the sentence in the translation process. The student may appear to be reasonably fluent when talking to other students or the teacher, and may have a fair amount of background knowledge of a subject, but still have trouble keeping up with reading or clearly expressing academic ideas through writing. English idioms and figurative language may be particularly challenging or confusing for ELL students.

Some fairly simple accommodations can help these students be more successful, including allowing extra time to complete work, giving them a translation dictionary, providing translation help (if available), and creating learning and assessment opportunities that provide concrete experiences rather than just verbal ones. For example, rather than having an ELL student read a table describing the characteristics of different unknown minerals prior to completing an assessment item that requires the student to sort rocks based on their physical characteristics, the student could handle and test representative minerals in a lab. To make accommodations that best meet students' needs, teachers must get to know the specialists who teach English as a second language (ESL) or the bilingual educators in the school or district. Teachers can work with specialists to select appropriate transitional standards, support and teaching methods for students as they make the transition from their home language to the language of school.[7]

Students With 504 Plans

Some students with disabilities do not require instructional modifications, but do need accommodations (e.g., lab tables they can reach from a wheelchair, additional time to write reports or to complete tests and assignments, an assistant to help them use materials). These students will have a plan developed under the guidelines of Section 504 of the Adults with Disabilities Act (ADA). The relevant accommodations will be spelled out for school personnel in the 504 plan, and the school must provide these accommodations for the student. Any ac-

[7]For more information on working with LEP students, read the book *Academic Competence* (Adamson, 1993).

commodations provided during the regular instructional process should also be available to students when they are doing classroom-based assessments and when they do standardized tests.

Students With Individualized Education Plans

Students whose disabilities interfere with their ability to learn or achieve in school have an individualized education plan (IEP). For these students, you need to discuss assessment and grading early in a course or school year as part of a conference with you, the student (if appropriate), the parents or guardians, and the IEP manager (usually a special education teacher or school psychologist). If the student can learn the same material when given *accommodations* (e.g., more time to complete work, reduced *numbers* of problems, shorter but equally difficult novels, help with comprehending social studies or science text, use of a Braille-writer, sign language interpreter, or educational assistant), then the standards for the quality of the work should be the same as for other students. For students who plan on college or other postsecondary education, this is the appropriate choice. The summary grade will show how well the student with a disability has met the same standards as her nondisabled classmates.

Some students with disabilities require *modifications* of instruction and assessment tools in order to succeed. These modifications might include different assignments, lower standards, different curricula, easier problems or books, and the like. You will need to discuss these modifications with parents or guardians early in the year so that parents/guardians know that grades do not reflect typical work for the other students in that grade level. Unless this is done, parents and students may erroneously assume that As and Bs on a report card reflect an ability to do work comparable to nondisabled peers, leading to stress and disappointment when the students and parents or guardians realize the truth.

At the same time, teachers, parents, guardians, and others who work with disabled students *must* guard against the impulse to unduly lower their expectations for these students' achievement. Children with disabilities should be given the opportunity to learn as much as they possibly can. Often such students can do much more than adults give them credit for, if they are given additional time, assistance, and other supports. Their success depends, in part, on the ways in which you fully include them in the life of your classroom. The best strategies for accomplishing this are going to vary by individual and should be taken into account when developing classroom assessment policies for each student. We address various ways to alter assessments for accommodations and modifications in Chapters 4 through 8.

RELIABILITY AND VALIDITY IN CLASSROOM-BASED ASSESSMENT

In the previous section, we made references to *reliability* and *validity*. The *Cambridge Advanced Learner's Dictionary* (2002) defines *reliable* as "dependable" and *valid* as "based on truth or reason." What do these terms mean in the classroom?

The terms *reliability* and *validity* are commonly used in the context of assessment—particularly in the context of standardized tests. We have found that, unless teachers can see the application of these concepts to their own teaching, the terms become words "memorized for a test" (Taylor & Nolen, 1996). Part of the reason teachers do not see how these terms apply to their own assessments is that the way psychologists first conceived of reliability and validity had more to do with the reliability and validity of experiments and experimental measures than with the life of the classroom teacher. Still, some aspects of these concepts are very important to your work as a teacher. Throughout this book we will return to the notions of reliability and validity as they apply to different types of classroom assessment tools and processes. However, we begin by creating an analogy.

Suppose you were the physical education teacher and you wanted to create a pretest for the unit on basketball. You know that students were introduced to basketball the previous year and you need to know what to teach this year. You put a trash basket on a chair. Then, one by one, your students throw a toy basketball into the trash basket. After one toss you decide whether students know how to throw the ball into the basket. Setting aside the ridiculousness of the test, would *one* toss be sufficient for you to make a dependable (reliable) decision about each student? Probably not. How many tosses would be sufficient for your test?

Suppose, in order to have sufficient evidence to make a reliable decision, you decide to have each student toss the ball into the basket ten times. You compute the total number of times the ball went into the basket as each student's score. Now you are likely to have a reliable test of throwing toy basketballs into trash baskets.

The next question is, "Can you really say anything about students' ability to play basketball based on your test?" Probably not. In fact, this test looks very little like basketball. The basketball pretest is an *indirect* measure of the knowledge and skills it is intended to assess. As such, you have to make giant leaps to *infer* that successful performance on the test predicts successful performance in a game of basketball. So what is a direct measure of students' knowledge and skills?

To design the most truthful and reasonable (valid) measure of basketball, one has to look at the overall game of basketball. Table 1–1 lists some of the knowledge and skills students must have to play the game of basketball. Suppose you used the list in Table 1–1 to build your test. What would the test look like?

You might test their knowledge of the rules of the game through a paper-and-pencil test. You might have them do 10 free throws, 10 lay-ups, 10 three-point shots, 10 jump shots, and try to catch 10 rebounds. You might have them run up and down the court several times passing and dribbling the ball. Finally, you might put them into small teams and have them use offensive and defensive strategies. Through these scrimmages and the passing/dribbling drills, you might be able to see how well they communicate as well as their strength, endurance, speed, and agility. Would this be a better pretest? Yes. Would it be the *best* pretest? That depends on what you want to know.

If you want to assess individual students on their individual skills, this more direct test is probably a reasonable way to have them demonstrate those skills. However, if you want to know how much they know about playing basketball, the most valid assessment will be to have them play the game. One game may tell you very little. Just as throwing one ball into a basket does not allow you to make a reliable judgment about whether students can repeat their performance, having students play a single game will not show how well they can play the game of basketball. They will have to play several games before you can make reliable judgments about each student.

Now, suppose you decide to use the even more direct assessment. You begin observing students as they play basketball games, and you find that you are watching some students more than others. Will you be able to depend on your observational notes? Probably not. Hence, if you are assessing students through observation as students play the game,

Table 1–1
Knowledge and Skills Needed in Basketball

Knowledge	Skills	Strategies	Teamwork	Personal Best
Rules of the game	Lay-ups Free throws Three-point shots Passing Dribbling Jump shots Rebounding	Defense • Zone • One-on-one • Stealing the ball Offense • Pick & roll • Coach-designed plays • Give & go Roles of position	Communication Sharing the ball Playing own position	Strength Endurance Speed Agility

you have to be very systematic to make certain that you see every student do every skill. You need some sort of assessment tool to record your observations. Using that assessment tool, you can be certain that you use the same performance expectations to assess each student's skills and knowledge (validity). You also need to make certain that the students know you are observing them so that they can do their best (reliability). Because systematic observations are a necessary aspect of the assessment, you become part of the assessment. You add to or detract from the reliability of the assessment through your consistency in observing each student and your consistency in holding all students to the same expectations. You add or detract from the validity based on the degree to which you are observing only the knowledge and skills of basketball and carefully recording what you observe for each student.

Last, as students play the game several times, you are likely to notice that their skills are improving. As you are assessing them, they are learning. Before too long, you will feel compelled to coach students—to give them points to work on and to tell them what they are doing well. At that moment, you are fully integrating assessment and instruction.

In summary, classroom teachers must make reliable (dependable) decisions about students using assessment tools that are as valid (direct, true, and reasonable) as possible given the amount of time we have available for assessment and the very real limitations of human observation and judgment. The dilemma, then, is how to balance the demands for reliability (dependability) and validity (truth) with the limitations of time and number of observers. We have found that the most effective way is for teachers to use real work as the basis for both instruction and assessment—providing feedback and coaching for students so that they can improve their knowledge and skills.

Clearly, ensuring the validity and reliability of classroom assessments is a process that takes some time and thought. In what follows, we describe a framework for validity and reliability for classroom assessments that builds on the basketball analogy.

Validity Framework for Classroom Assessments

In the classroom, validity encompasses (a) how assessments draw out the learning, (b) how assessments fit with the educational context and instructional strategies used, and (c) what occurs as a result of assessments, including the full range of outcomes from feedback, grading, and placement to students' self-concepts and behaviors to students' constructions about the subject disciplines. In the classroom context, you must know how to look at your own assessments and assessment plans for evidence of their validity, you must know where to look for alternative explanations of student performance, and you must consider the consequences of assessment choices on your students and yourself. The more you teach, the easier it is to evaluate the validity of your assessment tools and processes. The following is a validity framework that we developed for classroom-based assessments (Taylor & Nolen, 1996).

Validity Dimension 1: Do the concepts and processes required in the assessments really reflect the content of the subject area or discipline?   Before you can decide whether your assessments measure the content domain, you must be able to think clearly about the content areas or disciplines you teach. In Chapter 2, we discuss content standards and their role in developing learning objectives for your students. In your teaching, you must determine which concepts and processes are most important and which are least important in order to adequately reflect the breadth and depth of the subject area in teaching and assessment. One of the greatest sources of invalidity is over- or underrepresentation of some aspect of the discipline or subject area (Messick, 1989). For example, if you only assess the rules for the game of basketball through a paper-and-pencil test, you are not providing a valid assessment of your students' knowledge and skills in basketball. Therefore, validity of assessments begins with a clear focus on your learning goals and objectives (see Chapter 2). For each discipline, you must identify the critical knowledge and skills in a way similar to the chart in Table 1–1.

With clear learning goals and objectives, you can evaluate the first aspect of validity—whether the different assessments you use actually ask students to demonstrate *all* of the concepts and skills you want students to learn. You must ask yourself, "Have I included a way to assess all of the knowledge and skills I want my students to learn?" Because assessment is as much a function of how you assign scores or grades to students' work as it is whether the items and performances represent all the learning objectives, validity also has to do with the degree to which the way you evaluate student work and your strategies for summarizing grades reflect the targeted learning objectives. Scoring rules and grading summaries also have to be evaluated as to whether they give too little or too much value to certain concepts and skills. For example, although effective writing involves appropriate content, relevant ideas, logical organization, word choices, language usage, appropriate voice, and writing conventions (grammar, punctuation, spelling, and capitalization), many teachers focus their evaluation of students' writing only on writing conventions—which makes the assessment of writing less valid.

Validity Dimension 2: Do items actually draw out the targeted concepts and skills, and do students perform similarly on different assessments of the same knowledge and skills?   An important aspect of validity for classroom-based assessments is whether the assessments are actually assessing what you want students to learn. Standardized test makers use item tryouts to find out how the items function *before* they use the items on tests to give scores to students.

Most teachers do not have the luxury to do this with their own tests. Textbook tests are rarely tried out with students before they are published. Therefore, you need to develop ways to find out whether test items and performance directions actually tap the concepts and skills you think you are assessing. One way to do this is to ask students to explain their work or show their steps as they complete various tests, quizzes, or performances. In Chapter 7, we discuss ways in which you can have students explain their answers to test items so that you can see what they are thinking. You may discover that an item isn't really assessing what you thought—that the item is flawed in some way. To ensure that your assessments of students are valid, you must be willing to delete the scores from flawed assessments and generate new scores or grades.

Another aspect of this dimension of validity is comparing students' performance across different items or performances to see whether they are performing similarly on items or performances that are intended to measure the same learning objectives. For example, in Chapter 6, we introduce Ms. Steinberg, a science teacher. In her science test, she has more than one item measuring each science inquiry skill. As she scores the items on her test, she will quickly see whether students are performing similarly on items that are intended to measure the same thing. She will also be able to look at the written reports of students' science investigations and compare how they do on the reports with how they do on test items that assess the same inquiry skills. If student performances on different tasks measuring the same knowledge or skill are very similar, you can have more confidence that the test items or performance tasks are valid measures of the same learning targets. In short, Validity Dimension 2 requires time to review students' *performances* to see whether the directions or items are functioning well—in a sense, this is an opportunity for you to "test the test."

Validity Dimension 3: Do the assessments fit the instructional methods and work equally well across groups and settings? One of the most fundamental validity questions you must ask yourself is whether you actually taught what is being assessed, whether the way you assess fits the way you taught, and whether students had sufficient exposure to and practice with concepts and skills to be successful on the assessments. Recall the experiences of Mr. Hanks and Mr. Johnson. A mismatch between what is taught and what is assessed can not only lead to frustration for teachers and students, but can also result in invalid grades for students.

In addition to the fit with instruction, validity has to do with how well various assessment strategies meet the unique needs of your students. For example, a teacher once told Catherine that she could not use writing assessment with her new immigrant students because they had nothing to write about. When queried further, it turned out that the teacher was using standardized writing prompts that referenced contexts unfamiliar to some of her students (e.g., Write a story describing something that happened at Thanksgiving dinner.). Although students might have been able to write a story, the writing prompt prevented some of them from demonstrating their writing skills.

Validity Dimension 4: What are the relationships between assessments and other measures or background variables? One of the main threats to the validity of classroom assessments is when factors within the assessment prevent students from showing what they know and are able to do. For example, many language arts teachers want students to learn how to examine literature for character development, theme, plot development, and setting. Suppose all of the classroom assessments require students to read a novel and write a report. Also suppose that there are students for whom a selected novel is well above their reading level and students who cannot communicate their ideas through writing because of their limited English proficiency.

The validity question is whether the format of the assessment prevents some students from demonstrating their understanding of character development, plot development, theme, and setting. If these students could demonstrate their literary analysis skills after hearing a book (on tape) or could demonstrate their skills through an oral report, the written assessment is not valid for these students. Similar questions can be asked about any assessment. If the learned knowledge and skills *can* be demonstrated in a way other than through a given assessment (without changing the target for what is assessed) and if some students could show their conceptual understanding and skills through an alternate format, then using only one format for assessment is *biased* in favor of those who can perform in the chosen way and against those who cannot. In creating and selecting assessments, you must determine whether performance is influenced by factors irrelevant to the targeted learning objectives such as assessment format, assessment response mode, gender, language of origin, or other factors.

This validity dimension becomes increasingly critical as classrooms become more diverse and whole-group teaching becomes more difficult. You must learn how to adapt assessment to meet the needs of diverse students while still obtaining good evidence about student achievement related to your learning objectives. This aspect of validity also requires skill in writing scoring rules focused only on the targeted knowledge and skills rather than how well the student performed in a given assessment format. For example, if students are asked to demonstrate their understanding of character development, plot development, theme, and setting in an essay exam and the teacher evaluates the quality of students' writing, the assessment will favor students who are skilled writers and will be biased against students who are not skilled writers or who are English language learners.

Validity Dimension 5: Are there negative consequences of assessments and grading practices that could be prevented if assessments had been more valid? As we discussed earlier, assessments have effects on students. The nature of the assessments, feedback, and grading can all influence student learning, self-concepts, motivation (Butler & Nisan, 1986; Covington & Omelich, 1984), and perceptions of the subject areas and disciplines being taught. Therefore, the final dimension of validity for classroom assessments is related to how classroom assessments affect the students themselves. You can examine the consequences of your assessments and grading policies (see Chapter 9) to see how they affect students. If students are developing a notion of the subject area as a collection of facts that are to be memorized, this consequence is *mis*-educative. If some students get poor grades whereas others get good grades *because of invalidity in dimensions 1 through 4,* then the consequences that arise from those grades (promotion to the next grade level, placement in special programs, access to honors classes, etc.) are invalid consequences. Your ethical responsibility is to create and select valid assessments so that consequences are fair and are based on appropriate information. Throughout this book we describe specific strategies for ensuring that assessments and grading policies are valid and of sound technical quality.

Reliability Framework for Classroom Assessments

As we have discussed, some elements of reliability are critical to classroom assessment. Three dimensions of reliability relevant to the classroom are (1) whether you can make dependable statements about what students have learned in relation to your goals and objectives, (2) whether students know exactly what is expected on tests, performances, and other assessments, and (3) whether you are consistent in your assessment practices—across students and over time.

Reliability Dimension 1: Can I make a dependable statement about what students have learned in relation to my goals and objectives? Assessment experts often talk about reliability as consistency in performance. In the basketball analogy, we asked whether a single throw of the toy basketball was sufficient to make a dependable (reliable) statement about whether the student could throw the ball into the basket. Would the student perform in the same way a second time? Sometimes you will have opportunities to give repeated trials to students (as when they do multiple arithmetic exercises demonstrating a single skill). You may ask students to do similar tasks several times during a quarter or trimester (e.g., spelling tests, arithmetic worksheets). However, as with basketball, the more the assessment relates to real, valued performance, the harder it is to have students demonstrate performances consistently from one time to the next. As with basketball, practice and coaching make consistent performance over time unlikely. Students learn and change as they learn. Teachers wouldn't have it any other way. Therefore, reliability in terms of student consistency is not appropriate for classroom assessments. Still, it is possible that grading decisions made at the end of a marking period can be much more reliable than the individual assessments. For grades to be reliable, teachers must ensure that they have *sufficient, high-quality* assessment information from which to make reliable decisions about students. The reliability of grading decisions depends on the validity of the assessment tools and processes. If attention is given to validity dimensions one through four, then you can begin to ask whether there is sufficient information from which to make reliable decisions. Multiple, valid assessments are very likely to give reliable information about students. The more sources of valid assessment information you have at the end of a grading period, the more likely that your decisions will be ones that you and others can depend on.

You can use grading policies to organize your thinking about the sources of information you will use for making judgments about student learning (Chapter 9). Rather than using "averaging" techniques in grading, you can use your professional judgments to look at the range of evidence about student learning and make a "holistic, integrative interpretation of collected performances" (Moss, 1994, p. 7). Therefore, to address Reliability Dimension 1, you need to obtain as much valid information about students' achievement of your learning objectives as possible throughout a marking period.

Reliability Dimension 2: Do my test items or performance directions give clear, unambiguous expectations for students? When students are not clear about what they are being asked to do, they are less likely to produce the response you expect; they are more likely to respond in a way that is *inconsistent* with their own knowledge and skills or in ways that are inconsistent across tasks for which you have the same expectations. In contrast, when test items and performance directions are clear and explicit, students are more able to show what they know and are able to do. We have found, in our teaching and in the teaching experiences of our students, that when directions and items are clear and focused, the quality of student work is likely to be much better and easier to evaluate. In Chapters 4 through 8, we discuss how to write items and performance directions that will help you ensure that students are clear about your expectations. When students are clear, their performances and responses are more likely to reflect their true knowledge and skills.

Reliability Dimension 3: Am I consistent in making decisions across students and across similar types of work? As a teacher, you will generally use three types of assessment that could be affected by the consistency of your judgments about students' learning. You will create and use short-answer and performance items for tests (Chapters 7 and 8); you will assign projects and performances (Chapter 4); and you will give multiple assignments for which you have the same expectations (Chapter 6). In these three situations, the consistency of *your* judgments depends on (a) whether the rules for scoring short-answer items and performance items are consistently applied across students, (b) whether the rules for scoring extended performances are applied consistently across students, and (c) whether rules for scoring frequently occurring types of assessment are applied consistently across similar tasks and over time. In Chapters 4, 5, 7, and 8, we show you how to develop a variety of scoring rules (checklists, rating scales, and rubrics) that will help you be consistent in evaluating work across students and over time.

Throughout this book, we will return to these ideas about reliability and validity in the classroom as we present different assessment methods and processes. In Chapter 12, we discuss notions of reliability and validity as they apply to standardized tests. If you truly understand these ideas—both from the perspective of the classroom and from the perspective of standardized tests—you will be more able to help parents and school administrators understand how your assessments tell an accurate story about what your students have learned in your class.

SUMMARY

In this chapter we have introduced our philosophy of assessment as well as our deepest concerns about how assessments are used in schools. We have presented these ideas so that, as you read the forthcoming chapters, you can understand the perspective we take and the examples we use. In the next chapter we discuss the place of assessment in the instructional context. In a way, that chapter is an extension of our philosophy. To support students, you need to be very clear about what you want them to learn, how you will teach so that

they learn, and how you will assess to determine whether your instructional strategies have been successful. To select and create appropriate assessments tools, you must be equally clear about what is important for students to learn. Your assessment tools and processes will tell students your values, your expectations, and whether you can be trusted as a guide in their learning process. This book is intended to help you make assessment choices that will support your students and make your life as a teacher a positive experience.

REFERENCES

Adamson, H. D. (1993). *Academic competence: Theory and classroom practice—preparing ESL students for content courses.* White Plains, NY: Longman.

Anderman, E. M., Griesinger, T., & Westerfield, G. (1998). Motivation and cheating during early adolescence. *Journal of Educational Psychology, 90*(1), 84–93.

Butler, R., & Nisan, M. (1986). Effects of no feedback, task-related comments, and grades on intrinsic motivation and performance. *Journal of Educational Psychology, 78*(3), 210–216.

Cambridge Advanced Learner's Dictionary. (2002). Available: http://dictionary.cambridge.org/

Covington, M. V., & Omelich, C. L. (1979). Effort: the double-edged sword in school achievement. *Journal of Educational Psychology, 71*(1), 169–182.

Darling-Hammond, L. (2001). Apartheid in American education: How opportunity is rationed to children of color in the United States. In T. Johnson, J. E. Boyden & W. J. Pittz (Eds.), *Racial profiling and punishment in U. S. Public schools: How zero tolerance policies and high stakes testing subvert academic excellence and racial equity.* Oakland, CA: ERASE Initiative Applied Research Center.

Elkind, D. (2001). *The hurried child: Growing up too fast too soon* (3rd ed.). Cambridge, MA: Perseus Publishers.

Heath, S. B. (1982). What no bedtime story means: Narrative skills at home and school. *Language in Society, 11*(1), 49–76.

Lairon, M. (1991). Personal communication, April 10, 1991.

Levidow, B. B., Hunt, E., & McKee, C. (1991). The DIAGNOSER: A HyperCard tool for building theoretically based tutorials. *Behavior Research Methods, Instruments, and Computers, 23,* 249–252.

Lomax, R. G., West, M. M., Harmon, M. C., Viator, K. A., & Madaus, G. F. (1995). The impact of mandated standardized testing on minority students. *Journal of Negro Education, 64*(2), 171–185.

Martinez, M. E. (1990). *A comparison of multiple-choice and constructed figural response items.* Princeton, NJ: Educational Testing Service.

Maughan, B. (1994). Poor readers in secondary school. *Reading and Writing: An Interdisciplinary Journal, 6*(2), 125–150.

Messick, S. (1989). Validity. In R. L. Linn (Ed.), *Educational measurement* (3rd ed.). Washington, D. C.: American Council on Education, Washington, D.C.; National Council on Measurement in Education.

Minstrell, J. (2001). The role of the teacher in making sense of classroom experiences and effecting better learning. In D. Klahr & S. Carver (Eds.), *Cognition and instruction: 25 years of progress.* Mahwah, NJ: Lawrence Erlbaum.

Moss, P. A. (1994). Can there be validity without reliability? *Educational Researcher, 23*(2), 5–12.

Proulx, M. (1994). *Learning outcomes in mathematics: Performance assessment vs. traditional testing in constructivist classrooms.* Unpublished Masters, University of Washington, Seattle, WA.

Schoenfeld, A. H. (1988). When good teaching leads to bad results: Disasters of well-taught math courses. *Educational Psychologist, 23,* 145–166.

Self, T. C. (1985). *Dropouts: A review of the literature.* Monroe, LA: Project Talent Search: Northeast Louisiana University.

Shepard, L. A. (1991a). Psychometricians' beliefs about learning. *Educational Researcher, 20*(7), 2–16.

Shepard, L. A. (1991b). Will national tests improve student learning? *Phi Delta Kappan, 73*(3), 232–238.

Smith, M. L. (1991). Meanings of test preparation. *American Educational Research Journal, 28*(3), 521–542.

Standards for educational and psychological testing. (1999). Washington, DC: American Educational Research Association, American Psychological Association, National Council on Measurement in Education.

Taylor, C., & Nolen, S. B. (1996). A contextualized approach to teaching teachers about classroom-based assessment. *Educational Psychologist, 31,* 77–88.

Yen, W. M. (1993, June). *The Maryland School Performance Assessment Program: Performance assessment with psychometric quality suitable for high stakes usage.* Paper presented at the Large Scale Assesment Conference, Albuquerque, NM.

WHAT IS WORTH TEACHING
AND ASSESSING?

I n this chapter, we address one of the toughest issues in teaching—deciding what to teach and what to assess. Many teachers tell us that they have to cover all that is in a textbook so that (1) students will be ready for the next year or course in a sequence or (2) students will do well on standardized tests. The problem with coverage is that, quite often, students do not learn what is covered. Successful teaching is much more than covering important content. For example, international studies in mathematics and science have shown that depth rather than breadth leads to better mathematics and science performance on international tests (Cogan & Schmidt, 2002; Schmidt, McKnight, Houang, Wang, Wiley, Cogan, & Wolfe, 2001; Schmidt, Houang, & Wolfe, 1999). Successful teaching means that students have learned what is taught. Throughout this book we focus on what students are learning. This chapter is only the beginning of that focus.

We divide this chapter into three major parts. In the first part, we briefly discuss the role of assessment in the context of instruction. In the next part, we discuss how to decide which—of all the knowledge and skills you want students to learn—are most important and long lasting. In the final section, we describe different roles of assessment in the classroom. This chapter is intended to help you focus your instruction and assessment tools and processes so that you and your students get maximum benefit.

ASSESSMENT IN THE CONTEXT OF INSTRUCTION

It is hard to imagine thinking about assessment without considering the instructional context in which assessment occurs. Yet, lack of connection between instruction and assessment is too often the case.[1] Nearly everyone has experienced the test at the end of a unit or course that included items over content never taught. If assessment is to be supportive of students' learning, it must be developed to fit with the learning targets (goals and objectives) you have for students. Assessment must also be consistent with methods of instruction if it is to support student learning. Poor connections among learning goals, learning objectives, instruction, and assessment cause more than confusion and frustration. For students who have not developed intrinsic motivation to learn or for whom learning is a challenge, lack of consistency between instruction and assessment can lead to anger and/or despair.

Figure 2–1 shows the ideal relationship among learning goals and objectives, instruction, and assessment. In this chapter, we explain this relationship and give guidance on how to develop and improve the connection between these three critical aspects of teaching.

TEACHING TO MEANINGFUL LEARNING TARGETS: WHAT DO I WANT THEM TO LEARN?

Learning occurs when people change cognitively or behaviorally due to experience. Although teachers hope that students learn from teaching, much of what students learn comes from experiences outside of school. Therefore, you must decide not only what you want students to learn from their experiences in the classroom but also how to enhance or even alter that which students learn outside of school. Before you can assess students' learning (and

---

[1]Recall the experiences of Mr. Hanks and Mr. Johnson described in Chapter 1.

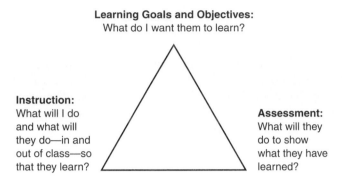

Figure 2–1
The Relationship Among Learning Targets, Instruction, and Assessment

your effectiveness as a teacher), you need clear ideas about what you expect your students to learn from your teaching.

When determining what you want students to learn, there are two useful questions to ask for each subject area you teach. The first is, "If they don't learn anything else from me this year, what are the five to six most important concepts, skills, and/or dispositions I want them to learn in this subject?" The second question is, "What are the two or three most important performances students should learn in this subject?" Both questions serve a valuable purpose.

In some subjects, such as mathematics, the primary purpose of instruction is for students to become mathematically literate and able to use mathematical knowledge and skills to solve real problems in life beyond school. An infinite number of real-world performances can show mathematical literacy and the ability to solve problems. A secondary purpose of instruction is for students to think mathematically so that they can pursue study in mathematical fields such as computer science, life science, physics, engineering, architecture, philosophy, economics, and higher levels of mathematics. Mathematics teachers may think more about the knowledge and skills they want students to learn than about any specific performances. Still, there are some performances that most teachers of mathematics want all of their students to learn. For example, any teacher of mathematics probably wants students to learn how to develop graphs, tables, and charts, and to interpret graphs, tables, and charts to obtain mathematical information about important topics or issues. Similarly, although all teachers of science want students to learn fundamental science concepts and processes, many also want students to know how to engage in systematic scientific inquiry.

In contrast, the language arts, as the name implies, are focused on the arts of language. Like visual and performing arts, the language arts are predominantly performance based. The overall goals of instruction are to help students develop the arts of reading and interpreting text, speaking and presenting, creative and informative writing, listening, and dramatic interpretation. While there are enabling skills and important knowledge (e.g., decoding skills, capitalization and punctuation rules, and verb conjugation rules), the knowledge and skills clearly relate to a variety of performances. At the same time, some teachers value knowledge in the language arts that does not relate to specific performances. For example, a teacher might want students to gain knowledge about the influence of particular writers on their genres (e.g., William Shakespeare, Ernest Hemingway, e e cummings, or Maya Angelou). Similarly, most visual arts teachers want students to learn how to create artistic works, and some arts teachers also want students to know the history of one of more art media or the influence of particular artists on a given medium.

To determine what you want students to learn, it is best to begin with your knowledge of the subjects (disciplines) you teach and combine that with your values as an educator. This may seem like a daunting, or even impossible, task; however, teachers do not work in vacuums. Most subject areas have state and national curriculum standards that are intended to establish targets for student learning. They provide invaluable assistance to teachers as they work to decide what *matters most*.

We say "matters most" because no period of time (be it a trimester, semester, or year) is sufficient for students to learn *all* that we want them to learn. Grant Wiggins (1989) makes this point in his paper entitled, "The Futility of Trying to Teach Everything of Importance." Learning takes time. Effective learning of anything of importance takes multiple examples, thoughtful reflection, and repeated practice with new concepts, skills, and performances.

One unfortunate outcome of the "factory model" of schooling (Feldman, 1999; Hennen, 1996) is that teachers hurry through content as they "cover" one topic after another. This rush for coverage leaves little time for thought, for internalizing ideas, and for making new concepts or skills a solid part of the students' cognitive or behavioral repertoire. One student in our assessment class reported hearing the phrase, "Hurry up and give me the test. I'm forgetting already." Phrases like this suggest that students memorize for tests but do not retain or value the information memorized. Clearly this is not evidence of learning. Research on students' retention of tested knowledge reinforces the preservice teacher's experience. Students retain little of what is taught in courses where content coverage takes precedence over deep understanding and mastered skills. In contrast, when deep understanding is the focus of instruction, students not only retain what they have learned, but also build on their understanding with or without explicit instruction in a given subject area. For example, Vokos (1999) found that students who learned physics principles and concepts through inquiry-based courses learned more and retained their understanding longer than their peers who were enrolled in traditional college physics courses—even though less content was covered.

If students cannot learn all that is taught, teachers must make wise choices about what *is* possible given a fixed period of time. We use the terms *learning goals* and *learning objectives* as labels for statements about what teachers want students to learn. Learning goals are broad statements about learning outcomes that reflect the ultimate aims of schooling. Learning objectives are focused statements about the knowledge and skills that help students attain the goals. We use the term *subjects* or *subject areas* to refer to the conventional titles given to content taught in school (e.g., reading, mathematics, science, social studies) and the term *disciplines* to refer to fields of study and work such as physics, economics, history, literary analysis, and biology. When thinking about both the conceptual understanding and the performances you want students to learn, it helps to think about the disciplines as well as the subject areas. It is easier to think about what work is valued and what knowledge and skills are essential if you consider both everyday life and the more academic work typical of each discipline. In what follows, we elaborate on these ideas.

Learning Goals

When you write the learning goals for the subject(s) you teach, you will define what you want students to attain from one or more years of schooling. Goal statements are broad generalizations often guided by national, state, or district standards documents. In the day-to-day reality of schools, goals may appear to be idealistic statements that are easily forgotten. Yet, goals must be kept in mind so that you do not lose sight of your real purposes for teaching. Before you begin to write your learning goals, take a moment to think about the subject area(s) you will teach and the disciplines within those subject areas. Ignore, for the moment, the goals and objectives provided in textbooks. Ask yourself:

1. What are the major dimensions of each *subject area* I will teach? Some of the dimensions of mathematics (defined by the "Principles and Standards for School Mathematics" from the National Council for Teachers of Mathematics, 2000) are number systems and number operations, mathematical communication, problem solving, reasoning and proof, and mathematical representations. In their document, "Science for All Americans," the American Association for the Advancement of Science (AAAS, 1989) includes dimensions such as understanding the physical world, the living environment, and the human organism; understanding the worldview of scientists; and scientific inquiry processes and scientific thinking.

2. Which aspects of these subject area dimensions are the *most important* for students to learn in *this* term or *this* year, and at what level of sophistication? Students will continue to work on these broad goals after they have moved on to other teachers, in what Bruner (1977) calls the "spiral curriculum." For example, a second-grade teacher may teach mathematical communication, knowing that the first-grade teacher taught them aspects of mathematical communication and that their fifth- or seventh-grade teacher will continue to teach more and more sophisticated aspects of mathematical communication.

3. What knowledge and skills within the *discipline(s)* will help students understand *how people work* in the discipline, *what people know* that helps them be successful in this discipline, and *how people think* in the discipline? State and national curriculum standards often separate *processes, conceptual understanding,* and *thinking skills.* For example, writers take their work through a *process* as they develop their work from initial ideas through various drafts to final published works. In addition, many writers (fiction writers, poets, historians, biographers, etc.) use their *knowledge* of various literary devices such as descriptive language, metaphors, symbols, and personification to create images, communicate themes, and improve understanding for readers. As a writing teacher, you may want your students to learn how to use an effective writing process to create high-quality work *and* develop understanding of the vocabulary and techniques used by writers.

4. What work do adults do (within the discipline and in daily life) that show they have met these larger goals? For example, scientists conduct systematic observations in natural environments as well as controlled experiments. They analyze the data resulting from these investigations and prepare research reports. They present their reports at conferences and publish them in journals. Are these important performances valuable to you so that you will want to teach students how to do them well?

These four questions can help you frame the learning goals for your teaching. Figure 2–2 gives examples of learning goals for different subject areas taught in school. In parentheses following each goal are the disciplines related to these goals. Although these certainly do not represent an exhaustive list of goals for each subject area, they are useful starting places for thinking about learning goals in different subject areas. For each subject area identified in Figure 2–2, there are goals focused on knowledge or conceptual understanding

---

Example Language Arts Goals

1. Students will learn how to use a writing process to improve their writing (any discipline that involves published written work).

2. Students will learn how to critically evaluate plot, character, theme, and setting in literary works (Literary Criticism, Comparative Literature).

Example Visual Arts Goals

1. Students will learn how to use design principles (shape, color, line, texture, etc.) to construct a work of art (Painting, Printmaking, Sculpture, Glass Blowing).

2. Students will learn the characteristics of works from dominant art movements during the 19th and 20th centuries (Art History).

Example Social Science Goals

1. Students will learn how to acquire, evaluate, and interpret historical information (History).

2. Students will learn historians' interpretations of the causes and effects of major historical events (History).

3. Students will learn how humans and environments interact to influence one another (Geography).

Example World Language Goals

1. Students will learn how to converse effectively in Spanish (daily speaking).

2. Students will learn the grammatical structure of the Spanish language (Linguistics).

Example Mathematics Goals

1. Students will learn processes for problem solving in mathematics (Theoretical Mathematics, Statistics, and everyday life).

2. Students will understand the fundamental concepts and procedures of algebra (Theoretical Mathematics and everyday life).

3. Students will effectively comprehend and communicate mathematical ideas and solutions (Theoretical Mathematics, Statistics, Architecture, Physics, Biology, Engineering).

Example Science Goals

1. Students will understand how to apply scientific research methods to investigate research questions (Basic and Applied Scientific Research).

2. Students will understand important structures, functions, and processes in the systems of living organisms (Botany, Zoology, Anatomy, Environmental Science, Farming, Genetics).

Figure 2–2
Example Learning Goals for Six Subjects Taught in School

(e.g., Students will learn historians' interpretations of the causes and effects of major historical events.) and goals that focus on work that is characteristic of professionals in the discipline(s) identified in parentheses (e.g., Students will learn how to acquire, evaluate, and interpret historical information.).

It is evident that each of these goals cannot be attained in one year or term of classroom learning experiences. Still, it is worthwhile to set valued goals as the ultimate focus of your teaching so that you keep in mind the overall purpose of the instructional activities and assessments you use. By choosing a few important goals you want to help students attain and teaching toward those goals, students have a better chance of learning and of making sense of what you teach.

Our former students tell us that when they use this strategy, students not only learn a great deal in the time they have available, but also look forward to and ask for more opportunities to engage in real work and to learn more substantive concepts. In contrast, when teachers simply walk through lesson plans without a focus on ultimate goals, students become confused about the purposes of their work. Some students may become permanently disconnected from school; others may simply wait until the "irrelevant" work of school is done so they can move on to the real world. As schools become more focused on helping students reach standards, school contexts are more likely to encourage teachers to work together across subjects and grade levels to help students achieve important goals.

Learning Objectives

Learning objectives guide the day-to-day work of teaching. They are more specific than goals and are statements of the knowledge and skills students will gain from instruction. Achievement of learning objectives helps student attain the broader goals. For example, the goal statement in Figure 2–2, "Students will learn how to converse effectively in Spanish," is very broad. What specific knowledge and skills do students need to learn, as they become effective speakers of Spanish? Is pronunciation important? Will they need to learn how to listen for main ideas rather than trying to translate another's speech word for word? Are there formal and informal conventions of speech they need to know so that they speak appropriately to peers and teachers? You can begin to frame your learning objectives by brainstorming a list of the knowledge (e.g., rules for when to use formal and informal conventions) and skills (e.g., listening for main ideas) that enable students to achieve particular goals.

Probably the most difficult aspect of choosing the learning objectives for each goal occurs when the goal is very broad. For example, the goal in Figure 2–2 that states, "Students will learn historians' interpretations of the causes and effects of major historical events," is very broad. How does the social studies or history teacher decide what major events to focus on? Sometimes these events are selected for the teacher as when a U.S. history course has a particular time frame (e.g., pre-Columbian to 1850). In this case, the teacher's job is to decide which of the many important events that could be taught in this period of time are most important—events that students should not leave school without knowing. If the teacher does not set priorities, then students will experience a broad survey of information without capturing the most important focus of the goal—*historians' interpretations* of *causes and effects*. In this case, not all knowledge of an event will help students achieve this goal. Only knowledge of causes and effects is important. In addition, the goal suggests that there may be multiple interpretations of causes and effects. Therefore, to write learning objectives for this goal, the teacher's job is to determine (1) which events matter more than any others, (2) what aspect of the events has to do with causes and effects, and (3) whose interpretations about the causes and effects of particular events will be included.

Framing Learning Objectives

An important question that has influenced education for nearly 50 years is how to frame learning objectives. Three strategies have been used in this framing process: *behavioral ob-*

jectives, *teaching objectives*, and *learning objectives*. Although this book uses a learning objectives frame, in what follows, we describe each of the three types of objectives. We explain why we believe that learning objectives can help teachers focus their teaching better than do teaching or behavioral objectives.

Behavioral Objectives   Beginning in the 1960s, mastery learning and behavioral objectives emerged as the panacea for solving educational problems (e.g., Bloom, Hastings, & Madaus, 1971). Objectives were written in terms of specific behaviors students would do by the end of a lesson; teachers were expected to write behavioral objectives for every lesson. Many district curriculum standards were written in terms of behavioral objectives. Behavioral objectives focused on tightly defined knowledge or skill and named the observable behavior that students would do to show they had learned the knowledge or skill. The behaviors were written in terms of specific verbs (e.g., identify, define, recognize) and often these verbs were derived from what could be assessed by way of traditional test items. The phrasing of behavioral objectives also implied how the knowledge or skill in question would be assessed.

The notion of behavioral objectives came from a learning theory called *behaviorism*. According to this learning theory, any important educational outcome (e.g., understanding scientific taxonomies) could be defined in terms of many specific behaviors (e.g., define the term *attribute*, sort by attributes, classify by attributes, name the different attributes used in scientific taxonomies, name the organs and structures in plants and animals, list the functions of organs in the circulatory system in plants and animals, identify the functions of bones in the skeletal system in animals, etc.). The key to successful teaching was to carefully analyze each important outcome in terms of all of the enabling skills and bits of knowledge needed, teach each skill or fact, and as students mastered the prerequisite skill or memorized the specific knowledge, they could combine these skills and knowledge to build toward the important outcome (Holland, 1961). The theory was derived from animal studies wherein animals were taught to do certain complex behaviors through teaching small parts and reinforcing each lesser behavior until animals could combine these behaviors into a complex performance (Skinner, 1938). Needless to say, these performances did not require complex cognition and were easily defined in terms of behaviors.

Generalizing this learning theory to human behaviors and human cognition has at least two problems. The first problem is that humans want to know *why* they are doing what they are doing. The piano student who is practicing scales, arpeggios, chord progressions, and etudes wants to know what this has to do with playing music. The second problem is that not all that is learned can be shown or defined in terms of overt and specific behaviors.

Along with the problems related to behaviorism as a human learning theory, behavioral objectives have limitations. First, when objectives are written in terms of specific behaviors, they tended to trivialize learning rather than focus on cognitive or behavioral changes that generalize beyond a specific lesson.

For example, suppose Mr. Ferrara is teaching language arts to his tenth-graders and he wants his students to write an essay explaining how authors use literary devices in their work. He found the following behavioral objective in the district's language arts standards, "Students will define metaphor, simile, symbol, imagery, and personification." Although this objective is measurable, it is very narrow. When faced with such a narrow objective, Mr. Ferrara asked himself, "Is the definition of these terms what matters? Will this show me whether students are ready to write a paper describing how authors use these devices in their writing?" To get at the latter understanding, he wrote, "Students will identify metaphors, similes, symbols, imagery, and personification in literary works." Mr. Ferrara then asked himself, "Does this objective go far enough? Does identifying a literary device in a literary work show me whether students can write a paper describing how authors use these devices in their writing?" Next he wrote, "Students will interpret the meaning of metaphors, similes, symbols, imagery, and personification in the works of William Shakespeare, Leo Tolstoy, and Charles Dickens."

Through this example of the thinking required to write behavioral objectives, the second limitation to behavioral objectives becomes clearer: a large number of objectives is required to get at an important understanding or skill. If each objective must name a very specific behavior that builds up to the larger understanding or skill he ultimately wants students to achieve, Mr. Ferrara will have to write dozens of behavioral objectives for the paper he wants students to write—not only several objectives for analysis of literary devices but also many behavioral objectives for each of the aspects of writing, such as topic sentences, supporting sentences, variety in sentence structure, paragraphing, sequence of ideas, informative titles, elements of bibliographies, and multiparagraph reports. The sheer number of behavioral objectives needed for everyday teaching—and the fact that the specificity of behavioral objectives generally demands that new objectives be written for each different lesson—often leads teachers to stop writing objectives altogether. This may be even more problematic because a lack of objectives can lead to unfocused teaching.

The third limitation of behavioral objectives is that many teachers confuse behavioral objectives with instructional activities. For example, we often read behavioral objectives that include such statements as, "Students will write in journals daily." "Students will work in small groups to complete homework assignments." "Students will complete a lab on acids and bases." Each of these statements refers to actions students will take. However, the behaviors do not give information about what students will learn. What is the purpose of daily journal writing? Do students learn how to write complete sentences? Do they learn how to develop personal responses to literature, how to record their critical reading of literature, or how to generate ideas for future creative writing opportunities? Similarly, what do students learn from completing an investigation on acids and bases? How to systematically test hypotheses under controlled conditions? How to measure acids and bases? The effects of acids and bases on reactive materials?

In summary, although behavioral objectives can help teachers focus their instruction and assessments, the limitations of behavioral objectives make them difficult to use in everyday teaching. Objectives must help you focus your teaching without adding unnecessary work.

Teaching Objectives   In contrast to behavioral objectives, some teachers have learned to write what are called teaching objectives. These are statements about what the teacher will do or what the teacher will have students do during each lesson. The objectives in the previous paragraph fit well into the category of teaching objectives. Suppose Ms. Abernathy wants students to learn critical ideas about acids and bases. She might list the teaching objectives in Figure 2–3 for her lesson on acids and bases.

Ms. Abernathy would use these statements to guide teaching and lesson planning. These statements are limited because they do not identify what students are to learn from the activities. One could infer from these three activities that students are to learn how acids and bases affect other matter, the chemical properties of acids and bases, and either the names of common acids and bases *or* how to test for acidity *or* how to read and interpret the

---

Lesson Objectives

1. Students will see a demonstration of the effects of acids and bases on four materials (metal, oak leaves, leather, and stone).

2. Students will listen to a lecture on the properties of acids and bases.

3. Students will test household materials for their pH level.

Figure 2–3
Ms. Abernathy's Teaching Objectives for a Lesson on Acids and Bases

pH scale. However, without a clear idea about what students are to learn, lessons can easily stray from their intended purposes or lack purpose completely.

Learning Objectives   In contrast to behavioral objectives and teaching objectives, learning objectives are statements about what is to be learned. Rather than write many different and narrow behavioral objectives for literary analysis, Mr. Ferrara's learning objective might be, "Students will learn how authors use literary devices (e.g., metaphor, simile, personification, imagery, symbol) to communicate ideas and feelings." Inherent in this learning objective is the requirement that teachers teach the meaning of terms used to describe literary devices, how to find these devices in literary works, and how to interpret them. How students show this understanding is not defined and can differ from assessment to assessment, class to class and from student to student. The determination of how students demonstrate their learning is part of the assessment plan, rather than the learning objective. Mr. Ferrara might also have objectives related to the strategies authors use to create settings, plots, themes, and characters (see objectives for goal 2 in Figure 2–4A).

Hence, learning objectives are statements about what students are to learn. Some learning objectives will refer to conceptual understandings (e.g., "Students will learn how the rules in the U.S. Constitution help to maintain a balance of power among the different branches of government." "Students will learn how the contents of the U.S. Constitution and the Bill of Rights reflect the concerns of and conflicts among the framers of the constitution."), whereas other learning objectives will refer to important skills (e.g., "Students will learn how to use a variety of prewriting techniques (group brainstorms, lists, and webs) to generate ideas for their own writing." "Students will learn how to use decoding skills (letter sounds; word patterns; meanings of prefixes, root words, and suffixes) to comprehend the meaning of text.").

So that teachers remember to teach to the larger idea, we recommend that teachers focus on broader statements of student learning rather than several specific behaviors or facts. Learning objectives can be written by identifying important component parts that communicate fundamental elements of learning objectives. For example, the learning objective, "Students will learn how to use a variety of prewriting techniques (group brainstorms, lists, and webs) to generate ideas for their own writing," has two elements. The first part is the idea that students will learn *prewriting techniques*. This identifies the type of skills students will learn. Second, the purpose of the prewriting techniques is to *generate ideas for their own writing*. Hence the techniques are not important for their own sake. They serve a writing purpose. For a second learning objective, "Students will learn how to use a variety of decoding skills (letter sounds; word patterns; meanings of prefixes, root words, and suffixes)

Goal 1: **Students will learn how to use a writing process to improve their writing.**

Objective 1.1   Students will learn how use prewriting strategies (such as lists, webs, charts, outlines) to generate and organize ideas for their own writing.

Objective 1.2   Students will learn to use ideas from prewriting to develop first drafts.

Objective 1.3   Students will learn how to revise their drafts to improve plot, character development, setting, and organization.

Objective 1.4   Students will learn how to revise their drafts to improve word choice, sentence variety, and voice.

Objective 1.5   Students will learn how to use proofreader's marks to edit their own and others' work for grammar, punctuation, and capitalization.

Goal 2: **Students will learn how to critically evaluate plot, character, theme, and setting in literary works.**

Objective 2.1   Students will learn how authors use symbols, action, imagery, and characters to develop themes.

Objective 2.2   Students will learn how authors use descriptive and figurative language to create setting.

Objective 2.3   Students will learn how authors use event sequence, conflict, and resolution to create plots.

Objective 2.4   Students will learn how authors use action, descriptive language, dialogue, and other strategies to develop characters.

Goal 1: **Students will learn how to use design principles (shape, color, line, texture, etc.) to construct a visual work of art.**

Objective 1.1   Students will learn how to use shape in developing a visual composition.

Objective 1.2   Students will learn how to use color in developing a visual composition.

Objective 1.3   Students will learn how to use texture in developing a visual composition.

Objective 1.4   Students will learn how to use line in a visual composition.

Objective 1.5   Students will learn how to use perspective to create depth in a visual composition.

Objective 1.6   Students will learn how to use symmetry and asymmetry to create balance in a visual composition.

Objective 1.7   Students will learn how to use design elements to move the viewer to different elements of a composition.

Goal 2: **Students will learn the characteristics of works from dominant art movements during the 19th and 20th centuries.**

Objective 2.1   Students will learn the characteristics of art from the cubist movement.

Objective 2.2   Students will learn the characteristics of art from the impressionist movement.

Objective 2.3   Students will learn the characteristics of art from the abstract expressionist movement.

Objective 2.4   Students will learn the characteristics of art from the surrealist movement.

Objective 2.5   Students will learn the characteristics of art from the pop art movement.

Objective 2.6   Students will learn the characteristics of art from the photorealist movement.

Figure 2–4
Examples of Learning Objectives for Various Subjects

Goal 1:   Students will learn how to acquire, evaluate, and interpret historical information.

Objective 1.1   Students will learn how to locate and select primary and secondary sources needed to answer historical questions.

Objective 1.2   Students will learn how to use primary and secondary sources to identify potential causes and effects of important historical events.

Objective 1.3   Students will learn how to use primary and secondary sources to identify common themes across historical eras and events in history.

Objective 1.4   Students will learn how to examine language and images for the presence of bias to determine the validity of information.

Goal 2:   Students will learn how humans and environments interact to influence one another.

Objective 2.1   Students will learn how humans adapt their food and shelter to the resources in an environment.

Objective 2.2   Students will learn how humans choose settlement locations based on the physical and climatic characteristics of an environment.

Objective 2.3   Students will learn how human behaviors affect the physical and climatic characteristics of an environment.

Goal 1:   Students will learn how to converse effectively in Spanish.

Objective 1.1   Students will learn how to use accents, word patterns, and letter sounds to enhance pronunciation.

Objective 1.2   Students will learn how to listen for main ideas to grasp speakers' meaning and intent.

Objective 1.3   Students will learn to use appropriate formal and informal conventions when speaking to peers and adults.

Goal 2:   Students will learn the grammatical structure of the Spanish language.

Objective 2.1   Students will learn how to conjugate regular and irregular verbs to indicate tense and number.

Objective 2.2   Students will learn to use pronouns to communicate the gender of speaker or object.

Objective 2.3   Students will learn conventions for telling time in Spanish.

Figure 2–4 (continued)

to comprehend the meaning of text," the important skills are *decoding skills*. These skills serve the purpose of helping students *comprehend the meaning of text*. Learning objectives that are focused on skills generally indicate not only *what* is to be learned but the *purpose* for the skills as well.

Both of the example objectives indicate that students will learn a *variety* of techniques or skills. This suggests that the teacher will teach more than a single technique. For each learning objective, the specific skills to be taught are given in parentheses. These lists can guide the instructional focus. If, through preassessment, the teacher discovers that the students already know how to use brainstorming and listing as prewriting strategies, the teacher

---

Goal 1:   Students will learn processes for problem solving in mathematics.

Objective 1.1   Students will learn how to define the problem to be solved.

Objective 1.2   Students will learn how to extract mathematical information relevant to solving problems.

Objective 1.3   Students will learn to apply a variety of concepts, procedures, and strategies to solve problems.

Objective 1.4   Students will learn to persist when faced with nonroutine problems.

Objective 1.5   Students will learn to adjust strategies when first efforts are not successful.

Goal 2:   Students will understand the fundamental concepts and procedures of algebra.

Objective 2.1   Students will learn how to use mathematical functions to represent relationships between variables.

Objective 2.2   Students will learn how to use coordinates, graphs, and formulas to represent mathematical functions.

Objective 2.4   Students will learn how to use graphs to solve for equalities and inequalities.

Objective 2.4   Students will learn how to use equations to solve for equalities and inequalities.

Goal 1:   Students will understand how to apply scientific research methods to investigate research questions.

Objective 1.1   Students will learn how to generate researchable questions that build on previous research.

Objective 1.2   Students will learn how to develop testable hypotheses relevant to their research questions.

Objective 1.3   Students will learn to select experimental and control variables relevant to their hypotheses.

Goal 2:   Students will understand important structures, functions, and processes in the systems of living organisms.

Objective 2.1   Students will learn the names and functions of organs in the human respiratory system.

Objective 2.2   Students will learn the names and functions of organs in the human reproductive system.

Objective 2.3   Students will learn names and functions of organs in the human circulatory system.

Objective 2.4   Students will learn the normal processes of the human circulatory, respiratory, and reproductive systems.

Figure 2–4 (continued)

can focus on webs and outlining as other valuable prewriting strategies. If students know several strategies but do not use them regularly in their writing, the teacher can focus instruction on how to use the ideas they generate through prewriting strategies in their written work.

Figure 2–4A through 2–4E give several learning objectives for goals listed in Figure 2–2. Note that, for each subject area, a content goal and a process goal has been listed along with its relevant objectives. Each learning objective that focuses on skills indicates what is to be learned and its purpose. Learning objectives that are focused on skills begin with "students will learn *how to*" and learning objectives that are focused on conceptual understanding begin with "students will learn." If you want students to know how to do something (e.g., use prewriting strategies, conduct systematic scientific inquiry), write the objectives to remind yourself that you must teach them *how*.

Note that the learning objectives focused on conceptual understanding do not include such phrases as "learn about" or "learn that." When you want students to learn *about* something, decide ahead of time what you want them to learn about the particular target. For example, suppose you wrote the following learning objective: "Students will learn about the Civil War." You should ask yourself, "What do I want them to learn about the Civil War?" Your answers might include the causes of the Civil War, the effects of the Civil War on the economies of Southern states, or the influence of the Civil War on 20th-century politics. If you write an objective that states "Students will learn that authors use plot, setting, characterization, and theme to create stories," this suggests that you want students to memorize labels for parts of a story. In contrast, a learning objective that states "Students will learn *how* authors use plot, setting, characterization, and theme to create stories" suggests that you will help them understand how authors use these techniques differently in different stories.

Note also that the lists of objectives given in Figures 2–4A through 2–4F do not include every possible objective for each of the goals; objectives may differ somewhat depending on the age of the students and the focus of a course or grade level. In fact, although some processes (e.g., mathematical problem solving) may be similar for all grade levels—varying only in the level of sophistication of the problem—learning objectives for older students are generally broader than learning objectives for younger students.

Developmental Issues in Writing Learning Goals and Objectives

Teachers of younger students may wonder if there is a place for disciplinary thinking when writing goals and objectives. What, you may ask, can first- or second-graders learn that is similar to the work of adults in the disciplines or even in the world beyond school? What big concepts can they learn when they are just beginning to read, write words, and add whole numbers? These are important questions but need not limit teachers' willingness to help students see themselves as writers, scientists, social scientists, critics of literature, or even mathematicians. We have known teachers who successfully engaged students, from diverse backgrounds and communities, in scientific research, writing workshops, and mathematical problem solving in first and second grades. The key is to take students from where they are and gradually build their skills and concepts toward bigger conceptual understandings and more sophisticated thinking and process skills.

For the young child, learning how our number system works is one key to successful work in later mathematics and in life beyond school. Therefore, puzzling over the number system and finding patterns and surprising connections among different parts of the number system is the child's version of what mathematicians do later in life. Similarly, making systematic observations (e.g., of the growth and development of a plant over time, of how electrical circuits work in a flashlight) mirrors what adult scientists do. Therefore, although the specific knowledge or skills may be simpler than what older students must learn, young children can still engage in the same kind of work as those in various disciplines to discover what is already known and accepted. Their discoveries can help them learn what we consider simple concepts and skills. The genuine pleasure that comes from discovery in one subject can sustain students when they struggle in other subjects.

Hence, when deciding what they want young children to learn, elementary and secondary teachers can adopt the same goals and then identify the knowledge and skills related to those goals that are within the developmental range of their students. For example, Figure 2–4E gives several objectives related to algebraic thinking. The focus of these objectives is on functions. As Ms. Jones writes mathematics learning objectives for her third-graders, she knows that representing linear relationships is not relevant to the cognitive development of her students. She asks herself, "What can third-graders learn that is relevant to algebra?" Her state standards indicate that students are to learn how to "recognize, extend, and create patterns" and that they must "learn how to solve for missing information in number sentences." Ms. Jones decides that solving for a missing number in an equation is the precursor to solving algebraic functions. She also understands that number patterns can be a precursor to functions. Figure 2–5 shows Ms. Jones's learning objectives for the goal, "Students will understand the fundamental concepts and procedures of algebra." As can be seen, Ms. Jones's learning objectives are much more concrete and represent concepts and skills relevant to third-graders.

Where to Find More Information About Goals and Objectives   Many teachers do not know why certain concepts or skills are given in district or state curriculum standards documents or where they fit into students' overall development. National standards documents are very helpful in giving explanations and examples to support these curriculum standards. Appendix A gives a list of Web sites that can be used to obtain national standards documents. Some standards, such as the *Principles and Standards for School Mathematics* (NCTM, 2000) can be downloaded from the Web. Others can be purchased from professional organizations. These documents also give standards by grade-level bands, which can help new teachers understand not only what they need to help students learn, but also how their learning objectives fit into the ongoing development of students' knowledge and skills. These documents do more than name important learning goals and objectives. They provide teacher-friendly information to help new teachers understand the reasons for the given standards.

Appendix B gives the names of professional organizations for teachers. Professional organizations help teachers stay current with recent research on students' learning as well as giving them access to methods that other teachers and researchers have found effective. Professional organizations publish and update curriculum standards, instructional ideas, assessment guidelines, and journals with information on recent research and practice in each subject area. Many states have state or regional chapters of national professional organizations that provide regular (annual or semiannual) professional development conferences and workshops to help teachers incorporate appropriate instructional and assessment strategies in their classrooms.

WHAT'S WORTH ASSESSING?

Once you know what you want students to learn, the next step is to plan instruction. Initial planning of instruction comes from three sources: your goals and objectives, the important performances you want students to learn how to do in your class (see Chapter 4 to learn more about how to assess valued performances), and the other forms of assessment

Goal 1:	Students will understand the fundamental concepts and procedures of algebra.
Objective 1.1	Students will learn the concept of pattern.
Objective 1.2	Students will learn how to determine the pattern rules for numeric patterns.
Objective 1.3	Students will learn how to apply rules to extend number patterns.
Objective 1.4	Students will learn how to solve for a missing value in a simple equation.

Figure 2–5
Example of Ms. Jones's Algebra Learning Objectives for Third-Graders

you plan to use. The link between goals and objectives and assessment is the teaching process. *When teachers know what they want students to learn and how students will demonstrate their knowledge and skills, they are more likely to plan instruction that will help students succeed.*

Important and valued performances can become central to instruction and can guide lesson planning as well as assessment processes. When valued performances are central to instruction, lessons move students toward better performances. Ongoing assessment is used to give students practice with the concepts and skills and to assess how well students are developing those concepts and skills. To help students learn how to solve mathematical problems, teachers give them meaningful and engaging problems to solve. Students learn various mathematical concepts *as they solve those problems*. In this way, students learn the mathematical concepts and skills as well as problem-solving strategies. By making problem solving central to the instructional process, students regularly practice the skills needed to solve problems and have practice in applying the targeted knowledge (concepts) and procedures.

If a teacher wants students to learn how to write effective research papers, he can help each student select an interesting issue and then teach students *how to* develop research questions about their chosen issues, obtain information, take notes, create outlines, and write interesting papers through which they share their new knowledge. By making performances the centerpiece of instruction, students are more likely to be interested in learning the note taking, outlining, and writing. Identifying valued performances, planning lessons, and organizing those lessons—so that students learn what they need to learn—are critical links in the relationship among learning goals and objectives, instruction, and assessment. Assessment must be part of the planning process from the very beginning.

In Chapter 1, we discussed assessment of understanding and assessment of expertise. In what follows, we elaborate on the variety of different assessment tools and processes that serve these two purposes by describing the instructional plans and assessment tools and processes used by one teacher. These plans, tools, and processes are guided by goals, objectives, and a focus on important valued performances.

Sizing Up Assessments

Mr. Jefferson, an eighth-grade social studies teacher, plans to teach his students how to do historical research in addition to important content related to world geography and state history. He begins the year by writing learning goals and objectives for his course and deciding what important performances students will do during the year. He decides to make historical research the centerpiece of his teaching and to help students learn important historical and geographical concepts through that research. Figure 2–6 shows Mr. Jefferson's goals and objectives for the first semester of the year—the semester focused on world geography.

To begin the year, Mr. Jefferson decides to do an instructional unit that will lay the groundwork for the rest of the year. The unit will include lessons on historical research skills, group work skills, and historical writing skills. He selects the first research project, sets expectations for the project, and plans lessons that are likely to help students learn the relevant skills and do well on the final performance. He decides that the first research paper will be fairly short (about four to five pages in length) so that students can work on their research and writing skills without becoming overwhelmed with a topic and without having to integrate ideas from too many sources.

Before he begins teaching, Mr. Jefferson wants to know what his students already know about conducting text-based research. He also wants to know whether students can work independently, whether they have appropriate skills for working in the library and in study groups, and whether they know how to use the library card catalog and Internet search tools. Finally, he needs to know whether his students know how to follow directions on assignments. Following Airaisian (1997), we call this "sizing-up assessment."

During the first week of school, Mr. Jefferson uses a series of *informal* assessment tools and processes to learn about his students (see Chapter 5 to learn more about informal assessments). He places students in small groups and gives them some tasks to do. He observes their work and makes notes about what they do well and what they need to work on in terms of social skills and group-work skills. He also gives them a paper-and-pencil preassessment of research skills to see if they know what tools to use to locate particular kinds of information and how to use the encyclopedia, the dictionary, and the card catalog. He has them play an Internet scavenger hunt game to see what they know about using search engines and he records what he sees. He has small groups of students work with primary documents (letters between two soldiers during the Civil War) and asks them to determine who these people are, when the event is happening, and what the writers' perspectives are. He observes to see how they interpret the documents and whether they use references to make sense of information that is unfamiliar to them (e.g., vocabulary, events, military ranks).

At the end of the week, Mr. Jefferson has a good sense of what he needs to include in his lessons. He shares what he has learned with his students and sets the stage for the research project. He guides students as they create a checklist for him to use to assess their skills in working independently and as effective members of a group. They create another checklist so they can self-assess their research skills as well as their skills in reading, interpreting, and evaluating primary and secondary sources (see Chapter 10 to learn more about self-assessment). Figure 2–7 and Figure 2–8 are the two checklists Mr. Jefferson and his students created together.

Before the end of the first week of school, Mr. Jefferson has accomplished three important tasks. He has involved students in their own assessment, communicated that he is working with students as an ally in their learning, and communicated many of his learning objectives to the students. Here assessment has served several different purposes besides the gathering of information to make grading decisions. Students are part of the process of defining expectations, which can help them take ownership of those expectations. In addition, students are conducting self-assessment, which can help to ensure that they are attending to the important criteria Mr. Jefferson wants them to focus on as they conduct research.

Goal 1:   Students will learn how geographical factors affect human movement and settlement patterns.

Objective 1.1   Students will learn how plate movements, volcanoes, and glaciers create landforms and bodies of water.

Objective 1.2   Students will learn how landforms and bodies of water influence human movement (e.g., transportation routes and migration patterns).

Objective 1.3   Students will learn how landforms and bodies of water influence human settlement patterns.

Objective 1.4   Students will learn how to locate information on maps using scales, grids, latitude and longitude, compass directions, landforms, highways, and keys.

Objective 1.5   Students will learn how to interpret recreational maps, population maps, topographical maps, political maps, road maps, and resource maps.

Objective 1.6   Students will learn different strategies geographers use to define regions.

Objective 1.7   Students will learn the names and locations of the continents, major oceans and seas, major rivers, and major mountain ranges.

Objective 1.8   Students will learn the geographic causes of major contemporary regional conflicts.

Goal 2:   Students will learn how to conduct original historical research.

Objective 2.1   Students will learn to identify issues they care about to focus their research.

Objective 2.2   Students will learn how to generate research questions about their issues that help focus their research.

Objective 2.3   Students will learn to how to locate primary and secondary sources relevant to their research questions.

Objective 2.4   Students will learn how to locate ideas and details from sources relevant to their research questions (including skimming, using headings and subheadings, etc.).

Objective 2.5   Students will learn how to summarize important ideas and details in their own words to avoid plagiarism.

Objective 2.6   Students will learn how authors use language, images, and data to influence readers' or listeners' opinions.

Objective 2.7   Students will learn how to organize ideas from diverse sources to create coherent informative reports and persuasive arguments.

Goal 3:   Students will learn how to work effectively in small and large groups.

Objective 3.1   Students will learn to listen to others' ideas and comments.

Objective 3.2   Students will learn to ask for clarification when confused.

Objective 3.3   Students will learn to offer relevant ideas to group work.

Objective 3.4   Students will learn how to take on different group roles.

Objective 3.5   Students will learn to monitor their own behaviors and make adjustments to support the efforts of the group.

Objective 3.6   Students will learn to work independently when necessary.

Figure 2–6
Three of Mr. Jefferson's Social Studies Goals and Associated Objectives

Group-Work Skills Observational Checklist

Check (✓) the box if the behavior was seen. Student Name	Offers relevant ideas	Adds to others' ideas	Asks questions, when needed, to clarify others' ideas	Adjusts own behaviors to help the group stay on task	Takes responsibility for own role in a group	Comments on ideas, not people	Follows directions independently without need of supervision	Attempts tasks before asking for help or advice

Goal 3: Students will learn how to work effectively in small and large groups.

Objective 3.1   Students will learn to listen to others' ideas and comments.

Objective 3.2   Students will learn to ask for clarification when confused.

Objective 3.3   Students will learn to offer relevant ideas to group work.

Objective 3.4   Students will learn how to take on different group roles.

Objective 3.5   Students will learn to monitor their own behaviors and make adjustments to support the efforts of the group.

Objective 3.6   Students will learn to work independently when necessary.

Figure 2–7
Group-Work Skills Checklist for Mr. Jefferson's Class

Research Skills Self-Evaluation Checklist

Student Name: _____ Date: _____

Use this checklist to guide your research work.

☐   I have a research question that is about an important geographic issue.

☐   I found more than one primary source related to my question.

☐   I evaluated the primary sources for language that suggests a bias.

☐   I evaluated the primary sources for images or data that suggest a bias.

☐   I found *at least two different* secondary sources relevant to my question.

☐   I evaluated the secondary sources for language that suggests a bias.

☐   I evaluated the secondary sources for images or data that suggest a bias.

☐   I accurately summarized the main ideas in each source in my own words.

☐   My summary includes important details from the source.

☐   I recorded the name of the source, the author, and other information I will need in a
    bibliography.

Goal 2: Students will learn how to conduct original historical research.

Objective 2.1   Students will learn to identify issues they care about to focus their research.

Objective 2.2   Students will learn how to generate research questions about their issues that
                help focus their research.

Objective 2.3   Students will learn to how to locate primary and secondary sources relevant to
                their research questions.

Objective 2.4   Students will learn how to locate ideas and details from sources relevant to their
                research questions (including skimming, using headings and subheadings, etc.).

Objective 2.5   Students will learn how to summarize important ideas and details in their own
                words to avoid plagiarism.

Objective 2.6   Students will learn how authors use language, images, and data to influence
                readers' or listeners' opinions.

Figure 2–8
Research Skills Checklist for Mr. Jefferson's Class

Ongoing Assessment

Mr. Jefferson now has some tools for continuous assessment of students' research skills as well as their ability to work in groups and independently during the research process. He plans to meet with his students on a periodic basis as they do their research project to give them feedback on their social and independent research skills and to see how they are progressing on their research. He can use the checklists to guide feedback during these conferences because they detail the expectations relevant to many of his objectives. Although these assessments are invaluable, Mr. Jefferson needs additional assessments to monitor students' development of report-writing skills as well as their ability to combine or organize information from a variety of sources to make a convincing argument. He uses a *process portfolio* approach to teach and assess students' skills (see Chapter 10 to learn more about process portfolios).

When Mr. Jefferson notices that students are still having trouble with group work, he has students participate in role-plays wherein they focus on positive and negative small-group behaviors. At the end of each role-play exercise, he has the students return to their group-work skills checklist to see what they might want to add or change to improve the checklist. Mr. Jefferson also notices that several students are nervous about working without his direct guidance. He gives these students encouragement when they work independently on any portion of the project. He hopes that, over the course of the unit, most students will develop more confidence in their own ideas and choices.

Each day, Mr. Jefferson gives mini-lessons on relevant aspects of the research process using what he learned from the sizing-up assessments in the first week. His mini-lessons include how to generate research questions, how to identify bias in sources, how to summarize rather than copy ideas, how to develop outlines, how to combine information from multiple sources to write about a subtopic, how to write transitional statements between ideas, how to cite sources within text, and how and when to use footnotes. Mr. Jefferson observes students during the mini-lessons to see whether they understand the examples. He slows down or modifies the lesson if necessary. Each mini-lesson takes about 10 minutes and has an accompanying handout that students put in their research notebooks. He organizes the mini-lessons so that they are relevant to the stage of their work.

After mini-lessons, students work on their research projects. Sometimes, he gives students small-group exercises to analyze good and poor examples of paragraphs, transition sentences, or other aspects of writing so that they can work to improve the examples. During these times, he walks around and observes their group-work behaviors using the class-developed checklist.

As students work on their own research papers, they turn in different stages of the work. He reads the work at each stage and gives students feedback so that they can make improvements before they go on to the next stage. For skills that are new to students, he is the only one who gives feedback. For skills that are more familiar to students (such as writing topic and supporting sentences, paragraphing, word choices, organization, spelling, punctuation, and capitalization, and bibliography), he has students give each other feedback, guided by peer evaluation checklists (see Chapters 4 and 10 to learn more about peer evaluation); however, he also looks at drafts of their work to ensure that all students are getting effective feedback.

In his written and oral feedback, Mr. Jefferson asks guiding questions, makes suggestions, and gives examples to guide students' thinking as they improve their work (see Chapter 3 to learn more about giving high-quality feedback). He then looks at revisions to see if students are simply editing their writing or are reflecting on the feedback and making thoughtful decisions about what is likely to improve their work. Sometimes, Mr. Jefferson places students with similar problems into small groups for feedback sessions so they can hear others' feedback or work together to solve research or writing problems. At other times, he observes small peer assessment groups to see whether he needs to add mini-lessons on particular skills or ideas. Occasionally, as he observes small groups, Mr. Jefferson finds that a mini-lesson did not work well and students are confused about an idea or skill. He then reteaches the skill or concept and adjusts his mini-lessons for the students in the next periods.

Summative or Formal Assessment

As students complete each step in their research project, they place the final draft, along with earlier drafts, into their process portfolios. At the end of the project, they have their research questions, notes and references, summaries, prewriting ideas, outlines, early drafts of topic paragraphs, drafts of the report (including Mr. Jefferson's and other students' feedback), and the final report. Giving a final score on the research paper turns out to be fairly easy. Because of the mini-lessons, small-group practice with ideas, independent work, in-depth teacher feedback at different stages, and peer feedback, most of his students do an outstanding job on their research papers. Mr. Jefferson uses several *scoring rubrics* to evaluate the final reports (see Chapter 4 to learn more about scoring rubrics). He gives them scores for quality of research, effective use of primary and secondary sources, the overall cohesiveness and accuracy of main ideas, details and examples, the organization of ideas including transitions, writing mechanics (grammar, punctuation, spelling, and capitalization); and documentation for research papers (citations, bibliography, and footnotes).

The research project takes three weeks. Therefore, by the end of the fourth week of school, Mr. Jefferson has created a classroom community focused on collaboration and mutual support. He has behaved more like a coach than an evaluator. Meanwhile students have learned important research skills, group-work skills, and writing skills. This sets the stage for the rest of the school year where Mr. Jefferson expects to have students do multiple research projects (some for papers, some for community presentations, some for formal debates) while they learn the important content of his eighth-grade social studies curriculum—world geography and state history. With each research project, he will increase the length and complexity of the assignment as students develop better and better research skills. He will also include lessons and practice needed for participating in debates and for giving effective presentations.

Social-Emotional Assessment

During the first week of class, Mr. Jefferson notices that Martin is having difficulty adjusting to his new freedoms and responsibilities. Regardless of the role-plays and individual feedback, Martin seems to have difficulty working independently. During independent research time, Martin often disturbs other students by asking questions or making jokes. When in small groups, Martin often takes the group off task by making jokes, singing, or grabbing other students' materials. Mr. Jefferson talks to Martin about his concerns during the one-on-one meetings; however, even though Martin says he wants to improve, there is no noticeable change in behaviors. After a few days, Mr. Jefferson goes to the school records and finds that Martin has had behavior difficulties in many classes. In addition, his standardized test scores suggest that he may have reading problems.

Mr. Jefferson decides to do an *individual assessment* of Martin's reading skills (see Chapter 4 to learn more about individual performance assessments). He chooses books at different reading levels and has Martin read several passages aloud. He finds that, although Martin can sound out words and letters and knows many high-frequency words, he has few skills for reading multi-syllable words or for making sense of new vocabulary words in context. These skills are critical for success in all subject areas in middle and high school. Mr. Jefferson contacts the school psychologist assigned to his school and asks that Martin be tested and given some reading support. Meanwhile, he finds materials that are easier to read and has Martin proceed with his research project. He simplifies the language in the peer evaluation checklists to make it easier for all of the students to read. He also works out a contract wherein Martin will be allowed to work with others as long as he does not distract other students and works on improving group-work skills. However, if Martin distracts other students in his group, he will be removed from the group and will work alone until he is ready to work productively. Mr. Jefferson notices that, although not always perfect, Martin begins to increase the amount of time he can stay in his group without distracting other students.

SUMMARY

A quick look at all of the different types of assessment Mr. Jefferson uses is very informative about the role of assessment in the classroom. Once Mr. Jefferson has established his *learning goals and objectives* and decided what important performances he wants students to learn, he does sizing-up or *preassessments* to find out what students already know about research, bias in sources, working in groups, and working independently. He does *ongoing assessment* to monitor quality of research, writing quality, social skills, and self-confidence in the research process. He monitors students during lessons and adjusts lessons as needed. He uses *observational assessments* of group work to see if students understand skills and concepts and adds lessons whenever needed. He uses assessment to adjust instruction for current and future students. He has students do *self-assessment* and *peer assessment* so they can understand his expectations and participate in their own assessment. He uses *scoring rubrics* focused on the targeted learning goals and objectives to *summatively* assess the final research reports. He *informally assesses* students and encourages movement toward independent work for those who are uncertain. He conducts an *individual assessment* of Martin's reading skills, refers him for special services, and develops a behavioral contract with Martin.

Mr. Jefferson's planning, lessons, and projects make sense because they are built on clear learning goals and objectives and clear ideas about important work students will do during the school year. His assessments include the range of formal and informal assessments that teachers do every day. He has clear ideas of what he wants students to learn and uses this focus to guide decision making so that he can help each student succeed. Although Mr. Jefferson may seem like an idealized teacher, these are the characteristics of effective teachers described in the research on high-quality teaching and learning (Corbett & Wilson, 2002; Demmon-Berger, 1986). Through the chapters in this book, you will learn many of the skills teachers like Mr. Jefferson use every day.

REFERENCES

AAAS. (1989). *Science for all Americans: Report on literacy goals in science, mathematics, and technology.* Washington, DC: American Association for the Advancement of Science.

Airasian, P. (1997). *Assessment in the classroom: A concise approach* (2nd ed.). New York: McGraw-Hill.

Bloom, B. S., Hasting, T. J., & Madaus, G. (1971). *Handbook on formative and summative evaluation of student learning.* New York: McGraw-Hill.

Bruner, J. S. (1977). *Process of education.* Cambridge, MA: Harvard University Press.

Cogan, L. S., & Schmidt, W. H. (2002). Culture shock—Eighth grade mathematics from an international perspective. *Educational Research and Evaluation, 8*(1), 13–39.

Corbett, D., & Wilson, B. (2002). What Urban Students Say About Good Teaching. *Educational Leadership, 60*(1), 18–22.

Demmon-Berger, D. (1986). *Effective teaching: Observations from research.* Arlington, VA: American Association of School Administrators.

Feldman, D. (1999). National policy, local interpretation: The American rural curriculum, 1897–1921. *Rural Educator, 21*(11), 8–14.

Hennen, J. C. (1996). *The Americanization of West Virginia: Creating a modern industrial state, 1916–1925.* Lexington: University Press of Kentucky.

Holland, J. G. (1961). *The analysis of behavior: A program for self instruction by James G. Holland and B. F. Skinner.* New York: McGraw-Hill.

NCTM. (2000). *Principles and standards for school mathematics.* Reston, VA: National Council of Teachers of Mathematics.

Schmidt, W. H., Houang, R. T., & Wolfe, R. G. (1999). Apples to apples. *American School Board Journal, 186*(7), 29–33.

Schmidt, W. H., McKnight, C., Houang, R. T., Wang, H. C., Wiley, D. E., Cogan, L. S., & Wolfe, R. G. (2001). *Why schools matter: A cross-national comparison of curriculum and learning.* San Francisco: Jossey-Bass.

Skinner, B. F. (1938). *The behavior of organisms: An experimental analysis.* New York: Appleton-Century Company.

Vokos, S. (1999, March). *Improving student learning at the introductory level and beyond: The role of research, Part II.* Paper presented at the APS Centennial Meeting/APS/AAPT Joint Meeting, Atlanta, GA.

Wiggins, G. (1989). The futility of trying to teach everything of importance. *Educational Leadership, 47*(3), 44–48, 57–59.

3

EFFECTS OF CLASSROOM-BASED ASSESSMENTS ON STUDENTS

MOTIVATION AND ASSESSMENT

Many people consider grades and assessments to be motivators. In some college classes, students request weekly quizzes so they will be "motivated to keep up with the reading." Teachers sometimes remind students of upcoming assessments to prod them to stay on task or to focus on particular information. We've all heard students ask, "Will this be on the test?" Teachers are usually people who have been successful in "playing the game of school" (Anderson, 1977), and often project onto their students the view that grades are important. But is this really the case? In this chapter, we will take a look at what motivates students, how different motivations influence student effort, the strategies students use to learn, students' interpretations of assessment results, how students' motivations can be influenced by the assessment practices and feedback they experience, and how teachers can use assessment practices to help create an environment where all students can be motivated.

Motivation and Student Goals

Researchers have found a more complex picture when studying student motivation than is represented in the brief scenarios above. Those who study students' reasons for learning have identified multiple goals driving students' learning and behavior in school. Here are some examples.

When students are *task-involved*, they pursue learning for its own sake. They feel successful when they are interested in a topic, learn something new, improve their skills, or perform their best. When students become *ego-involved*, they are concerned with demonstrating that they are smarter or better than others at a task, skill, or subject (Nicholls, 1989; Nicholls, Cobb, Yackel, Wood, & Wheatley, 1990; Nicholls, Patashnick, & Nolen, 1985; Nolen, 1988; Thorkildsen & Nicholls, 1998). There's a down side to ego involvement. What if students want to demonstrate that they are smarter or better but they aren't? Some researchers (Elliot & Harackiewicz, 1996) have identified a third goal related to involvement that they call *performance-avoidant*. The goal for performance-avoidant students is to do well in school in order to avoid looking *incompetent*. Students may also try to do well to please their parents, to bring honor to their families (Park & Nolen, 1998), or for some other reason extrinsic to the learning itself, such as getting a scholarship or admittance to a university. Of course, there are other goals that are not so focused on achievement, including social goals (Urdan & Maehr, 1995; Wentzel, 1999) and goals to avoid work without getting into trouble.

The kinds of motivation students have, their personal reasons for learning or for avoiding the appearance of failure, influence the way they engage in school. If a student wants to look more capable than others (or to avoid looking incompetent), he may try to give the impression that he is not working hard on a task that others can do more easily. If a student is focused on improvement or on learning new and interesting information, she is likely to see working hard as the appropriate means to that end. Again, the picture becomes more complex when students have a mixture of goals. For example, a student could be both task and ego involved if he wants to learn but also values being one of the best and brightest in class (Nicholls, 1989).

Motivation and Students' Interpretations of Assessments and Grades

Grades and assessments take on different meanings, depending on what is motivating students to learn. Suppose Keisha takes a high school psychology class. She is really interested in psychology and wants to learn as much as she can; she is task involved. To the extent that the scores on assessments, her grades, and other feedback give her important information about what she knows and what she needs to learn or improve, she will likely see them as useful tools. A score of 85% on a quiz focused on important psychological concepts and principles could motivate Keisha to study harder or differently—if she can determine from the quiz performance her own level of competence in psychology and what she needs to do to improve. On the other hand, if the teacher gives a quiz over superficial details, such as "What was the name of the client in the video tape of Rogerian therapy,"[1] or if Keisha is not helped to use the quiz results to guide her learning, the score of 85% may be seen as completely uninformative and even unfair. Keisha might decide that there are better ways to spend her time; she may find other ways to meet her learning needs and to receive feedback on her performance. If the quiz is too easy (not challenging enough) and doesn't really assess deep understanding of psychology, Keisha may see a score of 100% as having no real value.

Suppose Clarice is also interested in psychology and wants to learn as much as possible. However, she also sees school performance as a means to the ends of showing superior ability and getting into a good college. She might appreciate the information gained from a quiz that tested deep understanding and that gave her information on how to improve. But she may be more concerned that the score of 85% shows that she is not one of the best students in the class, especially if she studied hard for the quiz. She may also worry about the related extrinsic goal of getting into a prestigious college. However, if the test is over memorizable bits of information, she may be perfectly happy to get the "A" that Keisha devalued, especially if she is one of the few students to do well on the quiz.

Both Keisha and Clarice are likely to be very dissatisfied with a score of 70%. Lisa, on the other hand, is taking the class to fill a graduation requirement, but she doesn't really care about psychology. She doesn't much care what is on the quiz, as long as she passes the class, so a score of 70% may be perfectly acceptable and a signal to keep studying at a minimal level.

High school students are quite capable of separating the scores on assessments from the quality of the test and from their conceptions of their own ability. Young children, on the other hand, don't make these clear distinctions. In kindergarten, first grade, or second grade, children do not readily distinguish among effort, ability, and scores on assessments (Nicholls & Miller, 1983). Children who get good scores are smart and try hard; if they get low scores, they are not smart and haven't tried hard enough. Children believe that all they have to do is try hard and they will get smart and get good scores—a belief that is a boon to teachers trying to encourage their slower learners to keep at it. Young children believe that being smart and doing well are a matter of applying effort, so lower scores might increase their motivation (Nicholls, 1984, 1989; Nicholls & Miller, 1983, 1984). And children who announce, "I got one hundred percent correct!" after their spelling test may just be celebrating a happy event, not egotistically claiming superior ability.

Some young children, however, begin to notice that no matter how hard they try, they still don't do very well. They have a hard time explaining this to themselves and may withdraw from the unpleasant experience by avoiding work as much as possible. Patti, one of the first-graders in a study of motivation for literacy in young readers (Nolen, 2001) was a mas-

[1]An actual question Susan's daughter found on a psychology test.

ter at avoiding work. She had great difficulty in reading and writing, and generally did very little during independent work time. She had discovered that if she looked busy, she could avoid sanction by the teacher. During a writing session, while the teacher was busy with a reading group, Patti organized an elaborate game of princess and the dragon for the next recess period. When the teacher reminded the students that they only had a few minutes until recess, she quickly scribbled a sentence on her paper. Her teacher, knowing how she struggled to write and wishing to encourage any writing behavior, praised her and sent her off to recess, unwittingly reinforcing her avoidance behavior. Of course, Patti's skill at avoidance meant that she had fewer learning opportunities, made slower and slower progress, experienced more frustration, and so on in a downward spiral.

As children develop, they begin to see ability as a limiting factor in the usefulness of effort. The emergence of this conception is probably influenced by children's experience in school. In classrooms where high ability and performance are emphasized and rewarded, children quickly learn which children tend to repeatedly receive attention and are considered the best and the brightest. Children in these classes are more likely to develop the adult notions of ability and effort earlier. If children are in classes where relative ability is not made salient, they may develop this notion later, retaining their belief in effort as the cause of ability (Nicholls & Miller, 1983).

By about age 12, most children fully separate ability, effort, and scores. They realize that if they are not very good at something, effort will only go so far in helping them do well. This can lead them to devalue a subject or class and withdraw their effort. If they don't try hard, poor performance can be explained by lack of effort, rather than as an indicator of low ability. This is one explanation for why there is a drop in motivation for many children during the transition between elementary school and junior high/middle school (Nicholls, 1992). For these students, a low score or grade may or may not motivate them to try harder. Whether students try harder depends more on the goals that motivate them and the particular assessment and grading practices used.

INFLUENCING MOTIVATION THROUGH INSTRUCTION AND ASSESSMENT

Types of Motivation

Students tend to have general motivational tendencies, or theories of school learning, that they bring with them to class, and that influence their responses to teachers' attempts to motivate them (Thorkildsen, Nolen, & Fournier, 1994; see the research sidebar). But teachers can, through their instruction, assessment, and feedback, influence students' motivation. You may ask, "Which kind of motivation should I promote?" or "As long as students are working, does the kind of motivation matter?"

Ego Involvement Increasing ego involvement by calling attention to differences in ability may be useful in motivating the able students in your class. So how do teachers increase ego involvement? Seeing one's name at the top of a list of test scores or having one's project held up as an example of excellent work can be very satisfying to those who are able to achieve such success. The downside of ego-involving classrooms is that, by second or third grade, children realize that only the top students can reap these rewards. It is only in the fictitious

Research Sidebar 3.1:

CHILDREN'S VIEWS OF FAIR AND EFFECTIVE WAYS TO MOTIVATE STUDENTS

Thorkildsen, Nolen, and Fournier (1994) interviewed elementary school students from second through fifth grade in two very different schools. One was a public, urban Montessori school where teaching was inquiry focused and child centered, and children received neither grades nor extrinsic rewards for performance. The other was a public, suburban school practicing outcomes-based education, where outcomes are prescribed by the adults and children received grades and a mixture of rewards and recognition for high performance. The researchers were interested in students' views of the best ways for teachers to motivate students to do math.

They described three different "kinds" of learners (fast learners, who almost always finished and got all their problems right; slow learners, who worked hard but seldom finished and so couldn't get all the problems right; and kids who get distracted and fool around, not completing their work). Then they presented students with four types of feedback that teachers could use to motivate their students. The first two could only be earned by the fast learners: public praise for high achievement, with a suggestion to others that they work harder and extrinsic rewards for high achievement. Extrinsic rewards for effort were available to both fast and slow workers if they worked hard, but not to kids who fooled around. Finally encouragement, which combined a positive comment on their work with tailored assistance, could be applied to all three student groups. The fast learners got more challenging work, the slow learners got suggestions for different strategies to use, and the kids who fooled around were given more interesting math to do.

Surprisingly, the researchers found the same four orientations or student theories in each school. About half of the students in each school (53% in the urban inquiry-focused school, 44% in the suburban outcomes-based school) endorsed the theory that math should be meaningful, and that teachers should provide moderately difficult work that helped students engage and make sense of the math. About a quarter of the students (16%, 27%) saw learning as the students' duty, and that teachers' duty was to help make that happen. Both of these groups favored a feedback strategy that combined encouragement for work done well, as well as interesting work and suggestions for improvement. About a quarter of the students (27%, 25%) held an economic theory of school that favored extrinsic rewards for hard work. These students argued that learning was the student's work, and that it was fair and effective to "pay" them for this labor, just as teachers are paid for theirs. A very small number (4%) endorsed public praise for superior work, and felt that the suggestion that the other students work hard so they could be smarter was "mean." Some students (about 33%) said that extrinsic rewards for achievement might be effective, but was not fair because only the fast learners could get them. Most felt it was also likely to discourage other students who could not perform at that level.

The fact that a quarter of the students in the Montessori school, where rewards and grades were never given, preferred extrinsic rewards for effort suggests that students bring these theories of school learning and motivation with them to school. However, there were small differences in the proportion of students who articulated "meaningful math" theory, with more students in the inquiry-focused school endorsing this theory. More students in the suburban, outcomes-based school endorsed the "dutiful learner" theory. These differences may have been a function of the reasons for learning stressed in these two schools.

Lake Wobegon[2] that "all the children are above average." When highlighting high ability, by implication the teacher also highlights low ability.

Once students differentiate the effects of ability and effort, working very hard and still doing poorly—relative to others—may lead students to infer that they have low ability. Their peers are also likely to make the same inferences. Hence, in ego-involving classrooms, persisting in the face of task difficulty is risky; even if a hard-working student succeeds, others may do so with far less effort, again implying low ability. If the student withdraws effort with the excuse that the task is "dumb" or that she or he "had more important things to do," lack of effort may deflect such implications (Nicholls, 1989; Covington & Omelich, 1979).

Extrinsic Motivation   Theories about *extrinsic* motivation and external rewards for learning have a long and controversial history in education (Cameron & Pierce, 1994, 1996; Deci, 1978; Kohn, 1996; Lepper, Keavney, & Drake, 1996; Ryan & Deci, 1996). The research is consistent, however, in finding that, when people do something in order to get rewards, their intrinsic motivation to do the activity declines. Unexpected rewards, on the other hand, do not have this effect. In schools, scores and grades are seen by many educators as extrinsic reinforcers for learning. Comments such as, "If you study hard, you will get a high score on the test," or "If you contribute to the discussion, you will get participation points," are fairly common in schools. Teachers typically find that participation and effort increase, at least temporarily, under these conditions. Research on these strategies for motivating students suggests that, after the rewards are withdrawn, or sometimes if they don't increase, interest in the activity or subject declines (Lepper & Greene, 1975).

There is also the danger that when children are learning in order to get rewards, they tend to look for shortcuts to performance, even when they may sacrifice learning to do so (Condry & Chambers, 1978). Suppose an elementary teacher tells his students to write a story that is two pages in length, and that, when they are finished, they may do something more interesting. Many of his students may write whatever comes into their heads, using large printing and maybe leaving extra space, in order to fulfill the requirement and get the reward. It is unlikely that these students are thinking about improving their writing skills, making their story interesting, or trying out new ways of expression.

Task Involvement   In contrast to the scenario above, if the teacher indicates that his students are writing stories that will be "published" and shared with a real audience (an audience other than the teacher), and if he emphasizes improving so that the stories will be more interesting to the audience, his students are more likely to see the connection between effort, writing instruction, and a finished product to be proud of. When students are primarily task involved, younger and older children, as well as adults, see effort as the means to increased ability. What's more, students who are focused on learning and improving are more likely to persist in the face of difficulty, and more likely to pursue a subject after the course

[2]Garrison Keillor, "A Prairie Home Companion," Minnesota Public Radio and Public Radio International.

or unit is finished. A number of researchers have found that, unlike most of the other reasons for learning, students who are task involved tend to use and value learning strategies that lead to deeper understanding and improved retention of information (for a review, see Nolen, 1996). When task-involved students judge their own ability, they use *self-referenced comparisons;* they compare their current performance with what they used to be able to do, rather than to the performances of other students. This means that *all* students in a class can consider themselves able to learn and improve as long as they put forth effort. Even low-ability students can focus on their own increasing skill, rather than becoming discouraged that they are not as able as others (Nicholls, 1989, 1992).

As you can see, the choice of motivating strategies is not simple. Students will bring their own general tendencies toward various goals with them to the classroom. Although children will always be the ones to select their goals, a teacher can influence the kind of goals they adopt. Finally, different kinds of strategies for motivating students in the classroom can have unintended side effects, particularly for low-achieving students. Research suggests that task involvement has the most positive effects for the majority of students in a class, but creating a task-involved classroom requires looking closely at connections among instruction, assessment, feedback, and grading.

Creating a Task-Involving Classroom

In most school settings, the teachers set the daily curriculum and decide what students need to learn. Teachers usually set the standards for achievement and have the final say in assessing and evaluating student work. Students must do what teachers tell them to do in order to get high scores and good grades. This description of the typical classroom has the characteristics of an extrinsically motivating setting.

As children move through the school years, there are also increasing amounts of social-comparative information, such as tracking students into high- and low-achieving groups or offering honors classes for some but not for others (Eccles, et al., 1993). An emphasis on social comparison creates an ego-involving setting. When teachers emphasize relative ability by posting grades or using norm-referenced grading, students may have a harder time staying task focused. How does a teacher work against these institutional norms to establish a classroom where task involvement is encouraged?

Pushing Against the Norms   Clues about how to create a task-involving classroom may be found by looking at the characteristics of task-involved people. Task-involved individuals do not tend to measure their performance against the performances of others. When people are task involved, they strive for improvement in meaningful skills and knowledge—to become their own personal best (Nicholls, 1989). Instruction that leads to this improvement, as well as assessment and feedback that show students their progress toward competence, supports this goal.

Setting clear and meaningful standards for quality of work or levels of competence helps students judge their own work. These strategies also provide a framework for useful feedback and help students concentrate on their improvement. They know that their score or grade will reflect their level of competence and will not be compromised by that very able student who "warps the curve." Helping students track their increasing competence through the use of portfolios of work over time can provide powerful evidence of individual growth (see Chapter 10).

Matching Instruction and Assessment   As children move through the school system, they increasingly realize that teachers' assessments and grading policies are the best indicators of what is valued in that classroom. When there is a mismatch between teaching and assessment, the teacher-student relationship can be damaged by mistrust. In addition, if teachers use open-ended learning activities where students have a lot of choice in what they do, but grades depend on scores on multiple-choice tests with single correct answers, students soon begin to lose interest in the learning activities. Why get excited about something that doesn't "count"? In the example of the two middle school math classes given in Chapter 1, Mr. Hanks's students had clearly determined that the tests reflected the teacher's definition of achievement and that the hands-on activities didn't help them meet that expectation. In longitudinal studies of high school students, those who perceived their teachers' goals as increasing student understanding and independent thinking were more likely to be task involved at the end of the school year. One study showed that, in classrooms where students perceived their teachers this way, the students were also more likely to have higher scores on a districtwide, curriculum linked achievement test (Nolen, 2003).

Focus on Meaningful Work   In this book we argue against viewing assessment as something separate from instruction. When teachers select learning activities, they are also selecting opportunities for both informal and formal assessment. If students see the work as meaningful, they will be more likely to stay task involved. But what is meaningful work? Does it depend solely on individual interest in the topic or task? Even when students are not initially interested in a task, are there ways to make it more meaningful?

Level of Challenge   Task-involved people, left to their own devices, tend to select work that is moderately difficult: challenging, but not overwhelming (Nicholls, 1984, 1989). Such work provides the greatest opportunity for learning and improvement. Providing work at an appropriate level of challenge for all students can be difficult, given the wide range of ability levels most teachers find in their classes. Work that allows for multiple approaches or solution paths allows students to choose a path that makes sense to them, is more interesting, and increases their feelings of autonomy, a powerful motivator (Ryan & Deci, 2000). Providing varied levels of scaffolding for students is another way to adjust difficulty levels to meet the needs of individual students. Scaffolding can be provided by other students as well as the teacher. Elizabeth Cohen, in her book, *Designing Groupwork,* describes ways to set up small groups so that each student can make a meaningful contribution to group success (Cohen, 1986) regardless of her ability.

Interesting Work   Interesting work does more than increase student motivation; it can actually result in better performances (Hidi & Anderson, 1992; Schiefele, 1990). Work that allows students some choice in strategy, topic, or product inherently capitalizes on individual students' interests. However, there are other characteristics that make work interesting. Related to the notion of moderate challenge, the work should be complex enough to engage the student in higher-order thinking, but should not be needlessly confusing. When directions or scoring rubrics are unclear, students waste time wondering and worrying about what they are supposed to be doing, or worse, spend time doing something that is not at all what the teacher intended. Finally, if students are to be given some choice in their work, their ideas should be shared and taken seriously by the teacher and peers.

For example, surveying her high school integrated math/physics students, Ms. Simpson asked them to recall a time when they felt truly absorbed in a task in their classroom. Several students mentioned a task where they were given a Dixie cup and asked to figure out the volume without directly measuring it. A student described the experience of following her own ideas this way: "Since we chose such an [unconventional] method and my group was very determined to finish our project before the end of the period, we were 'in the flow.'"

The following is another example from a second-grade classroom. Ms. Jackson, a veteran primary-level teacher, is well-known for the quality of her math instruction. Working with a large group, she warmed up by asking students to show her various numbers using Unifix® cubes. By having everyone do all the problems, she gave all of her students a chance to practice. Students with different levels of sophistication in math chose different strategies, all visible to the teacher via the manipulatives. By allowing for multiple solution paths, Ms. Jackson took the first step toward task-involving instruction. At the same time, she was able to assess where her students were in their understanding of numbers. She could see who still counted up one cube at a time and who put groups of 10 cubes together, showing an understanding of place value. Then she asked students to share their solutions, exposing the less-skilled to new ways of thinking about numbers, while validating their own solutions.

Support for Autonomy   A large body of research shows that there are strong positive relationships among feelings of autonomy, relatedness, and intrinsic motivation (Deci & Ryan, 1985, 1987; Ryan, Koestner, & Deci, 1991). Even though most students find that teachers and other adults determine what, when, and how they will learn, and usually have the final say in whether they have learned, there are ways to support student autonomy. Helping students feel autonomous demonstrates a level of trust in their ability to choose wisely, which can improve the relationship between student and teacher.

Making Choices   Although scaffolding may be necessary, there are many ways to teach children how to work autonomously from kindergarten on up. In the examples described in Research Sidebar 3.2, students learn to choose what work to do (within appropriate limits), how to do it, and when to do it. Besides increasing motivation to learn, these practices prepare students for learning in settings such as college where they must take responsibility for their own work. There are other strategies for teaching autonomy. One of the most powerful is self-evaluation.

Self-Evaluation   Children and teens can be taught the standards for judging their own and others' work. If these standards reflect the way such work is judged in the real world, students will not only increase their autonomy, but also learn these aspects of the structure of the disciplines. Successful teachers of writing workshops teach students how to read and give feedback to their fellow writers. In learning these skills, they become more aware of the quality of their own writing and more able to set their own goals for improvement. Leslie Herrenkohl and her teacher colleagues (Herrenkohl, Palincsar, DeWater, & Kawasaki, 1999) reported teaching fifth-graders how to evaluate each others' hypotheses and theories

---

Research Sidebar 3.2:

SUPPORTING AUTONOMY BY TEACHING CHILDREN TO MAKE WISE CHOICES

Students in Jody Walmsley's kindergarten class spend the first half of the morning on literacy. When they are done with their morning journal writing, they may choose an activity to do until group reading instruction begins. Jody scaffolds their choices by limiting their choices to literacy activities during this time, ensuring that they continue to get literacy practice while allowing them to choose activities that interest them.

Primary students in Joshua Brewer's mixed-age, urban classroom learn to schedule their own independent work. Each student has a list of work to accomplish by the end of the week. Mr. Brewer asks them to schedule their time so that all the work gets accomplished, but children can decide whether to work on one task each day, or to work some on one task and switch to another. At the end of each day, they discuss that day's schedule and evaluate their scheduling strategies. Students decide whether to change strategies depending on their progress toward their weekly goals. For example, a student might have begun with a favorite activity only to find that he was unable to switch to a less-interesting activity when he had planned. That student could decide to start with the less-interesting activity and use the favored one as a reward for finishing. Mr. Brewer reports that, in the space of a week, most students master the task of scheduling—completing their work with more regularity and fewer reminders from the teacher to stay on task.

A sixth-grade teacher in one of Susan's classes found that her suburban, middle-class students were finding it impossible to complete their math homework. She tried extrinsic rewards, threats, pleading, to no avail. We discussed increasing the amount of autonomy her students had about what and how much practice they needed. She presented the following system to her students, emphasizing the relationship among doing homework, learning math, and getting better test scores. The teacher made up a notebook of all the worksheets she would normally give as homework, ordered by operation and difficulty and numbered. Each Friday, her students would put in an "order" for a minimum of five pages of their choice. She found that most students ordered one or two very easy worksheets, then picked three or four that related to the math they were currently learning. In fact, the same worksheets they would have been assigned under the old system. The teacher found that almost every student regularly turned in their five pages, and many asked for extra worksheets because "they weren't sure they really understood it yet."

---

by teaching specific critical roles for use by audience members. With scaffolding and practice, these students learned the difference between an observation and a theory—something that much older students have difficulty grasping.

They also learned something about the "syntactic structure" of science: that a theory had to be supported by evidence in a way that was convincing to the scientific community (Schwab, 1978; Wilson, Shulman, & Richert, 1987). A theory wasn't "right" just because the teacher said so or because it matched an explanation in a textbook. When students learn to self-evaluate, they are able to take charge of their own learning and work in partnership with their teachers toward mutually acceptable learning goals.

FEEDBACK AND TASK INVOLVEMENT

Students love positive feedback. Everyone likes to hear that they have been doing good work, working hard, and making progress. However, positive feedback that does not help students improve can backfire. When students realize that the feedback they receive does not help them see what they have done well or what they need to do to improve, they can begin to devalue it.

Students who have difficulty learning need to hear feedback that questions neither their effort nor their ability. Instead of encouraging these students to simply work harder, it is more effective to attribute their difficulties to possibly faulty learning strategies or lack of experience with new skills. This acknowledges their effort without leading to an inference of low ability (Clifford, 1986). In fact, low performance often *is* due to use of a faulty learning strategy and finding a better one will make learning easier. To be useful, the feedback needs to target specific strengths and weaknesses (Sommers, 1982; Wilson & Wineburg, 1993). In addition, however, the student must feel that there is a chance for meaningful improvement. Feedback that is given on an assignment that can't be revised or that is not clearly and specifically related to future work is unlikely to be seen as useful by the student. Policies that give only partial credit for revisions are little better than no-revision policies—why should the student spend time and effort revising something if the best he can hope for is a slight improvement in the grade, despite the fact that he now understands how to do the work? When the final score on an assignment does not reflect the student's actual skill or knowledge, a high score becomes an unattainable reward—meaningless in terms of the student's own learning.

In short, you can use a variety of strategies to increase students' intrinsic motivation to do well on their work and to learn. When you assess students' accomplishments in terms of standards rather than in comparison to other students' work, ensure a good fit between what is taught and what is assessed, help students develop autonomy by giving students opportunities to focus on their own interests in their work, and provide effective feedback on their performances, students can learn to be more task involved. In this way, assessments become tools for teaching as well as for assessing students' knowledge and skills. In what follows, we elaborate on the critical role of feedback in the assessment and instructional process.

Providing Effective Feedback

Consider learning to swim. At one level, you receive feedback from the activity itself. This type of feedback is called *autotelic* feedback (Csikszentmihalyi & Larson, 1984). If you can move from one place to another without touching the bottom, you are swimming. If you can do so with less and less effort, you are improving. The more knowledge you have of swimming, the more likely you will be to learn from this kind of feedback.

However, an instructor can provide feedback based on her greater knowledge of swimming technique and the fact that she can see what you are doing. This feedback can help you progress faster than you might on your own as you learn from the feedback. It can also have an effect on your motivation. If the instructor points out specific strengths in your current technique, and at the same time communicates confidence in your ability to improve by suggesting specific changes, you are more likely to feel encouraged and will be more likely to continue to work on your swimming. If the instructor *only* points out your weaknesses, or fails to provide suggestions for improvement, you may become discouraged and quit (Butler, 1987).

Providing effective feedback is one of the teacher's most powerful tools. Feedback on student work is an opportunity for individualized or group instruction based on students' current level of expertise or understanding. It can be part of the scaffolding provided as students learn to judge the quality of their own and others' work. It can be a regular part of the process students use to develop valued work. As with any other aspect of teaching, providing effective feedback requires attention to the learning goals and objectives, consideration of the characteristics of the students, and ongoing reflection on and revision of feedback strategies. Without thinking carefully about it, teachers are likely to give the kind of feedback they had as students. In all likelihood, the kinds of positive feedback teachers received as students came in the form of high scores on tests and performances, individual instances of "good work" or "nicely done," and high grades. Negative feedback typically came in the form of red ink on papers. Unfortunately, the red marks were probably edits on their work or vague comments such as "not clear" or "confusing" or other "rubber stamp" comments that could be used interchangeably from paper to paper (Sommers, 1982). In contrast, teachers can carefully structure feedback to move students from less skillful to more skillful performances—from less effective to more effective learning strategies.

Feedback can be nonverbal, oral, or written. Naturally, younger students will receive mostly oral feedback on their work, whereas intermediate, middle, and high school students will typically receive more written feedback. However, all students look for feedback from their teachers and interpret teachers' words and actions as information about their performance, whether or not the teachers are aware of it. A frown while looking at a student's drawing is feedback just as much as the words used to comment on the work. Asking a student a question in class and then doing something else while he is answering is also feedback; it tells the student that his response is not really important. Feedback is any action on the part of the teacher that provides information to his or her students about how the teacher views their ideas or actions. To be effective, feedback must be focused, timely, consistent with the demands of the assignment, and most important, must lead to opportunities for improvement based on the feedback.

Feedback That Is Clear and Focused on Important Aspects of the Task, the Subject, or Learning Process   Look at the example of feedback that Mr. Barnes and Ms. Kelsey gave to the same history essay in Figure 3–1. In the example, both teachers gave the essay the same letter grade. However, their summary comments were quite different, as were their ideas about how to help the student to improve. Notice the lack of specificity in Mr. Barnes's summary comments. How much information does he provide to the student to help him revise or to do better on the next essay? Compare his summary comment with Ms. Kelsey's. If you had been Mr. Barnes's student, would you have a clear idea of what strategies to use to improve your essay? In her feedback, Ms. Kelsey points out characteristics of the essay that are consistent with good historical writing, helping the student to recognize them in his own writing. Her criticisms are framed with the notion of historical argument; she uses feedback to teach the student how historians make their cases for a particular interpretation of historical events. She is leading toward a prepared performance of a set of skills employed in the real world.

One of the most important uses of feedback is to guide students toward learning to produce high-quality work. By developing rubrics based on appropriate standards for authentic work in the discipline, and keying feedback to the rubric, you have an excellent opportunity to teach students what makes work in that discipline "good" in the real world. As students internalize these standards, they will become more able to evaluate their own and others' work, instead of depending solely on you to judge quality.

A high school student wrote the following essay for a study on teacher assessment (Wilson & Wineburg, 1993). Students with a range of ability answered the prompt, forming a set of papers representative of a typical junior history class. Then the teachers participating in the study individually marked the essays and talked with the researchers about their feedback. Here is how two teachers from this study marked the same essay. The two teachers had similar backgrounds. Both had master's degrees in history from well-respected universities. Both had attended well-respected teacher education programs, though Ms. Kelsey had less experience in the classroom than had Mr. Barnes. As you can see from the grades given, both teachers saw room for improvement.

Student #7
U.S. History

When the French and Indian war ended, British expected Americans to help them pay back there wear debts. That would be a reasonable request if the war was fought for the colonies, but it was fought for English imperialism so you can't blame them for not wanting to pay. The taxes were just the start of the slow turn toward rebellion another factor was when parliament decided to forbid the colonial government to make any more money. Specie became scarcer than ever, and a lot of merchants were pushed into a "two way squeeze" and faced bankruptcy.

If I had the choice between being loyal, or rebelling and having something to eat, I know what my choice would be. The colonist who were really loyal never did rebel, and 1/3 support the revolution.

The main thing that turned most people was the amount of propaganda, speeches from people like Patrick Henry, and organizations like the "Association." After the Boston Massacer and the issuing of the Intolerable acts, people were convinced there was a conspiracy in the royal government to extinguish America's liberties.

I think a lot of people also just were going with the flow, or were being pressured by the Sons of Liberty. Merchants who didn't go along with boycotts often became the victims of mob violence. Overall though, people were sick of getting overtaxed, and walked on and decided let's do something about it.

Barnes's Summary Comment:

—your topic sentence is weak

—more factual detail would improve your essay

—note spelling and grammar corrections

C–

****

Kelsey's Summary Comment:

—The greatest strength of this essay is its outstanding effort to grapple thoughtfully with the questions, why did the colonists rebel? Keep thinking personally, "What if I were here?" It is a great place to start.

—To make the essay *work,* however, you need to refine your organization strategies significantly. Remember that your reader is basically ignorant, so you need to express your view as clearly as you can. Try to form your ideas form the beginning to the middle and then an end.

In the beginning, tell what side you're on: What made the colonists rebel—money, propaganda, conformity?

In the middle, justify your view. What factors support your idea and will convince your reader?

In the end, remind your reader again about your point of view.

Go back & revise & hand this in again!

Wilson, S. M., & Wineburg, S. S. (1993). Wrinkles in time and place: Using performance assessments to understand the knowledge of history teachers (p. 739). *AERJ, 30,* 729–769. Copyright 1993 by the American Educational Research Association, reproduced with permission from the publisher.

Figure 3–1
Examples of Teacher Feedback on a High School Social Studies Essay

Feedback That Is Consistent With Performance Expectations   To be sure that feedback is consistent with the assignments and with the learning objectives, you must begin by having identified learning objectives, a clear idea about the assessment tools and processes that will help you know whether students are achieving those targets, and appropriate standards for student work for the unit. The kind of feedback you give can then be grounded in the targets and standards and provide students with information about how well they are approaching them.

For example, Mr. Johnson directed groups to prepare an oral report on the geography of a country of the group's choice. His main goal was to increase his fourth-grade students' understanding of the relationship between geography and population growth, and his scoring rubric gave more weight to content than to the form of presentation. When students practiced their presentations, however, he gave feedback only on their presentation skills: visual aids, shared presentation, clear voices that could be heard throughout the room. Because of the feedback given during their rehearsals, students decided that it was more important to put in extra time on producing visual aids than to do more research. The group presentations were polished, but Mr. Johnson was disappointed. Most groups described the geography in detail, but barely touched on the relationship between geography and population. The students, in turn, were disappointed in their grades. What happened?

Throughout their rehearsals, Mr. Johnson was observing and assessing students' work. He had identified learning targets; however, as he observed, he was focused on the quality of students' presentation skills. Although these may have been important for him to teach, and he may need to add them to the learning goals and objectives he sets for his fifth-graders, the feedback Mr. Johnson gave was too limited. It did not help students focus their attention on what he felt were the most important aspects of the project. Students, in turn, didn't learn the central concept he was trying to teach, or at least they produced no evidence of that learning.

Clear, encouraging, and useful feedback supports students' task involvement by helping them master the skills and knowledge you have determined are most important.[3] When students misread or cannot determine the expectations, they must rely on their own hunches. This can lead to higher levels of performance for more assertive students—those likely to ask for additional help or input—and lower levels of performance from students who do not "just know" the expectations.

Timely Feedback   The longer the time between student work and feedback, the less effective it will be. This is especially true for younger children. Elementary teachers often spend much of their time walking around the classroom while the children are working, assessing their progress and giving immediate guidance and feedback. This practice is important for teachers of older students as well. Giving timely feedback requires that teachers avoid becoming buried in their students' work. When a student turns in an assignment, but doesn't receive feedback for days (for young children) or weeks (for older students), most of the opportunity for instructing through feedback is lost. Children have moved on, often with undetected, faulty

---

[3]In our own teaching, we often use actual words and phrases from the scoring rubrics when we give written feedback to our students. If students have weaknesses, we ask questions, provide suggestions, and ask for clarifications that can help in revisions or in future performances. We try to make sure that the feedback is based in the targets and standards as put forth in the rubrics, but we also tailor the feedback to the individual student's performance.

understanding, and they may have a difficult time remembering the specifics of their work. Reasonable turnaround times also demonstrate that you value students' efforts and their work enough to provide timely and therefore potentially useful feedback. To improve turnaround times, you will need to make certain that the volume of student work is manageable. Focusing on a few central performances, skills, and concepts can lessen the number of assignments, giving you more time to provide feedback on important work. You may also decide that not every assignment needs feedback (e.g., assignments done for practice).

Opportunities for Improvement and Relevance to the Student

Providing students with an opportunity to revise and improve their work is a good way of encouraging them to pay attention to your careful feedback. Students often have a difficult time seeing how the feedback given on one assignment relates to the next assignment, and so may not see teacher comments as useful for anything except justifying a grade. However, if the feedback can be put to good use on the current work, the student has a chance (and likely has more motivation) to put the suggestions into practice and compare the revised work with the original. This immediate practice with new strategies or skills helps students store them in memory with multiple associations; this makes them easier to transfer to similar situations later (Bransford, Brown, & Cocking, 2000).

Fewer assignments with opportunities for teacher or peer feedback during the preparation are ways to naturally incorporate a feedback loop or two into your students' work. Music teachers do this as a regular part of instruction. Each rehearsal is an opportunity to teach through the use of feedback on performance. By the time students reach the final performance before an audience, their work has been honed and polished. Any complex project or paper that is worked on over a period of time can have built-in feedback points (outlines, drafts, preliminary proposals for solving a problem, etc.). Students can learn many important skills and deepen their own knowledge if given opportunities to improve work already in a draft form—provided the feedback is focused on what the teacher wants students to learn.

Feedback can support task involvement by emphasizing continued learning and improvement. However, feedback is interpreted based on students' perceptions of its function in the classroom ecology. If students believe that the teacher is interested in their learning, improvement, and independent thinking, they are more likely to take suggestions for improvement in that spirit. If they see the teacher as controlling, as wanting students to adopt his or her standards and ideas without question, if they see the score on an assignment as a means of exercising power, then they are more likely to resent feedback as just one more example of social control. This is especially true of middle and high school students, who are beginning to develop their sense of autonomy and independent self (Eccles et al., 1993).

Students' interpretation or valuing of feedback also depends on their attitude toward the class or subject matter. If they see the learning activities and assignments as busy work, as irrelevant to their lives or interests, or as hoops to jump through in order to be passed to the next level, they will treat the feedback they received accordingly. Although this is not always under the teacher's control, much can be done to build assignments around real-world issues that are of interest to students. We will discuss this in later chapters of this book.

Praise Versus Encouragement

The wording of feedback can also make a difference in how students interpret teacher comments. For example, "This is great! You are really good at math," labels a child as having a permanent characteristic. This is what Rudolf Dreikurs and his colleagues (Dreikurs, Grunwald, & Pepper, 1982) called "praise," and what elementary students in one study (Thorkildsen et al., 1994) found generally unfair. This may not be as much of an issue for young children who can't compare themselves to group ability norms, but by third or fourth grade, this kind of praise can make the child being praised and children around her uncomfortable. Try saying "I like the way Jennifer is working hard!" to a room full of fifth-graders and watch many of them (including Jennifer) squirm.

On the other hand, Dreikurs suggests that "encouragement" focuses on the work or effort of the student. It is not necessary to wait until the child has done something praiseworthy to give encouragement; it can be given in process. "You are really concentrating on this, and I see that you are making progress. Let me know if you want help with different ways to tackle these kinds of problems," is an example of encouragement. So is, "This is a very interesting solution! I hadn't thought of that one, but it makes sense to me."

Wording can also reduce the discouraging effects of stereotype threat on motivation. Many stereotypes hold that certain groups tend to perform more poorly than others on academic assessments. For example, there are stereotypes that girls don't perform as well as boys in math; European males are not as good at math as Asian boys; African American students perform more poorly than European Americans on standardized tests, and the like. Claude Steele and his colleagues have found that invoking these stereotypes ("stereotype threat") can actually depress performance on assessments for the stereotyped group if they believe the assessment could be biased. When a white teacher gives critical feedback "across the racial divide," minority students may presume that the teacher is biased. Cohen, Steele, and Ross (1999) conducted two experiments on the effects of feedback on students' motivation to revise an essay. They found that African American students were less likely to trust feedback from a white evaluator, and less likely to spend time revising, than their ability-matched white peers. However, when the feedback was accompanied by information that high standards were used *and* by an assurance of the student's capacity to reach those standards, both groups responded positively to feedback. African American students were more motivated than any other group in the study to do additional revision, even though this was not for a class for credit.

Feedback has a crucial role in the assessment and instruction process. It goes hand in hand with well-prepared instruction and well-developed assessments to help students reach the goals we set for them. In the example of Mr. Barnes and Ms. Kelsey, we noted that the feedback that Ms. Kelsey gave was the kind of feedback that would help the student develop work that was like that of historians. Teachers' choices of what to attend to when giving feedback are the ways they tell students what they value in student work and what they want students to learn. Therefore, the assessments themselves can affect students—not only in their conceptions of themselves as learners and in their motivation to focus on their own learning, but also in their conceptions of the disciplines represented in the subject area.

EFFECTS OF ASSESSMENTS ON STUDENTS' CONCEPTIONS OF THE DISCIPLINES

One very powerful way to increase students' motivation and their task involvement is to give them work that is authentic and to help them learn how to do that work well. Assessment tools send powerful messages to students about what we value. They also help students form their ideas about the nature of the subject disciplines—What is science? How is history created? What is a good poem? How is our knowledge of biology organized? Wineburg (1991) compared the ways that bright Advanced Placement history students and professional historians used primary and secondary source material to reach conclusions about a historical event. After years of instruction in school, the high school students had learned that textbooks were the most trustworthy sources, to be consulted when one wants to know what "really happened" in history. They did not examine the purposes or perspectives of the various writers, including eyewitness accounts, contemporary accounts of the event, an excerpt from a novel about the event, and a standard high school textbook. On the other hand, the historians looked first at the author of a document, thought about what his purposes might have been, and how the author's relationship to the event might influence his perspective. They rated the textbook account as the *least* trustworthy, lower than even the historical novel. Clearly the very able high school students had no notion of how real historians work with documents to draw conclusions about what happened at a certain point in history. They believed that there was a single historical truth, and that these facts were to be found in their most oft-used sources, their history textbooks.

How did they come to this way of thinking about history? In most history classes, the textbook is the only source consulted. Assessments tend to be focused on comprehending and remembering important information from the textbook. Students may never be asked to construct a historical argument based on primary sources. Research projects often start with the "truth" as presented in the textbook, and students look for supporting (but not disconfirming) evidence in other secondary sources (other textbooks, encyclopedias, the Internet). Students are often taught simplistic ways of evaluating the information they find in other sources and may even learn to distrust those accounts that contradict the account presented in their history texts.

This doesn't have to be the case. High school students, and even middle school students, can learn to be critical readers of historical accounts, to look for both confirming and disconfirming evidence for their ideas about what happened during an event, and to take into account the probable perspectives of the authors of these sources. Similarly, students of all ages can learn to develop hypotheses and theories about everyday phenomena and to know the difference between the two (Herrenkohl et al., 1999). Upper elementary levels to high school students can also learn how to design systematic studies to investigate their hypotheses; they can learn how to examine differences in the results across a classroom of students investigating the same question. Students of literature can learn how to construct a sound argument for their own interpretation of a poem and can learn to thoughtfully compare their interpretation with those of professional literary critics. However, students can achieve these goals only if they are given learning activities and assessments that require them to think in these ways, supported by the feedback and other scaffolding provided by the teacher.

Teachers teach students how to conceptualize the various disciplines through the work they have students do in class, for homework, and on tests. As Schwab (1978) says,

> . . . methods are rarely if ever neutral. On the contrary, the means we use color and modify the ends we actually achieve through them. *How* we teach will determine *what* our students learn. If a structure of teaching and learning is alien to the structure of what we propose to teach, the outcome will inevitably be a corruption of that content. And we will know that it is. (p. 242)

SUMMARY

Each choice that we make as teachers can encourage our students to become more or less involved in their own learning. Assessment tools and processes have tremendous power in the lives of students—both in the ways that students come to judge their own abilities and in the ways that they communicate what is important to know and be able to do. Assessments serve a critical educational function. Given that students generally learn more and remain in school longer when they are task involved and intrinsically motivated, educators have a responsibility to create learning communities that foster these conditions. Through your assessment and instructional choices, through the types of feedback you give, and through the connections you make between what students learn and the world beyond school, you can create learning communities that benefit your students and that make your teaching experience positive.

REFERENCES

Anderson, R. C. (1977). The notion of schemata and the educational enterprise: General discussion of the conference. In R. C. Anderson, R. J. Spiro, & W. E. Montague (Eds.), *Schooling and the acquisition of knowledge* (pp. 415–431). Hillsdale, NJ: Erlbaum.

Bransford, J. D., Brown, A. L., & Cocking, R. R. (Eds.). (2000). *How people learn: Brain, mind, experience, and school* (expanded ed.). Washington, DC: National Academy Press.

Butler, R. (1987). Task-involving and ego-involving properties of evaluation: Effects of different feedback conditions on motivational perceptions, interest, and performance. *Journal of Educational Psychology, 79*(4), 474–482.

Cameron, J., & Pierce, W. D. (1994). Reinforcement, reward, and intrinsic motivation: A meta-analysis. *Review of Educational Research, 64*(3), 363–423.

Cameron, J., & Pierce, W. D. (1996). The debate about rewards and intrinsic motivation: Protests and accusations do not alter the results. *Review of Educational Research, 66*(1), 39–51.

Clifford, M. M. (1986). The comparative effects of strategy and effort attributions. *British Journal of Educational Psychology, 56*(1), 75–83.

Cohen, E. (1986). *Designing groupwork: strategies for the heterogeneous classroom.* New York: Teachers College Press.

Cohen, G. L., Steele, C. M., & Ross, L. D. (1999). The mentor's dilemma: Providing critical feedback across the racial divide. *Personality and Social Psychology Bulletin, 25*(10), 1302–1318.

Condry, J., & Chambers, J. (1978). Intrinsic motivation and the process of learning. In M. R. Lepper & D. Greene (Eds.), *The hidden costs of reward: New perspectives in the psychology of human motivation* (pp. 61–84). Hillsdale, NJ: Erlbaum.

Covington, M. V., & Omelich, C. L. (1979). Effort: The double-edged sword in school achievement. *Journal of Educational Psychology, 71,* 169–182.

Csikszentmihalyi, M., & Larson, R. (1984). *Being adolescent: Conflict and growth in the teenage years.* New York: Basic Books.

Deci, E. (1978). Applications of research on the effects of rewards. In M. R. Lepper & D. Greene (Ed.), *The hidden costs of reward: New perspectives on the psychology of human motivation* (pp. 193–203): Lawrence Erlbaum.

Deci, E. L., & Ryan, R. M. (1985). *Intrinsic motivation and self-determination in human behavior.* New York: Plenum.

Deci, E. L., & Ryan, R. M. (1987). The support of autonomy and the control of behavior. *Journal of Personality and Social Psychology, 53,* 1024–1037.

Dreikurs, R., Grunwald, B., & Pepper, F. C. (1982). *Maintaining sanity in the classroom: Classroom management techniques.* New York: Harper & Row.

Eccles, J. S., Midgley, C., Wigfield, A., Buchanan, C. M., Reuman, D., Flanagan, C., et al. (1993). Development during adolescence: The impact of stage-environment fit on young adolescents' experiences in schools and in families. *American Psychologist, 48*(2), 90–101.

Elliot, A., & Harackiewicz, J. M. (1996). Approach and avoidance achievement goals and intrinsic motivation: A mediational analysis. *Journal of Personality and Social Psychology, 70*(3), 461–475.

Herrenkohl, L. R., Palincsar, A. S., DeWater, L. S., & Kawasaki, K. (1999). Developing scientific communities in classrooms: A sociocognitive approach. *Journal of the Learning Sciences, 8*(3–4), 451–493.

Hidi, S., & Anderson, V. (1992). Situational interest and its impact on reading and expository writing. In S. H. K. A. Renninger, & A. Krapp (Eds.), *The role of interest in learning and development* (pp. 215–238). Hillsdale, NJ: Erlbaum.

Kohn, A. (1996). By all available means: Cameron and Pierce's defense of extrinsic motivators. *Review of Educational Research, 66*(1), 1–4.

Lepper, M. R., & Greene, D. (1975). Turning play into work: Effects of adult surveillance and extrinsic rewards on children's intrinsic motivation. *Journal of Personality and Social Psychology, 31,* 479–486.

Lepper, M. R., Keavney, M., & Drake, M. (1996). Intrinsic motivation and extrinsic rewards: A commentary on Cameron and Pierce's meta-analysis. *Review of Educational Research, 66*(1), 5–32.

Nicholls, J. G. (1984). Conceptions of ability and achievement motivation. In R. E. Ames & C. Ames (Eds.), *Research on motivation in education, Vol. 1: Student motivation.* New York: Academic Press.

Nicholls, J. G. (1989). *The competitive ethos and democratic education.* Cambridge, MA: Harvard University Press.

Nicholls, J. G. (1992). The general and the specific in the development of expression of achievement motivation. In G. C. Roberts (Ed.), *Motivation in sport and exercise* (pp. 31–56). Champaign: Human Kinetics Books.

Nicholls, J. G., Cobb, P., Yackel, E., Wood, T., & Wheatley, G. (1990). Students' theories about mathematics and their mathematical knowledge: Multiple dimensions of assessment. In G. Kulm (Ed.), *Assessing higher-order thinking in mathematics.* Washington: American Association for the Advancement of Science.

Nicholls, J. G., & Miller, A. T. (1983). The differentiation of the concepts of difficulty and ability. *Child Development, 54,* 951–959.

Nicholls, J. G., & Miller, A. T. (1984). Reasoning about the ability of self and others: A developmental study. *Child Development, 55*(1990–99).

Nicholls, J. G., Patashnick, M., & Nolen, S. B. (1985). Adolescents' theories of education. *Journal of Educational Psychology, 77,* 683–692.

Nolen, S. B. (1988). Reasons for studying: Motivational orientations and study strategies. *Cognition and Instruction, 5*(4), 269–287.

Nolen, S. B. (1996). Why study? How reasons for learning influence strategy selection. *Educational Psychology Review, 8*(4), 335–355.

Nolen, S. B. (2001). Constructing literacy in the kindergarten: Task structure, collaboration and motivation. *Cognition & Instruction, 19,* 95–142.

Nolen, S. B. (2003). Learning environment, achievement, and motivation in high school science. *Journal of Research in Science Teaching, 40,* 347–368.

Park, J., & Nolen, S. B. (1998, April). *The structure of motivational orientations among Korean and American adolescents.* Paper presented at the annual meeting of the American Educational Research Association, San Diego.

Ryan, R. M., & Deci, E. L. (1996). When paradigms clash: Comments on Cameron and Pierce's claim that rewards do not undermine intrinsic motivation. *Review of Educational Research, 66*(1), 33–38.

Ryan, R. M., & Deci, E. L. (2000). Self-determination theory and the facilitation of intrinsic motivation, social development, and well-being. *American Psychologist, 55*(1), 68–78.

Ryan, R. M., Koestner, R., & Deci, E. L. (1991). Ego-involved persistence: When free-choice behavior is not intrinsically motivated. *Motivation and Emotion, 15,* 185–205.

Schiefele, U. (1990). The influence of topic interest, prior knowledge, and cognitive capabilities on text comprehension. In J. M. Pieters, K. Breuer, & P. R. J. Simons (Ed.), *Learning Environments* (pp. 323–337). New York: Springer-Verlag.

Schwab, J. J. (1978). *Science, curriculum, and liberal education.* Chicago: University of Chicago Press.

Sommers, N. (1982). Responding to student writing. *College Composition and Communication, 33,* 148–156.

Thorkildsen, T. A., & Nicholls, J. G. (1998). Fifth-graders' achievement orientations and beliefs: Individual and classroom differences. *Journal of Educational Psychology, 90*(2), 179–201.

Thorkildsen, T. A., Nolen, S. B., & Fournier, J. (1994). What is fair? Children's critiques of practices that influence motivation. *Journal of Educational Psychology, 86,* 475–486.

Urdan, T. C., & Maehr, M. L. (1995). Beyond a two-goal theory of motivation and achievement: A case for social goals. *Review of Educational Research, 65*(3), 213–244.

Wentzel, K. R. (1999). Social-motivational processes and interpersonal relationships: Implications for understanding motivation at school. *Journal of Educational Psychology, 91*(1), 76–97.

Wilson, S. M., Shulman, L. S., & Richert, A. E. (1987). '150 different ways' of knowing: Representations of knowledge in teaching. In J. Calderhead (Ed.), *Exploring teacher thinking* (pp. 104–124). Sussex, England: Holt, Rinehart & Winston.

Wilson, S. M., & Wineburg, S. S. (1993). Wrinkles in time and place: Using performance assessments to understand the knowledge of history teachers. *AERJ, 30,* 729–769.

Wineburg, S. S. (1991). Historical problem solving: A study of the cognitive processes used in the evaluation of documentary and pictorial evidence. *Journal of Educational Psychology, 83*(1), 73–87.

ASSESSMENT OF VALUED PERFORMANCES

In this chapter, we elaborate on our definition of performance assessments as assessments of authentic work, including both live performances and the products of student work. Assessment of live performances—including speeches, instrumental solos, the process of scientific investigations, and debates—involves assessments of work that must be assessed during direct observation of students as they engage in the performance itself. Assessment of performance products—including written reports, short stories, poems, three-dimensional mathematical models, computer Web sites, and paintings—are assessments of the concrete outcomes of students' efforts. Here we describe how to identify ways for students to engage in work that is authentic to subject disciplines and to life beyond school—from small performances to multistage work prepared over a longer term. By creating opportunities for your students to do authentic work, you will help them see how the knowledge and skills they learn in school apply to real work. This way of thinking is helpful in planning instruction as well as assessments, and also in helping students develop the schema they need to make sense of what you teach.

We divide this chapter into nine major parts. In the first part, we explore the idea of authenticity in student work. Next, we discuss the differences among authentic performances at the primary level, the intermediate level, and the secondary level. In the third section, we explain prepared accomplishments and exit performances. Next, we describe how to develop an effective performance-based assessment, including both directions and scoring rules. In the next two sections, we discuss how to give appropriate feedback to students' work and the motivational issues in performance assessments. In section seven, we discuss adapting authentic work—either to make connections between subjects or to make accommodations and modifications for students with diverse needs. In the eighth section, we discuss how to use individually administered performance assessments to assess students' skills and strategies. In the final section, we look back at the ideas in this chapter through the lenses of reliability and validity.

AUTHENTICITY IN STUDENT WORK

What is authentic work? The answer to this question depends on the age of the student, the subject area, and the definition of *authentic*. We define authentic work as work that has relevance in the world beyond school. Some authentic work is scholarly work. Table 4–1 gives examples of scholarly work characteristic of different disciplines. These are types of work that students can do during the course of instruction. In each of these cases, the people doing the scholarly work are engaged in a process through which they apply a set of discipline-based strategies to ideas and evidence to explain or make sense of some phenomenon, event, or object.

A second type of authentic work is found in the everyday world. Table 4–2 gives some examples of authentic work in everyday life that students can do through the course of instruction. Needless to say, the number and variety of authentic performances is infinite. Teachers can select from these ideas (and many more) the types of work to teach in a

Table 4–1
Examples of scholarly disciplines and the authentic work of the scholars.

Scholars	Authentic Work
Research Science	Conduct experiments and investigations in order to create new knowledge about the natural world (e.g., the systems of the human body, the causes of diseases such as cancer, the structures and functions of the atom, and the composition of the universe).
Historians	Collect documents and artifacts from a period in time and write histories that explain the events and people of an era from the historian's point of view.
Mathematicians	Use procedures and algorithms to develop and examine mathematical models of real events or mathematical phenomena in number systems.
Literary scholars	Examine the relationship between the works of authors and their personal, historical, and social contexts; between themes in different works of a single author; or between different authors who write about the same themes.
Political scientists	Use documents and artifacts to examine the relationships between the values and choices of people and the course of political events or how political events influence the values and choices of a people.

Table 4–2
Examples of authentic work in everyday life and work.

Individuals	Authentic Work
Artists	Use the elements of design, form, and medium to create unique works of visual or performing arts.
Composers and musicians	Use patterns and progressions, melodies and harmonies to create or perform anything from a new song to a symphony.
Readers	Read to obtain useful information, to entertain themselves, and to complete tasks.
Economists, accountants, and everyday citizens	Work with numbers to create budgets, predict financial outcomes, and account for money.
Homemakers and chefs	Combine chemistry and mathematics to create tasty meals for families or customers.
Politicians	Examine claims and evidence to make informed decisions about whether to vote for a bill, support a foreign policy, or fund a particular initiative.
Citizens	Read the paper, watch TV news, and/or listen to radio news to make informed decisions about voter initiatives, to decide whether to vote for a certain candidate, to determine whether they will write letters to the newspaper or their legislators to express opinions on current issues, etc.

performance-based classroom. Authentic work has value because it helps students to make sense of the knowledge and skills teachers want them to learn.[1]

The challenge to the classroom teacher is to select work that is authentic, that is worth doing, and that incorporates the knowledge and skills you teach. Some textbooks present skills in isolation as if the skills or knowledge are the goals of instruction. We believe that authentic work should be the goal and that skills are best taught in the context of that authentic work (Wiggins, 1992). However, selecting the authentic work begins by answering three questions: What knowledge and skills do you want your students to learn? What performances are worth learning? What is appropriate for the developmental level of your students?

WORK WORTH DOING: DEVELOPMENTAL ISSUES IN PERFORMANCE ASSESSMENT

Authentic Work at the Primary Level

Children in kindergarten through second or third grade are faced with the greatest challenges in learning. They enter school with bright eyes, ready to learn to read, write, and do mathematics. Yet, for many, reading, writing, and computing are arduous tasks. Decoding letters, combining letters and sounds, seeing word patterns, recognizing the structures of print, as well as other essential elements of reading may not be fun—in the same way that practicing scales or chords are less enjoyable than playing songs on the piano. Still, the goal of reading instruction is not mastery of individual skills—the goal is reading fluently and understanding what is read.

Although writing letters, words, and sentences are important writing skills, children can communicate ideas in writing long before they know how to spell all the words they know and long before they have completely mastered the grammar of English. Similarly, children use money, measure time, and divide cookies evenly among friends long before they understand how to manipulate number symbols in addition, subtraction, multiplication, or division exercises. Finally, children come to school with varying degrees of skill in working with others. Learning how to be an effective member of a classroom or group takes time and practice. Children have many social skills to master in these first few years of schooling.

---

[1]One example of this link between skills and authentic performance we experienced as mothers. When our daughters were learning how to play soccer, they began with biweekly practice before the first scheduled game. The girls practiced passing balls, blocking balls, throwing the ball from the sideline, making long kicks, and scrimmaging in small teams. Then the girls played their first competitive games. They were confused. There were new children to play with. Yet they were expected to play competitively and win a game—to ignore their natural curiosity about the other children and simply play to win. They were to apply the skills they had been practicing and play nonstop until the end of a certain period of time. It took two or three games before the girls began to understand how to put all of the parts together—social as well as psychomotor—and truly play a competitive game. As they developed a better understanding of the purpose of the skill drills, they practiced harder and worked harder during scrimmages. In short, once they understood how to apply the skills, the skills themselves took on a new level of importance. If the girls had only practiced the skills, never having a chance to play a game, few would have stayed beyond the first few weeks of the soccer season.

In short, the most authentic tasks for primary level students are to read and understand what they read, to communicate through writing, to use mathematics in everyday situations, to explore the concrete world around them through their senses, and to become good citizens in their school community. The most important performance-based assessments of primary level children will be assessments of their reading skills, strategies, and comprehension; their application of addition, subtraction, and possibly multiplication to familiar situations; their communication through writing; their observations and thinking about events and objects in their world; and their work with others.

Authentic Work at the Intermediate Level

As children go from third through sixth grade, they begin to master some of the primary level tasks and can expand their expertise. Students at this age are curious about the natural world, about people, about body systems, about light bulbs and electricity. Their innate interest in order and classification leads them to collect stamps, coins, gum wrappers, insects, stickers, bottle caps, and soda pop cans. In short, making sense of the concrete world fascinates them. If they have developed basic reading, writing, mathematics, observational, and social skills and have some control over those skills,[2] then they are ready for authentic work that goes beyond school. With guidance, they can develop researchable questions and design scientific investigations about salmon, cars, simple machines, tide pools and other phenomena. They can use mathematics to design models of houses, playgrounds, and neighborhoods, to create artistic designs, to create a model economy in the classroom, or to organize the results of a survey. They can conduct social science research on local heroes, the origins of their hometown, or attitudes of the people in their neighborhood toward some local issue. They can write persuasive letters to the editor of the newspaper about issues they care about or participate in a debate about a controversial local issue using arguments and evidence. They can read books that have interesting characters and plots, and examine how the author created the characters or the plot. They can write their own stories with interesting characters and plots, using descriptive language and vivid settings. They can further develop their social skills by working together to accomplish a wide range of important work. They can make decisions and examine the outcomes of those decisions.

Some students at the intermediate level may still be struggling with basic reading, writing, and mathematics skills. However, most struggling students will still have the level of interest and cognitive development needed to engage in authentic work. They may need more support in obtaining information through text or in producing written performances. It may take them longer to complete authentic work; they may need more opportunities for feedback and revision. Yet, they can still benefit from engagement in authentic work as long as the work is *concrete* and *familiar*.

The most authentic performances for intermediate level students are those that give them opportunities to use their basic skills and more advanced knowledge and skills to do what most adults do—engage in the real activities of life and research. Work that is readily accessible to them will capture their attention and help them more readily understand the goals of the performance. As intermediate teachers plan for authentic performances in their

[2]When children have control over basic skills, they use reading strategies purposefully; know when to invent spelling and when to look for words in the dictionary; understand how our whole number system works, what number symbols mean, and when to add, subtract, multiply and divide; know how to carefully observe and record their observations; and can be intentional in their social behaviors.

teaching, they need look no further than what the parents of their students do for a living. In all likelihood, many interesting kinds of work are represented by the parents of children in the average classroom—ranging from homemaking to bus driving to electrical wiring to scientific research. Leisure activities are also candidates for authentic work—reading and talking about books, discussing characters or the plot in a TV show, mastering the physics of riding a bicycle, examining the interplay among organisms in the natural world around a campsite or playground. Therefore, the most powerful performance-based assessments of intermediate level children will be assessments of their use of basic knowledge and skills as well as subject specific knowledge and skills (e.g., scientific principles and processes, mathematical problem-solving and reasoning skills, literary analysis skills, social science research skills) as they engage in tasks that are similar to the work and play of adults in the real world.

One of the concerns often raised by highly creative teachers is whether focusing on familiar contexts that are easy to experience directly might limit elementary students' imagination, creativity, or thinking. Recently, for example, an elementary teacher told us that elementary students should be able to construct a three-dimensional model of the earth, moon, and sun relationship and to show or describe how this relationship creates night and day, phases of the moon, and seasons. Certainly, teachers can show students how to create a model of some phenomenon they are unlikely to ever see directly. In fact, current models of the earth, moon, and sun relationship have come from indirect observations. However, the question is not whether students can *reproduce* a model that teachers want them to know; but whether the students *understand* the model they have created. Identifying familiar contexts for student performances need not create limits. These are simply ways to start when conceiving what authentic work will be sensible to *all* students. If some students can *easily* engage in authentic work related to the concrete world, and are ready to expand into a more abstract world, they should be encouraged to do so. Probably the best way to know whether students are ready to deal with abstract ideas is to give them opportunities to generalize the abstractions to a new situation. If students can transfer an abstract concept or principle to new events and phenomena, then they probably understand that concept or principle. However, if students can only recreate a model demonstrated by the teacher or restate an abstract idea presented by the teacher, then they may not be ready for ideas that are that abstract, at least in that domain (Gobbo & Chi, 1986).

Concrete concepts and principles are not necessarily low-level ones. For example, the method for scientific classification of plants and animals began as a very concrete process. Yet, learning how to organize objects, events, and living things on the basis of physical properties and characteristics requires fairly sophisticated thinking. Using techniques of description, action, and dialogue to create a character in a story is also fairly sophisticated. So, selecting authentic work that is familiar and concrete does not mean that the work will be boring or will limit the possibilities of imagination.

Authentic Work at the Secondary Level

As students move through the secondary grades, teachers face many challenges. Students at this age are still curious about the natural world, simple machines, and body systems. They are also moving in an intensely social world at home and school; social issues command their attention. They are more sensitive to issues of justice, fairness, democratic ideals, the notion of laws, and other abstract social ideas. They become increasingly aware of and able to imagine a world far away and very different from their own. Some have traveled a long way to come to their community. Some have traveled widely with their parents. Others have never left their own community. They are generally more able to express themselves in writing and most have mastered basic reading skills and strategies. As mathematics becomes more abstract, many turn away, believing that they cannot understand the world of symbol manipulation (Schoenfeld, 1988). Some have already decided that school is the wrong place for them and are simply waiting until they can leave.

It is during these years that students increase their ability to take on ideas and engage in work they have never seen or have encountered only through movies or books. Authentic performances might include new types of work or more sophisticated versions of performances done during elementary school—acting in a play; participating in a simulated United Nations (UN) assembly or reenacting a constitutional convention; designing and conducting a scientific investigation or experiment; writing a history of a person, a place, or its people; participating in a civic action campaign to educate the public about some social or environmental issue; writing a play or a book of poetry. The list goes on and on.

Given that some students at the secondary level believe school has no value for them, authentic work that connects them to the real world becomes even more crucial. If they are to leave school understanding their roles as literate participants in a democratic society, they must have experiences that empower them to participate in events that affect their lives while they are still in school.

The most authentic performances for secondary level students are those that empower them and help them understand their roles in world beyond school. Work that is linked to issues of justice and equity will attract all students—even many who are disaffected. Scholarly activities will attract those who want to be prepared for college. Work that helps students answer their own questions and construct new knowledge for themselves will appeal to all students and empower them to independently find answers to their own questions beyond school.

As secondary teachers plan for authentic performances in their teaching, they need to consider the compelling concerns for adolescents. What compels one student may differ from what compels others; therefore, teachers must examine the curriculum standards and identify diverse performances that demonstrate the same knowledge and skills. A constitutional convention, a simulated World Trade Organization (WTO) conference, a simulated United Nations assembly, and a debate over a civil rights bill may all require the same research skills, the same skill in predicting the consequences of public policy, and the same applications of skills in debate and compromise. Yet a particular context may appeal more to one student than another. What is critical is that, as students engage in diverse performances, they demonstrate similar knowledge and skills so that teachers can be confident that students are all meeting the same standards.

In planning authentic work, teachers can consider the subject they teach and identify authentic work related to their own discipline. Alternately, they can work with teachers in other disciplines to identify authentic work that requires knowledge and skills across several disciplines.

In summary, the most powerful performance-based assessments of secondary level students will be assessments of how they apply their knowledge and skills to solve real problems, to develop new knowledge, and to address social and political issues that are relevant to their lives. For junior high and middle school students, these performances should be directly relevant to their own present and future lives, although the performances may include examination of abstract notions such as justice and equity. For high school students, the performances can be related to concepts, people, and issues far from their own experiences. Regardless of the level, however, the work must have value to the students.

PREPARED ACCOMPLISHMENTS AND EXIT PERFORMANCES

Although not all authentic performances are highly polished,[3] two special categories of authentic work described in performance assessment literature strongly affect how teachers teach: prepared accomplishments (Wolf, 1991) and exit performances (Wiggins, 1992). Prepared accomplishments are performances for which students have an opportunity to work through several stages to develop a prepared, final performance. Exit performances are performances that schools determine should be accomplished by *all* students by the time they exit a certain level of schooling. Exit performances are generally prepared accomplishments, but not all prepared accomplishments become exit performances. In contrast, impromptu performances mirror on-the-spot performances expected in life beyond school.

Prepared Accomplishments

Examples of prepared accomplishments that are common in many schools are listed in Table 4–3. The best performances for this type of assessment are those that will have *real audiences*. Here we define a real audience as individuals or groups beyond the teacher/ evaluator. Real audiences can be peers, the principal, parents at a science fair, judges at a math Olympiad, newspaper editors, younger children, a group of architects designing a remodel of the school, members of the school board, representatives to local government— even the President of the United States. As students participate in young author conferences, broadcast school news by closed-circuit TV, scientifically investigate community environmental issues, propose landscape designs using math skills, and perform in music concerts, they develop a sense that prepared work is the work that is seen by real audiences. Because the performance is not just prepared for a grade, but may have a real impact on the audience, students tend to value these performances more than those done only for the teacher.[4]

---

[3]For example, an impromptu speech or conversation in a foreign language may require different strategies and skills than rehearsed and polished speeches or plays in a foreign language.

[4]Susan unwittingly created a "real audience" for her high school students at the Oregon School for the Deaf, where she taught English and reading. Her students had grown up writing "weekend stories," mostly pieces of "creative" writing that were to be used as writing samples to assess whether students were applying the skills of the curriculum to their own writing. These generally took the form of, "I went home this weekend. I watched TV. I slept a lot. We went to eat pizza." Boring, boring, boring. Susan banned writing about weekend activities, and provided a box of "story starters," openings or plot beginnings that the students could choose to use to develop their own stories. At the same time, she provided an Authors' Board, and invited students to publish stories for their peers to read and enjoy (the decision whether or not to publish was left up to the student). The work did not have to be completely polished; deaf students often have great difficulty learning the nuances of English syntax, and to require perfection may have dampened the enthusiasm of those at the low end of English proficiency. The point was to get real feedback on their ideas from the people that counted most in their lives: their peers. It was a great hit. Students typically posted their work anonymously, so part of the attraction was reading the story and trying to figure out who wrote it. But there was evident delight in the stories themselves. Upon entering the classroom, most students made a beeline for the board to see if there were any new stories. Suddenly these students, who had spent their school lives writing only for their teachers, had a real audience. And it was a powerful motivating experience.

Table 4–3
Examples of prepared accomplishments.

Subject Area	Examples of Exit Performances
Science	• Conduct and present the report of a science investigation. • Write a paper to explain and justify the classification of a newly discovered organism. • Investigate and write a paper on the genotype of a simple organism. • Produce a videotape demonstrating Newton's laws.
Social Studies	• Create a travel brochure for a city, state, or nation. • Write a biography of a historical or contemporary figure. • Write a letter to the editor about an issue of concern. • Write a historical narrative. • Write a research paper on a historical question, issue, or problem. • Write a research paper on the geographic and political factors affecting human migration during a time in history. • Conduct research for and participate in a debate or forum.
Language Arts	• Write a short story. • Write an autobiographical account. • Write a poem. • Act in a play. • Write a play. • Write a literary analysis of a work of fiction. • Write a comparative analysis of two authors or two works by the same author.
Mathematics	• Design, create a floor plan, and build a three-dimensional model (to scale) of a building, a playground, etc. • Write a computer program for a common algorithm (e.g., mean, circumference of a circle, area of a circle, or area of any polygon). • Create a two- or three-dimensional design that fits given mathematical criteria. • Generate a question, collect data to answer the question, organize it graphically, and summarize the results.
Music	• Perform a vocal or instrumental solo. • Perform in a band or orchestra concert. • Write a simple composition.
Arts	• Paint a landscape, still life, or abstract painting. • Create a piece of pottery. • Sculpt or construct an abstract or representative sculpture. • Organize a collection of photographs around a theme. • Create a composite that communicates a theme (e.g., the tension between nature and technology). • Design the cover for a compact disk. • Design clothing for comfortable travel.

The degree to which children are expected to take all their work to a polished level depends on the age of the students. If primary level children must revise every performance and make it a polished piece, they could be derailed in their interest and joy of learning and discovery. Teachers and primary students might choose one or two important pieces per year as the focus for prepared accomplishments. For intermediate and middle school students, many performances merit sufficient attention to take students through various stages of revision to a prepared accomplishment. When students have some choice over which performances they polish, they are more likely to select those that hold some personal interest or an appropriate level of challenge, and thus to maintain motivation over the longer term. (We revisit this notion when we discuss portfolio assessment in Chapter 10.)

Prepared accomplishments for high school students could require multiple related performances leading up to a culminating event. For example, students may be expected to do a formal research paper on the social, political, and economic issues of a country and then represent the country at a simulated UN assembly or WTO conference. Students may be expected to do a background research paper on the studies already conducted related to their research question before designing and conducting their own scientific investigation. Students may grapple with solving and presenting solutions to smaller mathematical problems (abstract or concrete) before taking on the larger, more complex real-world problem that involves integration across mathematical domains (geometry, algebra, statistics, etc.). They may conduct and present research on a period in history prior to writing a play or short story about that period. These related performances could go through rounds of feedback and revision as students learn a genre of writing; the skills of argument, negotiation, and compromise; the skills of systematic inquiry and scientific communication; the skills and strategies used to solve mathematical problems; and the conventions for communicating those solutions. Therefore, the notion of a prepared accomplishment at the high school level could mean that students have opportunities to engage in several preparatory performances and receive feedback on those performances prior to some culminating event—a more complex, public performance.

Obviously, prepared accomplishments require students to integrate and apply a wide range of knowledge and skills to complete the performance. They help students understand the actions that take a performance from initial, rough versions to final performances that meet performance standards. They also give students an opportunity to learn while completing the performance. For example, when students conduct research and write reports, they learn and demonstrate research skills, organizational skills, data analysis skills, and writing skills, as well as developing their understanding of the content of the research. As students take initial observations or notes from the research and move them into an outline or a visual organizer (e.g., a web or table), they learn and demonstrate what they know about putting ideas together in a coherent way. As they take data and put it into charts, tables, graphs, or coherent paragraphs, they learn and demonstrate their skills in analyzing and organizing data and in using data to communicate information. As they write drafts, revise the drafts to clarify and elaborate on ideas, and check for spelling and grammar, they learn and demonstrate their skills in clearly communicating their knowledge and ideas. As they prepare their final drafts for publication and presentation to an audience, they learn and demonstrate their skills in presenting ideas in ways that are appealing to themselves and to their audience. Hence, taking one performance from the initial idea to a prepared accomplishment helps students practice diverse skills that are valuable for a lifetime. At the same time, students show what they have learned through the process. Teachers can use mini-lessons and other timely instructional activities to teach students what they need to know to move to the next stage of a prepared accomplishment. Instruction, learning, and assessment are integrated through the performance.

Exit Performances

As mentioned above, the major difference between a prepared accomplishment and an exit performance is whether the performance is established as an exit requirement for specific levels of schooling. An exit performance for the elementary level might be a short story, a science investigation, a research report, an artistic performance, or some other prepared accomplishment. In essence, an exit performance is a prepared accomplishment that is expected of *all* students by a certain grade level.

Establishing exit performances is one way to set standards for schools and to focus instruction on valued performances. When schools within a district work together to identify exit performances across school levels, the performance definitions can help guide a curriculum sequence so that all students develop the knowledge and skills needed to successfully complete the exit performances. The exit performances require more sophisticated skills at each developmental level.

For example, Figure 4–1 presents descriptions of exit performances in informational writing for students in the primary and intermediate school levels. Teachers in an urban elementary school wrote these two descriptions when they decided to focus on writing in their school. They had been struggling with state and district learning standards and needed concrete descriptions to guide their teaching. As can be seen, the primary level performance focuses mostly on the surface features of informational writing: coherent ideas, complete sentences, accurate spelling, and simple punctuation. The content of the paragraphs is not given any attention except that it needs to be coherent. For the intermediate level, the teachers increased the demands. The informational writing was to be a report including factual content, several coherent paragraphs organized into a unified paper, varied sentence structures, and a range of punctuation marks. Using these two descriptions, the teachers were able to focus their writing instruction so that students could work toward these desired performances as well as working toward the achievement of state curriculum standards in writing. Figure 4–2 presents descriptions of exit performances in scientific inquiry for elementary, middle school, and high school levels. Middle and high school teachers in the same urban district wrote these descriptions to guide their teaching, to focus performance assessments, and to create an articulated science inquiry curriculum for students. As with the descriptions in Figure 4–1, the expectations for the performances increase from one level to the next.

When exit performances are established, teachers are more likely to incorporate similar authentic work into their classroom activities on a regular basis; they are more likely to teach the knowledge and skills in state or district curriculum standards in a way that makes sense to the students. In short, they are more likely to teach the whole as well as the parts (Voorhees, 1994).

There are two types of exit performances: integrative performances and discipline specific performances. Schools might have one exit performance that integrates all subject areas (say a science or social studies investigation of the interplay between an environmental issue and the people in the community, including background text-based research, data collection, data analysis, written and oral presentation). Two integrative exit performances that are common in middle schools and junior high schools are "Project Reach" and the "I Search." For both of these performances, students examine their own histories and that of

---

Primary Benchmark Performance Description

By the end of primary level, the student will be able to write an organized informational paragraph that is composed of a group of sentences with one coherent thought. The paragraph will be written in complete sentences with accurate capitalization, basic punctuation, and spelling.

Intermediate Benchmark Performance Description

By the end of the intermediate level, the student will be able to write multiparagraph reports. Each paragraph will have a central thought that is unified into a greater whole with factual information that supports the paragraph topic. Topic areas for the report may be supplied by the teacher. The writing will be in complete sentences, in the student's own words, using correct capitalization and spelling, and including a range of punctuation marks.

Figure 4–1
Benchmark Performances in Writing to Inform

their families by integrating historical and geographical knowledge as well as reading and research skills. Students present their research findings using the conventions of writing and the social sciences.

Senior projects, a specific type of exit performance, are generally defined by students with guidance from teachers or other adults. Students work through a performance that links their knowledge and skills to the world beyond school—possibly to their planned profession.

Alternately, schools might require one or more exit performance in each subject area or discipline. For example, one state in the Pacific Northwest requires students to prepare at least three written works to earn their Certificate of Initial Mastery—one persuasive piece, one informational piece, and one narrative piece. Some schools and districts require students to participate in national social studies performances, such as Project Citizen, History Day, Model UN, and We the People, prior to graduation from middle or high school. Discipline-specific exit performances are often scholarly work that is characteristic of a given discipline,[5] whereas integrative performances are generally more connected to the world beyond school.

The major difference in the demands of exit performances as students move up the grade levels is the amount of guidance and support students receive as they complete the performance. At lower grade levels, the specific characteristics of exit performances are generally school- or teacher-defined and teacher guided. As students mature, teachers move further into the background and students make more decisions about the directions of their exit performances.

Until now, we have discussed the idea of authentic work as if this is a straightforward task of deciding what work is real and meaningful and then helping students accomplish the work. We described the benefits of engaging students in authentic work, from writing a haiku to carrying out a community project. Nearly any subject area, not to mention life itself, has authentic or meaningful work; therefore, identifying authentic work is not very difficult. New teachers can begin with some of the examples listed in table 4–3. As teachers

---

[5]Examples of discipline-specific exit performances are creating a work of art; creating a mathematical model; investigating the geographic, economic, and social factors that influence political conflicts; reading and reporting on a particular work of literature; writing a story or poem; and conducting and reporting on a science investigation.

Elementary Benchmark Performance Description

By the end of elementary school, students will observe a discrete event related to a given research question and describe the event using sensory observations and metric measurement. Research questions and events will be related to a scientific concept under study. They will present their observations using graphs and charts. Graphs and charts will be clearly labeled (including data source, units of measurement, and scale) and informatively titled. Students will interpret the data from their observations and offer explanations of the results as they relate to the scientific concept.

Middle School Level Benchmark Performance Description

By the end of middle school, students will complete a scientific investigation that includes:

- Formulating a hypothesis on a given problem or question
- Designing and setting up an experiment
- Conducting the experiment and collecting relevant data
- Displaying data in graphs, charts, and tables
- Analyzing data
- Formulating a conclusion
- Presenting findings to peers

Graphs, tables, and charts will be clearly labeled (including data source, units of measurement, and scale) and informatively titled. Reports will summarize results and show their relationship to hypothesis and/or relevant scientific concepts.

High School Level Benchmark Performance Description

By the end of high school, students will complete a scientific investigation that includes:

- Identifying a research problem or question
- Researching literature related to the problem or question, using at least three sources
- Formulating a hypothesis on the problem or question based on the literature
- Designing and setting up an investigation
- Collecting relevant data
- Displaying data in graphs, charts, and tables
- Analyzing data
- Formulating a conclusion
- Reviewing the experimental procedures and making suggestions for improvement and/or future research
- Presenting findings in standard scientific report format

Graphs, tables, and charts will be clearly labeled (including data source, units of measurement, and scale) and informatively titled. Reports will summarize results and show their relationship to hypothesis and/or relevant scientific concepts.

Figure 4–2
Benchmark Performances in Scientific Inquiry

grow in their profession, they will recognize even more types of work that are authentic to the disciplines they teach and relevant to their particular students.

In the previous pages we have addressed students' developmental needs and their interests as we suggested the kinds of authentic work that might become central to your instruction. The most important message is that students need to understand the purpose of work and see its relevance to their own lives. If students are personally engaged in the work, they will try harder, learn more, and do better work. The sooner students engage in real work, the better their understanding of why they need to learn what is taught in school.

We want to give a few words of caution, however. There are barriers to engaging students in authentic performances. One barrier is that students may resist hard work if prior expectations for their performances have been low. Another barrier is that teacher-defined performances may represent teachers' interests and experiences more than the interests and experiences of their students. To address the first barrier, teachers must build trust and feelings of confidence among their students from the beginning of the year and guide their students toward successful completion of challenging work. It is critical that students personally experience the sense of mastery that comes from doing well. This is a significant departure from the idea of 'coverage' wherein teachers move from topic to topic whether or not students learned the previous content and/or skills. To address the second caution, it is important that teachers begin with their own ideas for authentic work related to their disciplines and expand or adjust those ideas as they get to know their students and the work of the disciplines better.

Once schools, teachers, and/or students decide what the authentic performances are to be accomplished, the next stage in performance assessment development is to write directions for students and to develop rules for scoring student work. Writing directions and scoring rules is a very logical process. In our own teaching, we find that when directions and scoring rules are clear to students, the quality of student work far surpasses our expectations.

DEVELOPING PERFORMANCE-BASED ASSESSMENTS

Although many students engage in authentic work during instructional activities, the difference between a performance and a performance *assessment* is whether the performance goes beyond a set of directions (expectations) to guide all students' work and includes a set of rules for scoring (evaluating) the performance and/or the product of the performance. When performance is the centerpiece of instruction, rather than an add-on (for example, writing poetry as a daily part of students' work in a poetry unit or solving nonroutine or complex problems as daily part of instruction in linear equations), the performances chosen for assessment will not stand apart from the regular work of the classroom. Students will be prepared to engage in these authentic assessments—especially when the expectations for the quality and characteristics of the work (performance criteria) are known and practiced. This leads to the most important key to successful performances and performance assessment: clear expectations and directions to students.

Describing the Performance

Before setting performance expectations or writing directions for students, it is very useful to describe, in writing, a well-executed performance. It is best to describe any of the following that are relevant:

- ◆ The *steps* students must take to *prepare* the performance
- ◆ The *processes* (e.g., writing process, scientific process, thinking processes) they must *complete* to do the performance well
- ◆ What the *final performance* will probably look like, including how students will show what they have learned

---

Persuasive Letter to the Editor

Preparation: The student will identify and research a local controversial issue that is important to her or him. Research may include local newspaper stories, TV news stories, radio news stories, voter pamphlets, church bulletins, newsletters, interviews with parents/guardians and other neighborhood friends, and other local sources.

Steps in the performance:

1. The student will draft a letter to the editor including his/her position on the issue, two or more arguments to support her/his position, at least one example or piece of evidence to support each argument, and a conclusion calling for agreement with the position or a call for action.

2. The student will revise the draft to improve organization, elaborate as needed on ideas, delete unnecessary information, improve sentence structure and variety, and add persuasive language (appeals to conscious, language that communicates urgency, etc.).

3. The student will edit the work to improve spelling, grammar, punctuation, and capitalization.

Final performance: The final performance will be in letter format with an appropriate greeting and closing, including all improvements in persuasive language and form, organization, content and ideas, sentence structure, and writing conventions, using language that is appropriate for a newspaper editor.

Figure 4–3
Persuasive Writing Performance Description

Figures 4–3 and 4–4 give descriptions of two different performances: Mr. Keaton's sixth-grade persuasive writing performance (in this case, a letter to the editor) and Ms. McKinley's seventh-grade problem-solving performance (in this case, a statistics problem). As can be seen, each description includes not only the final performance, but also the steps the student will go through to complete the performance. The descriptions show that these can be authentic performances and could become prepared accomplishments. The steps in each performance provide multiple opportunities for teachers to collect stages of the students' work, assess, provide feedback, and ask for additional thinking, evidence, descriptions, and so forth.

Ensuring the Match Between the Performance and Learning Goals and Objectives

Once the performance is described, teachers should return to the learning objectives they have established for their classes (knowledge as well as skills) and identify which ones are to be demonstrated (and possibly learned) through the performance. If the performance demands knowledge and skills for which there is no planned instruction, the teacher must decide how to add the knowledge and skills to the lesson plans. If the performance does not require students to use some of the knowledge and skills that are valued and targeted by instruction, the performance assessment may be revised to include demonstration of addi-

---

Solving a Mathematical Problem With Statistics

Preparation: The student will research a community problem. Research sources may include local newspaper stories, TV news stories, radio news stories, the Internet, and interviews with parents/guardians and other neighborhood friends. The student will clarify the problem, generate one important question to be answered through analysis of data related to the problem, and identify the mathematical demands of the problem.

Steps in the performance:

1. The student will extract relevant data from the problem situation and organize the data in a way that helps her/him to develop a solution. Organization may be in a table, chart, graph, Venn diagram, or other logical organization for the data set.

2. The student will select appropriate tools and apply reasonable strategies and procedures to the problem.

3. The student will adjust tools, strategies, and/or procedures as needed when initial attempts are unsuccessful or ineffective.

4. The students will develop a viable solution to the problem by answering the question(s).

Final performance: The final performance will be a statement of the problem, the question(s) to be answered, a description (verbal, numerical, or pictorial) of the strategies used to solve the problem, and a discussion of the proposed answers to the question(s) including data organized in an appropriate way; references to specific data that support claims, inferences, and interpretations; and a discussion of how the data support claims, inferences, and interpretations. All descriptions, equations, tables, graphs, charts, or other graphic displays will be legible, be clearly labeled, and include appropriate scales or measurements.

Figure 4–4
Problem-Solving Performance Description

tional learning objectives. Or, if these omitted learning objectives are not appropriately demonstrated via the performance, additional assessments will be needed.

Figures 4–5a and 4–6a give learning goals and objectives defined by Mr. Keaton for his sixth-graders and Ms. McKinley for her seventh-graders. A careful comparison of the performances in Figures 4–3 and 4–4 and the learning objectives in Figures 4–5 and 4–6 shows that, in each case, some expectations in the performance descriptions are not included in the learning objectives for the class.

In the letter to the editor, the description of the performance indicates that the students are to "conduct research," use "persuasive language," and write in "letter form." None of these expectations matches the learning objectives for Mr. Keaton's class. Mr. Keaton must decide whether to add learning objectives for these expectations (all of which would likely relate to state or district curriculum standards) along with appropriate instruction. Otherwise, he must eliminate these as expectations. If Mr. Keaton plans to keep the expectations, a new goal and some new learning objectives would need to be added for the class. In addition, Mr. Keaton would have to plan some instructional activities that help students develop the relevant knowledge and skills. Figure 4–5b shows a new learning objective that Mr. Keaton could add to his language arts Goal 1.

Goal 1:   Students will learn strategies and techniques of persuasive writing.

Objective 1.1   Students will learn how to develop a position on a controversial issue.

Objective 1.2   Students will learn how to support positions with arguments.

Objective 1.3   Students will learn to support arguments with facts, data, valid examples, and other evidence.

Objective 1.4   Students will learn how to organize persuasive writing to build a strong case for their positions.

Goal 2:   Students will learn how to edit their own and others' writing.

Objective 2.1   Students will learn how to check written work for punctuation and capitalization.

Objective 2.2   Students will learn how to check written sentences for structure, tense, gender, and case.

Objective 2.3   Students will learn how to use tools to check the spelling of unfamiliar words.

Goal 3:   Students will learn how to effectively revise their own and others' writing.

Objective 3.1   Students will learn how to improve the organization of ideas in written text.

Objective 3.2   Students will learn to select ideas and examples that support the major thesis of a written work and eliminate ideas and examples that do not support the major thesis.

Objective 3.3   Students will learn how to improve sentence structure and variety in written work.

Objective 3.4   Students will learn how to use tools to improve word choices.

Objective 3.5   Students will learn how to adjust language and voice for audience and writing purpose.

Goal 4:   Students will learn how to prepare their own writing for publication.

Objective 4.1   Students will learn how to set margins and page layouts for different purposes of writing.

Objective 4.2   Students will learn how to select fonts for different purposes of writing.

Objective 4.3   Students will learn to use careful reading to proof final versions of written work.

Figure 4–5a
Goals and Objectives for Writing

GOAL 1: *Students will learn strategies and techniques of persuasive writing.*
Objective 1.5   Students will learn how to use language to create a sense of urgency, appeal to conscience, strengthen a case, and encourage action.

Figure 4–5b
Objective to Add to Goal 1 for Mr. Keaton's Class

The next box shows a new learning objective that he could add to his language arts Goal 4.

GOAL 4: *Students will learn how to prepare their own writing for publication.*

Objective 4.4   Students will learn to use an appropriate format for different purposes; for example, letters, essays, and research reports.

Figure 4–5c
Objective Added to Goal 4 for Mr. Keaton's Class

Adding these two learning objectives and developing instructional activities that helped students achieve these expectations in their letters would address two requirements for the letter to the editor. Figure 4–5d shows a fifth goal that Mr. Keaton could add to his language arts goals and objectives if he plans to have students conduct research on an issue prior to writing a persuasive peice about the issue.

GOAL 5: *Students will learn how to conduct systematic research related to their own research questions.*

Objective 5.1   Students will learn how to develop researchable questions.

Objective 5.2   Students will learn how to locate sources that are useful in answering their questions.

Objective 5.3   Students will learn how to take notes from text-based and video-based sources as well as from personal interviews.

Objective 5.4   Students will learn how to extract useful information from a variety of sources.

Objective 5.5   Students will learn how to detect bias and prejudice in different sources.

Figure 4–5d
Objective That Could be Added to Mr. Keaton's Language Arts Goals

As you can see, there are many skills relevant to research that would have to be taught so that students can complete the performance described by Mr. Keaton. All of these learning objectives have value for the students. The letter to the editor becomes a rich performance through which Mr. Keaton can teach persuasive writing, research skills, revision skills, editing skills, and publishing skills. If Mr. Keaton knows that students achieved some of these learning objectives during the fifth grade, the lessons related these learning objectives may be brief reminders to students. However, if Mr. Keaton has many students who have not learned how to do research, revise their work, edit their work, write persuasively, and publish their work, he will need to develop lessons for each of these goals and include specific activities that help students develop skills related to each learning objective. You may think that these are a lot of learning objectives to teach just so that students can write a letter to the editor. Although this may be the case, it is also possible that Mr. Keaton will have students do other research-related writing and publish their writing in various ways throughout the school year. Hence, adding these objectives to his year long goals and objectives only helps to ensure that students have the knowledge and skills needed to complete any performances that require research, a writing process, and publication of their writing.

A close look at Ms. McKinley's learning goals and objectives shows that there is a good match between her learning objectives and the expectations for a well-developed performance. However, although students' achievement of the mathematical communication, problem-

---

Goal 1: Students will learn how to solve open-ended mathematical problems.

Objective 1.1 Students will learn to clarify the problem to be solved including question(s) to be answered and information relevant to answering the question(s).

Objective 1.2 Students will learn a variety of ways to organize mathematical information to assist in problem solving (for example, sorting, graphing, ranking, and placing information in tables, charts, organized lists, and tree diagrams).

Objective 1.3 Students will learn to select or develop useful strategies for solving a problem.

Objective 1.4 Students will learn to adjust strategies and/or abandon unproductive strategies if necessary.

Objective 1.5 Students will learn to use tools and resources to help them approach, understand, and solve problems.

Objective 1.6 Students will learn to persist with problems until they find a satisfactory solution.

Objective 1.7 Students will learn to check solutions against their initial understanding of a problem.

Goal 2: Students will learn how to communicate mathematical ideas and results using language, graphics, equations, and symbols appropriate to the audience and purpose.

Objective 2.1 Students will learn to describe mathematical procedures, information, and results using words, diagrams, graphs, pictures, equations, and symbols.

Objective 2.2 Students will learn to label all mathematical information and representations with informative and appropriate titles, categories, scales, and measurement units.

Objective 2.3 Students will learn to select an appropriate scale to represent data in an unbiased way.

Goal 3: Students will learn statistical concepts, procedures, and representations used to analyze and represent data.

Objective 3.1 Students will learn how to organize data into tables and graphs (line graphs, bar graphs).

Objective 3.2 Students will learn how to compute the median and mode for a given set of data.

Objective 3.3 Students will learn how to select the appropriate statistic (median or mode) and/or graph (line or bar) for the type of data.

Objective 3.4 Students will learn how to use data to make predictions and draw conclusions.

Figure 4–6a
Goals and Objectives for Statistics, Mathematical Problem Solving, and Mathematical Communication

solving, and statistics objectives can be shown in the performance, there are additional requirements in the performance that are not generally included in the mathematics curriculum. Specifically, she expects students to "research a community problem" and, once they have done their mathematical work, write "a discussion of the proposed answers to the question(s) including. . . references to specific data that support claims, inferences, and interpretations; and a discussion of how the data support claims, inferences, and interpretations."

As with Mr. Keaton, Ms. McKinley has to decide whether she is going to add a research goal to her instructional plans. She also has to decide whether she is going to add a goal related to informational writing that involves supporting claims with statistical evidence. Although these are not typical mathematics goals, they are certainly appropriate in a middle school or junior high mathematics class that grounds mathematical concepts and procedures in real-world contexts. Alternately, she can change the demands of the performance. Figure 4–6b shows the additional objectives that Ms. McKinley adds to her mathematics objectives.

GOAL 2: *Students will learn how to communicate mathematical ideas and results using language, graphics, equations, and symbols appropriate to the audience and purpose.*

Objective 2.4   Students will learn how to make and support claims using mathematical evidence.

GOAL 3: *Students will learn statistical concepts, procedures, and representations used to analyze and represent data.*

Objective 3.5   Students will learn how to use a variety of strategies for systematically gathering data to answer research questions.

Figure 4–6b
Objectives Added to Goals 2 and 3 in Ms. McKinley's Class

We recognize that some assessment specialists would begin with learning objectives and then derive performances from the objectives. We find, however, that many teachers have difficulty working from parts to a whole. In fact, as mentioned in Chapter 2, the idea of learning objectives comes from early task analyses of important and valued performances. Therefore, it makes sense for teachers to use the same process as did early instructional theorists—beginning with valued performances, analyzing them for their parts, and then moving back and forth from performance descriptions to learning objectives to performance descriptions—checking at each point whether the two are congruent.

Writing Directions

Once the performance is clearly described, writing directions is a fairly simple task. The directions can be derived from the description. The major difference is that you want to make certain that your directions are written *to* the students rather than *about* them and that you have made all expectations explicit. We recommend that you begin directions

---

Directions for Your Letter to the Editor

You are going to write a letter to the editor of the newspaper. The letter will be about something important to you that is in the news these days. Your job will be to convince the people who read the paper to think about your point of view. Before you start writing, you are going to do some research to find out why it is an issue and what other people think about the issue. You may get information from the newspaper, TV, radio, magazines, or other printed material. You may also interview your friends, your parents, or people in your neighborhood. If you want to do an interview with neighbors, you must get your parents' permission. I will do some lessons on different ways to gather information about the issue.

When you finish your research, you will begin drafting your letter to the editor. You may do all of your drafting and revisions on the computer. In your letter:

    a. Clearly describe the issue (use your research to help you).
    b. State your position on the issue.
    c. Give at least two reasons for your position (use your research to help you).
    d. Give examples for each of your reasons (use your research to help you).
    e. Give a concluding statement that restates your position and tells the readers what they should do.

After you finish your draft, you will share it with your writing group to get some feedback. You will use the feedback and your own ideas to make whatever improvements you need to make. Keep the marked copy to turn in with your final letter. Things I will be looking for after your revisions include:

☐ Good ideas with good examples
☐ Logical organization of your ideas
☐ Different sentence types (simple sentences, complex sentences, and compound sentences)
☐ Language that might make the reader stop and think
☐ Language that is okay for the editor of a newspaper

When you finish revising your letter, I will make a photo copy so you can put it in your folder. Then you are going to edit your work. When you edit, I want you to check:

☐ Spelling
☐ Grammar
☐ Punctuation and capitalization

Last you will write your final version of the letter. Be sure your letter is typed, double spaced, and has at least 1-inch margins. You can use whatever font you want to use, but it should be easy for the editor of a newspaper to read your letter. When you turn in your final letter, include all of your notes from research, drafts, and marked copies.

Figure 4–7
Directions to Students for the Letter to the Editor

with statements like "You are going to . . . " and "You will . . . " and "You are expected to. . . ." Remember that you are likely to omit information the first few times you write directions. Your students will ask questions for clarification, so make notes about their questions on a copy of the directions and update the directions for the next time you have students do the performance.

Directions for Your Mathematics Report

You are going to do a report on an issue in our community. The report will be about something important to you that is in the news these days. Before you begin your research, write a statement of the issue as you understand it; write a question you have about the issue that can only be answered by using data; and decide what kind of data would best answer the question.

Next you are going to gather data that answers your question. You may get information from the newspaper, TV, radio, the Internet, or other sources. You may also interview your friends, your parents or guardians and people in your neighborhood. If you want to do an interview with neighbors, you must get your parents permission. I will do some lessons on different ways to gather information about your issue. Once you finish your research, you will begin analyzing your data. Be sure to:

- ☐ Collect only data related to your question.
- ☐ List the results in a way that helps you analyze them.
- ☐ Use your statistical skills to organize and analyze the data so that you can answer your question.

Sometimes researchers run into problems when they try to answer questions. You may need to try different ways to organize and analyze the data or you may need to do more research. That's okay, just check with me if you need help. When you have answered your question, you will write your final report. In your report you will include:

- ☐ A thorough description of the issue
- ☐ Your question about the issue
- ☐ An explanation of your choices for data sources, type of graph, and whether you chose the median or mode as the best statistic for the results
- ☐ A description of the process you used to analyze the data and answer your question (you may use words, labeled pictures, and/or numbers in your description)
- ☐ A summary of the data in a table, chart, or graph, including the median or mode (whichever is the best statistic for your data)
- ☐ The answer to your question (your conclusion), including specific results that support your conclusion and explaining how the results support your conclusion

You will turn in each part of your work at different times during the quarter so I can check your work and give you feedback. I expect you to use the feedback to improve the work.

Figure 4–8
Directions to Students for the Mathematics Report

Sometimes, students will ask for more direction than you want to give. You may want them to find their own issue or problem to focus on. You may want them to identify their own sources for their research. You may want them to choose a way to organize information or data. Students who are used to having teachers guide every step in their work may resist taking the risk of self-choice—especially if they have learned that teachers actually have *unwritten* expectations. In fact, we have found that students' resistance to self-choice most often comes from experiences in school or at home where self-choice has been discouraged or even punished. The best way to deal with this resistance is to give students experiences wherein they make smaller choices at first and are supported in their decision making. When students make unrealistic choices, teachers can gently guide them to more realistic choices by asking them to consider the amount of work required, the time it will take, the time available, and their own level of knowledge and skill. If *all* students are required to ask themselves these kinds of questions before finalizing their choices, then those who make unrealistic plans can learn from their self-analysis and that of their peers.

In contrast to aspects of performance wherein students make their own choices, there may be strict conventions that you want all students to follow. Make certain you know what decisions you want them to make and what decisions you want to make and include those differences in your directions.

Figure 4–7 shows the directions for the letter to the editor Mr. Keaton wrote for his sixth-grade students. Figure 4–8 shows the directions for the statistical problem-solving task Ms. McKinley wrote for her seventh-grade students. Each teacher has carefully written the directions so that the reading level is low. They both used words likely to be familiar to most of their sixth- or seventh-grade students. Both teachers refer to times when students will receive feedback. Their next task will be to make certain that the directions will lead students to complete the well-executed performances they have described. When students receive directions that leave them wondering what is expected of them, they tend to become frustrated and withdraw from the task. Needless to say, students will not be able to complete either task without instruction and teacher support.

Developing Scoring Rules

The next most important part of performance assessment development is development of scoring rules. Scores are any numerical or descriptive summary applied to a performance. Therefore, scores can be words, numbers, or even pictures for young children. Scores can be used in positive, neutral, or negative ways. For example, a score of 20 means nothing unless the student knows how many points are possible. Even then a score of 20 can be fairly neutral, unless students see the score as fixed—that they cannot change the score through improved work.[6] In this book, we hope to help you use scores in more useful and informative ways—both as feedback to students and as indicators of the standards you want your students to reach.

Some performance assessment experts begin with scoring rules and define performances based on the dimensions of a good performance. For example, the Northwest Regional Educational Laboratory has created a six-trait writing model (Cullum, 2000) to develop six scoring rubrics (one each for ideas and content, organization, voice, sentence fluency, word choice, and writing conventions) that are applied regardless of the writing purpose. The state of Oregon has developed mathematics rubrics for four dimensions of mathematics problem-solving performances (problem solving, communication, reasoning, and conceptual understanding) that are applied regardless of the type of problem students solve. These tools are useful ways to begin examining student work and to define the qualities of good work. These trait rubrics are used in large-scale testing programs wherein the types of writing and mathematical problems vary from year to year. Trait rubrics can also be

---

[6]Students who do not see the opportunity to improve are also less likely to read or use feedback from the teacher.

useful in the classroom as long as the traits are taught to all students, so that students can begin to internalize the meaning of the rubrics and apply them to their own work.

However, teachers also need to know how to develop their own scoring rules—rules that are general or specific depending on the needs of the students, the desires of the teachers, and the type of work. General rubrics are very useful when you want to assess overall qualities rather than specific conceptual understanding or specific skills. However, if the focus of your assessment is on whether students have learned some specific concepts or skills, you may need scoring rules that focus on the concepts or skills you want to assess. For example, if a third-grade teacher has been teaching students how to use punctuation in their stories and students are to use quotation marks, question marks, exclamation marks, periods, and commas, the teacher may find that a scoring rubric designed to assess writing conventions as a whole (capitalization, punctuation, spelling, and grammar) is not useful for her purposes.

Performance Criteria   Scoring rules come in many different formats. However, all scoring rules can be classified in one of three categories: checklists, rating scales, and scoring rubrics. All scoring rules begin with *performance criteria* or observable characteristics of student performances.

Performance criteria can be specific to a given assignment or general across a wide range of work that differs in minor ways. For example, Mr. Keaton's students are writing a letter to the editor; however, many of the criteria for letters to the editor are shared by other types of persuasive writing—a clear position, arguments supporting the position, factual evidence and examples that support each argument, anticipation of counterarguments, a call for action, and a logical flow of ideas. Writing conventions (correct grammar, punctuation, spelling, and capitalization) are also common to most forms of writing. On the other hand, some criteria are specific to letter writing—a letter form and language appropriate for a newspaper reading audience. Finally, some criteria are specific to a successful letter to the editor, such as a focus on a contemporary issue that is of importance to a broader reading audience.

To have an authentic performance assessment, the criteria on which the performance is evaluated must also be authentic. In the case of Mr. Keaton's task, the performance criteria must fit the definition of a good letter to the editor in the real world. A perusal of his checklist (Figure 4–9) shows that almost all the criteria for the product are ones an editor might use in deciding whether to print the letter. Table 4–4 shows performance criteria that are authentic to the scientific task of scientific research that involves developing a research question and hypothesis, designing an investigation to test the hypothesis, and writing up the results. Table 4–4 also shows authentic performance criteria for historical arguments. These examples could apply to the real world of scientists and historians.

Note that the performance criteria are not just a restatement of the directions for the performance. Performance criteria indicate what students will demonstrate in their performances related to the learning objectives. For example, Mr. Keaton's performance criteria for revision indicate that revisions *improved* the work. The performance criteria for ideas and content state that students *show understanding of the issue* and *urge agreement or action*.

Once performance criteria are determined, teachers can decide what type of scoring rule to use: checklists, rating scales, or rubrics. Each type of scoring rule serves a different instructional and assessment purpose.

Table 4–4
Performance Criteria for Scientific Research and Historical Argument

Performance	Performance Criteria
Scientific Investigation: The student will develop a research question and hypothesis; design one or more investigations to test the hypothesis; conduct the investigation; collect and organize data; prepare a written report including background research, question, hypothesis, summary of the steps of the investigation, results (in language and graphic forms), a conclusion, and one or more interpretations of the results, tying the results back to the original hypothesis and question.	• Summary of background research is accurate. • Question builds on what is already known. • Hypothesis is testable. • Hypothesis is grounded in what is known. • Investigation adequately tests the hypothesis. • Interpretation of results fits the data. • All parts of the report are included (question, hypothesis, investigative steps, results, and interpretation). • Data are accurately reported. • Displays communicate results. • Conclusion and interpretation(s) follow from results.
Historical Argument: The student will conduct research related to a controversial historical issue using original documents and artifacts; write a historical argument that includes background information on the issue, a position on the issue, at least two arguments to support the position, evidence and examples that support the arguments, and a conclusion that refers to the arguments to make a strong case for the position.	• Background information shows understanding of the issue. • Position on the issue is stated. • At least two arguments are given to support the position. • Specific evidence/examples from source documents supports arguments. • Counterarguments are given. • Counterarguments are refuted using evidence. • Essay builds a case for the position. • Conclusion summarizes the case.

Checklists and Rating Scales A *checklist* is simply a list of the performance criteria you expect to see in students' work along with a place to check whether each specific criterion is present or absent, right or wrong. Figure 4–9 is an example of a checklist that could be used to assess the letters to the editor written by Mr. Keaton's sixth-grade students. The checklist is set up with a place for the student's name, the date of the work, the name of the performance, and the list of performance criteria for the letter.

A *rating scale* is similar to a checklist except that, instead of indicating whether the criterion is present or absent, right or wrong, the teacher gives one or more of the performance

Student Name: _____ Date: _____

Check each characteristic that is present.

Persuasive Writing: Content and Ideas
☐ Shows understanding of the issue.
☐ Position is stated.
☐ Position is related to the issue.
☐ Reasons support the position.
☐ Factual evidence supports the reasons.
☐ Descriptive examples support the reasons.
☐ Information from research is used in reasons, evidence, and examples.
☐ Conclusion urges action or agreement.

Organization and Format
☐ Greeting is given.
☐ Ideas are organized logically.
☐ Closing is given.
☐ Name is typed and signed.
☐ Language is appropriate for letter to the editor.

Writing Conventions
☐ Words are spelled correctly.
☐ Capitalization is correct.
☐ Punctuation is correct.
☐ Grammar is correct.

Revision
☐ Revision improved persuasive language, if needed.
☐ Revision improved ideas and examples, if needed.
☐ Revision improved sentence variety, if needed.
☐ Revision improved organization, if needed.

Editing
☐ Edits improved spelling, if needed.
☐ Edits improved capitalization, if needed.
☐ Edits improved punctuation, if needed.
☐ Edits improved grammar, if needed.

Figure 4–9
Checklist for Letters to the Editor

criteria a rating on some scale. Rating scales can indicate how often something happens or how well something is done. The words chosen for the rating depend on the characteristics being rated. Figure 4–10 is a rating scale that could be used to assess the letters to the editor written by Mr. Keaton's sixth-grade students. In addition to the criteria given in the checklist, each performance criterion has a rating.

Ratings differ depending on the criterion. Performance criteria related to the content of the letter are rated for clarity and strength of argument. Performance criteria related to writing conventions are rated for number of errors. Performance criteria related to revising and editing are focused on whether changes were made and whether changes improved the letter. Because different ratings are more or less appropriate for different performance criteria, rating scales take more thinking to create than do checklists—specifically in selecting the words to describe the ratings used. For example, if Mr. Keaton had used ratings about accuracy to evaluate the content and ideas part of the letter, he would communicate a very different message in the rating scale. His message would be that there are *correct* positions, arguments, reasons, and examples. This is a very different message than he has given by focusing on the strength and clarity of the students' positions, arguments, and evidence.

Students who are to be scored for accuracy of positions, arguments, and reasons are more likely to become dependent on the teacher to figure out what the teacher believes are the "correct" positions, arguments, reasons, and examples. The terms selected for a rating scale are, therefore, very important in communicating teachers' values. Teachers need to think carefully about the words they choose so that they can help students become independent learners and so that they can provide feedback on levels of quality—something that checklists cannot do well. Generally, the highest rating for each criterion is set as the "performance standard" or the level of quality you want students to attain through your instruction and their hard work on the specific performance or similar performances.

Scoring Rubrics A *scoring rubric* is a descriptive, holistic evaluation of a performance. One or more rubrics can be applied to a given performance depending on the dimensions of work. Scoring rubrics combine the ideas about *quality* from rating scales and *performance criteria* into paragraphs that describe different levels of performance.

Scoring rubrics should have a limited number of levels—generally three to six depending on the complexity of the task—because holistic evaluations of students' work are the most subjective form of scoring. When the rubrics have a limited number of levels, teachers are less likely to add bias to their evaluations (Littlefield & Troendle, 1987).

Some teachers use the highest level in a rubric to establish the desired performance standard, whereas other teachers have a level *just above* the desired level of quality. Teachers who create rubrics with a level above the performance standard want to use the highest level to recognize students who have performed above or beyond what was expected. Although the desire to reward students who perform above expectations is understandable, it is important to treat such scores carefully. Teachers must ask themselves whether appropriate instruction could help *all* students achieve the higher level of performance. Teachers must also be certain that they are acknowledging the students' work rather than the work of an outside helper. Finally, teachers must use caution when using these rubrics in grading policies. Grading policies should not result in lower grades for students who consistently satisfy all performance criteria and meet teachers' expectations. If the performance standard is not the highest level on a rubric, it is important to give clear descriptions of the qualities

Student Name: _____ Date: _____

Circle a rating for each characteristic that is present.

Persuasive Writing: Content and Ideas

Shows understanding of the issue.	Clear	Understandable	Unfocused
Position is stated.	Clear	Understandable	Confusing
Position is related to the issue.	Strong	Adequate	Weak
Reasons support the position.	Strong	Adequate	Weak
Factual evidence supports the reasons.	Accurate	Mostly accurate	Little accuracy
Descriptive examples support the reasons.	Strong	Adequate	Weak
Information from research used in reasons, evidence, and examples.	Strong	Adequate	Weak
Conclusion urges action or agreement.	Strong	Adequate	Weak

Organization and Format

Greeting is given.	Yes	No	
Ideas are organized logically.	Logically	Minor flaws	Confusing
Closing is given.	Yes	No	
Name is typed and signed.	Yes	No	
Language is appropriate for a letter to the editor.	Well-chosen	Acceptable	Needs work

Writing Conventions

Words are spelled correctly.	All	Few errors	Many errors
Capitalization is correct.	All	Few errors	Many errors
Punctuation is correct.	All	Few errors	Many errors
Grammar is correct.	All	Few errors	Many errors

Revision

Revision improved persuasive language, if needed.	Improved	No improvement	No change
Revision improved ideas and examples, if needed.	Improved	No improvement	No change
Revision improved sentence variety, if needed.	Improved	No improvement	No change
Revision improved organization, if needed.	Improved	No improvement	No change

Editing

Edits improved spelling, if needed.	Improved	No improvement	No change
Edits improved capitalization, if needed.	Improved	No improvement	No change
Edits improved punctuation, if needed.	Improved	No improvement	No change
Edits improved grammar, if needed	Improved	No improvement	No change

Figure 4–10
Rating Scale for Letters to the Editor

of performances that meet the performance standard so students clearly understand what they are expected to accomplish.

Figure 4–11 is a set of scoring rubrics that could be used to assess the letters to the editor written by Mr. Keaton's sixth-grade students. There are five scoring rubrics for the letter to the editor so that Mr. Keaton can assess and provide feedback on different dimensions of the performance. He will use one rubric to score persuasive content and ideas and a second rubric to score organization and letter format. Students could have strong and effective content and ideas with poor organizational skills or poor use of the letter form. Mr. Keaton will use a third rubric to score writing conventions. As with the other two dimensions of performance, students may be stronger or weaker in writing conventions than in content, ideas, or organization. Mr. Keaton will use the fourth and fifth rubrics to score the students' use of the writing process—specifically their use of revision and editing skills as shown in the improven between drafts and the final version of the letter. Evaluating each aspect of the letter separately gives Mr. Keaton an opportunity to give feedback on different strengths and weaknesses.

Combining qualities and performance criteria to describe the highest and lowest performance levels is usually fairly easy. Writing the descriptions for the intermediate levels is

---

Student Name: _____ Date: _____

Circle the score for each rubric.

Persuasive Writing: Content and Ideas

- Shows understanding of the issue.
- Position is stated and related to the issue.
- Reasons support the position.

- Factual evidence and descriptive examples support the reasons.
- Information from research used in reasons, evidence, and examples.
- Conclusion urges action or agreement.

4 points   The issue is briefly and accurately described, showing solid understanding of the issue, and the student's position is strong and clearly related to the issue. All reasons, examples, and evidence are grounded in research, provide strong support for the position, and are well integrated into a convincing case for the position. Conclusion makes a strong case for action or agreement.

3 points   The issue is described accurately, although description may be too long or too brief. The student's position related to the issue is stated. All reasons, examples, and evidence are grounded in research and provide adequate support for the position, resulting in a reasonable case for the position. Conclusion asks for action or agreement.

2 points   The issue, if described, may be too long or too brief. The student's position related to the issue is stated or implied. All reasons, examples, and evidence provide adequate support for the position, although they may rely more on anecdote and opinion than on information from research. Conclusion asks for action or agreement.

1 point   It is difficult to determine the issue or the student's position in the letter. There may be examples, evidence, and reasons that are not clearly related to a position. Conclusion may not be given.

Figure 4–11
Rubrics for Letters to the Editor

Student Name: _____ Date: _____

Circle the score for each rubric.

Organization and Format

- Greeting is given.
- Closing is given.
- Name is typed and signed.
- Ideas are organized logically.
- Language is appropriate for letter to the editor.

4 points	The writing is in letter form with appropriate letter elements. Ideas are logically organized with language that is appropriate for audience.
3 points	The writing is in letter form, but specific elements may be missing. Ideas are mostly organized with language that is appropriate for audience.
2 points	The writing is in letter form, but specific elements may be missing. Ideas are mostly organized, with occasional use of slang or casual language not appropriate for audience.
1 point	The writing may not be in letter form. Organization of ideas is haphazard and use of slang or casual language detracts from the message.

Writing Conventions

- Words are spelled correctly.
- Punctuation is correct.
- Capitalization is correct.
- Grammar is correct.

4 points	Spelling, grammar, punctuation, and capitalization are excellent. Very minor errors do not detract from meaning or communication of ideas.
3 points	Spelling, grammar, punctuation, and capitalization are good. Several minor errors do not detract from meaning or communication of ideas.
2 points	Spelling, grammar, punctuation, and capitalization are fair. Errors detract somewhat from meaning or communication of ideas.
1 point	Spelling, grammar, punctuation, and capitalization need substantial work. Errors detract significantly from meaning or communication of ideas.

Revision

- Revision improved persuasive language, if needed.
- Revision improved sentence variety, if needed.
- Revision improved ideas and examples, if needed.
- Revision improved organization, if needed.

4 points	All revisions have improved the overall quality of work. Attention has been given to language, sentence variety, ideas, examples, and organization, where needed.
3 points	All revisions have improved the overall quality of work. Attention has been given to at least *three* of the following: language, sentence variety, ideas, examples, and organization, where needed.
2 points	Some revisions have improved the overall quality of work. Attention has been given to at least *two* of the following: language, sentence variety, ideas, example, and organization, where needed.
1 point	Some revisions have improved the overall quality of work whereas some may have lessened the quality. Attention has been given to at least *one* of the following: language, sentence variety, ideas, example, and organization, where needed.
0 points	No evidence of revisions.

Figure 4–11 *(continued)*

Editing	
• Edits improved spelling, if needed.	• Edits improved capitalization, if needed.
• Edits improved punctuation, if needed.	• Edits improved grammar, if needed.

4 points	All edits have improved the overall quality of work. Attention has been given to spelling, punctuation, capitalization, and grammar, as needed.
3 points	All edits have improved the overall quality of work. Attention has been given to at least *three* of the following: spelling, punctuation, capitalization, and grammar, as needed.
2 points	Some edits have improved the overall quality of work. Attention has been given to at least *two* of the following: spelling, punctuation, capitalization, and grammar, as needed.
1 point	Some revisions have improved the overall quality of work, whereas some may have lessened the quality. Attention has been given to at least *one* of the following: spelling, punctuation, capitalization, and grammar, as needed.
0 points	No evidence of edits.

Figure 4–11 *(continued)*

typically more difficult. These descriptions should be more than simply a rating scale in paragraph form. They should describe something about the overall quality of the work that is missed when looking at each criterion separately. Mr. Keaton's rubrics include various criteria; however, there is a sense that the whole is more important than the individual parts. For example, in the rubric for content and ideas, rather than evaluate the specific elements of a persuasive argument, Mr. Keaton is evaluating whether "All reasons, examples, and evidence are grounded in research, provide strong support for the position, and are well integrated into a convincing case for the position."

For the intermediate levels of performance, the language changes to whether the letter presents a "reasonable case" or is simply a position with arguments. A careful examination of each of the other rubrics shows the same kind of holistic thinking. Our experience has been that when creating rubrics, once they are applied to actual student work, the language for each level is slightly modified to reflect differences in quality that actually occur and to better reflect our values (see, for example, Taylor & Nolen, 1996).

Comparing Scoring Rules A careful look at the three types of scoring rules shows that performance criteria for the scoring rubrics are no different from the performance criteria for the checklist and rating scale. What changes is whether the performance criteria are evaluated separately or whether performance criteria and levels of quality are evaluated holistically. Hence, performance criteria are the crux of all scoring rules. Another common element of the three scoring types is that the students are given categories for the different scores. Mr. Keaton has organized all three types of scoring rules by content and ideas, organization, writing conventions, revision, and editing. In this way, he has identified his major goals for students' writing and communicated his values as a teacher.

Both the performance criteria and the categories for the scores come from the learning objectives. The teacher must be able to look back to the learning objectives and determine whether the criteria listed are what she or he intends to teach. Suppose Mr. Keaton had put in a criterion such as "shows creativity and wit in ideas and language." Teachers often claim that it is criteria like these that give them an opportunity to give points to those students who are bright and exceed expectations. Would this be a fair performance criterion? Can teachers teach creativity and wit? In fact, performance criteria like this one are *often* listed as criteria for students' performances, which can be a recipe for failure if students believe they are not creative or witty—whether or not their self-assessment is true. Teachers may need to find less threatening ways to acknowledge and celebrate students who exceed expectations without including these criteria in the score for a piece of work. This is one role of feedback.

By choosing to score revision and editing skills, Mr. Keaton makes it clear that he considers the performance to be more than a final product. He also values the skills students use as they develop the final product. Because his learning objectives include revision and editing, he wants to assess how well students are learning these skills. Needless to say, Mr. Keaton must look at the earlier drafts to see whether students improve their letters in the ways he has defined in his learning objectives. By evaluating the quality of revision and editing, Mr. Keaton communicates that he is not simply asking students to go through stages of revision but he cares what happens during those stages.

Cautions in Developing Scoring Rules   We have already described one caution in writing scoring rubrics—the potential for bias that comes with too many levels on the rubric. There are other problems that can arise when creating scoring rules.

BOX 4.1: *Rules for Developing Checklists and Rating Scales*

1. Make sure the checklist or rating scale has a clear focus, based on the performance criteria.
2. For checklists or rating scales for internal states (conceptual understanding, thinking skills, attitude, etc.), list the *behaviors* that will allow you to make the necessary inferences. Providing information on target behaviors will help students understand what they must do to demonstrate their competence. It is especially important if others (parents, aides, peers) will be using the rating scale.
3. For specific knowledge (e.g., knows letters of alphabet) or procedural knowledge (e.g., how to focus a microscope), list the specific knowledge or procedural steps used to complete the task you plan to observe.
4. Use checklists for aspects of the performance that are all or nothing: Use terms like "yes/no," "present/absent," or "observed/not observed."
5. Use rating scales for performance aspects that can be judged in degrees. Use words to anchor the points of the rating scale relevant to the dimension of the performance to be assessed. Dimensions may relate to quality (e.g., effective, adequate, unacceptable), opinion (e.g., strongly agree, agree, disagree, strongly disagree), frequency (e.g., often, occasionally, rarely, never), degree of support (well supported, adequately supported, needs more support), accuracy (completely, mostly, partially), and others. Think carefully about what you want to know and how you want to look at it before deciding which dimension to use for your rating scale.

BOX 4.2: *Rules for Writing Scoring Rubrics*

1. Use a different rubric for each of the identified performance dimensions.
2. Limit the rubric to 3 to 6 points indicating levels of competence. Create only as many levels as you can describe given the complexity of the work.
3. Begin with clear performance criteria related to each dimension of performance and related to your learning objectives.
4. Write clear descriptions of the performance levels represented by each point. These are general descriptions of each level of quality. Some rubrics give lists of discrete characteristics for different levels of quality; usually, however, these are simply rating scales disguised as rubrics since students might do well on one criterion but poorly on another. Therefore, if performance criteria are listed at the top of rubrics and then performance levels are holistic quality descriptions, rubrics are easier to apply.
5. Make certain that each performance level is distinct from each other level. Students should be able to see how their work matches the score received and what needs to be done to perform at a higher level.

Focus on Demonstration of Learning Objectives Possibly the most serious problem occurs when performance criteria are focused more on the completion of a task than on what knowledge and skills are shown in the work. For example, Figures 4–12 and 4–13 show two very different ways to write performance criteria for Ms. McKinley's mathematics problem-solving assessment. In the first version, the performance criteria are simply focused on task completion. These criteria are almost a restatement of the directions for the performance.

In the second version, the performance criteria are closely aligned with the learning objectives for each of the three goals: mathematical problem solving, concepts and procedures of statistics, and mathematical communication and representations. The performance criteria for problem solving delineate what defining the problem, using appropriate strategies and technology, and developing solutions look like in this performance. The performance criteria for concepts and procedures of statistics clarify the statistical concepts to be shown in this performance (selecting appropriate graphs and statistics, computing median or mode, using appropriate units of measurement). The performance criteria for mathematical communication clarify the types of communication important to this performance (titles and labels on graphs, unbiased scales, explanations and descriptions of mathematical ideas). Although some of the criteria in figures 4–12 and 4–13 are the same, others are quite different. It is essential, when developing performance criteria, to check that the performance criteria are *more than* task completion and that they clearly represent the learning objectives you have set for your student.

Observable Performance Criteria Vague performance criteria or rating scales can present problems. Performance criteria should be observable aspects of a performance. If part of a performance cannot be observed (e.g., thinking processes), teachers must either have the students describe those aspects and evaluate the description or omit the internal processes from the evaluation. Ms. McKinley's learning objectives include such statements as "adjust

Data Collection	Data Analysis	Final Report
◆ Writes a statement describing the issue. ◆ Writes a question about the issue. ◆ Identifies the kind of data that would best answer the question. ◆ Gathers data to answer the question: • Uses the newspaper, TV, and/or radio • Uses the Internet • Interviews friends • Interviews parents or guardians • Interviews neighbors • Gets parent permission for interviews with neighbors	◆ Analyzes data related to the question. ◆ Lists data in organized way. ◆ Uses statistics skills to organize and analyze data.	◆ Answers question. ◆ Turns in drafts of work. ◆ Uses feedback to improve work. ◆ Writes final report: • Describes the issue • Writes question about the issue • Explains the reasons for data gathered, type of graph, choice of median or mode • Describes procedures used • Summarizes the data in table, chart, graph, median, and/or mode • Uses specific data in summary • Explains how data supports conclusion

Figure 4–12
Math Problem-Solving Performance Criteria Focused on Completion of Task

strategies and/or abandon unproductive strategies if necessary," "persist with problems until they find a satisfactory solution," and "check solutions against their initial understanding of the problem." Each of these behaviors is very hard to observe. Ms. McKinley can *infer* whether students have checked their solutions against their initial understanding of a problem by looking at their conclusions and how they use data to support conclusions. If conclusions are disconnected from the question, then students have not "checked solutions against their initial understanding of the problem." In the case of persistence, Ms. McKinley can infer that students have persisted when she evaluates the final performance, though she can't tell if the student found the problem straightforward, requiring little persistence, or if the student had to struggle to come to a satisfactory solution. If the performance is complete and meets all criteria, then she can infer persistence. In this case, "persistence" does not mean "effort."[7] For the other learning objective, the only way that Ms. McKinley will know that students have abandoned or adjusted strategies is if they describe such behaviors when describing the processes they used. If Ms. McKinley has regularly shown students that mistakes and initial failures are expected, they are more likely to accurately describe their problem-solving processes. If Ms. McKinley has penalized students when they do not initially select the most effective or appropriate solution strategy, they are less likely to honestly describe their problem-solving processes. Finally, Figure 4–14 shows a checklist Ms. McKinley has developed for her students to use in their own assessment of their

[7]It's important to note that, given that students are working on the same type of problem, evaluating effort can put students who can easily work through a solution at a disadvantage. As noted elsewhere in the text, effort is very difficult to measure.

Criteria for Mathematical Problem Solving	Criteria for Math Communication and Representations	Criteria for Understanding of Statistical Concepts and Procedures
• Introduction shows understanding of the issue. • Research question is related to the issue. • Research question can be answered with data. • Selected resources are appropriate for the research question. • Data are organized in a way that helps to answer the question. • Selected procedures are appropriate for the data and research question. • Adjusts or abandons strategies that do not answer question. • Conclusion relates to research question.	• Graphs have informative titles. • Graphs are labeled. • All data are labeled in terms of measurement units. • Choice of scale avoids bias. • Conclusions are supported with mathematical evidence. • Uses mathematical language appropriate to the task. • Reasons given for choices communicate processes used.	• Selected graphs are appropriate for the data. • Selected statistic (median or mode) is appropriate for the data. • Median or mode computations are accurate. • Conclusions follow from the data. • Measurement units are appropriate for the data. • Reasons given for choices show understanding of statistical concepts.

Figure 4–13
Math Problem-Solving Performance Criteria Focused on Demonstration of Learning Objectives

work, and Figure 4–15 is the rating scale Ms. McKinley will use in scoring students' work based on her performance criteria.[8]

Inference and Trust Two important issues in assessment are *inference* and *trust*. Whenever teachers assess a learning objective through performance, they are not directly observing but are using evidence to make an inference. When Mr. Keaton evaluates students' letters to the editor, he makes inferences about whether students have learned how to make a persuasive argument, how to organize writing, how to use writing conventions, and how to edit and revise their writing. When Ms. McKinley evaluates students' final reports, she makes inferences about students' problem-solving and communication skills as well as their conceptual and procedural understanding in statistics. The more invisible the focus of the learning objective, the greater the inference that has to be made. Any assessment of students' thinking and reasoning requires greater inference than assessment of some observable outcome such as the ability to organize sentences into a paragraph with a coherent message.

The other issue is that of trust. Assessments are not neutral. When teachers select what to assess, they make a statement of their values. When teachers identify perform-

[8]Notice that Ms. McKinley's rating scale is formatted differently than the one used by Mr. Keaton. Ms. McKinley has combined performance criteria with similar ratings to create fuller, verbal descriptions rather than just single words.

Student Name: _____ Date: _____

Check each characteristic that is present.

Problem Solving

☐ Introduction shows understanding of the issue.

☐ Research question can be answered with numerical data.

☐ Research question is related to the issue.

☐ Selected resources are appropriate for the research question.

☐ Data are organized in a way that helps to answer the question.

☐ Selected procedures are appropriate for the data and research question.

☐ Solutions are based on the research question and data.

☐ Conclusion relates to research question.

Mathematical Communication

☐ Graphs have informative titles.

☐ Graphs are labeled.

☐ Data are accurately represented.

☐ All data are labeled in terms of measurement units.

☐ Choice of scale avoids bias.

☐ Conclusion is supported with mathematical evidence.

☐ Uses mathematical language appropriate to the task.

☐ Description of processes used communicates strategies and thinking.

Statistical Concepts, Procedures and Representations

☐ Selected graphs are appropriate for the data.

☐ Median or mode computation is accurate.

☐ Selected statistic is appropriate for the data.

☐ Measurement units are appropriate for the data.

☐ Conclusions follow from the data.

☐ Reasons given for choices show understanding statistical concepts.

Figure 4–14
Checklist Option for Ms. McKinley's Mathematics Problem-Solving Performance

ance criteria, they make another statement of their values. When teachers penalize students through assessment, they make yet another statement of their values. It should be apparent by now that we fundamentally believe assessments can and should be used to support students—that the purpose of assessment is to help students understand what is important to learn and what successful work looks like. When assessments are used to punish students, they no longer serve a positive educational purpose. Rather they become one more hurdle students must learn to jump as they work their way through school. Each assessment choice a teacher makes has the potential to build or undermine

Student Name: _____ Date: _____

Rate each criterion based on the description in the box.

Problem Solving	3	2	1	0
Introduction shows understanding of the issue.	Introduction shows a thorough understanding of the issue.	Introduction shows a superficial understanding of the issue.	Introduction shows a limited understanding of the issue.	Introduction shows no understanding of the issue.
Research question is related to the issue. Research question can be answered with numerical data.	Research question is appropriate for the issue and can be answered using numerical data.	Research question is marginally related to the issue and can be answered using numerical data.	Research question may or may not be related to the issue; responses will be difficult to record numerically.	No research question given.
Selected resources are appropriate for the research question.	A variety of resources provide appropriate data for the question.	At least one resource provides appropriate data for the question.	Resources used did not address the question.	No resources used.
Data are organized in a way that helps to answer the question.	Data are effectively organized to make graphing and statistical analyses easier to do.	Data are organized; however, organization could be more effective for the purpose.	Little attempt was made to organize the data.	No data were provided.
Selected procedures are appropriate for the data and research question. Solutions are based on the research question and data. Conclusion relates to research question.	Procedures, solutions, and conclusions are all relevant to the original research question and the type of data collected; corrections and/or adjustments show awareness of misfit.	Procedures, solutions, and conclusions are mostly relevant to the original research question and the type of data collected.	Procedures, solutions, and conclusions are partially relevant to the original research question and the type of data collected.	Procedures, solutions, and conclusions are irrelevant to the original research question and the type of data collected.

Figure 4–15
Rating Scale Option for Ms. McKinley's Mathematics Problem-Solving Performance

Mathematical Communication	3	2	1	0
Graphs have informative titles. Graphs are labeled.	Labels and titles are informative and appropriate for the graph and for the data.	Labels and titles are appropriate for the graph and data but provide limited information.	Labels and titles are partially appropriate for the graph and data.	Labels and titles are omitted.
Data are accurately represented.	Data in graphs and text are completely accurate.	Minor data errors in graphs and text do not detract from the purpose of the performance.	Significant data errors detract from the purpose of the performance.	No data presented.
All data are labeled in terms of measurement units. Choice of scale avoids bias.	Data and scales are labeled with measurement units; scale is accurate and appropriate.	Data and scales are labeled with measurement units; scale distorts data.	Data and scales are occasionally labeled with measurement units; scale is inaccurate.	No measurement units or scale presented.
Conclusion is supported with mathematical evidence.	Conclusion is well supported with mathematical evidence.	Conclusion is supported with some mathematical evidence.	Conclusion is not supported with mathematical evidence.	No conclusion given.
Uses mathematical language appropriate to the task.	All mathematical language is appropriate for the problem, the data, the analyses, and the results.	Most mathematical language is appropriate for the problem, the data, the analyses, and the results.	Some mathematical language is appropriate for the problem, the data, the analyses, and the results.	Mathematical language was not used.

Figure 4–15 (continued)

Statistical Concepts, Procedures and Representations	3	2	1	0
Selected graphs are appropriate for the data.	Graph is appropriate for the type of data—line graph for continuous data and bar graph for category data.	If multiple graphs are used, some but not all are appropriate.	Graph is not appropriate for the type of data—line graph for continuous data and bar graph for category data.	No graphs were given.
Selected statistic is appropriate for the data. Median or mode computation is accurate.	Statistic is appropriate for the data; computation is accurate.	Statistic is not appropriate for data; computation is accurate.	Statistic is not appropriate for the data or computation is not accurate.	No statistic selected. No computations done.
Measurement units are appropriate for the data.	Measurement units are all accurate for the data.	Measurement units are mostly accurate for the data.	Measurement units are not accurate for the data.	No measurement units given.
Conclusions follow from the data.	Conclusion follows from the results.	Conclusion mostly follows from the results.	Conclusion attempted but only minimally related to results.	No conclusion given.
Reasons given for choices show understanding of statistical concepts.	Shows solid understanding of statistical concepts.	Shows some understanding of statistical concepts.	Shows minimal understanding of statistical concepts.	Shows no understanding of statistical concepts.
Reasons given for choices communicates processes used.	Explanation thoroughly and clearly justified the choices made and explained the processes used.	Explanation minimally but clearly justified the choices made and explained the processes used.	Explanation justified the choices made or explained the processes used.	No explanations were given.

Figure 4–15 *(continued)*

students' trust. Therefore, when designing performance-based assessments, when writing performance criteria, when creating scoring rules, and when evaluating students' work, teachers should be conscious of the value statements they make and the potential of any assessment to detract from student learning and students' confidence in their independent ability to learn.

Assessments of Individuals Within Group Performances. One of the most common complaints from students, parents, and guardians concerns the idea of scoring a group product. Performance criteria, such as all group members contribute to the product, presentation flows easily from presenter to presenter, group members listen to each others' ideas, groups develop a consensus position, can cause anger and frustration. The group may fail to meet a criterion because of the behaviors of one or two individuals.

It is important that students learn how to work in groups to create performances and products. Many adult, real-world performances require cooperation among adults to complete performances and products. Yet, generally each person has unique responsibilities in the adult work. A publishing company generally has authors, style editors, typesetters, cover designers, and printers/manufacturers. Hence a book is the product of the contributions of many people. Each contributor has a unique contribution to the success of the whole. And each individual's contributions can be assessed. In much the same way, group products and performances are the work of many hands and minds. Teachers owe it to students to ensure that students' unique contributions are recognized. If one student does not do her or his part, teachers should not penalize all the students in the group because they are unlikely to have control over the contributions of any single individual. The following are several true stories about group work that exemplify our points.

> Maria, a seventh-grader, came home from school and said, "I never want to be in a group with boys again." When her mother asked why, she answered, "We had to do a report on the Revolutionary War and none of the boys did their research. So we got a C on the report. When I told Mr. Carson that Jackson and Colin didn't do their research, he said that we should have done it! That's not fair!"

Maria is right. It isn't fair. Not only that, Maria learned two unfortunate lessons: that group work with boys was a bad thing and that girls are expected to do the boys' work. Even though the same event could have happened in an all-girl group, the lesson learned was too late to be changed. Mr. Carson's nonchalant attitude toward the situation taught the wrong lesson.

> Ahmed, a tenth-grader, was fuming when his father got home from work. When his father asked what was wrong, Ahmed said, "I hate group work! We had to act out part of Hamlet in class today and Melissa and Joe totally flaked out. They made faces and acted like idiots. We got a D for the reading!"

Ahmed's anger is appropriate. He may have been doing exactly what was expected; however, the poor citizenship skills of two students resulted in a low grade for the other students acting out the scene. The lesson learned was that group work was bad. It is unlikely that the teacher intended to teach this lesson. In fact, she or he probably thought the lesson would be that students must behave themselves when doing oral readings. Unfortunately, in the power relationships among peers, Ahmed and his copresenters had little power over the behaviors of Melissa and Joe. Teachers can observe students during performances and identify the contributions of each individual rather than punishing an entire group for the behaviors of a few. For example:

> Corina, Tom, and Marcus, sixth-graders, were working on a research paper about China. The teacher gave the students six topics that had to be included in the report. Each student was to research two of the topics, including a bibliography for each topic. Each student was also required to add one visual aid to the report: a map, a time line, or table, graph, or chart. Finally, each student was required to contribute one part in the final report: a cover with the title and the group members' names, a picture of an artifact (photocopied or drawn) from the country they were researching, and a table of contents. When Corina didn't do one of her topics and forgot to make the time line, Ms. Jackson was able to give each student a fair score on her or his contributions even though parts of Corina's contributions were missing.

This latter example shows how work can be fairly divided so that each individual's contributions are assessed. If students are learning what teachers want them to learn, scores on products or performances that are created by a group should reflect what the individual students have learned or demonstrated rather than whether one or more students failed to complete a task or behaved in an inappropriate manner.

Using Scoring Rules   Both numbers and words can be used for scoring. For example, Mr. Keaton did not use numbers for either the checklist (Figure 4–9) or the rating scale (Figure 4–10). In contrast, Ms. McKinley used a scale of 0 through 3 on her rating scale (Figure 4–15). Some teachers are uncomfortable using numbers, whereas other teachers believe it helps students to make a summary judgment about themselves. These are choices teachers can make. Nevertheless, once teachers decide to use the scores from students' work in the summary grade at the end of a grading period, it is often easiest to transform qualities into numbers because numbers are easier to manage. Descriptive words, however, may be more useful in helping students to focus on the quality of their work rather than the points. If teachers use numbers, the scoring rule must indicate what the numbers mean. Figure 4–16 shows what Mr. Keaton's rating scale could look like if he decided to use numbers instead of words.

As you can see, the words that correspond to numbers are given above the numbers so that students will know what the numbers mean. There is nothing more frustrating to students than to get numbers that rate their work and not know what those numbers mean. Scoring rules should communicate, in some way, what students need to do to improve their work. Numbers alone cannot do that.

FEEDBACK AND PERFORMANCE ASSESSMENT

The extent to which teachers provide ongoing formative assessment, feedback, scaffolding, and opportunities to revise primarily depends on the type of performance assessment. In prepared accomplishments, teachers will probably want to provide more support, especially if the assessment is also a vehicle for students to improve their knowledge and skills. Ongoing formative assessment and feedback can take many forms: teacher-student conferences, written feedback on rough drafts, small-group discussions, or peer commentary. Feedback can even occur while the teacher is listening in on pairs or small groups as they work collaboratively on a project. When teachers ask clarifying questions and make suggestions, this

Student Name: _____ Date: _____

Circle a rating for each characteristic that is present.

Persuasive Writing: Content and Ideas	Clear	Understandable	Unfocused/Confusing
Issue is defined.	3	2	1
Position is stated.	3	2	1
	Strong	Adequate	Weak
Position is related to the issue.	3	2	1
Reasons support the position.	3	2	1
Descriptive examples support the reasons.	3	2	1
	Accurate	Mostly accurate	Little accuracy
Factual evidence supports the reasons.	3	2	1
	Effectively	Adequately	Minimally
Information from research used in reasons evidence, and examples.	3	2	1
	Strong	Adequate	Weak
Conclusion urges action or agreement.	3	2	1
Organization and Format	**Yes**	**No**	
Greeting is given.	1	0	
Closing is given.	1	0	
Name is typed and signed.	1	0	
	Logically	Minor flaws	Confusing
Ideas are organized;.	3	2	1
	Appropriate	Acceptable	Needs work
Language is appropriate for letter to the editor.	3	2	1
Writing Conventions	**All**	**Few errors**	**Many errors**
Words are spelled correctly.	3	2	1
Capitalization is correct.	3	2	1
Punctuation is correct.	3	2	1
Grammar is correct.	3	2	1
Revision	**Improved**	**No improvement**	**No change**
Revision improved persuasive language, if needed.	2	1	0
Revision improved ideas and examples, if needed.	2	1	0
Revision improved sentence variety, if needed.	2	1	0
Revision improved organization, if needed.	2	1	0
Editing	**Improved**	**No improvement**	**No change**
Edits improved spelling, if needed.	2	1	0
Edits improved capitalization, if needed.	2	1	0
Edits improved punctuation, if needed.	2	1	0
Edits improved grammar, if needed.	2	1	0

Figure 4–16
Rating Scale for Letters to the Editor Using Numbers

is a form of feedback. For exit performances, in which students are to demonstrate what they can do independently, teachers will probably provide less ongoing guidance; feedback is likely to be on an as-needed basis. However, the performance criteria, performance standards, and examples of previous students' successful performances should be available to help students understand the expectations and purpose of the work.

When we discussed the qualities of effective feedback in Chapter 3, we stated that it was important to provide opportunities to learn through feedback. One aspect of this function is particularly important for performance assessments. Feedback, used in conjunction with authentic performance criteria, can help students learn the criteria by which such performances are judged. If these criteria are rooted in the everyday activities of competent adults, they can provide additional connections to the real world, as in Mr. Keaton's letter-writing task. If grounded in the real work of a discipline, they become a way to teach students how good work is defined and evaluated in a particular discipline. For example, in a primary class, mathematics feedback might help students be more specific as they explain how their solution led to a correct answer, and how they know it is correct. This is an initial representation of the way mathematicians use proof to persuade the mathematical community of the validity of their work.

Using Feedback to Support Student Engagement

Feedback that helps students to learn and feedback designed to encourage students to persist in the face of difficulty share several characteristics. First, teachers point out the things students are doing well. This not only helps students feel that they have accomplished something, even when still in process, but also reinforces the notion that these strengths are important aspects of a good performance. Next, teachers ask questions about aspects of the work that appear to be problematic or that students have yet to complete. The information gained through questioning can help teachers with the third characteristic: pointing out problems and providing suggestions for improvement. To preserve the students' feelings of self-determination, it helps to frame these as suggestions rather than directions, when that is possible.

Figure 4–17 is an example of written feedback Mr. Keaton gave to a student about the rough draft of her letter to the editor. First, he pointed out that she has stated her points clearly and that her choice of words is likely to catch an editor's attention, reinforcing two important aspects of a successful letter to the editor. Then he asked her to clarify one of the reasons she has provided for her position saying, "Can you think of an example to add? . . . Maybe this sentence could be rewritten to focus on Native Americans' rights. You could ask Ms. Gonzalez for ideas." (Ms. Gonzalez is the social studies teacher.) He also notes lack of clarity when he says, "I'm not sure who 'they' are. The Bureau of Indian Affairs or the people building the plant. I think you should put in a name for each 'they.'" By describing how the word choices make it hard for him to follow her argument, Mr. Keaton provided an authentic reason for revision. He represented writing as communication, rather than as a formulaic exercise for making perfectly grammatical paragraphs. Note that each of his feedback comments—both positive and questioning—is related to specific criteria for the letter.

Finally, he suggested a general strategy, "Also, have a friend read it after your next draft to see if another person (who doesn't know the story) understands your points." Using questions and suggestions rather than directives leaves the student some control over the process. Students who believe they can make such decisions themselves are more likely to feel ownership over their performances; the work is less likely to become "the teacher's project," and students are more likely to remain personally invested in producing a good performance.

Elizabeth,
Good work
so far. Please
see my notes below
about how to make
this clearer. Also, read
have a friend read
Nov. 16, 2002   it after your
next draft
to see if another
person
(who doesn't
know the
story) understands
your points.
Mr. Keaton

Dear Editor,

Why would anyone ~~put~~ want
to put a toxic waste treatment
plant ~~near~~ on an Indian
Reservation?   It is a bad idea
for two reasons. First, at other
plants the waste got in the
soil. It made the soil poison.

Good! This will
catch
their
attention.

] Very clear
introduction
to your
points.

Can you think
of an
example
to add?

Second, Native Americans always
get bad things, They didn't
ask, all the people to vote. They're
going to put in the plant
even though many Native
Americans don't want it. The
government should stop making
people do things they don't
want to do!   Very clear ending.

Is there
a
better
word
than
"thing"?

Maybe
this
sentence
could be
rewritten to
focus on Native
Americans' rights.

You could ask
Ms. Gonzalez
for ideas.

Elizabeth Carpenter

I'm not
sure
who
"they"
are.
The Bureau
of Indian
Affairs or
the
people
building
the
plant.

I think
you
should
put in
a name
for each
"they".

Figure 4–17
Example of Feedback for a Letter to the Editor

113

Motivational Issues in Performance-Based Assessments

Performance-based assessments have a motivational advantage over many other types of assessments. As authentic performances, they seem more relevant to the real world or work in the discipline; they are complex and can provide opportunities for students to continue learning during assessment; and they have the potential of being shared with people other than the teacher. Yet it is possible, even easy, to undermine these advantages when constructing performance tasks. We have touched on some of these issues above. In the following section we will elaborate.

Comparability Versus Choice

Recall from our earlier discussion of motivation that task involvement is associated with working hard, using good learning strategies, and persistence in the face of difficulty. Task involvement requires that students are interested in the topic, are working on a challenging but not overwhelming task, and have an opportunity for learning or improving their competence. It is also important that students feel they have some self-determination in the process.

Before you exclaim "Right! So much for task involvement!," consider this. All these things are more likely if you provide students with some choice. If students choose a topic, for example, they are by definition more likely to be interested in that topic. In both Ms. McKinley's and Mr. Keaton's tasks, students are asked to choose an issue or problem that is important to them. When they choose from among different approaches to the performance, they are likely to select a task that is moderately difficult for them, if they see an opportunity to learn or improve. Again, in both example tasks, students are given some choice in how they gather data and shape their problem. Students who are more confident conducting interviews might choose more of those; students who have strengths in library research might emphasize that instead. And the provision of choice guarantees that most students will perceive at least some self-determination and control over their work. Performance assessments offer more scope for teachers to encourage task involvement than most other forms of assessment, but this requires planning.

Choice is powerful. In most schools, students have very little choice in what they study, how and when they study it, and how they show what they've learned. Elementary school teachers we know have given children the choice of whether they start a math worksheet at the top or the bottom. This tiny bit of self-determination was greeted by smiles and greatly increased motivation to complete the task. The fact that such a small choice got such a large response should tell us something about how little choice students feel they have in school.

Choice is good. On the other hand, teachers must make sure that the choices that they provide within a performance task still allow them to fairly evaluate all students on the learning objectives. For example, allowing students to choose either an oral presentation or a written report would not be appropriate if one or more of the learning objectives involved oral presentation skills. Ms. McKinley may need to monitor her students' choice of topic so that they select one that is neither too simple or narrow in scope nor too broad or complex. This may not be as much of a problem for Mr. Keaton's letter to the editor assignment. In one of her graduate classes, Susan noticed that some students selected topics for their term projects that bore little relationship to the course, or selected topics that depended almost exclusively on sources outside of the course readings. By the time students handed in their projects, it was too late to deal with this problem, and she was left trying to figure out how to evaluate students' ability to use the knowledge gained in the course to explore a problem of interest to students. Now she usually requires her students to write a one-page prospectus describing the topic for their term project, its relationship to the course, and a draft bibliography, due fairly early in the term. This gives her a chance to provide feedback to students on the scope and relevance of their project to the course while there is still time to modify the topic. For elementary and middle school or junior high school students, teachers can give students several options that are equivalent in difficulty and complexity to make certain that all students have manageable tasks.

Evaluation and Motivation

"I really love my senior project and I'm learning so much!" a student in a high school psychology class told Susan. "But I hate the fact that I have to write it up and present it." Heads nodded around the class. She felt that the evaluation process was an intrusion on her learning, a hoop to be jumped through that took the joy out of her project.

"Do you see the evaluation process as useful in any way?" Susan asked. The student shook her head. "Would it be better if the assessment part of the project gave you useful feedback?"

"Oh, yes," came the reply.

When students see the assessment of their performances as unrelated to their learning and improvement, it becomes an external judgment that doesn't help and might do a lot of damage, especially if students have had little feedback about their progress along the way or if they are unclear about the performance criteria. Even an exit performance can and should be a learning experience for students. Too often assessments are viewed by students as another chance for teachers to control them. The threat of evaluation can prevent a student from becoming too engaged in a project, and it can dampen the enthusiasm that interesting tasks engender. In contrast, useful evaluation can support student engagement, as well as enhance learning. If students know the performance criteria and receive feedback telling them they are making steady progress—especially if the feedback is authentic to the performance—they are less likely to fear the evaluation of a final performance.

Clear Purpose, Directions, and Scoring Methods

When a performance task is introduced, teachers should clearly explain the purpose of the assignment. Teachers should ask themselves the following questions: Why is it important? What will students learn? What will I learn about my students' grasp of the content? How will I use that information to support student learning? In the absence of clear explanations, younger students may go along out of obedience, trust, or to please the teacher. However, as students get older they become less willing to engage in tasks they perceive to be meaningless. The directions, standards, and scoring methods also must be clearly understood by students and should clearly relate to the purpose of the assignment. When the teacher's intent is cloudy, the expectations unknown, and the evaluation is looming on the horizon, students are more likely to resist, develop anxiety, or disengage. Only when expectations are clear do students have a chance to demonstrate their competence and to feel some control over the process. Public criteria and expectations are not only ethical, but also good educational practice, and they strengthen the trust in the teacher-student relationship.

Let's take another look at the directions and rubrics created by Ms. McKinley and Mr. Keaton. The directions in Figures 4–7 and 4–8 are clear; the students will know what they need to do and what their final product should contain. If the two teachers provide students with the scoring rubrics or checklists in advance, and perhaps with examples of previous students' work, students will have clearer ideas about how they are going to be evaluated. Teachers' purposes are not stated in the documents in Figures 4–7 through 4–11 and Figures 4–14 through 4–16. Nor is there information about how teachers will make use of the information to support student learning. This information will have to come from the way in which the assignment fits with the instructional unit and from verbal explanations given by the teacher. Purposes and use can be reinforced by the teachers' actions while students are working on the assignment.

INTEGRATION, MODIFICATION, AND ACCOMMODATION

Authentic performance assessments might be altered in three ways to adjust to local circumstances. Teachers might intentionally have students integrate their knowledge and skills across traditional subject area lines. This might require slight or major adjustments to performance expectations, directions, and scoring. Second, teachers might make slight changes in the ways that students are expected to show their accomplishments so that they can accommodate students who have mild disabilities. Finally, teachers may need to make substantive modifications of performance expectations to fit the individualized education plans (IEPs) for students with moderate to severe disabilities.

Integrating Performance-Based Assessments Across Subjects

In contrast to standardized tests and many textbook tests, authentic performances inevitably require integration of knowledge and skills across subject areas. For example, in conducting a scientific investigation and preparing a report on the results, students must use their scientific knowledge and their scientific investigative and communication skills. The mathematical skills of data collection and organization of data into tables, charts, graphs, and simple statistics (such as finding the most common [modal] or average [median or mean] result) are common aspects of scientific reports. In addition, although the writing style is particular to scientific reporting, good writing skills (organization, sentence fluency, word choices, spelling, grammar, punctuation, and capitalization) are also required. Finally, if students conduct investigations that are relevant to local, state, or national issues (such as the effects of toxicity levels in rivers and streams on fish populations), students may also use their social studies knowledge and skills.

When Mr. Keaton told Ms. Gonzalez, the social studies teacher, about the letter to the editor, they decided that it would be a good opportunity for them to have students do a joint project. One of the regular assignments in Ms. Gonzalez's class was to have students summarize the important ideas and details from a newspaper article about a current event. Her learning objectives related to the assignment were, "Students will learn strategies for reading and comprehending informational documents such as newspapers, magazines, and founding documents (e.g., the Declaration of Independence)," and "Students will learn how to extract main ideas and details from informational text." Other than selecting one article each week and writing an accurate summary, Ms. Gonzalez had no other requirements. Although she believed that reading current articles from newspapers and magazines was important, students seemed to be going through the motions of the assignment without really understanding its purpose. Mr. Keaton's letter to the editor assignment seemed a perfect time for Ms. Gonzalez to rethink this assignment and make it more interesting for the students. Before adjusting her assignment, Ms. Gonzalez reviewed her social studies learning goals and objectives. She decided that adjustments to her assignment didn't require any changes in the learning objectives. The method of assessment was what needed work.

Mr. Keaton and Ms. Gonzalez decided to adjust the letter to the editor performance to have students write about an issue they were following in the news as part of the current events aspect of their social studies class. To adjust her assignment, Ms. Gonzalez decided to have each student select one region of the world to study through newspapers and magazines, such as the Middle East, the Far East (China, Japan, and Korea), Western Europe, Eastern Europe, Australia and the Pacific Islands, Southeast Asia, West Africa, East Africa, and South Africa. Each week, students would find an article about their region of the world and write a one- or two-page summary of the important ideas and details in the article. As before, Ms. Gonzalez would check their summaries for whether they captured the important ideas and details.

Figure 4–18 gives the directions and a checklist that Ms. Gonzalez gave students to guide their written summaries of the newspaper and magazine articles. She used this throughout the term to quickly assess their summaries and to see whether the accuracy and completeness of students' summaries were improving over time.

Mr. Keaton adjusted his assignment by having his students write their letter to the editor using the ideas from one or more of the articles they had read. The new directions for his assignment are given in Figure 4–19. The changes are in italics. As can be seen, Mr. Keaton's modifications simply focused the letter to the editor on issues relevant to their work in another subject area. Other than that, changes were minor, simply giving the students a clearer focus. None of his scoring rubrics required any changes to fit the adjusted assignment.

Accommodations and Modification of Performance-Based Assessments

Authentic work that becomes a performance assessment can provide students with special needs an opportunity to demonstrate their knowledge and skill by using their strengths. For example, mechanical skill, musical ability, acting, or speaking may come more easily to some students than reading and writing in English. Performance assessments that require extensive reading and writing may put some children with special needs at a distinct disadvantage. It is important to make sure you know the strengths and limitations of your students so you can anticipate necessary adaptations and modifications.

In Chapter 1 we distinguished between *accommodations* and *modifications*. This distinction is important in instruction, but particularly in assessment and grading. An accommodation alters the administration of an assessment so that students who are ELL and students with disabilities can be assessed on the same learning objectives with the same criteria as other students in the class. Accommodations are necessary when the standard administration would measure the disability rather than the learning objectives, resulting in an *invalid* assessment. A modification, on the other hand, changes what is assessed and/or the criteria used to evaluate performance. Such a modification would mean that the performance would not be a valid assessment of the original learning objectives.

Mr. Keaton has a student, Amanda, with a profound hearing loss. She uses a sign-language interpreter in all of her classes. When Mr. Keaton designed a performance assessment where students prepared presentations about a topic they had researched, he included one of the accommodations specified in Amanda's IEP. Amanda signed the presentation and her interpreter "reverse interpreted" her signs into English sentences. Amanda was evaluated on all of the same criteria as the other students. Her grade of B+ meant the same thing as a hearing student's grade of B+ on the same assignment. Requiring Amanda to speak her presentation would likely lower her score, but the lower score would not reflect her achievement

Current Events: Directions for the Summary of a Newspaper Article

Choose one of the following regions of the world to be the focus of your current events work throughout the term:

Middle East (for example, Iraq, Iran, Saudi Arabia, Jordan, Israel, Lebanon)

Far East (Japan, China, and Korea)

Southeast Asia (Thailand, Cambodia, Laos, Malaysia, Philippines, Indonesia, Vietnam)

South Asia (for example, India, Pakistan, Uzbekistan, Afghanistan, Nepal, Sri Lanka)

Pacific Islands (for example, Fiji, Samoa) and **Australia**

West Africa (for example, Chad, Ghana, Senegal, Ivory Coast)

East Africa (for example, Egypt, Ethiopia, Sudan)

Southern Africa (for example, Zimbabwe, Zaire, Congo, South Africa)

Western Europe (for example, England, Ireland, Scotland, Germany, Norway, Sweden, Denmark, Netherlands, France)

Eastern Europe (for example, Rumania, Czech Republic, Slavic Republic, Slovenia, Serbia, Croatia, Hungary)

Each week, you will find a newspaper or magazine article about an event in the region you choose. I will supply newspapers, and you are expected to go to the library to find others. You will read the article and write a summary of the article.

- The summary will include the main ideas and important details in the article.
- The summary will be in your own words.
- The summary is to be *no more than two pages* hand written. Staple the original article to your summary.

Use the checklist to guide your summaries.

- ☐ The article is about an event or person in the region of the world I have chosen.
- ☐ The article is from a newspaper or magazine that was published in the past week.
- ☐ My summary includes the main idea of the article.
- ☐ My summary includes only the important details related to the main ideas.
- ☐ My summary is in a logical order.
- ☐ My summary is in my own words.
- ☐ If I quote a sentence from the article, it is in quotation marks.
- ☐ I included no more than two quotations from the article.
- ☐ The summary is no more than two pages hand written.
- ☐ I attached the article to my summary.

We will be creating a class list of events and issues in each region of the world. At the beginning of class each Monday, you will add what you have learned from your article to the list for your region of the world.

Figure 4–18
Directions and Checklist for Ms. Gonzalez's Article Summary Assignment

---

Directions for Your Letter to the Editor

You are going to write a letter to the editor of the newspaper. *The letter will be about an issue in the region you are investigating for your social studies current events assignment.* Your job will be to convince the people who read the paper to think about your point of view on the issue. *You will use the information you have gathered through your current events summaries.* In addition, you may also interview your friends, your parents, or people in your neighborhood to find out what they think about the issue. If you want to do an interview with neighbors, you must get your parents' permission. I will do some lessons on different ways to gather information about the issue.

When you finish your research, you will begin drafting your letter to the editor. You may do all of your drafting and revisions on the computer. In your letter:

- ☐ Clearly describe the issue, *why it is an issue* (use your research to help you), *and any background information necessary for the audience.*
- ☐ State your position on the issue.
- ☐ Give at least two reasons for your position (use your research to help you).
- ☐ Give examples for each of your reasons (use your research to help you).
- ☐ Give a concluding statement that restates your position and tells the readers what they should do.

After you finish a first draft, you will share it with your writing group to get some feedback. You will use the feedback and your own ideas to make whatever improvements you need to make. Keep the marked copy to turn in with your final letter. Things I will be looking for after your revisions include:

- ☐ *A clear focus on a specific region of the world*
- ☐ Good ideas with good examples
- ☐ Logical organization of your ideas
- ☐ Different sentence types (simple sentences, complex sentences, and compound sentences)
- ☐ Language that might make the reader stop and think
- ☐ Language that is okay for the editor of a newspaper

When you finish revising your letter, make a copy and put it in your folder. Then you are going to edit your work. When you edit, I want you to check:

- ☐ Spelling
- ☐ Grammar
- ☐ Punctuation and capitalization

Then you will write your final version of the letter. Be sure your letter is typed, double spaced, and has at least 1-inch margins. You can use whatever font you want to use, but it should be easy for the editor of a newspaper to read your letter. When you turn in your final letter, include all of your notes from research, drafts, and marked copies.

Figure 4–19
Directions and Checklist for Mr. Keaton's Letter to the Editor

of the learning targets. Instead, her achievement would be masked, in part, by her disability, rendering the assessment invalid.

If the performance assessment was meant to evaluate students' comprehension and evaluation of written source material through reading, Mr. Keaton would *not* have allowed Amanda's interpreter to sign the written material to her; she would have had to read it on her ability to present. If he allowed the interpreter to sign texts for a reading assessment, he would be changing the learning goals from reading comprehension to sign comprehension; this would be a *modification*. Unless Amanda's IEP specifies such modifications, Mr. Keaton should only use the accommodations necessary for her to be assessed.

Adaptations do not change the criteria or performance standards used to judge the quality of the work, and the final performance is presented in the same forms as are other students' performances. Some students may need extra time, others may need to dictate the written parts of their performance to an adult; some students may need to reduce the length of a performance to complete it within a certain time frame. Students with limited English proficiency may need both the use of a translation dictionary and additional time to complete their work. These and other adaptations should make it possible to provide a fair and valid assessment of students who do not require modifications. The students themselves, along with the specialists assigned to their cases, can be of great assistance in figuring out appropriate accommodations; these adaptations should be spelled out in the IEP as well. A sample of accommodations and modifications is presented in Figure 4–20. However, each must be evaluated against the specific learning targets to make the final determination of whether an adaptation changes the task or criteria.

Teachers must look at their learning targets and then at each criterion for a performance to decide whether the criterion is critical to the performance. For example, if an English teacher is assessing literary analysis, he must ask himself whether reading and writing are critical to the ability to do literary analysis. Probably not. Students can listen to novels on tape and present analyses orally while still demonstrating the ability to analyze character, theme, and plot development.

Some students' disabilities or limited English skills require modifications of the tasks, such as changing the criteria or lowering of the standards used to judge the work. The teacher may scaffold parts of the task, requiring the student with special needs to complete only certain parts. Teachers must be very clear about the purposes of the performance assessment and the learning objectives it is meant to assess. In collaboration with a specialist, perhaps, the learning objectives can be examined in the light of a student's IEP. Teachers must ask themselves which of these objectives is appropriate for this student. If an objective is appropriate, can it be reached in time to do this performance assessment? Is it better to reduce the standard for the performance on that target, or to eliminate the objective from consideration at this time? If targets are appropriate, but can't all be assessed at this time due to the student's limitations, which are the most important? These are questions that must be answered on an individual basis for each student. If students with special needs are to learn as much as possible, teachers must use only *necessary* adaptations. Modifying assessments unnecessarily can exclude students from opportunities to learn and be assessed on their learning.

Students with disabilities may also have their own learning objectives, set by the relevant specialist and documented in the IEP, that they are to work on in your classroom. Sometimes these can be worked into a performance assessment. For example, a student who is working on his social skills may work in a small group on a reduced portion of the task and also be learning or being assessed on his social skills. (The teacher will need to make sure that the small group, in this case, allows the student to do what he can, rather than relegate him to observer status.)

With appropriate accommodations or modifications, all students in your classroom can learn and be assessed. The goal is always that all students learn as much as they possibly can while they are in your charge, and that your assessments should allow them to show you what they have learned.

John is an 18-year-old senior. He takes Language Arts, US History, and Applied Math in the mornings at Central High School and also is successfully enrolled in diesel mechanics through a special "early entry" program at the local community college in the afternoons. His IEP lists his strengths as mechanics and his seriousness about his education: He is determined to both finish high school and earn his AA degree. He is also working on goals of self-advocacy, self-determination, and the use of reading and writing skills and strategies on real-world tasks. The IEP manager gave his high school teachers the following list of necessary accommodations and modifications, taken from his IEP.

Curriculum/Program Modifications or Supports for John's General Education Classes

1. May need assignments and test read to him and/or practice of reading strategies.
2. Check for understanding of instructions and assignments; may need specific process-based written instructions for tasks requiring multiple steps and due dates.
3. May need a scribe to write verbatim answers at times when processing is difficult for him so he can focus on the thinking task and not on the written language deficit. May need a notetaker or editor.
4. May need extra time to complete assignments when and if he is demonstrating responsibility by seeking extra help and doing homework.
5. Assignments and projects may be modified to focus on the mastery of core concepts of the course.

Mr. Keaton's letter to the editor assignment is a good opportunity for John to practice skills useful in self-advocacy, as well as working on real-world uses of reading and writing. In order to successfully complete the assignment, John would need both accommodations and modifications. The specific adjustments should be made in consultation with John (and perhaps his IEP manager).

Here are examples of specific accommodations and modifications John's teacher might use.

Accommodations (Same outcomes)

- Mr. Keaton's assignment instructions along with the social studies teacher's current events summarizing directions, support John's needs. Mr. Keaton will also require John to check in at specific points in the process (IEP #2). He will also read and comment on his first draft *before* John presents it to his writing group.
- John will gather appropriate newspaper articles himself, listen to radio accounts via radio websites and watch television news clips. He will be supported by a notetaker for audiovisual input and/or a reader for newspaper articles if needed for producing his summaries.
- John will use a computer for all drafting and polishing steps. He may use voice-activated dictation software (IEP #3).

Modifications (Different outcomes) and Specialized Instruction

- Mr. Keaton and John's learning resource specialist will teach reading strategies useful to glean information from the articles (IEP #1 plus special instruction on strategies).
- At the designated check-in points, Mr. Keaton will provide further instruction to John about (1) developing his position, (2) organization of information, (3) planning his initial draft, (4) the initial round of feedback (IEP #1). John will help establish the check-in dates (IEP #4).
- John will listen to his peers' letters and suggest revisions, but work with Mr. Keaton on editing instead of independently editing his work (IEP #3).

Figure 4–20

INDIVIDUALLY ADMINISTERED PERFORMANCE ASSESSMENTS

Much of what we have described thus far, in terms of assessments of valued performances, has been for performances that are given to all students at the same time. However, individually administered performance assessments are also important. Individual performance assessments can be used in any subject area where you want to have an opportunity to look closely at students' strategies and skills. For example, instrumental music teachers have students play individually so that they can listen for tone, watch position and posture, check fingering, etc. Language teachers interview students to see whether they can use the new language fluently, use their vocabulary in new ways, talk around words they do not know, and speak with a good accent (see Chapter 10 for an example of using interviews to assess foreign language students). Individualized assessments can be used in any subject area in which you are interested in obtaining a close, undiluted look at students' conceptual understanding and skill. If time is a factor, teachers can assess two or three students at the same time—if the behaviors that are the focus of the assessment can be seen as students perform in small groups (e.g., section practice for the middle school orchestra, reading circles in the elementary classroom).

Individually administered assessments are similar to group administered assessments in that the desired performance must be clearly described. So make sure to ask for what you want; directions to students should result in the desired performance, and scoring rules should be directly related to the learning objectives. For example, Figure 4–21 shows a scoring rule for an individual assessment of beginning students' skills and techniques while playing a musical instrument. Each behavior is rated in terms of how consistently the behavior is shown during the individual assessment. Because the scale is for use with beginning instrumental music students, the focus is on fundamental music skills and knowledge.

Two other important individually administered performance assessments are primary level assessments of reading and mathematics. During primary years, students develop their foundational reading, writing, and mathematics skills. Primary level teachers often have students read aloud to observe their reading skills and strategies (e.g., Running Records; Clay, 1993). It is also possible to assess students' problem-solving strategies and their understanding of mathematics concepts using individually administered assessments (e.g., Cognitively Guided Instruction; Carpenter, Fennema, & Franke, 1996).

Primary Level Individually Administered Reading Performance Assessment

There is no more authentic performance of reading than to have students read. Although most adult reading is silent reading, in order to assess students' reading skills and strategies, the most authentic performance for primary-aged children is reading aloud. Individual reading inventories (IRIs) or running records involve sitting with students as they read aloud from a book or reading passage that is *leveled*. Books and reading passages are leveled when there is a level of difficulty assigned to the books or passages based on grade level. For example, a reading passage might be considered appropriate for typical fourth-grade readers. While students read their book or passage, the teacher keeps a running record of students' reading strategies, word attack skills and corrections, and reading speed (the time it takes for the child to finish the passage is used to compute words per minute). When the child has finished reading, teachers ask students questions regarding the main

Instrumental Performance Scale

Read each item. Then circle the letter to indicate whether the behavior was shown consistently (C), occasionally (O), rarely (R), or not applicable (NA).

1. Has good posture	C	O	R	
2. Holds instrument correctly	C	O	R	
3. Uses correct finger positions	C	O	R	NA
4. Reads correct key signature	C	O	R	NA
5. Reads correct notes (pitch and duration)	C	O	R	
6. Uses correct time signature	C	O	R	
7. Stays in tune (neither sharp nor flat)	C	O	R	
8. Plays dynamics accurately	C	O	R	
9. Staccato is sharp and defined	C	O	R	
10. Mouth position is correct	C	O	R	NA

Goal 1:   Students will learn fundamental physical aspects of playing an instrument.

Objective 1.1   Students will learn to control their bodies (appropriate correct posture, correct finger position, and correct instrument position) as they play their instruments.

Objective 1.2   Students will learn correct finger positions for all major and minor scales.

Objective 1.3   Students will learn how to use mouth position and/or fingering to play notes in tune.

Goal 2:   Students will learn how to read instrumental music.

Objective 2.1   Students will learn how to read notes (i.e., pitch and duration).

Objective 2.2   Students will learn how to read time signature, key signature, and dynamic markings.

Objective 2.3   Students will learn how to play dynamically (e.g., slurs, sighs, staccato, crescendo, and decrescendo).

Figure 4–21
Rating Scale for Individual Assessment for Beginning Instrumental Music

ideas and details in the text and/or ask children to retell the story or relate the information from the text. Figure 4–22 shows an assessment tool that could be used to capture children's reading performances during an individualized reading assessment. Note that the form allows for a variety of information to be recorded about students as they read.

When using these types of individual reading assessments, teachers generally use both narrative and expository (informational) text, because children differ in their skills for reading different types of text. The purpose of individual reading assessments is to get a sense of whether students are learning how to read. There are published individual reading assessments with standardized passages. Some teachers use leveled books in their classrooms for regular assessments of children's reading.

Directions: Photocopy the text the student will read. Count the total number of words in the text. As the student reads (or while listening to an audiotape of the reading) note each of the following:

- Underline all decoding errors (spoken word differs from printed one).
- Circle any omitted words.
- Put a caret (∧) in the space if an extra word is added and write the extra word above the caret.
- If letters are reversed, mark with a ∿.
- Indicate self-corrections by putting a "C" above the word corrected.

Decoding

Decoding errors (D)   Count _____
Omitted words (O)   Count _____
Extra words (E)   Count _____
Reversals (R)   Count _____
Self-corrections (C)   Count _____

$$\text{Accuracy} = \frac{\text{Total words} - \text{Errors (D + O + E + R)} + \text{Self-corrections (C)}}{\text{Total words}}$$

On the marked text, put a slash (/) in the margin for each mistake in a line. Go back through the text and put a line through the slashes (X) where a mistake has been corrected or if the mistake shows understanding of meaning (for example, if the student uses an incorrect word but the word makes sense in the context).

$$\text{Meaningful mistakes} = \frac{\text{Total number of X's}}{\text{Total X's} + \text{Total /'s}}$$

$$\text{Speed} = \frac{\text{Total words} - \text{Errors (D + O + E + R)} + \text{Self-corrections (C)}}{\text{Time spent reading}}$$

Strategies

Uses pictures to figure out unknown words	Sometimes	Rarely	Never
Uses context to figure out unknown words	Sometimes	Rarely	Never
Makes reasonable predictions when asked		Yes	No
Asks questions about the information in the text		Yes	No

Comprehension (Retelling)

Maintains sequence		Yes	No
Includes main ideas or events	All	Some	Few
Uses names of main characters or name of topic		Yes	No
Includes important details		Yes	No

Objective 1   Students will learn to use prediction and questioning to make sense of text.
Objective 2   Students will learn the sounds of individual letters and letter blends.
Objective 3   Students will learn how to blend letter sounds into words.
Objective 4   Students will learn to read for main ideas and details.
Objective 5   Students will learn to use context clues and pictures to decode words and make sense of the text.

Figure 4–22
Example of a Running Record

For example, Ms. Wan, a second-grade teacher, spreads books around her classroom during the first two weeks of school and encourages students to browse among the books and select three books that interest them. She asks students to choose one book that is too hard, one that is too easy, and one that is just right. She gives them a "five finger rule" for deciding whether a book is too hard. As they read a book, they are to count each time they encounter something they cannot overcome. If they count five fingers on the first page, the book is too hard. A book that is too easy will require no effort at all. Finally, a book that is "just right" may require some effort but the student can read the entire book. When students have selected their three books, they meet with Ms. Wan, show her the books, and explain why each is too easy, too hard, and just right. Then they read aloud from each book. In this way, Ms. Wan can assess their reading skills and strategies, get a sense of their reading level, and assess their reading interests.

Primary Level Individually Administered Mathematics Performance Assessment

Individual mathematics assessments can be developed using research regarding how children learn mathematics (e.g., Carpenter, Fennema, & Franke, 1996). Children are given an array of manipulatives and are then given word problems. The difficulty of the word problems and the numbers used in the word problems differ depending on the grade level of the child and the types of operations students are learning. In a sense, the difficulty of problems is similar to leveled passages. Children then use whatever strategy they choose to solve the word problem. Some children will use manipulatives; some will use invented algorithms; some will write down the numbers and compute on paper; some will rely on recall of memorized number facts or algorithms. The purpose of the assessment is to see what different mathematical operations children have learned at the same time they are developing their understanding of mathematical operations and concepts.

Figure 4–23 is an example of an individual performance assessment tool for use in assessing children's understanding of addition and subtraction operations (based on the work of Carpenter, Fennema, & Franke, 1996). Each of the types of problems in the first column reflects a different aspect of addition (joining sets) and subtraction (separating sets). As with leveled books and passages, if students show skill and understanding with simple operations and numbers, they can be given more difficult numbers (e.g., two- or three-digit numbers, fractions, decimals), more difficult operations (e.g., multiplication, division), or both. For example, if a child shows solid understanding of addition with single-digit whole numbers, then the teacher can move on to double-digit whole numbers without or with regrouping (i.e., *borrowing* and *carrying*). If a different child shows comfort with addition, subtraction, multiplication, and division of single and multidigit whole numbers, the teacher can give the child simple word problems with fractions or other rational numbers. Teachers can observe students as they deal with the numbers and keep records of each child's understanding and skill.

Some might think that these simple word problems are not authentic performances, but remember that daily life is full of simple problems that are solved through arithmetic dealing with daily objects. For young children, figuring out the number of marbles during a game is a real-world problem.

Individualized assessments of young children are vital aspects of effective classroom instruction because they give clear ideas about what each student needs and how each student

Whole Number Addition and Subtraction Operations

For each of the problem types, identify which strategy or strategies (direct modeling, counting, or derived fact) the student used and describe how the strategy or strategies were used to arrive at a solution. Indicate the magnitude of the numbers used in each of the problem situations. Use 1 for numbers between 0 and 20, 2 for numbers between 20 and 100, and 3 for numbers greater than 100. Put whole numbers in a story context and vary the numbers and the context used in each problem. Ask students to do more than one story problem of each type and with different magnitudes of numbers. If a problem type is not assessed, leave the row blank.

Student Name: _____

Activity: _____Addition/Subtraction Word Problems_____ Number Level ___1___ Date: _____

Problem Type	Strategy Used			
	Direct Modeling (e.g., uses manipulatives)	Counting (e.g., uses counting technique)	Derived Fact (e.g., uses known facts mentally or symbolically)	Applies Operations (e.g., applies operations automatically)
Join Sets Oral problem given to student is in parentheses				
Result Unknown (Connie has 5 marbles. Juan gave her 8 more marbles. How many marbles does Connie have altogether?)		*Started counting at 5, 6, 7, etc. and stopped when she held up 8 fingers; then named the sum of 13.*		
Change Unknown (Connie has 5 marbles. Juan gave her some more marbles. Now she has 13 marbles. How many marbles did Juan give Connie?)	*Made a set of 13 counters to represent how many Connie had at the beginning and removed 5 of them; then counted the remaining counters.*			
Start Unknown (e.g., Connie has some marbles. Juan gave her 8 more marbles. Now she has 13 marbles. How many marbles did Connie start with?)	*Made a pile of 13 counters. She removed 8 counters to represent those Juan gave to Connie; counted remaining counters.*			

Objective 1 Students will learn how to solve whole number addition problems.

Objective 2 Students will learn how to solve whole number subtraction problems.

Figure 4–23
Record Form for Individually Administered Assessment of Addition and Subtraction Operations

is developing. Repeated experiences with reading aloud and with problem solving not only give teachers an opportunity to assess young children's learning, but are also learning experiences in themselves. As students read text and solve problems, they are developing skills and understandings at the same time.

RELIABILITY AND VALIDITY ISSUES IN PERFORMANCE-BASED ASSESSMENT

All the dimensions of reliability and validity described in Chapter 1 come into play when performance-based assessments are discussed. Many educators claim that performance-based assessments are more valid than traditional tests. However, this is the case only when the assessments meet certain quality standards. One quality standard is that the performances are ones that students can actually accomplish without undue support from others. This issue has been discussed extensively in the section on developmental appropriateness of assessments. A second quality standard is that the performance assessments reflect authentic work in the world beyond the classroom—the academic world, the world of work, and the everyday world (Validity Dimension 1). Therefore, when planning performance-based assessments, one question you should ask yourself is whether the work is a real-world performance. There are times when legitimate classroom activities have no counterpart in the real world.[9] However, if the goal is to help students understand where their knowledge and skills apply and why learning is valuable, students need the opportunity to engage in work that is real.

It is also important to ask yourself whether performance-based assessments truly reflect the learning targets (Validity Dimension 1). The process of checking performance descriptions against the learning objectives is one way to strengthen this relationship. In addition, as you check to make certain that your directions will result in the desired performance, you are checking for Validity Dimension 2.

Another aspect of Validity Dimension 1 has already been discussed extensively—that of the relationship between scoring rules and learning objectives. The extent to which you can make inferences about whether students have achieved your learning objectives depends on whether the scores assigned to student work reflect your learning objectives. If scoring rules are not aligned with the learning objectives, scores will not be a valid reflection of students' achievement of those objectives. Too often teachers and test developers create interesting performance assessments without sufficient attention to the scoring rules. Because the decisions you make about students in terms of grading and feedback usually are based on scores, you must be willing to take the time to ensure a close alignment among the learning objectives, the performance, and the scoring rules.

---

[9]For example, it is common practice for students to play sound-letter games when learning sound-letter correspondence. Although this may be an important strategy for teaching sound-letter relationships, it is not an authentic performance. Similarly, writing assessments that stress a particular type of writing (e.g., compare and contrast essays, descriptive essays) are often used to teach various rhetorical strategies; however, they are only a subset of the writing strategies adults use in larger written works. Teachers must clearly differentiate between performance-oriented learning experiences and authentic performances.

Another validity issue is the relationship between instruction and assessment (Validity Dimension 3). If students are expected to do authentic work, your instruction must prepare them for that work. Teachers can use two different strategies to link instruction with performance-based assessments. First, they can use the performance as a vehicle for students to learn important skills. For example, if data gathering and data analysis are to be shown in the performance described by Ms. McKinley, students could have mini-lessons on various data gathering and data analysis skills and then apply them to their own projects. Rounds of feedback could be used to further the instructional value of the performance. Alternately, teachers could give smaller assignments that are components of the larger work and then use the performance-based assessment as a culminating performance wherein students apply their knowledge and skill in a new situation. Fundamental to both strategies is that, to result in a valid assessment, performance-based assessment should be supported by instruction targeting the elements of a successful performance.

Another issue relevant to the validity of performance-based assessment is the degree to which adaptations you make for students with special needs results in scores that have the same meaning for all students (Validity Dimension 4). If a performance-based assessment is intended to assess writing skills—students must write to obtain valid scores. However, if the focus of the assessment is on conceptual understanding, research skills, thinking skills, reading skills, or similar learning targets, then writing is only one way to assess students' level of skill. Oral presentations or physical models might suffice to demonstrate the same knowledge and skills. Hence, you must ensure that the scores are truly a measure of the knowledge and skills you want to assess—and that the performance itself does not prevent valid assessment.

As you examine the directions for performance assessments to ensure that they will result in the performance you want, you are ensuring Validity Dimension 2. The final dimension of validity that applies to performance-based assessments relates to consequences of assessment interpretation and use (Validity Dimension 5). You must ask yourself whether the assessment process is likely to detract from students' conceptual understanding, skills, motivation, and understanding of the nature of the work. This dimension has been discussed in terms of trust and feedback. In addition, when assessing consequential validity, you must examine the extent to which the performances help students develop an accurate understanding of the subject disciplines and the extent to which evaluation processes and feedback might detract from students' scores and long-term learning.

Performance-based assessments also must be examined in terms of reliability. In a fundamental way, teachers are the test when they use performance-based assessments. Because assessments of performances require solid professional judgments, you must use a number of strategies to ensure that your judgments are reliable. The first dimension of reliability—that of dependability of scores—is difficult to accomplish in a single performance. This dimension has to do with sufficiency of evidence. If students do a single performance related to the learning targets, it is difficult to make any solid claims about their achievement. However, if you use feedback cycles for authentic work, you have more evidence than you would have otherwise. In addition, if authentic work is supplemented by other forms of assessment gathered over the course of a grading period, you can be more confident in the summary judgments they make about students. Hence, it is always a good idea to identify a variety of ways of assessing each learning objective—either through multiple similar performances or through alternate assessment strategies. Ms. Steinberg's unit assessment plan in Chapter 6 shows multiple ways to assess the same skills.

The performances for Mr. Keaton's and Ms. McKinley's classes involved fairly complex performances developed over time. Other less complex performances can be used during the same period of time to assess knowledge or skills with parts of the final performance to increase the reliability of decisions made about individual students. For example, if the formal performance (prepared accomplishment) in a science class was a final report from an independent scientific investigation, the teacher might assign and formally assess different aspects of scientific investigation through smaller performances (e.g., performances that show students' skills in writing research questions, developing testable hypotheses, and designing experimental investigations; performances wherein students take data from someone else's investigation, organize and analyze the data using simple statistics; present the data in charts, tables, and graphs; and write a summary of the results, including whether the results support given hypotheses). This way, even though the students are working on an independent research project, the teacher gives students opportunities to show their knowledge and skills in addition to the final performance.

The second dimension of reliability has to do with consistency of scores. Directions to students are a critical factor in obtaining consistent scores for performance-based assessments. Students must know what is expected of them. If teachers must clarify directions, all students must see or hear the clarifications so that all students are working under the same rules. The third dimension of reliability, that of consistency of scoring over time and across students, is best accomplished by using systematic scoring rules wherein even subjective judgments are guided by clear performance criteria. Careful attention to the development and improvement of scoring rules are essential to consistent scoring across time and students.

SUMMARY

Performance-based assessments are powerful assessment and instructional tools. Through performance-based assessments, not only do teachers give students clear ideas about the purposes of schooling, but students can develop the kinds of skills that make them independent learners beyond school. Performance-based assessments can be the centerpiece of instruction. Students can learn skills and knowledge while doing real work. Through valued performances, assessment can become an ongoing process as students work on prepared accomplishments and exit performances.

The critical elements of performance-based assessments—authenticity of the work, developmental appropriateness of performances, clear directions to students, appropriate scoring rules, and cycles of feedback and revision—require imagination, planning, practice, revision, and patience on the part of teachers. It has been our experience that, once teachers identify and define performances that have inherent value, they are much clearer about what to teach, how to teach, and what other classroom assessments to create. Most importantly, we find that using performance-based assessments can be rewarding for teachers as they see their students' growing sense of accomplishment, purpose, and pride. Helping students to accomplish a few meaningful performances can make teaching much more rewarding than hundreds of worksheets or assignments—each measuring a different discrete skill.

REFERENCES

Carpenter, T. P., Fennema, E., & Franke, M. L. (1996). Cognitively guided instruction: A knowledge base for reform in primary mathematics instruction. *Elementary School Journal, 97*(1), 3–20.

Clay, M. M. (1993). *An observation survey of early literacy achievement.* Portsmouth, NH: Heinemann.

Cullum, R. (2000). *6 + 1 Traits of writing: The complete guide.* Portland, OR: Northwest Regional Educational Laboratory.

Gobbo, C., & Chi, M. (1986). How knowledge is structured and used by expert and novice children. *Cognitive Development, 1*(3), 221–237.

Littlefield, J. H., & Troendle, G. R. (1987). *Effects of rating task instruction on consistency and accuracy of expert raters.* Paper presented at the annual meeting of the American Educational Research Association, Washington, DC.

Schoenfeld, A. H. (1988). When good teaching leads to bad results: Disasters of well-taught math courses. *Educational Psychologist, 23*, 145–166.

Taylor, C., & Nolen, S. B. (1996). A contextualized approach to teaching teachers about classroom-based assessment. *Educational Psychologist, 31*, 77–88.

Voorhees, S. C. (1994). *A study of teachers' initial responses to portfolio-based assessment.* Seattle: University of Washington.

Wiggins, G. (1992). Creating tests worth taking. *Educational Leadership, 49*(8), 26–33.

Wolf, D. P. (1991). Assessment as an episode of learning. In R. Bennett & W. Ward (Eds.), *Construction versus choice in cognitive measurement: Issues in constructed response, performance testing, and portfolio assessment*, pp. 213–240. Hillsdale, NJ: Lawrence Erlbaum Associates.

INFORMAL PERFORMANCE
ASSESSMENT

In the preceding chapter we described how to formally assess valued performances that have been developed over the course of instruction. Such assessments normally become part of a student's final grade, portfolios, or both. Informal assessments, on the other hand, can be used for a variety of purposes, from sizing up students' skills and knowledge at the beginning of the school year to monitoring whether students understand what they are supposed to be doing in an assignment to assessing students' progress toward a learning objective, or final performance. Before discussing this issue further, it is important to recall that there are assessment processes (strategies for gathering information and evaluating that information) and assessment tools (tests, quizzes, worksheets, directions for performance assessments, scoring rules, and so forth).

Most informal assessments occur as part of normal instructional activities. In its simplest form, informal performance assessment can consist of walking around and listening to your students as they work on a small-group task. Through daily observations, you can get a sense of whether students understand the task or underlying concepts. If problems arise, you can step in quickly to explain or provide direction. If problems seem widespread, you can stop the class for a brief explanation, to give students a chance to ask questions, or to give a new example—preventing lost time and confusion. (Of course, sometimes you may *want* students to struggle with a problem or issue to learn how to deal with confusing problems, to come up with their own unique solutions, or to build on later as you help students reflect on the struggle itself.)

You may want to gather information about students' developing skills and performances-in-preparation. The information you gather can be shared with students through written feedback or during individual conferences. The information can be used to plan targeted interventions for students who are struggling or not progressing, to guide future work, and to provide additional documentation for more formal assessments to come. As with formal performance assessments, informal assessments can be *observations* of students, assessments of *paper-and-pencil* work, or some combination of both observational and paper-and-pencil assessments.

INFORMAL OBSERVATIONAL ASSESSMENTS

The focus of observational assessments, as the label suggests, is on behaviors that can be observed when students are engaged in instructional activities or informal performances. Three ways to capture evidence of student learning are useful for informal assessment purposes: *checklists, rating scales,* and *anecdotal records.* We introduced checklists and rating scales in Chapter 4. In this chapter, we will discuss their use for informal purposes and introduce anecdotal records.

Any adult who has been prepared to do so can complete a well-developed observational rating scale, checklist, or anecdotal record to document a variety of student behaviors. You can observe behaviors relevant to important skills directly or you can infer conceptual understanding, attitudes and beliefs, or thought processes from behaviors that are indicators of those internal states and processes. If your students are old enough, they can be taught how to assess their own informal performances and behaviors during instructional activities. They can also assess the informal performances and behaviors of oth-

Name: Tracy Miller	Concept/Skill: area	Date: Jan. 17

Target	Notes
Problem-solving strategies	*Used repeated addition strategy* *Drew a picture*
Mathematics communication	*Identified only relevant information from problem* *Couldn't recall the term "area" when describing the solution to the problem*
Mathematical reasoning	*Gave a reasonable prediction of the area of the garden using estimation*

Figure 5–1
Ms. Chen's Anecdotal Record for Mathematics

ers. The thinking and techniques required to construct observational assessment tools are similar, regardless of the purpose to be served by them. Observers complete observational tools *while* students are engaged in some informal performance or instructional activity or *after* students have completed an informal performance or activity. Whenever possible, records should be made while observing since, in the busy school day, it is easy to forget details that may be important.

Informal Observational Assessment With Anecdotal Records

Anecdotal records provide a strategy for systematically recording notes about students' responses, ideas, and behaviors. Sometimes a written record of the specific behavior (verbal or nonverbal) can be more useful for diagnostic assessment than a simple checklist or rating scale. The notes recorded for each student are unique.

Figure 5–1 shows an anecdotal record for Tracy, a fourth-grade student in Ms. Chen's class during a measurement unit about area and perimeter. The notes were made while Tracy shared her problem-solving strategies on the board. As is shown in Figure 5–1, Ms. Chen's learning targets were very broad: mathematical problem-solving, communication, and reasoning. Still, it is better to have broad targets than to simply observe without any particular purpose in mind.

In her notes, Ms. Chen describes Tracy's strategies for finding the area of a garden, her ability to extract information from the problem situation, and whether she could use the information in the problem to predict the area of the garden before computing. The format of the record sheet allows Ms. Chen to identify the targets she is assessing and to write descriptions of her observations. The information at the top of the form shows that it can be used for different students, for different concepts or skills, and on different days.

The description of Ms. Johnson in Chapter 1 is another example of using anecdotal records. Her index card file with brief anecdotal records on each student helps her quickly note student progress in these skills, as well as her observations of each child's motivation level for reading and writing.

Anecdotal records can be used any time the teacher wants more detail about students than can be recorded on a checklist or rating scale. For example, after a writing conference, Mr. Scheurich, a language arts teacher, notes students' current goals for their writing, new or ongoing problems, as well as his suggestions for next steps. He reviews this information just before his next writing conference with students so that he can keep track of all 120 students he sees each day.

Some teachers keep anecdotal records on all students, focusing on a small group of important learning targets. Others may use anecdotal records for only a subset of students for whom the teacher needs additional information. For example, when a particular student is struggling with concepts, skills, or behaviors, anecdotal records can help document the nature and extent of the problems, the teacher's remediation strategies, and the results of those strategies. This is helpful for instructional planning. It is also important if the teacher refers the student to the multidisciplinary team, the English as a second language (ESL) teacher, a school psychologist, counselor, or school social worker. These records can often help narrow the search for the cause of the problem and help focus future remediation strategies more productively.

Anecdotal records are also useful when collecting data on student misbehavior. If a teacher notes the circumstances of the misbehaviors and the student's response, the cumulative record of notes can be used to help craft a strategy for working with the student, or to inform a referral for special education or counseling. The anecdotal records can also show a teacher that the behaviors are not as bad nor as frequent as the teacher believed and help her analyze the reasons behind her own misperception as well as identify possible strategies for getting the student back on track.

For example, Ms. Sawyer, a biology teacher, found that one of her students seemed to be laughing at her much of the time. Sam joked around with other students before and after class. He also asked questions that seemed to show resistance to the class activities. Ms. Sawyer decided that Sam was going to be a problem student and started monitoring him closely—correcting his behaviors and calling on him when he wasn't paying attention. One day, a guest speaker came to talk about service learning opportunities in the conservation corps. All through the talk, Sam looked at the speaker with his usual laughing face. As expected, he asked more questions than anyone else. At the end of class, Sam was the first student at the front of the room to sign up. He told the guest speaker that he could begin right away. Having assumed that Sam found the idea of a conservation corps amusing, Ms. Sawyer was completely surprised by his eagerness. She looked back on her observations and thought she might have been mistaken about Sam's behaviors.

For the next two weeks she wrote down what was going on in class when Sam was grinning as well as the context and content of his questions. To her surprise, she found that Sam was usually on task during class time despite the before- and after-class joking with other students. However, when he became particularly excited about something, his face lit up in a broad grin. Although he usually asked questions at the beginning of an assignment or class activity, his questions were always thoughtful. She realized that, because of her first impressions, she had missed Sam's genuine desire to understand the purpose of various assignments and activities and his excitement and had interpreted his behaviors as negative. Had Ms. Sawyer kept descriptive anecdotal records rather than quickly making inferences, she would have been less likely to make such a mistake.

1. Decide in advance what ideas, skills, understandings, and attitudes or feelings you are looking for, and list them on the form. Then, while observing, write down each student's behaviors that you believe are evidence for that child's ideas, skills, understandings, and attitudes or feelings.

2. Make certain that the student is in a situation that allows her/him to demonstrate what you are assessing and that the targets to be observed *can* be observed.

3. Write down exactly what you see that you believe is related to the targeted learning. You will make inferences based on these records, but the behaviors themselves must be recorded so that there is evidence for those inferences. For example, it is important to write on the anecdotal record form, "Maggie used her fingers to count out a solution to the problem" rather than "Maggie is at the concrete operational stage" or "Maggie has a weak understanding of the addition operation."

Figure 5–2
Rules for Creating Anecdotal Records

Figure 5–2 gives the rules for developing anecdotal records. Each of these rules will help you create an observational tool that helps you systematically observe your students. Rule 3, "write down exactly what you see," is the most important rule. Teachers, like other human beings, try to make sense of what they see, hear, and sense in other ways. However, humans are notoriously unreliable in the inferences we make if we jump from observations to inferences too quickly. Our own biases are likely to interfere with the inferences we make, and we are likely to see what will reinforce our biases, rather than noticing behaviors that are inconsistent with our biases as was the case with Ms. Sawyer.

Anecdotal records can be used to help define the behaviors and ratings for checklists and rating scales. This may be useful for novice teachers, who are still developing their sense of what their students can be expected to do. If you are not certain what behaviors to put on a checklist or rating scale for scientific inquiry, you can observe students who are doing exactly what you want them to do, write down the behaviors that show students know how to conduct a systematic investigation. Then use the behaviors to draft a checklist or rating scale. Anecdotal records of student misbehavior can be used to define the behavior and the situations in which problematic behavior occurs. This, in turn, can be used to develop checklists or rating scales to be used in teaching students to control inappropriate behaviors while developing new, more appropriate responses to those situations.

Informal Observational Assessment With Checklists and Rating Scales

Checklists and rating scales were introduced in Chapter 4. In this section we provide examples of checklists and rating scales geared toward informal assessment opportunities.

Sizing Up Students Prior to Instruction   Sizing-up assessment (Airasian, 1997) was introduced in Chapter 2. When teachers meet a new group of students at the beginning of the term or year, they often try to get a sense of students' attitudes, prior knowledge, and skills as quickly as possible so that they can plan instruction according to students' needs. Primary teachers often spend the first week of school establishing the routines of the classroom and the second week reviewing some of the critical concepts and skills students learned the previous year. Some primary teachers use informal assessments to get a sense of the students as a group; others use several individual informal assessments to make decisions about grouping students for reading or mathematics instruction. Experienced teachers quickly develop an initial sense of which children might need additional help with social and academic skills. However, as Airasian's (1997) research has shown, teachers must continue to size up their students as the year progresses so that students have an opportunity to change negative first impressions. Effective teachers make a point to continue sizing up their students as the school year progresses (Parnell, 2001).

Suppose a French teacher wants to know something about his students' attitudes toward learning a new language, learning French in particular, and their knowledge about French culture. In this case, he can develop a rating scale for students to complete, indicating their interest in various cultural topics, their feelings about their own ability to learn a new language, their feelings about public practice, or their reasons for taking the class. Because this survey would be aimed at getting a sense of the class as a whole, the teacher could ask students to complete the rating scale anonymously so that they are more likely to share their feelings honestly.

Teachers also want to know whether students have the skills and knowledge necessary to begin instruction. The required skills and knowledge vary by subject matter, of course, but also by the kind of instructional strategies the teacher wants to use. Mr. Fabian has students discuss literature in small groups. The success of this instructional strategy depends on students' discussion skills and their understanding of the elements of literature (e.g., theme, plot, character development, mood). He begins the year by assigning a short story the first day of class. Students start to read the story during class and finish it for homework. The next day, he has students break into five expert groups—one for each of five literary elements. He uses the checklist in Figure 5–3 to observe students' discussion skills and their understanding of the elements of literature he selected. Although he cannot assess every student's understanding of literary elements, he will get a sense of the class's understanding.

Ms. Frankl uses small-group work in several subjects she teaches to her fifth-graders. Her students come from several different fourth-grade classrooms, and she wants to know what kinds of small-group skills her students have. Some of her students speak English as a second language, and one student has an individualized educational plan (IEP) that specifies goals in social skills, particularly group work skills. She is particularly interested in whether some students tend to take control of group activities, while others are shut out of participating (see Cohen & Lotan, 1997).

If most students are relatively skilled, Ms. Frankl may not need to spend much time with the whole group going over appropriate strategies for working in groups. She may be able to focus on one or two aspects of group work that seem to be problems for the whole group. On the other hand, if many of her students have not learned how to work in groups or do not work well in groups, she will need to teach them group work skills before students can function well on their own. If only a few students need extra work on group skills, she can plan for small-group instruction and arrange for these students to work in groups with others who have strong group skills. If students with IEPs or who have limited English proficiency have trouble in small groups, she may want to consult with the IEP manager or ESL teacher.

Ms. Frankl begins the year with some science group activities that are related to the first unit she will be teaching but don't require extensive knowledge of the material. When she wants to keep a separate record for each student's file, she uses the checklist in Figure 5–4. When she wants to record observations for as many students as possible in a short amount of time, she uses the same checklist in clipboard form for ease of recording (see Figure 5–5).

Literary Analysis and Discussion Checklist

Literary element: _____ For each behavior, check (✓) if the behavior was observed. Student Name	Uses correct term for literary element (Goal 2)	Offers ideas about literary element (Goal 2)	Notes author's strategies related to literary element (Goal 2)	Supports ideas with evidence from the text (Obj. 1.3)	Links ideas to elements in other literary works (Obj. 1.5)	Adds relevant points to others' ideas (Obj. 3.2)	Challenges others' claims using textual evidence (Obj. 1.4)	Use appropriate language and tone of voice (Obj. 3.1)

Goal 1: Students will learn how to develop a literary argument.

Objective 1.1   Students will learn how to develop supportable literary claims and theses.

Objective 1.2   Students will learn how to support claims with reasonable arguments.

Objective 1.3   Students will learn how to support arguments with textual evidence and examples.

Objective 1.4   Students will learn how to use evidence to refute alternate explanations.

Objective 1.5   Students will learn to use outside sources (e.g., historical evidence, other literary works) to support or refute claims.

Goal 2: Students will learn how to critically evaluate plot, character, theme, and setting in literary works.

Objective 2.1   Students will learn how authors use symbols, action, imagery, and characters to develop themes.

Objective 2.2   Students will learn how authors use descriptive and figurative language to create setting.

Objective 2.3   Students will learn how authors use event sequence, conflict, and resolution to create plots.

Objective 2.4   Students will learn how authors use action, descriptive language, dialogue, and other strategies to develop characters.

Goal 3: Students will learn how to participate in civil discourse.

Objective 3.1   Students will learn to avoid personal statements about others.

Objective 3.2   Students will learn to build on others' ideas.

Objective 3.3   Students will learn to consider others' ideas before arguing points.

Figure 5–3
Mr. Fabian's Literary Analysis and Discussion Observational Checklist

---

Group Work Checklist

Student Name: _____   Date(s): _____

Check the box if the behavior was observed.

The student:

☐ Shared own ideas about work (Obj. 3.1)

☐ Appeared to listen to others' ideas (Obj. 3.2)

☐ Worked to incorporate others' ideas into the task (Obj. 3.2)

☐ Adjusted own behavior to support the group's goals (Obj. 3.3, 3.4)

☐ Contributed to completion of group's efforts (Obj. 3.5)

☐ Stayed on task/helped others stay on task (Obj. 3.5)

Goal 3:   Students will learn how to work effectively as a member of a group to solve problems, to learn new concepts, and to complete projects.

Objective 3.1   Students will learn to contribute relevant ideas and strategies.

Objective 3.2   Students will learn to consider the effectiveness of *all* ideas and strategies.

Objective 3.3   Students will learn to assess the impact of their own attitudes and behaviors on the other members of a group.

Objective 3.4   Students will learn to adjust their own attitudes and/or behaviors if they negatively impact group effectiveness.

Objective 3.5   Students will learn to work independently to complete tasks and projects.

Figure 5–4
Ms. Frankl's Group Work Checklist for Preassessment

When Ms. Frankl decides she wants to use a clipboard for her observations but also wants a record for each student, she transfers the information to individual checklists.

If Ms. Frankl's class needs additional instruction on group work strategies, she specifies those goals and objectives and plans for assessment. She may continue to collect checklist data for the first grading period, and then use those data to fill out a rating scale for each student to include as part of the information that is sent home with the progress report. In Figure 5–6, Ms. Frankl has listed the learning targets for small-group work and provided a rating scale that she uses to record the consistency with which students exhibit the relevant skills. As she moves into more complex topics in science, she adds two more skills related to applying concepts learned through instruction. She keeps a separate rating form in each student's file, but also uses a clipboard checklist set up similarly to the clipboard format shown in Figure 5–4 to make decisions about the whole class.

As part of her instruction in small-group skills, Ms. Frankl wants students to be able to evaluate their own and others' group behaviors. She decides to have each student in the group fill out one of the rating scale forms (Figure 5–4) for each of the group's members and use this information to inform both her whole-group instruction and, perhaps, interventions in individual groups.

	Shared own ideas about work (Obj. 3.1)	Appeared to listen to others' ideas (Obj. 3.2)	Worked to incorporate others' ideas into the task (Obj. 3.2)	Adjusted own behavior to support the group's goals (Obj. 3.3, 3.4)	Contributed to completion of group's efforts (Obj. 3.5)	Stayed on task/helped others stay on task (Obj. 3.5)
Date _____ Activity _____ ✓ = observed blank = not observed **Student Name**						

Figure 5–5
Ms. Frankl's Clipboard Checklist for Small-Group Work

Informal Assessment of Student Perceptions Using Paper and Pencil or Oral Assessment

Teachers can use several methods to check in with students before, during, or after instruction. Unlike the techniques described above, the processes and tools in this section are aimed at assessing students' own perspectives on the subject matter, assignments, social structure of the classroom, and understanding of specific topics or skills.

Almost all these processes and tools can be used with students from kindergarten on up. All the assessment processes and tools encourage students to reflect on and communicate their own experiences in relation to class activities, an important developing metacognitive skill. They communicate to students that their ideas and feelings are important to the teacher and worthy of class time. When students feel their ideas are valued and respected, they are more likely to engage in learning activities.

Brainstorming *Brainstorming* is a general technique used in discussions to get lots of ideas out on the table for consideration. The idea is to produce as many ideas as possible, without stopping to evaluate the merits of any idea. Once a list is produced, individual ideas

---

Group Work Scale

Student Name: _____ Date(s): _____

Activity: _____

For each behavior, indicate whether it was Consistently demonstrated (3), Usually demonstrated (2), Occasionally demonstrated (1), or Rarely or never demonstrated (0).

3	2	1	0	Shared own ideas about work (Obj. 3.1)
3	2	1	0	Appeared to listen to others' ideas (Obj. 3.2)
3	2	1	0	Worked to incorporate others' ideas into the task (Obj. 3.2)
3	2	1	0	Adjusted own behavior to support the group's goals (Obj. 3.3, 3.4)
3	2	1	0	Contributed to completion of group's efforts (Obj. 3.5)
3	2	1	0	Stayed on task/helped others stay on task (Obj. 3.5)

For each behavior, indicate whether it Showed solid understanding (3), Showed partial understanding (2), Showed little understanding (1), Not done (0).

3	2	1	0	Used concepts from readings, lectures, or other relevant sources to support ideas (Obj. 3.6)
3	2	1	0	Connected concepts to own prior knowledge and experiences as needed for the task (Obj. 3.6)

Goal 3: Students will learn how to work effectively as a member of a group to solve problems, to learn new concepts, and to complete projects.

Objective 3.1   Students will learn to contribute relevant ideas and strategies.

Objective 3.2   Students will learn to consider the effectiveness of *all* ideas and strategies.

Objective 3.3   Students will learn to assess the impact of their own attitudes and behaviors on the other members of a group.

Objective 3.4   Students will learn to adjust their own attitudes and/or behaviors if they negatively impact group effectiveness.

Objective 3.5   Students will learn to work independently to complete tasks and projects.

Objective 3.6   Students will learn to apply relevant concepts and skills to the completion of the task.

Figure 5–6
Ms. Frankl's Rating Scale for Small-Group Work

can be discussed and evaluated, if that is appropriate. Teachers can use brainstorming to informally assess students' understanding of an assignment, to find out about their interest in specific topics, or to find out what kinds of strategies they use for tackling a problem. These lists can also serve to help students firm up their understanding through seeing and hearing multiple examples.

Mr. Achebe read a book to his first-grade students about how friends behave toward each other. Then he explained that they would be writing a class book about friendship, with each student or pair of students contributing a page with a statement about friendship and an illustration. Showing them an example written by a former student, he explained that it was okay to have adults or other children write students' ideas on their pages.

Before beginning, he wanted to make sure that everyone understood what to do and had some possible topics for their page. He asked the group to brainstorm friendly behaviors, listing them on the board as they were suggested. He made a point of eliciting responses from children who were sometimes ignored or rejected by others and affording their contributions the same respect he gave to other children. Most of the students had ideas relevant to the assignment. As students moved off to start their work, he left the list on the board for reference and made sure to check in with the students who had not contributed to the brainstormed list to make sure they, too, understood what to do.

At the beginning of the school year, Ms. Gottlieb wanted to find out what her students knew about effective study strategies. She started by assigning a chapter in their history textbook; then she gave groups of four or five students about 5 minutes to share ideas about studying textbooks with each other. Once they were back in the large group, she asked them to brainstorm strategies for studying and learning from the text. The first suggestion, "Read it!" was greeted by giggles from the students. But she solemnly wrote it down on the board and said, "What else?" Although students had some ideas (read it over again, write down the vocabulary words, answer the questions in the back of the chapter), she was somewhat surprised by how few ideas these high school juniors had about how to study. Based on this informal assessment, she planned to build lessons on effective study strategies into her first units of study and revisit them throughout the year.

Freewrites   *Freewrites* tap into students' views, generally at the beginning or end of a lesson or event. In a freewrite, students are asked to write to a brief prompt for a short period of time (usually 5 to 6 minutes).[1] Teachers can use freewrites at the end of an event to find out, in an unthreatening way, what students learned from an activity or unit, what they are still confused about, what their reactions to a guest speaker were, and so forth. Because the teacher is trying to get a sense of the class as a whole, it is not necessary for the teacher to identify the responses of individual students and, often, anonymity increases honesty. Freewrites require that students be fairly fluent writers and are probably best used with upper-elementary and secondary students.

Quickshares   *Quickshares,* as the name implies, are another quick way to gauge the range of responses of the group. At the beginning of a discussion, the teacher might go around

---

[1]When Susan begins the first class period of her class, Dilemmas of Teaching and Learning, students are asked to take out a piece of paper and do a freewrite to the prompt, "What is real learning?" They are told to continue writing the whole time, without stopping, and without worrying about spelling, punctuation, or grammar. Susan watches to make sure everyone continues writing, even if it is only "this is a stupid thing, why do I have to keep writing." Often students will come up with more ideas to write if they keep pencil to paper, rather than pausing to try to find the "right" or "best" idea. Reading the anonymous freewrites prior to the next class gives Susan a sense of what her students' personal theories of learning look like. She can use this information to plan instruction in more formal theories of learning that relates to students' own existing ideas. She also uses them as discussion starters, asking students to share their ideas in a small group and look for similarities and differences. This primes the students' thinking, raising interest in the topic and raising questions to which students can find answers during the course.

the room, asking students for one response to the topic, passage, or event. For example, Ms. McKinley showed a film describing the importance of both privacy and group cohesion in Japanese culture to her students in Japanese II. At the end of the film, she asked each student in turn to give *one* response or question related to the film. As with brainstorming, discussion and comments on each other's ideas were not allowed. Students were able to "pass" if they could not think of anything to say. In 5 minutes, both teacher and students had a sense of the diversity of views, and Ms. McKinley was able to use their responses to start a lively discussion that capitalized on students' own interests and questions. Later she used the information she gained through listening to students' responses to both the film and the reactions of their peers to plan a learning activity in which students created skits based on their new knowledge of Japanese customs.

Journals   *Journals* take many forms, depending on the teacher's assessment and instructional purposes. Although all journals entail more or less regular entries in a notebook or journal over time, the contents of journals can be as variable as subject matter, development, and teacher and student purposes can make them.

A kindergarten teacher's literacy goals are likely to focus on children's developing phonemic awareness, their growing ability to write recognizable letters of the alphabet, and their emerging knowledge of sound–letter correspondences. The teacher may use daily or weekly journal writing to collect ongoing information about children's developing competencies in literacy. At the beginning of the year, kindergarteners might dictate a sentence to an adult and then illustrate it. As the children learn to write alphabet letters, the teacher may have them dictate, then copy the adult's writing onto their picture, then "read" it aloud. The child's recopying provides information about their progress in learning to write the letters of the alphabet.

Later, the teacher may assess students' emerging use of sound–letter correspondence by encouraging them to use invented spellings to communicate their ideas. In Figure 5–7, the teacher can examine the invented spelling used to write "My sestr hs a eer ekfashin today" (My sister has an ear infection today). It can be used along with other evidence to document that the author is developing good phonemic awareness and is making appropriate connections between sounds and letters. The use of "sh" in "ekfashin" and "ee" in "eer" suggest that she is also beginning to acquire some of the spelling patterns needed for correct spelling. By having students write regular journal entries, the teacher has a record of each child's literary development that can be used with other evidence to plan instruction, communicate with parents, and shape remediation, if necessary. The children themselves also value their journals as evidence of their own improvement in writing, contributing to their motivation to write.

Of course, the literacy goals and objectives for a seventh-grade language arts class will be different from the literacy goals and objectives created by the kindergarten teacher. Although both can use journals, they will serve different instructional and assessment purposes. Mr. Schmidt's goals for his students include developing a sense of how authors use story structure, plot devices, characterization, and the like to create particular responses in their readers. As part of his instruction, his students keep journals in which they record their responses to the literature they are reading as a group. When Mr. Schmidt teaches a lesson on a particular technique used by the author to create a response, he can anchor this discussion in students' independent responses. Students can refer to their recent journal entries and compare their responses to those of other students. Mr. Schmidt also periodically reads the journals, assessing their understanding and looking for areas that need additional instruction. To make this manageable, he collects journals from about 10 students per day

Figure 5–7
Example of Kindergarten Journal Entry

across his three seventh-grade language arts classes. In this way, he stays in touch with the group's progress and can respond individually to each student every 2 or 3 weeks.

Journals can be used in any subject to collect information on student learning. Ms. Simpson, a high school integrated math/physics teacher, has her students write in their journals once a week about what they have learned that week, and what still confuses them. She collects these at the end of the week and uses this information to plan both group instruction and extra assistance for individuals or small groups. In this way she often catches problems before they become obvious on assignments and tests, and while intervention may be the most effective. She also looks for strengths in students who may not contribute often, or whose responses tend not to be taken seriously by the class. She then capitalizes publicly on these strengths by asking these students to serve as mentors for others having trouble with those areas. This can call attention to these students' strong points without embarrassing them and can help increase their status among their peers (Cohen & Lotan, 1995).

Ms. Simpson occasionally prompts students to address a particular topic in an entry. For example, she became interested in enhancing their motivation. She explained the feeling of being "in flow"—high concentration, losing track of time, feeling completely engaged, moderately high challenge matched by moderately high skill level—based on Csikszentmihalyi's (1988) theory of optimal motivation. She asked her students to describe one out-of-school experience and one experience in the integrated math/physics class. She learned a lot about her students, and her students wrote that they enjoyed the novel experience of examining their own motivations.

The ability to reflect on one's own goals, purposes, and feelings is an essential part of what Corno (2001), Kuhl (1998, Kuhl & Kazen-Saad, 1988) and others call "volition": protecting one's intentions to achieve important goals despite low interest, competing goals, or other distractions. Volition is central to the self-control necessary as students become increasingly responsible for their own learning and achievement. Another way journals can be focused is to have a regular set of directions to use when making journal entries. For example, a social studies teacher might ask students to respond to each day's reading by writing one comment and one question about the information in the text. An art teacher might ask students to draw a sketch of an object or part of an object each day. A language arts teacher might ask students to briefly describe one event each day, including images, sounds, smells, feelings, and tastes. For each of these focused entries, the teachers can use the students' entries to assess what students are learning, their challenges, and their insights.

Homework   *Homework* is another potential source for informal assessment of students' understanding. As students complete homework assignments, they not only show what they know and can do, but also demonstrate how they go about making sense of new ideas. Ms. Mizokawa, a second-grade teacher, used students' mathematics homework to make anecdotal records about the strategies they used to do routine math exercises. Figure 5–8 shows her anecdotal record about Tina's strategy for regrouping in addition. She was not just finding out *whether* students could regroup, but *how* they regrouped.

This way of looking at homework requires that students are asked to show their thinking or their processes on homework assignments. In middle and high school, it may not be possible to look at every student's homework every day; however, using Mr. Schmidt's strategy of examining the work of 10 students each day can give more diagnostic information than can be obtained from homework scores—particularly if teacher's aids or peers score students' homework.

Student Name: ___*Tina*___

Activity: ___*Addition worksheet*___   Date: ___*Nov. 9, 1997*___

Describe behaviors demonstrated in class during whole-class or small-group work that show conceptual understanding.

Target	Behavior
Shows understanding of symbolic representations of 1s, 10s, 100s place (Obj. 1)	*Courtney invented an algorithm to add two-digit numbers two at a time. She created something that looked like this:* $$\begin{array}{r} 70 10 \\ 58 \\ +\ 23 \quad 1 \\ \hline 81 \end{array}$$ *This shows an understanding of place value in the 10s and 1s places.*
Regroups during addition (Obj. 2)	*Courtney's algorithm represented 5 and 2 in the 10s place as 50 and 20. Her algorithm also regroups 8 + 3 to 10 and 1. This shows understanding of regrouping during addition.*
Regroups during subtraction (Obj. 2)	*No evidence at this time.*

Objective 1   Students will learn place value in the base ten number system.
Objective 2   Students will learn how to apply place value understanding in number operations.

Figure 5–8
Example of Anecdotal Record for Recording Strategies in Homework

USING INFORMAL ASSESSMENTS TO TEACH AND PROVIDE FEEDBACK TO STUDENTS

We have talked about the importance of the feedback cycle to effective teaching in a standards-based model. Feedback that comes only at the end of the learning process, in the form of grades and comments on final performances, may come too late for many students. Despite the time and effort teachers put into these comments, students are unlikely to pay much attention to them, particularly if there is no possibility of revision. The task is finished, it's time to move on. Students may not see the connection between the feedback on this performance and future performances they know little about. As students learn, informal assessments can support that learning and motivation by providing opportunities for targeted instruction and encouragement *before* they are held accountable for that learning.

The information gained through informal assessments can inform you and your students, indicating progress toward learning targets as well as indicating areas where improvement is needed. Combining informal assessment and feedback creates a "teachable moment." Students have had an opportunity to use their skills and knowledge, have wrestled with the task, and have a basis for understanding the teacher's feedback. You can provide feedback that is targeted to each student's current level of competence, using scaffolding to make the task moderately challenging for each student. Tasks that are perceived as too easy or too difficult are least likely to support student motivation to learn (Nicholls, 1989). In addition to manipulating level of difficulty, you can provide encouragement to students tailored to their current strengths and weaknesses. Finally, if effective feedback is provided when students still have a chance to affect the outcome of their final performances, students are more likely to view those performances as successful learning experiences.

Informal assessment with feedback may be even more critical for students who lack confidence, have limited English proficiency (LEP), or have disabilities that interfere with their ability to carry out a task spanning days or weeks. Students with attention deficit disorder, for example, often have severe difficulty with organization and time management. Such students are likely to need for you to provide more scaffolding in organization and to check in more frequently to help with managing the collection, storage, sorting, and use of information. It can be useful to set proximal goals with students, providing built-in checkpoints as well as making a complex task seem less daunting (see Chapter 3).

For English language learners, you will need to monitor both the understanding of the assignment and the built-in barriers for those who are not native speakers. For example, the style that is appropriate for a letter to the editor in the United States may be different from the style used in other countries and cultures. Students who have been educated in Vietnam, for example, may believe that the direct argument format of a standard letter to the editor insults the editor's intelligence. In Vietnam, it is seen as more polite to write in a more indirect fashion, which assumes that the recipient is intelligent enough to read between the lines. Early and more frequent assessment of students who speak English as a second language can catch these differences while there is still time for additional instruction in local expectations.

Teachers sometimes become frustrated with students who check in too frequently, seeing them as overly dependent on teacher feedback and unwilling to work on their own. Although it may seem counterintuitive, it is often best to provide lots of positive feedback early on and then wean students away from this gradually as their confidence grows. May, a student in Mr. Fantetti's fourth-grade class was forever pestering him to check her math work. "Is this right?" she would ask after every problem. "Is this how you do it?" After a while, Mr. Fantetti decided that he needed to make May work more independently. He told May to stop asking, to just finish her work on her own. May would raise her hand for assistance, and he would ignore it as long as possible in an effort to get her to be more independent. But May would not move on until each problem had been checked. If he didn't stop at her desk, she would wait, doing nothing, and usually not finish her work. Clearly Mr. Fantetti's strategy was not working.

After some reflection, he decided to show her that she was more competent than she believed. He decided to help May set proximal goals, gradually increasing the number of problems she needed to do before checking in for feedback. First, he had her check in after completing the first problem in a set, to make sure that she understood how to approach it. If she appeared to understand how to tackle the problems, he asked her to do two problems before checking in. She could handle this modest increase, and Mr. Fantetti was prepared for her to appear at his elbow in a fairly short time. Gradually, Mr. Fantetti asked how many problems she thought she could do before checking in, gently encouraging her to do larger sets. Before long, May was asking for feedback at about the same frequency as other students in the class. At the same time, Mr. Fantetti began working with the whole class on strategies for checking the reasonableness of their own work.

Building in Planned Assessment/Feedback Points

Providing informal assessment and feedback takes time to do well, and time is a limited commodity in schools. In this section, we'll discuss tools that can be used to make this a feasible part of the teacher's overall instructional plan. Rating scales, checklists, and comments on drafts can provide informal assessment data and feedback. Informal assessment can be provided by the teacher, peers who have been taught how to provide feedback, and the individual student who learns to self-assess.

In Chapter 4, Mr. Keaton's letter to the editor project has informal assessment with feedback built in at several points. First, in the assignment handout, he provides students with descriptions of the process and final project in a checklist format, making it easier for students to self-assess as they work. Second, he requires students to present a draft of their letter to their writing group for feedback. Using the same points contained in the checklist he will use to evaluate the final drafts of students' letters to the editor, he constructs a checklist sheet to guide the peer feedback given by the writing groups (Figure 5–9). Not only does this focus the feedback on the important aspects he has incorporated into the final performance rubric (see Figure 4–9), it helps to reinforce all students' understanding of the characteristics of good persuasive writing and provides practice in evaluating it.

Finally, after students revise their letters based on the group's feedback, Mr. Keaton reads the revised letter and provides additional feedback using the checklist shown in Figure 5–10. It differs from the peer feedback checklist (Figure 4–9) only in the inclusion of writing convention. The informal assessment at this stage allows Mr. Keaton to find students who are still struggling with the content and structure of the essay and work with them *before* they must turn the final draft in for a grade. He may require some of these students to turn in a revised draft before they can move on to editing. For students who have successfully structured a persuasive essay, Mr. Keaton can provide encouraging feedback focused on their strengths and aspects to consider for final editing. All students receive information on their progress toward the goal of a successful finished product, as well as help in reaching that goal. Both are likely to increase student engagement in the task and the likelihood that they will achieve the standard.

In addition to providing opportunities for scaffolding and feedback to students, first drafts of students' work can provide a wealth of information about students' knowledge and skills. For example, one of our pre-service teachers was preparing a lesson on the Bill of Rights of the U.S. Constitution. His cooperating teacher told him that the students knew how to write a "five paragraph essay." Based on this information, he gave students an assignment in which they were to select one of the individual rights protected by the Constitution and write the first draft of a five-paragraph essay on why the right they chose was important in the 21st century. He planned to use the drafts to get a sense of students' current understanding of the Bill of Rights.

The next day, only two students brought their drafts. The class began with many questions and complaints about the assignment. Quickly, the student teacher realized that,

---

Writing Group Feedback: Persuasive Letters & Essays

Student Name: _____ Date: _____

Discuss each characteristic, making note of the group's suggestions.

Persuasive Writing: Content and Ideas

☐ Issue is defined.

☐ Position is stated.

☐ Position is related to the issue.

☐ Reasons support the position.

☐ Factual evidence supports the reasons.

☐ Descriptive examples support the reasons.

☐ Information from research is used in reasons or examples.

☐ Conclusion urges action or agreement.

Organization and Format

☐ Greeting is given.

☐ Ideas are organized logically.

☐ Closing is given.

☐ Name is typed and signed.

☐ Language is acceptable for letter to the editor.

NOTES

Figure 5–9
Checklist for Writing Group Feedback, Letter to Editor

whether or not they had been taught, students did not currently know how to write five paragraph essays. He quickly abandoned his lesson plans for the day and did a lesson on the structure and purpose of five-paragraph essays. The following day all students came to class with a first draft of their essays and were ready to participate in a class discussion on the Bill of Rights. He was able to use their first drafts to assess their understanding of how to write a five paragraph essay and their understanding of the concept of rights.

Draft: Persuasive Letters & Essays

Student Name: _____ Date: _____

Check each characteristic that is present.

Persuasive Writing: Content and Ideas

☐ Issue is defined.

☐ Position is stated.

☐ Position is related to the issue.

☐ Reasons support the position.

☐ Factual evidence supports the reasons.

☐ Descriptive examples support the reasons.

☐ Information from research is used in reasons or examples.

☐ Conclusion urges action or agreement.

Organization and Format

☐ Greeting is given.

☐ Ideas are organized logically.

☐ Closing is given.

☐ Name is typed and signed.

☐ Language is acceptable for letter to the editor.

Writing Conventions

☐ Words are spelled correctly.

☐ Capitalization is correct.

☐ Punctuation is correct.

☐ Grammar is correct.

COMMENTS

Figure 5–10
Checklist for Teacher's Review of Draft Letter to Editor

Summary

Informal assessments serve multiple purposes: They provide valuable assessment information about students at the beginning of a year or unit of instruction. During a unit, they can inform teachers about the effectiveness of their instructional strategies. They provide opportunities for feedback to students at a point when they are most likely to benefit from intervention. Informal assessments help teachers evaluate student progress and plan necessary modification in instruction or content. They can provide opportunities for teachers to call attention to the strengths of students who may not be valued by their peers.

Informal assessment is used by good teachers all the time, whether they are aware of it or not (Parnell, 2001) and whether or not they keep written records. Simply looking out at your students and seeing blank or worried faces can tell you that something is amiss with the teaching–learning process. This kind of assessment happens in the moment and can be difficult to summarize over time; it can also be difficult to remember specifically which students had difficulty with which activities. Regular records of informal assessments could be important in deciding whether to refer a student for evaluation by the school's interdisciplinary or child study team and can be used by that group to inform their decision making. With some additional planning, teachers can collect information over time or across individual students, using any of the methods described in this chapter.

References

Airasian, P. (1997). *Assessment in the classroom: A concise approach* (2nd ed.). New York: McGraw-Hill.

Cohen, E. G., & Lotan, R. A. (1995). Producing equal status interaction in the heterogenous classroom. *American Educational Research Journal, 32* (1), 99–120.

Corno, L. (2001). Volitional aspects of self-regulated learning. In B. J. Zimmerman & D. H. Schunk (Eds.), *Self-regulated learning and academic achievement: Theoretical perspectives* (2nd ed., pp. 191–225). Mahwah, NJ: Lawrence Erlbaum.

Csikszentmihalyi, M. (1988). The flow experience and its significance for human psychology. In M. Csikszentmihalyi & I. S. Csikszentmihalyi (Eds.), *Optimal experience: Psychological studies of flow in consciousness* (pp. 15–35). New York: Cambridge University Press.

Kuhl, J. (1998). Decomposing self-regulation and self-control: The Volitional Components Inventory. In J. Heckhausen & C. S. Dweck (Eds.), *Motivation and self-regulation across the life span* (pp. 15–49). New York: Cambridge University Press.

Kuhl, J., & Kazen-Saad, M. (1988). A motivational approach to volition: Activation and deactivation of memory representations related to uncompleted intentions. In V. Hamilton & G. H. Bower (Eds.), *Cognitive perspectives on emotion and motivation* (Vol. 44, pp. 63–85). New York: Kluwer Academic/Plenum Publishers.

Nicholls, J. G. (1989). *The competitive ethos and democratic education.* Cambridge, MA: Harvard University Press.

Parnell, C. J. (2001). *The landscape of teaching work: How teachers make educational decisions.* Unpublished doctoral dissertation, University of Washington, Seattle, WA.

INTRODUCTION TO CLASSROOM TESTING

In a writing study, students were given the following writing prompt: *There are certain subjects you are required to take in school. Write an essay telling what is good and what is bad about being required to take certain subjects.* Based on their written essays, it appeared that sixth- and seventh-grade students interpreted the prompt to mean: *Write an essay telling what is good and what is bad <u>about the subjects</u> you are required to study.* When discussing reading and mathematics, the students were very clear about their purposes. One typical student wrote, "You have to read because there are words everywhere. You have to read road signs, menus, contracts, and directions. You have to know math because you have to balance a checkbook and buy cars and houses. And you have to use math in lots of jobs." When discussing social studies and science, 70% of the students in this diverse sample said something like, "You study science and social studies so that when you grow up and someone asks you a question, you know the answer."

This last comment is a very telling one. Students use forms of assessment and classroom instructional experiences to make sense of school. Assessments play a critical role in helping students construct an understanding of why they study the subjects in school. Clearly, for this sample of sixth- and seventh-grade students, schoolwork in science and social studies had no real-world application. The purpose of learning was to do well on tests. Adult use of these subjects extended no further than playing a game of Trivial Pursuit®. You may ask, "How can this be avoided?"

In the previous two chapters, we focused on using authentic work as the centerpiece of instruction. Because students' performances on authentic tasks can be very similar to performances in life beyond school, assessments of that work—both formal and informal—can be the most effective and valid ways to assess students' knowledge and skills. These performances also give students a clearer picture of how the knowledge and skills they learn transfer to the world beyond the classroom.

In this and the next two chapters, we present more traditional forms of assessment. In this chapter, we describe how to build tests that truly assess what you want students to learn. In Chapter 7 we describe how to write traditional test items (multiple-choice, short-answer, true-false, matching, and completion items). In Chapter 8 we describe how to create performance items (essay items, performance tasks, and direct writing assessment) that teachers can use independently or in classroom tests. In each chapter, we describe the item types and give rules for writing each type of item. The rules are derived from research on what does and doesn't work if items are to actually measure what you want to measure. Although Chapters 7 and 8 have common elements, we see a significant difference between traditional test items and performance items—differences that will become apparent as we describe them. In this chapter, we describe how to design and build tests. We discuss the various problems that can arise in testing and how you can avoid the pitfalls that lead to poor test development.

Tests, as we know them today, have been used for nearly a century to quickly and efficiently measure knowledge and simple applications of skills. The advantage to tests is that students can complete many items in a short time; therefore, teachers can assess a broad range of facts, skills, and simple applications quickly. Tests have had widespread acceptance by teachers. They can provide closure to instructional units or a check-up on whether students have memorized a body of knowledge (such as a set of spelling words). One typical instructional cycle is to teach, assign homework for practice, test, and then move on to the next topic of study without looking back or revisiting a particular concept or skill. Although this strategy has some logic, it fits best within what has been called a "factory model" of education. Students are objects moving along the conveyor belt of school and teachers provide input—teaching this idea or that skill. The test is a check to be sure students "got" what the teacher taught. In this model, efficient tests are useful tools.

However, in a standards-based educational model, all students are supposed to meet standards. For some students with disabilities, standards may be established by each student's individualized education plan (IEP) team. For students in the regular education program and for many students with disabilities, standards are established by the district or state curriculum standards. Assessment tools and processes are used to find out whether students are meeting standards, to determine what to teach next if they are, and to adjust instruction if they are not. Therefore, test performance is used as part of the overall feedback cycle and, when students do not perform well on tests, teachers must ask themselves whether the problem lies in the assessment, the instructional strategies, or the students' learning. In the standards-based model, tests, quizzes, and worksheets can be used to determine what to teach (preassessments) or whether a particular instructional strategy was successful in helping students learn. Tests serve diagnostic and instructional planning purposes as well as grading purposes.

Teachers in standards-based classrooms often have students redo parts of quizzes and tests when the first performance is not up to standard. In one high school in the Pacific Northwest, the mathematics teachers use what they call a "100% completion and 90% competency" rule. In this school, students must fully complete all homework, tests, and quizzes and do so with 90% competency in order to earn credit. If students make errors on a test, quiz, or homework assignment, they must revise the work and correct the errors. If the errors are careless mistakes, students can simply fix them. If the errors are due to lack of understanding or skill, the students meet with the teacher to get extra help with the concept or skill and then redo the missed items on the test, quiz, or homework. Needless to say, students are less likely to forget what they have learned when teachers hold them accountable for learning everything that is tested.

Advocates of testing claim that teachers can generalize from the number of items students answer correctly on a test to what students know in a subject area as a whole. Although teachers might look at test performance for their students *as a group* to assess what they have learned, it is not appropriate to make this judgement for a single student. An individual student's performance on a single test can misrepresent that student's accomplishments by assessing mainly the knowledge and skills the student *has* learned while omitting the knowledge and skills the student *has not* learned. Alternately, another student may find that the test is focused on what she *has not* learned and omit what she *has* learned. In both cases, the test scores misrepresent the individual student's knowledge and skills in the subject area.

In addition, performance on tests does not necessarily generalize to performance in work beyond school. We cannot infer that students' knowledge is equivalent to students' ability to use that knowledge. Given that scores from tests of memorized knowledge and simple applications do not generalize well, performance items have become more and more popular for use in classroom assessments. The advantage to these latter types of items is that they are tightly controlled performances. Generally they require 5 to 20 minutes to complete and ask students to apply their knowledge and skills in ways that are similar to authentic performances or parts of authentic performances.

For example, suppose an elementary teacher was teaching students how to write research papers. One of her learning objectives might be "Students will learn how to summarize main ideas and details of text in their own words." She might give students essay items that ask students to write brief summaries of excerpts from magazine articles. The teacher could then assess whether students can write a brief summary of text, capturing the main ideas and important details. This could be an important preassessment to use before students begin to work on their own research papers wherein this skill is central to successful completion of the work. If a few students are still unable to summarize effectively, the teacher can provide individual guidance during library research time. If *most* students still need help with summarizing, the teacher will know that a particular lesson did not work. She can adjust the lesson and reteach the skill. A teacher can also use performance items to assess students' ability to do a component of a larger performance. For example, a teacher might give her students performance items wherein they must take data and put it into a graph or chart. This would help the teacher assess a skill that is part of writing a report from a scientific investigation.

Whatever the reason for using traditional and performance items in classroom tests, items must be well written to find out whether students have learned what they are supposed to learn. Well-written traditional and performance items are clear and straightforward. They do not contain tricks that prevent students from showing what they know and are able to do. They target the important learning objectives and are consistent with the methods of instruction.

BUILDING TESTS

Although tests begin with test items, it is sometimes easier to understand issues related to items by looking first at tests as a whole. The purpose of a test, quiz, or worksheet is to give you the information you need. In this section, we describe how to build a test, beginning with learning goals and objectives.

Building tests is an art and a science. The best tests are ones that are composed of well-written items, written *before* a particular unit or topic is taught, and in harmony with the instructional processes and content. The worst tests are composed of poorly or hastily written items, items of limited relevance to instruction, or items disconnected from the valued learning objectives.

Before building a test, you must think about what it is that you want students to learn and what it looks like when they have learned. Some of what you want students to learn may be efficiently assessed through traditional tests. If the learning objectives are stated in terms of learning a body of knowledge or a set of skills, then traditional items may be an appropriate way to assess. For example, if you want students to learn the meaning of vocabulary words, how to solve for x in an equation, or how to conjugate irregular verbs in Spanish, you can efficiently test this knowledge using tests that give students multiple items—each item assessing a different vocabulary word, a different algebra exercise, or a different conjugation of an irregular verb. If you want students to apply knowledge and skills in complex combinations, make an interpretation, synthesize information, or make an evaluation, traditional tests are not the best ways to assess. Learning objectives must guide decisions about tests.

Assessment Plans and Test Maps

An assessment plan is an overall guide for how you will assess students' learning of the knowledge and skills relevant to an instructional unit, quarter, trimester, or semester. A test map is a design for a single test that will be used during an instructional period. Prior to instruction, examine the learning objectives for the unit, quarter, or semester and determine the best ways to assess your objectives. You can judge which objectives can be efficiently assessed through traditional items, performance items, or formal performance assessments. Next, you decide how many performances and/or test items are needed to adequately measure each learning objective. Finally, you decide which item type(s) you will use to have students show the learning objectives.

Ms. Steinberg, a ninth-grade teacher, is beginning an earth science unit on water. She wants to assess students' understanding of the stages of the water cycle and physical properties of water in different states, as well as students' ability to design and conduct systematic scientific investigations, draw conclusions, make interpretations from data, and represent scientific results in data tables and/or graphs. First Ms. Steinberg decides that students' ability to design and conduct systematic investigations should be assessed through one or more performance assessments. She decides that some aspects of scientific investigation (e.g., drawing conclusions, making interpretations from data, and representing scientific results in tables and/or charts) can be assessed through both a performance assessment and on a test. She decides that assessing students' understanding of the water cycle and physical properties of water in different states are most efficiently assessed through a test. Figure 6–1 shows Ms. Steinberg's assessment plan for the water unit. Based on the assessment plan, she will have students do one formal performance, a test with three performance tasks (see Chapter 8), six multiple-choice items, one matching set, and two short-answer items (see Chapter 7). In the next section, we discuss how Ms. Steinberg could put her test together.

Test Layouts

Throughout this book, we have emphasized that, in a standards-based assessment system, all assessments should help you find out what students have learned related to the learning objectives that are the focus of instruction. This maxim is also important to consider when organizing items into a test or quiz. When the layout of a test or quiz prevents students from showing what they have learned, teachers cannot be sure what scores mean. This makes it difficult to adjust instruction to meet students' needs. For example, the following item was created by a teacher for a social studies test:

> The golden age of Greece was called the golden age because: (a) it was a time of great works of art, important philosophical ideas, and democratic ideals, (b) people found gold in the hills of Greece, (c) it was the 50th anniversary of Greek civilization, (c) all of the above.

This item, along with the other 19 items on the test, was printed on one side of a sheet of paper. Not only does the item violate several multiple-choice item writing rules, the layout of the item can present problems for students who understand the concept of "golden age" but who have reading difficulties. Although the teacher may have shown a good awareness of conservation of paper, he did not show understanding of what it takes for students to show their understanding through multiple-choice items.

Those who are familiar with standardized tests will know that answer choices are never laid out in the format shown in the example above. In fact, the layout of tests can have as much to do with student performance as does the quality of items. Some general rules for laying out tests are given below. Each rule is intended to help you create tests and quizzes through which students can show what they truly know and are able to do.

Objectives Students will learn:	Formal Performance Assessment		Unit Test		
	Design, Conduct, and Report on a Scientific Investigation	Performance Tasks (No. of tasks)	Multiple-Choice Items (No. of items)	Short-Answer Items (No. of items)	Matching Set (No. of sets)
How to design a simple investigation.	Design an investigation that tests the effects of different amounts of water on three types of plants. Be sure to include the research question, the materials you will use, the steps in the procedure, and what results you'll measure and how often.				
How to conduct a simple scientific investigation.	Conduct your investigation keeping detailed records of your results.				
How to represent data in graphs and/or charts.	Create a chart of the results of your investigation.	Given data, create a graph (2).	Given data, select the appropriate graph (2).		
How to use data to draw a reasonable conclusion.	Use the results from your investigation to draw a conclusion about the answer to your research question.		Given an investigation and data, identify an appropriate conclusion (2).	Given an investigation and data, identify and appropriate conclusion (1)	
How to make interpretations from the results of investigations.	Write a recommendation to someone who lives in the rain shadow of a mountain about what plants to buy for his yard.		Given an investigation and data, identify a reasonable interpretation (2).	Given an investigation and data, make a reasonable interpretation (1)	
The stages of the water cycle.		Draw a picture of the water cycle with the process (e.g., evaporation) labeled (1).			
The physical properties of water in different states.			Give a description of the physical properties of water and identify the state of water.		Match physical properties with states of water (1).

Figure 6–1
Ms. Steinberg's Assessment Plan for the Water Unit

Rule 1. Use print sizes and fonts that are easy to read. When students take tests and quizzes, they are often anxious about their performance. Minimize any problems students might have by making the text easy to read. For example, most tests are printed in New Century Schoolbook font in 12-point type. This is an easily readable font and size of type. Another popular font is Arial, although this font is typically used for tables, graphs, and charts rather than text. For very young children, 14- or 16-point Arial font is best because the letters will look more like hand printed letters than fonts such as Times New Roman and New Century Schoolbook.

Rule 2. Don't place too many items onto a single page. Along with the print size and font, the amount of space between items can affect the amount of stress students experience in the testing situation. If you need to save paper, use two-sided printing rather than squeezing too many items on a page.

Rule 3. Use capital letters to identify answer choices for multiple-choice and matching items when students must write letters to indicate their answer choices or must use a separate answer sheet rather than circle their answers. Capital letters are easier to decode when students have reading problems. If students must write their answers on a separate sheet of paper or on a line to the right or left of the items, it will be easier for you to decide whether a letter is an A or a D if they write capital letters. If you use a separate bubble answer sheet, capital letters are easier to see on the answer document.

Rule 4. Minimize the visual distractions for items. For older students, stack answer choices and put space between them so that students can clearly see *each* answer choice. All of the examples given in Chapter 7 show stacked answer choices except the items for very young children. Very young children are just learning to read left to right. Top-down formats in the items can cause confusion for them. As students get older, there is generally more text in the answer choices, hence the top-to-bottom format is best. In addition, space between answer choices makes clear distinctions between the choices.

Rule 5. Make certain that items don't provide clues to the answers for other items. This is a common problem in testing, especially when there are not sufficient ideas to warrant a paper-and-pencil test. Once a test is completed, go back through all items and make certain that you haven't clued the answer to one item in the set-up for another item.

Rule 6. Put items in a sensible order. When students must answer questions related to a reading passage, have them answer questions that ask about "big ideas" (e.g., main idea) before you have them go back and look at specific details. Similarly, when students are looking at stimuli such as graphs, tables, charts, and pictures, put "big idea" questions before questions focused on smaller details. When students are doing mathematics problems, put easier problems first. Make certain that all items related to a stimulus or reading passage follow the passage. Don't intersperse items that are unrelated to the stimulus materials with those that depend on those materials. Figure 6–2 shows Ms. Steinberg's test for the water unit. As can be seen, she has used questions that are related to stimulus materials such as data tables. Each item is formatted in a way that separates it from other items. There are no clues from one item to the next.

Name: _____

SCIENCE TEST

Read the investigation. Then do 1 and 2.

Mara and Jon did an investigation to look at the effects of different liquids on bones. Look at the steps in their investigation.

Question: What is the effect of different liquids on chicken thigh bones?

Materials:
Three 8-oz. cups
Cola
Orange juice
Water
3 clean thigh bones from chickens

Procedure:
1. Put 6 oz. of cola in one cup; 6 oz. of orange juice in one cup; 6 oz. of water in one cup.
2. Place a bone in each cup.
3. Observe bones over 7 days.
4. Record observations.

Observations:

Day	Bone in Orange Juice	Bone in Cola	Bone in Water
1	Off white	Off white	Off white
2	Off white	Slightly brown	Off white
3	Slightly yellow	Brown	Off white
4	Slightly yellow	Dark brown and rubbery	Off white
5	Yellow	Black and rubbery	Off white
6	Yellow and rubbery	Black with small holes	Off white
7	Yellow and rubbery	Black with small holes	Off white

1. What conclusion can Jon and Mara make from the data in the investigation?

   A. Different liquids have little effect on the chicken bones.

   B. The orange juice is the one liquid that changes bones' color.

   C. The acids in cola break down bones faster than the acids in orange juice.

2. Write a health recommendation to other students based on the results of this investigation. Use information from the observation table to support your recommendation.

Figure 6–2
Ms. Steinberg's Test for the Water Unit

Read the investigation. Then do 3 and 4.

Courtney and Cameron did an investigation to look at the effects of different amounts of light on bean plants.

Question: What is the effect of different amounts of light on plant growth?

Materials:
Six 6-oz. cups
Six bean seeds
Water
Potting soil

Procedure:
1. Soak the bean seeds in water for 2 days until the seed leaves begin to come out of the seed.
2. Fill each 6-oz. cup ¾ full of potting soil.
3. Place a seed in each cup and cover with ¼ inch of potting soil.
4. Place 3 cups near a window.
5. Place a cardboard box over 3 cups.
6. Add 2 oz. of water to each cup each day.
7. Observe the plants over a 2-week period.
8. Write down observations.

Observations:

Day	Bean Seeds in Sunlight	Bean Seeds Under Box
2	Tops of plants are showing	Tops of plants are showing
4	Plant is green; ½ inch high	Plant is light green; ½ inch high
6	Plant is green; 1 inch high	Plant is pale green; 1 inch high
8	Plant is green; 2 inches high	Plant is yellow; 2 inches high
10	Plant is green; more leaves; 2½ inches high	Plant is yellow; 2 inches high
12	Plant is green; more leaves; 3 inches high	Plant is white; 2 inches high; wilted
14	Plant is green; many leaves; 4 inches	Plant is white; wilted

3. Write *one* conclusion Courtney and Cameron can make from the data in the investigation. Support the conclusion with specific data from the table of observations.

4. Which of the following can be inferred from the data in the investigation?
   A. Put bean plants in sunny places in the garden.
   B. Give bean plants the same amount of water each day.
   C. Use potting soil in gardens when growing beans.

Figure 6–2 (continued)

Read the investigation. Then do 5 and 6.

Robin and Juan did an investigation to look at the effects of fertilizer on pea plants.

Question: What is the effect of fertilizer on plant growth?

Materials:
Six 6-oz. cups
Six pea seeds
Fertilizer
Water
Potting soil

Procedure:
1. Soak the pea seeds in water for 2 days until the seed leaves begin to come out of the seed.
2. Fill each 6-oz. cup ¾ full of potting soil.
3. Add ¼ teaspoon of fertilizer to 3 cups.
4. Place a pea seed in each cup and cover with ¼ inch of potting soil.
5. Add 2 oz. of water to each cup each day.
6. Observe the plants over a 2-week period.
7. Write down observations.

Observations:

Day	Pea Seeds Without Fertilizer	Pea Seeds With Fertilizer
2	Tops of plants are showing	Tops of plants are showing
4	Plant is green; ½ inch high	Plant is green; 1 inch high
6	Plant is green; 1 inch high	Plant is green; 2 inches high
8	Plant is green; 2 inches high	Plant is green; 3 inches high
10	Plant is green; more leaves; 2½ inches high	Plant is green; more leaves; 3½ inches high
12	Plant is green; more leaves; 3 inches high	Plant is green; more leaves; 4 inches high
14	Plant is green; many leaves; 4 inches	Plant is green; many leaves; 5 inches

5. What **conclusion** can Marta and Juan make from the data in the investigation?
   A. Fertilizer makes the growth spurt phase longer.
   B. Fertilizer makes pea plants grow taller.
   C. Fertilizer makes pea plants grow more leaves.

6. Which of the following can be inferred from the data in the investigation?
   A. Organic fertilizer is better than chemical fertilizer.
   B. Use fertilizer if you want plants to grow taller.
   C. Potting soil and fertilizer are both necessary for plant growth.

Figure 6–2 (continued)

7. Draw a picture of **six** stages of the water cycle in the space below. In your picture, be sure to:
   - Label each stage of the cycle
   - Use arrows to show how the process flows
   - Describe what happens to the water molecules at each stage
   - Use scientific terms for the processes at each stage

Read each situation. Then write the name of the state of water beside the situation.

Liquid	Gas	Solid

8. _____ State of water when the temperature is 32° F or 0° C

9. _____ State of water just after evaporation

10. _____ State of water during condensation

11. _____ State of water during precipitation

12. _____ State of water at 120° F or 100° C

Figure 6–2 (continued)

Look at the growth data in the table.

Height of Bean Plants for 7 Days

Day 1	Day 2	Day 3	Day 4	Day 5	Day 6	Day 7
1 cm	2 cm	4 cm	8 cm	10 cm	12 cm	13 cm

13. Use the data in the table to create a line graph. Be sure to:
    - Give the graph an informative title
    - Label both axes
    - Use an appropriate scale
    - Graph correct data

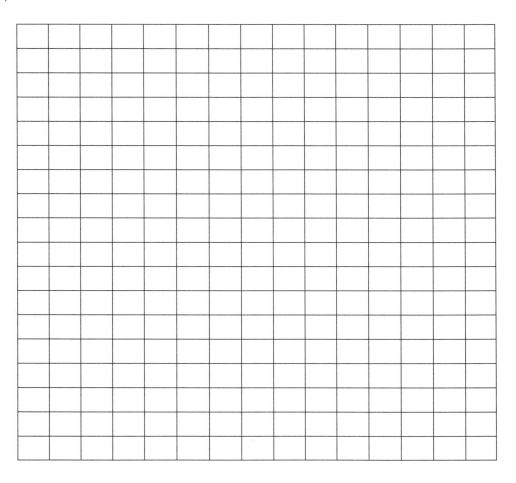

Figure 6–2 (continued)

Look at the rainfall data in the table.

Rainfall for a One-Year Period in Alabama

Jan.	Feb.	Mar.	Apr.	May	June	July	Aug.	Sept.	Oct.	Nov.	Dec.
9 cm	6 cm	5 cm	3 cm	2 cm	2 cm	1 cm	1 cm	1 cm	4 cm	8 cm	10 cm

14. Use the data in the table to create a line graph. Be sure to:
    - Give the graph an informative title
    - Label both axes
    - Use an appropriate scale
    - Graph correct data

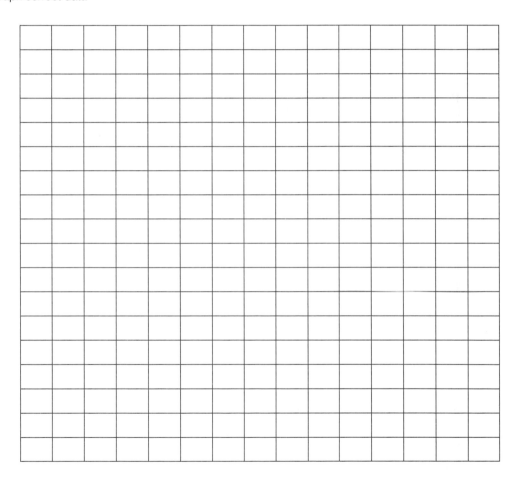

Figure 6–2 (continued)

For each multiple-choice item, circle the letter for the correct answer. Look at the data in the table.

High and Low Temperatures in Seattle Over a Seven-Day Period

	Day 1	Day 2	Day 3	Day 4	Day 5	Day 6	Day 7
High	52	58	60	54	50	50	52
Low	32	30	28	25	23	23	25

15. Which of the following graphs shows the trend in the **high** temperatures?

A.

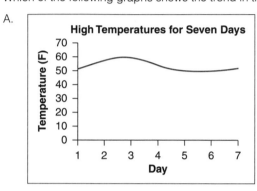

B.

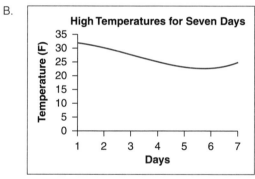

C.

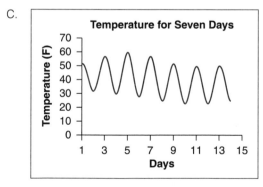

Figure 6–2 (continued)

Precipitation in Seattle Over a Seven-Day Period

Day 1	Day 2	Day 3	Day 4	Day 5	Day 6	Day 7
10 mm	10 mm	20 mm	30 mm	20 mm	10 mm	10 mm

16. Which of the following graphs shows the trend in the precipitation over seven days?

A.

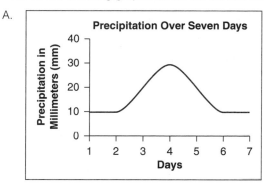

B.

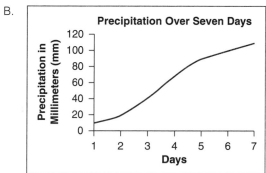

C.

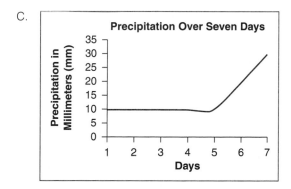

STOP

Figure 6–2 (continued)

Rule 7. Measure knowledge and skills using more than a single item.   A careful examination of Ms. Steinberg's test shows that she assessed some knowledge and skills using two or more items. Recall the basketball test described in Chapter 1. If we have students do something more than once, we can be more certain that their responses are typical of their performance.

Scoring Tests

Assigning scores to test items is much like assigning scores to performances. You must decide what kind of information you want to capture and create scoring rules that help you capture the information you need. In a traditional testing context, teachers often assign points to items without having scoring rules. The only feedback the student receives is the number of points earned for each item and a total score on the test. In a standards-based context, it is important to do more than just assign points to items. Teachers can use the points to communicate students' strengths and weaknesses. Teachers can also use the scores across students to decide whether test items worked well and whether students as a group learned specific knowledge and skills.

Ms. Steinberg had two choices when assigning scores to students' responses to performance items 7, 13, and 14. She could have simply created generic rubrics to give scores to students' responses to the performance items. Instead, Ms. Steinberg created scoring rules that provided more than a score for each item. Figure 6–3 shows the scoring rules Ms. Steinberg used for the test. The scoring rules include the answers to multiple-choice and matching items, brief scoring rules for the short answer items, and rating scales for the performance items. Because Ms. Steinberg wants to track students' performances related to her learning objectives, she has also created an individual student score sheet (see Figure 6–4) to record how each student performs on the items in terms of their relationship to the learning objectives. Finally, Figure 6–5 shows how Ms. Steinberg recorded performance across items so that she can decide what her classes as a whole learned well and what, if anything, they did not learn. Since inquiry skills were to be a semester long focus, Ms. Steinberg used the record sheet to track how each student did on the skills for inquiry. She will be able to use the rating scales for graphing throughout the semester. She will be able to use the results from this assessment, along with information from other assessments throughout the semester, to see whether students' inquiry skills are developing satisfactorily over time.

Avoiding the Pitfalls in Test Development

Find Ways to Assess All of Your Objectives, Not Just Those That Are Easy to Test   The most common mistake teachers make in test development is to assess only that which can be easily tested through traditional items. Many item types can be used in a test. Varying item formats to get optimum coverage of your objectives is one way to avoid misrepresentation of your objectives. Using performance assessments and performance items (see Chapter 8) also helps to ensure that you measure the thinking skills as well as knowledge and simple applications. Finally, take the time to write items that require students to think carefully, synthesize information, apply their knowledge, and interpret information, even in your traditional tests. With practice, and as you become clearer about what you want students to learn, traditional item writing will get easier.

Scoring Key

1. C

2. Provides a reasonable health recommendation (1 point) and ties the recommendation to the data (2 points). Example response: People should brush their teeth after drinking colas or orange juice because the liquids soften and discolor the teeth.

3. Provides a reasonable conclusion based on the data in the table (1 point) and compares the data from the table for the two conditions to support the conclusion (2 points). Example response: The plants needed sunlight to gain color and to grow. Even though the plants grew with and without the sunlight, after a few days, the plants without sunlight stopped growing and their color turned white. The plants in the sunlight kept growing and stayed green.

4. A

5. B

6. B

7. Picture accurately represents the water cycle (2 points), including six stages of the water cycle with a description of what happens to the water at each stage (1 point for each stage correctly named; 1 point for accurately describing the process at each stage)

Picture	Completely Accurate	Partially Accurate
Picture accurately shows the stages in the process	2	1
Arrows on the picture accurately show the flow of the process	2	1

Stage	Accurate Term	Accurate Description
Evaporation: water molecules are warmed up and rise into the air	1	1
Cloud formation: water molecules begin to cool and move closer together	1	1
Condensation: water molecules cool and become liquid	1	1
Precipitation: water molecules become heavy and begin to fall in the form of rain, snow, sleet, etc.	1	1
Water collection: water molecules collect as snow and/or ground water.	1	1
Transportation: water molecules move through groundwater or snowmelt into streams and from streams to rivers, lakes and/or oceans through watersheds	1	1

Figure 6–3
Scoring Key and Rules for Ms. Steinberg's Science Test

8. Solid

9. Gas

10. Liquid

11. Liquid

12. Gas

13 & 14.

Graph has an informative title	Informative (2)	Relevant (1)	Missing/Irrelevant (0)
An appropriate measurement scale is represented on one axis	Interval (2)	Ordinal (1)	Missing (0)
Times of observations are accurately represented on the second axis	Completely (2)	Partially (1)	Missing (0)
Titles for axes are accurate	Both (2)	One (1)	Neither/Missing (0)
Data is accurately represented in bars	All (2)	Some (1)	None (0)

15. A

16. A

Figure 6–3 (continued)

Test Concepts and Skills in More Than One Format   Another type of error teachers make in test development is inattention to the diverse needs of students. As we discussed in Chapter 1, students show their knowledge and skills in different ways. To find out what your students know and are able to do, you need to think about more than one format for assessing concepts and skills. Ms. Steinberg's test is only one of her unit assessments. She also has a formal performance that she can use along with the test to assess students' knowledge and skills. In addition, Ms. Steinberg had students identify graphs as well as create graphs, write a conclusion as well as recognize conclusions, and make an interpretation as well as identifying interpretations. In this way, students can show their knowledge and skills in more than one way. A short-answer format might allow some students to show what they know when a multiple-choice format does not. Alternately, students who are just developing an understanding of how to make interpretations, draw conclusions, and create graphs might be able to recognize them and not construct them. A variety of item formats will help you learn more about what your students know and are able to do.

     The validity of total scores from a test depends on the validity of scores from each item on the test. Once you are comfortable with the specific items on the test, you need to consider whether the items on the test reflect the range of knowledge, skills, and conceptual understanding you want students to learn. In Ms. Steinberg's science test, the items ranged in type and in coverage of her objectives. However, she did not rely solely on tests to assess students. In her unit assessment plan, she also included assessments of their lab work and of their research reports. Hence, at the time of grading, she will enhance the validity of the

Individual Score Sheet for Unit Test
The Magic of Water

Student Name: _____   Date: _____

Item Number	Learning Objective	Score							
1	Draw conclusion							1	0
2	Make inference (relate results to health)							1	0
	Support claims with data						2	1	0
3	Draw conclusion							1	0
	Support claims with data						2	1	0
4	Make inference							1	0
5	Draw conclusions							1	0
6	Make inference							1	0
7	Picture reflects water cycle including stages and process						2	1	0
	Terms are accurately used at each stage	6	5	4	3	2	1	0	
	Process at each stage is accurately described	6	5	4	3	2	1	0	
8–12	Accurately identifies states of water		5	4	3	2	1	0	
13	Graph has informative title							1	0
	Axes are correctly titled						2	1	0
	Time of observations are accurately represented						2	1	0
	Scale is appropriate for data						2	1	0
	Data are accurately represented in bars						2	1	0
14	Graph has informative title							1	0
	Axes are correctly titled						2	1	0
	Time of observations are accurately represented						2	1	0
	Scale is appropriate for data						2	1	0
	Data are accurately represented in bars						2	1	0
15	Graph accurately represents data							1	0
15	Graph accurately represents data							1	0

Figure 6–4
Individual Student Score Sheet to Help Ms. Steinberg and Students Identify Strength and Weaknesses

Grade 9—Period 3 Water Unit Test Date _____ Students' Name	Knows vocabulary for water cycle (Item 7; 6 points possible)	Understands processes of the water cycle (Item 7; 7 points possible)	Understands states of water (Items 8–12; 5 points possible)	Draws reasonable conclusions (Items 1, 3, & 5; 3 points)	Makes reasonable inferences (Items 2, 4, & 6; 3 points)	Uses data to support claims (Items 2 & 3; 4 points)	Gives graph an informative title (Items 13 & 14, 4 points)	Uses appropriate scale for the data (Items 13 & 14, 4 points)	Accurately represents times of observations (Items 13 & 14; 4 points)	Uses accurate titles for axes (Items 13 & 14; 4 points)	Accurately represents data (Items 13–16; 6 points)

Figure 6–5
Ms. Steinberg's Record Sheet to Track Student Understanding and Skill Shown on Water Unit Test

overall judgments of students' knowledge, skills, and conceptual understanding because her information about each student came from multiple measures.

As with any assessment, validity of the resulting scores depends on whether students are actually taught what you assess. It is critical at the time you create a performance item or a performance test that you review your teaching plans and what actually occurred when you were teaching to make sure that all you assess has been taught. Although we believe that any test should be written before instruction begins, in these days of high-speed desktop publishing, tests can be modified to more accurately reflect what was taught.

USING STUDY GUIDES TO HELP STUDENTS BE SUCCESSFUL ON TESTS

One of the best ways to help intermediate through high school students to be successful on your tests is to use study guides. Study guides generally come in three types: (1) lists of the knowledge, conceptual understandings, thinking skills, and demonstrations teachers expect students know and be able to do at the time of the test, (2) examples of performance items that represent the types of work teachers will expect on the test, and (3) a set of items and tasks from which teachers choose to be included on the test. Study guides give students foreknowledge of what they are to study to prepare for a test. However, to prepare study guides, you need to make certain you are clear about your learning objectives and that the study guide reflects all that you want students to know and be able to do.

If your learning objectives are focused on specific knowledge and/or applications of algorithms (e.g., five causes of the U.S. Civil War, three effects of Reconstruction on African Americans in the Southern states, at least two themes in each novel studied, six major techniques used to create a visual composition, how to apply the quadratic equation, how to factor polynomial equations), the type of study guide that *lists* the important knowledge and skills is very effective. If your learning objectives are focused on deep understanding of concepts, complex integration of skills to solve problems, communicate effectively, analyze situations, and represent information in systematic ways, then study guides that give examples of the types of items and/or actual items that may be included on the test are more useful.

We have used both the second and third types of study guides in our teaching. When you give the students items similar to the items you will use on the test, students can practice doing the types of thinking and performances you will expect them to learn in the course. For example, suppose you plan to have students analyze excerpts from literature for how the authors use literary devices such as simile, metaphor, symbols, and alliteration to create effects, you can give students examples of literary excerpts and the type of items you would give them on a test. They can use the study guide to practice the analysis needed or to practice developing effective responses to performance items.

When you give actual items to students, it is important to give students more items than they will actually be expected to do on a test in a fixed time period. Some teachers give the study guides as take-home tests; however, students who have more support at home are likely to do better on take-home tests than students who lack support at home. In addition, some students merely copy others' responses to items, making it difficult for the teacher to judge who has learned and who has copied.

We have found that when the items require thoughtful and effective application, analysis, synthesis, and evaluation using the knowledge and skills we teach, the time students spend preparing for the full range of items on a test is a powerful opportunity to learn. Students can work individually or together to complete the study guides. If students are practicing with items similar to the ones to be on the test, we discuss their practice answers in class so that they can clarify their understandings and check to see whether responses to performance items are acceptable (e.g., have sufficient examples to support claims). We also allow time in class to work on study guides so students can work with others or ask questions to clarify their understandings. Because the time spent working on the study guides is time spent learning, study guides are simply another tool for teaching. We find that, by using these strategies, when students finally come to the test situation, most have developed a deep understanding of that which we are testing. In fact, the preparation is really more important than the test. Of course, as with other standards-based assessment practices, we give students opportunities for revision on their tests so that they can demonstrate their accomplishments once they have met all standards.

In the opening paragraph of this section, we noted that study guides are useful for students in intermediate through high school grades. Young children have difficulty seeing the big picture of what they are to learn as a list of discrete bits of knowledge or the elements of a study guide. Their big picture must be related to the real world in which they live. Hence, developmental issues must be considered before you decide when and how to use tests in your classroom.

DEVELOPMENTAL ISSUES IN TESTING

Before deciding when and how to use tests, you need to consider whether tests are developmentally appropriate for the students you teach. For example, field tests of multiple-choice items with kindergarten and preschool children have shown that the children had a great deal of difficulty dealing with the notion of discrete test items (see for example, *Early School Assessment Level I Teachers Guide,* Macmillan McGraw-Hill, 1990, p. 6). Even though the tests were largely pictorial and students only had to circle the correct picture, numeral, or letter, the children tried to turn the test items into a story, which led to errors in their responses. Given that most of their time with reading and mathematics instruction had been contextual (e.g., reading simple stories, creating pictographs as part of a unit on apples), their confusion was quite understandable. Children *learn* to respond to discrete items—it is not an inherent ability. Therefore, the age of children is an important consideration when you decide whether to use tests and what item and test formats are most appropriate.

If possible, avoid using paper-and-pencil tests with young children; instead, assessments should be as much like children's concrete experiences as possible. However, if you plan to give paper-and-pencil tests to young children, create or select items that are supported by pictures. Print sizes should be large enough so that beginning readers or prereaders can distinguish letter shapes. There should be no more than four or five items on a page. Children should be able to circle their choices for multiple-choice items rather than filling in bubbles and draw lines between answer choices in matching items rather than writing letters (see examples in Chapter 7). Children should have access to manipulatives when taking mathematics tests that assess number-numeral correspondence, properties of geometric figures, addition, subtraction, and other concrete concepts. Testing time should be limited so that children's performance is not affected by fatigue. For example, in most standardized tests, testing time for preschool through first grade is 10 to 20 minutes per test with substantial breaks between testing sessions (see for example page 5 of the *Early School Assessment Level I Examiner's Manual,* Macmillan McGraw-Hill, 1990).

Test items generally ask for one skill, strategy, application, or understanding at a time. As children mature, they are more able to manage the discrete nature of items on tests, although it is always more effective to assess students' knowledge and skills when used in a context (see Chapters 7 and 8 for ideas about how to create items that are connected to a context). As they learn to read, they are more able to manage larger amounts of information presented in print. At the intermediate level (grades four through six) pictures, diagrams, and figures are still very helpful when assessing science, mathematics, or social studies; however, reading and writing can be assessed without the support of graphics. The reading load for mathematics and science items should be limited where possible—although word problems, tables, graphs, and charts are all critical aspects of science and mathematics assessments. One way to minimize the reading load is to use simple sentences and to minimize the use of polysyllabic words unless they are critical to the subject being tested. For example, a teacher may want to assess students' understanding of the relationship between *perimeter* and *area* or their understanding of how our *government* ensures *democracy.* These italicized terms are critical to the subjects of mathematics and social studies, respectively; therefore, the vocabulary should be taught, used regularly in class, and used in test items. However, specialized vocabulary that isn't critical to measuring the targeted concepts can be avoided. A mathematics word problem that includes information about musical instruments (trumpets, xylophones, cymbals) could be changed to one that is about fruit (apples, oranges, bananas). At the intermediate level, teachers should still use reasonable print sizes and avoid crowding too many items on a page. Testing time can be longer; however, students should sit for no more than 45 minutes or an hour when taking a test. By the intermediate level, most students can mark their answers to items on separate answer sheets; however, this can increase the chances of careless errors that do not represent students' true understanding, knowledge, and skills. Finally, students at the intermediate level can respond well to performance items (short-answer items, brief essay items, performance tasks, and writing assessments; see Chapter 8) as long as the teacher does not expect highly sophisticated answers. If performance items are used in mathematics, social studies, reading, and science tests, teachers should ignore students' writing skills (grammar, punctuation, spelling, and capitalization). Students must be able to show their conceptual understanding, knowledge, and skills without worrying about writing conventions when taking a test—writing skills should be considered only when testing students' writing skills. If students are still struggling with communication through writing, students should be encouraged to use diagrams, pictures, and other nonverbal strategies to show their knowledge, skills, and conceptual understandings in performance items.

By the middle years (grades six through eight), most students are able to deal with traditional test and item formats. Reading skills have generally solidified, and students can focus on a test for an hour without undue stress. It is still important to use simple sentence structures when testing and avoid using difficult vocabulary that is not critical to the knowledge, skills, and conceptual understanding that are the focuses of the test. Middle school students can respond to information presented in several sources together (e.g., a graph, a brief passage, and a picture presenting information about a historical event). As with younger students, middle school students will do better work when concepts and skills are tested in a context rather than as disconnected items. Teachers can expect more complex responses and more effective communication of ideas in performance items; however, some students may still need to use figures, diagrams, pictures, and other nonverbal strategies to communicate their knowledge, skills, and conceptual understandings. Finally, as will be discussed in Chapter 7, although it is sometimes easier to write items where students identify incorrect information, students from kindergarten through eighth grade have difficulty dealing with negatives, opposites, and inverses. Therefore, it is important to avoid items that include the word *not* in the stem.

High school students (grades nine through twelve) are generally very sophisticated test takers. Many have been tested annually with standardized tests and nearly all have been tested monthly if not weekly in school. Many have also become very skilled at identifying flaws in test items and in using test-taking skills (test wiseness) to figure out correct answers when they do not know the answers. Whenever possible, it is a good idea to use performance items when testing high school students. They can read, analyze, and interpret much more complex information (as long as it is reasonable given the time length for the test), and they can develop more sophisticated responses to essay items, performance tasks, and writing assessments (see Chapter 8).

RELIABILITY AND VALIDITY ISSUES FOR CLASSROOM TESTS

Recall from Chapter 1 that there are several dimensions of validity that are important in classroom-based assessments. Some of these aspects will be discussed in the chapters that follow (e.g., scoring rules that clearly target the learning described in the learning objectives). However, two dimensions of validity are important to tests as a whole. Validity Dimension 1 relates to the degree to which the collection of items on the test truly represent the breadth of knowledge and skills to be learned and the discipline you teach. To help ensure that your tests are valid, you must be clear about the learning objectives that are the target of instruction and then make certain that the items on the test fairly represent what you want students to learn. The most effective way to do this is to create a test map or test blueprint, which is similar to Ms. Steinberg's assessment plan. The right hand side of her assessment plan maps out the number and types of items she will put on her tests. Creating a test map is generally an iterative process. You begin with the learning objectives and instructional plans, create some items to measure the learning objectives, and adjust the map as necessary if you discover that some learning objectives are not easily assessed through traditional or performance items or if some objectives are more easily assessed through a test than you expected. Ultimately, the test map should represent the breadth of your learning objectives. Because the most important validity issue is whether the overall grade for a course or subject area truly represents students' knowledge and skills related to your objectives, be sure to identify ways to measure all of your objectives using a variety of measures rather than limiting yourself to tests.

As students move through school and on to college or work, they need a clearer sense of how the knowledge and skills they are learning apply to the world beyond school. This is important for both motivational reasons and because knowledge learned in the context of real-world performances is more likely to transfer to the real world. Teachers also need to know whether students can transfer what they are learning to more authentic contexts. Well-developed performance items require more thinking, problem-solving, and generalization than do traditional multiple-choice, true-false, matching, and completion items. In addition, 'test wiseness' strategies become irrelevant when students construct their own responses. You might ask, "What about college entrance tests? Don't they have to know how to take those?" Our response is that teaching students how to take college entrance tests may be important to successful admission to college for those who are college bound. However, students' future success will not depend solely on how well they take tests. High school teachers can test in authentic ways—using assessments aligned with state and national standards—and teach test taking strategies separately.

Dimension 3 of validity refers to the degree to which assessments match the methods of instruction. As you build your tests, be sure to have your unit and lesson instructional plans in front of you so that you are thinking about *how* students will learn as well as *what* students will learn. If you plan to use hands on explorations of concepts, a test assessing recall of facts may not be a good fit of what students have learned. Recall Mr. Hanks's and Mr. Johnson's teaching experiences described in Chapter 1. Had Mr. Hanks aligned his assessment with his instruction, he may have had more success using hands on instructional methods.

Dimension 4 of validity is about the effect of background variables on students' performances on assessments. As you build your tests, be sure that you consider multiple ways to assess concepts so that all students may show what they know and can do—avoid using the same item type throughout the test. Also, use the test layout information described earlier in this chapter to help ensure that all students can access the test items. Finally, as you write items, watch out for misrepresentations or stereotypical representations of any social or cultural group. Misrepresentations and stereotypes can cause students to feel marginalized by the testing experience, which can affect their motivation to do well on the test.

Dimensions of reliability also apply to testing. In the chapters on writing test items, we discuss the clarity of directions and scoring rules (Reliability Dimension 2) and the role of teacher consistency in applying scoring rules (Reliability Dimension 3) as these dimensions apply to items. At the test level, the degree to which you can depend on any judgments you make about your students becomes important (Reliability Dimension 1). Recall that in the basketball example, the teacher needed more than one observation of a skill to be certain about any judgments made about students' basketball skills. Ms. Steinberg has helped increase the reliability of test scores by having students demonstrate their knowledge and/or skills in multiple ways—both within the test and across assessments. She has 3 items that assess drawing conclusions, 3 that assess making inferences, and 4 that assess converting data to graphs. In the performance item assessing students' knowledge of the water cycle, she assesses their understanding through a labeled diagram *and* through the verbal descriptions that accompany the diagram. For states of water, she has 5 matching items that assess students understanding of the 3 states of water. In addition, she has used a record sheet to capture information about each of her students at the objective level. In this way, she has more diagnostic information about their knowledge and skills.

As you can see, careful test building is the first step in helping to ensure valid and reliable scores from students' performances on tests. Hasty test building and simply using tests from published instructional materials, regardless of whether they match instruction, are less likely to result in valid and reliable scores on tests.

MOTIVATION AND TESTING

Issues of validity are at the heart of student motivation. Students who feel that they are being tested fairly over content they were taught are more likely to be open to using the results to guide their further efforts, learning from their mistakes. Students who believe that the test questions were vague, did not match the content of lessons, or were purposefully tricky will be more likely to dismiss the results as irrelevant. Using poorly constructed tests is a way of breaking trust with your students.

Consider your own testing experiences: Most people have taken tests that seem to bear no resemblance to what was taught, tests in which items were written to capture trivial aspects of the content, or tests that seem to arise from the teacher's desire to see them fail. An item one of our daughters encountered on an introductory psychology test required students to remember the name of the fictitious couple in a textbook example of Rogerian therapy. Not only is this an item that sheds no light on students' understanding of counseling psychology or therapy, it creates the feeling that it will be impossible to study effectively for future tests. Under these conditions, students are likely to see their efforts to study to be in vain. When students come to believe that studying does them no good, they can develop what some psychologists call "learned helplessness" (Abramson, Seligman, & Teasdale, 1978; Elliott & Dweck, 1988; Miller, 1986; Seligman, Kamen, & Nolen-Hoeksema, 1988). They have learned that they are helpless to do well and are likely to reduce both their efforts and their interest in the subject.

We can't guarantee that writing excellent tests will ensure that your students will look forward to taking them, or that they will thank you for your efforts. However, when students are tested over the material they were taught and see assessment results as useful information that can help them improve, they are more likely to continue to try and to direct their efforts more effectively.

ADAPTATIONS FOR CHILDREN WITH SPECIAL NEEDS

Adaptations of tests and testing procedures depend on the goals of the students, as well as their individual needs. Students, especially in middle and high school, who are planning on postsecondary educations, who have 504 plans (rather than IEPs), or who are English language learners, may need to be given *accommodations*. Accommodations help students overcome the limitations of a disability or English skill level and show what they know and can do in a subject area. Students with IEPs (individualized education plans) that specify modified learning objectives will need *modifications* of test item content, format, and/or testing conditions to assess those individualized objectives. You may want to review Figure 4–20 in Chapter 4, which provides examples of different types of accommodations and modifications.

Before considering adaptations, however, the teacher must first examine the test to make sure that items are clearly written, and are not unintentionally difficult for any student due to poor item writing quality. This will help all the students in the class by ensuring that you are testing the learning targets and not their ability to decipher confusing items.

Accommodations for Traditional Testing

Students whose learning objectives are not different from the ones teachers hold for the rest of their students may still require somewhat different conditions of testing to accommodate their disabilities. The difficulty of the items and the standards used to evaluate performance tasks and essay items should not be changed. However, students with disabilities or limited English proficiency may work more slowly than other students because processing or translating the sentences takes more cognitive effort. These students will need more time to complete tests and/or fewer items. Some of these students, particularly those who must work harder to decode text and those with attention deficit disorder, may need to take breaks during the examination period. Students with visual disabilities may require the use of fewer items per page, larger fonts, or more clear space around each item.

Students with limited English proficiency may also need translation help during a test to show whether they have met the learning targets. If the test is *not* an assessment of reading ability, students with LEP and students with reading disabilities may need items or parts of items read aloud or translated. If the test includes items assessing knowledge of vocabulary, translators must be told which words they should *not* translate. For example, in a matching set where students match vocabulary words to their definitions, translators might translate the definitions but not the vocabulary words themselves. For LEP students, translation dictionaries (Spanish/English; Russian/English, etc.) can help students complete test items if a translator is not available. Likewise, if you are interested in whether a student can think analytically about a passage, rather than whether she can decode it, those items can be tape-recorded so that the student can listen (repeatedly, if necessary) while reading. All of these methods will require extra time; some may require a change in testing location so that students do not disturb one another.

Students with reading disabilities may need changes in the format of the test. For example, making sure items are surrounded by plenty of white space will make it easier to concentrate on a specific item. You can also teach students strategies such as using a piece of scratch paper to cover up the part of the page they are not working on, to reduce the visual distraction. Matching sets may need to have fewer items, or to be broken into smaller chunks. Students with learning disabilities or attention deficit disorder may find it difficult to keep the target word in mind while reading ten possible definitions. Breaking the set into two five-item sets would still test the knowledge of vocabulary without disadvantaging these students.

Students with physical disabilities affecting fine motor control can be allowed to point to an answer or dictate to a scribe, rather than laboriously writing a response. Sometimes students may have special equipment for communicating that can be used during testing. For students who use Braille, tests and other assignments can be reproduced in Braille. Students can also listen to items on tape and respond orally or using a Braille-writer or computer. Many modern laptop or desktop computers can be programmed to read print passages aloud; these could be used rather than tape recorders, and students could type their responses right into the test document.

Hearing-impaired students often have difficulty with language proficiency as well as hearing and speaking. If children are born deaf or lose their hearing soon after birth, they are not exposed to the extensive oral language experience received by hearing students or those who lose their hearing later in life. To participate fully in public school settings, these students will usually have a sign-language interpreter. Teachers may erroneously believe that since reading and writing are visual processes, hearing-impaired students will have no difficulty with them. Unfortunately, the lack of constant aural English input can prevent students from developing fluency and control of the grammar and syntax of English. These students may need the sign-language interpreter to act much like any language interpreter, reading items where decoding is not being assessed, translating definitions so that students can match them to vocabulary words, and so on.

Modifications for Traditional Testing

Students for whom IEPs require modified learning objectives should be assessed in ways that allow them to show whether they have met those objectives. The nature of these objectives should be determined by the teacher in collaboration with the IEP manager, the parent or guardian, and, if appropriate, the student. Students should always be encouraged to learn as much as possible of the standard curriculum. If some or all of this curriculum is beyond the capability of the student, learning objectives should be tailored to encourage maximum learning within the limitations of the disability. For some students, these objectives may be social rather than academic, and their assessment should be discussed with the IEP manager.

Some students may be able to learn similar content but at a less-sophisticated level. For example, a typically developing child may be able to analyze a short story for the strategies and devices the author used to move the plot from beginning to conflict to climax. A student with a moderate to severe cognitive disability may require modifications to simplify this task to identification of the story elements themselves. As another example, most fifth-graders can work on fractions and ratios, whereas a child with Down's syndrome may need to work to understand the concept of division into equal parts. Other students may have entirely different learning objectives. For example, a child with a reading disability in a third-grade classroom may work on decoding strategies while other children are working on comprehension monitoring strategies such as self-questioning, summarizing, and clarifying the meaning of unfamiliar words. Assessments for these students would reflect these differences.

In summary, testing students with special needs requires attention to those needs. Teachers may need to either adjust the testing process to allow assessment of the same knowledge and skills tested in other students (accommodation) or align the tests to the requirements of students' IEPs (modifications). In a standards-based educational system, educators must make every effort to find out what *all* students know and are able to do in relation to curriculum standards. Teachers must be sensitive to potential barriers and work to remove them.

HOW AND WHY TO USE FEEDBACK, REVISION, AND RESUBMISSION WITH TESTING

Typically, feedback on tests has consisted of a total score and marks showing which items were answered incorrectly. Essay items might also have the number of points earned for each item. Students can glean some information by inspecting this minimal feedback; seeing which items were correctly and incorrectly answered can give students clues about what they have learned and what they have not (presuming, of course, that they believe the test to be a measure of what they have learned). Tests are often one-time assessments; unless the same content is to be tested in the future, students may have little incentive to use this feedback to learn more about the content. If they have learned to play "the game of school" (Anderson, 1977), they may use the opportunity to learn more about how their teacher tests, including the kinds of items favored and the type of content included (e.g., details or overarching concepts, computation or problem solving, etc.)

Teachers can go beyond this minimal approach to help make tests into opportunities for students to learn more about the content, as well as about which kinds of skills and knowledge are valued by the teacher. In this section we will discuss the kinds of feedback that students find useful, ways teachers can teach students about how to use this feedback, and ways to enhance student motivation to continue learning after the test.

Feedback on Tests

We begin with an example of discouraging feedback. Figure 6–6 shows the actual feedback given to Chipper, a student who clearly has difficulty with spelling. Just as clearly, we see a teacher who is frustrated, is angry, and has decided that the student is willfully refusing to learn by not trying hard enough. Research on teacher grading has shown that teachers give lower grades to students whom they believe are underachievers (who could do better if they tried harder) (Covington & Beery, 1976) . Late in the year, this teacher has clearly come to the end of her patience.

Visual effects   Several visual aspects of the feedback could be improved. The first is simple: It is not necessary to visually emphasize the possible affective component of a score or grade using variations on the "smiley face." Although those who earn one may feel encouraged, those who, instead, receive a "frowny face" like the one drawn by Chipper's teacher are only further shamed.

Negative affect can also be elicited when teachers cover the page with their own writing. The teacher's note in Figure 6–6 draws the reader's attention immediately away from the student's work and how it might be improved. The sheer volume of teacher writing in this example is overwhelming, especially to a younger child (even if the content is more supportive than it is in the example.) For younger students especially, extensive feedback is easier to digest in small chunks. For more complex tasks, this is important for older students as well. In Chapter 3 we contrasted the summary comments of two high school history teachers (Figure 3–1). In that case, Ms. Kelsey's comment, though extensive, was broken into meaningful units to help the student make sense of and later refer to different aspects of the feedback.

Crossing out student work and replacing it with the teacher's can seem disrespectful or even antagonistic. After a lesson on giving appropriate feedback, a teacher intern in Susan's class once brought an example of a lesson plan that had been turned in to another instructor. This instructor had scrawled feedback and suggestions in a purple felt-tip marker all over the lesson plan, resulting in what the student said felt like "a sea of purple ink." The majority of the feedback was corrective rather than encouraging. After wading through this sea, I was surprised to see that in the end, the lesson plan had received a good grade. The effect of this piece of positive feedback was lost on the student, as well: Instead

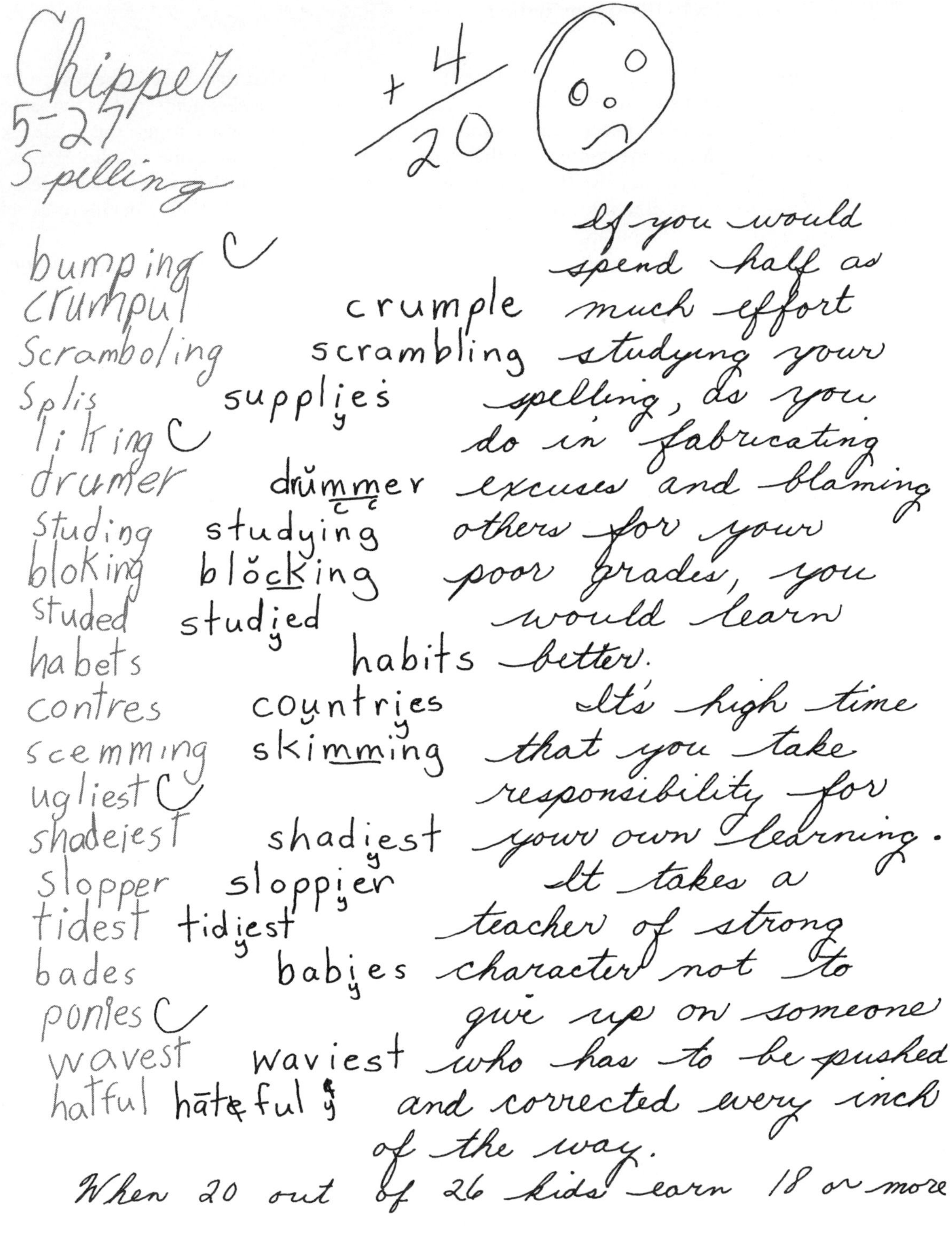

Chipper
5-27
Spelling

$\frac{+4}{20}$ ☹

bumping ✓
crumpul   crumple   If you would spend half as much effort studying your spelling, as you do in fabricating excuses and blaming others for your poor grades, you would learn better.

Scramboling   scrambling
Splis   supplies
liking ✓
drumer   drummer
Studing   studying
bloking   blocking
studed   studied
habets   habits
contres   countries   It's high time that you take responsibility for your own learning.
scemming   skimming
ugliest ✓
shadejest   shadiest   It takes a teacher of strong character not to give up on someone who has to be pushed and corrected every inch of the way.
slopper   sloppier
tidest tidiest
bades   babies
ponies ✓
wavest   waviest
hatful hateful

When 20 out of 26 kids earn 18 or more

Figure 6–6
Chipper

180

+9
/18

Learn to spell:
<u>listening</u>

Chipper
5-27
Listning

1 cat
2 c~~recurls~~ its tong
3 w~~p~~ith its tongue

I even had you spell this word out loud as I wrote it on the board. You spell it to me every time ~~it~~ we do listening. Cant you please copy correctly from the board ??

1 Because ~~that~~ <u>their</u> ~~slips~~ <u>died</u>
2 ~~when~~ when ~~thay are~~ ~~alon~~ lonely
3 ~~tays~~ <u>they</u> sing
4 Why Wolves Howl

1 elevator
2 the street and the town
3 The mini fire truck drove around inside the
4 ~~A~~ A Small Fire ~~🖊~~ factory
The Small Fire Truck   'building.

points out of 20, that shows that your low grades are not my fault. They are your fault and it's time you realize the truth and act upon it. I don't understand why your parents listen to your excuses.

Figure 6–6 (continued)

181

of encouraged she felt disrespected and angry. How likely was she to pay attention to the teacher's suggestions?

In Figure 6–6, the effect of the teacher's writing is so overwhelming, it is easy to miss the fact that she *did* follow another simple strategy for improving the visual effects of feedback: instead of marking incorrect answers, she marked correct ones. Receiving a test back with a sea of red marks can itself be very discouraging. (Another familiar example is the term paper with every spelling and punctuation error circled in red.) In addition, if students are allowed to make corrections and resubmit their tests, those red marks can never be erased and must remain even after revisions. A more encouraging strategy is for the teacher to use a "C" to mark correct answers and leave incorrect answers blank. Then when students correct their errors, the teacher can add Cs. The resulting paper looks no different than that of a student who got all the items right on the first try. Figure 6–7 illustrates the use of more appropriate visual techniques.

Error analysis   For a teacher to provide useful feedback, she needs to examine the test for patterns in the errors. In Chipper's case, his spelling errors seem to be phonetic: he is using the same techniques to spell words as young children use when they are allowed to use "invented spelling." The fact that a student of his age is still spelling this way is a clue that there may be an underlying disability making it difficult for Chipper to learn to spell. Examining the words further, it is clear that Chipper is hearing all the sounds of the words and connecting them to letter symbols. This is an important prereading skill. If his errors had shown that he could get the first sound but not the subsequent sounds, the teacher would need to help Chipper learn those sound–letter patterns before she could hope to teach him to spell the kinds of words included in the spelling test. In fact, although Chipper turned out to have a reading disability that prevented him from learning to spell, he had quite a few underlying strengths that could be built on in working on his spelling. Further examples of using error analysis to inform feedback and remediation with performance and essay items will be discussed in the next chapter.

Students can also learn to analyze patterns in their errors. Students' errors in mathematics often reveal one or two "buggy" approaches to problem solving (Brown, Day, & Jones, 1983). If students can work through the problems they missed, noting where they made their errors, they can often correct a single flaw that results in being able to correctly answer many of the missed problems. This gives students a sense of control over their performance that is necessary if students are going to continue to put forth effort. It also reinforces the notion that mathematics is logical rather than magical: that algorithms are not incantations that magically produce correct answers. For example, Twyla received her second algebra test back and was dismayed by the low score. After setting it aside for a few days, her teacher asked her to work through each exercise, figure out what she had done wrong, and write it down. Twyla had made two consistent errors: errors in computing with negative numbers and errors in computing with fractions. After analyzing and writing about her errors, Twyla finished the course without making the same mistakes again.

Comments   Written comments are not as frequent on traditional tests as they are on performance assessments, papers, and essays. However, if comments help point students in the direction of error analysis, or provide an error analysis for them, they can help guide students

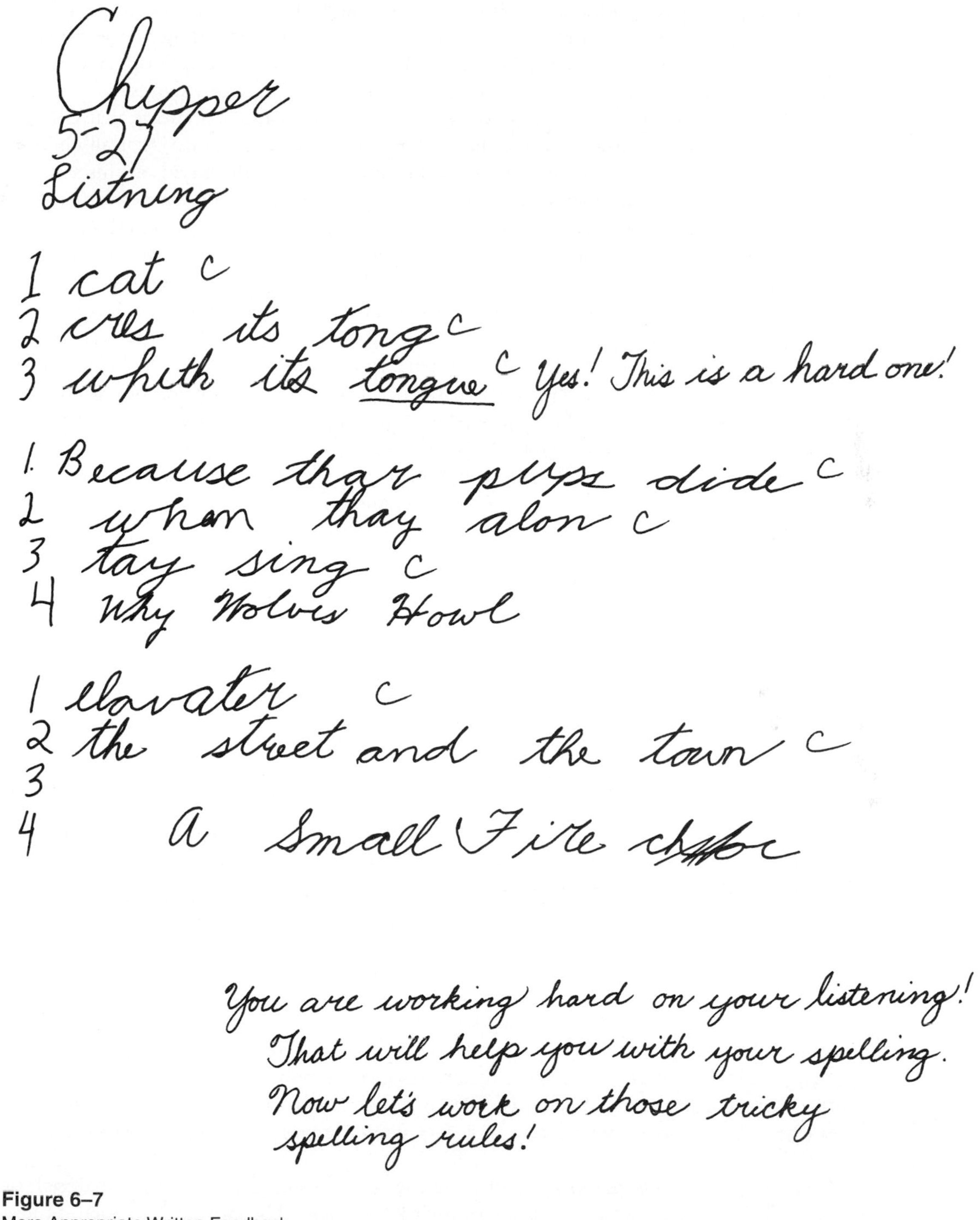

Chipper
5-27
Listning

1 cat ᶜ
2 crls its tong ᶜ
3 whith its <u>tongue</u> ᶜ Yes! This is a hard one!

1. Because thay plys dide ᶜ
2 whan thay alon ᶜ
3 tay sing ᶜ
4 Why Wolvs Howl

1 elavater ᶜ
2 the street and the tawn ᶜ
3
4   a Small Fire ch̶i̶p̶e̶r̶

You are working hard on your listening!
That will help you with your spelling.
Now let's work on those tricky
spelling rules!

Figure 6–7
More Appropriate Written Feedback

in their further studying. Elementary school teachers may write a few overall comments when a student has done well; these can be applied to a range of scores depending on the student's previous performance. Writing something like, "You are really improving!" can remind students that they are making progress, even if they are not getting perfect scores.

In Chipper's case, the teacher has not analyzed the errors and is unaware that Chipper may have an underlying disability. She may believe, as some teachers do, that all children should be able to memorize spelling words if they practice enough. Based on this assumption, she concludes that Chipper's poor performance is caused solely by poor effort, and she labels Chipper's explanations as excuses. Given this diagnosis, her strategy is to shame Chipper into trying harder. If Chipper is actually trying as hard as he can, he may develop what some psychologists call "learned helplessness" and begin to withdraw from the task. If he has enough experiences where his efforts do not improve his performance, he may begin to withdraw from school in general (Dweck, 1986; Schunk, 1989). This will reduce his opportunities to learn, leading to deteriorating performance and perhaps to maladaptive behaviors. In studies of elementary students, children tend to rate the teacher strategy of telling poor-performing students "You need to try harder" as ineffective and unfair in motivating students to learn math (Nolen & Nicholls, 1993; Thorkildsen, Nolen, & Fournier, 1994). Effort is, in fact, very difficult to judge, especially when those efforts occur at home.

Beliefs about the relative importance of ability and effort is, in part, culturally based. In many Asian cultures, effort is believed to be more important than ability as a cause of good performance. In most Western cultures, the opposite is true (at least by late elementary school). This does not mean that attributing poor performance to lack of effort is necessarily motivating if the student is already trying as hard as she can, even in cultures where effort is the norm. A more effective strategy is to suggest to students that the reason their efforts are not successful is because they are using ineffective strategies (Clifford, 1986). Strategies can be taught, tried, and modified; because this is under the control of the learner, feelings of helplessness are diminished and hope is restored.

Getting a Second Chance: Revising and Resubmitting or Retaking Tests

Allowing students to revise or retake tests is consistent with a standards-based focus on using assessments to support student learning. Sometimes students' first realization that they are not learning something comes when they get a test back and see a poor grade. Perhaps due in part to insufficient opportunities for constructive feedback during the learning process, it is not uncommon for students to claim, "I think I know the material, but I have no idea how I did on the test." Most students have experienced that sinking feeling when, after handing in a test, they go over their notes and realize that they made the same procedural mistake in several problems. They know how to do the problems, but because they applied this "buggy" algorithm to the whole set, they also know the answers were incorrect and their grade will suffer. Others have received tests back only to find that their answer, although correct from a certain point of view, is not the keyed-correct answer. If only they could explain why they chose their answer, they could demonstrate their understanding to the teacher!

Students may do poorly on a test because they truly don't understand the material, or because the test was not a valid measure of their knowledge. The latter can happen if there is a mismatch between content taught and content tested, if the teacher made item-writing mistakes, or if directions were difficult or misleading. Because many teachers have had little or no instruction in how to construct valid tests, they have difficulty telling the difference between validity problems and lack of learning. Students who press their claims that the test is at fault may be interpreted as argumentative, whiny, or unable to take responsibility for their own performance. The teacher may be unsympathetic and exhort the students to work harder or pay closer attention.

There are several more effective ways of dealing with items or directions that students perceive to be faulty. For poor directions, students may be allowed to retake that portion of the test, once they know what was expected. When faulty items are discovered, the teacher may drop the item scores from the test score. However, this may mean that a learning target is not reliably assessed. An alternative is to have students who believe the answer they gave was defensible, even if it was not the keyed-correct answer, explain in writing why their response was correct *and* why the keyed-correct response is not the best answer. If the answer is faulty, the teacher will be able to evaluate the explanation to see whether the student truly understands the tested concept. If he does, the student should be given credit for the item. More often, during the process of writing out their explanations, the students will come to realize why the answer they chose was not correct and accept the consequences.[1]

At the end of a course or grade level, the teacher must make a judgment about students' knowledge and skills in the subject matter area(s). If a standards-based philosophy of teaching is employed, it does not matter whether students learn a concept or skill by a particular point in the term, only that they learn it by the end of their work with that teacher. Often, however, students who could master material, if given more time, are penalized by having to complete assessments before they are ready. For example, a student may not have learned to conjugate regular verbs in Spanish by the first test. If he fails that portion of a test and then learns the content in the next week or two, the score on the test does not reflect his true mastery of the subject.

This leaves teachers with a dilemma. Should they provide opportunities to retake or revise and resubmit tests once the content is mastered? There are at least two frequent objections to this strategy. First, revision can clearly make more work for overworked teachers. Second, and perhaps more difficult to resolve, is whether allowing retakes or revisions is fair to those students who knew the material at the time of the original test. Let's take the second problem first.

Fairness to Others   The question about whether it is fair for students to retake tests or revise their responses to test items is bound up in two notions inherent in Western culture: the notion that schools are venues for identifying top students and the notion that ability is

---

[1]Susan used to give "fuzzy-item sheets" out with every test. Students then had the opportunity to catch poorly written items and write out their reasoning, but during the test instead of after. This has the advantage of allowing students to get credit if they figure out the correct response while writing out their explanation. If the item was faulty and the student's reasoning correct, she could give them credit for their reasoning before the tests were handed back. After implementing this strategy, students in her classes were much less argumentative and felt that their concerns would be listened to. This contributed to their perception of the tests as fair.

the most important determinant of performance. If all students can earn high scores, the thinking goes, then students who learn quickly will not be rewarded or stand out as being the top students. The second notion—that a person who can perform at the same level as others with less work is more able—is held by the majority of adults and adolescents in the United States and other Western countries. The idea of a meritocracy based on ability is deeply seated in Western cultures. More talented professional athletes, for example, earn higher salaries than those of lower ability, and this is seen as just by most sports fans. Similarly, if some students can learn more quickly than others, some teachers believe that their grades should reflect this higher ability. Conversely, if their students retake tests and improve their scores, some teachers believe that they should not earn full points, even if they now understand the material as well as those who performed well on the original test.

A competitive environment is probably not the best environment for learning, however (Ames, 1984; Ames & Archer, 1988; Nicholls, 1989). In a study of ninth-grade science classrooms, for example, Nolen (2003) found that when students perceived their classrooms as ability-based meritocracies, their performance on a districtwide, curriculum-based test was compromised. Students in other classes who saw teachers and peers to be focused on mastery and independent thinking performed significantly better on the district test.

For teachers who embrace the standards-based philosophy that assessments should support the learning of all students, penalizing students for needing more time to learn particular skills and concepts is inappropriate. This practice can reduce students' motivation to try to master content after the first test, even while teachers are feeling generous for allowing the retest or revision. The following example illustrates this point and also shows how assessment practices meant to give students a second chance can be undermined by a grading policy that penalizes students for accepting the opportunity.

Ella failed a math test, receiving a 64%. Her teacher allowed retakes, if completed within a week of the original test. Ella got extra help in learning the content, practiced, and increased her score to 80% correct, demonstrating a much better grasp of the material. The teacher's grading policy decreed that, in fairness to those who did well on the original test, no matter how well a student did on the retest, she would not raise their score to more than 80%. Her strategy for this was to multiply the retake score by 80%. So despite the fact that Ella clearly showed evidence of mastering the material, she received a failing score of 64%, the same score she received on the original test. When asked what she learned from this experience, Ella replied that if she didn't learn the material as quickly as others in her class, she may as well give up. This was doubly unfortunate, given the fact that this course was sequential: mastery of earlier content was necessary for success on later material. Instead of encouraging her students to master mathematics, the teacher unwittingly sent Ella into a downward spiral of low motivation, withdrawal of effort, and poor performance.

As a teacher, you will have to decide which you value more—the time it takes to become proficient or the level of proficiency achieved in relation to the standards, regardless of how long it takes. Clearly the purpose of this book is to advocate for teaching to standards of quality rather than time.

How to Allow Retakes and Resubmissions Without Being Overwhelmed by Extra Work

Teachers can allow retakes and resubmissions of traditional tests and still manage their workload. The following strategies are a sample, arranged from most to least additional work.

Parallel Forms If students are given the same items to complete on a retest, they may have memorized the answers without really learning any more of the underlying skills or concepts. Teachers who wish to provide students an opportunity to be retested on the same content, but not the same items, can develop what are called "parallel forms" of the test. This is the same technique that large test companies use to develop alternate forms of standardized tests. To create two forms, consult your testing plan and develop twice as many items for each objective as you would for a single test. Look at Ms. Steinberg's assessment plan in Figure 6–1. To develop parallel forms, she would create four items measuring how to represent data in graphs and/or charts, six items on how to use data to draw a reasonable conclusion, and six on making interpretations of results. She could then flip a coin to assign each item within an objective to either form A or form B. This method requires some extra work up front, especially the first time a test is given on this topic. If Ms. Steinberg keeps these items in a file or on her computer, however, she can use them again the next time she teaches the unit. She may add new items in subsequent years, or revise or replace old ones. In any case, it becomes simple to generate alternate test forms after the initial set of test items is developed, as long as both tests have the same number and formats of items for each learning objective. With traditional test items, the extra work is in item development because traditional tests are quickly and easily scored.

Revision With Explanations Teachers who do not want to take the time to generate enough items for alternate forms may want to consider allowing students to revise their original responses to a test. This must go beyond changing the answers, however, because students will have been told the correct answers when the tests were handed back and discussed in class. To ensure that students understand the content and can apply the skills, teachers can ask for justifications or explanations for each changed answer. (This is a variation on the "fuzzy-item sheet" strategy discussed in footnote 1.) You can require students to explain both why their original response was incorrect, as well as why the keyed response is correct. For some subjects, it may be appropriate for students to analyze and explain a pattern of errors, and why the revised strategy results in correct answers (see Twyla's experience described on page 184). A satisfactory explanation is evidence of the student's mastery of the content. Revision with explanation requires a bit more time for teachers to evaluate students' work, but avoids having to generate extra items for parallel forms.

Cumulative Examinations Many teachers give cumulative exams as a way to ensure that students have retained the material learned earlier in the course or term. Cumulative exams provide a natural way to give students a second chance to demonstrate mastery of content. A cumulative final exam, for example, will assess learning of objectives from the first half of the course as well as from the second half. The items in the first half can be scored twice: Once as a "retake" of the midterm, and once as part of the score for the final exam. If the score received on the midterm portion of the final is higher than that received on the midterm itself, this is evidence that students have increased their mastery of the material. The new score can replace the original midterm score for purposes of computing the course grade. No extra time or work is generated in this method, other than what would naturally be done in creating the final exam, and students are encouraged to keep trying to master the material from earlier in the course. The midterm itself can be seen as a tool to help students to see how much they have learned and what concepts and skills need more work. This is particularly important for students who are struggling to master content and who do not expect to do well on the first test: they do not have to give up hope of success in the course overall.

SUMMARY

In this chapter we have presented information about the business of testing, how to plan for tests, how to lay out tests so that students will not feel undue stress, how to create and use study guides, how to accommodate or modify tests for students with special needs, how to ensure the validity and reliability of scores from tests, and issues related to feedback and revision in testing. The following chapters can guide your efforts in writing and evaluating items so that they help you know what students have learned rather than presenting barriers for students and painful experiences for you. In each chapter we introduce the types of items and their purposes. Then we give rules for each type of item along with positive and negative examples. Finally, we discuss issues related to students with special needs and how to ensure the reliability and validity of scores from your items.

REFERENCES

Abramson, L. Y., Seligman, M. E. P., & Teasdale, J. D. (1978). Learned helplessness in humans: Critique and reformulation. *Journal of Abnormal Psychology, 87*(1), 49–74.

Ames, C. (1984). Competitive, cooperative, and individualistic goal structures: A cognitive-motivational analysis. In R. Ames & C. Ames (Eds.), *Student motivation* (Vol. 1, pp. 177–207). New York: Academic.

Ames, C., & Archer, J. (1988). Achievement goals in the classroom: Students' learning strategies and motivation processes. *Journal of Educational Psychology, 80*(3), 260–267.

Anderson, R. C. (1977). The notion of schemata and the educational enterprise: General discussion of the conference. In R. C. Anderson, R. J. Spiro, & W. E. Montague (Eds.), *Schooling and the acquisition of knowledge* (pp. 415–431). Hillsdale, NJ: Erlbaum.

Brown, A. L., Day, J. D., & Jones, R. S. (1983). The development of plans for summarizing texts. *Child Development, 54*(4), 968–979.

Clifford, M. M. (1986). The comparative effects of strategy and effort attributions. *British Journal of Educational Psychology, 56*(1), 75–83.

Covington, M. V., & Beery, R. G. (1976). *Self-worth and school learning.* New York: Holt, Rinehart.

Dweck, C. S. (1986). Motivational processes affecting learning. *American Psychologist, 41*, 1040–1048.

Elliot, E. S., & Dweck, C. S. Goals: An approach to motivation and achievement. *Journal of Personality & Social Psychology, 54*, 5–12.

Macmillan-McGraw-Hill (1990). *Early School Assessment Level 1 Examiner's Manual.* Monterey, CA: CTB/Macmillan McGraw-Hill, 5.

Macmillan-McGraw-Hill (1990). *Early School Assessment Level 1 Teacher's Guide.* Monterey, CA: CTB/Macmillan McGraw-Hill, 6.

Miller, A. (1986). Performance impairment after failure: Mechanism and sex differences. *Journal of Educational Psychology, 78*, 486–491.

Nicholls, J. G. (1989). *The competitive ethos and democratic education.* Cambridge, MA: Harvard University Press.

Nolen, S. B. (2003). Learning environment, achievement, and motivation in high school science. *Journal of Research in Science Teaching, 40*, 347–368.

Nolen, S. B., & Nicholls, J. G. (1993.) Elementary school pupils' beliefs about practices for motivating pupils in mathematics. *British Journal of Educational Psychology, 63*, 414–430.

Schunk, D. (1989). Self-efficacy and achievement behaviors. *Educational Psychology Review, 1*(3), 173–207.

Seligman, M. E. P., Kamen, L. P., & Nolen-Hoeksema, S. (1988). Explanatory style across the life-span: Achievement and health. In E. M. Hetherington, R. M. Lerner, & M. Perlmutter (Eds.), *Child devel-opment in life-span perspective* (pp. 91–114). Hillsdale, NJ: Erlbaum.

Thorkildsen, T. A., Nolen, S. B., & Fournier, J. (1994). What is fair? Children's critiques of practices that influence motivation. *Journal of Educational Psychology, 86*, 475–486.

TRADITIONAL ITEM
DEVELOPMENT

In this chapter we focus on traditional tests and traditional items. First we introduce and closely examine different item types (multiple-choice, true-false, completion, matching, and short-answer items), how they are best used, and rules for writing effective items of each type. Finally, we discuss how to use traditional items in a standards-based assessment context including how to assess English language learners and students with special needs and how to use feedback and revision with traditional tests.

In a standards-based assessment system, the purpose of traditional tests and quizzes is to determine, in an efficient way, whether students have learned what you want them to learn. If students have only a tenuous handle on what an item is testing or if they have had too little exposure or practice with concepts or skills, they may need more time, instruction, and practice in order to deeply understand. Hence, the results of assessments should tell you what to do next. The bottom line is that you must decide whether the efficiency of traditional testing strategies is an appropriate trade-off for the assessment information you can obtain through more direct methods of assessment such as essays and performance tasks (Chapter 8) and assessments of valued performances (Chapter 4).

DEVELOPING AND EVALUATING TEST ITEMS

In this chapter, we introduce five types of traditional items: multiple-choice, true-false, matching, completion, and short-answer items. Each serves a different purpose in assessment. True-false, matching, and completion items tend to be most useful in measuring recall of knowledge such as facts and definitions as well as simple comprehension and analysis. Multiple-choice items and short-answer items are the most flexible and can measure knowledge as well as simple creations, applications, analysis, and reasoning. The rules and information presented here are derived from many sources, including measurement textbooks and research on effective item development. These rules, if carefully followed, *help* ensure that worksheets, quizzes, and tests assess what you want students to learn. However, making certain that items measure the learning objectives takes careful reflection on what items are truly asking students to do.

You may ask, "Why spend time worrying about how to write test items when I can use tests, quizzes, and worksheets provided by publishers of our textbooks?" This is a question many teachers ask and the answer is fairly straightforward. If you really want to know what your students learned in relation to *your* learning objectives, you must create and select items that will draw out what you want to know. Not all published items will target your learning objectives. Look to see whether the published items really fit with the learning objectives you have set. In addition, not all items are equally effective as assessment tools, even in published materials.

For example, students should not get right answers for the wrong reasons. Poorly written answer choices in multiple-choice or matching item sets lead students to select right or wrong answers for the wrong reasons. If students can figure out the answer to an item or question because of clues in the item or the test or because of problematic item formats, then you will not know what students truly understand. Alternately, if students become uncertain about their own knowledge because an item has unnecessary distractions or the language is unclear, then you are unlikely to find out what students have really learned. Tricks that prevent students from showing us what they have learned will not tell you about the success of your instruction.

Ultimately you will determine whether traditional items are well developed, match your learning objectives, and fairly assess students. If you create or use poor items or items that don't really assess what you want students to learn, then tests, quizzes, and worksheets will give poor information, making it hard to adjust instruction to meet students' real needs. If you create or use well-developed items, you can assess some of your learning objectives fairly well—within the limits of the type(s) of items you choose. This chapter will help you create and evaluate traditional items.

Traditional items can be used in preassessments to quickly determine what students already know prior to instruction; they can be used in tests and quizzes to check the success of instruction. A traditional item can stand by itself and assess discrete knowledge. Alternately, items can be written so that students must *apply* their knowledge and skills to analyze, evaluate, or interpret a *stimulus* such as a reading passage, diagram, chart, table, graph, picture, or problem. When items are attached to one or more stimuli, it is easier to assess cognitive processes that are similar to the real work of life beyond school. Therefore, you must know *what* you want to assess before creating traditional items and then work to select and create items that actually elicit the knowledge or skills you want to assess. Assessments should not be random or haphazard. Decide what ideas, facts, principles, analyses, evaluations, and so on that you care about and make sure each item truly asks for what you value *and* what you taught. In the following sections, each item type is introduced along with how it is best used and the rules for writing the particular type of item.

Developing and Evaluating Multiple-Choice Items

Multiple-choice items are the most popular, most flexible, and most widely used of the traditional items. They are popular for many reasons. First, multiple-choice items are very flexible. They can be used to assess knowledge, comprehension of text, simple applications of principles and formulas, recognition of examples of concepts, and recognition of reasonable analyses or evaluations of stimulus materials. They can require simple recall in order to respond correctly, or they can require careful thinking. What a multiple-choice item assesses depends on how the item is written. Second, multiple-choice items can be used to assess students' ability to distinguish between good and poor examples of concepts, interpretations, inferences, or principles. In this case, students must not only recognize the correct answer, but also reject the incorrect answers.

For example, each of the items in Figure 7–1 assesses the objective "Students will learn the differences between primary and secondary sources." To answer the questions, students must complete three steps: (1) read the two passages, (2) read the item *stem* and the *answer choices,* and then (3) decide which choice accurately explains the classification of the relevant passage. The student cannot simply recall the definition of a primary or secondary source. Nor does the student simply identify which passage is primary and which is secondary. He must apply that knowledge to determine what makes Passage 1 *qualify* as a secondary source and what makes Passage 2 *qualify* as a primary source.

The general format for multiple-choice items is to have a *stem* and *answer choices* or *response choices.* The stem is typically a question; however, stems can be incomplete sentences as they are in Figure 7–1. The question is answered or the sentence is completed by one of the answer choices. Test makers call the correct answer the *keyed* correct answer because an answer key is used to score the students' responses to the items. When too many students

---

Passage 1

The Indian exerts his spirit upon the world by means of religious activity, and he transcends himself in a sense; he expands his awareness to include all of creation, and in this, he is restored as a man and as a race. Nothing in his universe is exclusive of him, but he is part of all that is and forever was and will be.

There is remarkable esthetic perception, which marks in the Indian world, a sense of beauty, of proportion, and design.

Passage 2

Do you all see me? . . . Do you all help me?

My words are tied in one with the great mountains, with the great rocks, with the great trees, in one with my body and my heart.

Do you all help me with supernatural power, and you, day, and you, night! All of you see me one with the world.

Yokuts' Prayer
Excerpts from *The World of the American Indian,* (1989, pp. 24–25). Reprinted by permission of the National Geographic Society.

1. Passage 2 is a primary source because
   A. It gives one person's personal opinion about nature.
   B. It is a direct translation of a Native American prayer.
   C. It gives factual information about Native Americans.
2. Passage 1 is a secondary source because
   A. It is one writer's generalization about Native Americans.
   B. It identifies the primary sources used to draw conclusions.
   C. It gives factual information about Native Americans.

Figure 7–1
Examples of Items That Require Analysis of Stimulus Materials

answer incorrectly, test makers first check to make sure the answer key is correct. If it isn't, this is called a *miskey.* Wrong answers, called *foils* or *distractors,* are most effective when they represent common errors or misunderstandings.

For example, choice A of the first item in Figure 7–1 represents one type of common error made when interpreting text—choosing an answer that could be correct in a general sense—primary sources often contain personal opinions—but is not correct in this specific instance. Choice C represents a misconception about primary sources—that they are factual.

Rules for Writing and Evaluating Multiple-Choice Items   There are several accepted rules for writing multiple-choice items. Each of these rules is derived from extensive research on multiple-choice items that has been conducted over the past century of multiple-choice test use. Figures 7–2 through 7–9 give different versions of items to demonstrate each of the multiple-choice item writing rules. The column labeled *inappropriate* gives versions of items that are flawed in some way. The column labeled *appropriate* gives a revised version of the item that fits the rules.

Rule 1: Decide whether the learning objective is best assessed through a multiple-choice item. If you want to assess simple recall of several related facts (e.g., definitions of related terms such as potential energy, kinetic energy, and thermal energy), a matching item set (see page 213) might be more effective than a multiple-choice item. If you want to understand students' thinking, a short-answer item (see page 206) or essay item (see Chapter 8) might be more appropriate. If you want to assess a complex concept and think that students may recognize an example of the concept but might have trouble generating their own examples, a multiple-choice item may be the most effective assessment tool.

Rule 2. Make certain that the stem poses a problem complete enough that the student knows what is expected before reading the answer choices. In Figure 7–2, each of the items in the column labeled *inappropriate* has an unclear stem. Students must read each of the answer choices *before* they know what the item is asking for. In contrast, the items in the column labeled *appropriate* give a clear focus. A clear stem makes it easier to write comparable answer choices and easier for students to know what to look for in the answers. For item 1, the inappropriate version has a vague focus and the answer choices are descriptions of very different situations involving the relationship between the atmosphere and other variables. To fix the item, a situation is described in the stem and then students must predict the impact on the atmosphere. The inappropriate version of item 2 has answer choices that are focused on widely different possibilities—forms of government, vocabulary problems, sources of ideas, and economic systems. To fix the item, the stem is focused on students' understanding of a characteristic of representative democracy. The inappropriate version of item 3 has a vague stem and the answer choices focus on different aspects of topic sentences, whereas the appropriate version of the item asks about the *function* of a topic sentence.

Finally, for the inappropriate version of item 4, the reader might think the stem is asking for a description of the main idea; however, choice A is a statement about where main ideas are located, choice B is a main idea statement, and choice C is an evaluation of how well the author developed the main idea. Hence, the student must read each answer choice, reevaluate the stem in light of the answer choices, and decide which one is more accurate. In the revised item, all answer choices are about potential main ideas.

Rule 3. To assess recall of facts, literal comprehension, or simple applications of algorithms or rules, it is usually best to ask questions that begin with which, who, what, where, or when. Sometimes you may want to know whether students recall particular facts they were to learn. When did a certain event occur? Who behaved in a certain way, had a particular motive, or made a particular discovery? Where did a certain event happen? What was the immediate effect of a particular event? These types of questions are also useful if you want to know whether students can read and literally comprehend written text, tables, graphs, charts, diagrams (e.g., Who was the main character of the story? Where did the story take place? How did the main character solve his problem?).

Rule 4. To assess thinking, use questions that begin with why, how, or which of the following. Anytime you want to go beyond simple recall or literal comprehension, questions must ask for some kind of thinking. Thinking skills can range from simple applications (e.g., How many more students liked apples than oranges?) to explanations (e.g., Why did the main character pick a fight with his father?) to evaluations (e.g., How does the addition of a second control variable improve the investigation?). Another variation is when the item asks students to identify examples of some phenomenon or an appropriate prediction or interpretation

Item	Inappropriate Versions	Appropriate Versions
1	What happens to carbon in the Earth's atmosphere? A. It increases because of all of the burning forests and fuel. B. It decreases because of all of the burning forests and fuel. C. It increases because it is one of the building blocks of all living organisms. D. It stays about the same, but is recombined in different molecules.	If humans continue to burn forests and fuel, the carbon in the atmosphere will A. increase somewhat in amount. B. transform into nitrogen ions. C. be used up by living organisms. D. recombine into different molecules.
2	Democracy is A. our form of government. B. a political party. C. based on the writings of Voltaire. D. capitalism.	Which of the following is an example of representative democracy? A. Senators and Congressmen, elected by citizens, enact laws. B. Lawyers represent defendants and plaintiffs in court. C. Supreme Court judges decide whether laws are constitutional. D. The President selects cabinet members who enforce laws and policies.
3	A topic sentence A. always comes first in a paragraph. B. must have supporting sentences. C. is not essential for all writing.	What is the function of a topic sentence? A. to tell what the paragraph is about B. to summarize the information in a text C. to give details about the topic
4	As Maria walked with her father, she felt awkward and didn't want to tell him about her feelings, her thoughts, her ideas. They had always talked before. What happened? Why had he changed? He was gone only a short time, and yet there was something different about him. Maria wondered if *she* was the one who had changed. Had she grown apart from him in these past few months? The main idea of this paragraph A. is provided in the first sentence. B. is that people change. C. is not well developed.	As Maria walked with her father, she felt awkward and didn't want to tell him about her feelings, her thoughts, her ideas. They had always talked before. What happened? Why had he changed? He was gone only a short time, and yet there was something different about him. Maria wondered if *she* was the one who had changed. Had she grown apart from him in these past few months? What is the main idea of this paragraph? A. Maria is confused about her relationship with her father. B. Maria and her father are going for a very long walk. C. Maria and her father were once best friends but he has changed.

Figure 7–2
Examples of Inappropriate and Appropriate Multiple-Choice Item Stems

Item	Inappropriate Versions	Appropriate Versions
1	The part of the flower that holds the eggs is called an A. stamen. B. pistil. C. ovary.	The part of the flower that holds the eggs is called A. a stamen. B. a pistil. C. an ovary.
2	Which branch of the government is responsible for enforcing laws? A. Legislative B. Executive C. Federal and state courts	Which branch of the government is responsible for enforcing laws? A. Legislative B. Executive C. Judicial

Figure 7–3
Examples of Item Stems That Do and Don't Give Grammatical Clues

(e.g., If trends continue as they are in the graph, which of the following is likely to happen in 10 years?).

The demands of the item rather than the words used in the item determine whether it requires simple recall or higher-order thinking skills. Not all questions that begin with "what" are factual questions. A question like "What is likely to happen if . . . ?" will assess students' ability to make predictions—a higher-order thinking skill. Alternately, a "why" question may only ask for a memorized fact. For example, an item that asks, "Why did the Southern states want to secede from the Union?" could be asking for recall of a memorized fact. If students read an excerpt from a historical document and then are asked, "Based on the information in the text, why did the Southern states want to secede from the Union?" then the item is asking for comprehension. Finally, if students are given more than one document and then are asked, "Based on the information from all three documents, what is the main reason the Southern states wanted to secede from the Union?" then the item requires higher-order thinking. In this latter case, the student is asked to compare the information from multiple texts before answering the question. From these examples, it is clear that, when writing multiple-choice questions, the specific interrogative is less important than the kind of thinking demanded by the item. Nevertheless, rules 3 and 4 can help you remember to think about how you ask questions.

Rule 5. Make certain that grammar in the stem does not give clues to the answer. Grammar can give clues to correct answers in several ways. The inappropriate version of item 1 in Figure 7–3 shows how the article *an* can give clues to an answer choice. The inappropriate version of item 2 shows how a stem can suggest a singular answer (*which branch*). Because one of the answer choices is plural (Federal and state courts), students can eliminate that answer choice. Improving each item requires simple changes.

Rule 6. Answer choices should all be viable, reasonable choices. Probably the best way to decide whether multiple-choice items are effective is to create short-answer items and then use students' responses to generate multiple-choice answer choices in the future. In this way, each answer choice reflects errors students really make. Standardized tests usually have the same number of answer choices for all items. This is necessary because, when separate answer documents (sometimes called *bubble sheets*) are used, there is less confusion about which bubble to fill in if all items have the same number of answer choices. For classroom assessments, students generally respond on the test; therefore, teachers can use the appropriate number of choices for the item. It is better to have one clearly correct answer and two effective distractors than to spend time trying to create a third distractor that is useless or ridiculous.

Rule 7. Answer choices should be similar in length, grammatical syntax, and conceptual complexity. The issue of answer choices is closely tied to the quality of item stems. It is evident from the items in Figure 7–2 that poor item stems often have nonparallel answer choices. Well-focused item stems often help in writing parallel answer choices; however, this is not always the case. Making answer choices similar in complexity, length, and syntax will cause less confusion. In addition, students cannot use the structure of the item to figure out the correct answer.

All of the inappropriate items in Figure 7–4 have well-focused stems; however, the answer choices are very different in grammar, complexity, or length. For item 1, the process of making the answer choices parallel simply required putting the answer choices into sentences. For item 2, to make the answer choices parallel, changes had to be made to the cognitive complexity of the answer choices—all of the revised answer choices are compound sentences with a cause and an effect. For the inappropriate version of item 3, the answer choices all refer to activities; however, the grammatical structure is very different. All that it took to fix the items was to begin each phrase with the past tense form of the verb.

The best way to write comparable answer choices is to write a focused stem and the correct answer. Then write wrong answers that are about the same length, that use the same grammatical structure, and that tap into misconceptions or common errors. This may take some work, back-and-forth, to make certain that the answer choices are really comparable. However, once you have the hang of it, writing items and answer choices becomes easier and easier.

Rule 8. Make certain that there are no clues to the correct response given in the stem. It is fairly easy to give clues to answer choices in the stems of multiple-choice items. Key words are the usual source of a clue. For the inappropriate version of items in Figure 7–5, the words in italics give clues to the test taker about which response is correct. In the appropriate versions, the items have been revised to eliminate the clues. Therefore, once you have put your quiz, test, or worksheet together, it is important to double-check for clues both within and across items. When students who do not know a concept, principle, idea, or fact use clues to figure out the correct answer, teachers get a false idea about what students know and are able to do.

Rule 9. Avoid answer choices that are designed to trick students into responding incorrectly. Teachers often tell us that they use standardized tests, such as the *SAT I: Reasoning Test* or the *American College Admissions Test (ACT)*, as models for item writing. Although it is true that these tests are well developed and have benefited from item tryouts and years of item development research, the purpose of standardized, norm-referenced tests is very different from the purpose of classroom assessments. The purpose of the SAT, ACT, and similar tests is to clearly distinguish between students of similar ability. Items are designed so that even high-achieving students are likely to select incorrect answers. For example, in those types of tests, the answer choices for vocabulary items are often very close

Item	Inappropriate Versions	Appropriate Versions
1	Body structures and fossil records are used to group gorillas, chimpanzees, and humans together in the taxonomic order of primates. Which information supports the conclusions that these animals had a common ancestor? A. a common diet B. they engage in similar behaviors C. DNA	Body structures and fossil records are used to group gorillas, chimpanzees, and humans together in the taxonomic order of primates. Which information supports the conclusion that these animals had a common ancestor? A. They eat similar foods. B. They have similar behaviors. C. They have similar DNA.
2	What was Huck Finn's conflict as he and Jim moved down river? A. He wanted to help Jim but was afraid to break the law. B. He was lost. C. He felt guilty about reporting the Duke to the Sheriff. D His father was after him.	What was Huck Finn's conflict as he and Jim moved down river? A. He wanted to help Jim, but he knew it was against the law. B. He knew his father was chasing him, and he was afraid he'd get caught. C. He turned the Duke into the Sheriff, and he felt guilty. D. He thought he was lost, but he was afraid to tell Jim.
3	What did President Roosevelt do to bring America out of a depression? A. spend federal money on work programs B. a war C. subcontracting federal projects to private businesses	What did President Roosevelt do to bring America out of a depression? A. He spent federal money on work programs. B. He started a war with Germany and Japan. C. He subcontracted federal work to private businesses.

Figure 7–4
Examples of Items With Nonparallel and Parallel Answer Choices

to being correct—different from correct by nuance rather than by everyday usage. Figure 7–6 gives an example of an item that has more than one plausible correct answer; however, only one *correct* answer according to the context.

As teachers, your purpose in assessment is different from that of a test designed to distinguish between similar students. Your job is to teach so that students learn. Assessments should help you find out whether you have been successful. In the age of standards, teachers and students are increasingly evaluated based on how well students achieve state and national standards. Therefore, items should measure whether students have learned. If the state standards include higher-order thinking skills, items can ask for higher-order thinking and still be fair to all students. Items do not have to be tricky to ask for critical thinking. As you write or evaluate multiple-choice items, be sure to ask yourself whether the knowledge and skills you *taught* and students have *studied* and *practiced* actually prepared them for the demands of every item on a test or quiz. If some other skill (e.g., the ability to spot a trick)

Item	Inappropriate Versions	Appropriate Versions
1	Tom and his three friends went to the movies. Movie tickets cost $8.50 *times* each person. Which equation shows how much money they needed? A. $8.50 × 4 B. $8.50 × 3 C. $8.50 + 4 D. $8.50 + 3	Tom and his three friends went to the movies. Movie tickets cost $8.50 per person. Which equation shows how much money they needed? A. $8.50 × 4 B. $8.50 × 3 C. $8.50 + 4 D. $8.50 + 3
2	Mia wanted to paint her bedroom light blue. She needed to know how much paint would cover *the whole area of* the walls and ceiling. Which of the following should she do before she goes to the paint store? A. Find the perimeter of the walls and ceiling. B. Find the circumference of the walls and ceiling. C. Find the area of the walls and ceiling.	Mia wanted to paint her bedroom light blue. She needed to know how much paint would cover the walls and ceiling. Which of the following should she do before she goes to the paint store? A. Find the perimeter of the walls and ceiling. B. Find the circumference of the walls and ceiling. C. Find the area of the walls and ceiling.

Figure 7–5
Examples of Multiple-Choice Items With and Without Clues to Correct Answers

Read the sentence. Then choose the word that *best* completes the sentence.

1. The boy had been hiding for so long that he had a _____ look.
   A. frightened
   B. haunted
   C. hungry
   D. worried

Figure 7–6
Example of an Item Designed to Differentiate Between Students of Similar Achievement Levels

is required, then the item is probably not a valid measure of the learning objective. In Figure 7–7, the first item is a "trick" item from a college biology test. Although the instructor may have wanted to make sure that students knew the names and discovery of these two scientists, he only assessed whether they could spell one of the names correctly. The revised item comes closer to assessing whether students had memorized this fact.

Rule 10. Don't create distractors that are partially correct or that overlap with the correct answer. Generally when teachers use traditional item tests, they are *not* trying to test whether students can read the items but whether students have knowledge and skills the items assess. When answer choices overlap or are partially correct, you are testing students' reading skills and their ability to tease apart different answer choices rather than whether they can locate the correct answer. The inappropriate version of item 1 in Figure 7–8 has four answer

	Inappropriate Version	Appropriate Version
	The team who discovered the double-helical structure of DNA was A. Watson and Cruck. B. Watson and Crack. C. Watson and Crick. D. Watson and Crock.	Watson and Crick discovered A. that genes cause cystic fibrosis. B. the double-helical structure of DNA. C. that genes can have natural mutations. D. the function of messenger RNA.

Figure 7–7
Example of Trick Item Testing Trivial Differences Rather Than the Objective

Item	Inappropriate Version	Appropriate Version
1	From farthest to nearest, what is the order of the following objects in the night sky? A. Galaxies, stars, planets B. Galaxies, stars, the moon, earth C. Stars, the sun, galaxies D. Planets, stars, the moon	Which of the following objects is closest to the earth? A. A galaxy B. The sun C. Planets D. Stars

Passage

The Navajo do not speak the names of the dead. There is a belief that if one mentions the name of a person who is dead, he invites the person's ghost to haunt the living. So the appropriate way to talk about someone who died is to say, "That man who died," or "The one who died."

If a person dies in a hogan, the family will no longer use the hogan and must build a new one. The hogan is now the home of the ghost. If a person enters a hogan inhabited by the dead, she can get ghost sickness and must participate in a ceremony to cleanse herself. This is called returning to "hozro" or the "Navajo Way." The Navajo Way is at harmony with all that is.

Item	Inappropriate Version	Appropriate Version
2	How do the Navajo handle the ghosts of the dead? A. They do ghost dances and abandon ghost hogans. B. They do not mention the name of the dead person. C. They cleanse themselves of the memory of the dead person. D. They build new hogans and do ceremonial dances.	What is one way the Navajo handle the ghosts of the dead? A. They do ghost dances and invite ghosts to dance with them. B. They cleanse themselves if they get ghost sickness from a ghost hogan. C. They try to forget everything they learned from the dead person. D. They destroy their hogans to drive the ghost away.

Figure 7–8
Examples of Items With and Without Answer Choices That Overlap or Are Partially Correct

choices. All three distractors overlap with the correct answer. This can cause unnecessary confusion among students. The appropriate version of item 1 has only one correct answer; the other choices do not overlap. The two items measure the same concept; however, the revised version doesn't create a reading burden for the student.

The inappropriate version of item 2 has distractors that are partly correct and partly incorrect. Again, this is unnecessary during testing situations. Anxiety is usually high during testing times. Students are likely to feel the pressure of time and, upon recognizing an answer that contains partially correct information, they may make a careless choice. If you want to ask for careful thought, multiple-choice items are probably not the most efficient means for assessing thinking. The revised version of item 2 has one completely correct answer and three answers that are completely incorrect but that might be chosen by someone who only skims the reading passage.

Rule 11. Do not use "none of the above," "all of the above," "a and b," or similar answer choices. Answer choices such as these make testing unnecessarily difficult for students. Students have learned that tests are full of tricks. They are often assessed over content that was *not* taught. When "all of the above" or a similar choice is given, even students who have studied the material carefully can distrust their memories under the stressful conditions of testing. They may think they have missed something or that they are being tested over content they were not taught.

Teachers sometimes use the "all of the above" strategy when they find that it is easier to write correct answers than incorrect answers. This is typically the case when several traits or characteristics are relevant to an event, character, or phenomenon (e.g., a novel has multiple themes; major events in history have multiple causes; mammals have multiple characteristics). The more complex the thinking or ideas related to the correct answer are, the more difficult it will be to write wrong answer choices. Figure 7–9 gives two examples of items in which this is the case. Although it is best to create incorrect answers, it may be difficult to write incorrect answers that are attractive to those who do not understand a concept but who have been exposed to the material. In this case, there are several alternative approaches that may be more effective than using the "all of the above" strategy.

One alternative is to use such stems as "All of the following rights are protected by the U.S. Constitution EXCEPT . . . " or "Which of the following is NOT a right protected by the U.S. Constitution?" This format tells students to look for an *incorrect* answer. The first alternatives for the two items in Figure 7–9 show examples of how the inappropriate item can be rewritten using "All of the following EXCEPT . . . " or "Which of the following is NOT."

Although both of these item stem formats can help when teachers have difficulty writing incorrect answers, they also add a cognitive load to the test-taking experience. Data from standardized testing programs suggest that younger students have a great deal of difficulty with *reverse* thinking. Even into middle and junior high school, when faced with these types of items, the majority of students select the first correct example. Therefore, these item stems should be used only with high school students—especially because the purpose of the testing situation is to find out what students know and are able to do rather than whether they can think in reverse. Of course, as is shown in the second alternative in Figure 7–9, one can take the time to create good *incorrect* answers.

Inappropriate Versions	Appropriate Version 1	Appropriate Version 2
Which of these is a theme of Jane Austin's *Sense and Sensibility?* A. Money helps to ensure that women will marry. B. Women who keep their feelings to themselves win husbands. C. Improper behaviors can cause social ruin. D. All of the above.	All of these are themes of Jane Austin's *Sense and Sensibility* EXCEPT: A. Money helps to ensure that women will marry. B. Women who keep their feelings to themselves win husbands. C. Improper behaviors can cause social ruin. D. Women have personal power and control equal to that of men.	Which of these is a theme of Jane Austin's *Sense and Sensibility?* A. Proper behavior keeps one respectable; improper behavior causes ruin. B. Women have personal power and control equal to that of men. C. Men are more dishonest and manipulative than women.
Which of these is a function of the legislative branch of the federal government? A. Propose and enact federal laws. B. Develop the federal budget. C. Check the power of the president. D. All of the above.	Which of the following is NOT a function of the legislative branch of the federal government? A. Propose and enact federal laws. B. Develop the federal budget. C. Check the power of the president. D. Enforce federal laws and policies.	Which of these is a function of the legislative branch of the federal government? A. Propose and enact federal laws. B. Decide the constitutionality of laws. C. Enforce federal laws and policies.

Figure 7–9
How to Deal With Item Stems With More Than One Reasonable Answer

A third alternative for teachers who are having difficulty writing more than one incorrect distractor is to use short-answer items and ask students to list a certain number of traits, examples, characteristics, and so forth. In addition, teachers can give students multiple-choice answers that are all correct and ask students to select and defend their choice. This strategy would not work for selecting one correct fact (e.g., one right protected under the U.S. Constitution), but it would work when you want students to take positions and support them (e.g., "Which of the following is the most important right protected under the U.S. Constitution? Support your choice using evidence and examples from your reading.").

Rule 12. Distractors are most useful in assessment if they are examples of misconceptions or common errors. Figure 7–1 showed examples of how misconceptions and common errors can be used to create distractors. Figure 7–10 gives two additional items that show how distractors can be used to assess misconceptions or common errors. The first version of item 1 in Figure 7–10 has three distractors with no particular logic to warrant their use. When distractors like these are given, students may select the correct answer simply because the distractors are not viable. In contrast, the second version of item 1 has very intentional distractors. Choice A is the correct answer. Choice B is what students might choose if they

Item	Version 1: Random Distractors	Version 2: Common Error Distractors
1	Tom and his three friends went to the movies. At the movies, they each bought popcorn and sodas. Tickets cost $7.00, popcorn cost $3.75, and sodas cost $2.50. Which equation can be used to figure the total amount they spent at the movies? A. 4 ($7.00 + $3.75 + $2.50) = x B. x + $7.00 = ($3.75 + $2.50) 4 C. $7.00 − ($3.75 + $2.50) = 3$x$ D. $7.00 − 3$x$ = $3.75 + 2.50	Tom and his three friends went to the movies. At the movies, they each bought popcorn and sodas. Tickets cost $7.00, popcorn cost $3.75, and sodas cost $2.50. Which equation can be used to figure the total amount they spent at the movies? A. 4 ($7.00 + $3.75 + $2.50) = x B. 3 ($7.00 + $3.75 + $2.50) = x C. 4 * $7.00 + $3.75 + $2.50 = x D. 3 * $7.00 + $3.75 + $2.50 = x

Look at the picture of the balance. Two objects are on opposite ends of a board that is resting on the triangle-shaped block. Right now, the forces acting in this situation are in balance.

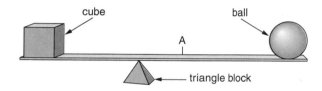

Item	Inappropriate Version	Appropriate Version
2	What will happen if the triangle block is moved to the right and placed under point A on the board? A. The balance will tilt *down* on the left. B. The balance will tilt *up* on the left. C. The balance will remain the same.	What will happen if the triangle block is moved to the right and placed under point A on the board? A. The balance will tilt *down* on the left because the cube has greater mass than the ball. B. The balance will tilt *up* on the left because the cube has greater mass than the ball. C. The balance will tilt *down* on the right because the ball has greater mass than the cube. D. The balance will remain the same because both objects have the same mass.

Figure 7–10
Distractors That Do and Don't Provide Information About Common Errors or Misconceptions

do not include Tom in the information they extract from the word problem. Choice C is what students might choose if they do not understand the order of operations. Choice D is what students might choose if they do not understand the order of operations *and* extract the wrong number of people from the word problem.

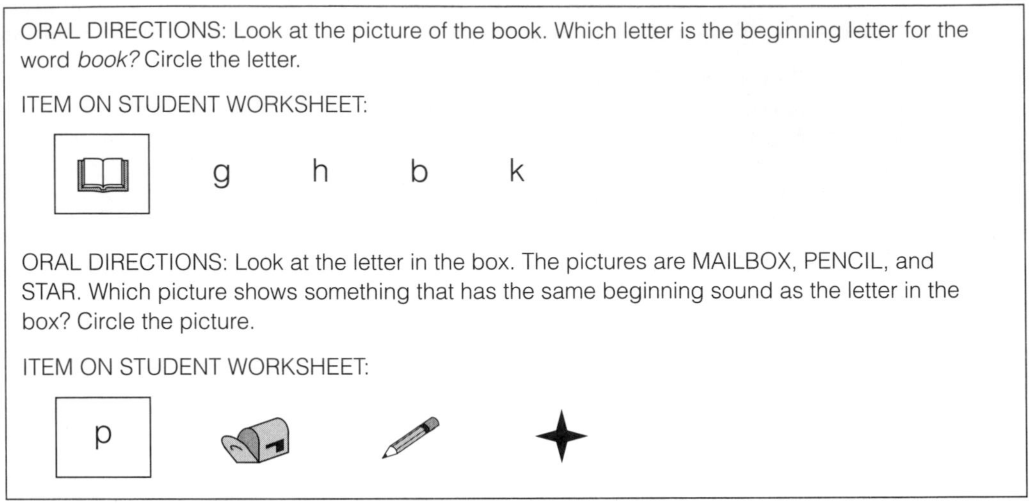

ORAL DIRECTIONS: Look at the picture of the book. Which letter is the beginning letter for the word *book?* Circle the letter.

ITEM ON STUDENT WORKSHEET:

[book]   g   h   b   k

ORAL DIRECTIONS: Look at the letter in the box. The pictures are MAILBOX, PENCIL, and STAR. Which picture shows something that has the same beginning sound as the letter in the box? Circle the picture.

ITEM ON STUDENT WORKSHEET:

p   [mailbox]   [pencil]   [star]

Figure 7–11
Examples of Item Formats Appropriate for Very Young Children

For the first version of item 2 in Figure 7–10, the answer choices are acceptable; however, they do not tell the teacher *why* the student has made a particular choice. In the second version, the student has to choose a reason for the expected change or lack of change. This helps the teacher assess why the student made a particular choice. Choices B through D are all misconceptions that lead to problematic predictions.

Rule 13. Use oral directions for young children (K–2 or 3 depending on the content). When assessing conceptual knowledge in domains other than reading and language, reading can interfere with performance (see Figure 7–11).

Rule 14. Use art for young children (K–2) unless you are assessing reading comprehension. Even for reading comprehension, keep multiple-choice items as simple as possible. Have the children circle or point to answers rather than mark bubbles or write letters designating the answers. The two multiple-choice items in Figure 7–11 are formatted for young children.

Variations on Multiple-Choice Items   Typically multiple-choice items have only one correct answer and a correct response is awarded one point. Sometimes teachers use multiple-choice items that have more than one right answer (also called a multiple-response item). When this type of multiple-choice item is used, teachers can use several strategies for giving students scores. One common scoring strategy is to treat each answer choice as a true-false item. Students receive one point for each correct answer they mark and one point for each *incorrect* answer they *don't* mark. For a four-choice item, students could earn up to four points. Another common scoring strategy for multiple-response items is to give students one point if they get all of the choices right and zero points if students make any mistakes.

Research comparing these two scoring strategies (Wu, 2003) shows that they both work equally well when looking at the total test scores earned by students; however, the strategy of giving points for each correct choice can give more classroom-based information. There

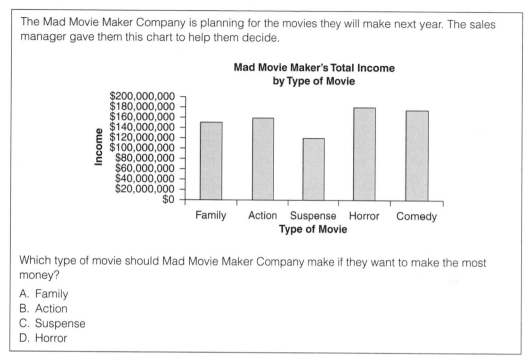

The Mad Movie Maker Company is planning for the movies they will make next year. The sales manager gave them this chart to help them decide.

Mad Movie Maker's Total Income by Type of Movie

Which type of movie should Mad Movie Maker Company make if they want to make the most money?

A. Family
B. Action
C. Suspense
D. Horror

Figure 7–12
Example of Flawed Item

is clearly a difference between a student who has partial understanding and a student who has no understanding. The "all or none" scoring strategy will not differentiate between these two students.

A useful extension of the multiple-choice item is to have students explain their choices in a short-answer follow-up item. This is very useful if you want to know the students' reasoning for their answer choices. No matter how much attention you give to writing multiple-choice items, there are times when you will not see flaws in items. These flaws may lead students to make choices that are correct from the student's perspective. Figure 7–12 shows an example of a flawed item that could lead students to an incorrect response. According to the introduction, the graph shows the profits from different movie types. The teacher's guide says that the correct answer is D—Horror Movies. However, there is no information about how many movies of each type were made by the company or about how much different movies cost to make. Therefore, the data in the graph cannot be used to make decisions. If children are allowed to explain their choices, then teachers have a chance to see if student choices are sensible.

Another way that short-answer follow-up questions can help is when students have misconceptions. Explaining a choice helps the teacher see whether misconceptions are widely shared or whether they are limited to a few students. Finally, when students explain their choices, they sometimes realize the error in their thinking and change their initial choices. Hence, although the use of multiple-choice items may lead to guessing, asking students for follow-up explanations can help them focus better on the answer choices.

Objective: Students will learn how to use idiomatic phrases effectively in written and oral language.

Item on students' test:

Define *modismo* and give one example.

Information in teacher's scoring guide:

Scoring rule: 1 point for correct definition and 1 point for an example

Example response: A modismo is an idiomatic phrase, a phrase that has meaning because of the cultural context. An example of a modismo in Spanish is "¿Qué no?" which can be literally translated as "What no?" but means, "Don't you think?" in Mexico.

Figure 7–13
Example of a Short-Answer Item That Does Not Match the Relevant Learning Objective

Developing and Evaluating Short-Answer Items

Short-answer items are questions or prompts with responses that can range from a few words or numbers to a few sentences to a geometric proof. They are useful for assessing knowledge; application of knowledge, concepts, principles, and equations; comprehension and simple analysis of text, graphics, and other stimulus materials; and simple explanations. Short-answer items are brief, standardized items that usually require no more than 2 minutes to complete. They can be used in all subjects to assess knowledge and simple applications that are not easily assessed through multiple-choice, true-false, matching, or completion items. Short-answer items are commonly used in workbooks and worksheets. They can be used with multiple-choice or true-false items to have students justify or explain their choices. Several short-answer items can be used with passages, graphics, or other stimulus materials to allow for individual interpretations of the stimulus materials.

Short-answer items can cause confusion for students if the question is not worded clearly. When writing short-answer items, it is important to have the correct responses or the expectations for responses clear in your mind (or written on paper alongside the item) so that you can check to make certain you have asked for what you want students to do. Whether there are specific correct answers or a range of effective responses, you must create scoring rules with which to judge the adequacy of student responses. Scoring rules are rules for assigning points or judgments to students' responses. Scoring rules may include the knowledge that must be shown; any writing conventions that must be used; the types of thinking that must be exhibited; the concepts, formulas, or principles that must be correctly described or applied; or any other expectations for which you will evaluate students' responses. The following item-writing rules will help you to write short-answer items with fair scoring rules for tests, quizzes, and worksheets.

Rules for Writing and Evaluating Short-Answer Items

Rule 1. Be sure the item asks for knowledge or skill relevant to your learning objectives. Although this may seem obvious, it is just as likely that a short-answer item can be disconnected from your learning objectives as a multiple-choice item. Figure 7–13 gives a learning objective and a short-answer item. The learning objective is focused on the use of idioms

Inappropriate Version	Appropriate Versions
What is the digestive system?	Name *three* organs in the digestive system.
	Describe *two* functions of the digestive system.

Figure 7–14
Inappropriate and Appropriate Versions of Short-Answer Items

in spoken and written language, but the item asks for a definition and an example. The intent of the learning objective is for students to use idiomatic phrases, not to define the term *modismo* and give a decontextualized example. The foundation of validity in assessment is to make certain that every item targets learning objectives in a precise way.

Rule 2. Make certain that the question or prompt is simple and clearly indicates what you want to know. Students should not have to read your mind to find out what you want to know. If you want students to create a list, ask for a list. If you want five examples, ask for five examples. Figure 7–14 shows inappropriate and appropriate examples of how to use a short-answer item format to assess students' knowledge of the digestive system. The revised versions give clearer expectations for students.

Rule 3. Make certain short-answer items are appropriate for the needs of young children. Keep the language of directions or questions very simple. You may need to read directions for items aloud to students. In addition, you can allow students to draw pictures or use manipulatives rather than writing their responses—even for reading comprehension items. Figures 7–15 through 7–17 show three short-answer items for young children. The item in Figure 7–15 assesses comprehension of a reading passage. The item in Figure 7–16 assesses understanding of multiplication. For the items in Figures 7–15 and 7–16, students can show their understanding in pictures. Finally, the item in Figure 7–17 assesses fundamental understanding of numbers and their symbolic representations. For this item, students use manipulatives to show their understanding.

Rule 4. For short-answer items that have one or a few limited responses, list all *the possible correct answers.* Listing all possible answers will help you clarify whether you have clearly asked for what you want to know. For example, if you want students to list the major components of the digestive system, write down all of the major components (mouth, esophagus, stomach, small intestine, large intestine) and ask for as many as you want students to list.

Rule 5. If short-answer items have no absolutely correct responses but do have key words or ideas that are to be represented in the response, list the key words and ideas and write at least one sample response that includes the key words or ideas. Using the scoring rule and a sample response, you can determine whether you have asked for all that you want in your question or prompt. Figure 7–18 shows a short-answer item for which three key ideas are expected. Once the key ideas were written, the teacher revised the prompt for the short-answer item to ask for all key ideas. Although you should write sample responses for every item, the main purpose of these sample responses is to check the quality of your item and the scoring rules for the item. You will not give the sample responses to your students. It is useful, however, to teach students your expectations for responses to short-answer items. You might give an example

Read the story.

Benny hid behind the bushes at the back of the playground. He saw Sam step off his bus and run to the school. He did not want Sam to find him. Every day Sam chased Benny around the playground. He grabbed Benny and pushed him down in the dirt. The teachers never saw. Today Benny decided he would run away from school. He walked behind the bushes toward the back gate. Suddenly he saw Mr. Jackson standing by the gate.

Mr. Jackson sat down on a stump. "Hi Benny," he said. "Do you like your new school?"

"No," said Benny. He would not look at Mr. Jackson.

"Has something happened?" asked Mr. Jackson.

Benny's eyes filled with tears. He told Mr. Jackson about how lonely he felt and about Sam. Mr. Jackson listened carefully. Then he said, "It's hard to make new friends, Benny. But I think I can help." He took Benny's hand and they walked to the school building. Benny didn't feel alone anymore.

Tell why Benny hid behind the bushes. Use words or pictures.

Teacher scoring guide:

2 points	Response shows understanding, through words or pictures, that Benny is afraid of Sam or that Benny has decided to run away from school.
1 point	Response shows comprehension of another part of the story (e.g., Mr. Jackson near the gate; Benny being sad).
0 points	Response shows no relationship to the story.

Figure 7–15
Appropriate Response Options for a Short-Answer Reading Item (Grades 2–3)

Explain why 6 × 7 = 42. Use words or pictures.

Teacher scoring guide:

2 points	Response shows understanding of multiplication; student describes or draws a diagram, picture, or array that shows seven groups of six or six groups of seven.
1 point	Response shows partial understanding of multiplication; student describes grouping or arrays but does not note the necessity of equal-sized groups or arrays; draws a diagram or picture that shows grouping or arrays but not all groups or rows in the array are of equal size.
0 points	Response shows no understanding of multiplication.

Figure 7–16
Appropriate Short-Answer Response Options for a Mathematics Item (Grades 2–3)

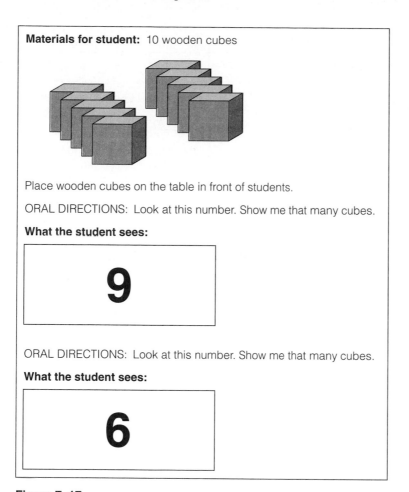

Materials for student: 10 wooden cubes

Place wooden cubes on the table in front of students.

ORAL DIRECTIONS: Look at this number. Show me that many cubes.

What the student sees:

9

ORAL DIRECTIONS: Look at this number. Show me that many cubes.

What the student sees:

6

Figure 7–17
Appropriate Response Option for Short-Answer Mathematics Item (Grades Prekindergarten – Kindergarten)

item and one or more sample responses that show the level of quality and completeness you expect in their work as well as the diversity of correct or defensible answers. You should then go over the sample and give students a chance to clarify your expectations.

The idea of adjusting items to give all expectations is one that some teachers resist. Teachers may ask, "Aren't we giving away the answer?" This is an important issue in the use of performance items. When do directions give students the answer and when do they give guidelines for answering correctly? The example in Figure 7–18 does not tell students what sentences to write or what ideas to write about—only what the rules are for writing those sentences. If they don't know the unit vocabulary, how to adjust articles for nouns, or how to conjugate verbs, they will not be able to do well on the item. This is similar to a game of basketball. No two games are alike; however, the rules of the game, the size of the court, and the skills and strategies applied are the same from game to game. We would not expect students to play basketball without knowing the rules, the strategies, and the skills.

First Draft of the Item	Scoring Rule
Write *two* complete sentences using your Spanish vocabulary.	Key ideas: Use of appropriate articles for gender—el, la, las, and los (1 point for each sentence) Use of appropriate conjugation of verbs *to be* (estar and ser) (1 point for each sentence) Use of nouns and verbs related to travel (1 point for each sentence)

Figure 7–18A
Example of a Short-Answer Item That Does Not Communicate All Expectations

Revised Item	Scoring Rule
Write *two* complete sentences in Spanish. Be sure to use: • the correct article for each noun, • the correct conjugation of the verbs *estar* and *ser,* • verbs and other vocabulary from the unit on travel.	Key ideas: Use of appropriate articles for gender—el, la, las, and los (1 point for each sentence) Use of appropriate conjugation of verbs to be (estar and ser) (1 point for each sentence) Use of nouns and verbs related to travel (1 point for each sentence)

Figure 7–18B
Example of a Revised Short-Answer Item Adjusted to Scoring Expectations

Teachers might say, "Students should *just know* that I want correct articles, correct conjugation of verbs, and the vocabulary from the unit." If students *just know* expectations, then they have been blessed with teachers who all have the same expectations for students. In reality, students move from teacher to teacher and adapt their performances to the expectations of different teachers. One teacher might *not* worry about whether students use vocabulary from the unit on travel as long as the sentences are grammatically correct. For this teacher, students learn to focus on getting the grammar right rather than on developing vocabulary. Another teacher might be more concerned with attempts to use vocabulary from the unit in new sentences and have less interest in the accuracy of conjugations—as long as the verbs taught in the unit are used at the correct location in a sentence. For this teacher, students learn to focus on developing their vocabulary and learn grammar at a slower pace.

Each teacher has ideas about how students learn a new language, and each teacher will use those values to determine how to assess students' responses to performance items. Students should not have to guess about your values or read your mind—they should be working on what you want them to learn and demonstrating that learning through the assessments you use. The same argument can be made for work in any subject area (e.g., qualities expected of graphs in a math class, grammar expectations in an assessment of reading comprehension, citations expected in a social studies test). Expectations must be clearly stated in the question or directions.

Objective: Students will learn how to solve systems of equations.

Item on students' test:

Solve for X and Y using the equations below. Be sure to show how you solve for X and Y:

$3X + Y = 4$ and $2Y - 2X = -8$

Information in teacher's scoring guide:

Scoring rule:

Solves for X and Y (2 points).

Demonstrates appropriate steps to solve for X (1 point).

Demonstrates appropriate steps to solve for Y (1 point).

Example response: $3X + Y = 4$

$Y = 4 - 3X$

$2(4 - 3X) - 2X = -8$ Substitution

$8 - 6X - 2X = -8$

$8 - 8X - 8 = -8 - 8$

$-8X = -16$

$-X = -2$

$X = 2$

$3(2) + Y = 4$ Substitution

$6 + Y - 6 = 4 - 6$

$Y = -2$

Figure 7–19
Example of a Scoring Rule for the Steps in the Solution to an Algebra Problem

Rule 6. Create scoring rules that take into account the degree of complexity expected in students' responses. Although the traditional item types are usually scored as 1 (correct) or 0 (incorrect), short-answer items may have more than one point value due to the ideas or skills shown. When writing scoring rules for key words or key ideas, give point values for each item and indicate where the points come from. For the example in Figure 7–18, the teacher gives 1 point for each sentence if the articles are correctly used; 1 point for each sentence if travel vocabulary is correctly used; one point for each sentence if the verbs are correctly conjugated. The total number of points for the item is 6. Figure 7–19 shows a multistep mathematics item with points for different steps in the solution process. The scoring rule does not demand that the student use one particular strategy for solving the equations, only that the solutions be correct and that the strategies be appropriate. Solving the problem using appropriate strategies is worth 4 points.

Rule 7. If short-answer items are open-ended and subject to many different valid responses, create a brief scoring rubric, focused on the relevant learning objective, to score the responses. Make sure the scoring rubric targets the understanding you want to assess and is related to the directions in short-answer item. Figure 7–20 shows a short-answer item intended to assess students' ability to extract main ideas and details from a reading passage. The *inappropriate* scoring rule (rubric) is too vague to be used. There is no guidance for what makes a response excellent versus good. Such a scoring rubric could lead to unintentional bias in scoring. A

Objective: Students will learn how to read for main ideas and details.

Reading passage and item on students' test:

The Navajo do not speak the names of the dead. There is a belief that if people mention the name of a dead person, they will be inviting the person's ghost to haunt them. So the appropriate way to talk about someone who died is to say, "That man who died," or "The one who died." If a person dies in a hogan, the Navajo will no longer use the hogan. The hogan is now the home of the ghost. If a person enters a hogan inhabited by a ghost, she or he can get ghost sickness and die. To prevent death, the person must participate in a ceremony to cleanse herself or himself. This is called returning to "hozro" or the "Navajo Way." The Navajo Way means being at harmony with all that is.

In contrast, the Zuñi see death as a time when the spirit of the person goes to join the kachina spirits. When a person dies, the people bury the person as quickly as possible and give the person food and water for the 4-day journey to join the kachina spirits.

1. Write a brief summary (3 to 5 sentences) to describe how the Navajo view death and how the Zuñi view death. Use at least two details from the passage to demonstrate the differences.

Information in teachers's scoring guide:

Example Answer:

For the Navajo, life after death is not good. Ghosts are to be feared because if a person gets in touch with a ghost, s/he is in danger. For Zuñi, it seems like life after death must be seen as a very good thing since the kachina are the spirits that bring all good things to the people.

Inappropriate Scoring Rubric: (Too vague; no clues as to performance criteria)	**Appropriate Scoring Rubric**
3 = excellent 2 = good 1 = poor 0 = unrelated to passage or prompt	3 = shows <u>accurate comprehension</u> of passage and uses <u>at least two appropriate details</u> to support claims. 2 = shows accurate comprehension of the passage with <u>only one appropriate detail</u> to support claims **OR** shows <u>mostly accurate</u> comprehension of the passage with <u>at least two appropriate details</u> to support claims. 1 = shows partially accurate comprehension of the passage with <u>only one appropriate detail</u> to support claims. 0 = shows little or no comprehension of the passage

Figure 7–20
Example of Short-Answer Item With Appropriate and Inappropriate Scoring Rubrics

teacher might focus on the clarity of the response or the quality of the writing, rather than the accuracy of the comprehension. In contrast, the appropriate scoring rubric is focused on the accuracy of comprehension.

Rule 8. Determine whether the number of points given to an item is reasonable given the total number of points on the test and the demands of the other items. The example item in Figure 7–18 is worth 6 points. This may seem like too many points for one item requiring students to write only two sentences. However, writing sentences is more difficult than filling in blanks with correct words or recognizing sentences that are correct. If, after careful examination, you still think that the number of points assigned to an item seems like too many or too few for a single item (when compared to the points given to other items on the test), you can give ½ point for each key element or 2 points for each key element. The decisions about how to assign points should be made after an entire test is written so that each item is evaluated in relation to the other items on a test.

In a standards-based assessment system, what students learn, rather than the number of points, is the critical issue. While it is appropriate to look at whether the number of points assigned to an item makes sense in the context of the test as a whole, it may be more important to spend your time helping students who do not earn all of the points learn what they need to learn in order to answer all of the items correctly. As was discussed in Chapter 6, you can return tests, quizzes, and worksheets to students and have them revise their work if they do not earn all of the points the first time. This would be especially useful for short answer items, because revisions would be improvements on the students' own ideas and work rather than corrections of multiple-choice, true-false, matching, or completion items with explanations.

Rule 9. Write all correct answers, sample answers, scoring rules, and scoring rubrics before you give items to students. It is important that you have clear ideas of what you are looking for *before* you give any performance items to students. Although you may have to adjust your scoring rules once you see how students interpreted the items, it is best to begin with clear answer keys and scoring rules so that you keep focused on what you want to know about your students' knowledge and skills. Note that, for the short-answer item in Figure 7–18, word order is not being scored. If a student put an adjective in the wrong place in relation to a noun, the student should not be penalized. If the teacher discovered, after administering the item, that she wanted students to use correct word order for adjectives, she could adjust the item for the *next* time she used it and create a new scoring rule. It would not be valid or fair to change the expectations without changing the item itself.

Developing and Evaluating Matching Item Sets

Matching item sets are a compact way to simultaneously assess a set of related knowledge. They are actually a compact set of multiple-choice items wherein the same answer choices are available for each item stem. Matching item sets work well for matching paired information such as facts (e.g., state capitals with states or key events with their dates), definitions (e.g., vocabulary words or science concepts with definitions), knowledge of concepts (e.g., concept names with examples), and simple applications (related math computations with answers). Matching items provide a list of stems (definitions, phrases, pictures, or other stimuli) and a list of answer choices (words, phrases, pictures, numbers, etc.). Matching item sets are used for efficient measurement of knowledge rather than depth of understanding or strength of skill. The following rules help to create useful matching sets.

Rules for Writing and Evaluating Matching Sets
Rule 1. Make sure the knowledge you are assessing is best measured in a matching item set. If you find that the ideas are too complex to be easily listed in columns, other forms of assessment are probably more appropriate.

Rule 2. Select a closely related set of knowledge to assess in each matching item set. Teachers frequently make matching sets that give long lists of definitions and/or descriptions with equally long lists of terms and/or names. This can lead to a great deal of error in assessment because students vary in their skill at managing long lists. If a student makes an initial choice, marks it as "used," and then changes her mind, she may become confused, use a choice more than once, or omit choices. When teachers create traditional item tests, the goal is usually efficiency in assessment. Therefore, matching item sets should be created to achieve that goal. Anything that adds an unnecessary reading burden or cognitive complexity to the matching item set works against the goal of efficiency and assessment accuracy. Hence you are likely to get more accurate information about your students' knowledge from several separate matching item sets—each with a cohesive set of stimuli and responses—than from one long matching item set.

Rule 3. Make sure the number of stimuli and response choices in the matching item set is appropriate for the developmental level of the students. Students in grades 5 and above can usually manage 8 to 10 items in a set; whereas very young children may be able to manage only 3 or 4 items.

Rule 4. Make certain that the concepts you test within a matching item set are very similar in type. Don't mix definitions with concepts with activities of famous people, and so forth. The purpose of assessment is to find out what students have learned (or, in the case of preassessment, what they already know prior to instruction). When matching item sets contain a wide mix of stimuli, students may figure out the correct match through the clues in the type of information assessed rather than because of real knowledge. Figure 7–21A shows a matching set that combines people, products, and cities. Students have a 50/50 chance of selecting the correct response for most of the stimuli just by the nature of the stimulus. For one stimulus (beef), students are highly likely to select the correct response even if they have never studied Missouri. Figure 7–21B shows how the set would be revised to focus on similar facts.

Rule 5. For older students (grades 5 and above), provide more options than there are blanks so that students cannot choose by process of elimination. When students have partial knowledge, they are typically able to eliminate enough choices in a matching item set that they can select effectively from the remaining choices, even if they don't know the particular knowledge assessed. The

---

Match the answers with the definitions.

Column A   **Column B**

	St. Louis	A. The capital city of Missouri
	Jefferson City	B. Author of stories about life on the Mississippi River
	Beef	C. A major commerce center in Missouri
	Harry Truman	D. Born in Independence, Missouri
	Mark Twain	E. A major export of Missouri

Figure 7–21A
Inappropriate Matching Item Set

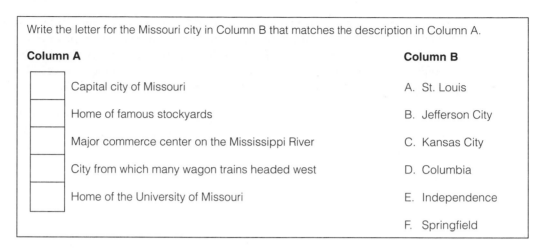

Figure 7–21B
Appropriate Matching Item Set

matching item set in Figure 7–21A has the same number of choices as stimuli. A student who knows some of the information is likely to figure out the remaining answers through mixed content and eliminations. The revised set in Figure 7–21B has more choices than stimuli.

Sometimes teachers tell us that they don't really mind if students can find answers by process of elimination. When probed, two reasons are given for this laissez faire perspective: (1) the facts don't matter that much or (2) process of elimination is a good thinking skill. Our response to these ideas should be fairly obvious by this time. First, if the facts don't matter that much, don't bother to waste your time or the students' time by testing them. Second, the purpose of assessment is to find out whether students have learned what you taught. If you value the process of elimination as a thinking skill, then teach it and assess it. If you want students to learn particular facts, then teach and assess those facts. Be clear about your learning objectives and make sure the instruction and assessment reflect those objectives.

Rule 6. Give clear and developmentally appropriate directions for how to mark responses to the matching item set. Tell students simply and exactly how to respond. Wordy directions will be hard for young children and poor readers to follow. The terms *right* and *left* are confusing for many young children. Vague directions can cause confusion about what is expected. The matching item set in Figure 7–21A has directions that are very vague. Because there is no question, some students won't know what is meant by "answer." Students may be confused about how to match the stimuli with the responses. Some may write letters, some may draw lines. The revised set in Figure 7–21B has clear directions.

Rule 7. Write the definition, example, or problem in the left-hand column and the term, concept, or solution in the right-hand column. When students respond to matching sets, they generally follow the left-to-right, top-to-bottom strategy they use in other reading situations. If terms or answers are on the left and definitions or problems are on the right, students tend to read the information in the left-hand column and then read all of the responses in the right-hand column. This can add greatly to the reading load. However, if students read a definition and look for a term or read a problem and look for the solution, then the matching item set works like a multiple-choice item wherein students know what to look for as soon as they read the stimulus.

This lowers the reading burden for the students. Adding an unnecessary reading burden to the matching item set works against the goal of efficiency. The matching item set in Figure 7–21A violates Rule 7. The matching set in Figure 7–21B has been reorganized so that the definitions are on the left and terms on the right. A careful look at the matching item set in Figure 7–21B shows that it is a clearer tool and more likely to assess students' knowledge.

Rule 8. Make certain that the stimuli and the responses do not contain clues to correct answers. As with multiple-choice items, this happens easily and can usually be fixed by changing a word or two. Clues are more likely when the stimuli include very different stimuli than when the stimuli are all of a similar class. For example, Figure 7–22A shows a matching set that has two major clues. By including "fraction" as a response choice and "a type of rational number" as a stimulus, students who know that fractions are ratios have a clue to the meaning of the term *rational number* even if they don't know the meaning of the term. Figure 7–22B is a revision of the matching item set that eliminates clues by eliminating "fraction," which was unlike the other terms in the set.

Rule 9. Lay out the matching item set to make it easy for you to score. Older students can write the letter of a choice in a blank. Younger students may have trouble with this abstraction; therefore, they can draw lines between their choices. Letters are easier to score when the matching set has many choices. You must choose between what is easiest for you to assess and what is most appropriate for the students to do. If letters are to be used in the response, it is generally easier to score matching sets if the blanks are on the far left and in a straight column. The Tables utility in most word processing software can be used to lay out matching sets in an easy-to-score format.

Rule 10. For young children, use art and/or simple words and oral directions to eliminate unnecessary reading. Figures 7–23A and 7–23B show two simple layouts for matching item sets for young children. As can be seen, the directions for the kindergarten/first grade

Write the letter for the term in Column B that matches the description or definition in Column A. Each term is used only once.

Column A	Column B
☐ A number divisible only by itself and one	A. Numeral
☐ A symbolic representation of a whole number	B. Fraction
☐ A number that can be represented by a ratio of whole numbers	C. Irrational number
☐ A kind of rational number	D. Integer
☐ A positive or negative whole number	E. Rational number
	F. Prime number

Figure 7–22A
Matching Item Set With Clues to Correct Choices

Write the letter for the term in Column B that matches the description or definition in Column A. Each term is used only once.

Column A

☐	A number divisible only by itself and one
☐	A symbolic representation of a whole number
☐	Number that can be represented by a ratio of whole numbers
☐	A positive or negative whole number

Column B

A. Numeral

B. Prime number

C. Irrational number

D. Integer

E. Rational number

Figure 7–22B
Matching Item Set With Clues Eliminated

ORAL DIRECTIONS: *(Place matching picture on overhead.)* Look at the pictures of squares *(point to column of squares)* and the numbers *(point to column of numbers)*. Draw a line from the squares to the number that tells how many squares. The first one is done for you.

ITEM ON STUDENT WORKSHEET:

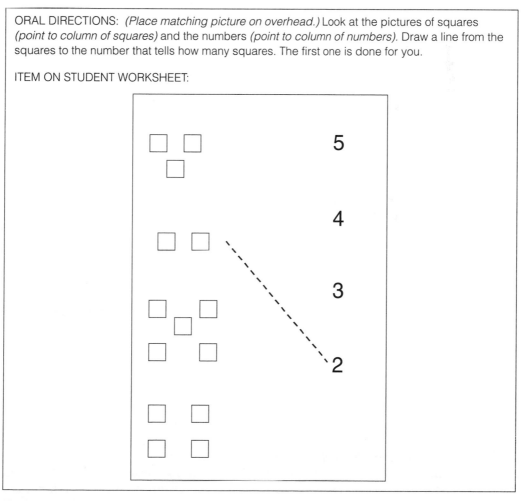

Figure 7–23A
Appropriate Matching Item Set for Grades K–1

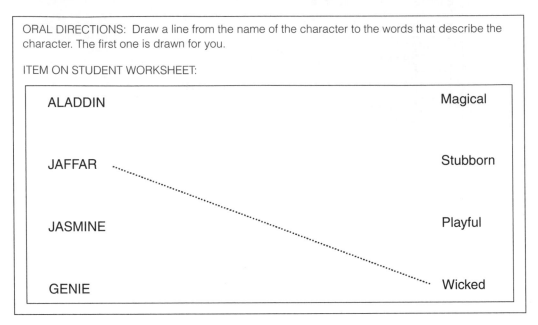

ORAL DIRECTIONS: Draw a line from the name of the character to the words that describe the character. The first one is drawn for you.

ITEM ON STUDENT WORKSHEET:

ALADDIN   Magical

JAFFAR   Stubborn

JASMINE   Playful

GENIE   Wicked

Figure 7–23B
Appropriate Matching Item Set for Grades 2–3

matching item set indicate that the teacher will show students what is meant by squares and numbers and gives an example to show how it is to be completed.

Variations in Matching Item Set Formats   You may find it easier to write matching items by listing key ideas or terms at the top of the page and having students write the word or idea next to the definition. Another format is to have several examples of two or three concepts and ask students to select the term that best fits each example. Figure 7–24 shows this latter format.

Developing and Evaluating True-False Items

True-false items typically test knowledge of concepts or facts, or they may test recognition of the correct applications of principles, algorithms, or rules. True-false items can be used with graphics, passages, or other stimulus materials when these stimulus materials yield correct or incorrect inferences, analyses, or comprehension. When used with stimulus materials, the items assess whether the students can correctly read and comprehend the stimulus and then apply rules for inference, analysis, or comprehension relevant to the subject area (e.g., given a picture of the setup for a scientific investigation, can the student identify the independent and dependent variables). As with multiple-choice and matching items, true-false items are best used when you want to narrow the focus of assessment and control the nature of students' responses.

Rules for Writing and Evaluating True-False Items
Rule 1. Make certain that the true-false format is the most appropriate way to assess the targeted knowledge.   Use true-false items to assess information that is either true or false and not debatable. Opinions, interpretations, and principles that are still under debate by scholars should not be assessed through true-false items.

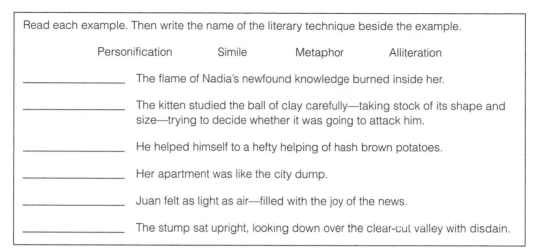

Read each example. Then write the name of the literary technique beside the example.

Personification   Simile   Metaphor   Alliteration

_____   The flame of Nadia's newfound knowledge burned inside her.

_____   The kitten studied the ball of clay carefully—taking stock of its shape and size—trying to decide whether it was going to attack him.

_____   He helped himself to a hefty helping of hash brown potatoes.

_____   Her apartment was like the city dump.

_____   Juan felt as light as air—filled with the joy of the news.

_____   The stump sat upright, looking down over the clear-cut valley with disdain.

Figure 7–24
Alternate Format for Matching Item Sets

Item	Inappropriate Versions	Appropriate Versions
1	T F Jefferson City is *not* the capital of Missouri.	T F St. Louis is the capital of Missouri.
2	T F Houston is one of the locations of NASA and is the capital of Texas.	T F Houston is one of the locations of NASA. T F Houston is the capital of Texas.
3	T F St. Louis is one of the most important cities in the United States.	T F St. Louis has been an important city for U.S. commerce because of its location on the Mississippi River.
4	T F French should be spoken by all citizens of Louisiana.	T F Many believe that French should be a state-recognized language in Louisiana.

Figure 7–25
Inappropriate and Appropriate True-False Items

Rule 2. Do NOT insert the word not *in a true statement to make it false.* False statements should be misconceptions or misapplications. Students too easily miss the word *not* in a true-false statement. In addition, negations in a true-false item add an unnecessary cognitive load to the assessment situation. Figure 7–25 shows inappropriate and appropriate true-false items. For item 1, the word *not* has been inserted in an otherwise true statement. The appropriate version of item 1 simply gives an incorrect statement. Not only is this statement incorrect, the city chosen to make the statement incorrect is one of the two largest cities in Missouri and, therefore, represents a common mistake.

Rule 3. Do NOT combine true and false information in a single item. Write statements that are entirely true or entirely false. Combining true and false information in the same statement

ORAL DIRECTIONS: Find Number 1. Look at the words YES and NO. I'm going to read a sentence. Circle the YES if the sentence I read is true and circle the NO if it is *not* true. "The word *apple* begins with the letter *A*."

ITEM ON STUDENT WORKSHEET:

1. YES   NO

Figure 7–26A
Appropriate True-False Item Format for Beginning Readers

presents a trick item to students who are in a stressful (and usually timed) testing situation. Students are likely to read the true information and mark their answer choices without reading the entire statement. Again, if the purpose is to find out what students have learned, tricks and distractions must be avoided in assessment. The inappropriate version of item 2 in Figure 7–25 is partly true and partly false. There are two appropriate alternatives given for that item.

Rule 4. Never lift sentences directly from a textbook. Students with good memories can answer correctly without understanding the concept.

Rule 5. Make certain that items test factual statements; do NOT put value judgments into true-false items. The assessment reasons for this rule are obvious. However, another important issue arises whenever testing value judgments and opinions. If students do not agree with a tested value judgment or opinion, they have a valid right to appeal the assessment. It is, however, acceptable to test whether students recognize an opinion held by others. In such a case, the true-false statement must indicate that this is the opinion held by others. Items 3 and 4 in Figure 7–25 show two ways to deal with assessment of opinions or value judgments in true-false items. For item 3, the inappropriate statement is changed to a true statement about the importance of St. Louis. For item 4, the inappropriate statement is changed to indicate that a certain opinion is held by a group of people in Louisiana.

Rule 6. Avoid terms that will provide clues to the true-false item. Terms such as *all, always, never, none,* and *every* are all-inclusive. Since few facts apply to all situations, terms that are completely inclusive or exclusive provide clues that a statement is false.

Rule 7. For young children who are not yet reading or reading minimally, use oral directions and simple art or simple words for true-false items. Figures 7–26A and 7–26B show two true-false formats for young children. In each case, reading is minimal or unnecessary.

Developing and Evaluating Completion Items

There are two types of completion items used in tests: *sentence completion* items and *cloze* items. Sentence completion items are isolated sentences with one or two missing words, numbers, or symbols. Sentences can be broadly interpreted to include number sentences and equations as well as verbal sentences. Completing the sentences shows knowledge of facts, terms, symbols, definitions, formulas, or simple applications. Sentence completion items measure memorized facts or, in the case of grammar exercises, very simple applications of knowledge. Cloze items are designed to assess passage comprehension or language usage. As such, they generally occur in longer passages with several missing words in the overall passage. In the section that follows, we separate rules for sentence completion items from rules for cloze items.

ORAL DIRECTIONS: Find Number 1. Look at the pictures. You can see a smiling face and a frowning face. I'm going to read a sentence. Circle the smiling face if the sentence I read is TRUE. Circle the frowning face if the sentence I read is NOT true. "When you are in a lightning storm, it is safe to get under a tree."

ITEM ON STUDENT WORKSHEET:

1.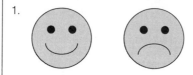

Figure 7–26B
Appropriate True-False Item Format for Beginning Readers or Nonreaders

Rules for Writing and Evaluating Sentence Completion Items

Rule 1. With certain exceptions, the blank should be at or near the end of the sentence. Blanks at the beginning or in the middle of the sentence create a reading comprehension problem for students. Students should be able to read the information in the stem and determine what is needed to complete the blank without having to use any puzzle thinking. The three exceptions to this rule are English and foreign language usage items, cloze items (see next section), and the ability to solve simple equations. Figure 7–27 shows appropriate and inappropriate completion items. The inappropriate version of item 1 has the blank at the beginning of the sentence. In this case, the students must read the entire sentence and then work backward to complete the missing information. This adds an additional cognitive load to the testing process that is unnecessary. The revision of item 1 assesses the same fact; however, the sentence has been restructured to place the blank at the end of the sentence. In most cases, it is possible to change the syntax of sentences to ask for the same knowledge in a more accessible format.

Rule 2. The omitted words should be significant—a central concept to be assessed. Assessment is wasted when students are expected to complete a sentence with trivial information rather than a critical fact. The inappropriate versions of items 2 and 3 in Figure 7–27 assess unimportant information while important facts are included in the sentence. The revisions simply required placing the blank at a different place in the sentences.

Rule 3. Do NOT lift a sentence out of a textbook and simply leave out important words. Students who have good visual memories may recall sentences even though they do not understand the important ideas in a text. Given the limitations of completion items, it is important to use them as effectively as possible. This means that students should be able to transfer ideas from one situation to another.

Rule 4. Leave only one or two blanks in the sentence. The student should not have to read your mind to respond to the item. The more blanks, the more students must infer about the missing information and the more likely their responses will not show their true knowledge. The inappropriate version of item 4 in Figure 7–27 clearly has too many blanks and the student must make too many assumptions to complete the sentence. The revision focuses on the central concept in the sentence.

Item	Inappropriate Versions	Appropriate Versions
1	_____ was where the colonists wrote the Declaration of Independence.	The city where the Declaration of Independence was signed is _____ .
2	A major transportation route for grains and livestock is the Mississippi _____ .	To move grain and livestock from St. Louis to the Gulf Coast, a major transportation route has been the _____ River.
3	The colonists protested against taxes at the _____ Tea Party.	The Boston Tea Party was a protest against taxation without _____ .
4	The major system in humans necessary for _____ _____ throughout the body is the _____ _____ .	The major system in humans necessary for moving nutrients throughout the body is the _____ _____ .
5	Maria _____ en _____ casa bonita.	Write the correct article: Maria vive en _(un/uno/una)_ casa bonita. Write the correct conjugation of the verb: Maria _(viver)_ en una casa bonita.

Figure 7–27
Inappropriate and Appropriate Completion Items

Rule 5. To use completion items to assess grammar usage in English or other languages (e.g., verb conjugations), be sure that each item focuses on only one concept at a time. This rule relates to rule 4. If too many blanks are given in the item, students must comprehend the sentence before determining what language is appropriate to complete the sentence. Figure 7–27 shows an inappropriate Spanish grammar item and two appropriate versions of the item.

Rule 6. For young children, leave enough room to write the entire response. Older students can write their answers on a separate sheet of paper. This is simply a developmental issue. Young children have difficulty transferring their answers to separate answer sheets.

Rule 7. For very young children (K–2), avoid completion items requiring reading and writing. Because reading and writing are required in the typical completion item, and young children may still be struggling with reading, a written format is not really possible. It is best to create an oral sentence that is open-ended and ask students to finish the sentence. Figure 7–28 shows an example of a sentence completion item format for very young children.

Rule 8. Write all possible correct responses for any blank in the completion item and include that with your answer key. Teachers often discover that students interpreted the items differently than intended. If students complete a sentence with a viable answer, be sure to give them credit. For example, in example 5 of Figure 7–27, without a cue for the verb, students might use a verb that fits the sentence but was not the intent of the teacher (*to play* rather than *to live*). Without the cue for the article, students might use a different but viable article (*la*

ORAL DIRECTIONS: Look at the three pictures. They are SUN, BOX, and PUZZLE. Now, listen to this sentence. "The fox in socks got into the _____ ." Circle the picture of the word that rhymes to complete this sentence. "The fox in socks got into the _____ ."

ITEM ON STUDENT WORKSHEET:

Figure 7–28
Example of Completion Item Format for Very Young Children

rather than *una*). If you find there are very many possible answers, you want to use a different item format.

Rules for Writing and Evaluating Cloze Items As mentioned earlier, cloze items assess students' reading comprehension and language usage. They can also be used to assess second language learning. The focus of cloze items is to have students complete sentences using their comprehension of what they have read and their understanding of the structure of language.

Rule 1. Make sure all passages chosen for cloze items are at a difficulty level that students can read. If the focus is on comprehension, make certain that the cloze passage is at the same reading level as the reading level you are trying to assess. If the focus is on grammar, use passages that are at a reading level below that of the students so that students are focused on grammar rather than comprehension.

Rule 2. Give children sufficient context to figure out missing words. Needless to say, the more blanks in the text, the more difficult it will be for students to figure out what is expected in the blanks. Figure 7–29 shows an inappropriate cloze passage wherein there are so many blanks that students cannot know what is expected.

Rule 3. Omit words or phrases strategically. If the goal is to assess grammar, make certain to omit only key grammar. If the goal is to assess whether students can use contextual information to predict missing information in a sentence, make certain the context is sufficient to make the appropriate prediction. In the appropriate cloze passage, the student can predict that the first missing word is *pencil* or *pen* based on the activity (spelling) and the presence of paper. The student can predict the words in each of the remaining sentences based on the overall contextual information. For example, "I looked in my backpack. I didn't _____ one there." clearly contrasts looking but not finding or seeing. For "The store was _____, so I had to go somewhere else," the reader can infer the store was closed because the writer had to go somewhere else.

Inappropriate Comprehension Cloze Passage:

I needed to practice my _____ . I had _____ , but I didn't have a _____ .

I looked in my _____ . I didn't find one there. I went to the _____ . The store

_____ closed. I had to _____ somewhere else. Finally, I found what I needed

in a surprising _____ . I found them at the _____ station.

Appropriate Comprehension Cloze Passage:

I needed to practice my spelling. I had paper, but I didn't have a _____ . I looked in my

backpack. I didn't _____ one there. I went to the store. The store was _____ , so

I had to go somewhere else. Finally, I found what I needed in a surprising _____ . I found

them at the _____ station.

Figure 7–29
Examples of Inappropriate and Appropriate Comprehension Cloze Items Assessing Reading
Comprehension

Rule 4. Accept any reasonable word that completes the sentence. Students may interpret text differently but appropriately. If the response given by a student fits the sentence based on the context, the student should receive credit whether or not the answer choice fits the answer key.

VALIDITY AND RELIABILITY ISSUES FOR TRADITIONAL ITEMS

For traditional items, validity refers to whether the item measures what it is supposed to measure. Reliability refers to whether the item will result in consistent performances from an examinee if she were to respond to the item again. When creating traditional items, it is important to recheck to make certain that you can depend on the *scores* (no matter who does the scoring) and that the items actually *ask for* what you want to measure.

General Strategies for Assessing Traditional Test Items for Validity and Reliability

Check That the Answer Key for Each Item Is Correct   Reliable *scores* are fairly easy to obtain from traditional items because, for the most part, scoring is a matter of correct or incorrect responses. Hence the reliability of item scores depends on the accuracy of the answer keys (for multiple-choice, true-false, completion, and matching items) as well as the clarity and precision of the scoring rules for short-answer items. The greatest threat to reliability of scores for short-answer items is the degree to which teachers systematically apply the same scoring rules to every student's response.

Check the Match Between Items and Learning Objectives   Although this message was part of the rules for every item type, it is important to recheck your items to make certain that they truly are consistent with your learning objectives. In other words, attend closely to the

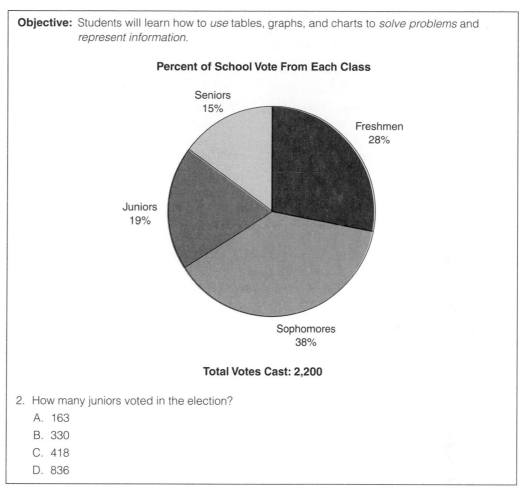

Objective: Students will learn how to *use* tables, graphs, and charts to *solve problems* and *represent information.*

Percent of School Vote From Each Class

Seniors 15%

Freshmen 28%

Juniors 19%

Sophomores 38%

Total Votes Cast: 2,200

2. How many juniors voted in the election?
   A. 163
   B. 330
   C. 418
   D. 836

Figure 7–30
Example of a Mismatch Between an Item and an Objective

validity of your items. To write or select items that measure your objectives, you must be very clear about what it is you want students to learn and what it looks like when they have learned. The most common error in traditional testing is use of items that do not match learning objectives.

Figure 7–30 is an example of this mismatch. The learning objective, "Students will learn how to *use* tables, graphs, and charts to *solve problems* and *represent information*" says that students will use graphs in complex ways—to solve problems and represent information. Although the item is, indeed, a graphing item, it does not relate to solving problems. Nor does it ask the student to represent information. Hence, the item does not measure the objective. It may take some practice, but careful analysis of items can help you decide whether items are appropriate for your objectives. Compare the content, thinking skills, and type of response required by items with your objectives. If there is a mismatch, either select a more appropriate item or write one that meets your needs.

Make sure all of the requirements for an item are clear and straightforward. The clearer the item, the more likely the students will respond in the same way if they see the item again and the more likely they are to demonstrate what they know and are able to do. If students do not know what items are asking them to do, they are unlikely to show their true knowledge or skills.

Test the Items Before Using Them to Test the Students   Some of the technical rules for writing traditional test items are regularly ignored by teachers and educational publishers. This does *not* mean that these rules are unimportant. It means that item writers are ill-informed. In fact, items in textbooks and supplemental materials are often published without being *tried out* on students; therefore, the impact of violation of item-writing rules is unknown.

Carefully writing or selecting items with attention to the item-writing rules in this chapter can help you avoid most of the problems that occur with traditional items. Although teachers generally can't do formal item tryouts, you can look at the results of tests and delete items that are problematic. If the content measured by the items is important, you can improve problematic items for the next use or create another way to assess the content.

Once you have found an effective way to assess, you can create additional items using a similar format. In Ms. Steinberg's test (Chapter 6), she used one format for items that measured the same skills (graphing data, drawing conclusions from results, making inferences from results). Once she found an item format that worked, she simply used it again and again. This not only helps to ensure that the items are effective, but also means that Ms. Steinberg doesn't have to invent each item anew. Good assessment is really a matter of finding strategies that work and using them again and again. This is as true for traditional items as it is for formal performance assessments.

Validity Issues in Using Traditional Items to Assess Students With Special Needs

Three aspects of item writing are particularly important for students with reading disabilities or with limited English proficiency (including some hearing-impaired students). Paying attention to these issues can increase the validity of your tests.

Needlessly Complicated Syntax   Good items are written using simple, active, declarative sentences. Unless you are testing students on their ability to understand complex sentences and passive voice, these should be avoided in writing items. In Figure 7–31, the item stem is written in the passive voice, with an implied subject rather than a specific one ("The study of living animals and fossil records is used to . . . "). In the second sentence, "these animals had a common ancestor" is a sentence embedded in another: a subordinate clause. This is a complex sentence, and is more difficult to read. Compare this stem to the second version of the stem in Figure 7–31 ("Scientists study . . . "). The subject (scientists) is specified and comes before the verb, making this an active, declarative sentence. In the second version of the item, the clauses for the second sentence have been separated into simple sentences.

Length   Notice, however, that the second version of the item stem in Figure 7–31 is longer than the first. In fact, teachers often use passive, complex sentences to make stems shorter than the same information given in simple, declarative sentences. Length of stems is an

---

Complex: The study of living animals and fossil records is used to group gorillas, chimpanzees, and humans together in the taxonomic order of primates. Which information supports the conclusion that these animals had a common ancestor?

   A. They eat similar foods.

   B. They have similar behaviors.

   C. They have similar DNA.

Simple, active, declarative: Scientists study living animals and fossil records to group animals into taxonomic orders. They have put gorillas, chimpanzees, and humans together in the order primates. Some scientists claim that these animals have a common ancestor. Which information supports this conclusion?

Simple and shorter: Some scientists claim that gorillas, chimpanzees, and humans all have a common ancestor. Which information supports this conclusion?

Figure 7–31
Avoiding Overly Complicated Syntax

important consideration in designing tests; the more students have to read before they can answer the item, the longer it takes to complete the test. This can be particularly problematic for students with disabilities or who have limited English proficiency. It is also of general concern for all students because longer items mean fewer of them can be included, possibly reducing the reliability of the test. The creator of the original item put the first sentence in to give a little background for the item. However, background is not necessary to answer the question. When writing a test, appropriate ordering of items (see Chapter 6) can provide sufficient context. In that case, the third version of the item shown in Figure 7–31 should be sufficient.

Vocabulary, Context, and Idioms   Sometimes items require that students have met a learning target *and* that they have specialized knowledge that was *not* taught in class because it is not a learning target. Students in your class come from a variety of cultures and backgrounds. Those who have outside experiences that provide the knowledge necessary to complete the item will be unfairly advantaged, whereas students without those experiences will be blocked from showing that they have met the learning target. Figure 7–32 shows two items measuring the same understanding of ratio. Figure 7–32A is framed in a baseball context and uses specialized vocabulary such as "at-bat" and "batting average." Students who are familiar with baseball and its statistics will be more likely to get the answer correct, even if they don't completely understand the behavior of rational numbers. Students who understand rational numbers but who are not familiar with baseball may not be able to decipher the item stem so that they can display that knowledge. Figure 7–32B shows a similar item measuring the same underlying knowledge of rational numbers, but the context and vocabulary are more likely to be familiar to all students.

Idioms are more subtle but can be just as confusing to students with limited English proficiency. The item in Figure 7–33 contains several idioms as well as sports slang that may mask a student's knowledge of the math. For students who are not familiar with basketball, the italicized terms could cause confusion.

Bob and José are on the same baseball team. José has played in 10 games and he has 30 *at-bats*. Bob has played in 5 games and has 20 *at-bats*. Both players have a *batting average of .350*. In the next game, both players have 4 *at-bats* and get 3 *hits*. At the end of the game, how did their *batting averages* compare?

   A. Bob's *batting average* was higher than José's, because he had fewer total *at-bats*.

   B. José's *batting average* was higher than Bob's, because he had more total *at-bats*.

   C. Their *batting averages* were still equal, because both boys got three *hits* in the game.

   D. There is not enough information in the problem to answer the question.

Figure 7–32A
Example of a Math Item in a Context Requiring Specialized Knowledge

Bob and José are in the same class at school. All students turn in 20 homework assignments by the end of the semester, but the teacher doesn't care when they turn them in. José has turned in 10 homework assignments so far. Bob has turned in 5 homework assignments. Both boys have an average of 75% correct for their homework so far. What will happen to their overall average if both boys get 100% on their next homework?

   A. Bob's average will be higher than José's, because he had turned in fewer homework assignments.

   B. José's average will be higher than Bob's, because he had turned in more homework assignments.

   C. Their averages will be still equal, because they got the same score on the quiz.

   D. There is not enough information in the problem to answer the question.

Figure 7–32B
Revised Item With Math Item in a Context That Is Familiar to All Students

Bob and his dad are *shooting hoops* at the park. Bob thinks his dad is *over the hill,* so he challenges him to a *free-throw contest*. Bob *bets* his dad that he can *shoot twice as many baskets* as his father. If his father *shoots 5 baskets* in 10 tries, how many *baskets* will Bob need to *shoot* to *win the bet*?

Figure 7–33
Example of an Item Requiring Knowledge of American English Idioms

     Addressing each of these three issues while writing items will help to ensure that you do not need to make significant changes in the content of your items when they are used in tests. Often what is helpful for students with special needs is also helpful for all students. Testing can be a stressful situation, but clear, simply worded items without unnecessary linguistic hurdles are likely to make the testing situation less stressful.

SUMMARY

In this chapter we have described the purposes of traditional test items and rules for writing or evaluating them. Throughout the chapter, issues of reliability and validity have been woven into the decisions made while writing items and building tests. Finally we discussed how to adapt traditional tests for students with special needs, including English language learners. In the next chapter, we discuss performance items (essay items, performance tasks, and direct writing assessments). Together, these two chapters can help you create good tests that help you and your students assess what has been learned, and what still needs time, different instructional strategies, or both.

REFERENCES

Wu, B. C. C. (2003). *Scoring multiple true-false items: A comparison of summed scores and response pattern scores at the item and test levels.* Paper presented at the annual meeting of the National Council on Measurement in Education, Chicago.

PERFORMANCE ITEM
DEVELOPMENT

The purpose of performance items is to have efficient ways to assess whether students can apply knowledge and skills to solve problems, analyze situations, represent information and ideas, and do other work that can be demonstrated through student responses to standardized prompts. The major differences between performance items and formal performance assessments are length and breadth. A performance item takes less time to complete and typically assesses only part of a more complex, authentic performance. For example, an *essay item* on a literature test might ask students to demonstrate part of what they would show in a formal paper (e.g., analyze a theme in a work of literature; synthesize ideas across two works by the same author). A *performance task*, for which students create a graph using data (as in Ms. Steinberg's test shown in Chapter 6), is one part of an overall report in a scientific investigation. Performance items serve a similar purpose as scrimmages in sports—they ask students to apply some of the skills necessary for the authentic performance.

One benefit of performance items over formal performances is repeatability. For both of the examples described above, students can demonstrate application of a few skills to more than one performance item, whereas formal performances generally require use of a broader range of skills to a single, authentic task. Used in combination with formal performance assessments, performance items can help you determine what learning objectives to teach as students work toward completion of a formal performance. For example, a teacher could have students write a brief, informative paragraph before beginning to write reports. If they show adequate control over writing paragraphs, then the teacher knows he doesn't have to teach students how to write paragraphs. However, if the teacher finds that students can organize sentences in sequence but don't know how to write topic or concluding sentences, he can teach students these skills before teaching them how to write multiparagraph reports.

Performance items can also give you more than a single observation of students' accomplishment of a skill or set of skills. A close look at Ms. Steinberg's overall assessment plan in Chapter 6 (Figure 6–1) shows that she will combine three types of assessments: (a) observations of students as they conduct their investigations, (b) assessments of the reports they write regarding their investigations (including the investigation design; observations; organization of results into tables, graphs, or charts; conclusions from and interpretations of results), and (c) assessments of their performance on the unit test. She will have multiple opportunities to assess whether students have achieved the learning objectives.

In this chapter, we introduce and closely examine different performance item types (essay items, performance tasks, and direct writing assessments), how they are best used, and rules for writing effective items of each type. Next, we describe how to use performance items alone or as part of tests and quizzes. Finally, we discuss how to use performance items in a standards-based assessment context, including how to assess English language learners and students with special needs and how to use feedback and revision with performance tests.

DEVELOPING AND EVALUATING PERFORMANCE ITEMS AND TASKS

In this section, each performance item type is introduced along with the rules for writing the particular type of item. Some writers call performance items "constructed response" items to distinguish them from multiple-choice, true-false, and matching items, wherein students simply recognize a correct answer rather than supplying a response. We use the term *item* to reflect the diversity of ways we ask students to produce a response. For example, an item might be a *question* (e.g., Alpha Rentals charges $20 per day and 10¢ per mile and Beta Cars charges $40 per day with unlimited mileage. Which car rental company gives the best deal for a 2-day, 500-mile trip?). Alternately, an item might be a set of *directions* students must follow in order to respond (e.g., Use the data in the table to create a graph. Be sure to give the graph an informative title, label the axes, use an appropriate scale, and accurately record the data.). Finally, an item might be a fairly open-ended *prompt* (e.g., Suppose you found a brown cardboard box with your name on it. Write a story telling where you found the box and what happened next.).

The three types of performance items described in this chapter are essay items, performance tasks, and direct writing assessments. Each serves a different assessment purpose. Essay items tend to be used in language arts and social studies tests to assess students' analyses, syntheses, interpretations, or evaluations of information from literature, primary documents and artifacts, and/or textbooks. Performance tasks are used in nearly all subjects when students are asked to demonstrate application of knowledge and skills in a novel situation (see Ms. Steinberg's science test items requiring graphing skills in Chapter 6, Figure 6–2). Performance tasks may or may not require written language in the students' responses. Finally, direct writing assessments are used when we want students to demonstrate their English or foreign language writing skills. An example of this type of item would be the prompts used in district and state testing programs (such as the one described above); however, teachers also use writing assessments in their classrooms as preassessments and to assess students' progress in writing skills in a standardized way.

Performance items are standardized (all students do the same task following the same set of directions in the same amount of time) to give teachers more control over the assessments than they have with formal performance assessments. As with the chapter on traditional items, the rules and information presented here are derived from many sources, including measurement textbooks and research on effective item development. Although performance items come closer to authentic performances than do traditional items, it can be more difficult to write performance items that effectively draw out students' knowledge, skills, and thinking. In addition, evaluating students' performances requires careful and systematic application of scoring rules.

The power of performance items is that they can show understanding and skills better than traditional items. The weaknesses of performance items are that (a) if they are unclear, they can be interpreted differently by different students and (b) if the scoring rules are absent or inadequate, evaluations of students' work can be biased and unreliable. Most of us have taken an essay test in which we thought we answered the questions, only to find that we did not know what the teacher wanted. The most common question we are asked about writing performance items is, "How do I ask questions or present prompts to find out what my students know and are able to do without giving them the answers?" We believe that you can create effective performance items that are clear, that students understand, and that give you the information you seek without giving students the answers. This chapter will help you create and evaluate performance items and performance tests.

As with traditional items, performance items can be used in preassessments to determine what students already know prior to instruction and in tests to check the success of instruction. Individual performance items can be used alone as a way to check for the success of a lesson on a particular skill, concept, or process. Performance items are best when they are linked to a stimulus such as a picture, a reading passage, a set of data, a set of documents or artifacts, or a problem situation. When items are attached to one or more stimuli, it is easier to assess knowledge, skills, and processes in ways that are similar to authentic performances. However, performance items can also be used to assess recall and simple application through lists of words, diagrams, or a few sentences. Because performance items give you a chance to assess parts of valued performances, you should use these items whenever possible to assess higher-order thinking skills (e.g., creation of new products, application of standard procedures, interpretation and evaluation of ideas and text). Therefore, you must know *what* you want to assess before creating performance items and then work to create items that actually elicit the knowledge or skills you want to target in the assessment. Assessments should not be random or haphazard. Decide what ideas, skills, principles, analyses, evaluations, and so forth that you care about and make sure each item truly asks for what you value *and* what you taught.

Essay Items and Performance Tasks

Essay items and performance tasks are very popular among teachers who want students to think critically and apply their knowledge and skills in diverse situations. Students are presented with a question or directions and students write one or two paragraphs or complete a brief performance in response. Essay items ask for written responses; performance items ask for written work, graphics, and/or brief live performances. Essay items and performance tasks are carefully standardized (all students do the same task following tightly controlled directions) to give teachers more control over the student responses than they have with assessments of valued performances. Responses to performance items may take 5 to 20 minutes to complete, depending on whether the items stand alone or are part of a test. These types of assessment tools are more authentic than traditional items; however, they are simpler than work that is authentic to various disciplines. We have combined these two types of performance items into one section because the rules for writing them are the same. In what follows, we distinguish between essay items and performance tasks. Then we give the rules for writing both types of assessment tools.

Essay Items   If students must write a coherent essay in one or two paragraphs, it is called an essay item. Essay items may ask students to summarize, synthesize, evaluate, make judgments, reason, or do other complex processes that are typically shown through writing. For example, an essay item might ask students to write an essay defining one of the classic conflicts found in literature using supporting examples. Essay items can be used along with performance tasks so that students can describe the decisions, thinking, and/or process they used to complete a task. Several brief essay items measuring different concepts can be organized into a test. In this case, each item would take no more than 5 to 10 minutes to complete.

Performance Tasks   The major differences between an essay item and a performance task are the amount of writing and the type of writing. If students must do a brief performance or part of a complex performance (e.g., draw a floor plan, create a chart, write a dialogue using a foreign language, draw a shape using perspective, write the dialogue for a skit) or do a brief performance that is one example of other, similar performances (e.g., write a haiku, sketch a still life), the work is called a performance task. Performance tasks may ask students to represent information or ideas in graphic forms (e.g., graphs, drawings). They may ask students to complete a brief authentic performance that must be written (e.g., write a haiku). In both of these cases, composed writing is minimized or writing is unnecessary in the performance.

A set of performance tasks can be developed to represent different parts of a larger, more authentic performance. For example, scientific research could be divided into several smaller performance tasks—each as an independent item—and the teacher could assess students' understanding of the different aspects of scientific investigation (e.g., designing an experiment to test a given hypothesis, organizing observations into a data table, reporting data in graphs, analyzing the data presented in graphs or statistics to draw a conclusion, making an overall generalization, and developing a new hypothesis). Each task could be used independently during an instructional unit to assess whether students were learning parts of the larger performance or the tasks could be combined into a test. Ms. Steinberg's test (Chapter 6, Figure 6–2) included performance tasks related to graphing; however, she could also have included performance tasks for designing investigations, organizing observations into data tables, or summarizing results. Several brief performance tasks measuring different applications of a learning objective can be combined into a single test (e.g., two items asking students to write haiku, two items asking for four lines of poetry in iambic pentameter, and two items asking for free verse). If performance tasks are combined to form a test, each task should be brief—each requiring only 5 to 10 minutes—so that students will have time to complete the test.

Some performance tasks are live performances. For example, if a teacher wants to find out whether students can do a dramatic reading, he could give students several poems or excerpts from plays, have students select one, read through the piece, and then perform the work aloud. If a teacher wants to find out whether students can systematically conduct investigations, she could give students an investigation and observe as students follow the procedures to see whether they are systematic in following procedures and in recording observations. Hence, performance tasks are not necessarily paper-and-pencil tasks, whereas essay items are always written.[1]

Although young children can do performance tasks, it is not developmentally appropriate to ask young children or students with limited English proficiency (LEP) to write responses to essay items. The cognitive demands of writing the response would interfere with students' ability to show their knowledge and thinking skills.

Rules for Developing and Evaluating Performance Items

Essay items and performance tasks take time, thought, and practice to develop. These types of items can cause confusion for students if the question or prompt is not clearly written or is incomplete. As you select, revise, and create essay items and performance tasks, you will learn from students' responses what works and what doesn't. In time, the task will become easier as you develop more skill and find effective formats that can be repeated. The following rules will help you develop and select effective, interesting essay items and performance tasks.

Rule 1. Make certain that your item measures the targeted learning objective. Performance items are very useful, in all subject areas, for assessing students' problem-solving, reasoning, and communication skills, as well as their skill in doing dramatic interpretations or creating new works in the language, visual, and performing arts. Review your

---

[1] A reasonable exception to this is when students have writing disabilities. A teacher could have the student dictate her response and the teacher or a teaching assistant could write down the essay for the student.

learning objectives for a unit before writing or selecting essay items or performance tasks. Create or select essay items or performance items to assess whether students have achieved learning objectives that are performance oriented. For example, if your learning objectives are focused on what students are to learn how to do (e.g., "Students will learn *how to use* algebra to solve problems." "Students will learn *how to use* primary and secondary sources to interpret historical events." "Students will learn *how to use* excerpts from literature to support literary claims."), then the learning objectives are ideal for authentic performances and for performance items. In contrast, if your learning objectives are geared toward acquisition of knowledge (e.g., "Students will learn the major turning points in the American civil war." "Students will learn the quadratic equation." "Students will learn the major themes in the works of Edgar Allen Poe."), then performance tasks and essay items are less effective for measuring students' learning. Once you have written or identified performance tasks and/or essay items, carefully examine the items to ensure that they are truly asking for what you intended to assess. For example, Figure 8–1 presents a learning objective and two items. The first item asks for a list of ideas, whereas the second item asks students to apply their knowledge and the information given to make a graph. Which one is the better measure of the learning objective?

Rule 2. Questions or prompts posed to students should be clear and concise so that students know exactly what they are being asked to do. All expectations should be clearly stated. Your students should not have to guess or read your mind to know what you want them to do. Figure 8–2 shows several performance items that are inappropriately written because the expectations are too vague. In the second column the items are revised to be appropriate for eliciting the students' understanding. Item 1 is a combination of a performance task (drawing a labeled diagram) and an essay item (explaining how the bones, joints, and muscles function in the lever) for a science assessment. The inappropriate version does not ask students to show or explain how the chosen system works like a lever, making it hard to be sure of students' understanding.

Item 2 is an essay item that might be found in a social studies classroom. The revised version more clearly focuses the comparisons to be made between Woodrow Wilson and Harry Truman. Rather than the broad range of comparisons, possible from the inappropriate version, the two presidents are to be compared in terms of their foreign policies and their approaches to U.S. involvement in war. Item 3 is a science essay item and, as with item 2, the revised version gives a clearer focus for the comparisons between humans and monkeys. Finally, item 4 is a performance task for a Spanish class. The revised version makes all expectations for the dialogue clear. By indicating that people in the dialogue are a student and a teacher, the student must attend to cultural conventions regarding formal and informal speech. In addition, the directions give clear expectations for grammar (gender, verb conjugations) and for vocabulary (two irregular verbs and four vocabulary words about school).

It is best to use formats and directions consistently across different items rather than change the expectations for every item. For example, Ms. Steinberg's test (see Figure 6–2 in Chapter 6) uses the same item format for each of the graphing items. Her expectations, which are the same for both graphing items, are clearly stated in the directions. There are two advantages to using the same format for items measuring the same learning target: (1) you will find that performance tasks and essay items are easier to write once you have a format that works with your students and clearly communicates your expectations; and

---

Objective 1   Students will learn how to represent mathematical information in a variety of forms including symbols, tables, graphs, and pictures.

Inappropriate Item

Name and describe three ways to represent data.

Appropriate Item

Mr. and Ms. Warren are planning a camping trip. They decide to rent a minivan for a week rather than drive their own car. They contact two rental companies to find out what it will cost to rent the vans. Outdoor Adventures charges $400 per week with 100 free miles and then 20¢ per mile for each additional mile. Camper Corner charges $300 per week and 25¢ per mile. They think they will drive between 500 and 1,000 miles on their trip.

Create a graph that will help the Warrens estimate and compare the costs to rent a minivan from each rental company.

Figure 8–1
Example of Inappropriate and Appropriate Performance Items for a Learning Objective

(2) as your students become accustomed to the format, they will be more likely to show their thinking and skills if they are not trying to decipher your expectations. Notice that, for all four of the revised versions, while the directions in the items clearly state expectations, they do not "give away" answers. Only students who have learned the relevant knowledge and/or skills will be able to successfully perform in response to these items.

Rule 3. Avoid writing performance items that give a series of questions or too many directions.   Too often we see essay or performance items that give a series of questions or directions that are intended to prompt student thinking but result in disconnected responses. The inappropriate examples in Figure 8–3 demonstrate this problem. Students who are in an assessment situation (even if you have worked to help them understand that you support their learning) find these types of items confusing. Some students respond by answering each question separately. Others become bogged down in the number of words and lose the point of the work—generating responses very different from what the teacher was hoping to obtain. The series of questions in the inappropriate version of item 1 of Figure 8–3 do not help the language arts student see that the point is to link the excerpt from *Hamlet* to Hamlet's conflict. The "think about" statements in the inappropriate version of item 2 take the focus away from creating an artistic image that communicates feelings about an event and place the focus on composition, medium, and techniques.

Rule 4. Clearly state in the question, prompt, or directions, any criteria that will be used for scoring responses (e.g., content, examples, grammar, spelling, punctuation, organization).   One of the most frustrating experiences for test takers is when the expectations for responses are not given. Figure 8–4 shows a prompt that is very open-ended. It is evident from the sample answer that a thoughtful and complex response is expected. Writing a sample answer and a scoring rule can help you become clearer about the expectations. The revised version of the item includes all of the expectations.

Item	Inappropriate Version	Appropriate Version
1	The back of a hammer can be used as a lever to remove a nail from a board. Describe one lever system in the human body and include all the parts in the description.	The back of a hammer can be used as a lever to remove a nail from a board. Describe one lever system in the human body. Be sure to: • draw a labeled diagram of the human body lever system • describe or show how the human body lever works • explain roles of bones, muscles, and joints in the system
2	How were Woodrow Wilson and Harry Truman the same or different?	Write an essay comparing the administrations of Woodrow Wilson and Harry Truman in terms of their approaches to war in Europe. Be sure to tell <u>how their foreign policies were the same or different</u> and <u>how their approaches to American involvement in the wars were the same or different</u>. Give at least <u>two</u> examples from the readings to support your ideas.
3	How are chimpanzees and humans different?	Describe <u>two</u> ways that chimpanzees and humans have differed in their adaptations to their environments. Include: • <u>two</u> specific environmental conditions to which both chimpanzees and humans have had to adapt • the differences between how chimpanzees and humans have adapted to <u>each</u> environmental condition.
4	Write a dialog between two Spanish speakers.	Write a brief dialog between a teacher and a student. Be sure to include: • Two irregular verbs correctly conjugated • At least four of the new vocabulary words about school • Appropriate use of formal and informal language • Correct use of gender in articles and nouns

Figure 8–2
Inappropriate and Appropriate Examples of Essay Items and Performance Tasks

Rules 2 through 4 are focused on how to write effective directions, prompts, or questions for performance tasks and essay items. As we have said in a number of places in this book, assessments should draw out what students have learned. If the format of an item or directions given in an item prevent students from showing what they know and are able to

Item	Inappropriate Versions	Appropriate Versions
1	Read the excerpt from *Hamlet*. What is Hamlet thinking about at this point in the play? What are his concerns? What does he want to change? What are his fears?	Read the excerpt from *Hamlet*. Then write an essay describing how this excerpt relates to one of Hamlet's conflicts in the play. Be sure to include: • Your ideas about his conflict. • The feelings and thoughts he shows in the excerpt. • How his feelings and thoughts relate to his conflict.
2	Create an image that communicates how you feel about a current event in the world today. Think about what medium will best show your feelings. Think about what images are most appropriate. Think about how to use composition, movement, and repetition to communicate your feelings. Think about how to use texture and color to communicate your feelings. Think about how to represent the event and your feelings in the same image.	Think about a current event in the world today about which you have strong positive or negative feelings. Then create an image that communicates your feelings about the event. Be sure to: • Help the audience understand the event and your feelings. • Use the medium, techniques, and design elements that best communicate your feelings. You may want to make several drafts as you develop the image.

Figure 8–3
Examples of Essay Items and Performance Tasks That Give Too Many Directions or Questions and Appropriate Revisions

do (because expectations are not explicit, language is too complex, or directions are confusing), then students' performance will be a better indication of the quality of the assessment than students' knowledge and skills. As was mentioned earlier, students need to know the rules of the game. In a standards-based education system, the goal is to find out what students know and are able to do so that they can learn what they haven't learned and move on when they have learned. Barriers to successful demonstration of their knowledge, skills, and conceptual understanding must be removed.

Rule 5. Write a model response for each essay item or performance task.   Model responses will help you determine whether you have asked for all that you want. As is shown in Figure 8–4, the model response is focused on the reasons the Southern states wanted to secede and the Northern states wanted to maintain a union—not the "causes of the Civil War." Hence, the model response helps to clarify expectations and to write a clearer prompt. Model responses are not written for students. This would, indeed, give students your expected response. They help you write better items and they help you see how long it takes for you to compose a response. Remember that it will take students longer than you to respond to each item. However, if you want to help students understand how to write or create quality responses to your test items, you *can* create an example item with a sample response. Reviewing this before a test helps to ensure better responses from all students.

> **Essay Item Before Sample Response and Scoring Rule Are Written**
>
> What were the causes of the U.S. Civil War?
>
> **Sample Response and Scoring Rule for Civil War Item**
>
> **Sample Response:** The leaders of the Southern states were angry because they believed that states should have more power than the federal government. For example, they thought states, rather than the federal government, should decide whether to have tariffs on imported goods. They were frustrated with Congress's attempts to control trade with tariffs (which favored Northern manufacturers). They also thought that the federal government should allow states to decide whether to have slavery. They were frustrated by Northern abolitionists' insistence on prohibiting slavery in new territories when the Southern economy depended on slavery. The Northern states wanted to maintain the Union because of national pride and because the Union would be stronger if it was politically and economically united. For example, the Union was fairly young and there was great pride in having such a large country governed by constitutional law. Unionists also believed that, together, the North and South could be economically self-sufficient and could resist external threats. They had just won the Mexican-American War and were very proud of their strength.
>
> **Scoring Rule:** The student will include *tariffs* and *slavery* as reasons why the Southern states wanted to secede (2 points) and *national pride* and *economic and military strength* as reasons why the Northern states wanted to maintain the Union (2 points). Examples to support each reason are worth 1 point each (4 points).
>
> **Revised Item After Writing a Sample Response and Scoring Rule**
>
> Discuss *two major reasons* the Southern states wanted to secede from the Union and create the Confederate States and *two major reasons* the Northern states wanted to maintain the Union. Support each reason with at least one example from the text.

Figure 8–4
Evolution of an Item

Rule 6. Decide which one of three scoring methods (key words or ideas, scoring rubrics, or analytic checklists or rating scales) works best for each item. *Key words or ideas* are those key elements you expect students to write about in their essays or show in performance tasks. This type of scoring is most common for very short essay items and when there are correct terms or ideas that the students must include. Responses to the revised item in Figure 8–4 will be evaluated using a key idea scoring rule. The students must include four key ideas to earn four of the eight possible points for the item.

   Scoring rubrics are rules for assigning scores based on the quality as well as the accuracy and/or completeness of the response. Rubrics usually have four to six levels with a description of each level. Sometimes teachers create scoring guides wherein they create or select examples of performances at each level to help them judge students' work. *Analytic checklists* or *rating scales* provide diagnostic information about the exact strengths and weaknesses of the essay. Both rubrics and analytic checklists/rating scales are derived from the *performance criteria*. Performance or scoring criteria come from your learning objectives.

   Figure 8–5 gives an essay item with two different scoring rules: a rubric and a rating scale. The performance criteria for both scoring rules are the same—the only difference is

Item	Write an essay in which you describe and interpret:
	• The main character in your chosen novel.
	• The main character's conflict in the story and how it is resolved.
	• How the conflict relates to one of the themes in the novel.
	Be sure to give *at least two* examples of events in the story that show the conflict.
Sample Response	In the book, *Sense and Sensibility,* the main character is Elinor Dashwood. Elinor and her family are forced out of their home after Mr. Dashwood dies, because the estate is entailed to his son, John Dashwood. Elinor is the sensible member of the family. She is in love with Edward Ferrars but finds out that he is secretly engaged to another woman—Lucy Steele. Elinor is very controlling of her own feelings. Even though she is brokenhearted, she keeps it to herself and suffers alone. She believes that survival as a woman depends on behavior that does not bring disrespect. She hides her feelings while trying to caution her mother and sister, Marianne, to do the same. For example, when Marianne is falling in love with Willhoby, Elinor tells Marianne that her feelings are much too open and public. In the end, Edward is free of Lucy and asks Elinor to marry him. She wins what she wants (marriage) by being careful and controlled, but she loses the chance to be honest and get support from her family in the process. She represents the idea that to win a husband, one has to put proper behavior ahead of feelings.
Possible Scoring Rule: Rubric	**Performance Criteria** • Name of the main character • Accurate, detailed description of the main character • Desription of the character's major conflict • Interpretation of the relationship between the conflict and a theme • At least two examples that support ideas about the conflict and theme **Scores** 4 The essay presents an accurate and detailed description of the main character and insightful interpretation of his/her conflict in relation to a theme. Well-chosen examples provide effective support for the writer's view of the character's conflict and theme. 3 The essay presents an accurate description of the main character and a reasonable interpretation of her/his conflict in relation to a theme. Examples support the writer's view of the character's conflict. 2 The essay presents a partially accurate description of the main character. The character's main conflict or theme is named or inferred. Examples give some support for the writer's view of the character's conflict. 1 The essay gives a partially accurate description of the main character. Events in the story are accurately described; however, there is no interpretation of the conflict or theme. 0 The essay shows no understanding of character or conflict.
Possible Scoring Rule: Rating Scale	**Performance Criteria** Name of the main character Yes (1) No (0) Description of the main character Accurate/Detailed (3) Accurate (2) Partially Accurate (1) Inaccurate/Missing (0) Description of the conflict Accurate (2) Partially Accurate (1) Inaccurate/Missing (0) Interpretation of theme in relation to conflict Insightful (3) Reasonable (2) Identified/Named (1) Missing (0) Examples to support ideas Well chosen/strong support (3) Support (2) Some support (1) Missing (0)

Figure 8–5
Example of Two Types of Scoring Rules for the Same Essay Item

how scores are applied. The rubric requires a holistic evaluation of the response; the rating scale requires evaluation of each element of a response. The rating scale is more analytic and may help students understand where their responses need more work; however, it takes more time to rate each item than it takes to make a holistic judgment. Figure 8–6 gives a performance task with two different scoring rules: a checklist and a rubric. As with the essay item in Figure 8–5, the performance criteria for the two scoring rules are the same. Note that the performance criteria for the essay item in Figure 8–5 aligns closely with the directions for the item, whereas the performance criteria for the performance task in Figure 8–6 is focused on more general problem-solving skills. See Chapter 4, Assessment of Valued Performances, for more information on developing checklists, rating scales, and rubrics.

Rule 7. If you use scoring rubrics, it is important to create separate scoring rubrics for each dimension of performance you want to target.   As with any performance, performance items may ask for different dimensions of performance. For example, a teacher who uses the essay item in Figure 8–5 might be concerned about students' use of grammar, spelling, punctuation, or capitalization. If he included the performance criteria for spelling, punctuation, capitalization, and grammar in the rubric shown in Figure 8–5, it would be very difficult to use the rubric. A student might have an effective description and interpretation of the character's conflict and a theme in the novel but use poor writing conventions. Alternately, a student might have excellent command of writing conventions but have difficulty developing interpretations or supporting interpretations with examples from the novel. In such a case, a second rubric for writing conventions would be more appropriate. Similarly, if a teacher was concerned about mathematical communication as well as mathematical problem solving, she might create a second rubric to evaluate how effectively students communicate mathematical information in their responses (e.g., systematic representation of solutions, clarity of claims and evidential support, appropriate use of symbols, equations, visual representations, and mathematical terms).

Rule 8. Whenever possible, use generic rating scales or rubrics to evaluate work that students are likely to repeat over time.   When generic checklists, rating scales, and rubrics are used regularly, students get a clear sense of your expectations and are more likely to focus their efforts on the important learning targets. The scoring rules for the performance items in Figures 8–5 and 8–6 are focused on important learning targets in the language arts and mathematics, respectively. They are also flexible enough that they could be used for many performance items. When scoring rules can be used with many performance items, you will save time in item writing and you can more easily focus the requirements of your performance items. For example, one of the performance criteria for the performance task in Figure 8–6 is "supports claims with data from the problem." If the checklist or rubric for this problem were to be used with other mathematics performance tasks, the teacher would have to make certain that the problem asked for a conclusion, a claim, an interpretation, or inference related to the solution to the problem. Some examples of generic scoring rules are given in Figures 8–7 through 8–9. Using generic scoring rules such as these can help you focus the directions you give to students for types of performance tasks or essay items that are likely to be repeated during different lessons and units.

In the next section, we describe a special type of performance item: direct writing assessments. Generic scoring rules are commonly used in direct writing assessments; therefore, we will return to the issue of generic scoring rules in what follows.

Item	The students at Mountlake High School have decided to have a candy sale to raise money to buy uniforms for the high school marching band. There are two candy companies from which to buy the candy. Mountain Candy Company charges $1,000 and then $1.00 for each candy bar. Sweet Nothings Candy Company charges $1,500 and then 50¢ for each candy bar.
	For what number of candy bars will the cost to the school be the same for both companies?
	For what number of candy bars is it most cost effective to choose Mountain Candy Company? Give an example to support your answer.
	For what number of candy bars is it most cost effective to choose Sweet Nothings Candy Company? Give an example to support your answer.
	Show all the steps you use to solve the problem.
Sample Response (table and graphic responses also acceptable)	$y = \$1,000 + \$1.00x$ $y = \$1,500 + \$0.50x$ $\$1,000 + \$1.00x = \$1,500 + \$0.50x$ $\$1.00x = \$1,500 - \$1,000 + \$0.50x$ $\$1.00x - \$0.50x = \$500$ $\$0.50x = \$500$ $x = 1,000$ The school must buy 1,000 candy bars for it to cost the same for either company. If the students sell more than 1,000 candy bars, it is most cost effective to use Sweet Nothings Candy Company. For example, if the students sell 1,200 candy bars, it will cost ($1,000 + 1,200[$1.00]) = $2,200 to buy candy from Mountain Candy Company and it will cost ($1,500 + 1,200[$0.50]) = $2,100 to buy candy from Sweet Nothings Candy Company. If the students sell less than 1,000 candy bars, it is most cost effective to use Mountain Candy Company. For example, if the students sell 900 candy bars, it will cost ($1,000 + 900[$1.00]) = $1,900 to buy candy from Mountain Candy Company and it will cost ($1,500 + 900[$0.50]) = $1,950 to buy candy from Sweet Nothings Candy Company.
Possible Scoring Rule: Rubric	**Performance Criteria** • Develops a solution to the problem • Addresses all requirements of the prompt • Uses data to support all claims 3 The student develops a complete and viable solution to the problem using appropriate strategies. Detailed support is given for all claims using data from the problem. 2 The student develops a viable solution to the problem using appropriate strategies. Claims are accurate but may not be supported with data. 1 The student attempts to solve the problem using reasonable strategies. Claims, if given, are accurate based on solution. 0 The student shows no understanding of how to solve the problem.
Possible Scoring Rule: Checklist	**Performance Criteria** ☐ Develops viable solution ☐ Uses appropriate strategies ☐ Response is complete ☐ Supports claims with data from problem

Figure 8–6
Example of Two Types of Scoring Rules for the Same Performance Task

Critical Reading Scale
Thoughtfully/thoroughly done (T), Superficially/partially done (S), or Omitted altogether (O).
T S O   Has major position on the work
T S O   Includes two or more major arguments to support the position
T S O   Includes references to text that support position

Figure 8–7
Example of a Rating Scale for Use With Students' Responses to Text

Journal Writing Scale
Regularly (R), Occasionally (O), Infrequently (I), or Never (N).
R   O   I   N   Takes risks in writing
R   O   I   N   Writes about ideas, questions, reactions
R   O   I   N   Tries new writing strategies

Figure 8–8
Example of a Rating Scale for Use With Students' Writing Journals

Lab Report Scale
Accurate and clear (3), Mostly accurate and clear (2), Significant problems with accuracy and/or clarity (1), or Not done or disconnected (0).
3   2   1   0   Graphs, tables, charts are accurate based on data
3   2   1   0   Graphs, tables, charts include label, title, and scale
3   2   1   0   Procedures are completely documented
3   2   1   0   Written summary reflects investigation and results
3   2   1   0   Conclusions drawn follow from results
3   2   1   0   Generalization to principal or new hypothesis follows from conclusion

Figure 8–9
Example of a Rating Scale for Use With Students' Science Lab Reports

DIRECT WRITING ASSESSMENTS

Direct writing assessments are standardized writing assessments. They are called direct writing assessments because efforts have been made to create indirect measures of writing skills. For example, multiple-choice tests of language mechanics and language expression have been used to predict students' writing skills. Figures 8–10 and 8–11 give multiple-choice items that are similar to ones used on standardized tests of language mechanics or language expression. Direct writing assessments ask students to write effectively rather than to simply recognize features of effective writing.

Read the paragraph. Then complete questions 1 and 2.

The first step is to gather all ingredients, bowls, baking dishes, and utensils. The second step is to turn on the oven and set the oven temperature. The next step is to measure the ingredients. Once all ingredients are measured, follow the directions for the order in which ingredients are mixed together. Put the mixed ingredients into the appropriate baking dish and place it in the preheated oven. Then set the timer for the amount of baking time in the recipe. When the timer rings, the dish is ready to remove from the oven.

1. Which of the following is the best **topic sentence** for the paragraph?
   A. Cooking is really a matter of following a recipe in order.
   B. Once a dish is cooked, you can serve the dish to your friends.
   C. If you pick a nice baking dish, the food can be served in the dish.
   D. Before you start, go to the grocery store and buy the ingredients.

2. Which of the following sentences will add **useful information** to the paragraph?
   A. I've never really liked to cook new recipes.
   B. If you don't like it, you can always start over.
   C. Your friends will love to taste your home cooking.
   D. Be sure to test the dish to make certain that it is ready.

Figure 8–10
Example of Two Items That Indirectly Measure Language Expression

---

Read each sentence. Then decide which punctuation mark should be used in the sentence.

1. John sat with his mother and father at the picnic _____
   A. **?**
   B. **,**
   C. **.**
   D. **;**

2. If you want to go with us _____ you'll have to pack your bags quickly!
   A. **?**
   B. **,**
   C. **.**
   D. **;**

Figure 8–11
Example of Two Items That Indirectly Measure Language Mechanics

Direct writing assessments serve as "proxies" for more complex writing performances. For example, a teacher might ask students to write an informative essay with a topic sentence, supporting ideas, and a conclusion, or write a persuasive essay with a clear position, supporting arguments, and a convincing conclusion. These are both proxies for more complex written works, such as research papers and position papers, respectively. Essays that are intended to assess students' skill in actually developing a research-based position paper, a research report, or a complex literary analysis should be considered formal performance assessments and should be given in a context that allows students time to review their work to fulfill all criteria effectively. Such complex work is beyond the scope of a standardized, direct writing assessment.

At times, however, district and state assessment programs include assessments of writing skills in a standardized way and in a fixed period of time. In such contexts, teachers may use direct writing assessments in their classrooms to *prepare* students for district or state writing assessments when regular classroom writing is poetry, research papers, and/or writing for other authentic purposes.

Well-developed direct writing assessments begin with a writing prompt. A writing prompt is not as detailed as a performance item asking for demonstration of specific knowledge or skills; it is more open-ended. However, the prompt generally includes clues that help the student adjust the writing to purpose and audience. For example, a direct writing assessment might include a prompt such as "Sometimes teachers aren't fair. Describe a time when a teacher wasn't fair." In this prompt, the purpose is descriptive; however, because students are describing an event, the purpose is also narrative. Students must narrate an event and use descriptive language to help the audience see, hear, and feel the event. No explicit audience is given; therefore, students must assume that the audience is the teacher or, in the case of a state or district writing assessment, the audience is the rater who assigns scores to the students' written work.

Research on direct writing assessments has shown that narrative writing is the easiest for students; expository (informative) writing is more difficult; and persuasive writing is the most difficult. There are variations on writing purposes. Some state and district testing programs have assessed as many as eight different writing purposes (how-to writing, descriptive writing, explanatory writing, persuasive writing, narrative writing, informative writing, etc.). For each purpose, the prompt must include a cue word to help students know how to focus their writing. At times, the audience is explicitly given through cue words. For example, the prompt "Write a letter to the editor of your local paper to explain why students drop out of school" has two cue words: *editor* and *explain*.

For such open-ended prompts to work, students and teachers must know the criteria expected in the students' writing. For example, the rubrics developed for the "Six Traits of Writing" (Northwest Regional Educational Laboratory) are used nationwide to guide students' writing. These rubrics define six traits (dimensions) of writing: ideas and content, and organization, voice, word choice, sentence fluency, and conventions. Students receive a score from 1 to 5 on each of the six traits (see Figures 8–12 through 8–17 for the scoring rubrics for Six Traits of Writing).

In some testing programs, students' writing is scored on a different rubric for each writing purpose (e.g., Texas Assessment of Academic Skills; California Assessment Program). In this case, each rubric is called a "focused holistic rubric"—in other words, the rubric is focused on a particular writing purpose but looks at students' writing holistically; many dimensions of writing are assessed simultaneously. Figure 8–18 is a focused holistic writing rubric from the California Assessment Program (California Department of Education, 1990). The purpose is to evaluate students' autobiographical writing. Content, organization, and style elements are all incorporated into a single rubric. A separate rubric would be used for scoring writing conventions or mechanics.

When district or state testing programs are in place, teachers generally teach the rubrics to the students, have students apply the rubrics to their own and others' writing, and use these rubrics to evaluate students' writing in their own classrooms. This helps students internalize the performance criteria or expectations for their writing. As long as students are taught the criteria prior to participating in a direct writing assessment, then open-ended prompts are effective writing assessment tools. However, if criteria are not taught, then direct writing assessments are unfair to the students, and hence, invalid. Direct writing assessments can be used in any subject area where the teacher is focused on improved student

IDEAS AND CONTENT (Development)

5 *This paper is clear and focused. It holds the reader's attention.*
Relevant anecdotes and details enrich the central theme.
A. The topic is **narrow** and **manageable.**
B. **Relevant, telling, quality details** give the reader important information that goes **beyond the obvious** or predictable.
C. Reasonably **accurate details** are present to support the main ideas.
D. The writer seems to be writing from **knowledge** or **experience;** the ideas are **fresh** and **original.**
E. The reader's questions are **anticipated and answered.**
F. **Insight**—an understanding of life and a knack for picking out what is significant—is an indicator of high level performance, though not required.

3 *The writer is beginning to define the topic, even though development is still basic or general.*
A. The **topic is fairly broad;** however, you can see where the writer is headed.
B. **Support is attempted,** but doesn't go far enough yet in fleshing out the key issues or story line.
C. Ideas are **reasonably clear,** though they may not be detailed, personalized, accurate, or expanded enough to show in-depth understanding or a strong sense of purpose.
D. The writer seems to be drawing on knowledge or experience, but has **difficulty going from general observations to specifics.**
E. The reader is **left with questions.** More information is needed to "fill in the blanks."
F. The writer **generally stays on the topic** but does not develop a clear theme. The writer has not yet focused the topic past the obvious.

1 *As yet, the paper has no clear sense of purpose or central theme. To extract meaning from the text, the reader must make inferences based on sketchy or missing details. The writing reflects more than one of these problems:*
A. The writer is **still in search of a topic,** brainstorming, or has not yet decided what the main idea of the piece will be.
B. Information is **limited** or **unclear** or the **length is not adequate** for development.
C. The idea is a **simple restatement** of the topic or an **answer** to the question with little or no attention to detail.
D. The writer has **not begun to define the topic** in a meaningful, personal way.
E. **Everything seems as important as everything else;** the reader has a hard time sifting out what is important.
F. The text may be **repetitious,** or may read like a collection of **disconnected, random thoughts** with no discernable point.

Figure 8–12
Scoring Rubric for Ideas and Content of Writing
Source: Figures 8–12–8–17 are reprinted by permission of Northwest Regional Education Laboratory from http://www.nwrel.org/assessment/pdfrubrics/6plus1trait.pdf

writing. Direct writing rubrics, such as the Six Traits rubrics, are often used across the curriculum and across most grade levels.

Direct writing assessments can also be used in language classes (including English language classes for English language learners) to see how well students put together their vo-

ORGANIZATION

5 *The organization enhances and showcases the central idea or theme.*
The order, structure, or presentation of information is compelling and moves the reader through the text.

A. An **inviting introduction** draws the reader in; a **satisfying conclusion** leaves the reader with a sense of closure and resolution.
B. **Thoughtful transitions** clearly show how ideas connect.
C. Details seem to fit where they're placed; **sequencing is logical** and **effective.**
D. **Pacing is well controlled;** the writer knows when to slow down and elaborate, and when to pick up the pace and move on.
E. The **title,** if desired, is **original** and captures the central theme of the piece.
F. Organization **flows so smoothly** the reader hardly thinks about it; the choice of structure matches the **purpose** and **audience.**

3 *The organizational structure is strong enough to move the reader through the text without too much confusion.*

A. The paper has a **recognizable introduction and conclusion.** The introduction may not create a strong sense of anticipation; the conclusion may not tie up all loose ends.
B. **Transitions often work well;** at other times, connections between ideas are fuzzy.
C. **Sequencing** shows **some logic,** but not under control enough that it consistently supports the ideas. In fact, sometimes it is so predictable and rehearsed that the **structure takes attention away from the content.**
D. **Pacing is fairly well controlled,** though the writer sometimes lunges ahead too quickly or spends too much time on details that do not matter.
E. A **title (if desired) is present,** although it may be uninspired or an obvious restatement of the prompt or topic.
F. The **organization sometimes supports the main point or storyline;** at other times, the reader feels an urge to slip in a transition or move things around.

1 *The writing lacks a clear sense of direction. Ideas, details, or events seem strung together in a loose or random fashion; there is no identifiable internal structure. The writing reflects more than one of these problems:*

A. There is **no real lead** to set up what follows, **no real conclusion** to wrap things up.
B. Connections between ideas are **confusing** or not even present.
C. **Sequencing needs** lots and lots of **work.**
D. **Pacing feels awkward;** the writer slows to a crawl when the reader wants to get on with it, and vice versa.
E. **No title is present** (if requested), or if present, **does not match** well with the content.
F. Problems with organization make it **hard for the reader to get a grip** on the main point or story line.

Figure 8–13
Scoring Rubric for Organization of Writing

cabulary and grammar to create a cohesive written piece. As with direct writing assessments in English, students in language classes must know the expectations for the direct writing assessment. They must have had practice composing with their new language before they are tested. Even beginning language learners can compose paragraphs in the new language if given practice and tools (e.g., translation dictionaries).

VOICE

5 *The writer speaks directly to the reader in a way that is individual, compelling, and engaging. The writer crafts the writing with an awareness and respect for the audience and the purpose for writing.*

A. The tone of the writing **adds interest** to the message and is **appropriate for the purpose and audience.**

B. The reader feels a **strong interaction** with the writer, sensing the **person behind the words.**

C. The writer **takes a risk** by revealing who he or she is consistently throughout the piece.

D. **Expository or persuasive** writing reflects a **strong commitment** to the topic by showing **why** the **reader needs to know this** and why he or she should care.

E. **Narrative** writing is **honest, personal, engaging** and makes you **think about and react to** the author's ideas and point of view.

3 *The writer seems sincere, but not fully engaged or involved. The result is pleasant or even personable, but not compelling.*

A. The writer seems aware of an audience but discards personal insights in favor of **obvious generalities.**

B. The writing communicates in an **earnest, pleasing, yet safe** manner.

C. Only **one or two moments here or there** intrigue, delight, or move the reader. These places may **emerge strongly for a line or two, but quickly fade away.**

D. **Expository or persuasive** writing **lacks consistent engagement** with the topic to build credibility.

E. **Narrative** writing is **reasonably sincere,** but doesn't reflect unique or individual perspective on the topic.

1 *The writer seems indifferent, uninvolved, or distanced from the topic and/or the audience. As a result, the paper reflects more than one of the following problems:*

A. The writer is **not concerned with the audience.** The writer's style is a **complete mismatch** for the intended reader or the writing is **so short** that little is accomplished beyond introducing the topic.

B. The writer speaks in a kind of **monotone** that flattens all potential highs or lows of the message.

C. The writing is **humdrum and "risk-free."**

D. The writing is **lifeless or mechanical;** depending on the topic, it may be overly technical or jargonistic.

E. The development of the topic is **so limited** that **no point of view is present**—zip, zero, zilch, nada.

Figure 8–14
Scoring Rubric for Writer's Voice

DEVELOPMENTAL ISSUES FOR PERFORMANCE ITEMS

It is fairly obvious that essay items are not appropriate for children in the early primary grades. Short answer items (see Chapter 7) can serve the same purpose as essay items if you want to have students write sentences to communicate their thinking about a concept, issue, question or problem. Once students can compose paragraphs, essay items become more appropriate.

WORD CHOICE

5 *Words convey the intended message in a precise, interesting, and natural way. The words are powerful and engaging.*

A. Words are **specific** and **accurate;** it is easy to understand just what the writer means.

B. The words and phrases **create pictures and linger in your mind.**

C. The language is **natural and never overdone;** both words and phrases are **individual** and **effective.**

D. **Striking words and phrases** often catch the reader's eye—and linger in the reader's mind. (You can recall a handful as you reflect on the paper.)

E. **Lively verbs** energize the writing. **Precise nouns and modifiers** add depth and specificity.

F. **Precision** is obvious. The writer has taken care to put just the right word or phrase in just the right spot.

3 *The language is functional, even if it lacks much energy. It is easy to figure out the writer's meaning on a general level.*

A. Words are **adequate and correct in a general sense;** they simply **lack much flair and originality.**

B. Familiar **words and phrases communicate,** but rarely capture the reader's imagination. Still, the paper may have **one or two fine moments.**

C. **Attempts at colorful language** show a willingness to stretch and grow, but sometimes it goes too far (thesaurus overload!).

D. The writing is marked by **passive verbs, everyday nouns and adjectives, and lack of interesting adverbs.**

E. The words are only occasionally refined; it's more often, **"the first thing that popped into my mind."**

F. The words and phrases are **functional**—with only a moment or two of sparkle.

1 *The writer struggles with a limited vocabulary, searching for words to convey meaning. The writing reflects more than one of these problems:*

A. Language is so **vague** (e.g., *It was a fun time, She was neat, It was nice, We did lots of stuff*) that only a **limited message** comes through.

B. **"Blah, blah, blah"** is all that the reader reads and hears.

C. **Words are used incorrectly,** making the message secondary to the misfires with the words.

D. **Limited vocabulary** and/or frequent **misuse of parts of speech** impair understanding.

E. **Jargon or clichés** distract or mislead. Persistent **redundancy** distracts the reader.

F. Problems with language **leave the reader wondering** what the writer is trying to say. The **words just don't work** in this piece.

Figure 8–15
Scoring Rubric for Word Choice in Writing

In addition to cautions about the writing burden, students from second grade through early middle school years are less able to follow complex or multi-step directions. Careful scaffolding of responses can help students be successful in response to complex items. For example, the item in Figure 8–5 has a series of bullets that set expectations for students' responses to items. Children as young as third grade can think about and respond to this type of item; however, each component of the item should be asked separately with room for students to respond immediately after the component. In that way,

SENTENCE FLUENCY

5 *The writing has an easy flow, rhythm, and cadence. Sentences are well built, with strong and varied structure that invites expressive oral reading.*

A. Sentences are constructed in a way that underscores and enhances the **meaning.**

B. Sentences **vary in length as well as structure.** Fragments, if used, add style. Dialogue, if present, sounds natural.

C. Purposeful and **varied sentence beginnings** add variety and energy.

D. The use of **creative and appropriate connectives** between sentences and thoughts shows how each relates to, and builds upon, the one before it.

E. The writing has **cadence;** the writer has thought about the sound of the words as well as the meaning. The first time you read it aloud is a breeze.

3 *The text hums along with a steady beat, but tends to be more pleasant or businesslike than musical, more mechanical than fluid.*

A. Although sentences may not seem artfully crafted or musical, **they get the job done in a routine fashion.**

B. Sentences are **usually constructed correctly;** they **hang together;** they are **sound.**

C. Sentence beginnings are not ALL alike; **some variety is attempted.**

D. The reader sometimes has to **hunt for clues** (e.g., connecting words and phrases like *however, therefore, naturally, after a while, on the other hand, to be specific, for example, next, first of all, later, but as it turned out, although,* etc.) that show how sentences interrelate.

E. Parts of the text **invite expressive oral reading;** others may be stiff, awkward, choppy, or gangly.

1 *The reader has to practice quite a bit in order to give this paper a fair interpretive reading. The writing reflects more than one of the following problems:*

A. Sentences are **choppy, incomplete, rambling, or awkward;** they need work. **Phrasing does not sound natural.** The patterns may create a sing-song rhythm, or a chop-chop cadence that lulls the reader to sleep.

B. There is little to **no "sentence sense"** present. Even if this piece were flawlessly edited, the sentences would not hang together.

C. Many **sentences begin the same way**—and may follow the same patterns (e.g., *subject-verb-object*) in a monotonous pattern.

D. Endless connectives (*and, and so, but then, because, and then,* etc.) or a **complete lack of connectives** create a massive jumble of language.

E. The text **does not invite expressive oral reading.**

Figure 8–16
Scoring Rubric for Sentence Fluency in Writing

students can be sure to respond to each part of the item directions. Figure 8–19 shows the item from Figure 8–5 reformatted for younger students.

Although essay items are difficult for emerging writers, performance items that require drawings, figures, diagrams, and similar visual representations are easier for younger children to do. Children as young as second grade can summarize the most important events in a story using pictures. First and second graders can draw pictures to show mathematical understanding or create diagrams to show scientific understanding (e.g., interdependence between plants and animals). When working with young children, we have found that they

CONVENTIONS

5 *The writer demonstrates a good grasp of standard writing conventions (e.g., spelling, punctuation, capitalization, grammar, usage, paragraphing) and uses conventions effectively to enhance readability. Errors tend to be so few that just minor touch-ups would get this piece ready to publish.*

A. **Spelling is generally correct,** even on more difficult words.

B. The **punctuation is accurate,** even creative, and guides the reader through the text.

C. A thorough understanding and consistent application of **capitalization** skills are present.

D. **Grammar and usage are correct** and contribute to clarity and style.

E. **Paragraphing tends to be sound** and reinforces the organizational structure.

F. The writer **may manipulate conventions** for stylistic effect—and it works! The piece is very close to being **ready to publish.**

GRADES 7 AND UP ONLY: The writing is sufficiently complex to allow the writer to show skill in using a wide range of conventions. For writers at younger ages, the writing shows control over those conventions that are grade/age appropriate.

3 *The writer shows reasonable control over a limited range of standard writing conventions. Conventions are sometimes handled well and enhance readability; at other times, errors are distracting and impair readability.*

A. **Spelling** is usually **correct or reasonably phonetic on common words,** but more difficult words are problematic.

B. **End punctuation is usually correct;** internal punctuation (*commas, apostrophes, semicolons, dashes, colons, parentheses*) is sometimes missing/wrong.

C. **Most words are capitalized correctly;** control over more sophisticated capitalization skills may be spotty.

D. **Paragraphing is attempted** but may run together or begin in the wrong places.

E. **Problems with grammar or usage are not serious** enough to distort meaning but may not be correct or accurately applied all of the time.

F. **Moderate** (a little of this, a little of that) **editing** would be required to polish the text for publication.

1 *Errors in spelling, punctuation, capitalization, usage and grammar, and/or paragraphing repeatedly distract the reader and make the text difficult to read. The writing reflects more than one of these problems:*

A. **Spelling errors are frequent,** even on common words.

B. **Punctuation** (including terminal punctuation) is often **missing or incorrect.**

C. **Capitalization** is **random** and only the easiest rules show awareness of correct use.

D. **Errors in grammar or usage are very noticeable,** frequent, and affect meaning.

E. **Paragraphing is missing, irregular, or so frequent** (every sentence) that it has no relationship to the organizational structure of the text.

F. The reader must **read once to decode,** then again for meaning. **Extensive editing** (virtually every line) would be required to polish the text for publication.

Figure 8–17
Scoring Rubric for Writing Conventions

Score Point 6—Exceptional Achievement

Incident. Writer narrates a coherent and engaging story that moves the narrative toward the central moment. The narrative tells readers what they need to know to understand what happened and to infer its significance to the writer. The writer of a six-point essay will use some of the following strategies:

- Naming (specific names of people or objects, quantities, numbers)
- Describing visual details of scenes, objects, or people (size, colors, shapes, features, dress)
- Describing sounds or smells of the scene
- Narrating specific action (movements, gestures, postures, expression)
- Creating dialogues, interior monologues, or expressing remembered feelings of insights at the time of the incident
- Slowing the pace to elaborate the central moment in the incident
- Creating suspense or tension
- Including the element of surprise
- Comparing or contrasting other scenes or people

Rather than minimizing events, the writer of a six-point essay dramatizes the incident, using strategies like those above.

Context. Writer locates the incident in a particular setting and orients the reader to scene, people, and events. The writer goes beyond simply identifying or pointing to the scene or people using carefully chosen details relevant to the incident. The writer may devote considerable space in the essay to orientating readers, describing the scene and people, and providing background or context for the incident—but not at the expense of a well-told incident. In a six-point essay, there is balance between static context and dramatic, narrated incident.

Significance. The essay reveals why the incident was important to the writer. This significance can be either implied or stated. If the significance is implied, the reader can infer it confidently. The significance may be apparent in the writer's insights at the time of the incident or in the reflections from the writer's present perspective. Those insights and reflections may appear integrated into the narration or in the conclusion to the essay. The reflections may be humorous.

Voice and Style. In a six-point essay we hear an authentic voice that reveals the writer's attitude toward the incident. A six-point essay includes well-chosen details, apt words, and graceful, varied sentences. It often includes word play and imagery. A six-point essay engages the reader from the start and moves to a satisfying closure.

Score Point 5—Commendable Achievement

Incident. As in a six-point essay, the incident is coherent and engaging. The essay moves toward a central moment but with less drama than a six-point essay. A five-point essay relies on a narrower range of narrative strategies. A five-point essay may be structurally more predictable than a six-point essay, and it may be less focused than an essay graded six points, especially toward the end. Still, a five-point essay tells a clear, engaging story.

Context. The five-point essay has an appropriate and adequate context as in a six-point essay. Context does not dominate the essay at the expense of incident.

Significance. Significance can be either implied or stated but will be clear, either through remembered or present reflections. The reflections may be less well integrated into the essay than in a six-point essay; they often appear at the end. Reflections may not be as perspective as those in a six-point essay, but they will not be superficial. The reflections will be insightful but not as probing as those in a six-point essay.

Voice and Style. As in six-point essay, we hear authentic voice in a five-point essay. The essay is competent stylistically but may not have the grace, surprise, or sparkle of a six-point essay. Like a six-point essay, a five-point essay begins engagingly and closes in a satisfying way.

Figure 8–18

Rhetorical Effectiveness Scoring Guide for Autobiographical Incident From the California Assessment Program, 1990. Reprinted by permission from Writing Assessment Handbook, Grade Eight. Copyright 1990, California Department of Education, P.O. box 271, Sacramento, CA 95812–0271.

Score Point 4—Adequate Achievement

Incident. Incident is well told but may lack the coherence of a five-point essay. There may be digressions, but the story comes back on track quickly. Some four-point essays are smoothly told yet unrealized dramatically. Limited use of strategies.

Context. Context will be adequate to orient readers to the incident.

Significance. Significance is either implied or stated. Reflection is not as insightful as those in a five-point essay and may be only tacked on at the end.

Voice and Style. We usually hear the voice of an earnest storyteller. Predictable sentences and word choice.

Score Point 3—Some Evidence of Achievement

Incident. Essay relates a specific incident. Very limited use of narrative strategies. Story is competently told but told more briefly than the story in a four-point essay. Essay is flat and unfocused. Incident may be presented as a loosely connected series of events.

Context. The writer of a three-point essay may either devote too much space to context while neglecting the narrative or begin abruptly without necessary orientation.

Significance. Significance is implied to some degree or briefly stated. We have an idea why the incident was memorable, although reflections may not be especially insightful.

Voice and Style. Writer does not seem to be seeing the incident as it happened. Writer relates incident in uninvolved way. Predictable sentences and word choice.

Score Point 2—Limited Evidence of Achievement

Incident. The essay may fail to focus on an incident, or it may tell an incident without orientating context or significance. Essay is usually quite brief. If longer, it may be rambling, fragmentary, or may not include details. Writer attempts to construct the incident but fails to do so because of omissions, erratic jumps in time or space, or breakdown in cohesion.

Context. The context may be limited or even missing.

Significance. The writer of a two-point essay includes few reflections, if any. Reflections may seem superficial.

Voice and Style. Writer does not seem to be relating specific details about the incident. Evidence of personal involvement in incident is minimal. Sentences may be too short or long in disorderly way.

Score Point 1—Minimal Evidence of Achievement

Writer responds to prompt but usually only briefly.

Incident. The writer of a one-point essay may refer to an incident without identifying it specifically or may only imply the incident in the context. May point to an incident without developing it conclusively. Reader may need to infer the incident. In the essay, writer may focus on others instead of himself or herself.

Context. In the one-point essay, context is limited or even missing.

Significance. Little or no significance is implied or stated.

Voice and Style. The writer of this essay communicates little or no evidence of personal involvement in incident. Lapses in sentence control or diction interfere significantly with the sense of the paper.

Score Point 0—Inappropriate Response

Figure 8–18 (continued)

253

Write about the story you read.

Who is the story about?

_____

_____

What does she look like and how does she act?

_____

_____

_____

_____

What is the problem she has to solve?

_____

_____

_____

What does she do to solve her problem?

_____

_____

_____

Figure 8–19
Scaffolded Essay Item for Young Children

enjoy showing and explaining their ideas more than finding right answers in a multiple-choice format. We have also found that their responses to performance tasks give us much richer information about the level of their conceptual understanding than when they respond to traditional items—largely because of the limitations of traditional items. If you choose to use performance items with younger students, use oral directions and have students complete only two or three items at one time.

Students from elementary through early high school need practice working with multi-step performance tasks and essay writing before they face performance items in a test format. As students mature and as they have practice with essay and performance items, they are more likely to be successful in responding to them. However, when students write about conceptual understanding, analysis of a situation, explanations about how a phenomenon works, and other ideas in essay formats, the quality of their writing is likely to decrease as they focus on communicating their ideas. Therefore, it is important to separate quality of writing from essay responses if students are early in the development of their writing skills.

If students focus too much on the quality of their writing, the content of their responses is very likely to suffer. Only mature writers are able to handle writing quality and the content and thinking demands of essay items simultaneously.

RELIABILITY AND VALIDITY ISSUES IN THE USE OF PERFORMANCE ITEMS

As has already been emphasized a number of times in this chapter, the first step in ensuring the validity of scores that students earn from your performance items is whether the items actually draw out the knowledge, skills, and/or conceptual understandings at the heart of the learning objectives. There are four steps required to determine whether items truly measure your learning objectives. First, careful attention to your learning objectives, both when writing the objectives and when developing items to assess them, will help you make certain that you are targeting those learning objectives in your assessments. Second, scoring rules must clearly relate to the learning objectives; therefore, use your learning objectives to guide the writing of scoring rules—key words and ideas, checklists, rating scales, and rubrics. Third, writing sample answers will help you ensure that you are truly asking for what you want in the questions, directions, or prompts and that what you want truly relates to your objectives. Many times our students have looked at us with chagrin once they realized their sample answer showed no relationship to their learning objectives. Finally, carefully comparing questions, prompts, and directions with your sample answers and scoring rules, and making adjustments as needed, will help you to ensure the validity of the scores that result from the students' work. Although this may seem like a time-consuming process, recall Ms. Steinberg's test. Rather than create many different items, she focused her assessment on critical concepts and skills. Item formats and rubrics for her performance items were repeated—simplifying the development process considerably. As we have said elsewhere, the more you practice writing items and rubrics, the sooner you find effective item formats for your learning objectives, and the easier (and faster) the writing process will become.

The reliability of scores depends on the clarity of your items (do students know what is expected), the quality of your scoring rules (can they be applied in a systematic way to all students' work), and how systematically you apply scoring rules. Sometimes you may have to evaluate students' work over several days. In that case, look back at how you have applied the scoring rules to previous students' work before looking at the current batch of work, especially when using rubrics and rating scales. We find that if we use a checklist alongside a rubric, we are more likely to apply rubrics consistently across students. Although rubrics generally focus on overall quality, checklists can guide your judgments over time so that your reasons for determining overall quality remain focused on the learning objectives rather than some aspect of performance that is unrelated to the learning objectives (for example, if you are concerned about students' conceptual understanding shown in test items, grammar and spelling might distract you from focusing on the conceptual understanding shown). We often tell our students, "You are the test." In fact, each of you will *be* the test your students must face. If your test items are carefully developed or selected and target your learning objectives, if your scoring rules are aligned with your objectives and are well developed, if your tests represent the range of your objectives and only what you taught, if you apply your scoring rules systematically and fairly, students will see you as an ally in their education. If your items are poorly developed or selected and don't measure what was taught, if the scoring rules focus on factors unrelated to the learning objectives, or if you are inconsistent in your application of scoring rules, students will see you as an obstacle to overcome. Whether your tests are good or poor, they represent your choices. Hence, you are the test.

PERFORMANCE ITEMS AND STUDENTS WITH SPECIAL NEEDS

We described adaptations for students with special needs in the preceding chapter on traditional items. All of these suggestions apply to performance items as well. Students must understand questions and prompts if they are to demonstrate what they know. As with other kinds of assessment, students with special needs, including those with limited English proficiency, may need accommodations (translation assistance, extra time to complete the test, specialized equipment) or modifications (different learning goals with assessments to match).

Items that require written responses place an extra burden on students for whom writing in English is difficult. Students with writing disabilities may have difficulty with handwriting, forming clear sentences, spelling correctly, or planning what they want to say (skills that are especially important for essay items). Young students who have writing disabilities may have difficulty keeping in mind what they want to say while they struggle to form letters and words. These children can be given a scribe (teacher, aide, volunteer, or older student or peer) who will write to their dictation. This frees up their working memories to focus on the substance of the task.

Older students may benefit from using a computer, which can provide spellchecking, grammar checking, and easier editing. Many teachers construct their tests on computers and print them out for students. Students could just as easily be given a copy of the test document on a computer and be allowed to type responses (any diagrams or drawing required can be done on paper). Recent research suggests that training students to use dictation software (where their spoken words are automatically typed on the computer) can improve the quality of written performances for low performing students (Quinlin, 2002).

Students who have a limited command of English, including many students with hearing impairments, may also make errors of spelling and sentence structure. They may be able to respond appropriately to the demands of the task but lack the vocabulary to show what they know. Teachers can provide translation dictionaries or provide needed vocabulary words when asked. Performance items that encourage or require drawings or diagrams, rather than completely verbal responses, may also help English language learners reveal their understanding and skill.

Evaluation of the written products of students with special needs requires that teachers be clear about their learning targets. Even when the learning targets and scoring rubrics do not emphasize writing skill, it is easy to be swayed (both positively and negatively) by students' writing. Poor writing can get in the way of communication, and demand that the reader work extra hard to understand. It is understandable when teachers with stacks of papers to evaluate become irritated when they have to wade through confusing syntax or poor handwriting. Unfortunately, this can lead teachers to judge such papers more harshly, even when writing skill is not being assessed. The reverse is also true: When a student turns in a beautifully written paper, teachers' attention can be drawn away from the skills and knowledge being assessed.

Clear and detailed scoring rubrics, rating scales, and checklists can help prevent these problems. If certain aspects of writing will be judged, that should be spelled out in the scoring rule and students should have an opportunity to learn how to write appropriately. If writing is not one of the learning objectives being assessed, having a clear scoring rule focused on the learning objectives will provide a way for you to control your biases toward good writing ability. When writing is a target, the teacher must consider how this will affect students with IEPs or whose English skills are limited. If the student's IEP specifies a reading or writing disability, accommodations should be made so that the student's score is not affected by his or her disability. For example, there is no reason that literary analyses must be shown in writing. A student who can narrate her analyses of theme, plot, or character development to a scribe or to a computer with voice recognition software, can demonstrate the same level of critical reading skills as the student who has no writing disability or a student with no limitations in English proficiency.

As always, consult with the IEP manager or special education teacher when developing accommodations and modifications for students in special education. For English language learners, work with the ESL or bilingual education teacher to develop appropriate supports. This can lead to better interventions and provide more opportunities for the students to progress. Working with the specialists in your building will not only help you adjust your assessments and teaching, but also educate the specialist in the requirements for students in your class. This will, in turn, help these teachers work with your students more productively.

MOTIVATION AND FEEDBACK ISSUES WITH PERFORMANCE ITEMS

Much of the discussion of motivation and feedback related to traditional test items applies to performance tasks as well. In fact, many tests include both types of items. For some students, the chance to write at some length about what they know is preferable to answering multiple-choice items. Through explanation, they believe that they can demonstrate that they have learned. Of course, for students who believe they are not good at writing or at constructing their own responses, the idea of producing a response is not motivating at all. As we have discussed above, for students who have disabilities or limited English proficiency, essay items may be a barrier to showing what they know.

Performance tasks can provide some of the task-involving benefits we discussed for performance assessments. They may be seen as more interesting or relevant because they represent real-world performances. Teachers can provide some choice of topic or format, increasing students' feelings of self-determination and allowing students to make choices that enable them to better show what they know and are able to do. Items and tasks that require more than a single word provide more scope for teachers to provide helpful feedback. We discuss these issues below.

Motivation and Performance Items

Teachers of older children and adolescents sometimes assume that their students know how to respond to essay items and performance tasks. For example, the answers to essay questions are often summaries of material read or presented in class. But without instruction, most students don't develop useful strategies for summarizing (Brown, Day, & Jones, 1983). As we discussed in Chapter 4, to have a valid assessment, students must have an opportunity to learn how to produce an accomplished performance. The same is true of essay items and performance tasks. Good responses to essay items and performance tasks require both an understanding of what is being asked in the item and knowledge of how to formulate such a response. However, tests generally do not include the built-in feedback cycles that are inherent to "prepared accomplishments." Students must produce a response on the spot, during the test, in a fixed amount of time, with perhaps one chance at revision.

Writing clear and complete directions for these items helps, but students will not always have clear and complete directions in all of their classes. Therefore, it is also important to *teach* students strategies for interpreting prompts and directions, as well as strategies for writing the response. Not only is validity increased when students know how to respond, but motivation can also increase. Students often feel that they know the material, but can't effectively respond when they are not sure what the teacher wants. When students feel that they are able to respond successfully to an item, their motivation to do so increases along with their self-efficacy (Schunk, 1989). They are also able to concentrate on their response rather than worrying about whether they are giving the teacher what he wants. This is especially important for those students who are less fluent in their writing—a group that will include both students who have been identified as having special needs and those who simply struggle with written communication.

Encouraging Interest and Task Involvement for Performance Items

There are two important ways to encourage interest and mastery motivation in response to performance items: authenticity and choice. Each of these is described more fully in what follows.

Authentic Tasks   Performance tasks can draw on some of the same sources of interest as performance assessments. To the extent that performance tasks ask students to perform aspects of valued performances—those that you want your students to be able to do in the real world—interest can be enhanced. Suppose the following directions are given to students in a math class, "Your mother has asked you to buy bread, butter, milk, and orange juice at the store. Each item costs less than $3 and more than $2. How much money do you need to take to the store so you have enough money for all four items? Show all the steps you use to solve the problem." Such an item can assess students' number sense, estimation skills, and ability to apply their knowledge in the real world. A science teacher might ask students to "Design an experiment to answer one of the following research questions." This item not only assesses students' knowledge of experimental design, but also increases the chances that students will be interested by providing a choice of research questions. The teacher could use knowledge of which topics might be interesting to students to capitalize on their existing motivations and background knowledge. Similarly, when essay items ask for more than a summary of learned information and can relate to students' interests, they are more likely to capture students' interest and motivation.

Choice   Choice within items can give students opportunities to select areas of interest and strength for their response. (e.g., "Identify one theme from Kingsolver's *Poisonwood Bible*. Then briefly describe three events in the novel that demonstrate the selected theme," or "Identify one of the individual rights protected under the constitution. Then write an essay to describe how the right applies to an event that has occurred in the past year. Include details about the event and explain its connection to the constitutional right."). One of the traditional places to find choice on a test is in essay items. Students may be allowed to choose "two from the following four essay questions." This allows students to choose a topic that may be interesting, or one they feel more able to adequately address. Whereas this kind of choice can increase students' engagement, teachers must use caution in creating the choices. Will the knowledge and skills taught be adequately assessed no matter which essay topics students choose? Are the topics equally important to have mastered? If the answer to these questions is yes, choice can increase motivation without decreasing the validity of the test. If the essay is meant to assess writing skills rather than topic knowledge, students can choose a topic or identify their own topic. If the choice is wide open, some students may not be able to independently generate a good topic, especially if there is time pressure. These students can be helped by providing a list of topic ideas.

There are other cautions about choice, however. First, not all prompts or questions are equally difficult. Even simple word changes can radically change the difficulty of a performance item (Wiser & Lenke, 1987). Therefore, if you want to use choice to increase task orientation, it is best to use performance items that you have used before and for which you know how students performed in the past. Second, students do not necessarily choose wisely. Students may choose items that are more difficult (because they like a challenge), begin to do poorly, and run out of time before they can adequately tackle a different item (Fitzpatrick & Yen, 1995). One way you can address these two issues is to select prompts or questions that are similar in difficulty (e.g., suppose you know that last year nearly all students got full credit on these two performance items and about three-fourths of the students got full credit on these two performance items). Then let students choose one prompt or question from a pair based on known difficulties.

Providing Encouraging Feedback on Performance Items As with performance assessments, performance items provide greater scope for feedback than do traditional test items. Feedback that gives information on students' current level of performance, coupled with a chance to improve, can encourage a mastery or learning focus. If teachers also engage seriously with students' ideas, they can fan the flames of interest, as well. All of the suggestions given previously for providing feedback hold here as well. To help students improve and learn the standards for performance, feedback must be related to the task requirements. To be useful, feedback has to provide enough information for students to figure out what needs to be done to improve. Vague comments such as "needs theme" or "spelling" are unlikely to be as useful as more specific comments, such as "I follow your argument up to here, but then I get lost. A concrete example might help," or "I think you're on the right track! Now you need to provide more evidence from your research findings to convince the reader of your interpretation." Questions that lead students in the right direction without giving them the answers can help students take the next step (e.g., "I'm not sure how you solved this. Can you explain why you _____?" or "You used 'really' several times in your essay. Can you think of some other words to use that would make it more interesting and powerful to the reader?" "What scale on your graph would result in equal intervals between numbers?")

Performance items allow teachers to assess both content mastery and communication skills. Feedback must make clear the relative importance of these two broad categories. If content knowledge is the primary focus, that should be the primary focus of feedback as well. If feedback focuses on clarity of communication, students will learn that this is the most important aspect of the assessment. When both are important, feedback should make this clear. In a conference with young children, it is inappropriate to discuss all of the weaknesses in the same session. Young students are likely to become confused or overwhelmed if there are too many comments, leaving discouraged and without knowing what they need to do to improve.

As with other forms of assessment, revision opportunities provide reasons for attending to feedback and a sense that the teacher is interested in student mastery. It also provides a way for students to immediately practice new skills in a known context, which is likely to improve chances that they can transfer those skills to new tasks.

SUMMARY

Performance items provide an opportunity to assess students' thinking related to important ideas, their recall of complex information, their ability to apply knowledge and skills to important tasks, and their ability to represent information in a variety of ways. After the invention of the multiple-choice item, performance items were rarely used in standardized tests. Eventually, they became scarce in classrooms. However, in the past decade or two, research on how to effectively develop performance items has helped bring a new kind of respectability to their use. In addition, teachers have become aware of the immense amount of information about students' understanding that is available through performance items; information that cannot be obtained from traditional items. Most important of all, performance items can be developed to allow students to do parts of valued performance—scrimmages for the game to be played.

This chapter has introduced each type of performance item, presented rules for writing them, and presented guidelines for adapting them for students with special needs. As you create your own assessments, these rules and guidelines can help you develop assessments that will measure valued standards. Because of the preponderance of multiple-choice item tests, you may be unfamiliar with performance items or you may have had experiences that led you to believe that they are unfair (e.g., essay tests with no guidelines or rubrics to help you understand the expectations). With practice, you can create performance items that come closer to your learning objectives. You can also create performance items to use as classroom exercises as students learn to grapple with real problems, real representation, and real opportunities for expression prior to or in place of traditional tests. Finally, you can combine several performance items into a test. In this chapter we have attempted to help you consider ways to make these assessments interesting and motivating to students. If done well, you may find yourself in the situation where students can't wait to take the test—not because they are afraid of forgetting the information but because they are excited to show you what they have learned.

REFERENCES

Brown, A. L., Day, J. D., & Jones, R. S. (1983). The development of plans for summarizing texts. *Child Development, 54*(4), 968–979.

Fitzpatrick, A. R., & Yen, W. M. (1995). The psychometric characteristics of choice items. *Journal of Educational Measurement, 32*, 243–259.

Quinlan, T. (2003). *Speech recognition technology and the writing process of students with writing difficulties.* Paper presented at the 2003 meeting of the American Educational Research Association. Chicago, IL.

Schunk, D. (1989). Self-efficacy and achievement behaviors. *Educational Psychology Review, 1*(3), 173–207.

Wiser, B., & Lenke, J. (1987, April). *The effects of wording on the difficulty of writing prompts for the Metropolitan Achievement Tests writing assessment.* Paper presented at the annual meeting of the National Council on Measurement in Education, Washington, DC.

GRADES AND GRADING PROCESSES

In this chapter we describe the business of giving grades. Most people have two images when they hear the word *grade*: a letter mark on an assignment and the grades given at the end of a quarter, trimester, or semester during the school year. In this chapter we want to distinguish clearly between these two notions. The first is really the same as giving scores to students' work as discussed in previous chapters. The second is the focus of this chapter.

Many teachers who are focused on the successes and needs of their students avoid thinking about the process of giving grades. They plan instruction. They work to create important and valuable assignments for their students. They set up learning experiences for their students. They regularly assess their students' work. Yet, when the end of a marking period—quarter, trimester, or semester—arrives, teachers must make some kind of summary decision about what students have individually accomplished: what they have learned, what skills they have developed, what work they have done.

Giving summary grades is another form of assessment, and it is one of a teacher's most important professional responsibilities. It is through progress reports or grade cards that teachers make public statements to students, parents or guardians, and school administrators about students' accomplishments. Ethical grading practices are ones in which teachers use their best professional judgments to determine what students have learned and communicate those judgments to others. Unethical practices occur when teachers add their own biases to the grades, use faulty information in figuring the grades, have too little information with which to make accurate statements about students' progress, compute grades mathematically without examining their meaning, or use grades to reward or punish students for attitudes or efforts.

In this chapter, we hope to set the stage for fair and professional grading practices that fit with the overall messages in this book: (1) do no harm, (2) use assessments to support students' learning, and (3) assessments that detract from or misrepresent students' achievement are not valid assessments. We believe it is important to summarize what others have said about grading before we present our own views. We do this because your colleagues will have many different views on the business of giving grades and because we want you to make informed choices. We provide an example of a grading policy—statements to students and parents or guardians about how the teacher plans to organize achievement information for grading purposes—and we show how to organize information and compute grades. We also describe how you can use grading policies to communicate what you want students to learn as well as your standards and expectations for work. We take into account the motivational consequences of grading choices, and we take up issues regarding grading students with disabilities and students who are English language learners.

WHY GRADE?

Grades are assigned for two broad reasons: to communicate with students, parents or guardians, and school administrators about students' achievement and to make gatekeeping decisions.

We believe that the most important purpose of summary grading is to provide feedback to students and their families. Different grading models provide different kinds of information for students and their families to use in monitoring progress and modifying learning strategies. Norm-referenced grading, described first, provides information about how a student performs relative to other students in the same course. The second grading model we present, criterion-referenced grading, provides information about a student's absolute level of performance, regardless of the performance of others. Although one could look at such a grade and see that a student had earned 95% of the possible points in a course, this alone does not indicate what was learned, whether the work was difficult or easy, or the level of a student's competence in a subject or skill. Thomas and Oldfather (1997) quote Nicki, a seventh-grader who moved from a nongraded elementary school to a graded junior high:

> At [my old school], like the conferences, they have a paragraph written about each subject and the strengths and the weaknesses of each child. [But now at my junior high], a B could say that you're turning in all of your homework and you're doing a good job on your homework and your quizzes, but when it comes to tests, that you really can't do it. Or it could be saying that I have a lot of strengths in applications and word problems, but when it comes to computation, I'm very careless. It is just a letter. It doesn't really tell you that much. (p. 108)

The third model we present, standards-based grading, is similar to criterion-referenced grading. Teachers judge student performance against a set of performance criteria rather than by comparing students. Unlike criterion-referenced grading, however, standards-based grading depends on public standards, which include descriptions of the levels of competence attained.

Gate-keeping and placement decisions are made to prevent individuals from advancing to work for which they are unprepared or to place students in particular programs or courses. Such decisions include moving to the next grade, advancing to a higher level of mathematics or French, graduation, and entry into colleges and universities. The same issues discussed above arise when considering the gate-keeping and placement function of grades. Different models of summary grading provide different kinds of information for gate-keeping decisions.

If one is selecting for the "best and the brightest," norm-referenced grading is one way to make such a determination. Criterion-reference grading gives information about whether the teacher believes that the students have mastered the material taught and are ready for the next level of work. Standards-based grading provides more information for gatekeepers who want to know specifically *what* the student learned and *how well*.

In the next section, we present the three models of grading. Each provides different kinds and amounts of feedback. Following their description, we discuss the issue of feedback via summary grades in more detail.

MODELS FOR ASSIGNING GRADES

Norm-Referenced Grading

Norm-referenced grading is the practice of giving grades based on how students compare to one another. It is called norm-referenced grading because students are compared to a "norm group"—students like themselves. It is more frequently called "grading on the curve" and is often used in college courses. The beliefs that underlie norm-referenced grading are from the late 19th century when psychologists developed ways to describe and quantify individual differences between people. Advocates of norm-referenced grading claim that comparison is the fairest way to assign grades (see, for example, Mehrens & Lehmann, 1991). Their arguments are these:

1. Some of what teachers hope students will learn in school (writing, artistic expression, mathematical reasoning) depends more on aptitude than instruction. Teachers are not able to teach these abilities well; therefore, the best way to evaluate students' performances is by way of comparison.

2. Teachers are not sophisticated enough in test development to control the difficulty of the items on tests; therefore, the only way to evaluate performance on tests is to determine how students compare to the mean or average score. Students will be either below the mean (below average), at or near the mean (average), or above the mean (above average) on a given test.

3. Norm-referenced grading converts test scores to the same scale, based on the standard deviation units in a set of scores. Tests will differ in the number of raw score points. Before converting scores on tests to final grades, they have to be converted to the same point system. If this is not done, then points alone will make some tests worth more than others in contributing to the final grade. Using standard deviations automatically converts scores on different tests and quizzes to the same scale. Teachers can then weight the scores to control how much each test or quiz contributes to the total score for the term.

To do norm-referenced grading, scores are converted to a common number system and then students' relative performances are either averaged across tests to get a final ranking of all students (if all tests count the same toward the final grade), or weighted and summed (if different tests are worth different amounts). Figure 9–1 shows scores on four tests for the 26 students in Ms. Sanchez's U.S. history class. The scores on each test have been translated into z-scores. Z-scores tell how many standard deviations above or below the mean each score is.[1] For example, Yoonsun was 1.6 standard deviations above the mean on Test 1, she was 1.11 standard deviations above the mean on Test 2, 1.03 standard deviations above the mean on Test 3, and she was 1.77 standard deviations above the mean on Test 4. She was well above average on all four tests. Once z-scores were computed, Ms. Sanchez computed a mean z-score for each student. Last of all, she decided how to translate the mean z-scores into grades.

There is not one correct or conventional way to decide what grades to assign to students based on their z-scores. In some classrooms, teachers distribute the grades so that the smallest percent of students earn As and Fs (say 10% As and 10% Fs); the next larger percent earn Bs and Ds (say 20% Bs and 20% Ds), and the very largest percent earn Cs (the remaining 40%). Other teachers set B as the most common grade and give very few Ds or Fs. Still other teachers use natural breaks in the z-scores to determine what grades to assign to each student. Ms. Sanchez used natural breaks in z-scores to assign grades. She gave the top 15% of students (4 students) As, the next 65% (17 students) Bs, the next 15% (4 students) Cs, and the lowest 4% (1 student) a D. The z-score range for Bs is between $z = .50$ and $z = -.50$, meaning that 65% of the students were between ½ of a standard deviation above and ½ of a standard deviation below the mean. Students above $z = .50$ were given an A; students with z-scores between -1.00 and $-.50$ were given a C, and the student with a z-score below -1.00 was given a D.

---

[1] For more information on how to use score means and standard deviations to compute z-scores as the common scale, see Mehrens, W. A., and Lehmann, I. J. (1991), *Measurement and Evaluation in Education and Psychology, Fourth Edition*, Fort Worth, TX: Holt, Rinehart, & Winston, 218–220, 232–233.

Student Number	Student	Test 1 Score	Test 2 Score	Test 3 Score	Test 4 Score	Test 1 z-score	Test 2 z-score	Test 3 z-score	Test 4 z-score	Mean z-score	Grades
26	Yoonsun	44	50	25	100	1.60	1.11	1.03	1.77	1.38	A
4	Britney	32	46	25	100	−0.06	0.49	1.03	1.77	0.81	A
25	Will	42	48	25	92	1.32	0.80	1.03	−0.04	0.78	A
15	Nikki	43	48	25	91	1.46	0.80	1.03	−0.27	0.76	A
24	Tess	32	49	25	91	−0.06	0.96	1.03	−0.27	0.41	B
7	John	28	49	25	93	−0.62	0.96	1.03	0.18	0.39	B
22	Tameka	27	50	23	95	−0.76	1.11	0.32	0.64	0.33	B
5	Gabriel	38	48	23	89	0.77	0.80	0.32	−0.72	0.29	B
6	Jen	42	50	21	88	1.32	1.11	−0.38	−0.95	0.28	B
16	Pat	39	49	24	86	0.91	0.96	0.68	−1.40	0.28	B
20	Seon	30	41	22	96	−0.34	−0.28	−0.03	0.86	0.05	B
8	Juan	27	47	23	91	−0.76	0.65	0.32	−0.27	−0.01	B
21	Tai	28	40	21	98	−0.62	−0.43	−0.38	1.31	−0.03	B
13	Michael	41	43	17	94	1.18	0.03	−1.79	0.41	−0.04	B
1	Anna	35	40	25	87	0.35	−0.43	1.03	−1.18	−0.06	B
2	Betsy	28	42	24	89	−0.62	−0.12	0.68	−0.72	−0.20	B
10	Lia	33	38	18	98	0.07	−0.74	−1.43	1.31	−0.20	B
14	Michelle	45	41	15	93	1.74	−0.28	−2.49	0.18	−0.21	B
12	Matt	33	39	18	96	0.07	−0.59	−1.43	0.86	−0.27	B
17	Paula	25	50	23	85	−1.04	1.11	0.32	−1.63	−0.31	B
23	Tara	29	29	24	93	−0.48	−2.13	0.68	0.18	−0.44	B
19	Ronnie	21	38	22	92	−1.59	−0.74	−0.03	−0.04	−0.60	C
3	Caitlin	23	41	21	90	−1.31	−0.28	−0.38	−0.50	−0.62	C
9	Lee	31	35	19	92	−0.20	−1.20	−1.08	−0.04	−0.63	C
11	Lin	25	30	20	95	−1.04	−1.98	−0.73	0.64	−0.78	C
18	Tan	23	32	21	83	−1.31	−1.67	−0.38	−2.08	−1.36	D

Figure 9–1
Test Scores, Score Ranks, and Grades Using Norm-Referenced Grading for Ms. Sanchez's U.S. History Class

Criticisms of Norm-Referenced Grading   Many educators argue against norm-referenced grading. Probably the most important argument is that norm-referenced grading is not appropriate in a context wherein teachers and students are engaged in purposeful activities. Many educators believe that most hardworking, well-taught students can learn what is taught. Therefore, simply ranking to determine who is best is not appropriate. Rather, students should be able to attain standards that reflect high-quality work.

Although one argument for norm-referenced grading is that grades should reflect differences in *aptitude*, that which is called aptitude may simply be a product of the educational environment in the home. A talent for artistic expression may result from exposure to works of art at galleries and concerts, community art classes, and family discussions about the arts. A talent for writing may result from experiences in a highly verbal family whose members use a broad vocabulary or have a penchant for storytelling. Excellent reasoning skills may come from being asked to explain, describe, and justify ideas and choices at home. The argument against including apparent aptitude in grades is that effective instructional practices and supportive educational environments can help students develop the skills that some learned at home.

The second argument against norm-referenced grading is that the ranking process seems to make classroom learning a competitive venture. Researchers have found that, when grading is competitive, students are less likely to work cooperatively (Ames, 1984; Johnson & Johnson, 1985). In addition to academics, students also learn important social skills while working with their peers in a mutually supportive learning environment.

Third, norm-referenced grades show how students rank but do not tell parents, guardians, or students much about what the students know and what they are able to do. For example, look at test scores for John, Tess, and Tameka (students numbered 7, 24, and 22, respectively) in Figure 9–1. Except for the first exam, their scores on each subsequent test were very high. This would suggest that these students are learning what these tests are testing; yet, the overall grade is a B. Note also that Tan, an ELL student, has gradually improved his performance over the term—moving from less than half the points on the first test to 64% of the points on the second test to over 80% of the points on the third and fourth tests. Yet, using the norm-referenced grading process, his grade for the course is a D. Clearly, it is not what Tan has learned that is the basis of his grade, but rather whether he came to the class with the same knowledge and skills as his peers. If students excel in their assignments (as happens when standards and expectations are clear, when students have study guides for tests, and when students can revise work to improve quality or demonstrate further learning), then ranking becomes a pointless and potentially undermining act.

The final argument against norm-referenced grading is that the model tends to limit the types of assessments used in the classroom. Ranking is only appropriate when comparing students across many classes. Ranking *within* classrooms could mean that high-achieving students earn low grades when compared with other high-achieving students. If scores from different classes are combined, then ranking is possible in fairly large schools with common tests across many classes. However, when the same test is used in multiple classes, tests must be kept secure (e.g., students from first period must be prevented from talking with students in third period) and teachers lose the option of designing assessments to build on the interests of individual students or groups of students.

Throughout this book we describe how to use feedback to teach students how to improve their work and move toward performance standards. If students are to be ranked, teachers have little incentive to provide feedback and students have little incentive to improve their work and meet higher expectations. If everyone improves, the curve moves upward and individual rankings become muddled. Ranking students based on their performance also encourages ego involvement and makes it difficult for students to remain or become task involved. Students at the lower end of the curve may see no point in trying when their chances of a higher grade are very small. Withdrawal of effort may lead to ever poorer learning, making improvement an increasingly remote possibility.

Children with special needs, who have individualized education plans (IEPs), 504 plans, or speak English as a second language, are at a particular disadvantage with norm-referenced grading. Limited English proficiency, learning disabilities, developmental delays, behavioral disabilities, and some medical conditions can all make it difficult for students to learn from instruction and to perform well on assessments. If modifications are made, teachers must decide how modifications will be taken account of in establishing the curve. Are such students guaranteed a permanent position at the bottom of the grade distribution? If their scores are adjusted to compensate for difficulties beyond their control, is this fair to other students in the distribution? Some of these problems must be dealt with regardless of the teacher's grading method, but they are particularly problematic when using norm-referenced grading.

Criterion-Referenced Grading

Criterion-referenced grading is the practice of giving grades based on whether students meet certain criteria. The beliefs that underlie criterion-referenced grading derive from the mastery learning movement of the 1960s and 1970s. Advocates for criterion-referenced grading claim that criterion-referenced grading fits with the purposeful nature of schooling. Their arguments are these:

1. Given sufficient time and practice along with focused instruction, students can learn what teachers want them to learn.
2. Specific learning objectives or targets identify what students are to learn; therefore, learning objectives are blueprints for instruction, assessment, and grading.
3. Criterion-referenced grading methods tell teachers not only whether students have achieved, but also whether their instruction has been successful.
4. Criterion-referenced grading communicates expectations to students. Students know what they are to accomplish in order to achieve the highest grade.

To do criterion-referenced grading, scores from various assignments are collected as points or as percentages. If collected as points, teachers generally give fewer points for assignments such as homework and practice exercises and more points for more important assignments such as tests, projects, and research papers. When using percentages, teachers convert points on different assignments to a common percent scale before summarizing for grades. Mr. Williams is a fourth-grade teacher. He uses the scores in Figure 9–2 to compute grades for the language arts part of the progress report. Only 10 students are included for illustrative purposes.

There are 10 assignments: two vocabulary tests, two book reports, four homework assignments to practice writing complex sentences, and two in-class writing assessments. The scores on each assignment have been translated into percentages prior to computing the final grade. Figure 9–3 shows the five-level holistic rubric Mr. Williams uses to evaluate writing assignments.

Student Number	Student	VT 1	VT 2	HW 1	HW 2	HW 3	HW 4	W 1	W 2	BR 1	BR 2	Tentative Grades	Final Grades
1	William	9	9	5	4	5	5	4	4	20	20	A	A
	%	90	90	100	90	100	100	90	90	100	100	94.75	
2	Betsy	10	10	3	2	4	5	5	5	20	15	A	A
	%	100	100	80	70	90	100	100	100	100	75	93.50	
3	Abraham	8	9	2	3	4	4	4	5	15	15	B	B
	%	80	90	70	80	90	90	90	100	75	75	83.25	
4	Robin	8	10	0	4	4	5	5	5	15	20	B	A
	%	80	100		90	90	100	100	100	75	100	89.50	
5	Gabriel	7	7	4	3	5	5	4	4	14	16	C	B
	%	70	70	90	80	100	100	90	90	70	80	79.25	
6	Jeff	6	7	3	3	3	3	2	3	13	15	C	C
	%	60	70	80	80	80	80	70	80	65	75	71	
7	Corina	7	8	3	4	4	5	4	5	14	17	B	B
	%	70	80	80	90	90	100	90	100	70	85	82.50	
8	Jin	5	10	5	5	5	5	4	5	18	20	A	A
	%	50	100	100	100	100	100	90	100	90	100	90.50	
9	Kate	7	8	3	3	4	5	3	4	15	18	B	B
	%	70	80	80	80	90	100	80	90	75	90	81.75	
10	Lee	8	8	4	4	4	5	3	4	17	18	B	B
	%	80	80	90	90	90	100	80	90	85	90	87.50	
Points Possible		10	10	5	5	5	5	5	5	20	20		

VT = vocabulary tests   HW = homework   W = writing assignments   BR = book reports

Figure 9–2
Language Arts Scores, Percent Scores, and Grades Using Criterion-Referenced Grading for Mr. Williams's Class

Performance Criteria for Writing
- Ideas and content are focused on one main idea
- Details and examples support the main idea
- Ideas are organized in a logical or sequential way
- Sentences are varied and have appropriate structure
- Capitalization and punctuation are correct
- Common words are spelled correctly

Scoring Rule:

Levels	Descriptors
Excellent	The work is organized with one central idea and supporting examples. Sentences are varied and show excellent understanding English grammar. Few or no errors in capitalization, punctuation, and spelling of common words.
Very good; could use minor improvements	The work is organized with one central idea and supporting examples. Simple sentences show good understanding of English grammar. Few or no errors in capitalization, punctuation, and spelling of common words.
Good; improvements needed in content and ideas	The work is organized with one central idea; could use more supporting examples. Sentences show good understanding of English grammar. Writer *may* need to improve capitalization, punctuation, and spelling of common words.
Fair; needs some revision; possible need for editing	The work has a main idea and examples, but problems with organization, rambling, sentence structures, or grammar may cause confusion for the reader. Writer may need to improve capitalization, punctuation, and spelling of common words.
Unacceptable; must be rewritten or have major revisions	It is difficult to find the main idea, and problems with examples, organization, sentence structures, or grammar may cause significant confusion for the reader. Writer may need to improve capitalization, punctuation, and spelling of common words.

Figure 9–3
Mr. Williams's Five-Level Holistic Writing Rubric

As can be seen, he has combined content, organization, grammar, and mechanics into one holistic rubric, which he discovered was difficult to apply. He decided he would change the scoring of writing assignments during the next term, but that it would have been unfair to his students to make the change this term. Mr. Williams did not use points on the rubric but, rather, descriptive statements. If he simply converted his descriptions to a scale of 1 through 5 and divides each student's score by 5 points, students who have done moderately well with a score of 3 will have only 60% of the points possible. In the typical criterion-referenced grading scheme, 60% is generally considered to be nearly failing work. So, Mr. Williams decided that he would use the following percent conversion for each score on the rubric: 5 = 100%, 4 = 90%, 3 = 80%, 2 = 70%, and 1 = 60%. He also decided to use the same rule for converting the homework scores to the percent scale. This way, students who attempted homework would get at least a score of 60%.

Because the assignments differed in their importance in the grade, Mr. Williams has decided to weight the homework as 10% of the grade, the vocabulary tests as 25% of the grade, the book reports as 40% of the grade, and the writing assessments as 25% of the grade. Once he had a weighted total for each student, he assigned the grades based on the total percentage of points earned.

Note that Mr. Williams has two columns for grades. One has the grade that corresponds to the percent cut points he has established for language arts (90–100 = A; 80–89 = B; 70–79 = C; 60–69 = D; and 59 or less = F). These are tentative grades based on weighted averages. Mr. Williams also wants the grades to reflect student improvement.

For example, Robin is on the borderline between a B and an A. Robin has done well on all assignments except for the first one in each category. For example, if she had turned in the first homework assignment—even if she had only received one of the five possible points—her percent grade would have been 91%. Mr. Williams knows that Robin's sister was born during the first week of school. So Mr. Williams takes into account her whole record and gives her the A grade. Gabriel is on a borderline—between a C and a B. A careful look at Gabriel's record shows that he has been consistently working at a B level, even though he has only been speaking and writing in English for 3 years. However, the 25% weight on the vocabulary tests has lowered Gabriel's overall weighted average. Mr. Williams looks back at Gabriel's writing and book reports and notes that he is using the new vocabulary words in his writing. In looking at Gabriel's work on the vocabulary tests, Mr. Williams notices that his errors may be due to the items on the test. The sentence completion items, for example, included vocabulary that may have been unfamiliar to a student who is learning English as a second language. Therefore, Mr. Williams decides to move Gabriel's grade to a B. Mr. Williams decides that, in the future, he may want to give less weight to vocabulary tests and focus more on whether students are using the vocabulary in their own writing. He also decides that he will revise the items on the published vocabulary tests before using them again.

The decisions Mr. Williams makes about converting rubric scores to a percent scale, weighting different types of assignments, setting cut points for grades, and giving credit for improvement are generally in the hands of the individual teacher. Teachers assign percents for different levels of rubrics based on their knowledge of the rubrics (which we will explain in more detail later). They give weights for different types of work based on their knowledge of the assignments and how well each one shows what students have learned. Homework is generally given less weight because not all students get equal help with the homework. Many writers recommend excluding homework and practice work from grading summaries. Research has shown that teachers want to give students credit for their homework and practice work, even if it is a small amount of credit (Cross & Frary, 1999; Frary et al., 1993).

Cut points for grades are also set by individual teachers—unless there are department, school, or district policies. Mr. Williams's cut scores for grades are the ones most commonly used in schools. At the elementary level, grade categories may have other labels besides the familiar letter grades (e.g., Excellent, Satisfactory, and Needs Work). Still, teachers must decide what cut points to use for assigning grades.

Criticisms of Criterion-Referenced Grading   Some educators argue against criterion-referenced grading. The most critical argument is that teachers cannot easily control the difficulty of assignments and grades may have more to do with the quality of the assignments than with students' achievement. For example, students in Mr. Williams's class seemed to have the most difficulty with the vocabulary tests. Suppose the vocabulary on these tests is too abstract or advanced for fourth-grade students. In contrast, nearly all students earned 100% on the fourth homework assignment. Does this mean that instruction on the sentence types was successful or that the practice exercise was too easy? Critics say that to use a criterion-referenced model, teachers must have some confidence that the tasks placed before students are neither so difficult that students cannot achieve nor so easy that the assessments are not a measure of what students have learned from instruction. In addition, they should be confident that all assignments in a category are of equal difficulty if they are going to average scores within that category. For example, are both of the writing assessments in Mr. Williams's class of equal difficulty? Were the requirements for both book reports the same or were they a bit more stringent for the second book report?

The second argument against criterion-referenced grading is that expectations for students may become too low in order to ensure that all students earn good grades. Some studies have shown that when criterion-referenced practices are used, minimum levels of performance become the expectations for all students—thereby placing limits on the educational experiences of bright students (Mangino & Babcock, 1986; Marion & Sheinker, 1999; Rogers, 1991).

The same can be true of deciding where to set cut points for students with special needs. If a teacher sets low minimum standards, is she providing opportunities for success, or limiting students' opportunities to learn as much as they can? Is she sending a message to these students that they are doing well in English, when their B was earned by getting a 40% average?

Despite these criticisms, criterion-referenced grading practices are widely used in elementary and secondary schools. There are ways of handling the problems raised in these criticisms. In terms of task difficulty, teachers can look at students' performances on assignments and evaluate whether the assignments are too difficult, too easy, confusing to students, or flawed in some other way. They can eliminate an assignment from the final grade if the assignment is inappropriate for one reason or another.[2] They can look at students' responses to parts of assignments, such as test and quiz items, eliminate parts that are problematic, and recompute the overall score.

The issue of lower expectations because of criterion-referenced grading practices is more difficult to handle. Teachers want all students to be successful. Still, some students come to school with less external support and lacking some fundamental skills. Setting lower standards will not serve these students' needs, because the demands of life beyond school require thinking, skilled, and knowledgeable individuals. On the other hand, some students with disabilities may never be able to attain the same high standards as their peers. Therefore, the question of expectations brings us to the question at the heart of teaching—how do teachers support all students to achieve high standards?

Standards-Based Grading

Our perspective is similar to the criterion-referenced view of grading; however, we place grading in the larger context of instruction. Neither the norm-referenced nor the criterion-referenced grading policies described thus far address issues we have raised in earlier chapters, such as selecting a few central performances and concepts as the centerpiece of

---

[2] Poor performance is frequently caused by unclear directions or insufficient instruction related to the demands of the assessment.

teaching, using feedback selectively to help students work toward high-quality prepared accomplishments that serve both instructional and assessment purposes, allowing students to continue to grapple with important concepts and develop deeper understanding, and giving students more control over their educational experiences. Both of the previous models places the onus of grading on the teacher and both models depend on mathematical computations as the basis of final grading decisions.

In contrast, we believe that any evaluation of students must serve a feedback purpose; therefore, students should be part of the grading summary process. We also believe that repeated exposure to and practice with substantive ideas and skills leads to deeper, more lasting understanding and generalizable skills. Thus we propose a *standards-based* model for grading.

In a standards-based grading model, teachers and students work together as partners in a learning endeavor. Teachers serve as coaches, guides, and resources while students develop conceptual understanding and complex skills. In this model, each assignment serves a purpose; there are fewer, more substantive assignments that require reflection as well as action; students are allowed to work toward deeper understanding and more generalizable skills over time; and all students can engage in different work while demonstrating the same standards. Finally, because students can use feedback to thoughtfully improve their work, all students can reach high standards and demonstrate deep understanding.

The assumptions of the standards-based model are:

1. Teachers (independently and with students) establish important learning objectives (targets) and gear all teaching and assessment toward students' achievement of those objectives.
2. With encouragement and support, students naturally want to learn and develop mastery in areas they find interesting or valuable.
3. All subjects have important and valuable performances that appeal to students and through which students can learn and demonstrate critical knowledge and skills.
4. Conceptual understanding and complex skills may take more time for some students and less time for others; however, the goal is that all students develop understanding and important skills.
5. Grades reflect what students have accomplished by the *end* of an instructional period.
6. Grades reflect what students learn through instruction, practice with ideas, and improvement based on feedback rather than one-shot attempts with new ideas.
7. Grading policies and practices are used as tools to communicate teacher expectations and values to students and their parents or guardians.
8. Parents or guardians, students, and teachers are partners in helping students to achieve high standards.

For standards-based grading, teachers collect scores as they would for any other grading policy. The main difference is that students are allowed to replace lower scores with higher ones as they learn more and improve the quality of their work. Ms. Henry uses standards-based grading in her seventh-grade mathematics classes. Each quarter, Ms. Henry focuses instruction on a few key mathematical concepts and procedures. Her goal is for students to deeply understand these concepts and procedures by the end of the quarter. During the quarter, students have four main types of assignments: homework, exams, projects, and group problem solving.

For homework, students practice with the concepts and procedures they have examined or explored in class. They complete 5 to 10 exercises from the textbook or from those created by Ms. Henry and then choose 2 to examine in detail. For the two chosen exercises, they show or describe the process they went through to find a solution (using words, labeled pictures, labeled diagrams, or numbers), identify mathematical concepts that are related to the procedure or concept under study, and describe how these concepts relate to the specific exercise.

For projects, students tackle real-world problems that require application of the concepts and procedures they are studying; use of appropriate mathematical language, symbols, and figures to communicate mathematical processes and conclusions; and use of mathematical reasoning and problem-solving skills to approach and reason through the problem.

Each day, students work in small groups on several simple problems or one complex problem. The problems are related to the concepts and procedures under study. Ms. Henry uses an observational rating scale to assess their group work skills and mathematical understanding.

During exams, students do exercises similar to their homework (describing or showing procedures, identifying related concepts, and describing how the concepts apply to the exercises) and do performance tasks wherein they apply the mathematical problem solving, concepts, and procedures to brief, real-world problems.

Public standards and expectations, feedback, student revision, and student growth in understanding and skill over time are key aspects of Ms. Henry's classes. She expects students to improve in their ability to analyze homework exercises and make mathematical connections (for example, using mathematical concepts and procedures from different areas of mathematics such as geometry and measurement to solve a problem), communicate mathematical ideas, work effectively in groups, and apply mathematical concepts and procedures to complex, real-world problems.

At the beginning of the year, she gives students her rubrics for problem solving and reasoning, making connections, and mathematical communication. She has them apply the rubrics to anonymous students' work (from previous classes) and discuss their impressions and experiences. After 2 or 3 weeks, students begin applying the rubrics to their own work. The students contribute to development of an observational rating scale to use when they are in groups (see Figure 9–4).

These early teaching efforts are intended to set course expectations and to help students internalize them. Involving students in creating a rating scale teaches the standards and skills necessary for self-evaluation. Practice in applying rubrics to their own and others' work helps students internalize the rubrics and better understand their meaning. Students don't have to wait for the teacher to evaluate their work but can give themselves frequent feedback; therefore, they are more likely to maintain their task involvement. In addition, when students have ownership in the standards, their intrinsic motivation to work toward those standards is increased.

Ms. Henry gives feedback on assignments, *teaches her students how to examine feedback*, and requires them to revise their projects based on feedback. She also gives students the option of revising their homework and exams based on feedback. She is careful to provide feedback on a few key aspects of the work so that students can focus their revisions and build understanding and skill over time. She monitors any common misconceptions shown in their homework and group work; she then plans lessons to help students develop deeper, more sophisticated understanding. If students need individual help, she is available before school, during lunch, and after school for study sessions, and she has individual conferences

Group Work Rating Scale				
Name: _____ **Date:** _____				
Circle the rating for each of your group work behaviors for today's class.				
1. Offered own ideas about problem	Usually	Occasionally	Rarely	Not done
2. Listened to others' ideas about problem	Usually	Occasionally	Rarely	Not done
3. Asked others for their ideas	When needed	Occasionally, when needed	Rarely, even when needed	Not done
4. Tried others' suggestions or explained why they might not work	Usually	Occasionally	Rarely	Not done
5. Made suggestions for improvements or changes	When needed	Occasionally, when needed	Rarely, even when needed	Not done
6. Did assigned group role	Usually	Occasionally	Rarely	Not done
7. Helped group stay on task	Usually	Occasionally	Rarely	Not done

Comments about the problems or the group: _____

_____

_____

_____

_____

_____

Figure 9–4
Jointly Developed Group Work Rating Scale for Ms. Henry's Class

with each student throughout the year. She teaches the students how to give each other feedback so they can help each other understand concepts better.

Ms. Henry is available for students to get help with their homework. That way all students have access to help as they begin working with a concept. She has students turn in first drafts of their projects for feedback before they complete them for a score. For complex projects, she breaks the project work into steps and has students turn in drafts of each step so they can make revisions along the way. Students can continue to make revisions as long as they are making progress and not depending on their peers or Ms. Henry to do the work for them.

In addition to observing students in groups, Ms. Henry has students use the class-developed rating scale to evaluate their own group work skills during group work. She discusses their progress as effective group members during individual conferences. She may encourage students to contribute more if they are shy or uncertain. She may encourage students to ask for others' ideas and contributions if they tend to dominate or take control.[3]

Ms. Henry uses the grade book to track students' scores over time to see whether they are improving and whether, based on the evidence she has collected, students have achieved the goals for the quarter. She hopes that all students will meet her standards.

In the events described above, there is no mention of grades—only standards, rubrics, and scores. Yet, even in a standards-based classroom, teachers generally must convert their students' scores to grades at the end of a term. When each term ends, Ms. Henry has three different judgments to make about students: (1) their understanding of mathematical concepts, (2) their ability to think mathematically and use procedural skills (reasoning and problem solving, communication, and connections across mathematical concepts), and (3) their group work skills. Although the conceptual focus will change during the year, the thinking, problem-solving, communication, connections, and group work skills will be taught all year. Her expectation is for students to be consistent in their use of effective group work skills by the end of the first semester and to be skilled at using mathematical processes by the end of the year. The following are the steps she uses to assign end-of-term grades:

1. Using the collection of scores (evidence) for conceptual understanding from homework, projects, and exams, she determines based on *all* of the evidence whether students fully understand the concepts (4.0), mostly understand the concepts (3.0), or still maintain some misconceptions (2.0).

2. The group work skills rating scale has seven items (see Figure 9–4), each of which is rated from 0 (not done) to 3 (usually or when needed) for a total group work skills score of 21 points. Ms. Henry averages the self-evaluations and her own observations to assign a score for each week. Each quarter, she sets a target score (performance standard) for students to achieve. By the end of the second quarter, she wants students to achieve a score of at least 15. Using the collection of scores from group work, she determines whether students have met and are maintaining the group work skills target (4.0), are close to meeting the target (3.0), or still need some work on their group work skills (2.0). She uses the last three scores for the quarter to assign the 4, 3, or 2 rating.

3. For mathematical problem solving and reasoning, mathematical communication, and connections, Ms. Henry uses rubrics that have five levels. Each quarter, she has a particular rubric score that she hopes all students will attain. The first quarter she wants them to achieve at least a level 3; the second quarter she wants them to achieve at least a level 4; the third and fourth quarters she wants them to achieve a level 5. Using the collection of scores from their homework, projects, and exams, she determines whether students have met or are maintaining these target scores (4.0), are very close to meeting the target scores (3.0), or still need to improve their use of these skills (2.0). For these mathematical processes (connections, communication, and problem solving and

---

[3] For more information on using small groups effectively, see Elizabeth Cohen's 1986 book, *Designing Groupwork: Strategies for the Heterogeneous Classroom*, New York: Teachers College Press.

reasoning), she bases her judgment on later work more than on the earlier work in the term.

Figure 9–5 shows the scores that seven of Ms. Henry's students earned on each assignment during the second quarter. There were 8 group work scores, 8 homework assignments, 2 exam scores, and 2 project scores. Homework (H1 to H8) receives two scores: one for conceptual understanding and one for mathematical connections. She has decided to include homework in the grade because she has been available for extra help if any students needed it; however, she gives homework a very small weight in the grade. Exams (E1 and E2) receive three scores: conceptual understanding, mathematical connections, and problem solving and reasoning. Projects (P1 and P2) receive three scores: conceptual understanding, problem solving and reasoning, and communication. Group work skills (G1 through G8) receive eight scores.

From the homework, exams, and projects, Ms. Henry has evidence about students' conceptual understanding during the term. From the homework and exams, she has evidence about students' ability to make connections among mathematical concepts. From students' exams and projects, Ms. Henry has evidence about students' mathematical problem-solving and reasoning skills. Finally, from students' projects, she has evidence about students' mathematical communication skills.

Figure 9–6 shows the final scores for the seven students in one of Ms. Henry's seventh-grade mathematics classes at the end of the second quarter. Her goals were that, by the end of the quarter, students earn a score of at least 15 on the group work skills rating scale, a level 4 on each of the mathematical process rubrics [Connections (Conn.), Problem Solving and Reasoning (PS/R), and Communication (Comm.)], and a level 4 on the major mathematical concepts (Conc.) that were taught that quarter (the relationships among geometric and measurement concepts and procedures). Ms. Henry assigned a final score based on whether each student met her end-of-quarter standards. For example, Ernalita, an ELL student, made steady progress toward the second quarter performance standard of 15 points for the group work skills score (see Figure 9–5). In the last three weeks of the quarter, Ernalita earned 13 points each week. Therefore, since she was "close to meeting" the group work skills target, she earned a 3.0 as a final score for group work skills.

Ernalita's average conceptual understanding score on homework was 4 (the target for the quarter), and her last four connections scores for homework were 3, 4, 4, and 5. Therefore, having met the performance standard on the rubric in both aspects of homework, Ernalita earned a 4.0 for conceptual understanding and a 4.0 for mathematical connections. For exams, Ernalita met the performance standard for conceptual understanding and made progress in mathematical connections and in problem solving and reasoning. Therefore, she earned a 4.0 for conceptual understanding and a 3.5 for both of the mathematical processes. A similar strategy was used to assign a final score for Ernalita's projects.

Although this may sound like a complicated way to summarize grades, Ms. Henry is able to handle the different scores because she clearly understands her learning targets and has thought clearly about how to combine different types of information into one summary grade. She also knows that, if any student wants to know how he is doing on different aspects of mathematics, she can give very specific feedback about areas of strength and areas that still need improvement.

When computing the final grades, Ms. Henry first computes a final score for each assignment type. For each exam and each project, the conceptual understanding score

Group Work Skills Scores / Homework Scores / Exam Scores / Project Scores

Student	G1	G2	G3	G4	G5	G6	G7	G8		H1	H2	H3	H4	H5	H6	H7	H8		E1	E2		P1	P2
Ernalita	9	8	13	12	13	13	13	13	Conc.	3	3	3	4	4	5	5	5	Conc.	4	5	Conc.	4	4
									Conn.	1	2	3	3	3	4	4	5	PS/R	3	4	PS/R	3	4
																					Comm.	4	5
Haven	8	9	15	14	13	14	15	15	Conc.	3	3	3	4	4	5	5	5	Conc.	3	4	Conc.	4	4
									Conn.	2	3	4	3	3	3	4	4	PS/R	3	4	PS/R	3	4
																					Comm.	3	5
Jared	9	8	12	16	14	15	16	16	Conc.	3	3	4	4	4	5	5	5	Conc.	4	5	Conc.	4	4
									Conn.	1	2	2	3	3	4	4	4	PS/R	3	4	PS/R	3	4
																					Comm.	4	5
Li	9	10	14	16	15	16	18	18	Conc.	2	3	4	4	4	5	5	5	Conc.	4	5	Conc.	4	4
									Conn.	1	2	2	3	4	5	5	5	PS/R	4	5	PS/R	4	4
																					Comm.	4	4
Leslie	5	7	8	8	10	12	14	13	Conc.	4	3	3	4	4	5	5	5	Conc.	4	5	Conc.	4	4
									Conn.	3	2	3	4	4	4	5	5	PS/R	4	4	PS/R	4	5
																					Comm.	4	5
Marc	9	10	15	13	19	18	18	19	Conc.	3	4	3	4	4	5	5	5	Conc.	4	5	Conc.	4	4
									Conn.	2	2	3	3	4	4	5	5	PS/R	4	5	PS/R	4	5
																					Comm.	4	4
Min	10	9	14	14	18	18	19	18	Conc.	3	3	3	4	4	5	5	5	Conc.	4	5	Conc.	4	5
									Conn.	2	1	2	3	4	5	5	5	PS/R	4	4	PS/R	4	5
																					Comm.	4	5

G1–G8 = Social Skills   H1–H8 = Homework   E1 and E2 = Exams   P1 and P2 = Projects
Conc. = Concepts   Conn. = Connections   Comm. = Communication   PS/R = Problem Solving & Reasoning

Figure 9–5
Mathematics Scores for Different Assessments in Ms. Henry's Class

Student	Group Work Skills (15%) Final Scores	Homework (10%) Learning Targets	Final Scores	Exams (35%) Learning Targets	Final Scores	Projects (40%) Learning Targets	Final Scores	Grade
Ernalita	3.0	Conceptual	4.0	Conceptual	4.0	Conceptual	4.0	3.86
		Connections	4.0	Connections	3.5	Problem Solving	3.5	
				Problem Solving	3.5	Communication	4.0	
Haven	4.0	Conceptual	4.0	Conceptual	4.0	Conceptual	4.0	3.86
		Connections	4.0	Connections	3.5	Problem Solving	3.5	
				Problem Solving	3.5	Communication	4.0	
Jared	4.0	Conceptual	4.0	Conceptual	4.0	Conceptual	4.0	3.91
		Connections	4.0	Connections	3.5	Problem Solving	3.5	
				Problem Solving	4.0	Communication	4.0	
Li	4.0	Conceptual	4.0	Conceptual	4.0	Conceptual	4.0	3.96
		Connections	4.0	Connections	4.0	Problem Solving	4.0	
				Problem Solving	3.5	Communication	4.0	
Leslie	3.0	Conceptual	4.0	Conceptual	4.0	Conceptual	4.0	3.85
		Connections	4.0	Connections	4.0	Problem Solving	4.0	
				Problem Solving	4.0	Communication	4.0	
Marc	4.0	Conceptual	4.0	Conceptual	4.0	Conceptual	4.0	3.96
		Connections	4.0	Connections	4.0	Problem Solving	4.0	
				Problem Solving	3.5	Communication	4.0	
Min	4.0	Conceptual	4.0	Conceptual	4.0	Conceptual	4.0	4.00
		Connections	4.0	Connections	4.0	Problem Solving	4.0	
				Problem Solving	4.0	Communication	4.0	

Figure 9–6
Final Scores and Grades in Ms. Henry's Class

comprises one-half of the grade and the average of the mathematical process scores comprise the other half of the grade. Like Mr. Williams, Ms. Henry then applies weights to the summary scores in each category before computing the final grade. Group work skills are 15% of the grade; projects are 40% of the grade; exams are 35% of the grade, and homework is 10% of the grade. Figure 9–6 has the summary score for each type of assessment and the final grades for each of the students after Ms. Henry applies the weights to the final scores for each assessment.

Leslie presented a special problem for Ms. Henry's system. Leslie has an IEP for a behavior disorder, and she has been working on her social skills. Group work was especially difficult for her at the beginning of the year. Ms. Henry met with Leslie, her parents, and the special education teacher responsible for managing Leslie's IEP. Together they decided that, because Leslie hoped to continue her education after high school graduation, she should be held to the same standard as the other students in the class. At the beginning of the first quarter, Leslie earned scores of 1 or 2 points on each component of group work skills. She made slow progress, but continued to work both in her math class and with the special education teacher on developing better group skills. A look at her group work skills scores for the second quarter shows that things started to improve early in the quarter, and that Leslie came close to meeting the standard by the end of the quarter. Because of this visible progress over time, both Ms. Henry and Leslie feel confident that she will meet standard the following quarter.

A standards-based grading method requires careful planning, clear targets for learning, and instruction that is focused on those targets. Given the central role of feedback in the instructional process, teachers must give fewer assignments and ensure that each requires students to think deeply about concepts and carefully practice their thinking and communication skills. If Ms. Henry gave too many assignments, if she planned assessments at the last minute, and if she was not clear about what she wanted her students to learn, she would have difficulty helping her students achieve the goals she has set. Her grade book has become not only a place to record scores on assignments, but a rich source of information about each student's progress toward the conceptual group work and mathematical process standards for her class.

Criticisms of Standards-Based Grading The criticisms of standards-based grading are similar to those for criterion-referenced grading. The most important concern about standards-based grading is that teachers will set the standards too low so that all students can achieve them. A secondary but related concern is that teachers will not know their subject matter well enough to be able to set reasonable standards or to identify the central concepts and skills for the subject area. These are legitimate concerns. Teachers who are successful teaching to standards do not work in isolation. They reach out to other teachers and to professional organizations to help them develop the expertise they need and to get external feedback on their expectations for students. The resources listed in Chapter 2 play critical roles in helping teachers develop reasonable standards and/or a deeper understanding of their subject areas.

Another criticism is that such a system does not acknowledge important differences among students. For example, in Ms. Henry's class, Li, Min, and Marc consistently earn higher scores than the other students listed. Is it fair to give them the same final grade as students who struggled more in the beginning? Again, this is an important question, and our answer is grounded in our fundamental beliefs about the purpose of schooling. If schools are intended to sort and identify the brightest students, then standards-based grading practices are not appropriate. However, if, as we believe, schools are intended to help all children be successful in life beyond school and to participate knowledgeably in a democratic society, then teaching to, assessing for, and reporting successful achievement of standards through a standards-based grading policy is appropriate for all students. Our experiences suggest that advanced students also benefit from the learning environment described here. With clear standards, advanced students tend to take work beyond expectations and to seek guidance in how to further improve their work. They also see that performance-based standards provide challenges even for them, especially when standards are based on deep understanding and high-quality performances rather than memorized facts, principles, and concepts.

The issue of individual differences is also a problem when students with disabilities or students who have limited English proficiency may have difficulty attaining the same high standards as their classmates. Here the teacher should work with the student, if appropriate, and with guardians and special educators to decide whether the same standards are appropriate, as in Leslie's case, or whether modifications of standards are necessary. We will discuss these choices later in the chapter.

DEVELOPMENTAL ISSUES: GRADING KINDERGARTEN AND PRIMARY-GRADE STUDENTS

Teachers who work with young children tend to think in ways consistent with standards-based grading. They are concerned with whether students learn the concepts and skills necessary to move on to the next grade level. These teachers, perhaps even more than those working with older students, are often interested in encouraging students' interest in school subjects and in their sense of competence and self-worth. The variety of report card systems (skill checklists, narrative reports, developmental timelines, as well as the familiar S+, S, S−, N scales) used to communicate students' progress to parents and students attests to the differences between the kinds of information relevant for younger students and the more traditionally academic progress reports created for older students.

Many teachers are uncomfortable with the thought of grading children who are so naturally variable in their developmental timelines. For example, it's perfectly normal for some children to learn to read in kindergarten, whereas others may not master the decoding along with comprehension until second or third grade. With this range of "normal" development, how can a teacher reasonably assign a summary grade? At grade card time, some teachers consider their memories of the students' work in a subject over the grading period. Based on this gestalt, they assign a 1 (excellent) or a 2 (satisfactory), an S (satisfactory) or S−, and consider their job done. In contrast, some teachers have very detailed lists of competencies that they expect students to learn and note which ones have been mastered at the time of each progress report. These teachers generally use individualized assessments to determine students' status in the week or two just prior to the time they must complete report cards and prepare for parent–teacher conferences.

Grades based on memory alone are difficult to justify to parents. They can be influenced by a student's general behavior, their work in subject areas other than the one for which the teacher is writing the report, their position in the class hierarchy,[4] or whether the teacher thinks they have support at home.

Parents and guardians of very young children depend on the information they receive from teachers to monitor their children's progress in schooling, to know when and what to work on at home, and to know whether their child needs special assistance. Finding out that a child has academic problems early can help parents and the teacher prevent later, more serious problems through early intervention. However, this can only happen if the information is presented to parents and other teachers in ways that are useful. Because of its focus on learning objectives and evidence, standards-based grading can be particularly useful in this regard.

As in standards-based grading for older children, kindergarten and primary teachers need clear learning goals and objectives, reliable and valid evidence of student achievement, and a way of summarizing this information appropriately in order to fairly report students' progress. Teachers can draw on many sources when developing learning goals and objectives and performance standards: district and state curriculum standards; national standards suggested by organizations such as the National Association for the Education of Young Children (NAEYC), National Council of Teachers of Mathematics (NCTM), and the National Council for the Social Studies (NCSS); and teachers and their colleagues' knowledge of the expectations for work in their own schools at the next higher grade level.

Once learning goals and objectives and performance standards have been determined, the teacher's task is to collect sufficient evidence of students' performance on these concepts and skills to make summary judgments. One of the best ways to do this is to keep collections of student work over time, as described in Chapter 10. Collecting samples of student work over the course of a reporting period provides the teacher with the evidence necessary to assess both students' growth and their current status in relation to your learning goals and objectives when filling out report cards. Teachers can supplement collections or portfolios with observational records of other kinds of assessments. Running records of children's reading proficiency, notes on which phonemes children can distinguish in which word position, checklists of social competencies, observational notes of math problem-solving strategies, and the like, can all inform summary judgments of growth and skill.[5]

Records and collections of student work are very useful in parent–teacher conferences. Most parents and guardians want to know three things about their children's work in school: What is my child learning? Is she learning as well as other students at this age? Is she getting along well with other children? They also want to know what kind of support to provide at home or, if they cannot provide support, what kinds of services they need to ask for

---

[4] One of our daughters received a C− in second-grade reading "because she was in the low reading group." When asked whether it meant that she was doing poorly relative to a standard, the class as a whole, or the reading group, the teacher replied, "I give *every* student in the low reading group a C− *so their parents will know where they are.* Your daughter is doing very well and is at the top of the low group." Needless to say, that is not what the grade communicated to her parents.

[5] A sixth-grade teacher Susan knew used to send these collections home along with the report cards. Parents could view the work and get concrete information about where students' strengths and weaknesses lay, and how those related to the grades received. Collections were signed by the parent and sent back to the teacher, letting her know parents had had an opportunity to inspect their children's work.

when their students are in extended day programs or with grandparents or babysitters. Having the evidence at hand makes explaining children's progress to parents and guardians much easier.

To answer the first three questions, teachers have to be very clear about what they expect students to learn—both academically and socially. With those clear targets laid out, teachers can select representative pieces of work and observational records over time to show parents and guardians whether the child is meeting standards and how their child's knowledge and skills have improved over time. The following is an excerpt from a parent–teacher conference Ms. Barlow, a second-grade teacher, had with Miranda's grandmother at the November parent–teacher conferences:

> "By the middle of second grade," Ms. Barlow explains, "we hope that all students can read a book at their reading level independently and answer comprehension questions about plot and character. Miranda is able to do this now when she reads books at this level (shows sample books). My goal for her reading is to get her reading somewhat harder books, like these (shows books), with similar comprehension."
>
> Miranda's grandmother looks a little surprised. "At home she reads harder books than these! Last week she finished *Little House on the Prairie,* and we checked out the next book in the series."
>
> "Hmm! If that's the case, maybe we should push her a little harder at school," replies Ms. Barlow. "I'll have her read a little bit from *Little House on the Prairie* to me, and then ask her to tell me about the plot and characters. Then we may be able to set some more ambitious goals for her reading. Maybe we can do some work around the 'Little House' series, since she seems interested in it."
>
> Ms. Barlow paused and then said, "Since Miranda moved here in September, she's had some difficulty getting into group activities. There are other children in the class who like these books. Maybe I can set up a book club group for these children."

By showing Miranda's grandmother concrete evidence regarding her reading level, she was able to learn something about Miranda she didn't know, but that would inform her later instruction. Getting an S in reading on her report card and an S− in citizenship would not have resulted in such an informative discussion.

FEEDBACK THROUGH SUMMARY GRADES

We have discussed the motivational consequences of feedback in many places in this book. For some students, summary grades provide meaningful feedback. One of Thomas and Oldfather's (1997) student co-researchers started at a graded elementary school and transferred to the nongraded school Willow. He stated:

> I would have liked to have grades at Willow because it's just very, very reassuring to get grades. And know what you're doing, rather than not really knowing whether you're ahead of or below everybody else. (p. 119)

This quote points out the power of grades to seep into a student's identity. Another seventh-grader in Thomas and Oldfather's research stated it this way:

> It's like, "okay, that grade, that's me. I am the grade. I did that. That's my grade. That's me." (p. 119)

For other students, grades are not at all useful as feedback. Sally, an 11th-grader, compares school to society. In her view, it's just

> . . . how you sell yourself out to get good grades. . . . School is just work and control. Like I said before, you can learn nothing and get an A and learn everything and get an F. (p. 120)

The motivational consequences of grades depend on their meaning to the students who receive them. Sally had clearly decided that grades did not reflect how much she had learned in a class; they were just a means of external control. On the other hand, for the student who missed having grades at Willow, grades were information that he could use in an ego-involved way to measure his achievement against the achievement of others. Of the three models we have presented, standards-based grading offers the most scope for providing meaningful feedback on a student's strengths and weaknesses. It is probably not as informative as careful narrative evaluations, but in situations where there is not sufficient time to produce narrative reports for every student, standards-based grading can provide useful information about student learning.

Standards-based feedback can focus on the learning as the most important aspect of student work, supporting and promoting task involvement. Combined with grading policies that allow students to differ in how they reach those standards (different work that requires demonstration of the same standards, more or less time, or additional instruction), every student in a class can be encouraged to improve.

As we argue in this chapter and elsewhere, the knowledge and skills that teachers teach and assess are statements of values. Students look to grading policies to see those values and, if the policy is clear and detailed, students can use it to plan their efforts wisely. Grading policies can also set the stage for task involvement, ego involvement, or extrinsic involvement, or some combination. They can also lead to student withdrawal of effort, if grades are seen as irrelevant or worse, or if good grades seem unattainable. In some cases, ways of dealing with late or missing work can lead students to sacrifice learning in order to earn points toward a grade.

Grading policies that stress learning and progress toward clear standards—coupled with encouraging written and oral feedback on work that points out both strengths and weaknesses, and suggests strategies for improvement—support student task involvement. Policies that punish students for learning more slowly or differently, or for not being sufficiently responsible, can quickly lead to disinterest and devaluing of the grade, the class, and the subject area.

CREATING A GRADING POLICY

Grading policies are carefully stated plans for how you will combine assessment information to make grading decisions. Many grading policies you will see in the schools are one-page letters to students that tell them behavioral expectations and how different parts of their work will be weighted to form a grade. We believe that grading policies can also serve as tools of communication among students, parents or guardians, and teachers. Because grades are usually important to students, and often used by students to judge the degree to which they can trust teachers, students and their parents or guardians are more likely to read grading policies than other documents. Therefore, we encourage teachers to take advantage of the importance of grades to communicate your expectations. The tone of a grading policy also communicates whether the teacher will be a dictator, a director, a coach, or a partner in the learning process.

There are six elements of a grading policy that serves as a way for teachers to communicate their goals and expectations to students and parents or guardians: (1) an introductory statement of your grading philosophy or grading model, (2) a description of the major types of work students are expected to do, (3) information about how work will be evaluated, (4) how much weight each type of work will contribute to the grade, (5) clear guidelines for how absences, late work, and extended illness will be handled, and (6) information about how scores on different work are to be combined into a grade. Each element can be used to communicate about a class and to set expectations. Figure 9–7 is an example of a two-page grading policy for Mr. Warren's ninth-grade humanities class.

Introductory Statement

As can be seen in Figure 9–7, the introduction can set the stage for the relationship between teacher and students; it can give an overview of the expectations teachers have for their students and communicate other important ideas the teacher wants to share. Mr. Warren states up front that he has expectations and that he wants all students to meet those expectations. He states that he wants the work in the class to be real. He makes it clear that students are to improve their work based on feedback. Hence, he has set himself up as a coach with expectations that students achieve the course goals.

Types of Work

Giving a brief overview of the types of work that go into a final grade can help students *begin* to understand the expectations for a class or teacher. Throughout their years of school, students must learn to adjust to the different demands of different teachers. Most people know that, even in courses with the same names at the same grade level, experiences can be very different. Too often in the daily events of a school year, students know little about what the expectations are, what work counts and what doesn't, and how different content and activities are linked. A brief description of the types of work that will be done can help students organize their thinking about what they will be expected to do. Teachers can use these brief descriptions to give a rationale for the work and to set initial expectations.

Mr. Warren's grading policy lists five types of work: class contributions, essays, projects, presentations, and a portfolio. He briefly describes each type of work, tells why it is important, and, where possible, gives some criteria for the work. Needless to say, to create this part of a grading policy, teachers need to think ahead about what matters, what they want students to accomplish, and what their general expectations are for each type of work. We have found that some teachers fear that such descriptions will limit their ability to "go with the flow." Yet, Mr. Warren's descriptions are general enough that he can move in any direction from them. A good grading policy should allow for this kind of flexibility while still helping students and teachers keep their eyes on the overall purposes of the class.

How Student Work Will Be Evaluated

Criteria for evaluation can be given as general guidelines, or specific criteria can be included within descriptions of the types of work. We prefer to include the criteria with the descriptions, because we find that expectations differ from one type of work to another. A careful examination of Mr. Warren's criteria shows that he has thought ahead about his general expectations for each type of work. He is giving students and their parents or guardians clear

HUMANITIES GRADE 9

Grading Policy

This is a class about the humanities and about the real world. I want everyone in this class to succeed; therefore, I will be grading you based on how well you achieve the goals of the class. I will make certain that you know all expectations before you do any assignment so you can meet course and assignment expectations. *You are expected to improve your work using feedback from me and from other students before any grades are assigned.*

Quarter grades will be based on several types of work:		Grading Scale
Contributions to the class	15% of grade	A = 90–100%
Essays	25% of grade	B = 80–89%
Presentations and demonstrations	20% of grade	C = 70–79%
Projects	25% of grade	D = 60–69%
Portfolio self evaluation	15% of grade	F = 0–59%

Contributions to the class (15%)

Sharing ideas and working with others to develop group products are essential skills for adults. Most of you already know a lot about what makes an enjoyable class or group; however, there is always more to learn. In the first week of school we will create a list of behaviors that set expectations for your contributions in class. When you are in class, you will assess yourselves and I will observe you to help you make progress in developing your skills. Contributions are assessed based on *individual behaviors* and I will be looking at your improvement over time. A checklist for contributions might look like this:

- ☐ Offered ideas for group projects
- ☐ Listened to others' ideas
- ☐ Gave useful feedback
- ☐ Did own share of work
- ☐ Was prepared for group work (did the readings, brought materials)

Essays (25%)

You will learn how to write like people who are professionals in the social sciences and the humanities. Good writing skills can help you throughout your life. So, even though you will be learning how to write as a social scientist or literary critic, the skills you learn will apply to many other kinds of writing. Two scores will be assigned to each essay: one for content and one for writing skill. Content expectations will vary for each essay. Scoring rules for writing skills will be based on the following criteria:

- ☐ Logical/sequential organization
- ☐ Effective use of language, sentence structures, and word choices
- ☐ Effective use of grammar and other language conventions

You will *revise* all essays based on feedback before turning them in for final scores.

Presentations and demonstrations (20%)

Clear verbal communication is an essential part of effective job performance in just about every field. For this class, you may do group presentations or individual presentations; however, assessment of presentation skills will be based on your individual performance. I will assess both content and presentation skills. You will practice presentations and receive feedback before any formal presentations are given a score. My expectations are:

Figure 9–7
Mr. Warren's Grading Policy

Content Criteria:	Presentation Criteria:
☐ Takes a clear position on an issue ☐ Supports position with evidence and examples ☐ Links ideas to readings or research ☐ Uses visual or other support to enhance ideas presented	☐ Makes eye contact with audience ☐ Speaking is clear and at a reasonable pace ☐ Volume is appropriate for audience and context ☐ Uses organizational strategy that is effective for purpose ☐ Uses organizational strategy that is effective for purpose

Projects (25%)

Projects will be similar to the work of people in the social sciences and the humanities. Through the projects you will get a chance to use your knowledge and skills in authentic ways. Since most real work is complex and requires many different skills, you will have opportunities to work through big projects in stages and get feedback along the way so you can improve the final work. Scoring rules for projects will vary and will be distributed at the time the project is assigned.

Portfolio (15%)

Reflective adults are more likely to use good judgment in their lives. At the end of every quarter, you will select four performances from the class that you think best show your knowledge and skill. You will write a self-evaluation about what you have learned, how the contents of the portfolio show your accomplishments, and what goals you have set for yourself for the next term. The portfolio will be assessed based on the following criteria:

☐ Thoughtful evaluation of own work in relation to the class goals
☐ Clear connections between the work in the portfolio and your self-evaluation
☐ Setting appropriate goals for next term based on work and self-evaluation

Late work and absences

You may turn in work one day late without penalty. If you will be more than one day late, we will set up a schedule for completion of the work. Late work beyond one day will receive a score that is 10% lower than the score earned. If lateness becomes a habit, I will send a notice home to your parents/guardians. You will have one week to make up missed work during brief absences. For extended absences, an individual contract will be developed and signed by both parents/guardians and the student. All work must be completed one week before the end of the quarter to be considered in the quarter grade. I need time to look at your work and give you the feedback you deserve.

Grade Summary

Once all of your assignments have been scored, I will summarize a score for each type of work. Then, using the weights for each type of work, I will compute your overall grade. The table below shows an example of a grade summary.

Type of work	Summary Score	Weight	Weighted Score (summary score times weight)
Class contributions	.89	15%	$.89 \times 15\% = 13.35\%$
Essays	.95	25%	$.95 \times 25\% = 23.75\%$
Presentations	.92	20%	$.92 \times 20\% = 18.40\%$
Projects	.96	25%	$.96 \times 25\% = 24.00\%$
Portfolio	.85	15%	$.85 \times 15\% = 12.75\%$
		Total	$92.25\% = A$

Figure 9–7 *(continued)*

messages about what students are expected to learn and do. For class contributions, he gives examples of expected behaviors. For essays, he indicates the expectations that will be consistent across all assignments and that there will be unique content expectations for each assignment. For presentations, he gives all expectations for presentation skills. For projects, he indicates that each assignment will have different expectations but that students will have all expectations when the project is assigned. He has set the stage for his class, suggesting that the basis for grades will be public and consistent with the purpose of the work.

Weighing the Evidence

Whether an elementary teacher giving a reading grade or a secondary teacher giving a language arts grade, all teachers face this question: "How do I take the collection of evidence for each of my students and make a fair summary decision that is also consistent with what I have said is important for students to learn?" Determining weights for different types of work is one of the most difficult tasks in the grading process. To assign weights, you will have to address seven aspects of grading: (1) the importance of a given category, (2) how much instructional time you will give to a certain category, (3) how much control you have over students' achievement in a given category, (4) the sufficiency of evidence in a given category, (5) your grading philosophy, (6) how to address effort and citizenship, and (7) your gut feelings about whether the final grades you assign to all of your students are fair and truly represent students' level of accomplishment when you finish summarizing.

Importance of the Work   The importance of a given type of work comes down to teacher values and the nature of the work. Although many would advise teachers to avoid expressing their own values in teaching, such a charge is impossible to accomplish. Each time you write a test item, create an assignment, or focus a lesson, you are expressing a value. Teachers may be guided by state or district curriculum standards in terms of what they teach, but the individual teacher determines the amount of weight given to each assignment or curriculum standard. Hence, while some teachers may place greater weight on the development of artistic techniques or facility with addition and subtraction facts, other teachers may place greater weight on artistic compositions or math problem solving. Rather than avoid this inherent responsibility, teachers owe it to students and their parents or guardians to make these values public. If the relative importance teachers place on different learning targets is not what parents or guardians value, teachers can open the door for dialogue and possible compromise. It is even possible for students and teachers to work together to determine the relative weights of different types of work, based on the needs of the students in a certain class.

Weighting also depends on how well the work is likely to provide good evidence about students' achievement. Assessment experts generally recommend that homework and work done for practice or preparation be omitted from the grade because this type of work shows developing skills and knowledge rather than expertise. On the other hand, teachers (especially teachers of secondary students) claim that students will not complete work unless there is a score attached. Whether teachers include homework, in-class practice work, or work done for preparation depends on two things: (1) how likely it is that students can do the work on their own and (2) whether the work is truly for practice or is part of a larger project or task.

Work done for practice could be omitted from the grade because later work will probably reflect any lack of practice. Early in the school year, teachers can intentionally give students the opportunity to discover the role of practice by setting up and *debriefing* an experience wherein students must have done the practice work to be successful on some later task. If teachers do this when they are creating the classroom expectations, they teach directly to the intrinsic worth of practice work.[6] Such an activity may lead students to complete the practice work for its own sake rather than to accumulate points for an external reward—the grade. Not every student needs the same amount of practice to learn a concept or skill. Helping students decide how much practice is necessary allows for individual differences, as well as helping them learn how to make good decisions about their education. A key element of an activity designed to teach the value of practice would be to debrief it, eliciting from students the connection between the practice work and the later work. A focused experience like this is especially important when teachers are helping students to gain control over their own success in school.

Some students with disabilities or who have limited English proficiency need additional time to complete their homework and may even need extra practice with concepts and skills. This can make it difficult for students to be successful because the demands are greater, unless accommodations can be made to meet their specific needs. Here again, working with the special education teacher assigned to manage the student's IEP or the ESL/bilingual specialist, the parents or guardians, and the student, a reasonable strategy can be devised, tried, and adjusted as necessary. A student who has difficulty reading and writing, but who is competent in mathematics, might be expected to do fewer mathematics exercises for homework, but to explain her strategies for solving these problems to the teacher or peers. In this way, the student has more time for the reading and writing homework.

In contrast to practice work, some individual work may be necessary to prepare for a later activity (for example, research that should be done before group work can proceed). In this case, it may be entirely appropriate to include an assessment of this work in an overall grade since it has to do with "Did own share of work" and "Was prepared for group work" (see Ms. Henry's criteria for group work and Mr. Warren's criteria for contributions to class). If students do not have a place to work outside of school or do not have access to resources outside of school, teachers must provide the workspace, the time for preparation, and the resources needed to ensure that *all* students can do the individual work before including it as a significant percentage of the grade. Again, the length of time some students need to complete preparation work may be greater than for many of their peers. Providing extra time to work on these assignments and possibly additional individual assistance can help students with special needs be more successful.

In contrast to work done for practice or preparation, there is other work that is clearly more important and should receive more weight. Most teachers consider formal performance-based assessments, examinations, substantive projects, research papers, and other major assignments as the most important. If well developed, these assignments are also most likely to demonstrate students' achievement of the learning targets set by the teacher. Therefore, teachers must look at each type of work and determine its value in providing evidence about students' learning. Work that provides strong evidence should be weighted more than work that provides weak evidence.

---

[6] Unfortunately, as students move through their years of schooling, they may learn that there is no relationship between homework and success in a class. An intentional exercise to teach the value of practice work in *your* class may be essential to the success of your teaching experience.

Amount of Instructional Time   Related to this issue of importance is the amount of in-structional time spent on a given category of work. Suppose a teacher has focused on sci-entific vocabulary, science concepts, and scientific investigation skills as the major goals for science. Suppose further that vocabulary is assessed through end-of-week tests, scientific concepts are assessed through the connections students make as they draw conclusions in their lab reports, and investigation skills are assessed through observational assessments and assessments of the lab reports. If the majority of instructional time is spent on experimen-tation and examination of concepts, but little instructional time is spent examining and working with the vocabulary words, the vocabulary test scores should have less weight than the other assessments. Needless to say, teachers generally give more instructional time to those learning goals they value the most.

Teacher Control Over Student Achievement   Most experienced teachers recognize that, re-gardless of the amount of work they put into the students' educational experiences, teachers have limited control over what students learn. On the other hand, teachers have more control over what students accomplish in class than they do over work done outside of class. Students' performances on homework often depend on the amount of external help students receive. Although some parents and guardians help students with their homework, other parents and guardians are not able to give extra help because of work schedules, language barriers, or other barriers. In addition, some students come into a class with more background knowledge and skill in a given area than teachers provide through instructional experiences. Teachers must consider whether students' achievement in a given category of work is due to their prior knowledge and skill or home tutoring, or due to instructional experiences in the classroom. Teachers must ask themselves, "Have *all* students been given sufficient opportunity to learn the material?" Teachers must take care not to give undue weight to that which students bring to a class or to work for which students are likely to get more or less help from home.

Sufficiency of Evidence   One question that must be answered prior to giving weights is whether the amount of evidence you will have at the time of grading is sufficient to make a summary decision about any individual student. Types of work with more evidence should receive more weight than types of work with scanty evidence. The concept of reliability was introduced in Chapter 1 and revisited in chapters about specific kinds of assessment tools. In the chapters on performance-based assessment, the focus was on the reliability of teach-ers' assessments of individual pieces of student work. In the context of grading, reliability means *sufficiency*. At the time grades are figured and entered into the students' permanent records, you need to make certain that you have *sufficient* evidence to make a summary statement about any one student. There are generally two ways to obtain sufficient evidence: (1) multiple assignments and (2) tracking the progress of a few important works over time.

   If you have several pieces of work in one category (say, for example, several still-life drawings, several freehand sketches, or several exercises with perspective for a visual art class; several quizzes or several lab writeups for a science class), you can get a sense of a stu-dent's overall accomplishment in that category. On the other hand, if students have worked for an entire term on one or two prepared accomplishments or exit performances (say an oil painting or sculpture for an art class including initial sketches and various stages of the work or a science research paper or fully implemented scientific investigation including background research, investigation design, implementation, results, and a written scientific paper), and you have seen various stages of the work, a single work may be sufficient for making a summary judgment in a category. The key in this latter situation is for the teacher to have *seen and assessed* various stages of the work for relevant criteria (see Chapter 4) so that the summary judgment isn't based on the final observation alone.

Grading Philosophy   The grading philosophy can guide the weighting and summarizing process. Within each weighted category, teachers generally include several assessments. The most common strategy is to compute an average score for each category of work, apply some predetermined weight to that category, and then add the weighted category scores together. This strategy is generally used for norm-referenced and criterion-referenced grading. A second strategy is to give more weight to later work than to earlier work—assuming that students' improvement is a result of instruction and practice with concepts and skills.

Some teachers may use both strategies, depending on the type of work. For work that is unique and not repeated (say, vocabulary tests or tests over particular sets of mathematics concepts), averaging across assessments may be an appropriate strategy because the content assessed differs for each test. However, for knowledge and skill that develops over time (say, story writing, scientific inquiry, mathematical problem solving, social science essay writing, group work skills, etc.), teachers may want to give more weight to later work than to earlier work.

Effort and Citizenship   Many assessment specialists say that effort and citizenship should not be included in grades. Effort grades are particularly problematic, for two main reasons. First, it is nearly impossible to assess student effort reliably and validly. Effort can sometimes be inferred from obvious action, yet only in gross terms. For example, if students go well beyond an assignment, a teacher can infer effort. The teacher still doesn't know, however, whether the effort required to do this extra work was more or less than the effort required for other students to do the original assignment. Second, because students come to school with a range of prior knowledge and ability, some students will need to apply almost no effort to reach a standard, whereas others need to work extremely hard. Grading effort does not fit with standards-based grading wherein teachers are not sorting students by aptitude.

Yet, research on the predictive power of grades and SAT scores for college success suggests that grades are better predictors of college success than SAT scores. The reasons for this are obvious. Some of the skills that lead to success in school (study skills, attentiveness, effort, good citizenship) are also skills that lead to success in college and life beyond school. We believe that, if teachers create public criteria related to citizenship and teach students how to be good citizens in the classroom community, then assessment of this aspect of achievement can be fairly included in grades. On the other hand, we believe that effort will naturally influence students' overall grade. The trick is to ensure that students *see* the connections between effort and success.

Mr. Warren has indicated that students are expected to use feedback to revise their work before he will assign a grade. Focused feedback can help students improve their knowledge and skills so that higher scores result. Earlier in this chapter, we discussed the idea of intentionally giving students experiences where success depends on practice and then debriefing that experience. Both of these kinds of teacher strategies can help students see the relationship between effort and success. Effort can then become a natural part of the assessment process, rather than an extra grade or score. If students revise their work thoughtfully, their efforts will pay off in higher scores.

Citizenship can also be taught and assessed in a systematic way. In the chapter on informal assessment (Chapter 5) we introduced the idea of assessment of students as they work in groups or in class as a whole. Some of that assessment may be of students' conceptual understanding that is not shown in their paper-and-pencil performances. Other aspects of the assessment may be related to their contributions in class and in their groups. As with effort, you cannot assume that students know how to be good citizens. Statements like "do unto others . . . " may be too vague for students to know what to do. This is especially true of some recent immigrants who bring different cultural understandings to group work. Students with some disabilities may not have mastered appropriate group work skills because they have difficulty reading social cues or controlling their emotions. In Ms. Henry's class, Leslie needed time, scaffolding from the teacher, and extra work outside of class to develop better group work skills.

Teachers can develop lessons that focus on how to work effectively in groups, distribute the work, assign roles, stay on task, listen to others, and contribute effectively to group efforts, all of which are critical life skills. Teachers can work with students to debrief these lessons and develop observational checklists that students use to monitor their own progress in citizenship skills. Teachers can meet with students to give them feedback about their progress in citizenship skills. If these steps are taken thoughtfully and consistently, then teachers can fairly include summary assessments of students' citizenship skills learned through the course of the term in grading summaries. Once teachers are confident that they are providing sufficient instruction and guidance, and are fairly assessing citizenship and effort, these elements of performance carry a weight in the overall grade, either directly, when a percent of the grade is given to group work and citizenship skills, or indirectly, when students make an effort to revise and resubmit work to improve their performance.

Gut Feelings   The final issue in weighting for grade summaries has to do with a gut feeling about whether the grades earned by students truly represent the quality of their work and your experience with your students. One task we often assign to our preservice teachers is to invent a grading summary for an imaginary student. Our students can take any one of the students they know in the field and predict what that student's scores will be on a variety of assignments. Then, applying a set of tentative weights, they do a grade summary for their imaginary student. They compare the summary grade with the individual scores to see if the results "feel right." Weights can then be adjusted to ensure that the various kinds of work get appropriate weights.

It is critical that such exploratory weighting happens *before* a class starts and not at the time you assign grades.[7] Use of a grading software or a spread sheet program will allow you to easily test different weights for several different imaginary students with different combinations of scores. The goal is to find the weights that you feel are most appropriate—and then to stick with the weights, even if the resulting student grades in a given term aren't consistent with your expectations. We have found that it may take more than one year's experience with a subject or course to find the weights that best reflect the importance and value you want to place on students' work. The most critical idea is that, even if we are not happy with the results, we live with our current weights until the next grading period, whereupon we adjust the weights and inform our next group of students of the new weights.

As you can see, assigning weights to different sources of evidence is a balancing act. You must weigh your values, your level of control, the importance of the work, and your sense

---

[7] One of the most unethical grading practices known to occur is when teachers adjust weights so that students they like get higher grades than students they don't like. Sadly, this does happen.

of whether the quality of the work develops over time. You must decide whether you will have sufficient evidence to make a summary decision in a given category. You must be good professional judges of the various factors likely to affect grades. Some teachers want to avoid the processes we have described here; however, avoiding the decision-making process is likely to lead to capricious grading practices and unfair assessments of your students.

Throughout the previous text on weighting different sources of evidence, much of what we have discussed is fairly straightforward. There are some judgments to be made, but the task is one that beginning teachers can do. The quality of the judgments is likely to improve over time as teachers become clearer about their instruction and their values.

Absences, Illnesses, and Late Work

When planning for grades, one issue teachers have to consider is what to do when students don't turn assignments in on time. Late work is a problem for teachers no matter what causes it. Illnesses are a very real problem in schools. When a flu virus hits a school, children cycle in and out of the classroom with regularity. A particularly virulent virus can lead to absences for days or even weeks. If students come back to school too soon, this leads to more widespread infections. Yet, absences due to illness can disrupt the normal flow of schooling. For example, if the daily lesson plans include a group presentation and one member of a group is ill, the presentation may be delayed. If students fall behind because of illnesses or absences, when they return, they must catch up on previously missed work while completing current assignments. This doubly punishes students: first with illness and then with a landslide of missed work. Teachers need to think ahead about these potential disruptions and build into their grading policies fair ways to deal with them.

In a standards-based classroom, the *amount* of work is not the central purpose of schooling. Teachers are teaching to desired outcomes. Therefore, policies must be developed that focus on the desired outcomes rather than the number of completed assignments. Teachers also need contingencies for unexpected disruptions in the routine. For example, if a student is ill on the day of his group's presentation and the presentation cannot be rescheduled, the student might be required to write a paper over the content of the presentation, or give his part of the presentation to the teacher outside of class. If a student misses several days due to an illness, the teacher should find alternate ways for her to develop the knowledge and/or skills that were the focus of the missed experiences. Too often, assignments take on a life of their own—giving students the idea that completion rather than competency is the goal of an assignment. Identifying appropriate alternatives in the case of illness or absences requires a clear focus on the targets of instruction.

Late work, due to illness or any other factor, can also disrupt the flow of schooling. Teachers may expect students to have certain work finished before they can move on to the next stage in a process. Teachers may find themselves reading student work that is days or even weeks out of sync with the current focus of the class. Finally, teachers may find themselves reading piles of late work just before the end of a grading period as students scramble to finish everything before grades are due. It is worth noting that what makes each of these delays a problem has more to do with the teacher's agenda than with the students' needs.

There are as many reasons for late or missing work as there are students in a classroom. Students may lack motivation for a particular assignment; they may lack the skills needed to complete a particular task; they may be overwhelmed with other assignments (especially in middle school and beyond as they must navigate the demands of multiple teachers); they may have personal issues that interfere with completing homework assignments. Some teachers consider late work an indication of poor attitudes or lack of effort. Teachers may use the grading process as a way to punish students for late work. Such a response is limiting in two critical ways: it places the focus on completion rather than achievement and is likely to block communication between students and their teachers. Again, a clear focus on the end goals of instruction can help teachers deal with issues of late work.

Mr. Warren has taken a moderate approach to absences and late work. He makes it clear that he expects students to complete assignments, yet he indicates that he is willing to set up a separate contractual arrangement if there are extended absences. He treats the issue of late work in a balanced manner. He gives students a one-day grace period but then notes that there will be a penalty for work that is later. He notes that chronic lateness will result in a contact with parents. Finally, he sets a deadline for all work to be turned in one week prior to the end of any grading period so that he has sufficient time to look at it. His policy is respectful of students and of himself.

Grade Summary

By a certain age, probably beginning in the intermediate grades, students need to know how their work will be summarized into a single score or grade for the term. Providing an example of a grade summary in the grading policy will help to make the summary process more public. Unfortunately, when grading is an invisible process, students soon come to believe that it is an unfair one. Mr. Warren has included a table at the end of the grading policy that shows how he will combine scores from different types of assignments into one grade.

Summarizing Grades

Although it may seem obvious that a single letter grade or number is inadequate to communicate the fullness of students' accomplishments, the conventions of schooling usually demand that teachers make one summary judgment about each student using a collection of evidence. At the elementary level, teachers may be able to give different judgments for reading, writing, spelling, and vocabulary, but at the secondary level, teachers must give summary grades for the language arts as a whole. Some elementary progress reports separate mathematics concepts from communication and problem solving; however, secondary grade cards generally require a single summary grade for all of mathematics. Other subjects (physical education, social studies, sciences, arts, music) generally require a single grade or evaluation at all levels.

Before you can make a summary decision about students, you have three steps to take. First, you need to convert all work into a *common scale*. Second, you have to apply *weights* to the scores for different types of work. Third, you need to summarize the weighted scores into a total score for the overall grade. Before assigning grades, you need to decide how you will handle specific issues such as late work, missing work, revisions and retakes, and what to do in the case of students who are on the borderline (for example, Mr. Williams's decision to move Robin and Gabriel's borderline grades to the next level because of special circumstances). You also must decide how you are going to treat students with special needs.

Common Scale The number of possible points may differ from one assignment to another. You may use a five-level rubric for one writing assignment and 100 points for an end-of-unit exam. Adding these points together would make the writing assignment worth less than

$1/20^{th}$ of the overall number of points. Some teachers simply multiply scores for an assignment times some number to make different work equivalent in overall value. For example, a teacher might multiply the rubric score on the writing assignment times 20 to make it worth the same value as the 100-point test. Other teachers convert scores on assignments to some common scale. For example, Mr. Warren has converted scores to decimal values by dividing the students' scores by the number of points possible to obtain a decimal score for each type of assignment. In other words, each summary score tells the fraction of the total points possible a student earned in each category.

The disadvantage to using total points in grading summaries is that you have to know ahead of time the exact number of assignments and the number of points for each assignment so you can fairly weight different assignments by giving them the number of points necessary to balance their worth with that of other assignments. This may not always be possible. Such a strategy means that it is difficult to make changes in assignments (e.g., adding points, subtracting points, eliminating assignments because of lack of time, adding a new assignment because of a teachable moment).

Therefore, it is most effective to convert scores to a common scale. Teachers typically use three common scales to summarize grades: decimal scales (indicating the decimal fraction of the points earned in each category from 0.0 to 1.00), percent scales (indicating the percentage of points earned in each category from 0% to 100%), and grade point scales (indicating the score in a given category on a 0.0 to 4.0 scale). Each of these is fairly easy to compute.

To compute the decimal scale, one simply divides the total number of points earned by the total number of points possible. This gives the decimal fraction of the total number of points possible that were earned by the student. This can be done for each assignment, making it easy to combine scores across assignments. The percent scale takes the decimal values one step further. After obtaining a decimal value (which may be difficult for students to understand), the value is multiplied times 100 to get a percentage of points earned. Again, this can be done for each assignment and then combined across assignments, regardless of the original number of points in each assignment. The grade point scale is simply the decimal value multiplied times 4.0, which can be done assignment by assignment before summarizing for a grade. Because young children are not familiar with the idea of a grade point, it makes more sense to use the percent scale for younger students.

The advantage to using decimal values, percent values, or grade point values, rather than total points in grading summaries, is that you can be more flexible in the teaching process. For example, sometimes Catherine finds that circumstances have made it impossible for students to do a planned assignment. She simply drops that assignment and computes the grade without it because she converts all scores to a common scale before summarizing.

Regardless of the method of converting scores to a common scale, teachers must examine the types of scores available. A five-level rubric will not convert directly to any common scale—even if the scores earned by students are multiplied by 20 to equal 100 points. Figure 9–8 gives two five-level rubrics: one for the content of a position paper and one for the writing conventions for the position paper. The description of each level on the rubrics indicates the quality of work associated with the score. A level 5 for the content rubric is an outstanding level of performance indicated by terms such as "accurate, complex understanding of issue" and "thoroughly supports arguments." A level 4 is a very good level of performance indicated by terms such as "accurate, complex understanding of issue" even though the student "needs more support for arguments *or* conclusion." Clearly level 4 work is very good work because weaknesses in support do not apply to both arguments *and* con-

Performance Criteria for Content

- Presents two or more perspectives on issue
- Supports perspectives with arguments and evidence
- Draws own conclusion and supports conclusion with examples and evidence

Scoring Rule:

Points	Descriptors	Computed %
5	Thoughtful; shows accurate, complex understanding of issue; thoroughly supports arguments and conclusion	100%
4	Shows accurate, complex understanding of issue; needs more support for arguments or conclusion	80%
3	Shows accurate, but fairly simple understanding of issue; needs stronger arguments or a stronger conclusion	60%
2	Shows some understanding of issue; lacks adequate arguments, support, or conclusion	40%
1	Shows weak understanding of issue; little or no support given	20%

Performance Criteria for Writing Conventions

- Clearly organized (introduction, body, conclusion)
- Appropriate transitions between ideas
- Correct writing conventions (grammar, punctuation, spelling, paragraph structure)

Scoring Rule:

Points	Descriptors	Computed %
5	Complete; meets all criteria; excellent quality	100%
4	Complete; meets important criteria; superior quality	80%
3	Complete or mostly complete; meets many important criteria and most lesser criteria; expected quality	60%
2	Partially complete; meets some important and lesser criteria; minimal quality	40%
1	Attempted; meets few important criteria and lesser criteria; poor quality	20%

Figure 9–8
Problems With Converting Rubrics to Percent Scores: Example Rubrics for a Position Paper

clusion. Finally, a level 3 performance is a decent level of performance indicated by terms such as "accurate, but fairly simple understanding of issue"; however, the student "needs stronger arguments *or* a stronger conclusion." A glance at the percent scores in the third column of each rubric shows what will happen if the rubric score is simply divided by the highest level of the rubric. Excellent work is, of course, converted to 100%; very good work is converted to 80%; good but simple work is converted to 60%.

As mentioned earlier, the most common conversion of percent scores to letter grades is the one used by Mr. Warren. Using his policy (from the first page of his grading policy in Figure 9–7), the rubric score for the student who does very good work would convert to a borderline B/C grade and the rubric score for the student who did good but simple work would convert to a borderline D/F. Needless to say, it is unlikely that the mathematical conversions of rubric scores are what the teacher who wrote these rubrics had in mind. One fairly simple way to solve the problem of rubric conversions is to change the relationship between the percent and letter grade. Canady and Hotchkiss (1989) suggested that it might make more sense to use the following conversions: 0–20% = F; 21–40% = D; 41–60% = C; 61–80% = B; 81–100% = A. Although this might solve the problem with the rubrics, many teachers would reject such a solution because it lowers the standards for all of the letter grades.

A second way to solve the problem is to use meaning and logic to make the conversion of rubric scores to percent scores. Suppose the teacher believes that the meaning for each level of the rubric corresponds to a different letter grade. Then he might convert level 5 to 100%, level 4 to 90%, level 3 to 80%, level 2 to 70%, and level 1 to 60%. In this way, even the lowest score on the rubric is a D. Other rubric score to percent score conversions are possible. The choices must be left to the professional judgment of the teacher. As with other issues related to rubrics described in Chapter 4, teachers develop better judgment about what rubrics mean as they use them over time.

Some might criticize the subjective nature of these logical conversions; however, in the case of converting rubrics to percent scores, strict use of mathematics is likely to be a misrepresentation of student work. For example, look at Figures 9.9 and 9.10A. Figure 9–9 gives Robin's scores for all of her work in a single term. As can be seen, she does well on quizzes but seems to have more difficulty with homework (6 or 7 out of 10 possible points) and tests (scores of 79 and 82). Her essay scores (using the content and conventions rubrics shown in Figure 9–8) begin low and improve by the second essay. Her final project scores, also scored for content and writing conventions, are 4 and 4, respectively. Hence, she has improved writing position papers and has developed strong skills over the term. Yet, if her teacher uses arithmetic to convert her rubric scores to fraction scores and then applies the weights (shown in Figure 9–10A), her overall grade is likely to be a C+, despite her level of achievement. Clearly this final grade misrepresents her actual level of accomplishment. In contrast, Figure 9–10B shows what Robin's grade summary would be if conversion from the rubric to a percent score were based on meaning and logic for both the content and conventions rubrics. The rubric scores were converted from 5 to 100%, 4 to 90%, 3 to 80%, 2 to 70%, and 1 to 60%. Her grade based on the "*meaning conversion*" is a solid B, which is a better reflection of her overall performance during the term.

We firmly believe that all grading is an act of professional judgment—hence subjective to some extent. The major differences between the subjectivity that many assessment professionals fear and the kind of good judgment we advocate are that good judgments are made in advance, are publicly presented rather than subjective and hidden, and can be scrutinized for whether they make sense logically and ethically. This can lead to judgments that are fair and professionally responsible.

Once conversion to an appropriate scale is done for all assignments, teachers must decide how to collect multiple sources of evidence across different types of work to compute a summary grade. Inherent in this summary process is another form of professional judgment discussed previously—that of deciding how much weight to give to different types of work.

Student	Quiz 1	Quiz 2	Quiz 3	Quiz 4	Essay 1		Essay 2		HW 1	HW 2	HW 3	HW 4	Test 1	Test 2	Final Project	Grade
Robin	9	9	9	9	3	3	3	4	6	6	7	7	79	82	4	
Tyler	9	9	10	10	5	5	0	0	9	9	10	9	92	90	5	

Figure 9–9
Students' Scores on All Assignments

Source	Fraction of Points Earned by Category	Weight by Category	Weight times Percent Earned	Weighted Value
Homework	.650	10%	.650 × 10%	6.50
Quizzes	.900	15%	.90 × 15%	13.50
Tests	.805	20%	.805 × 20%	16.10
Essays	.750	25%	.75 × 25%	18.75
Project	.800	30%	.80 × 30%	24.00
Total		100%		78.85 = C

Figure 9–10A
Summary for Robin With Conversion of Rubric Scores Based on Arithmetic

Source	Fraction of Points Earned by Category	Weight by Category	Weight times Percent Earned	Weighted Value
Homework	.650	10%	.650 × 10%	6.50
Quizzes	.900	15%	.90 × 15%	13.50
Tests	.805	20%	.805 × 20%	16.10
Essays*	.825	25%	.825 × 25%	20.63
Project*	.900	30%	.90 × 30%	27.00
Total		100%		83.73 = B

Rubric conversions for essays and project based on the following:
5 = 100%   4 = 90%   3 = 80%   2 = 70%   1 = 60%

Figure 9–10B
Summary for Robin With Conversion of Rubric Scores Based on Meaning

Missing and Late Work   Teachers often say to us, "In the real world, you aren't allowed to be late," and then they give examples of newspaper deadlines, heart transplants, or similar urgent situations. Both of us worked in the "real world" before we began teaching adults. We found that the real world has realistic expectations. For every case of a firm deadline that cannot be missed, there are thousands of deadlines that are not so firm. Therefore, penalizing students for late work or for missing work may be teaching the wrong lesson.[8]

The real world has strategies for dealing with late and missing work. First, adults decide whether the late or missing work is essential. For example, if a news bulletin is an optional

[8] We know parents who let their children stay home from school (with a sick call) to give them time to finish an assignment that was delayed by an illness, a soccer tournament, a death in the family, or some other real-world event. Clearly something is wrong when parents must lie for their children to help them be successful in school.

Type of Work	Fraction of Points Earned by Category	Weight by Category	Weight times Percent Earned	Weighted Value
Quizzes	.950	10%	.95 × 10%	9.5
Homework	.925	15%	.925 × 15%	13.88
Tests	.905	20%	.905 × 20%	18.10
Essays*	.500	25%	.50 × 25%	12.50
Project*	1.00	30%	1.00 × 30%	30.00
Total		100%		83.98 = B

*Rubric conversions for essays and project based on the following:
5 = 100%   4 = 90%   3 = 80%   2 = 70%   1 = 60%

Figure 9–11A
Tyler's Summary Grade Including Zero for Essay 2

communication tool from a firm or agency, pressing business may take precedence and delay the newsletter or eliminate it altogether. Therefore, the late or missing news bulletin is not considered in performance appraisals. Second, adults set priorities. Not all work is equally important. If some work is late but more important work is completed on time, then this is usually considered an acceptable outcome.

Critical to these different responses to late or missing work is negotiation. Competent adults meet with their colleagues to discuss the consequences of late or missing work, to determine whether the work is essential, and to determine the impact of delay. If delay is not possible, other responsibilities are set aside in order to meet deadlines. In the case of an unavoidable delay, there may be consequences. Employees may have to work overtime resulting in higher labor costs; materials may have to be shipped overnight resulting in higher shipping costs. In short, in most situations, even essential work may be delayed by unforeseen events; however, in the real world, people pay penalties—they are *not* told that the work was not done.

Teachers who are focused on important learning targets ask students to do important work. However, even in the standards-based classroom, not all work is essential. The ultimate judgment about whether students have attained the standards must come from the quality of work rather than the quantity of work. In the case of missing or late work, teachers can (a) determine how important the missing or late work is, (b) decide whether the delay merits a penalty, and (c) teach students how to negotiate and set priorities. If work is not essential to making a summary judgment, teachers can omit missing work from consideration when they summarize grades. If work is essential and delays or omissions have affected others, then penalties for late work can be instituted (as Mr. Warren has indicated in his grading policy). If missing work has not affected others, but it is important, teachers can set up contracts to help students finish incomplete work.

If at all possible, teachers should avoid figuring zeros in the grade. Figures 9.11A and 9.11B show what could happen for a student (Tyler) who has one missing essay assignment. Although Tyler's work throughout the term has been excellent (see Tyler's scores in Figure 9–9), her summary grade in Figure 9–11A is a low B because of one missing assignment. If

Type of Work	Fraction of Points Earned by Category	Weight by Category	Weight times Percent Earned	Weighted Value
Quizzes	.950	10%	.95 × 10%	9.5
Homework	.925	15%	.925 × 15%	13.88
Tests	.905	20%	.905 × 20%	18.10
Essays*	.975	25%	.975 × 25%	24.38
Project*	1.00	30%	1.00 × 30%	30.00
Total		100%		95.86 = A

*Rubric conversions for essays and project based on the following:
5 = 100%   4 = 90%   3 = 80%   2 = 70%   1 = 60%

Figure 9–11B
Tyler's Summary Grade with a 10% Deduction in Scores for a Late Essay

the focus of the missing grade is on the ability to write position papers using effective language conventions, Tyler has demonstrated excellent work on both Essay 1 and the Final Project. Hence, the missing score would add nothing to the grade that isn't already known through the other two assignments. Based on the rubric applied, an examination of Tyler's written essay and final project would suggest she can write position papers to a high standard. Hence, given the rest of her scores, a low B is not an accurate reflection of her accomplishments. On the other hand, if another purpose of the essay is to demonstrate conceptual understanding about the controversial issue under study, then the missing essay must be completed in order for Tyler's teacher to assess her achievement.

A policy of "one day late—no credit" communicates that turning in something (anything!) is more important than achievement. Such policies discourage students from taking time to do high-quality work on daily assignments or from finishing work that has been started but delayed. In the case of Tyler, if her work is of the same quality as previous work but has been delayed, a penalty rather than a zero would be a more ethical response. Figure 9–11B shows what Tyler's summary grade would be if she turned in her essay late, did the same quality of work, and had to pay a 10% penalty for the delayed work (Scores of 4.5 and 4.5 for content and conventions, respectively). For teachers who are worried that students will not do all assignments if they believe that missing work won't be counted, this latter strategy is the most ethical.

Communication with students is essential when dealing with late or missing work. Students have dozens of reasons to avoid talking to teachers about their late or missing work. Therefore, as the adults in the teaching situation, teachers have the responsibility to create a climate of trust, to seek out errant students, and to determine the causes of delays. In the event that none of the adult strategies work and students have substantial amounts of late and missing work, teachers then need to contact parents/guardians as well as the school counselor, school psychologist, or school social worker because it is likely that missing and late work is symptomatic of other issues. The grade summary is not the place to vent frustrations with errant students.

Revisions and Retakes

Related to the issue of late work is the question of how to grade work that has been resubmitted after an initial grade, or a test or quiz that students have retaken. Some teachers allow only partial credit for such work. Retakes and revisions are generally associated with criterion-referenced and standards-referenced grading policies. Policies for how to deal with retakes and revisions should be consistent with the grading philosophy inherent in the model. If the purpose of grades is to communicate achievement, teachers are likely to give students full credit when revisions or retakes demonstrate better achievement. However, it is common practice for teachers who espouse criterion-referenced grading philosophies to put a ceiling of 80% on anything retaken or resubmitted, allow only a fraction of the grade earned, or average the first and second efforts together. These policies can have serious motivational side effects. If improvement is not recognized, students will be discouraged from taking advantage of retakes or revisions. Some policies may inadvertently punish students for their revisions or retakes.[9]

The rationales behind various partial-credit strategies are similar to those behind various late-work policies. "It's not fair to those who did a good job the first time" is a throwback to proponents of norm-referenced grading. Our response to this is to consider your philosophy of teaching and grading. If grades are meant to stand for the student's level of competence at the end of the quarter, semester, or year, teachers must ask themselves, "Does it matter how quickly they reached competence? Does it matter if it took extra feedback or a second revision?" If teachers see their role as gatekeeper and their function to sort students into fast and slow learner groups, then partial credit strategies make sense.

Another argument for reducing credit for retakes is that, if students can take advantage of revisions and retakes, their first efforts will be of poor quality. We have heard teachers say, "If they can retake the quiz and earn full credit, they won't try as hard the first time, doubling the teacher's work," or "They'll just keep resubmitting their written work until we drown in papers." This is a very real concern. We have both dealt with these problems in our own "no-penalty" policies for retakes and resubmissions. For papers, one solution is to require that students clearly address our feedback in their revisions. Students who are not interested enough to do this careful work will find that neither their work nor their grade improves. If students are just avoiding doing good work in the first place, they will not want to put forth the effort to write a paper twice. For retakes of quizzes or exams, teachers can limit students to a single retake on a parallel form of the test (same concepts and skills, but different items). It then behooves students to make sure they understand the concepts and skills before they retake the tests. One way teachers can avoid the extra work associated with retakes for tests and quizzes is to give a cumulative exam at the end of a term, where the earlier material is naturally retested. If the score on the earlier material improves, the teacher can substitute the score for the more recent performance for the original score. Other than

---

[9] A high school student we know received a 67% (an F) on a math test. Her teacher allowed retakes, so she studied hard and scored an 80% (a B–) on the second try. Her teacher's grading policy stated that students could earn a maximum of 80% on a retake, which might have resulted in an improved score in the grade book. Unfortunately, the 80% limit was implemented by multiplying the retake score by .80, which reduced the student's score to 64%, a lower grade than the student started with and an inaccurate reflection of her knowledge and skill. In effect, the teacher was merely punishing her for not having learned the material well enough the first time.

Components of Science Grade		
Weight	Type of Work	How the Work Will be Scored
30%	Science Lab Reports (1 every other week)	**Scored by a six-level rubric:** 6 = 100% 5 = 93% 4 = 85% 3 = 75% 2 = 65% 1 = 55%
20%	Science Journal (1 entry each week)	**Scored by a three-level rubric:** 3 = thoroughly understood concepts (100%) 2 = partially understood vocabulary (70%) 1 = attempted but did not understand concepts (50%) 0 = did not attempt
30%	2 Projects (Research Paper and Independent Investigation)	**Each scored with a 20-item rating scale for a total of 40 points**
20%	2 Exams	**Each scored as percent of total possible points**

Figure 9–12
Components of the Science Grade for a Nine-Week Quarter

ensuring that the content assessed is consistent for the different tests or quizzes, almost no additional work from the teacher is necessary. If you decide to implement one of the other no-penalty revision or retake policies, we suggest that you set final dates for resubmitting or retaking to prevent an avalanche of work arriving at the very end of the term.

Example Grade Summary

Once you have determined the weights you wish to give to different types of work and the common scale, computing grades is a fairly straightforward process. As a simple example, Figure 9–12 lists the different types of work that Robert Little's teacher will use to give a science grade for her fifth-grade students at the end of a quarter. These include biweekly lab reports, weekly journal entries, two projects, and two exams. Notice that Robert's teacher does not include homework in her grading summary. She believes that homework is done for practice and that the students' in-class work is better evidence of their achievement than is homework. Also given are the weights for each type of work and the conversions for rubrics used to evaluate homework and lab reports.

Figure 9–13 gives the scores earned by Robert Little. We have divided the grade book into sections to make the scores for each type of work easier to see. The first step Robert's teacher must make is to convert the rubric scores to percent scores so that she can use a percentage-based grading system. Figure 9–14 gives Robert's scores for each assignment again; however, the rubric scores for journal entries and lab reports have been converted into percent scores. To be most efficient, Robert's teacher would write the rubric score on

Student	Lab 1	Lab 2	Lab 3	Lab 4
Robert Little	2	4	5	6
Rubric Levels	6	6	6	6

Rubric conversions: *6 = 100%*   *5 = 93%*   *4 = 85%*   *3 = 75%*   *2 = 65%*   *1 = 55%*

Student	J1*	J2	J3	J4	J5	J6	J7	J8
Robert Little	1	2	1	2	2	3	3	3
Rubric Levels	3	3	3	3	3	3	3	3

*J = Science Journal
Rubric conversions: *3 = 100%*   *2 = 70%*   *1 = 50%*

Student	Project 1	Project 2	Exam 1	Exam 2
Robert Little	32	37	27	30
Points Possible	40	40	30	30

Figure 9–13
Robert Little's Scores on Each Science Assignment

Robert's work but would enter the percent score into the grade book. This simplifies the summarizing process.

Notice that Robert's teacher has used the exact values for the conversion. This is very important. Although not all students who earn a 4 on a six-level rubric will have exactly the same quality of work, if Robert's teacher tried to differentiate among students who earned a level four—giving some of them 86% and others 80%, research suggests that the teachers would be highly likely to add some bias into the assessment process. As we discussed in Chapter 4, when teachers use rubrics, they must limit the number of levels in the rubric to ensure that they limit their subjectivity and prevent bias.

Once percent scores are assigned for the lab reports and journal entries, the next step is to add up all of the scores for each type of work and divide by the total points possible. For journal entries and lab reports, the teacher added the percentage points earned and the percentage points possible. For the projects and exams, the teacher used the number of points earned and the total points possible. Because each of these types of work has many points possible, it is not necessary to do any meaning conversions. The column second from the right in each row gives the total points or percents earned and the total points or percent possible. The column farthest to the right gives the decimal value that results when dividing points or percent earned by points or percent possible. As you can see, all of the different types of work have been placed on one common scale that ranges from .00 to 1.00.

Student	Lab 1	Lab 2	Lab 3	Lab 4	Total Earned	Decimal Value
Robert Little	65%	85%	93%	100%	343% of 400%	.86

Student	J1	J2	J3	J4	J5	J6	J7	J8	Total Earned	Decimal Value
Robert Little	50%	70%	50%	70%	70%	100%	100%	100%	610% of 800%	.76

Student	Project 1	Project 2	Total Earned	Decimal Value
Robert Little	32	37	69 of 80	.86

Student	Exam 1	Exam 2	Total Earned	Decimal Value
Robert Little	27	30	57 of 60	.95

Figure 9–14
Robert Little's Percentage Grade Summary

Robert's decimal values range from .76 to .95. His lowest performance is in the journal entries and it is evident that he had a more difficult time with journal entries at the beginning of the grading period than at the end. However, because each journal entry assignment was focused on different science concepts, Robert's teacher is computing an average across all of the entries.

A close look at the lab report scores shows that, for the most part, Robert did quite well. His rubric scores increased from 2 to 6 during the quarter. Because the focus of each lab was on different science content and Robert's teacher was not assessing inquiry skills, she computed an average score across all of the labs. Robert's performance in the labs is well correlated with his performance on homework assignments. The content at the beginning of the quarter may have been more difficult for him. Alternately, he may have had a personal issue that affected his performance at the beginning of the quarter.

Robert did well on the projects and earned 69 out of 80 points. He did very well on exams and earned 57 out of 60 points.

Once the decimal values were computed for each type of work, the teacher multiplied the decimal values times the weight for each type of work. Figure 9–15 shows the weighting process. The first column names the type of work; the second column gives the decimal value Robert Little earned. The third column gives the weight, and the fourth column shows how to compute the weighted total for each type of work. The last column shows the weighted total for each type of work. In a way, this weighted value shows how much of the weight (for example, how much of 20%) the student earned. Robert Little earned .95 of the possible points for exams; therefore, he earned 19 of the 20 percentage points assigned to exams.

Type of Work	Decimal Value	Weight	Decimal Value × Weight	Weighted Component Score
Lab Reports	.86	30%	.86 × 30	25.80
Journals	.76	20%	.76 × 20	15.20
Projects	.86	30%	.86 × 30	25.80
Exams	.95	20%	.95 × 20	19.00
Total		100%		85.80

Figure 9–15
Robert Little's Decimal Scores and Weighted Total

The bottom row of Figure 9–15 shows the totals. The sum of the weights must always be 100%. The sum for the weighted totals should be less than or equal to 100%. Robert has earned 85.8% out of 100%. If his teacher uses the same scale as did Mr. Warren, Robert has earned a B in science for this term.

There are several computer programs that will do grading summaries for teachers once they indicate the types of work and the weights. These programs are useful when teachers need to assign grades to large numbers of students. Care must be taken to ensure that the scores are correctly entered into the program, and teachers should manually compute a few students' grades to ensure that the program is working correctly. Remember, however, computer programs are not a substitute for professional judgments about students. They are only tools. The programs only do mathematical computations; they cannot think about the meaning of rubrics, whether all assignments are of equal importance, or whether students are making progress over time. If teachers choose standards-based grading policies and wish to use grading programs, the weighting process becomes a bit more complex because later performances for some types of work should receive more weight than earlier work.

Had Robert Little's teacher been assessing skills that grow over time in the journals and labs (e.g., specific scientific thinking and communication skills applied in journal entries and inquiry skills during labs), she would have divided the weights to reflect expected growth. For example, there are eight journal entries worth 20% of the grade. J1 through J5 might be worth only 8%, whereas J6 through J8 might be worth 12%. Similarly, the lab reports are worth 30% of the grade. If the teacher wanted to give more weight to later lab reports than to earlier ones, she might give the first two lab reports a weight of 10% and the later two lab reports a weight of 20%. These are nuances that teachers must think carefully about as they set up the grading programs to reflect their personal grading philosophies.

GRADING STUDENTS WITH SPECIAL NEEDS

Grades pose a special set of problems for students with disabilities and those for whom limited English proficiency makes it difficult to learn the material or demonstrate that learning. Should the summary grade reflect their achievement of the same standards as other students, or should some compensation be made for the fact that learning and performance are much more difficult for some students? If a learning-disabled fourth-grader reads at the first-grade level, should he be penalized for not understanding the material in the social studies text? What if, instead of completing the full page of math problems assigned to her peers, a student does only a quarter of the problems, but does them well?

English Language Learners

Grading policies for students with limited English proficiency may be a matter of school, district, or state policy. Even so, it may be possible to tailor the implementation of those policies to fit the situation. As we described in Chapter 1, English language learners (ELL) may have good conversational skills but still struggle with academic texts and writing. The specialists in teaching English as a second language in your school or district can help with both designing accommodations and setting grading standards for students as they work on improving their fluency in English. The grade card or progress report should indicate any modifications that were made so that parents or guardians and school administrators better understand the meaning of the grades.

Students With 504 Plans

Students with 504 plans do not have disabilities that have been judged to interfere with learning, but need other accommodations because of (usually) physical limitations. This may include special equipment, an aide to assist with physical tasks, but not modifications to the standards used to judge work (exceptions to this may include penmanship or other tasks made difficult by a physical limitation). Although the student may have some accommodations for taking tests or completing work, which are spelled out in the 504 plan, the work will be graded on the same standards as the rest of the class.

Students With Individualized Education Plans

Students with individualized education plans (IEPs) will likely need either accommodations or modifications in assessment and grading. As mentioned in Chapter 1, assessment and grading should be discussed early in the course or year as part of a conference with the teacher, the student (if appropriate), the parents or guardian, and the IEP manager (usually a special education teacher or school psychologist). If the student can learn the same material when given *accommodations,* then the standards for grading should be the same as for other students. The summary grade will show how well the student with a disability has met the same standards as her nondisabled classmates. It is particularly important for secondary students planning on postsecondary education to choose this option; this will give them information about whether they can succeed in later schooling with the accommodations available.

If, in order to succeed, a student requires *modifications* of instruction and assessment that include different assessments, lower standards, different curricula, easier problems or books, and the like, then grading systems should also be modified to provide reasonable expectations for student work. It is critical, however, that all the adults, and at some point, the student, are clear that these modifications mean that the A Fred earns does not mean he is achieving the same level of competence as his peers who do not have disabilities. It is neither honest nor fair to such students to lead them to believe they can do work at the same level as other students if they cannot. Such students may enroll in community college or technical school and find out after much expense and embarrassment that the As and Bs they earned in high school did not mean they could do postsecondary work. As with English language learners, the grade card or progress report should indicate any modifications that were made so that parents or guardians and school administrators better understand the meaning of the grades. Both accommodations and modifications should be documented in the IEP.

In all cases, decisions regarding assessment and grading should be made collaboratively with, at minimum, the teacher, parent or guardian, and the IEP manager or ESL specialist. The initial decisions should be made early in the year, and revisited if it becomes clear that they need to be modified. The goal for these students, as for all of your students, should be to learn as much as possible at as high a standard as possible, free from unreasonably low or high expectations.

SUMMARY

Our goal in this chapter was to bring the dilemmas of grading to teachers and to supply examples of how to deal with those dilemmas. Assigning summary grades is an important way in which we communicate with students, parents or guardians, and school administrators about students' accomplishments. As professionals, we must use our best judgment in each stage of the process. We cannot simply put numbers into a computer program and let the program make decisions for us. We owe it to our students and their families to make the rules fair and public.

We also know that this is not an easy process and takes time to do well. Summary grades begin with clear learning goals and objectives, focused teaching, and high-quality assessments. If you begin with clear learning targets and make certain you teach to them, if you develop high-quality ways of assessing your students, then summary grades are easier to compute. If you are clear about the learning targets, you are more likely to establish weights that are consistent with your overall goals for students. Finally, if you are focused on students' success, you are more likely to establish grading policies that are fair and ethical rather than capricious and unethical.

REFERENCES

Ames, C. (1984). Competitive, cooperative, and individualistic goal structures: A cognitive-motivational analysis. In R. Ames & C. Ames (Eds.), *Student motivation* (Vol. 1, pp. 177–207). New York: Academic.

Canady, R. L., & Hotchkiss, P. R. (1989). It's a good score! Just a bad grade. *Phi Delta Kappan, 71*(1), 68–71.

Cross, L. H., & Frary, R. B. (1999). Hodgepodge grading: Endorsed by students and teachers alike. *Applied Measurement in Education, 12*(1), 53–72.

Frary, R. B., Cross, L. H., & Weber, L. J. (1993). Testing and grading practices and opinions of secondary teachers of academic subjects: Implications for instruction in measurement. *Educational Measurement: Issues & Practice, 12(3)*, 23–30.

Johnson, D. W., & Johnson, R. T. (1985). Motivational Processes in Cooperative, Competitive, and Individualistic Learning Situations. In C. Ames & R. Ames (Eds.), *Research on Motivation in Education* (Vol. 2, pp. 249–286). New York: Academic.

Mangino, E., & Babcock, M. A. (1986). *Minimum competency testing: Helpful or harmful to high level skills?* Paper presented at the annual meeting of the American Educational Research Association, San Francisco.

Marion, S. F., & Sheinker, A. (1999). *Issues and consequences for state level minimum competency testing programs: State assessment series: Wyoming Report 1.* Washington, DC: Council of Chief State School Officers.

Mehrens, W. A., & Lehmann, I. J. (1991). *Measurement and evaluation in education and psy-chology* (4th ed.). Forth Worth, TX: Holt, Rinehart, & Winston.

Rogers, N. (1991). *High stakes minimum skills tests: Is their use increasing achievement?* (No. 90.25). Austin, TX: Austin Independent School District Office of Research and Evaluation.

Thomas, S., & Oldfather, P. (1997). Intrinsic motivations, literacy, and assessment practices: "That's my grade. That's me." *Educational Psychologist, 32*(2), 107–123.

PORTFOLIO ASSESSMENT

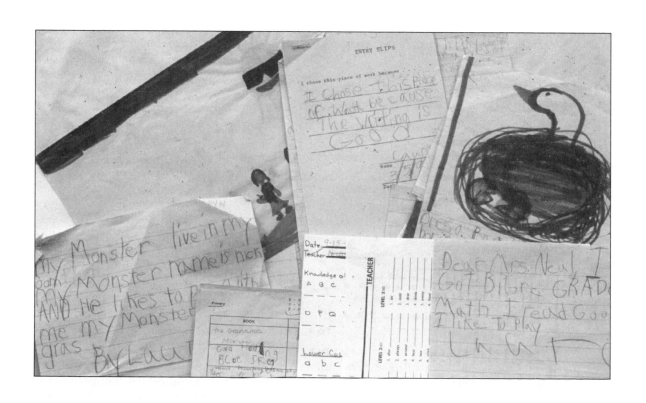

portfolio is "a purposeful collection of student work that tells the story of the student's effort, progress, or achievement in (a) given area(s)" (Arter & Spandel, 1992). The use of portfolios in education meets a number of educational needs. For example, portfolios provide a richer (and sometimes more accurate) picture of students' accomplishments than can be obtained from school grades. The use of portfolios has been found to help students take ownership of their own learning processes. In some states, portfolios are used in assessment programs as an alternative or supplement to standardized test scores. When done well, portfolios can be powerful assessment tools that help students to understand their strengths and weaknesses, to see their own growth, and to document their progress toward meeting standards. Alternately, if done poorly, portfolios can be annoying burdens for teachers and students. This chapter presents information about how to create portfolios for different purposes, how to engage students in using portfolios for their own learning, motivational issues with portfolios, and managing portfolios in the classroom. However, before we begin, it is valuable to elaborate on the definition of portfolios given by Arter and Spandel (1992); a definition that truly captures the power and possibilities of portfolios.

Purposeful is one of the key words in the definition of portfolios provided by Arter and Spandel. Portfolios have a number of different purposes, each of which presents a different picture of students. The most common purposes are (a) showcasing students' accomplishments, (b) demonstrating students increasing skill and/or knowledge in a particular subject, (c) demonstrating the process students have used to move from an initial set of ideas to a final, polished performance, and (d) creating a cumulative record of students' accomplishments so that future teachers can adjust instruction to students' needs. Each of these purposes results in different information about students. In addition, these purposes are not mutually exclusive. Teachers can apply one or more of these purposes in a given class or subject area depending on what the teacher hopes that students will learn.

Story is another key word in Arter and Spandel's definition of portfolios. Portfolios are powerful adjuncts to grades. While grades are a summative *statement* about how well students have achieved specific learning objectives during a particular marking or grading period, portfolios tell *stories*—about what grades mean, what growth has taken place, and what kind of effort students have applied to their work. Grades are generated almost exclusively by teachers; however, most portfolios are developed jointly by teachers, students, and even parents since each has her or his own version of the story to be told.

The decision to use portfolios as assessment tools requires a different sort of commitment to students' education. Teachers who use portfolios successfully make a commitment to find the time and space to help students *collect* their work in an organized way, *select* from their collections the work that shows their accomplishments, *reflect* on their work, and *set goals* for future accomplishments. Each of these steps in portfolio development requires teaching students how to do the given step. It has been our experience that students' choices in terms of portfolio entries, as well as their reflections on the work in the portfolios, help them develop a strong sense of accomplishment and a sense of closure at the end of a grading period in ways that final exams and grades do not (Taylor & Nolen, 1996b).

Although collections of student work can be vehicles for telling stories about students' accomplishments, a random collection of assignments that lacks purpose will not tell much of a story. The choices that students make as they put together their portfolios and the comments they and their teachers make about the work contained in the portfolios make the story more complete. In this chapter our goal is to help you develop effective ways to use portfolios so that you and your students benefit from them.

PURPOSES OF PORTFOLIOS

The primary reason teachers use portfolios is to document students' achievement through solid examples of their work rather than relying exclusively on grades. However, before you can begin to use portfolios in your classroom (or school), you need to be very clear about the purpose or purposes you want the portfolio to serve. In what follows, we discuss each of the different purposes in more detail to help you decide what purposes are appropriate for your classroom.

Working Folders

A working folder is not really a portfolio at all. It is an intermediate step in portfolio development. As students complete schoolwork, they collect that work in a folder or notebook. A working folder can include any work the teacher wants students to retain—early drafts, revisions, and final versions of performances; photographs; videotapes, audiotapes, and CDs; quizzes and tests; papers and projects; and homework. The primary purpose of the working folder is to provide a place to hold students' work until they are ready to select examples to be put in a portfolio. If you plan to use portfolios, it's important to move beyond working folders to one of the next four types of portfolios.

Showcase Portfolios

Showcase portfolios tell the story of what students have accomplished, in relation to a set of learning objectives, during a given period of time. For example, a showcase portfolio in the language arts might be a collection of a student's best written work from a grading period or school year. Valencia and Place (1994) discuss their observations of children as young as first and second grade who use showcase language arts portfolios to show their reading and writing skills. A showcase portfolio in mathematics might include a collection of work that shows a student's ability to use problem-solving skills to solve problems in different mathematical areas (number sense, measurement, geometry, algebra, statistics, or probability) *or* a collection of work that shows the student can combine mathematical knowledge and skills across mathematical areas to solve complex, real-world problems.

A showcase portfolio in the visual arts might include students' best drawings, paintings, and/or photographs; photographs of students' best sculptures, pottery, and/or compositions; or other artistic works. On the other hand, an arts portfolio might show the students' best applications of particular techniques (e.g., repetition, symmetry, perspective) or their best work in the certain medium (e.g., watercolors or charcoal). Note that, for the latter type of visual arts portfolio, two different showcase purposes were given: (1) demonstrating the student's best applications of certain techniques and (2) demonstrating the student's best use of one or more media.

Showcase portfolios can be used in any subject area as long as the purpose is clear; teachers must know what they want students to showcase. Figures 10–1 and 10–2 are graphic representations of two types of showcase portfolios. The right column shows the learning targets and the left column represents student entries. Figure 10–1 represents a showcase of

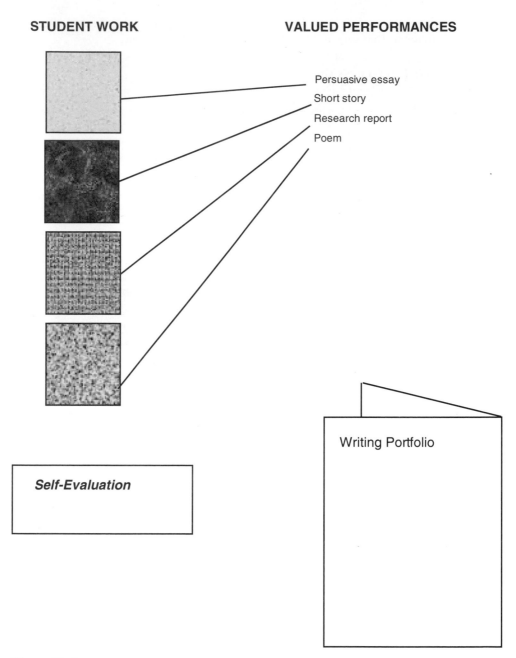

STUDENT WORK

VALUED PERFORMANCES

Persuasive essay

Short story

Research report

Poem

Self-Evaluation

Writing Portfolio

Figure 10–1
Representation of a Showcase Writing Portfolio

312

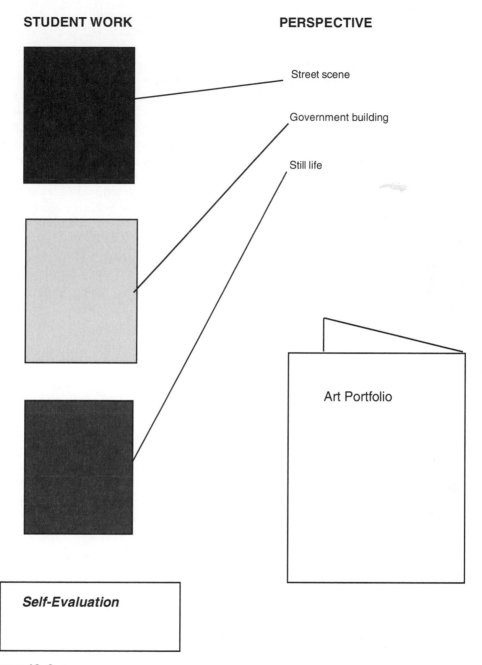

STUDENT WORK

PERSPECTIVE

Street scene

Government building

Still life

Art Portfolio

Self-Evaluation

Figure 10–2
Representation of a Showcase Art Portfolio Demonstrating Students' Best Works Using Three-Point
Perspective

students' best writing for several different writing purposes. To use such a portfolio, students would need multiple opportunities to write for each purpose so that they can select their best of each. Figure 10–2 represents a showcase of three entries that show the student's best work using three-point perspective.

Showcase portfolios provide the opportunity to teach students what counts as good work within the subject area. If students are to select their best work, they must learn the criteria used to judge such performances in the real world. Teachers can select criteria that are within the student's developmental level while keeping in mind the ultimate learning goals. For example, in a middle school history class, students can begin to judge their historical essays using versions of disciplinary criteria [what Schwab (1978) calls the "syntactic structure" of a discipline.] They could learn that good historical essays include evidence from a variety of sources, for example. A high school history student could learn more sophisticated criteria for judging their work—such as an expectation that an essay must include different points of view about an event, with an argument for interpreting these differences.

When creating showcase portfolios, the student, teacher, and/or parent or guardian can select entries. Anyone who selects an entry is asked to write a reflective piece (*entry slip*) telling why the particular piece was chosen. For example, Elman Middle School required all students to select their best written work to put in a language arts portfolio. RaeAnne selected a book report and an essay on Romeo and Juliet. The teacher selected a social studies report. When the parents were asked to select something to add to the portfolio, RaeAnne's father selected a short story and a poem. His comment about his choices was, "RaeAnne, I know that this isn't your best work, but I think you should do more creative writing. I noticed that you only had two pieces in your folder that were creative. I think your teachers should give you more chances to write stories and poems so you can learn to *play* with language."

Figure 10–3 represents a mathematics showcase portfolio that was used in middle school in the Pacific Northwest. The right column lists the mathematics goals. Students were to select four assignments from their notebooks that showed their best work in mathematical problem solving, communication, and reasoning; using mathematics in real-world contexts; and understanding of the concepts studied during the grading period. Lyle, an eighth-grader, selected four entries for his showcase portfolio. The left column represents his entries:

1. A homework assignment to show problem solving and reasoning skills applied to real-world problems
2. A second homework assignment to show communication about his algebraic understanding through writing
3. A test over solving linear equations through graphs, tables, and equations to show conceptual understanding and mathematical communication (graphic and symbolic representations)
4. A "problem of the day" to show his use of algebra to solve a real-world problem

Showcase portfolios are very flexible; however, their main purpose is to showcase what a student has learned—what the student knows and is able to do. Therefore, you need to define the focus of a showcase portfolio before you or your students select entries. Figure 10–4 shows the different focuses for showcase portfolios and the reasons teachers might want to choose each.

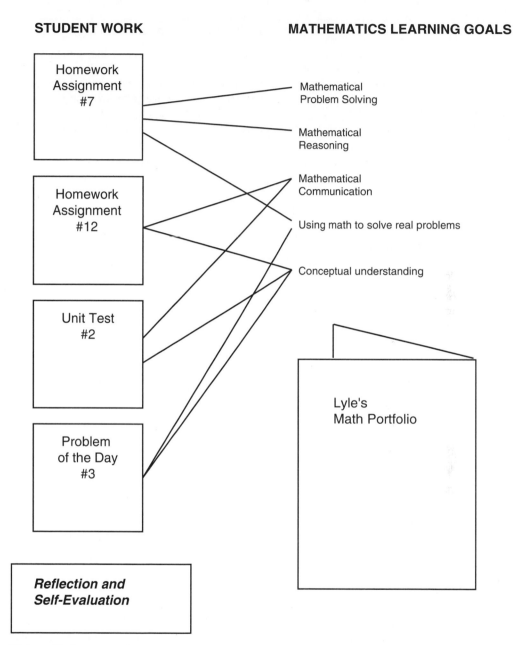

STUDENT WORK   **MATHEMATICS LEARNING GOALS**

Figure 10–3
Representation of a Mathematics Showcase Portfolio

Growth Portfolios

Growth portfolios tell the story of students' improvement over time. This type of portfolio is particularly important for students who are struggling learners or students who are learning something new and challenging, such as a new language or how to read. Figure 10–5

Focuses for Showcase Portfolios

1. *Showcasing students' best examples of different performances.* In a standards-based classroom, students generally have more than one opportunity to work on valued performances (e.g., writing for different purposes, solving mathematical problems, conducting scientific investigations, writing historical accounts and arguments, writing book reports) because teachers are not simply moving through a curriculum—they are committed to helping students accomplish important learning targets. This is an ideal context for using showcase portfolios wherein students present their best version of each valued performance.

2. *Demonstrating students' best work in relation to one or more learning objectives.* At times, teachers are focused on students' accomplishment of critical learning objectives. For example, a third grade teacher's most important writing objectives might be, "Students will learn how to write simple, compound, and complex sentences," and "Students will learn how to improve their writing for grammar and word order." This is an ideal context for using showcase portfolios focused on particular learning objectives. The portfolio entries might include worksheets, daily exercises in editing sentences, as well as drafts and final versions of written work—each showing the students' best work related to sentence writing, grammar, and word order. When objectives are the focus of the portfolios, it is best to have two or more examples of work for each objective.

3. *Demonstrating students' best work in relation to course goals.* Teachers may have some fundamental course goals upon which they base all of their instruction. For example, a science teacher might have two major goals: "Students will understand how all natural phenomena are the result of chemical, physical, earth, space, and/or living systems, their components, and the interconnections among components and systems," and "Students will learn how to use the processes of scientific inquiry." This is an ideal context for the use of showcase portfolios focused on course goals. The entries in the portfolio could include exams, lab reports, concept maps, and other evidence of these two major goals. Each entry may show more than one goal, as is shown in Lyle's portfolio in Figure 10.3.

Figure 10–4
Focuses for Showcase Portfolios

represents one type of growth portfolio, in this case, growth in scientific inquiry. Each of the three entries shows Tony's development of the skills related to inquiry. The right column shows the teacher's learning objectives for scientific inquiry.

Tony's first entry is a lab report showing his first effort at conducting an investigation and summarizing the results. It is very common for teachers to give students a research question, have them conduct a standard investigation (from a textbook or supplemental resource), record observations, and organize and summarize the results. Students can show only a few of the learning objectives relevant to inquiry through such pre-planned inquiries. The second entry is a lab report showing that Tony has generated a hypothesis, conducted an investigation, and summarized the results including comparing the results to his hypothesis. In this case, Tony has added his first attempt at writing his own hypothesis about the answer to a research question and has compared the results to his hypothesis. Developing hypotheses is a more difficult skill than conducting, observing, recording, and summarizing. It requires students to think critically about the research question, assess what they already know, and make a prediction with some sound reasoning for that prediction. Tony has now shown his first attempt at this skill. In addition, comparing the results to the hypothesis is what scientists do

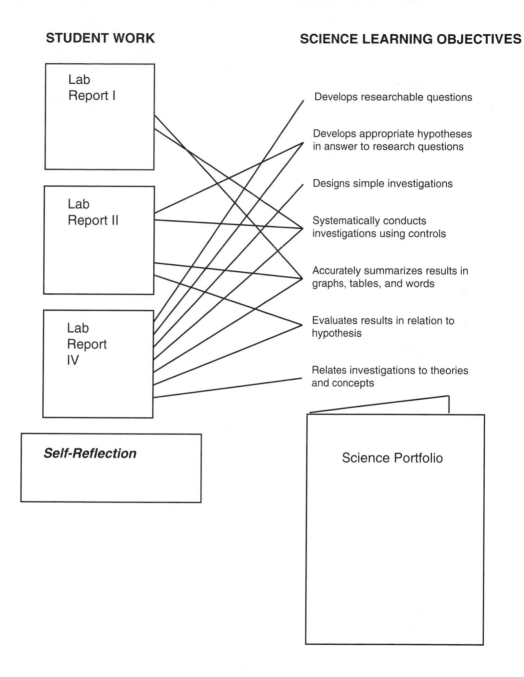

STUDENT WORK

Lab Report I

Lab Report II

Lab Report IV

Self-Reflection

SCIENCE LEARNING OBJECTIVES

Develops researchable questions

Develops appropriate hypotheses in answer to research questions

Designs simple investigations

Systematically conducts investigations using controls

Accurately summarizes results in graphs, tables, and words

Evaluates results in relation to hypothesis

Relates investigations to theories and concepts

Science Portfolio

Figure 10–5
Representation of a Science Growth Portfolio

every day. This step can lead to a new hypothesis and more investigative efforts. Hence, the second entry of Tony's growth portfolio shows that he is making progress in his inquiry skills.

In addition to showing Tony's new skills, Tony and his teacher can also assess whether he has *improved* in the skills of conducting an investigation, observing, recording, and summarizing the results. Tony's third entry is a lab report that shows that he can plan and conduct a complete investigation including developing a research question, generating a hypothesis, designing and systematically conducting the investigation, and drawing conclusions about the results in relation to the hypothesis and to the scientific concept under study. In the final entry, Tony has shown *new* skills: generating a research question, designing an investigation, and relating results to the concept under study. The idea of researchable questions related to a concept or theory is at the heart of scientific inquiry; therefore, the skill requires higher-level thinking than following directions or summarizing. In addition, designing an investigation requires carefully identifying the variables, selecting appropriate tools and materials, figuring out how to control sources of error, determining a set of logical steps to follow, and deciding what and when to measure/observe outcomes. Tony's entry shows that his research skills are growing in number. As with the second entry, the third entry can help Tony and his teacher examine growth in terms of the development of new skills and increased proficiency in previously learned skills.

This notion of growth can be used in any subject area and can become a tool to help increase students' motivation to continue working with new knowledge and skills. We have seen teachers use growth portfolios in writing, science at all levels, world languages, and elementary reading. (See Figure 10–7 for a summary of the typical focuses of growth portfolios.) The power of the growth portfolio is in giving students a concrete picture of their improvement, rather than an average across the work as summary grades often do. Growth portfolios could easily accompany Ms. Henry's (see Chapter 9) standards-based grading process as evidence that grades have captured whether students have met standards. This can be particularly important in helping parents and guardians understand the meaning of grades and the progress students have made.

Process Portfolios

Process portfolios are useful for documenting students' process through an important authentic performance. In Chapter 4, we discussed a range of different types of work that are authentic to the disciplines and to life beyond school. One of the most effective ways to help students accomplish real work, and to learn from the work, is to take them through a process from initial ideas or understandings to a final *prepared accomplishment* (Wolf, 1991). A process portfolio documents the steps students take to make this journey. The process portfolio communicates that there is value in the journey as well as the destination. As students work on an essay, a research paper, a short story, or another performance, each stage of the work is retained in a folder or notebook. For example, a process portfolio for a research paper might include initial ideas (e.g., freewrites, webs, lists), evidence of research skills (e.g., notes, an annotated bibliography describing the validity, reliability, and usefulness of each source), outlines or other organizing tools, drafts, revisions, feedback from the teacher and peers, comments about why certain decisions were made, and/or other artifacts that document the journey to the prepared accomplishment. Process portfolios help the teacher and student capture the student's thinking and ability to use a variety of skills to reach the final performance. Much of what students will use

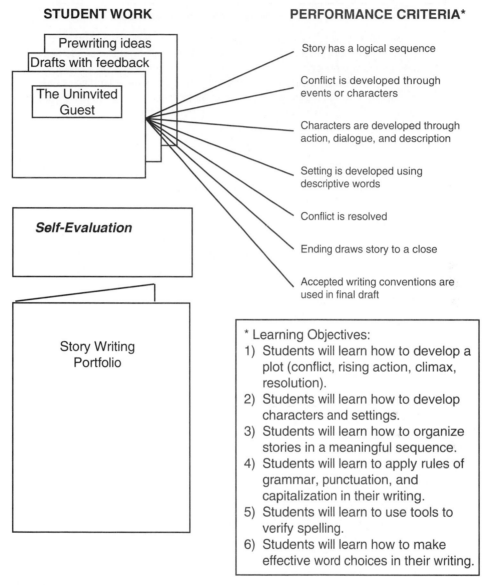

STUDENT WORK   **PERFORMANCE CRITERIA***

Prewriting ideas

Drafts with feedback

The Uninvited
Guest

Self-Evaluation

Story Writing
Portfolio

Story has a logical sequence

Conflict is developed through
events or characters

Characters are developed through
action, dialogue, and description

Setting is developed using
descriptive words

Conflict is resolved

Ending draws story to a close

Accepted writing conventions are
used in final draft

* Learning Objectives:
1) Students will learn how to develop a
   plot (conflict, rising action, climax,
   resolution).
2) Students will learn how to develop
   characters and settings.
3) Students will learn how to organize
   stories in a meaningful sequence.
4) Students will learn to apply rules of
   grammar, punctuation, and
   capitalization in their writing.
5) Students will learn to use tools to
   verify spelling.
6) Students will learn how to make
   effective word choices in their writing.

Figure 10–6
Representation of a Process Writing Portfolio

again and again in life beyond school are the skills it takes to initiate, implement, and complete important performances in thoughtful and effective ways; therefore, process portfolios are powerful tools for documenting the stages between ideas and final performances. Figure 10–6 represents a process portfolio for writing a short story. The student has kept the prewriting ideas, drafts of work (with feedback from others), and the final story. Figure 10–7 gives different types of performances that might be the focus of process portfolios.

Focuses for Growth Portfolios

1. *Demonstrating growth in the ability to do valued performances.* Growth portfolios are ideal for helping students document and see their growth in challenging work such as reading, speaking a new language, writing expository or persuasive essays, conducting scientific inquiry. The criteria for the performances remain the same over time and students demonstrate, through the growth portfolio, their increased skill in meeting the performance criteria as well as the increased quality of their performances.

2. *Demonstrating students' growth in relation to one or more learning objectives.* As with showcase portfolios, sometimes teachers are focused on students' growth related to a few critical learning objectives. The third-grade teacher who has focused on sentence writing and written grammar (see Figure 10–4) could also use a growth portfolio to help students see their growth in the variety of the sentence types they use in their writing and the use of revision to improve the grammar in their written work. The portfolio entries might include several written pieces that show students' growth related to both learning objectives.

Focus for Process Portfolios

1. *Recording the processes taken to complete any valued performance.* Process portfolios can be used for any valued performance that requires several stages of work to bring the work from initial ideas to a prepared accomplishment. Valued performances might include short stories, collections of poetry, research reports, science investigations, dramatizations, chamber music, instrumental or vocal solos, paintings, and more. Performances might also include application of knowledge and skills to complete a real-world performance such as using physics principles to design a bridge; applying mathematical understandings to conduct a survey, and to analyze, represent, and interpret the results; creating a brochure to represent a state or country; creating a newspaper to represent a time or place in history. In short, the focus of process portfolios can be any performance that requires multiple stages of work through which students learn and through which they demonstrate their developing thinking and procedural skills.

Figure 10–7
Focuses for Growth and Process Portfolios

The process portfolio is a vehicle for communication: between the teacher and the student, between the student and himself or herself; between teacher and student and the student's parents or guardians. In the best sense, a process portfolio unites instruction and assessment into one, seamless whole. As students do the work that is captured in the portfolio, they are learning and are demonstrating what they have learned just as the basketball players described in Chapter 1 learned while playing the game. Teachers can look at process portfolios to see whether instructional strategies are leading to successful development of thinking skills and procedural skills. They can "coach" students through feedback. Students have a record of what steps it takes to complete a performance, and parents can learn the specifics of the processes being taught. Process portfolios can also help students learn to be systematic in their work rather than haphazard. Finally, performances that have been developed through process portfolios can be entered into showcase portfolios because they are likely to be some of the students' best work.

An essential element of the process portfolio is the reflection and self-evaluation by the student—judging the final work based on the performance criteria (see Chapter 4), as well as reflecting on what was learned in the process itself. Reflection on the process allows students to take a step back from their work and examine their own learning process. In this way, a process portfolio also has elements of a growth portfolio; however, the growth is applied to one significant performance.

Cumulative Portfolios

In a sense, a cumulative portfolio is a showcase portfolio and a growth portfolio combined. The entries in a cumulative portfolio show students' best work over more than one school year. These portfolios stay with students' cumulative records and exemplify students' progress over the school years. Cumulative portfolios allow teachers to get a sense of each student's competencies and growth *before* the school year begins. Cumulative portfolios can be used for any or all subject areas; however, there are limits to what can be stored in a school building. The decision to use cumulative portfolios is generally made by the faculty in a school building or by district administrators, although a group of teachers in an academic department could decide to maintain cumulative portfolios on their own.

In districts or states where performances are included when determining eligibility for high school diplomas, students' work gathered over time can help to determine whether students have met the performance expectations defined in the standards. For example, at Eastman High School, students must demonstrate proficiency with seven different writing purposes each year. Their best written piece for each purpose is retained in the cumulative portfolio, and students must meet the standard for each writing purpose to graduate.

As with any other type of portfolio, cumulative portfolios must have a focus. The focus might be purposes of writing (as in the example above). The focus might cross curricular areas and include a variety of valued performances (e.g., a history report, a creative work, a report of a science investigation, a math project). The contents of the portfolio are used to communicate students' accomplishments to audiences beyond the classroom.

The major challenges in using cumulative portfolios are (a) determining the purpose(s), (b) selecting representative work for each purpose, (c) culling the work over time, and (d) storage of individual student portfolios at the school or district. Needless to say, Eastman High School's writing portfolios would require quite a bit of storage space if students had to maintain seven examples of their writing each year. Therefore, students (along with their teachers) must review the portfolios each year to identify which written pieces to retain and which to replace with better writing samples. This culling process is a critical part of cumulative portfolios, especially if similar work is to be collected every year. On the other hand, it is possible that a school might decide to have students collect different types of work in the cumulative portfolio each year (for example, a middle school might ask students to select a social studies research report in sixth grade, a science report in seventh grade, etc.). Again, determining the purpose of the portfolio is a critical aspect of what is included in portfolios and whether entries will be replaced over time. One school district in the Pacific Northwest color codes the cumulative portfolios based on when students entered the district. In this way, teachers know which students have had an opportunity to learn how to use their cumulative portfolios to represent their work. In addition, teachers use the portfolios to quickly get a sense of what learning opportunities students have had. One teacher in the district claimed, "The portfolios have changed the way we think about students. We focus on whether they are meeting standards not just whether we *cover* [italics added] the standards [in our teaching]." (Anonymous teacher comment during assessment training workshop in Kent, Washington, September 1998).

REFLECTION AND SELF-EVALUATION

Each of the portfolios represented in Figures 10–1 through 10–5 has a box labeled self-evaluation. There are two types of self-evaluation students can do in relation to their portfolios. One is to reflect on their work; the other is to evaluate whether their final performances meet a performance standard. Reflection and self-evaluation are two of the most powerful elements of portfolios. Self-evaluations give students an opportunity to examine their work to identify the strengths and weaknesses. Reflections give students an opportunity to think about what they have learned, the decisions they have made or are making, and the processes they have used.

Reflection and Self-Evaluation for Showcase and Cumulative Portfolios

How students use reflection and self-evaluation depends on the purpose of the portfolio. For a showcase or cumulative portfolio, the student's reflection and self-evaluation tell the audience (the student herself, the teacher, a portfolio review committee, the parent, etc.) what the individual entries show about the student's accomplishments. Students must explain why each entry was selected for the portfolio. A student might say, "I selected this for my portfolio because it shows I can do a haiku by myself" or "I selected this for my portfolio because it shows that I know how to use problem-solving steps to solve math problems that don't have right answers." In both of these examples, the statements are not evaluative—they are simply descriptions of what the entry shows. By definition, however, the reflections in showcase or cumulative portfolios should include elements of self-evaluation because the entries reflect the students' best work. Hence students must explain *why* an entry is their *best* work—an evaluation. Therefore, students who wrote statements like those above would have to *add* a statement about why the haiku or math problem is the *best* example of their haiku, poetry, math problems, and the like.

Figure 10–8 shows a cover sheet for a showcase portfolio in writing for third and fourth-graders. The purpose of the portfolio is clear from the cover sheet: to show the students' best story, poem, and written report and to show the students' best use of a writing process. The cover sheet also has criteria that help students to examine their own work. Catherine used a cover sheet like this one with third-graders with pleasing results. The children were asked to go through their written work and select entries for their portfolios. Catherine asked the children to use the checklist to evaluate each of their possible entries and to check the areas that were strong. The teachers were familiar with the students' work so they could help students identify strengths and weaknesses during a portfolio conference.

The following is an excerpt from an interview with a 10-year-old about the portfolio conference:

Interviewer:	What did you think of this process?
Corina:	I really liked knowing what I did well and what I needed to work on. When teachers write "very good" or "needs work" on my paper, I don't know what to do.
Interviewer:	Do you think other kids would like to do this?
Corina:	Yeah. Kids will find out what they do well. Some kids might not want to do it at first because they're not very proud of themselves. But if they do, they'll find out that they do some things really well and they'll know what to do to get better.

Writing Portfolio

Name _____Corina_____ Date ___May 14, 2001___

Teacher's Name ____Mr. Williams_____ Grade ___3_____

Story ☒ I developed the main character. ☐ I described a setting. ☒ I have a sequence of events. ☒ I have a conflict. ☒ I have a resolution to the conflict. ☒ I used my own voice. ☒ I used describing words.	**Title of Best Work** The Uninvited Guest
Report ☒ I have one subject for the report. ☒ I have factual information about the subject. ☐ I have an introduction. ☒ I included at least three topics related to the subject. ☒ I organized my ideas and the facts. ☐ I have a conclusion.	**Title of Best Work** The Salmon Cycle
Poem ☒ My poem is about an image, a feeling, or an experience. ☒ I used sense words (smell, taste, sound, touch, sight).	**Title of Best Work** My Favorite Memory
Writing Process ☒ I used prewriting strategies to come up with ideas. ☒ I used my prewriting ideas in my drafts. ☒ I revised my writing to organize my ideas better. ☒ I revised my writing to add more interesting words. ☒ I edited my work for spelling, capitalization, and punctuation.	

Figure 10–8
Third-Grade Writing Portfolio Cover Sheet

Out of the mouths of babes. Clearly, selecting portfolio entries and reflecting on each one helped Corina develop a better understanding of what it takes to write reports, stories, and poems. This dialogue shows the potential of portfolios to help students develop a better understanding of the criteria for different types of writing, to identify strengths and weaknesses, and to set goals.

For the portfolio represented in Figure 10–3, Lyle was pretty sure he had selected his best work; however, he didn't know how to write about his choices. His teacher had decided to use portfolios and had given students criteria for selection; however, she had not taught students how to write evaluations of their selections. In Lyle's case, he said, "This is the first time I've heard these words—reasoning, communication, concepts. I'm not sure what they mean." Students have to be taught how to reflect on and evaluate their work.

You can hold a conference with young children to help the children make selections and write their entry slips (Figure 10–9), as Catherine did with Corina. For older students, you can model how to select entries and how to write an entry slip.

Figure 10–9 shows a student entry slip, and Figure 10–10 shows a teacher entry slip. The sentence starter on the student entry slip (more appropriate for young children) helps the students to focus on the purpose of the entry slip—to describe what the student has learned. When students do not understand the purpose of entry slips, they are less likely to take them seriously. In one school that was experimenting with portfolios, the most common reasons for including an entry in a portfolio were "because I like it" and "because I worked hard on it." To make selections that truly showcase the students' accomplishments, students must know how to look for evidence of the objectives and criteria in their work.

Successful showcase and cumulative portfolios require students to understand what they are to learn and the criteria for good work so that they can reflect on their work, evaluate it, and set goals for themselves. In addition to modeling and coaching, you can have students work together to make initial selections, compare reflections, and get another student's perspective on their evaluations. The teacher entry slip includes a space to record district or state standards relevant to the entry. This is particularly important as schools focus their efforts on helping all students reach the standards. The teacher does not need a sentence starter; however, he has space to give descriptive and evaluative reasons for the selection.

Reflection for Progress Portfolios

For progress portfolios, the purpose of reflection is for each student to describe what the entries show about his areas of improvement and growth as well as to set goals for his future growth. For students to reflect on their growth, they must know what growth to look for. As with showcase portfolios, you can meet with young children individually and in small groups to help them understand their areas of growth. You can model reflection on growth for older students. The key to reflecting on growth is to have specific targets for growth.

For example, Figure 10–11 shows Señor Gutierez's learning goals and objectives for his Spanish I class. He has three broad goals: communication, vocabulary, and grammar. The way his goals are worded suggest that even grammar and vocabulary have a communicative purpose—they are not ends in themselves. Figure 10–12 represents a Spanish-language progress portfolio, and Figures 10–13A through 10–13C are the quarterly reflection sheets for the growth portfolios Señor Gutierez uses in his class.

ENTRY SLIP FOR STUDENT

Name: _____ Date: _____

Entry Name: _____

I chose this for my portfolio because it shows: _____

_____

_____

_____

_____

_____

_____

_____

_____

I think this is my best work because: _____

_____

_____

_____

_____

_____

Signed: _____

Figure 10–9
Example of an Entry Slip for a Student-Selected Portfolio Entry

Each week of the year, Señor Gutierez briefly interviews each student in his Spanish class and tapes the dialogue. He keeps a tape for each student. At the end of each grading period, Señor Gutierez asks students to listen to their tapes and reflect on their growth. At the end of the first quarter, he guides their listening task so that they will know how to listen for growth. He asks them to listen for improvement in pronunciation, use of a wider range of vocabulary, and attention to formality when speaking to an adult (Figure 10–13A). At the end of the second quarter he asks them to add to their reflections by listening for attempts to use Spanish in new ways (sentences not found in the textbook) and improved use of case and gender for nouns, pronouns, and articles (Figure 10–13B). By the end of the year, he

---

ENTRY SLIP FOR TEACHER

Student Name: _____   Date: _____

Entry Name: _____

Proficiency (District/State Standard) shown: _____

_____

Reason for the Selection: _____

_____

_____

_____

_____

_____

_____

_____

_____

_____

_____

_____

_____

Teacher Signature: _____

Figure 10–10
Example of an Entry Slip for a Teacher-Selected Portfolio Entry

asks them to reflect on their use of circumlocution (talking around unknown words) and responsiveness to what others are saying, in addition to various grammatical features of language (Figure 10–13C). As can be seen, Señor Gutierez has carefully selected which objectives to focus on each quarter. By having students listen for communication and vocabulary early in the year, he has communicated to students that he values their communication more than grammatical precision. He has used the growth portfolio to help them hear their progress in different aspects of language usage and to learn critical attributes of good oral communication.

Spanish I Goals and Objectives

Goal 1:   Students will develop effective oral communication skills.

Objective 1.1:   Students will learn to use Spanish pronunciation rules.

Objective 1.2:   Students will learn how to listen for main ideas rather focusing on details.

Objective 1.3:   Students will learn how to respond appropriately to peers and adults (formality).

Objective 1.4:   Students will learn how to listen for English cognates as a way to interpret unfamiliar words.

Objective 1.5:   Students will learn strategies for communicating meaning even when they don't know every word (e.g., circumlocution, synonyms).

Objective 1.6:   Students will learn to take risks (try new words, sentence structures, etc.) in their speaking

Goal 2:   Students will develop a broad Spanish vocabulary in order to communicate ideas.

Objective 2.1:   Students will learn vocabulary related to greetings.

Objective 2.2:   Students will learn vocabulary related to school and daily life.

Objective 2.3:   Students will learn vocabulary related to number, color, and shape.

Objective 2.4:   Students will learn vocabulary related to travel.

Objective 2.5:   Students will learn vocabulary related to food and holidays.

Objective 2.6:   Students will learn vocabulary related to sports and entertainment.

Objective 2.7:   Students will learn common irregular and regular verbs.

Objective 2.8:   Students will learn articles and pronouns.

Objective 2.9:   Students will learn common idioms

Goal 3:   Students will learn how to use Spanish rules of grammar to effectively communicate.

Objective 3.1:   Students will learn how to conjugate irregular verbs using present and past tense.

Objective 3.2:   Students will learn how to conjugate regular verbs using present and past tense.

Objective 3.3:   Students will learn to use Spanish word order.

Objective 3.4:   Students will learn to adjust articles and pronouns for case and gender.

Figure 10–11
Señor Gutierez's Goals and Objectives for Spanish I

Reflection and Self-Evaluation for Process Portfolios

For process portfolios, reflection is an ongoing part of the process. Students make reflective decisions at many stages of the work. Students often communicate reasons for those decisions. Sometimes reflections are recorded as editing or revision marks (circling words for which the student isn't certain of the spelling, capitalizing a word, adding punctuation, etc.). Sometimes those reflections are recorded as comments on a particular work—thinking out loud on paper, responses to others' feedback or comments, notes to the self about ideas or thoughts about the work. Finally, teachers may ask students to defend choices in a more

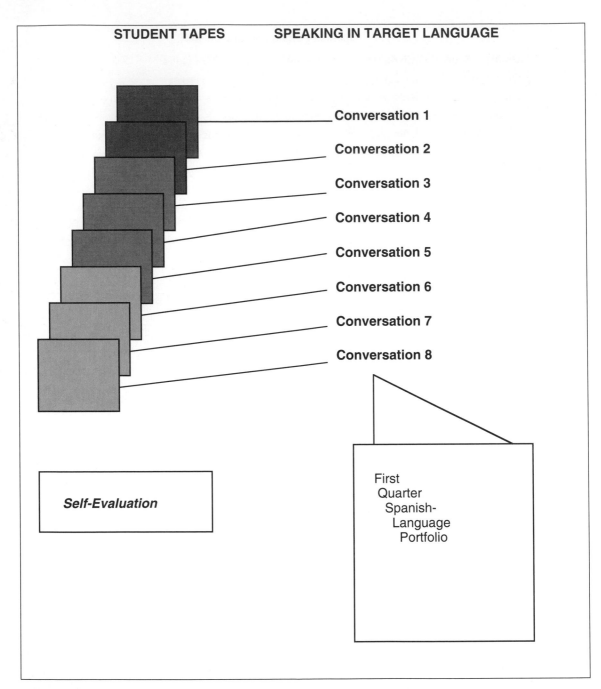

STUDENT TAPES   SPEAKING IN TARGET LANGUAGE

Conversation 1

Conversation 2

Conversation 3

Conversation 4

Conversation 5

Conversation 6

Conversation 7

Conversation 8

Self-Evaluation

First
Quarter
Spanish-
Language
Portfolio

Figure 10–12
Representation of a Spanish-Language Progress Portfolio

Listen to the tape of our conversations this quarter. As you listen, find the ways you have **improved.** Check the areas where you think you have **improved.** Be honest: *give yourself credit for your successes.* Then write a brief description to justify the checks you have made—explain *how* you have improved in each area. Use specific details from our conversations in your explanation. Your reflections are due: _____

☐ The range of vocabulary used

☐ The accuracy of pronunciation

☐ The appropriateness of teacher-student formality

Explanation of growth: _____

_____

_____

_____

_____

_____

_____

_____

In the space below, write two or three goals for improvement in Spanish for next quarter.

_____

_____

_____

_____

Figure 10–13A
Reflection Sheet to Guide Students' Reflections on Their Growth in Speaking Spanish During the First Quarter of Spanish I

formal way.[1] A science teacher might ask students to add a paragraph defending a research question based on the background research before they submit their questions. An elementary teacher might ask students to describe how they have used poetic devices (e.g.,

[1] For example, in our teaching, we ask students to write rationales for instructional and assessment decisions in terms of how instruction will help students learn knowledge and skills stated in their learning objective(s), how the assessment will draw out students' knowledge and skills related to the learning objective(s), and how the scoring rules relate to the knowledge and skills detailed in the learning objective(s). In short, *our* students must think through each assessment and instructional decision, in light of the learning objectives they have established for *their* students. We have found that when students write reflections as they develop first drafts of their assignments, they discover their own misconceptions or disconnections.

Be honest: *give yourself credit for your successes*. Then write a brief description to justify the checks you have made — explain *how* you have improved in each area. Use specific details from our conversations in your explanation. Your reflections are due:_____

☐ The range of vocabulary used

☐ The accuracy of pronunciation

☐ The appropriateness of teacher-student formality

☐ The variety of sentences (getting outside the textbook)

☐ The appropriateness of gender (male/female) and case (plural/singular) in pronouns, nouns, and articles

Explanation of growth:_____

In the space below, write two or three goals for improvement in Spanish for next <u>quarter</u>.

Figure 10–13B

Reflection Sheet to Guide Students' Reflections on Their Growth in Speaking Spanish During the Second Quarter of Spanish I

rhyme, simile, alliteration) in the first draft of a poem. The purpose of these formal reflections is to help students focus their work on the learning objectives. However, it is possible that too much reflection early on can limit imagination (e.g., when writing a short story or creating a visual work of art); therefore, you will have to be judicious about when to require formal reflection and when to make reflection a natural part of the process of creating a valued performance through feedback-revision cycles and stages of editing.

Figure 10–14 is a cover sheet for use with a science process portfolio. The purpose of the cover sheet is to guide students' reflection, after they have completed an investigation, on the overall process of moving from a question to a conclusion. The checklist for each stage is intended to guide the students' thinking as they reflect on their work. Implicit in the use of the checklist is a self-evaluation—students who complete the checklist will be determining whether they have met a set of performance criteria.

Figure 10–15 is an excerpt from the science process portfolio wherein Ms. Stone, the teacher, and Tony, the student, are "conversing" about Tony's conclusion from the investigation. The dialogue is an opportunity for Ms. Stone to teach Tony about how to draw a conclusion. Through this dialogue on paper, Ms. Stone can focus on Tony's specific issues, and Tony can indicate what she understands and doesn't understand about the process of drawing conclusions using data. Tony's response to Ms. Stone's first comment suggests that she knew how to incorporate data. Yet making recommendations based on the results was a stretch for her. She continued the dialogue in order to clarify what she should do next. In

Be honest: *give yourself credit for your successes.* Then write a brief description to justify the checks you have made — explain *how* you have improved in each area. Use specific details from our conversations in your explanation. Your reflections are due:_____

☐ The range of vocabulary used

☐ The accuracy of pronunciation

☐ The appropriateness of teacher-student formality

☐ The variety of sentences (getting outside the textbook)

☐ The appropriateness of gender (male/female) and case (plural/singular) in pronouns, nouns, and articles

☐ Conjugations of irregular verbs

☐ Conjugations of regular verbs

☐ Responses to what the teacher has said

☐ Talking around words I don't know

Explanation of growth:_____

In the space below, write two or three goals for improvement in Spanish for next year.

Figure 10–13C
Reflection Sheet to Guide Students' Reflections on Their Growth in Speaking Spanish During the Fourth Quarter of Spanish I

the final version of her conclusion, Tony had improved her conclusion by supporting it with data and by using the information in the investigation to make recommendations to the community. For the process portfolio, Ms. Stone had asked students to add a reflective piece to discuss decisions made during the revision process. Figure 10–16 is an excerpt from Tony's reflection on the changes.

Reflection and self-evaluation are essential elements in the use of portfolios. They give students an opportunity to think about their own learning processes. They help students internalize the criteria for good work. They help students to identify their strengths and weaknesses so that they can set goals for future learning. In short, reflection and self-evaluation are what make portfolios more than a collection of assignments. Our work with students, from 9-year-olds to adults, has helped us see that self-evaluation and reflection are often the most critical aspect of portfolios (see also Valencia & Place, 1994).

Science Research Process Portfolio Cover Sheet

Complete the checklist below as you review the materials for each stage of your research project. Once you have reviewed a stage, write an evaluation of your work at that stage. Include what you have done well and what you could improve in your next research project.

Stage
Research Focus (check one) ☐ Used own knowledge and experience to come up with my own topic ☐ Asked others about ideas for a topic ☐ Asked my teacher to give me a topic
Location of background information (check all that apply) ☐ Textbook ☐ Other texts ☐ Science journals ☐ Internet ☐ Interviews with scientists
Evaluation of Sources (check all that apply) ☐ Checked all information for relationship to research question ☐ Checked to see if more than one source gave similar information (reliability) ☐ Checked to see if previous studies were conducted systematically and with controls (validity) ☐ Checked to see whether claims are backed up with data
Organization of Information from Research (check all that apply) ☐ Took notes from each source in my own words ☐ Documented sources including author, publisher, date, etc. ☐ Used web, outline, graphic, or other strategy to organize ideas
Research Question (check all that apply) ☐ Follows from background research ☐ Can be investigated systematically ☐ Can be investigated in the amount of time available ☐ Can be investigated with materials available or materials that can be easily obtained
Investigation Design (check all that apply) ☐ Has hypothesis that follows from research question ☐ Has variables and conditions relevant to hypothesis and research question ☐ Includes sufficient control variables (times, measurements, frequencies, materials, etc.) ☐ Has one dependent variable with specific units of measurement identified ☐ Has a control condition or control group ☐ Has one experimental control variable
Observations/Measurements (check all that apply) ☐ Were systematic ☐ Followed planned design ☐ Were carefully recorded
Results (check all that apply) ☐ Are summarized statistically (frequencies, percents, means, etc., as appropriate) ☐ Are summarized in table(s), graph(s), chart(s), as appropriate ☐ Are summarized in written form
Conclusions and Discussion (check all that apply) ☐ Related to research question and hypothesis ☐ Supported with specific references to data results ☐ Adds to what is known from background research

Figure 10–14
Process Portfolio Cover Sheet for Science Research Project

Discussion and Conclusion

Based on the results of the study, it appears that dissolved oxygen levels impact the survival of salmon in this stream. If the community has to protect salmon from extinction, they will have to do something about the dissolved oxygen levels in their streams.

Ms. Stone, I don't know what to say after this.   Tony

Tony,
I think you are on the right track with your conclusion. You need to use some data to support the claim that DO levels impact survival of salmon. Include data from your investigation to support this statement. See if you can use data from your investigation to make suggestions about what the community can do to protect the salmon. Are there actions you think they should take based on what you learned?   Ms. Stone

Ms. Stone, Okay, I know how to add data. But I'm not sure about how to make suggestions about what they should do. Do you mean that the variables I looked at should be changed somehow?   Tony

Tony,
Yes, you should use the variables from the investigation. What are the variables that seemed to predict decreases in DO levels? What can the community do to control those variables? For example, the streams near housing developments seemed to have higher nitrogen levels which helped the algae to grow. In your conclusion, discuss what the algae does to the DO levels and why. Also, discuss what probably caused the higher nitrogen levels. Finally, does your background research help you know where the nitrogen comes from?   Ms. Stone

---

Figure 10–15
Teacher–Student Dialogue About the Conclusion for Tony's Final Report

---

I added the data on the difference in dissolved oxygen levels and the difference in the number of salmon hatchlings that survived in Clark Creek and Bench Creek. That gave support to my conclusion that the dissolved oxygen level was the reason there were fewer salmon hatching in Bench Creek than in Clark Creek. I already knew how to do that from math class so it was easy to add data.

The other data I had was about the amount of algae in both streams. Ms. Stone reminded me to look at my research on what caused algae in streams. The research says that when there is a lot of runoff from fertilizer, the nitrogen goes in the streams. That helps the algae grow and use up the oxygen. So, I added some stuff about what the people in the housing development could do about their lawns. I think I learned a lot about how to use data to support my claims. But I also learned to use the background research, which I never thought about before. I guess I always thought background research was just a requirement. I never thought about using it to make sense of my investigations.

Figure 10–16
Tony's Reflection on Revisions to Her Final Report

Motivation and Feedback in the Use of Portfolios

The use of portfolios creates many of the conditions for a task-involving classroom. All portfolios are reflections of students' individuality and, when combined with student participation in goal setting, can be powerful tools for engagement and learning. They are, of necessity, individualized instruction at least to some extent, and allow for specific, encouraging, and useful feedback that can sustain student motivation through difficult challenges. The focus of all portfolios is student accomplishment, represented in concrete terms rather than summarized abstractly with a grade. Students can *see* what they can do.

Growth portfolios can be especially powerful at showing students just how much they have learned over time. Often students are astonished when they see how far they have come; growth portfolios can provide a kind of time-lapse view of students' increasing mastery, making the invisible visible. The focus on a *self-referenced* notion of mastery inherent in growth portfolios is also important in promoting task involvement: It is not necessary to compare one student's work with other students' work. It is only important to see how the level of an individual's current work compares to her former abilities.

This self-reference is especially valuable for students who struggle with a subject. A student with a learning disability may not reach the highest level of competence compared to his peers, but he can still take pride in his accomplishments and learn how to set realistic goals. Portfolios can also provide a record of how specific strategies have worked in helping struggling students make progress, which is useful in planning future instruction and in working with the IEP manager or multidisciplinary team. More frequent feedback and scaffolding can help students with disabilities, as well as students who are still learning English. Portfolios provide a means for doing this without calling undue attention to these students as different.

An important element of successful process portfolio use is the feedback teachers give to students about their work, their progress, and their processes. Ms. Stone's feedback in Tony's process portfolio has several aspects of encouraging and useful feedback. First, Ms. Stone encouraged Tony by telling her she was "on the right track." Next, she gave Tony some specific things to think about as she worked on her report. However, she did not tell Tony precisely what to do next; nor did she edit Tony's work. She pointed Tony in a direction, with enough scaffolding to support Tony in learning how to write a report. Tony continued the conversation with Ms. Stone until she understood what her teacher was recommending (this conversation could also have occurred in person after Tony received the first response from her teacher). Then Tony had to take the next steps on her own, learning the function of different parts of the scientific process in communicating the results of her research and recommendations that might result in policy or behavioral change in the suburban neighborhood.

Feedback can be both oral and written, depending on the age of the student and the efficiency of one method over another. Young children may not be able to read extensive written feedback, but a sentence or two that they can read can be very encouraging. A kindergarten teacher Susan knows makes a point of engaging students' ideas: instead of a general "good job!" she comments on an aspect of the student's work. "That sounds very exciting! What did you do next?" Teachers of young children may need to do most of the feedback in one-on-one portfolio conferences. Middle and high school students may also need face-to-face discussion as part of the feedback mechanism, especially early in the term when students are learning the criteria for good work and the processes for producing it. Mr. Gutierez used early conferences with students to show them *how* to reflect on their growth. It may be necessary to give oral feedback to older students who have difficulty reading or who need more one-on-one instruction. Much of the feedback for secondary students, however, can be in written form.

Portfolios, Goal Setting, and Motivation

Portfolios can also provide an opportunity for students to set their own goals within the teacher's framework of learning goals and objectives. Portfolio conferences can be a chance for student and teacher to discuss the student's progress and for them to jointly set goals for the next phase of work. Ownership of goals for writing, language competence, mathematical thinking, and the like can be a powerful motivator for students facing difficult work; when students are helped to set short-term goals, they have even more motivation (Bandura & Schunk, 1981; Schunk, 2003; Schunk & Swartz, 1993).

When a person has only long-range goals (e.g., "I'm going to lose 20 pounds in the next year," or "My ultimate goal is skiing the most difficult slopes."), it is very difficult to see progress. Setting only distant goals can lead students to believe they are making no progress at all. This can, in turn, lead to lack of commitment and effort, which slows progress even more. In schools, students with disabilities can despair of making progress that "counts," feeling that they will never be able to accomplish what other students seem to do so easily.

Short-term goals allow people to set short-term targets against which to measure their own progress (e.g., "I'm going to lose 2 pounds every 2 weeks," or "I'm going to learn to do parallel turns on the easy slopes next month."). The fact that students are often surprised when faced with their own improvement over a semester suggests that they have not had short-term goals, and so have not been able to monitor and take pride in their accomplishments. For much of what students learn, they may not know how to set short-term goals because they don't know what is feasible in a given time span. For some students, competence can seem an unattainable goal. With ways to measure intermediate progress, however, they can experience the feelings of accomplishment that keep learners wanting to learn more.

Goal setting is a skill that can be taught[2] and portfolios provide a great opportunity to teach students how to set goals, how to monitor progress, and how to revise or extend future goals. Bolstered by the confidence that comes from accomplishing goals and seeing progress, students are motivated to continue. Teachers, too, can be buoyed up by the

---

[2] Susan once asked students in a high school drop-out rehabilitation program to participate in a panel discussion for her class of beginning teachers. She was especially interested in any advice these students might have for preventing other students from making the decision to drop out of school. Several students talked about how they had been taught to look at their possibilities and set goals for what they wanted to be able do after high school. They stated that they had never been able to imagine life after high school, and so had very diffuse goals or no goals at all. In the program, the students were taught strategies for setting proximal goals, as well as for how to achieve those goals. Combined with accelerated courses to help them remove failing grades from before the students dropped out, these goal-setting techniques helped many reenter the regular program and succeed despite difficulties.

progress their students have made. In short, portfolios provide a concrete set of perform-ance data teachers can use to teach their students how to evaluate their own work and set goals for the future. This not only sets the stage for more motivation in the present, but also teaches important life skills that have application in the real world of work and adult life.

ASSESSING PORTFOLIOS

Portfolios are important tools for telling stories about students' progress, accomplishments, and processes. However, each teacher must decide whether she or he will assess the portfolio beyond the scores already assigned to the work in the portfolio. Showcase, progress, and cu-mulative portfolios typically hold work that has already been scored or evaluated in some way. There are times when teachers have students work on a variety of individual pieces (say, in a writing workshop) and then ask students to pick four or five to finalize for the showcase port-folio. In this case, assessment of the portfolio makes sense. However, if the work housed in the portfolio has already been scored or evaluated, another score for the portfolio makes lit-tle sense. Students who have done well will get yet another score in the grade book showing that they have done well. Students who have struggled will have yet another score in the grade book showing that they have struggled. So, why are portfolios considered assessment tools?

First and foremost, portfolios allow students to *assess themselves* and reflect on their own learning and accomplishments. Second, portfolios give teachers an opportunity to see what students understand about what they are learning. Still, there are times when it makes sense to assess the portfolios themselves.

One way that teachers assess portfolios is to look at students' reflections to determine whether the students demonstrate conceptual understanding in what they say about their work. For example, if a mathematics teacher asks students to select the work that shows their best understanding of fractions, the reflections on that work (via the entry slips) can help the teacher know whether the students actually understand fractions. In this case, the re-flection can be another tool for assessment.

If teachers have goals and objectives related to self-evaluation and goal setting, teach-ers can look at students' reflections and self-evaluations to see whether they have an accu-rate picture of their knowledge and skills and whether they can set reasonable goals. The grading policy described in Chapter 9 includes an evaluation of a portfolio. The criteria on which the portfolio was to be evaluated were (1) thoughtful evaluation of own work in re-lation to the class goals, (2) clear connections between the work in the portfolio and your self-evaluation, and (3) setting appropriate goals for next term based on work and self-evaluation. If the students met all three criteria, they receive full credit for the portfolio. The rubric in Figure 10–17 is one that could be used to evaluate students' portfolio reflections.

Process portfolios result in a final, prepared accomplishment. Therefore, an assessment of the final performance is a natural part of the process. You may also wish to assess students' use of the processes shown in the portfolio. For example, one high school in the Pacific Northwest developed a set of rubrics to evaluate students' use of writing processes. The process portfolio cover sheet shown in Figure 10–14 has criteria for each stage of scientific investigation. These criteria could easily be turned into an evaluative tool such as a rating scale or several brief rubrics. If you choose to evaluate students' use of a process, it is criti-cal that your students know they will receive one or more process scores, that they are taught

---

Self-Evaluation Rubric

Performance Criteria

- Self-evaluation is provided for each entry
- Self-evaluation is a serious consideration of the strengths of each entry in relation to one or more learning objectives
- Self-evaluation is a serious consideration of the weaknesses of each entry in relation to one or more learning objectives
- Personal goals follow directly from assessed strengths and weaknesses

Rubric

4 points	Self-evaluation is a thoughtful, complete, and accurate consideration of strengths and weaknesses. Personal goals follow directly from the self-evaluation.
3 points	Self-evaluation is a technically complete and accurate consideration of strengths and weaknesses. Personal goals make sense based on the self-evaluation.
2 points	Self-evaluation is a partially complete and accurate consideration of strengths and weaknesses. Personal goals are generally related to self-evaluation.
1 point	Self-evaluation shows attempt to evaluate strengths and weaknesses. Personal goals, if given, are somewhat related to self-evaluation.
0 points	Self-evaluation was not seriously attempted; off task, not completed.

Figure 10–17
Example Rubric to Evaluate Final Portfolio

how to use each step of the process, and that they understand the expectations (criteria) for each step.

For cumulative portfolios that are used for high school graduation, evaluation is typically external to the classroom. In most cases, each piece in the portfolio has been evaluated by a teacher before being chosen for the portfolio. Therefore, the external judgment is about whether the collection shows that the student has met an overall performance standard. In many cases, this assessment is simply a yes/no assessment.

MANAGING PORTFOLIOS

Portfolios can be labor intensive for the teacher. Whether oral or written, thoughtful feedback takes time and effort on the teacher's part. If portfolios are to be used successfully, you need to be able to manage evaluation and feedback without being buried in folders or binders. This is especially true for middle and high school teachers who may see 120 to 150 students a day. One simple strategy is to allow for variation in submission dates, so that all of the students' portfolios don't arrive on the same day. To prevent having them all show up on the *last* day, create a list of possible due dates with a limited number of slots for each date and have students sign up in advance. This can have the advantage of helping you teach students to plan ahead and budget their time, while allowing some flexibility for them to work around due dates in other classes, school trips, and so forth.

Different types of portfolios require different amounts of feedback. In a showcase portfolio, feedback has already been given for the pieces selected. Entry slips give a final chance for teachers (and parents) to provide feedback on the students' selection of entries. Teacher selections and their entry slips can reinforce important learning goals and objectives by pointing them out in student work. Process portfolios probably require the most frequent and extensive teacher feedback, but they also provide the most opportunities for teaching students important processes and criteria for good work.

Once you decide which type or types of portfolios to use, you have to decide when to introduce them to your students. Working folders can be introduced at the beginning of the school year for students at all ages. In this way, they can get in the habit of storing their work for future selection. Young children are already learning management skills for school (e.g., returning homework, taking papers home to parents and returning them, organizing work in folders or notebooks); therefore, collecting work is a natural part of the process. Showcase and progress portfolios can be introduced later in the school year when students have generated a variety of work related to each learning objective or valued performance. Process portfolios may be introduced early in the year. You might choose to use process portfolios several times in a school year as students work through different valued performances. In an elementary classroom, although it is possible for students to have more than one process portfolio at a time, it is probably more effective for students to focus on one important performance at a time. They are more likely to learn from the process if they focus their reflections on the decisions and processes relevant to a single performance. Cumulative portfolios can be introduced late in the school year as students select entries to be stored in their cumulative records and passed along to next year's teacher(s).

Portfolios should be stored so that students and teachers have access to them at all times. For elementary students, teachers can keep folders in the classroom. If students are likely to have many potential entries from which to choose, accordion folders will be most useful—with different sections for each type of work or school subject. Once it is time to select entries for the portfolio, legal-sized folders can be laminated so that they last longer and stapled on the edges so that students' work doesn't fall out. You can use portfolio cover sheets as tables of contents inside the portfolio. Plastic crates to hold portfolios can be placed in different locations in the classroom so that students don't have to crowd around a single location to access their portfolios. Crates can be organized alphabetically, by work groups, or by any other system that helps you and your students know where to look for the students' portfolios.

Middle school and high school students can keep their work in binders until it is time to select items for portfolios. Time must be spent at the beginning of the school year to help students (particularly middle school students) learn how to store their work in systematic ways. Once it is time to select work for portfolios, you will need plastic crates or filing cabinets to hold students' portfolios. Crates or filing cabinets can be color coded for different periods. In addition, portfolios should be stored alphabetically, by last name, so that students can easily find their work. As with elementary students, a cover sheet, similar to those in Figures 10–8 and 10–14, can be used as the table of contents for the portfolio.

We offer two cautions about the storage of portfolios. The first is that students must learn to respect the privacy of other students' portfolios. Students may choose to share their work with other students; however, students should be able to trust that other students will respect their work and leave it alone. It is your responsibility to create a learning environment that builds trust among students and that establishes consequences for students who violate that trust. It is always a good idea to hold a class meeting to discuss privacy issues, to establish rules for use of portfolios, and to determine the consequences for breaking these rules. Students may have better ideas for meaningful consequences than adults do.

The second caution has to do with ownership. When portfolios are well executed, students develop pride in their work. If a student has worked hard on a piece and put it in his portfolio, he will feel anger and a sense of betrayal if his work disappears or is damaged. The portfolio is a holding place for the students' accomplishments. The work belongs to the student, not the teacher, other classmates, the school, or the district. Therefore, students' work should be treated with the same care shown to other private property. For example, Maria left her portfolio in the classroom at the end of the school year. She returned to pick it up the next week and discovered that the janitor had thrown out all of the papers that were left in the classroom—including her portfolio. Maria was angry at the janitor and heartbroken because all of her work was lost. When you embark on using portfolios, be sure to take students' rights and privacy into account as you make your plans. Be sure to communicate the importance of students' work to anyone who has access to your classroom.

Using Portfolios

As the representations in Figures 10–1 through 10–3, 10–5, 10–6, and 10–12 demonstrate, the focus of portfolios can vary depending on what the teacher wants students to capture and have students demonstrate. Figure 10–18 gives the steps required to use portfolios in a classroom, school, or district. Each step is necessary, but not sufficient for creating showcase portfolios. The final ingredient for success is the belief that a critical part of the instructional process is helping students internalize the purpose of their education and helping them become active partners in their own education. Following these steps would be an ordeal for teachers and students if that primary commitment were not the driving force behind using portfolios.

Decide whether you will evaluate the portfolio itself and what will be a fair basis for evaluation (e.g., the quality of reflection [Figure 10–13], use of process, or the quality of final unscored work). We have used process portfolios in our teaching for many years. There were moments when the amount of work seemed overwhelming. Guiding students through the drafts of their work and helping them think about their choices has meant that we take a "less is more" approach to our teaching (see Wiggins, 1989, *The Futility of Trying to Teach Everything of Importance*). Use of process portfolios meant that we had to make hard choices about what mattered most and what could be taught in a finite amount of time. We had to decide what our students were likely to learn on their own once they deeply understood some principles and had meaningful practice with critical skills. We had to figure out how to evaluate students' work, how to assess a final portfolio, and how to manage the process so that all of us (students and teachers) benefited from the process portfolio (Taylor, 1997).

While young children tend to embrace the creation of portfolios as well as reflecting on their own work, older students who have not had opportunities to benefit from portfolios may resist them. Some resist because they do not want to work hard or think hard. They may not appreciate the power of reflecting on their own learning processes. Some resist because they do not understand why they are doing the work. For us, this has meant that we adapted our teaching to make the purposes clearer. Some students resist because reflection on their own progress comes naturally to them; therefore, they dislike the formality of a

---

Steps to Using Portfolios

1. Establish a clear purpose for the portfolio. If you plan to have more than one purpose (e.g., showcase and process), be sure you are clear about the unique characteristics and purposes of each.

2. Decide whether to focus on students' demonstration of valued performances (Figure 10–1 and 10–5), particular learning objectives (Figures 10–2 and 10–4), learning goals (Figure 10–3), or processes through which students demonstrate thinking and procedural skills (Figure 10–6).

3. If performances are the focus of the portfolio, develop and/or identify clear criteria for high quality performances; if objectives are the focus of the portfolio, clearly define the objectives in language students understand; if process is the focus of the portfolio, clearly identify the stages of the work.

4. Identify the work or stages of the work from which students may *choose* AND/OR the work that *must* be included in order to demonstrate students' learning. Entries may be common to all students, unique to each student, or a combination of common and unique work.

5. Determine the number of entries to be included in showcase, cumulative, and growth portfolios. If learning objectives are the focus of the portfolio, you will need at least two entries for each learning objective. This will increase the realiability of decisions made about students using the portfolio.

6. Make sure the learning objectives, goals, or the criteria for performances are public and are in language that is understandable to students, their parents, and other audiences.

7. For showcase, growth or cumulative portfolios, allow students to participate in choosing the work to be included in the portfolio. Even if the work a student chooses is not her/his best work or the best example of growth, student choice is central to student ownership of the portfolio.

8. Teach students (through modeling and/or coaching) how to select work that exemplifies the learning objectives, goals, performance criteria, or process.

9. Create tools to help students reflect on their portfolio entries (e.g., Figures 10–9 and 10–13).

10. Teach students (through modeling or coaching) *how* to reflect on their work orally (for very young children) or in writing.

11. If the portfolio is a showcase, growth or cumulative portfolio, include work that *you* believe is the best. Teachers are generally better than students in judging the quality of work.

12. Make certain that each entry in a showcase, growth, or cumulative portfolio has an entry slip. You may write entry slips; students may write them; students may dictate them to you (if they are too young to communicate their ideas through writing); or you may help students write their entry slips during a portfolio conference. If parents or IEP team members will select entries, they should complete entry slips giving the reasons for their choices.

Figure 10–18
Steps for Effectively Using Portfolios in the Classroom

process portfolio. Our research has shown, however, that our students deeply understand the concepts and demonstrate their understanding and skill long after they leave us, crediting the reflective elements of the portfolio for their success (Taylor & Nolen, 1996b). Reading the final reflections on their portfolios has been inspiring—leading to ongoing renewal of our commitment to use portfolios in our teaching.

SUMMARY

We began by saying that portfolios can be powerful assessment tools. The ideas in this chapter will help you be successful in using portfolios and in avoiding some of the pitfalls. The purpose for the portfolio should reflect your assessment needs and goals. However, the labor intensiveness of different approaches must be considered as well when deciding which type of portfolio to use. We suggest that you experiment with portfolios at first by using them in one class (for secondary teachers) or one subject (for elementary teachers). This will give you a chance to try out different approaches and develop one that both meets your assessment needs and is survivable. We also recommend that you begin with a narrow focus (e.g., a process portfolio on a fairly simple performance or a small collection of assignments for a showcase portfolio) and work up to more complex focuses as you learn how to use portfolios and as you experience the sheer joy of discovering just how much students can understand about their own learning.

REFERENCES

Arter, J. A., & Spandel, V. (1992). NCME instructional module: Using portfolios of student work in instruction and assessment. *Educational Measurement: Issues and Practice, 11*(1), 36–44.

Bandura, A., & Schunk, D. H. (1981). Cultivating competence, self-efficacy, and intrinsic interest through proximal self-motivation. *Journal of Personality and Social Psychology, 41*, 586–598.

Schunk, D. H. (2003). Self-efficacy for reading and writing: Influence of modeling, goal setting, and self-evaluation. *Reading and Writing Quarterly: Overcoming Learning Difficulties, 19*(2), 159–172.

Schunk, D. H., & Swartz, C. W. (1993). Goals and progress feedback: Effects on self-efficacy and writing achievement. *Contemporary Educational Psychology, 18*, 337–354.

Schwab, Joseph J. (1978). Education and the structure of the disciplines. In *Science, curriculum, and liberal education*. Chicago: University of Chicago Press.

Taylor, C. S. (1997). Using portfolios to teach teachers about assessment: How to survive. *Educational Assessment, 4*(2), 123–147.

Taylor, C., & Nolen, S. B. (1996a). A contextualized approach to teaching teachers about classroom-based assessment. *Educational Psychologist, 31*, 77–88.

Taylor, C. S., & Nolen, S. B. (1996b). What does the psychometrician's classroom look like? Reframing assessment concepts in the context of learning. *Educational Policy Analysis Archives [electronic version], 4*(17).

Valencia, S. W., & Place, N. (1994). Portfolios: A process for enhancing teaching and learning. *Reading Teacher, 47*(8), 666–669.

Wiggins, G. (1989). The futility of trying to teach everything of importance. *Educational Leadership, 47*(3), 44–48, 57–59.

Wolf, D. P. (1991). Assessment as an episode of learning. In R. E. Bennett & W. C. Ward (Eds.), *Construction versus choice in cognitive measurement.* Hillsdale, NJ: Lawrence Erlbaum.

COMMUNICATING WITH OTHERS
ABOUT STUDENT LEARNING

Once you have collected assessment data and evaluated student achievement, you must report that achievement to the student, parent or guardian, and other school professionals. Written reports and report cards are sent to students and their parents or guardians and filed in the students' official school files. But communication can and, we argue, should go beyond these end-of-term reports. To be effective, communication needs to occur many times during a term or year of school.

In the chapter on grades and grading, we describe the various choices that go into summarizing assessment data and their effects on student learning and motivation. We discuss the importance of communicating your grading policies to students and their parents or guardians at the beginning of a year or course, so that students have a chance to meet standards, and parents have a chance to support their students' learning. Grades are used by other professionals, including a child's future teachers and any specialists currently providing special assistance. If students transfer to other schools, the grades recorded in their cumulative files travel with them (at least, ideally!).

The chapter on portfolio assessment provides an alternative to achievement summaries that can be used with or instead of summary grades. Portfolio assessment can show students' progress over time and their current levels of performance in concrete ways, by including examples of actual student work. Students, and their parents or guardians, learn what constitutes good performance in a subject area or areas. Student entry slips provide an opportunity for students to reflect on and evaluate their own work, and give parents and teachers a chance to examine those reflections. Other professionals, including the teachers who will be working with each student in the future, specialists, and schools receiving a transfer student, can see what was learned and the level of student performance in concrete terms. In this sense, portfolios can provide much more detailed information about student achievement than report cards can.

In this chapter we describe different strategies and tools for communicating about students: parent–teacher conferences, multidisciplinary child study teams, progress reports, newsletters, and other venues for communicating about students' achievements. We also discuss the ethics of this kind of communication and the federal laws governing the sharing of information about student achievement.

Several audiences need to know about students' accomplishments and progress. They include, but may not be limited to, students, parents and guardians, other teachers, educational specialists, and school administrators. Each of these audiences has different information needs, and part of your responsibility as a teacher is to have a plan for communicating with each of these audiences. Throughout this book we have described how to provide useful and encouraging feedback to students as a central aspect of instruction and assessment. In this chapter, we also discuss the needs of other audiences and how to prepare for and communicate with them. For some audiences, communication should be brief, informative, and serve a collegial purpose. For other audiences, detailed communication is critical to students' ongoing success in your class.

This chapter is divided into two sections. In the first, we describe purposes and tools for providing assessment and evaluation information to parents and guardians and students. We describe communicating for different purposes, at different developmental levels, using a variety of tools, including conferences and report cards. In the second section we discuss communicating with other educational professionals about student learning. We begin by describing ways you can communicate effectively about student learning to administrators, teachers who will be teaching your students in the future, and specialists assigned to monitor the progress of students with special needs. Finally, we consider how teachers can be effective problem-solving partners with other professionals when students may need special assessment and interventions.

COMMUNICATING WITH PARENTS AND GUARDIANS

Parents and guardians bring their own notions of schooling with them when they enter your classroom, and their interpretation of what they see and hear depends on those ideas and expectations. Parents and guardians of elementary students may have only partial memories of their own early educational experiences. Some may have very specific expectations about what students should learn and how they should learn, based on their own school experiences or those of their older children. Others may remember school as unnecessary or unpleasant. You will have to be prepared to communicate with parents and guardians whether they have professional degrees or a less than a high school education.

Parents and guardians will need to understand both your goals for their children and the children's progress toward those goals. Parents can be kept in the loop through a number of communication strategies, including postcards, e-mails, phone calls, parent–teacher conferences, and progress reports. Progress reports are generally identical to grade reports, but they are given as an intermediate indication of students' achievement. Again, the value of early communication with parents or guardians lies in enlisting their help in supporting student learning. Communication doesn't have to be one-way, from teacher to parent. Often parents and guardians can provide additional information about their child that can help you make needed adjustments; they have known their child longer and in more situations than you have.

To the extent that the learning objectives can be related to real work (see Chapter 4), parents and guardians will better understand what students need to learn. For example, Mr. Willis, a first-grade teacher, has focused on student learning of reading: knowledge and skills that range from the sounds of letters or combinations of letters (letter blends) to word reading to reading strategies to reading comprehension. He also expects students to learn how to write letters, words, sentences, and paragraphs. He has learning objectives related to a wide range of mathematical concepts and skills such as number names, number patterns, number-numeral correspondence, number operations (whole number addition, subtraction, and multiplication), simple measurement tools and concepts, the names of geometric shapes, how to represent data in bar graphs, how to solve problems, and how to communicate their mathematical knowledge. Finally, he wants students to learn to share their ideas, work and play well with other students, and follow school rules.

If Mr. Willis's communication to parents and guardians, whether in a newsletter or face-to-face, included a list of learning objectives written in educational language, many parents and guardians would not know what these terms and ideas meant. Therefore, he includes examples of work the students have completed that demonstrate the targeted knowledge and skills. He also includes examples of student-written sentences and paragraphs, student-created bar graphs, a list of stories students are reading in class, and an observational checklist he is using to observe students' social and communication skills as they work in groups and their social and motor skills as they play on the playground.

Just before conference time, Mr. Willis has students post their bar graphs and their favorite writing samples around the classroom. During conferences, he shows parents and guardians a 2-minute videotape of their child reading aloud, and then he describes the reading skills and strategies the child is using. In this way, the learning objectives take on meaning as the child sounds out words and letters, figures out the meaning of unfamiliar words, self-corrects reading errors, as well as retells a story and answers questions that show comprehension of the story. He shows another brief videotape of the child counting blocks and writing numerals for each number of blocks, using manipulatives to solve word problems, and sorting shapes by different attributes such as shape, color, and size. He presents one or two of the child's writing samples to parents and guardians. Finally, he shares his observations (using his observational checklist as a guide) regarding their child's skill in working and playing with others, the child's confidence in sharing ideas with the class, her ability to follow directions, and her developing motor and communication skills.

Parents and guardians need to have a clear sense of their children's progress so that they can be effective partners in their education. In the next section we discuss some of the differences among grade levels in the type of information and evidence parents and guardians need.

Developmental Considerations

The kinds of information you will provide to parents and guardians, the form that information takes, and the role of students in the process will depend, in part, on the grade levels you teach. Conferences about kindergartners and conferences about sixth-graders, for example, will both include information related to transitions into new school settings. The nature of the concerns, the information needed, and the implications of that information, however, will be quite different.

Information Needs Parents and guardians are interested not only in what students have accomplished at a given point in time, but also in how students are progressing and whether the progress is satisfactory. What constitutes acceptable accomplishments and progress differs for students at different levels of schooling.

Teachers of primary level children (i.e., prekindergarten through third grade) are concerned about students' academic, physical, social, and emotional development in school. The learning objectives teachers establish include those related to traditional academic areas (reading, writing, mathematics), as well as learning objectives for how children work and live with others, how they take care of themselves—from tying their shoes to asking for help—and how their motor development affects their abilities to complete school-related and self-care tasks. Young children are also learning to follow directions, to take materials home, and to bring materials to school—in short, they are adjusting to the routines of school. Teachers of young children must be very clear about the reading, writing, and mathematics learning objectives for their grade level so that they can communicate about whether students are progressing satisfactorily. They must also have clear and purposeful learning objectives for the skills and strategies students need to be successful in the school community. All of these objectives must be considered when communicating with others about primary level students' accomplishments and progress.

Teachers of students in the intermediate and middle school levels are generally more focused on academic work than they are on social, emotional, or physical development. However, if students are not adjusting well to school, working with others, or caring for themselves, teachers have an obligation to communicate this information to parents and guardians, and potentially with other professionals. As the purposes of study in some academic subjects become less obvious (e.g., "Why do I have to learn the names and locations of all the states in the United States?"), it is the teacher's job to explain those purposes to both students and their families. As we have emphasized throughout this book, teachers need to have clear notions of what academic knowledge and skills they want students to learn, why, and how students are likely to use that knowledge and those skills. Only then can they effectively communicate those learning objectives to others along with students' progress toward achieving those objectives. As children move from preadolescence to adolescence, the social skills necessary for group work, hallways, and social activities may be similar, but students' views of those skills (and their own competence) may change. Most intermediate and middle school teachers have learning objectives about discussion skills, group roles, dividing and sharing tasks, and classroom citizenship. Some teachers may have learning objectives related to individual and team sports or physical fitness. In developing a communication plan, it is wise to think about how you will help your students and other audiences understand your learning objectives and students' progress toward them.

High school teachers are generally focused on academic or career-related knowledge and skills, including both oral and written discourse skills. Some high school subjects, although required, are difficult to explain to lay audiences. Therefore, being clear about how the knowledge and skills students learn in high school relate to the world beyond school is prerequisite to communicating with families about their students' accomplishments and progress. In Chapter 4, we discussed using authentic performances as the centerpiece of teaching and assessment. When the knowledge and skills taught can be used in the context of authentic work, students and their parents or guardians can more easily see the value in what students are learning, which is an important first step in communication about students' learning. If students and parents or guardians do not see the value of what students are to learn, they may be less concerned if students do not accomplish the learning objectives. Figure 11–1 is an example of what we call a *goals and objectives rationale*. We have our students write rationales similar to these so that they can help students and their families understand the value of what they are learning. Of course, when such rationales are given, teachers must then help students apply the knowledge and skills in similar real-world contexts so that students' experiences are consistent with the rationales.

The Role of Students in Communicating Their Learning   Students can play a role in the communication process that ranges from recipient of the teacher's evaluation and goals to active participant. Many teachers require students to be present during conferences so that they can participate in the process. Some teachers involve students in the assessment and evaluation of their own work and in communicating what they have learned to parents, guardians, and others. When teachers have clear learning objectives and standards, and if they teach their students how to evaluate strengths and weaknesses in their work, students can be eloquent spokespersons for their own learning. They can also help to set goals for future learning, a process that is both motivating and an important life skill.

Young children's participation in a parent-teacher conference may be limited to selecting favorite pieces of art or written work from a portfolio and explaining them to their parent or guardian or giving a demonstration of math skills using manipulatives. If concrete evidence of their performance is available, as in progress portfolios (see Chapter 10), older primary students can talk about areas of strength or weakness in reading, writing, or math

> **Goal: Students will understand the fundamental concepts and procedures related to algebraic functions.**
>
> Objective 1: Students will learn how to use coordinates, graphs, and formulas to represent numerical functions.
>
> Objective 2: Students will learn how to use graphs to solve for equalities and inequalities.
>
> Objective 3: Students will learn how to use equations to solve real-world problems.

> **Example Rationale:** Functions are predictable relationships between events. When one event happens, the next event follows in a predictable way. Mathematics is a language used to describe these relationships. One way that adults work with functions is to represent them in formats that are acceptable in the mathematical community (Objective 1). Adults use the particular format that is most useful at the time. A researcher might create a scatter plot showing the relationship between students' hours of TV watching and their grades in school. A mathematician might represent relationships with equations or formulas. Adults not only use graphs to represent algebraic functions, they also use graphs to solve problems that involve multiple potential solutions. Graphing helps adults compare two or more alternatives to decide which one is more effective or beneficial under a given set of circumstances (e.g., car rental costs for a 1000 mile, 3 day trip). Adults also use functions to predict or describe what will happen next or to select from competing alternatives such as investment plans, credit purchases, or similar events and activities (Objective 3). Meteorologists use relations between barometric pressure and rainfall to predict weather, and scientists use patterns of plant growth to evaluate the different effects fertilizers have on specific plants or plant species. Finally, adults use algebra to solve problems in situations wherein there are multiple potential solutions within known boundaries. For example, a person buying an automobile might use algebra to select an automobile and an insurance company when she can spend no more than $20,000 (Objective 2).

Figure 11–1
Example Rationale to Explain Purpose of an Algebra Goal and Associated Learning Objectives

and help to set goals for the next grading period. This works best when children are used to talking about their strengths and weaknesses in a constructive fashion, and when they are used to thinking about what they want to improve. Young students can also participate in evaluating and setting goals for their own social and classroom behavior skills. A youngster who has difficulty concentrating during independent work can help identify some of the distractions and, with the help of the adults, make plans for minimizing them.

Intermediate and older students can be taught to analyze the quality of their own work based on the learning objectives. In the world beyond school, competent adults are responsible for monitoring their learning and performance, seeking guidance or information when necessary, setting their own goals, and developing useful strategies for meeting their goals. This is as true on the job as it is in postsecondary education. If teachers make sure that students understand the goals of instruction and are clear about standards of work, students can take an increasingly active role in communicating about their strengths and weaknesses with parents. Again, students' competence in this kind of self-reflection is enhanced by the availability of concrete evidence of their progress over time. Of course, there is some information only the student can provide during conferences: What made a chosen historical theme particularly interesting or relevant, why she used specific word or phrase choices in her writing, how confident she is in her grasp of certain concepts in math, why she was less than satisfied with her group work in science. Involving students in the discussion of their work and progress supports feelings of autonomy and provides an opportunity for students to feel that their views and choices are respected. As we have mentioned throughout this book, this can be powerfully motivating.

Communication Before Parent–Teacher–Student Conferences

Teachers have a variety of tools available to them to help keep communication flowing between school and home before and between parent–teacher conferences. Teachers who take the time to establish a rapport with families and to get to know their concerns find that when problems arise, parents and guardians are more likely to be willing to work with them to find a solution. Much information about the curriculum, assignments, standards, grading policies, and classroom management can be delivered to parents and guardians via group meetings, newsletters, Web sites, and notes to the home. Information about specific students and their learning, on the other hand, requires individual attention. Some of the more popular avenues of communication are described in the following sections.

Open House/Curriculum Night   Most schools have an evening when parents and guardians are invited to come and visit the school and meet their children's teachers, usually during the first few weeks of the school year. You will have a chance to talk to parents and guardians about your class, your goals for their children's learning, and perhaps some other items, but the main point is to begin the process of ongoing communication between home and school. Although the general principles are the same, the format of curriculum night looks different at different levels of schooling, and creates different constraints on what can be communicated.

If you are an elementary school teacher, you will generally have more time to talk with parents and guardians than secondary teachers do, because at this level children usually have one main teacher. On the other hand, you will have more to communicate: You will describe more subjects, explain your social goals, solicit classroom volunteers, and discuss social expectations. As in any kind of teaching, decide in advance the most important things you want to communicate during this short period. There are several ways to do this and keep the attention of family members (and students).

As families enter, they can examine the room and classroom artifacts that communicate important information. Elementary teachers generally display student work in the various subject areas, making sure that every child has work represented. During the first few weeks of school, as you are getting to know your students, you may want to have them complete short-term projects that result in a displayable product. This provides an enjoyable way to introduce your students to subjects they will be studying, as well as an opportunity for sizing-up assessment in a variety of academic and social skills.

Once parents and guardians have explored the room and seen their children's work, teachers often address the group as a whole. Remember that your most important task is to appear supportive and accessible, inviting parents and guardians to communicate and providing the information they need to do so. If you have families who speak another language at home, you should arrange for an interpreter. Before curriculum night, prepare written material with your name and school contact information for parents and guardians to take with them. They will want to know some of the things their students will be learning in different subject areas, and ways they can help at home. Avoid educational jargon. Select four or five important and overarching learning goals rather than listing an overwhelming number of learning objectives. Much of this information can also be put in a newsletter that you can distribute at curriculum night and send to missing parents.

Finally, take the time to solicit parent volunteers. The parents and guardians who attend curriculum night may be the ones most likely to volunteer, so it is important to provide a way for them to express interest. Provide a variety of ways parents and guardians could give their time, keeping in mind that many parents and guardians may be unable to come to school during the day, at least on a regular basis. When parents or guardians volunteer in your class, you have a terrific opportunity to help them understand exactly how you are teaching their children. This is especially important when you are teaching in ways that may be unfamiliar, and it can also help parents and guardians learn how to help their children at home.

After your presentation to the group, there may be time to meet families individually. Listen carefully to any concerns they may have or any information they may be able to tell you that will help you understand their child's needs. When parents and guardians feel that you will listen to them, they are more likely to contact you when they have a problem or question, and they may be more likely to listen to you carefully when you call.

In secondary schools, parents and guardians have only a short amount of time to visit each of the classrooms, so time is particularly precious. If you have students who speak English as a second language, find out if the school or district can provide an interpreter and let families know that one will be available. As in elementary school, it's best to have the important information, including your contact information, to hand out in written form. This handout can be an outline of your most important learning goals and a copy of your grading policy. In the 15 or 20 minutes you are allotted, parents and guardians will want to know something about your goals for their students' learning and how you work to support those goals. Once they have this information, they will have a context in which to understand your brief description of the major assignments and grading policy. Parents or guardians may want to share concerns or information that can help you work more productively with their student. Take note if this happens, although there won't be much time. It's important, then, to stress that you would welcome further questions or concerns by phone or e-mail. Finally, you may want to provide a blank postcard for parents and guardians to address. Later in the term, use these to quickly send positive notes home about their student and to pass along early warnings (e.g., Rita hasn't been turning in her homework regularly; big test next Friday, etc.). It's fast, easy, and will be much appreciated.

Although secondary teachers are less likely to be blessed with parent volunteers, there are other ways to keep families informed of ways they can assist their students. Positive calls home, brief monthly newsletters, a Web site, or a "homework line" where parents and guardians can call in and listen to a recorded message about the week's homework can all help.

Positive Phone Calls   One of the most effective ways to establish a productive relationship with parents and guardians is to make positive phone calls to the home. At or near the beginning of the school year, you can establish ties by introducing yourself to the parents or guardians and providing a brief positive observation about their daughter or son. Positive observations can be as simple as, "I'm really enjoying having Nguen in my class this year," "La Shonda has been working very hard in language arts and has written some wonderful poems," or "Juan is really helpful to me and to other students." If families do not have telephones, home visits may be arranged through the school administrator, or notes can be sent or mailed home. Many teachers at all grade levels believe that it is well worth the initial investment of time and energy to make their first call to parents and guardians a positive one. Secondary teachers can divide up the calls into batches of four or five and spread them out over the first few weeks of school.

During these brief calls, the parents or guardians may also be able to tell you any concerns they have or provide you with information about any special needs their children may have. You may also want to ask for information after making your positive comment. For example, "Austen is a quiet worker, but he often helps his table partners when they get stuck in math. That helps me a lot. Lately, I've noticed he seems kind of tired, especially in the mornings. Have you noticed this at home?" If you have made positive contact with parents and guardians, a call to discuss problems is more likely to be received as a request for help than as criticism of the child. As the year progresses, you can continue to make positive phone calls, even if you also have to phone to discuss problematic situations. Positive phone calls can also provide an opportunity to tell parents and guardians positive results when you are working together to help their child overcome a problem.

Newsletters, Web Sites, and Voicemail   To keep families informed about new units of study, upcoming tests, field trips, special projects, and due dates, you can use a variety of media. When choosing a format, keep in mind that students and their families do not all have access to the same resources; avoid making your attempt to communicate another barrier for families without computers or for parents or guardians who do not speak English. You or your district administrators may have access to community resources that can assist you in translating newsworthy information for parents and guardians who do not read English.

Newsletters Periodic one- or two-page newsletters can help parents and guardians keep abreast of their child's life in school. When parents and guardians are informed, they are better prepared to capitalize on opportunities to enrich their child's learning by making connections to the world outside of school. Newsletters can include tips for ways to help students do better in school, such as providing a quiet space for study, modeling reading for pleasure, discussing the mathematics of prices and purchasing decisions, and the like. To help parents and guardians understand the learning objectives, you can include examples of classroom activities and assessments. Newsletters can also tell parents and guardians about other important events at the school. Finally, students can contribute to newsletters by writing articles, poetry, stories, and other pieces to share with parents and guardians.

Web Site You can also put a variety of information on a Web site, where you have the advantage of being able to supply helpful links to sources of information for parents, guardians, and students. Remember to have a paper version of the information and the resources for parents and guardians who do not have easy access to the Internet. If you have a class Web page or electronic newsletter, you can include the Web address for parents and guardians in a newsletter. For students whose parents or guardians do not speak English, you may be able to translate or have translated at least a portion of the information. Some students will be able to read the items from the newsletter and translate the information for their parents or guardians.

Voicemail Homework lines can make use of district-supplied voicemail systems to provide brief updates about homework and assessments. Parents and guardians (or students) can call in to find out what schoolwork or studying students should be completing at home. This is a good alternative to Web sites for parents, guardians, and families who don't have access to the Internet.

Keeping Things Current For newsletters, Web sites, and voicemail, it's important to keep the material up to date. Pick a period between updates (or newsletters) that makes sense given your plans and your opportunities to make changes, but that still provides useful information. Web sites, because they remain open to those with access, can contain information that covers an entire grading period: Major assignments and evaluation criteria, grading policies, test dates, topics of study, and associated resources need not be amended very often. The Web site can also include a section for news or updates that can be quickly edited to provide updates for material that changes more rapidly. Newsletters can be sent on a regular basis to build understanding of the current events in the classroom.

Parent–Teacher–Student Conferences

From time to time you will meet with students and their parents or guardians to discuss academic or behavioral issues. Elementary schools generally schedule individual progress conferences for all students twice a year, in the fall and spring (see Scheduled Progress Conferences). Some smaller and alternative middle and high schools also schedule such conferences; however, it is more likely that secondary teachers will have conferences only when there is a problem to resolve. Some aspects of conferences are common to both types, but there are also important differences. One of the common aspects is the need for assessment information. In what follows, we begin by suggesting types of assessment data and effective ways to present it. Next we will discuss regularly scheduled "progress" conferences, and finally, additional considerations for holding "problem" conferences.

Choosing and Communicating Assessment Evidence for Conferences To conduct an effective conference, you will need to clearly explain each child's academic and social-behavior status. Social-behavior evidence needs to be more than just a general description of whether the student is a "pleasure to have in class." Academic evidence goes beyond showing samples of student work and a report card. In addition to detailed evidence, be prepared to explain your learning objectives and expectations for valued performances, so that parents and guardians will have a context within which to understand their students' progress. Writing a goals-and-objectives rationale, as described above, is a good way to make sure you are prepared to explain, not only what you expect, but also why. This is especially important when the work students do in your class is different from the work parents or guardians may have experienced in the past.

If you have laid the groundwork by communicating objectives and standards through curriculum night, newsletters, grading policies, and written criteria for assignments, many parents and guardians will have an idea of what you are teaching and your expectations. As with open house/curriculum night, having student products at hand provides a way

for parents and guardians to get a quick sense of learning objectives and valued performances. Displaying work in the hallways helps parents and guardians who are waiting their
turn to meet with you get a sense of the range of students' work before the conference
begins.

Academic Evidence Choose examples of student work that illustrate students' progress on
your most important learning objectives and valued performances. Complex performances
can communicate both learning of academic content and organizational, social, and communication skills. Progress portfolios can be especially effective in helping parents and
guardians focus on the growth students have made in knowledge and skills during the term.
Especially in the early grades, students are often as surprised as their families at just how
much they have improved since the beginning of the year.

It is also important to have concrete examples of work that meet your standards, especially if a student's work is either well below or well above the target. Making this comparison will provide parents and guardians with important information to use in discussing
whether special assistance or additional challenge might help a child.

Evidence of Social Skills and Classroom Behavior In the preschool through eighth grades,
schools serve an important role in socializing children—teaching them how to work and
play appropriately in social groups. Students in preschool through first grade may be expe-
riencing their first structured social situation outside the family. Children bring a wide variety of family customs and social structures to school, and teachers are charged with helping
all of these children adjust to the demands of school. Teachers of younger children will have
social and behavioral goals and standards for their students, and parents and guardians need
to be informed of their children's progress. Older children and adolescents will be learning
cooperative group skills, time management, and work strategies that are just as important
as their learning in the subject areas. Their status in relation to these skills will also be important to communicate.

In Chapters 4 and 5 you learned about using checklists, rating scales, and anecdotal
records for formal and informal assessment. Applied to social and behavioral learning objectives, these tools can be useful in preparing for and conducting progress conferences. For example, Ms. Francetti collects observational data on her sixth-grade students as they work in
small groups, prepare complex performances, and carry on large-group discussions. She uses
these tools to keep track of each student's progress toward mastery of these objectives and
to give them feedback on their group work skills. At the same time, she is concerned that
observational assessments are somewhat difficult to use directly in talking with parents and
guardians. She also wants students to learn to monitor and evaluate their own work in these
areas. When she prepares for parent–teacher–student conferences, she sits down with her
checklists, rating scales, and anecdotal records and composes a paragraph or two summarizing each student's progress. She asks each student in her class to do the same. These two accounts then form a basis for discussion and goal setting by student, parent, and teacher.

It is especially important to have sufficient data when students are having difficulty
meeting social and behavioral expectations. Records of problems, including when and
where they occurred, what the consequences were, and the effects of those consequences
on subsequent behavior are invaluable when trying to figure out causes and solution strategies with parents and guardians. Records can also be very important when you meet with
other professionals to resolve long-standing problems and make decisions about possible re-

ferrals for special services. This will be discussed in more detail in the last section of this chapter.

Scheduled Progress Conferences Scheduled progress conferences provide an opportunity for teachers to inform parents and guardians of their students' progress in both academics and social behaviors. It's also a time for parents and guardians to ask questions, and for parents, guardians, and teachers to discuss possible strategies for helping students improve. For some parents or guardians of young children, the parent–teacher conference will be the first extended contact with the school system. Even with "veterans" of multiple discussions with teachers, you have an opportunity (and responsibility) to establish or maintain a constructive relationship between families and the school for the benefit of students. Sometimes novice teachers dread interacting with parents and guardians, fearful of possible confrontations or criticisms. Although this occasionally happens, it is not the rule. Parents and guardians can be some of your most important allies in the education of your students.

Preparing for Conferences: Gathering Assessment Data The primary purpose of the progress conference is to share assessment data and evaluations with parents, guardians, and students. Inevitably, parents and guardians will ask, "Is my child reaching the standard?" "Is my child keeping up with other students?" or "Is my child doing as well as he should be?" All of these questions demonstrate parents' and guardians' concerns about whether their children are okay. For this reason, parents and guardians need to hear about how well their child is progressing regardless of his current status in relation to the learning goals and objectives. They need to know if he is making steady progress, closing the gap between his current performance and the standard; or whether he is exceeding the standard and may need additional challenges.

In preparing for the conference, you will want to assemble evidence of students' current work toward your most important learning objectives and standards. Scheduled progress conferences are generally quite short (around 20 minutes), and there is not time to discuss every aspect of a student's progress, so selection is important. (In addition to your learning objectives, refer to the section on kinds of information needed by parents and guardians at different grade levels, earlier in this chapter.)

Scheduled progress conferences are generally arranged over a period of a few hours over several days. Teachers usually have five to ten conferences in a single afternoon or evening, arranged one after the other. Because of limited time during and between conferences, organization, time management, and careful selection of evidence are important. Prepare by making notes of both strengths and weaknesses for each child, and refer to them during the conference. You may want to assemble similar items for each child, arranged in a folder in the order you want to address them, with the set of folders organized in order of appearance on the schedule. Anything you can do to avoid wasting time searching for materials will allow you to maximize the time you spend discussing children's progress. Make sure to leave time for questions and for parent concerns.

Find out if parents and guardians will need an interpreter at the conference, and arrange for one if necessary. Remember that translation takes time, so the conference will take more time to communicate the same amount of material. You may want to schedule conferences with an interpreter in larger time slots, or at the end of the session so that you can take the time you need without inconveniencing other parents and guardians.

Student-led conferences take additional preparation. Students need instruction and practice in reflecting on their work and producing self-evaluations. They may also need help staying within the allotted time and focusing on the central learning objectives. If you wish to implement student-led conferences, it is important to teach the necessary skills over time in the context of learning and instruction, rather than to try to quickly teach them right before conferences.

Conducting the Conference Arrange the conference setting to help students and their families to be as comfortable as possible. Everyone will need a relatively comfortable place to sit; for teachers of young children this may mean borrowing larger chairs. Avoid putting a desk or table between you and the parents or guardians; this can create a symbolic barrier, making it more intimidating for parents and guardians who may already be uncomfortable in a school setting. Have the student's work at hand and organized for easy access. You will need to keep an eye on the clock without parents and guardians feeling rushed, so either place parents and guardians so that the wall clock is behind them, or place a clock where you can look at it without looking away from the parents, guardians, and student.

During a conference, stay positive and productive and make it easy for the parents or guardians to participate rather than doing all the talking yourself. Avoid using educational jargon; use language with which a parent is comfortable and check for understanding. Concrete examples of students' progress and current status are good ways to help communicate complicated ideas. Beginning and ending with the child's strong points, discuss both the child's accomplishments and her difficulties related to your learning objectives. Try to state weaknesses in a way that avoids blaming or shaming the child. "Mindy is a very poor reader, I'm worried that she may need to be retained," is enough to frighten or anger many parents or guardians (and their children). This kind of message communicates lack of confidence in the child and can contribute to a sense of helplessness. Instead a teacher could say, "Mindy has been working hard in reading, but she has been having trouble in certain areas. I have started to work with her more one-on-one, and we'll see if that helps. I have some suggestions for things that you can do with her at home that would give her some extra practice." Even if a child is progressing satisfactorily, be prepared to give parents and guardians strategies for helping their children improve—simple strategies that parents can do whether they are busy professionals, single parents or guardians working two jobs, or working at home to take care of the home and family. Even the least educated parents and guardians can help children at home, if only by limiting television or sibling-care duties so that their children can have time to work on their own.

If there are problems to resolve, you may not have enough time to formulate a workable plan in such a brief conference. In that case, try to arrange for a longer conference in a few days. In either case, plan for a follow-up conversation to discuss progress. If a plan is agreed upon, make sure everyone knows their role in the plan and feels comfortable carrying it out. At the end of the conference, thank the parents or guardians for coming and encourage further communication to ensure their child's success. This is a good time to remind them of the various options for communication (voicemail, e-mail, etc.).

Postconference Make notes at each conference. Notes can be jotted down on the same page as the list of strengths and weaknesses you prepared for each child and kept in a folder, or you may want to jot down notes on index cards and keep a file for each student. Given the number of conferences teachers must conduct on a single afternoon or evening, the details of individual conferences will tend to blur if not recorded. Once conferences are over for the day, take some time to examine your notes and add or clarify material while it's relatively fresh in your mind. Reflecting on the process and making notes of what went well as well as what proved difficult can help you improve your techniques for the next set of conferences.

Problem Conferences   Later in the year, you may need to talk with a student's parents or guardians to ask for their help with a problem or to report a behavior that may become serious if not addressed. If the problem is not yet serious, and the main purpose of the conversation is to exchange information, it may be most efficient and least threatening to start with a phone call. If the problem continues after the contact has been made, you can call back and ask for a meeting with student and parent or guardian to work out a plan for resolving the problem.

Telephone Conferences   Even though you are calling about a problem, it is still a good strategy to start with a positive comment about the child. Often parents and guardians are taken by surprise when they hear that their child is having problems; positive comments ease the transition from whatever the parent has just been doing to thinking about problems at school. Some parents and guardians may have had many phone calls to report inappropriate behavior or academic problems and think school personnel are too ready to blame their student. If you have started the year with a positive call home, parents and guardians may be more willing to give you the benefit of the doubt. Starting with a positive comment can help them feel that you see some value in their son or daughter.

Teachers generally call home after they have tried unsuccessfully to resolve the issue with the student. You may feel frustrated, or that you have tried everything within reason and believe the problem must lie with the student, parent, and/or guardian. However, parents and guardians may know information that will help you to understand the root of a problem and may even be able to suggest strategies that have worked in the past. In any case, a good way to impart information about a problem can be to ask a question; this is likely to sound less like an accusation and more like you are trying to help.

Maria has been turning in work late or not at all in Mr. Cho's seventh-grade social studies class. Although she sometimes actively participates, lately she has become more and more withdrawn. Instead of doing her written work in class, Maria seems lost in space; staring at nothing or putting her head down on her desk. Mr. Cho wants to know if her parents are aware of any underlying problems that may be contributing to this, or whether Maria has struggled in the past with social studies. He decides to start with a phone call home. Maria's mother attended curriculum night, where she and the other parents and guardians filled out a card with Maria's name, her parents' names, and the best way and time to contact them. Maria's mother cannot take calls at work and has indicated that the best time to call is between 7 and 8 P.M. Mr. Cho dials the phone, and Mrs. Hinajosa answers.

> "Hello, Mrs. Hinajosa, this is Mr. Cho, Maria's social studies teacher."
>
> "Oh. Hello." After a pause, a worried Mrs. Hinajosa asks, "Has she done something wrong at school?"
>
> "No, I just wanted to talk with you a bit about her work in social studies. Is this a good time, or should we make an appointment to talk later?" asks Mr. Cho.
>
> "No, now is okay. But why are you calling?"
>
> "I've enjoyed having Maria in my class. She has some great ideas and gets involved when we have class discussions. But I wonder if she has said anything to you about any difficulties she may be having in social studies? Sometimes she has trouble concentrating when we are doing written work and lately she has been turning work in late."
>
> "Oh, no, she says she likes social studies. She has always been a good girl," replies her mother. "I will talk to her and tell her she must do better!"
>
> "Thanks, Mrs. Hinajosa, I was just a little worried. She seems so tired, I asked her if she was feeling okay, but she didn't want to talk about it."

Mrs. Hinajosa considers this. "Well, we have been very worried about her grandfather. He's been sick in the hospital for several weeks, and I know Maria has had trouble sleeping. She has also been watching her brothers while I am at the hospital in the evening, and sometimes she can't start on her homework until I get home."

Now Mr. Cho has information he can use to understand the problem and to come up with new strategies. It doesn't seem to be a problem of Maria's ability to do the work or lack of interest, but a temporary situation that, unless adjustments are made, may cause Maria to miss content she needs to be able to succeed later in the year. Mr. Cho continues to talk with Mrs. Hinajosa, and they agree that she will try to find another relative to help with babysitting, and Mr. Cho will talk to Maria and work out adjustments to assignments and due dates to help Maria get over this temporary hurdle.

Even when the purpose of the telephone conference is primarily to share information, sometimes parents and guardians may become defensive or angry. If it becomes clear that the phone conference is not going to be productive, it is best to terminate the call. Suggest that it would be better to have a face-to-face conference where there is more time to explain the situation and work on an acceptable solution. When the call ends, make notes of what happened during the phone call. If you have not arranged a time to meet, schedule a time to call back in a day or two. If the parent or guardian was confrontational, you may want to have an administrator or other appropriate staff member attend the conference.

Conferences at School Conferences to deal with student problems may be called by either the teacher or the parent or guardian. A student may have talked at home about difficulties in your class of which you are unaware. A progress report might trigger a worried or even angry phone call from home. You may have an issue that will require a face-to-face meeting rather than a phone call, or where it is preferable that the student, parent or guardian, and teacher discuss the problem together.

The first step in collaboratively resolving a problem is to collect information about the problem. Be prepared to describe the problem clearly and dispassionately and to provide evidence that will help the parents or guardians understand the issue, why it is a problem, what you have tried to do to resolve it, and what the results of those attempts have been. If it is an academic problem, have examples of student work and models of good performances with which to make comparisons. You will need records of grades and missing or late work, along with a copy of the grading policy to explain the impact of the problem on the student's success in the class. If it is a behavior problem, you will need records, too. It is not sufficient to say, "Bobby is a real problem in my class, and he needs to straighten up." Bring behavior checklists, anecdotal records made at the time of each incident, information about when the behaviors occur, and the consequences to the student and to others. Plan a possible strategy or two that you would be willing to implement, though the appropriate solution may change during problem discussion.

Decide whether other school personnel need to attend the conference. The most straightforward arrangement is to have teacher, parents or guardians, and the student, if appropriate. An interpreter may also be necessary. Depending on the problem, however, the meeting may include an administrator, other teachers who are having similar problems with the student, the school counselor, nurse, or special education teacher. The more people attending the conference, the more complex the group dynamics can be. Parents and guardians may feel overwhelmed by a large group of professionals. You may need to consider the power dynamics and conflicting agendas of the school personnel as well. If other staff members will be attending, meet with them prior to the conference to discuss common goals for the conference, and whether all need to be present. This will help you stay focused and consistent.

If you are asking for the conference, contact the parents or guardians to arrange a meeting. Again, start the phone call on a positive note. Ask for information; has the student said anything at home about problems at school? Then briefly and clearly describe the problem in general terms. The parent or guardian may have questions about the problem; provide answers but avoid conducting the conference on the phone (remember, you have decided that a phone conference would not be sufficient for this problem). Make it clear that you hope to be able to work with the parent and student to resolve the problem, and ask for a meeting time. Intermediate aged children and adolescents will often attend the conference as well. Unless there is a specific reason to exclude them, their inclusion helps ensure that everyone has heard all of the conversation about the issue and has had a chance to contribute to the solution. Keep in mind that many parents and guardians work during school hours, and that it may be necessary to meet outside of your work day. (Your school or district may have a policy governing this.)

If this is the first time you have met the student's family, you may want to meet them at the school office and walk them to the room where you are meeting. Introduce yourself, thank them for coming, and express your hope that you can all work together to work through the problem. Do not discuss specifics until you are in the meeting room. If other staff members are present, introduce them to the family. Be aware of the inherent power dynamics likely in such a conference. If there are several staff members and one parent, make sure that seating is *not* arranged with the parent on one side of a table and everyone else on the other.

As the conference gets under way, try to keep the tone constructive and nonconfrontational. Describe the problem clearly and use your assessment materials to help parents or guardians understand the issues. Treat the parents or guardians (and student) with respect. The parents or guardians may be worried or upset with you, the student, or both. They may need time to vent their emotions, ask questions, and express their concerns. If emotions are high, it is unlikely that you will be able to resolve the problem, but listening carefully and nondefensively will help an emotional parent feel heard and understood. Make sure everyone has had a chance to discuss the problem before moving to a solution plan, so that all are more likely to feel ownership of the solution. Remember that parents or guardians will often have good ideas about the best strategies to try. Once a plan has been agreed upon, it is important that everyone involved knows their role(s) and responsibilities. Plan a followup meeting or phone conversation to check on progress and revise the plan as necessary. If possible, provide each participant with a written version of the plan, detailing the various roles, after the conference. As with scheduled progress conferences, take a moment after it is over to reflect on the process and make notes to help you plan for your next conference.

Formal Progress Reports and Term Grades

Progress Reports Progress reports are used in some schools to help parents and guardians monitor the progress of their children throughout a grading period. These reports generally list the most recent assignments, whether the student has completed the assignments, any missing work, and any concerns the teacher has about the student's academic performance. In some schools, students are required to take these progress reports home, discuss them with their parents or guardians, have their parents or guardians sign them, and return them to school. In other schools, progress reports are mailed to the parents and guardians. The purpose of these reports is to keep parents and guardians informed; however, they can also serve as a motivational force for students, because they have to inform their parents or guardians about their current progress. These tools are easy to prepare. Simply list the assignments for an instructional unit, quarter, or trimester. Then check those that are completed. A space can be provided at the bottom of the sheet for brief comments from the teacher, for the parents' or guardians' and students' signatures, and for comments by parents, guardians, or the students. When mailing progress reports, unless the progress report is only to inform parents and guardians of their child's status with no expectation of return, it may be a good idea to send a postage-paid, return envelope so that parents or guardians can return their signed copy.

Term Grades   The most familiar communication tool is the grade card that is part of the regular school routine. If you have followed a systematic communication plan, there should be no surprises when the time comes for grade cards. Curriculum night, newsletters, and Web sites (if available) inform parents and guardians about your learning goals and objectives and prepare them for the types of work students will be doing. Progress reports help keep parents and guardians up to date about their children's current status. Parent–teacher–child conferences give you a chance to show students' progress toward meeting the learning goals and objectives. Problem conferences allow you to intervene on concerns before they become problems. Therefore, grade cards are simply a formal way of recording what is already communicated in many other ways. They become part of the students' cumulative records.

Grade cards differ from district to district and, in some cases, from school to school. Elementary grade cards generally provide much more information than do secondary grade cards. Elementary grade cards often include details about the standards to be attained by students within each subject area. In addition, they usually include a section on social skills, classroom behaviors, and study habits. Figure 11–2 shows a Grade 3 report card from a school district in the Pacific Northwest. The importance of school behaviors is evident in the fact that the section parents and guardians are likely to see first is the one entitled Life Skills, such as "follows school rules and accepts responsibility for personal actions." Next comes Communication Language Arts followed by Science, Mathematics, Health, Art, Fitness, Music, and Library.

Also note that learning objectives or content standards are given for each category. This makes it apparent to teachers, parents, and guardians alike what the learning objectives are for this school district. Finally, the key at the top describes the levels of proficiency that teachers are to assign to students' overall performance for the grading period ranging from E for excellent to N for not at grade level.

Figure 11–3 shows a grade card for a middle school in the Pacific Northwest. It is clear that communication about learning goals and objectives is up to the teachers—they will not be represented on the grade card. In addition to a space for summary academic grades in each subject, the grade card also includes a column for teacher comments. Giving space for these aspects of students' classroom behaviors allows teachers to communicate about effort and attitude without including these aspects of performance in the academic grade.

Grade cards, as summary tools, provide little information about students' learning. Therefore, it is your responsibility to make certain that the meaning of grades is clear to students and parents and guardians through grading policies (Chapter 9) and your other communication tools.

LAKE WASHINGTON SCHOOL DISTRICT PROGRESS REPORT: LEVEL 2
Third Grade

This represents an evaluation of your child's work over the course of the last grading period. Various classroom assessments were used during this reporting period to determine academic achievement at one of the following grade level expectations:

Overall Achievement reflected by a letter grade of: E = Excels at or above grade level expectation **S** = Satisfactorily meets grade level expectation **N** = Not at grade level expectation **P** = Passing **NP** = Not Passing **I** = Incomplete
Skill and Concept Development reflected by: 4 = Exceeds standard **3** = At standard **2** = Approaching standard **1** = Not at standard **I** = Not evaluated at this time

Student: *3rd Grade Student* **Grade Level:** 3
Teacher: *Sample Teacher* **School:** *Demo School*

Period	1st	2nd	3rd	Totals	Period	1st	2nd	3rd	Totals
Days Absent	0	0	0	0	**Days Tardy**	0	0	0	0

LIFE SKILLS: *These behaviors are representative of a successful system of personal conduct. It is the expressed intention of the LWSD to ensure all graduates demonstrate these life skills, which lead directly to increased student achievement.*
***"Exceeds standard (4)" does not apply to this section.**

GRADING PERIOD	1st	2nd	3rd	GRADING PERIOD	1st	2nd	3rd
Follows school rules and accepts responsibility for personal actions				Demonstrates respect for personal and community property			
Communicates in a respectful and courteous manner				Demonstrates quality work			
Attentive and follows directions				Cooperates while working in groups: • Supports others • Accepts differences			
Accepts suggestions and opportunities for improvement				Demonstrates self-confidence: • Asks questions • Lets needs be known			
Works well independently				Uses time wisely			
Completes classroom work carefully and on time				Completes homework carefully and on time			
Speaking: Effectively verbalizes ideas				Organizes work space and materials			

COMMUNICATION/LANGUAGE ARTS: *Effective communication involves the skills of reading, writing, spelling, listening, and speaking. It is the window to basic literacy and academic excellence.*

GRADING PERIOD	1st	2nd	3rd	GRADING PERIOD	1st	2nd	3rd
Overall Achievement—Writing							
Traits of Writing: Organization				Traits of Writing: Style (fluency, voice, word choice)			
Traits of Writing: Content/ideas				Traits of Writing: Conventions			
Forms of Writing: •Recount •Narrative •Report •Procedure •Explanation •Persuasive				Displays legible information: • Uses a variety of tools • Uses technology • Uses cursive writing			
Overall Achievement—Spelling							
Weekly tests				Application of spelling in daily work			
Overall Achievement—Reading							
Comprehends fictional materials (recalls and summarizes main ideas and details)				Utilizes fictional materials (applies, analyzes, infers, synthesizes, and evaluates information)			
Comprehends non-fictional materials (recalls and summarizes main ideas and details)				Utilizes non-fictional materials (applies, analyzes, infers, synthesizes, and evaluates information)			
Reads orally: •fluency •accuracy •phrasing				Vocabulary development: •contextual clues •decoding			
Projects/Units Completed:							

Figure 11–2
Sample Elementary School Report Card

Student:	*3rd Grade Student*			Grade Level:	3		
Teacher:	*Sample Teacher*			School:	*Demo School*		

SCIENCE: *Students build their understanding of science through investigation, supportive scientific information, and evidence. Topics of study in Level 2 include aspects of the following: earth science, life science, and physical science.*

GRADING PERIOD	1st	2nd	3rd	GRADING PERIOD	1st	2nd	3rd
Overall Achievement							
Demonstrates understanding of concepts and skills				*Uses communication skills to obtain and report scientific information*			
Uses appropriate technology to research, present, and display information							

Projects/Units Completed:

SOCIAL STUDIES: *Students develop the knowledge and skills they need to participate as responsible and effective citizens in an increasingly complex world. Topics of study in Level 2 include: history, geography & environment, culture, civics, and economics. Each of these areas is studied through the specific content areas of diverse communities, regional relationships, and formation of a nation.*

GRADING PERIOD	1st	2nd	3rd	GRADING PERIOD	1st	2nd	3rd
Overall Achievement—Social Studies							
Investigates historical and current issues, topics, and events				*Demonstrates understanding of the skills and concepts presented in history, geography, culture, civics, and economics*			
Uses a variety of tools and technology skills to research, present, and display information							

Projects/Units Completed:

MATHEMATICS: *Mathematics enhances people's ability to understand the world by providing a language for describing, explaining, and communicating about patterns. The use of mathematics enables people to solve problems, make decisions, and design models and systems.*

GRADING PERIOD	1st	2nd	3rd	GRADING PERIOD	1st	2nd	3rd
Overall Achievement—Mathematical Content / Processes							
Computation: *Computes fluently and makes reasonable estimates*				**Number Sense:** • *Understands numbers, ways of representing numbers, relationships among numbers, and number systems* • *Understands the meaning of operations and how they relate to one another.*			
Algebra: • *Investigates numerical and geometric patterns and relationships* • *Expresses them mathematically in symbols and in words*				**Geometry:** • *Explores spatial objects, relationships, and transformations* • *Develops more precise ways to describe shapes by learning specialized vocabulary* • *Locates points, creates paths, and measures distances within a coordinate system*			
Probability and Statistics: • *Generates questions about self and environment, collects and organizes data, and compares data sets* • *Predicts and confirms outcomes through experiments in probability*				**Measurement:** • *Measures the attributes of a variety of physical objects* • *Measures more complex attributes including area, volume, and angle*			
Problem Solving: • *Uses mathematical strategies to define and solve word problems* • *Recognizes when an approach is unproductive* • *Able to determine when an answer is reasonable*				**Communication:** • *Expresses ideas and processes using words, models, pictures, and/or symbols* • *Organizes and clarifies mathematical information through reflection and discussion*			
Projects/Units Completed:							

Figure 11–2 (continued)

Student: *3rd Grade Student*   **Grade Level:** 3
Teacher: *Sample Teacher*   **School:** *Demo School*

HEALTH: *Students establish the concepts and skills necessary for safe and healthy living by promoting active lifestyles, personal development, healthy choices, and behaviors.*

	GRADING PERIOD	1st	2nd	3rd
Actively participates in projects and discussions in the classroom				

ART: *Students acquire the knowledge and skills necessary to create, perform, and respond effectively to the arts. Topics of study include aspects of drama and visual arts.*

GRADING PERIOD	1st	2nd	3rd	GRADING PERIOD	1st	2nd	3rd
Completes assignments / demonstrates effort in classroom art lessons				*Expresses ideas and inventiveness of visual forms and techniques*			

FITNESS: *Students acquire the knowledge and skills necessary to maintain an active life. Topics of study include movement and fitness. Physical education grade reflects student's efforts to learn as well as cooperative and active participation.*

	GRADING PERIOD	1st	2nd	3rd
Overall Achievement—Physical Education				
Comments and Content:				

MUSIC: *Students acquire the knowledge and skills necessary to create, perform, and respond effectively to the arts. Topics of study include aspects of dance, drama, music, and visual arts. Music grade reflects student's efforts to learn as well as cooperative and active participation.*

	GRADING PERIOD	1st	2nd	3rd
Overall Achievement—Music				
Comments and Content:				

LIBRARY: *Students acquire skills to support lifelong learning by developing research and information skills, and a love of reading.*

	GRADING PERIOD	1st	2nd	3rd
Overall Achievement—Library				
Comments and Content:				

Figure 11–2 (continued)

COMMUNICATING WITH OTHER PROFESSIONALS

In addition to parents, guardians, and students, you will also be communicating assessment information to other professionals. This will include typical progress information (in report cards and other student records), justifying new approaches to teaching through evidence of student learning, documenting your own growth as a professional, and communicating with specialists when students need extra help.

Prereferral and Referral Decisions

Mr. Smith is a third-grade teacher in an urban elementary school that serves poor to working-class families. He feels comfortable working with students at a variety of skill levels and who come from a range of family backgrounds. He finds that for most students, once he spends a little time with them "sizing up" their current levels and interests, he can help them be successful in his class. This year he has a particularly needy group. Two children have Down's syndrome; a couple of children seem to have poor social skills; and two students are recent immigrants who speak Russian and very little English. Fred is another concern: He seems to have increasing difficulty with reading as the year progresses. He consults Fred's second-grade teacher, who says that, although Fred seemed a bit slow to "crack the

---

Student: *3rd Grade Student*   **Grade Level:**   3
Teacher: *Sample Teacher*   **School:**   *Demo School*

Teacher Comments
First Reporting Period:

Second Reporting Period:

Third Reporting Period:

YOUR CHILD IS IN A SUPPORTIVE PROGRAM IF ONE OF THESE AREAS IS CHECKED:

☐ SPECIAL EDUCATION SUPPORT IN:

☐ SAFETY NET SUPPORT IN:

☐ ENGLISH AS A SECOND LANGUAGE SUPPORT IN:

☐ QUEST

Figure 11–2 (continued)

code" in reading, he did not read poorly enough in second grade to qualify for special education. He talks with Fred's mother, who has not noticed Fred having difficulties with reading. "In fact," she tells him, "he likes to read to his younger brother." This is promising, but Mr. Smith knows that the instructional materials in third grade require students to read at higher levels. Students also are reading more informational text. Mr. Smith feels that he needs additional assistance to be able to meet Fred's needs; however, he wonders whether he should refer him for special education testing. What will this mean for Fred, now and in the future?

In the next section, we outline the process that schools and districts should have in place to assess children who may need special assistance, and to determine the most appropriate combination of placement and services. This process is based on federal law, and something similar should be in place in all schools in the United States. As a teacher, you will play an important role in this process, both in assessment and in designing instruction. But you will work as a member of a team of professionals, in collaboration with parents or guardians.

Professional Discussions About Students: Purposes and Processes

The primary purpose of prereferral[1] and referral[2] meetings is to find the *best educational approach* for students with special needs. Sometimes the best approach is for the teacher to

---

[1] Child Study Team (CST) or Building Assistance Team (BAT)
[2] Multidisciplinary Team (MDT)

STUDENT GRADING REPORT

SCHOOL DISTRICT	PERIOD ENDING
EDMONDS SCHOOL DISTRICT NO 15	06/23/95

SCHOOL
MEADOWDALE MIDDLE SCHOOL MM

TOTAL DAYS ABSENT	TOTAL DAYS UNEXCUSED
0	

GRADE LEVEL
7

HOME ROOM OR STUDENT ADVISOR
34

THANKS FOR MAKING THIS ANOTHER SUPER YEAR!
THE 1995-96 SCHOOL YEAR STARTS TUESDAY, SEPT. 5TH
(7TH GRADE AND NEW 8TH GRADERS ONLY) AND THURSDAY,
SEPT. 6TH, ALL 7TH AND ALL 8TH GRADERS.
SEE YOU THEN AND HAVE A GREAT SUMMER!

STUDENT NO.   STUDENT NAME   PARENT OR GUARDIAN

COURSE / TEACHER	PRD	GRADE / LEVEL 1ST 2ND TERM	CREDITS	ABS.	UNEXC. ABS.	TEACHER'S COMMENTS
DEN700 12 ENGLISH 7TH	1	C+	1.00			HAS NOT COMPLETED ALL ASSIGNMENTS EXCELLENT CLASS PARTICIPATION WORKS WELL INDEPENDENTLY A PLEASURE TO HAVE IN CLASS
DSS700 21 SOCIAL STUDY 7TH	2	D+	1.00			EXCELLENT CONDUCT EFFORT IS INCONSISTENT
DSC700 33 LIFE SCIENCE	3	B+	1.00			GOOD EFFORT GOOD CONDUCT GRASPS CONCEPTS AND SKILLS, USING THEM EFFECTIVELY SHOWS AN EAGERNESS TOWARD LEARNING
DMO781 41 ORCHESTRA	4	A-	1.00			COOPERATIVE AND POLITE GOOD EFFORT
DXR700 34 SILENT READING 7	5					A PLEASURE TO HAVE IN CLASS
DMA800 62 MATH 8TH	6	C-	1.00			GOOD EFFORT GOOD CONDUCT
DHE700 73 HOME EC 7TH	7	A-	1.00			EXCELLENT EFFORT CONSISTENTLY DOES HIGH QUALITY WORK CONSCIENTIOUS AND DEPENDABLE
DXW780 81 LIBRARY USE STAFF	8					
DPE701 2 EARLY PE 7TH	9	A	1.00			EXCELLENT EFFORT EXCELLENT CONDUCT

** FINAL GPA = 2.857 BASED ON 7.00 CREDITS ATTEMPTED

Figure 11-3
Sample Middle School Report Card

make accommodations for a student's disability in the regular classroom. For others, help from an educational assistant in the classroom is sufficient. Some students may need more specialized assistance in a pull-out program or study skills class. The only way a placement or assistance decision can be made is through discussion with all relevant parties.

Although federal laws govern the processes for placement decisions, each state and each district will have specific policies used to conform to those requirements. In general, the process looks like Figure 11–4. Your job as a teacher in this process is critical in two ways:

1. You are the expert in your classroom context; you know the social context, your teaching methods, and academic expectations. The student's problem is not "all in the student," but a function of the student's characteristics interacting with the characteristics of the environment in which he must succeed.

2. You will be one of the primary assessment data collectors, both pre- and postreferral. The collection of valid evidence of a student's functioning in your class is essential to determining the scope of the problem, evaluating interventions, and developing IEPs and 504 plans.

Level 1 At the top level of Figure 11–4, Mr. Smith becomes aware that his typical approaches and typical adjustments are not successful with Fred.[3] Fred has difficulty using the homework notebook required for all students, and often loses his assignments. His running record shows that he reads slowly and makes many errors; he also has very poor spelling skills. As Mr. Smith begins to observe Fred during language arts activities, he uses a checklist to keep track of his activity level. Over a period of several days, he notices that Fred avoids reading during "Silent Sustained Reading" time, often choosing books that are too easy or too difficult, flipping through the pages rather than reading. Alternately, he may try to engage others in whispered conversations. Mr. Smith also finds that Fred is almost always on task during science and math—offering good ideas and alternate solutions to problems. Mr. Smith checks his assessment records for small-group skills and finds that Fred is cooperative, but further observation shows that he avoids reading and writing tasks and favors drawing, diagramming, or calculation instead.

Mr. Smith begins with his "sizing up" data on Fred, but as he notices problems he focuses on collecting data relevant to the problem. This evidence is essential in establishing a baseline against which intervention results can be compared later. Mr. Smith may consult with Fred's former teachers, or informally with a special education teacher, counselor, or school psychologist to get ideas for different strategies to try. He keeps careful records of the strategies he tries and how those strategies affect Fred's functioning in the classroom.

Sometimes this process results in a successful adjustment of a teacher's strategies, and no further assistance is necessary. In this case, the teacher should keep a record of the successful strategies, along with information about the context in which those strategies worked

---

[3] Parnell (2001) found that teachers in her sample often showed signs of concern (altering their routes across the classroom to "check in" on specific students, keeping an eye on them during group tasks) before they were even aware of noticing a problem. Once these moves became a pattern, teachers recognized their concern and gathered more information, often in the form of trying out small interventions or other changes to see if the student could be brought back within a typical range of performance or behavior.

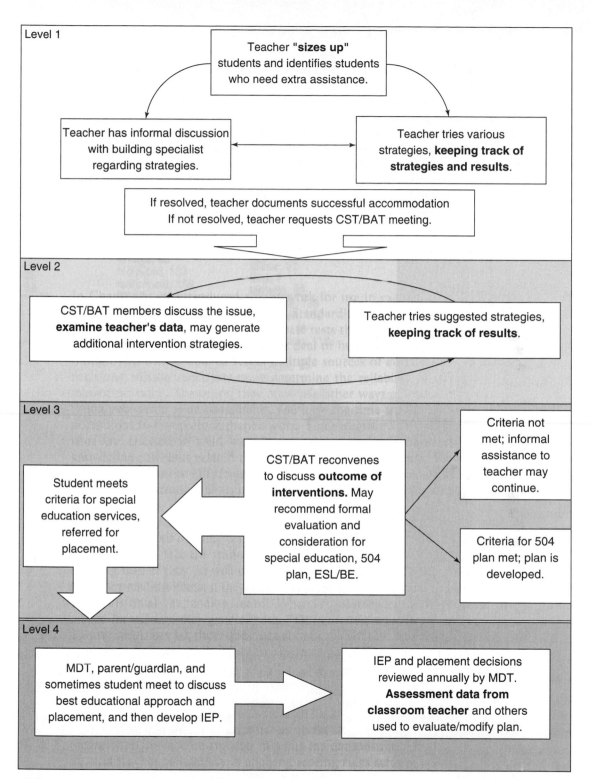

Figure 11–4

The Prereferral to Referral Process and the Role of Teacher Assessment (e.g., providing extra assistance with organization of assignments, an optional "quiet spot" the student can choose to use when distracted during reading time). This information can be passed on to the next teacher, easing the transition to a new class.

It is also important to document these adjustments so that if, later on, the student is referred for evaluation for special education or 504 services, this documentation can provide evidence that accommodations have been necessary in the past. It is common for students to do well in elementary school with these informal accommodations; it comes as a shock to students, parents, and guardians when "suddenly" a problem emerges at the next level of schooling. Keeping parents, guardians, and future teachers "in the loop" regarding necessary accommodations is essential in providing the information necessary to make future decisions about the best educational approach. It is also important to remember that if a student goes on for postsecondary education and needs disability services, the student must be able to document that they received such accommodations in the past.

Level 2   In Fred's case, Mr. Smith has tried spending extra time reading with him and has given him extra assistance in organizing his notebook. However, he is not satisfied with Fred's progress. Mr. Smith doesn't feel he has enough time to provide the extra assistance Fred needs to meet his needs; he fears that waiting longer will cause Fred to fall further behind. Mr. Smith's next step is to request a meeting of the Child Study Team (CST).[4] The CST generally includes the classroom teacher or teachers, a special education teacher, a school counselor and/or school psychologist, a school nurse (for health-related issues), and an administrator. This group meets to evaluate the data provided by the teacher and to decide the appropriate next steps. Sometimes alternate strategies are generated for the teacher to try in the classroom before a referral is considered. Mr. Smith and the CST members look at Fred's behavior and academic performance, using the records Mr. Smith provides, which include running records of reading performance, samples of Fred's written work from his portfolio, behavioral checklists Mr. Smith used to track Fred's behavior during language arts and group work, and anecdotal records of Fred's difficulties with his notebook. The team agrees that one or two more strategies should be tried. Once again, Mr. Smith tries the strategies and collects data on their effectiveness.

Level 3   When the CST reconvenes, Mr. Smith shares his assessment data. Although one of the strategies was helpful in improving his organization, Fred still has difficulty with reading and spelling that interfere with his work in all of his subjects. The CST agrees to refer Fred for formal testing by the school psychologist and a special education evaluation by the Multidisciplinary Team (MDT). The MDT includes many of the same people who served on the CST. The classroom teacher(s), a special education teacher, a school psychologist, and an administrator will attend, along with other professionals who have contact with the student in question. In addition, the parent or guardian and (optionally) the student will attend. Most MDT meetings should include students by the time they are in high school.

At the initial meeting, the MDT members recap the findings of the CST, particularly the interventions tried and their outcomes in terms of Fred's behavior and academic performance. Again, Mr. Smith's records of classroom assessments, strategies tried, and results

---

[4] Labels for these teams differ from district to district and state to state.

observed are central to the discussion. On the basis of this evidence, and with the consent of Fred's parents, the MDT decides to refer Fred to the school psychologist for testing for a possible reading disability. Once the test results are returned, the MDT reviews all the evidence and determines whether a student qualifies for special education services or a 504 plan. If not, the teacher may still receive informal assistance in teaching the student in the classroom, often in the form of consultations with the school psychologist, counselor, or special education teacher. In this case, the teacher should continue to document intervention strategies and results, both to give to future teachers and for possible reconsideration by the MDT later on.

Level 4   If a student qualifies for special education services, processes specified in the federal Individuals with Disabilities Education Act (IDEA) must be followed. The law provides for the broad involvement of parents or guardians, the student when appropriate, and other school professionals in the educational decisions made. It also ensures that all parties have access to due process in the event that an agreement cannot be reached. In Fred's case, the members of the MDT determined that Fred qualified for special education services. Together with the parents, they determined that the most appropriate placement, in the "least restrictive environment" (as specified by IDEA), was to remain in Mr. Smith's classroom and receive support from a classroom aide already present to work with other students with disabilities. Fred will also receive 30 minutes of additional reading instruction per day (provided by the special education teacher). These provisions, along with other information about Fred's disability, are included in an individualized education plan (IEP), which becomes the legal documentation of the decision. At the end of the school year, the MDT will evaluate the effectiveness of Fred's placement, using assessment information provided by Mr. Smith and the special education teacher. Mr. Smith will bring Fred's language arts portfolio, as well as records of Fred's spelling test performance and documentation of his time on task during reading activities. This information, along with formal reading assessments, will be used to modify the IEP for the following year.

The stages in the process described above are important and rely on good observations, assessment tools, and record-keeping processes. This is critical if all students are to meet standards. For many students, the process will illuminate ways that accommodations can be made to ensure that able students can work around their disabilities and learn important content and skills. For others, it will become clear that modifications are needed—that some students will not meet all standards. The role of assessment in determining what kinds of interventions are needed cannot be overstressed. The techniques presented in this book can help to ensure that you are a significant player on a child's team rather than a passive observer.

SUMMARY

Communication with parents and guardians, students, and other educators about students' progress and accomplishment is a central responsibility for teachers. In this chapter we have introduced many strategies that can open up the lines of communication between you and others. Although these strategies may seem like a lot of work, lack of communication can lead to many hours of frustrating meetings with parents or guardians, your colleagues, and your students.

Developing a communication plan before you begin a school year, getting the features of the plan in place, and enlisting help from parents or guardians and students in implementing that plan are all ways to make the work easier. As with writing goals and objectives, planning instructional units, and developing assessments before you begin teaching, a communication plan will make your job easier. When you, your students, and their parents and guardians are all working together, you will all feel more successful.

REFERENCES

Parnell, C. J. (2001). *The landscape of teaching work: How teachers make educational decisions.* Unpublished doctoral dissertation, University of Washington, Seattle, WA.

USING INFORMATION FROM STANDARDIZED TESTS

Two types of standardized tests are administered by schools, districts, and states to obtain measures of what students know and are able to do in relation to state, district, or national standards: *norm-referenced* tests and *criterion-referenced* tests. Norm-referenced tests give information about how students perform when compared with students who took the test in the same grade level and at the same time of year. Criterion-referenced tests (also called *standards-based* tests) give information about whether students are learning the knowledge and skills that states and school districts want them to learn. These are very different purposes. Teacher-made tests are almost always criterion-referenced tests in that they reflect what individual teachers want their students to learn. Norm-referenced and criterion-referenced tests that are mandated by school districts and states are called *standardized* tests because the tests are administered using the same testing conditions for all students and are scored in the same way for all students. Classroom tests can also be standardized tests if the teacher gives the same test to all students, under the same testing conditions (time limits, access to tools, seating arrangements, etc.). In this chapter, however, we focus on standardized tests that are *external* to the classroom.

When used *appropriately*, external, standardized tests can provide very useful information. If the information about individual students is supported by information from classroom assessments, standardized test scores can help to identify students who are successful, those who are at risk, and those who have an array of special needs. If patterns of scores for individuals are consistent over several years, then you can be more certain that the scores have meaning. When average scores for a classroom, school, or district are examined for patterns over time, the information can give clues as to the strengths and weaknesses of classroom instructional practices and the strengths and weaknesses of school or district curricula.

When used *inappropriately*, as when decision-making about the quality of schools is based solely on scores from external tests, there are many negative impacts on schools, teachers, and students. If teachers become too focused on test scores, research has shown that they seek to raise test scores by narrowing instruction to the tested content, teaching test-taking skills, and using instructional materials that mirror the types of items on the test (Nolen, Haladyna, & Haas, 1992; Smith, 1991). This may raise test scores; however, the scores have little meaning. When the test scores, rather than student learning, become the focus of instruction, students can learn less even as scores are increasing (Lomax et al., 1995; Shepard, 1989, 1991b).

In this chapter we present information that can help you understand how to use scores from external standardized tests thoughtfully and appropriately. We also include information about how to prepare students for these tests without giving in to a "teach the test" mentality. When students truly learn what they need to learn to be successful in school and life beyond school, and when teachers do what it takes to help their students succeed, external test scores will take care of themselves. You may need to prepare students for the item formats on tests (because these can seem very alien to students), but you need not focus your instruction on the specific content on tests. Nor do you need to spend an inordinate amount of time teaching test-taking skills. In this chapter, we describe how standardized tests are created, why they can be used to make inferences about how much students have learned, and how the scores can help you make decisions about the instructional needs of your students. The key is to have no fear so that you do no harm!

A Brief History of Standardized Testing[1]

To understand the current state of standardized testing, it helps to know how we got here. Standardized testing on any large scale has a very short history—as human history goes. People have used examinations for many centuries to select people for various purposes. Examinations were used in ancient China to select bureaucrats for government. Examinations have been used to select individuals for universities for several centuries. However, the particular form of mass testing used in the United States is a fairly recent invention. The multiple-choice item was invented during World War I out of a need for an efficient way for the armed forces to identify which men were literate and able to do arithmetic. A big problem was solved simply. At the same time, immigration to the United States was at peak levels and schools were needed to quickly turn immigrants into citizens. Standardized tests were seen as efficient, unbiased (compared with written examinations), and objectively scorable (i.e., all questions had right answers). The tests were norm-referenced. Although educators didn't know the limits of human capability, they could compare examinees' performances and rank them based on their scores in a way similar to ranking people on their height or weight. Norm-referenced tests were constructed to have items that ranged from very hard to very easy. In this way, all examinees could be ranked on the same test. Few would get all of the items right and few would get none of the items right. The same test could be used to measure all examinees in the same way that a 12-foot tape measure could measure the height of all men—even the tallest professional basketball player.

Time passed. Most of the time, the scores were simply used to see whether schools and students were on track. Students were tested every few years (e.g., at the end of elementary school or the end of junior high school) to see how they were doing. Little attention was paid to the scores unless a student did exceptionally well or exceptionally poorly.

During the 1960s, educational psychologists invented *programmed instruction* or *mastery learning*—a method of instruction based on behavioral learning theories. Important academic work, such as writing and reading, was broken down into multiple skills through a process called *task analysis*. Students were taught the parts of this real work and tested over the parts. Once they had mastered a particular set of skills, they could move on to the next, higher level of skill. This type of teaching and learning depended on criterion-referenced tests—tests that could tell whether students had mastered the knowledge and skills before they moved on. These tests differed from norm-referenced tests. First, they were focused on what students had learned rather than on how students compared with others. Second, there was no expectation that students' performances would result in a normal distribution of scores. As Bloom, Madaus, and Hastings (1971) said, "There is nothing sacred about the normal curve. It is a distribution best associated with chance; education is not a chance activity, and we seek to have the students learn what we have to teach. If we are effective in our instruction, the distribution of achievement should be very different from the normal curve. In fact, we may even insist that our educational efforts have been *unsuccessful* to the extent that the distribution of achievement approximates the normal distribution" (p. 52–53, emphasis in the original). The need for criterion-referenced information was so widespread that even the publishers of norm-referenced, standardized tests

---

[1] Really, it's pretty interesting!

began to offer scores for the objectives embedded in the tests. In this way, the scores could provide *diagnostic* information on the tested objectives while still providing norm-referenced scores.

At the same time that mastery learning and criterion-referenced tests were emerging, real efforts were being made to counteract poverty throughout the United States through President Lyndon Johnson's "War on Poverty." One significant way of addressing poverty was to ensure that students were learning what they needed to learn. If poor students came to school lacking the knowledge and skills of their more affluent peers, schools could receive federal aid to provide extra support for these students. The Elementary and Secondary Education Act of 1972 (Title I) provided a method for granting money to schools based on the test scores for these students. Essentially, for schools to retain Title I funding, poor, low-performing students had to make gains more quickly than their more affluent peers. Norm-referenced tests were the most efficient standardized way to measure gains. The federal law mandated that Title I students be tested in the fall and spring of each year to see whether the programs were helping to close the achievement gap. Testing companies rose to the occasion and developed tests for each grade level with fall and spring *norms.*[2]

During the late 1970s, educators and legislators in many states became concerned that students were moving from grade to grade and were graduating from high school without the knowledge and skills they needed. *Minimum-competency testing* was seen as a way to ensure that students had at least the minimum skills they needed. Minimum-competency tests were criterion-referenced, tests that assessed basic knowledge and skills. Most were multiple-choice; however, direct writing assessment was initiated in some states. Proponents of competency testing argued that, if policymakers wanted to ensure that students learned basic skills, tests measuring those skills would drive teachers to teach the skills—especially if the scores on these tests were available to the public (Popham, 1993). Together the need for scores for Title I funds and the push for minimum-competency testing of basic skills led to a dramatic increase in the testing of school-aged children.

A backlash against multiple-choice and norm-referenced testing began in the mid to late 1980s. Researchers found that scores on norm-referenced tests were being inflated through instructional practices that raised test scores without increasing student learning (Haladyna, Nolen, & Haas, 1991). Other researchers saw that quality teachers were leaving the profession because of pressure to raise test scores (Shepard, 1991b). Some of the criticism was aimed at the notions of behaviorism (Shepard, 1991a; Wiggins, 1989). If teachers only taught discrete skills in the formats used on tests, students were less likely to develop the schemata needed to know how to apply those skills when needed. Critics of minimum-competency testing claimed that minimums had become maximums; that teachers were teaching only the minimums in order to ensure that test scores were high. The tedium of drills on tested skills occurred more often in schools where Title I funds were most needed, in order to increase test scores and retain funding. Curriculum researchers claimed that textbook publishers organized instructional materials around the kind of thinking and skills found only on multiple-choice tests (Apple, 1990).

---

[2] Data tables that indicated how a nationally representative sample of students had performed on the test at each time of year.

Two responses emerged from this backlash. The first was a demand to eliminate multiple-choice testing. The second was the development of curriculum standards intended to raise expectations for students to "world class" levels.

Critics of multiple-choice tests claimed that much of what is valued cannot be measured in multiple-choice formats (e.g., Wiggins, 1989). They claimed that, if teachers teach to the test, tests should include assessments of valued student performances. Direct writing assessment was the first and most widely used type of performance assessment (see Chapter 8 for more information about direct writing assessment). However, in response to criticisms, test developers also began to create a variety of types of performance assessments ranging from simple short-answer items to complex science investigations. Tremendous efforts were made to develop clear scoring rules and to train raters to systematically apply these scoring rules to student work. Over time, the costs associated with administering and scoring complex performance led to a middle road. Standardized test items still remained predominantly multiple-choice; however, short-answer and performance items were added to assess more complex conceptual understanding, thinking skills, and processes. The technology and methods used to score students' responses to short-answer and performance items became very sophisticated—lessening the costs and improving the reliability of scores.

At about the same time of the backlash against multiple-choice tests, the standards movement began. The National Council for Teachers of Mathematics (NCTM) published the first version of the *Curriculum Standards for School Mathematics* in 1985 (NCTM, 1985). These standards were developed by teachers and other educators and were designed to refocus instruction in mathematics toward (1) student understanding of mathematical concepts and procedures and (2) their ability to solve problems involving mathematical information, reason logically, and represent mathematical ideas through language, symbols, and graphics. During the latter half of the 20th century, other professional teacher organizations developed curriculum standards. Each set of standards provided benchmarks in terms of what students should know and be able to do by the end of a particular developmental span. For example, the NCTM *Standards* set benchmarks for grades K through 3, grades 3 through 6, grades 6 through 9 and grades 9 through 12. Students were expected to learn the knowledge and skills described in the curriculum standards over a period of several years.

When the Elementary and Secondary Education Act (ESEA) was reauthorized in 1992, the Title I requirements changed from assessment based on norms to assessment based on curriculum standards. This led states to adopt or develop content (curriculum) standards and tests that would assess those standards. Some states retained the use of norm-referenced tests because of their focus on basic skills. However, many states developed their own assessments designed to measure their own state's content standards.

In 2002, the Elementary and Secondary Education Act was again renewed. At that time, the law made sweeping changes in the roles of standards and tests. The new law required each state to establish content standards and proficiency standards (cut-scores) for the tests. Schools were to ensure that *all* students met standards within 12 years. Assessments were to consist of multiple measures, including multiple-choice, short-answer, and performance items. Schools that did not succeed in bringing all students to the standard would be classified as "failing schools." Students in failing schools could be transported to successful schools at the request of their parents. If the school district did not have successful schools or if the successful schools were full, districts had to transport students to successful schools in other school districts. These rules applied to all students in regular education programs, all English language learners, and all but a very small proportion of students with disabilities. Projections (Heuschel, personal communication, 2002) showed that, in most states, all schools with diverse populations of students would be classified as failing schools within seven years.

As mentioned previously, research has shown that when teachers feel pressure to raise test scores, instruction is narrowed to the content on the test (Haladyna, Nolen, & Haas, 1991; Nolen, Haladyna, & Haas, 1992; Shepard, 1991b; Smith, 1991). In addition, when the focus of instruction is on raising test scores rather than student learning, scores can be increased without increases in student learning (Haladyna, Nolen, & Haas, 1991; Lomax, et al., 1995; Shepard, 1989, 1991b). Finally, research has consistently shown that, when high stakes (such as graduation, promotion, or labeling schools) are placed on test scores, school drop-out rates increase (Madaus & Clarke, 2001; Reardon, 1996). At the time of this writing—schools, districts, and states were still trying to determine how to protect their standards without relegating all of their schools to the status of failing schools.

Given the pressure to raise test scores, what is the solution for the teacher who has a classroom of diverse students? Many of the strategies described in this book can help you create a successful classroom without teaching to standardized test items. Beginning with standards, teaching in a way that students actually achieve those standards; teaching students how to obtain information, think about that information, and communicate effectively; and helping students understand the qualities of good work are the foundations of success. Teaching disconnected skills, expecting students to memorize bits of knowledge, and giving assessments without adequate instruction are recipes for frustration and disappointment. However, if standardized tests are only indirect measures of what we want students to know and be able to do, how can they be used as measures of student learning? In what follows, we describe how these tests are developed, how scores for criterion-referenced and norm-referenced tests are generated, how to use the scores from standardized tests in useful ways, and how to prepare students for taking standardized tests without compromising your values and ethics as a teacher.

HOW STANDARDIZED TESTS ARE DEVELOPED

In many ways, the methods used to develop criterion-referenced and norm-referenced tests are very similar. The most important differences are in the decisions made about what content should be included on the tests. Selection of content for standardized, criterion-referenced tests is similar to that for classroom tests. Before criterion-referenced tests can be developed, there must be well-defined content standards (what we call learning objectives). These standards define what students are to know and be able to do at a given grade level. For states or districts, content standards are often written by committees composed of teachers and other educators. Educators bring knowledge of students and of the content to be tested to the deliberation process. Often the committees consider standards from other districts, states, or national professional organizations such as NCTM. The content standards then determine the knowledge and skills that will be assessed to determine whether students are learning what they should know and be able to do.

Norm-referenced tests provide *national norms* [3]; therefore, selection of content for norm-referenced tests generally requires a survey of several sources of information. For each grade level, norm-referenced test developers examine national curriculum standards; the content standards for populous states (e.g., California, New York, Florida, Texas); content standards for large cities (e.g., Los Angeles, New York); the knowledge and skills included in widely used mathematics, science, social studies, and language arts text books; and the content included on other norm-referenced tests. From all of these resources, norm-referenced test developers identify the content standards at each grade level that are represented most widely—a *common curriculum*.

Designing the Test

Once the content standards are identified, test developers for both types of tests must decide *how* to assess the standards. Some standards cannot be assessed through paper-and-pencil tests (e.g., speaking and presenting skills, group work skills, scientific investigations); therefore, part of test planning is determining which standards will be tested on a paper-and-pencil test and which standards will be assessed through more complex performances.[4]

Choosing Item Types   Once the methods of assessment have been determined, test developers decide what types of performances, test items, and scoring rules (see Chapter 4, 7, and 8) are best for measuring the targeted knowledge and skills described in the content standards. For example, suppose a science content standard was: "Students will understand the meanings of scientific terms." The test developer would have to decide whether the terms would be tested through vocabulary items or through application of the concept represented by the term. Figures 12-1 and 12-2 show two different ways to measure the meaning of the term *potential energy*. The item in Figure 12-1 asks students to find a synonym for potential energy. The item in Figure 12-2 asks students to apply their understanding of states of energy to determine the energy state of the I-beam. Both items require vocabulary knowledge; however, the item in Figure 12-2 goes beyond definition to application.

The types of items used to measure content standards in standardized tests are often misunderstood. It is a common lament that standardized tests only measure knowledge. In fact, with the exception of vocabulary knowledge and arithmetic facts, most standardized test items measure applications of knowledge.[5] In most cases these applications are quite simple; however, they are still applications. For example, standardized tests rarely ask students to identify the rule regarding which punctuation mark to put at the end of a sentence (knowledge). Instead, students are asked to identify, from a selection, which punctuation mark to put at the end of a sentence that has no ending punctuation. The reasoning of the

---

[3] Scores that allow for comparisons of individual students' performance with that of a national sample of students. In the next section, we elaborate on how these norms are determined.

[4] More often than not, assessment of complex performances is left to classroom teachers while paper-pencil tests are used for district and state assessments.

[5] A notable exception would be Advanced Placement exams that are aligned with a specific curriculum. External norm referenced and criterion-referenced tests typically must represent a hypothetical common curriculum; hence, the focus cannot be on specific knowledge.

Which of the following is the best definition of *potential energy*?
A. stored energy
B. energy of motion
C. heat energy
D. electrical energy

Figure 12–1
Example of a Multiple-Choice Item Measuring Definition of Potential Energy

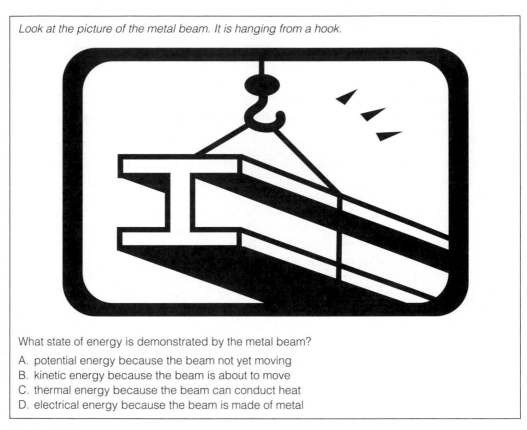

Look at the picture of the metal beam. It is hanging from a hook.

What state of energy is demonstrated by the metal beam?

A. potential energy because the beam not yet moving
B. kinetic energy because the beam is about to move
C. thermal energy because the beam can conduct heat
D. electrical energy because the beam is made of metal

Figure 12–2
Example of a Multiple-Choice Item Measuring Application of the Concept of Potential Energy

test maker is, "When a writer gets to the end of a sentence, he should know which punctuation mark to put there. Therefore, if an item presents the examinee with a sentence that has no ending punctuation, the skilled writer should know which punctuation mark (from a set) he should put at the end of that sentence."

To successfully avoid the "teaching to the test" trap, it is essential to understand the nature of standardized tests. Earlier in this chapter we mentioned that mastery learning models used behaviorism to design instructional programs based on task analysis of important work. In much the same way, test makers use task analysis to decide which types of items are best for measuring those standards. They identify important work, task analyze that work, and develop items to measure discrete parts of the work. Even computation tests are mostly composed of applications of computational skills rather than knowledge alone. Figures 8-10 and 8-11(see Chapter 8) show items that require simple applications of writing skills. The items shown in Figure 8-10 assess whether students can identify an appropriate topic sentence for a paragraph and a sentence that would add information to the paragraph. The items shown in Figure 8-11 assess whether students can select the appropriate punctuation mark for a particular location in a sentence. Each of these items reflects a small part of what makes up good writing—writing effective paragraphs and using appropriate punctuation marks.

Figure 12-3 shows items that a standardized test developer might use to assess research skills. If the task of conducting research were broken down into steps, some of those steps would include locating information in various resources and locating resources in a library database. The items in Figure 12-3 assess whether students know how to apply these skills. Figure 12-4 shows items that assess students' reading comprehension. These items represent various reading skills—comprehending important ideas and details, making interpretations and simple inferences, and figuring out the writer's tone or perspective. For each of these examples—writing skills, research skills, and reading comprehension—if students are engaged in real work in the classroom that involves reading, researching, and writing, they will learn the skills necessary to do well on items that measure these skills.

In other words, test developers strive to create tests that assess whether or not students can apply learned knowledge and skills in *new* situations. Teachers, on the other hand, tend to assess students' recall of knowledge.

For example, teachers at all levels commonly select a novel, play, or set of poems, have students read them, have class discussions over the relevant literature, and then test students over the details in the selected novel, play, or set of poems. Hence, rather than asking students to apply the literary analysis skills learned—through reading and class discussion—to *new* works, students must *recall* details, main ideas, and themes from the already-studied literature. Needless to say, teachers may find that students have learned what was taught (the content of the literary work); however, the teachers will *not* know whether students can read, comprehend, interpret, analyze, and critique literary text on their own. In contrast, standardized tests assess whether students can read, comprehend, and analyze *new* text. If teachers focus on knowledge and external standardized tests focus on applications of knowledge and skills, students will *not* have learned what they need to learn to perform well on the standardized tests.

Therefore, the best way to avoid teaching to the test is to figure out what real work the test items represent and then teach that work. If students have developed strong skills; if, as we have described throughout this book, they know what they are supposed to learn and can evaluate their own learning in relation to your learning objectives, then external standardized tests are less likely to be a problem for them. However, if students have only practiced with discrete skills and have not used them in authentic ways, if they have memorized information to prepare for classroom tests, it will be very difficult for them to transfer their knowledge and skills to the applications demanded by standardized tests.

In short, the selection of item types is one of the most critical aspects of standardized test development. For teachers, understanding what these items represent is critical for helping students achieve standards without teaching to the test items.

Use the following information to complete numbers 1 through 4.

INDEX
baseball 3, 29-35
  positions 29
  rules 29-30
  statistics 30-31
  World Series 32-35
basketball 3, 36-41
  NBA 36
  defensive strategies 38
  history 40-41
  positions 36
  offensive strategies 37
  rules 36
bodybuilding 65
boxing 3, 17-20

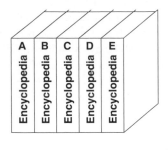

Honig, Donald. *Baseball: The Illustrated History of America's Game.* NY: Crown Books, 1990.
TOPIC: baseball, sports
548 pages
nonfiction

Voingt, David, O. *American Baseball.* 3 vols. Philadelphia: Pennsylvania State University Press, 1983. First published in 1966.
TOPIC: baseball, sports
1098 pages
nonfiction

1. On what page would a researcher look for information about the history of basketball?
  A. page 3
  B. page 36
  C. page 40

2. On what page would a researcher look for information about the positions in baseball?
  A. page 3
  B. page 29
  C. page 35

3. In which volume of the encyclopedia would a researcher look to find information about sports equipment used in baseball?
  A. Volume S
  B. Volume M
  C. Volume B

4. What is the most efficient way to find information about baseball in the library database?
  A. Look for resources by topic
  B. Look for resources by author
  C. Look for resources by publication data

Figure 12–3
Examples of Items Measuring Research Skills

Overall Test Design (Test Map)   Once the types of items for each standard are determined, test developers create test maps similar to Ms. Steinberg's assessment plan for her water unit (see Figure 6-2 in Chapter 6). The test map for a standardized test indicates which content standards will be included on the test, as well as how many items and what types of items will be used to assess each standard. When using criterion-referenced tests, test users generally want to know whether students are achieving each content standard as well as how

Read the passage. Then complete numbers 1 through 4.

It doesn't take creativity to make a quilt. It takes patience, persistence, and really good eyesight. My second cousin, Wilma, made quilts for a living. She lived on a farm in Missouri. The farm provided all of the food they needed and her quilts provided the money to buy other things. Usually she made the quilts from beginning to end. However, sometimes wealthy women from the city would piece together the top of the quilt and then send it to her to make the final quilt.

Piecing together the top is the easy part. Long ago, it was done by hand. More recently people sew the pieces together with a sewing machine. There are many beautiful patterns for quilts but even simple ones can be very beautiful. Once the top is pieced together, the really hard part begins. First Wilma had to lay the cloth that would be the back of the quilt on the floor. Then she put down a layer of cotton batting. Then she put on the top. She had to pin all the parts together before she began quilting.

Quilting is tedious work. She had to make tiny stitches to attach all the layers together. Sometimes she made fancy designs with the stitches—like circles or curlicues—but mostly the stitching was very plain.

She had an ancient quilting rack to hold the quilt off the floor and keep it straight while she did the stitching. Her quilting rack was very simple. It had long boards that were four inches by four inches on the ends. These boards sat on top of a frame that kept them off the floor. She would take one end of the quilt and roll it onto one of the long boards, leaving enough unrolled to stretch across the frame. She tacked the other end of the quilt to the second board on the opposite side of the frame. Then she'd start to stitch. She didn't just sew one line and then start another. Instead she started about 20 threads and worked her way across the quilt a little bit at a time—first moving forward with one thread, then another, then another, and so on. When I would visit Wilma, I was always amazed at all the needles lying on top of the quilt, waiting for her to get to work.

Once the top of the quilt was stitched onto the back through the batting, Wilma added the edging to finish the quilt. A single quilt took weeks to make. When they were finished, however, they were always works of art. After spending time watching Wilma work, I always wanted to make quilts. A few years ago I took the time to make one. I learned that I'm not the type of person who could make a living as a quilter. I did most of the work on the sewing machine. I found that I'm not patient enough to do all that stitching by hand. Even though it isn't a work of art, it makes me happy to look at it when I make my bed. It still has that homespun look that Wilma's quilts had.

1. What is the main idea of the passage?
   A. Cousin Wilma struggled hard to make a living.
   B. Making quilts is hard work, but they are worth it.
   C. A farmer's life is tedious and uninteresting.

2. Why is the quilting frame an important tool for quilting?
   A. It helps the quilter put together the smaller pieces of the quilt top.
   B. It keeps the quilt straight while the stitching is being done.
   C. It holds the quilt on the wall after it is completed.

3. All of the following words could be used to describe the author's voice in this passage. Choose the word you think best reflects the author's voice and explain your choice using information from the passage.

             Wistful   Amazed   Appreciative

   _____

   _____

   _____

4. Why do quilters need *patience* and *persistence*?
   A. Quilting is enjoyable and leaves the quilter with good feelings about the work.
   B. Quilting is an old fashioned job that people no longer have the time to do.
   C. Quilting has many detailed parts; it takes a long time to finish the work.

Figure 12–4
Examples of Items Measuring Reading Comprehension Skills

Standard	Number of Multiple-Choice Items (1 point each)	Number of Short-Answer Items (2 points each)	Number of Essay Items (4 points each)	Total Number of Points
Literal Comprehension of Narrative Text	4 items	1 item		6 points
Literal Comprehension of Informational Text	4 items	1 item		6 points
Inferential Comprehension of Narrative Text	2 items	2 items		6 points
Inferential Comprehension of Informative Text	2 items	2 items		6 points
Analysis and Interpretation of Narrative Text	1 item	1 item	1 item	7 points
Analysis and Interpretation of Informative Text	1 item	1 item	1 item	7 points
Critical Thinking about Narrative Text		2 items	1 item	8 points
Critical Thinking about Informative Text		2 items	1 item	8 points
Totals	14 items	12 items	4 items	54 points

Figure 12–5
Possible Test Map for Standardized Criterion-Referenced Reading Test

they are doing in the subject area as a whole. For example, suppose the reading standards for a state were literal comprehension, inferential comprehension, analysis and interpretation of text, and critical thinking about text (e.g., evaluation of author's purpose). Although an overall reading score is useful, scores for each reading standard would be more useful for planning individual or group instruction.

To provide scores for each content standard, criterion-referenced test developers try to include as many points as possible for each content standard included on the test. The more score points for a given standard, the more reliable or dependable students' scores will be for that standard. Of course, the test developer must balance the number of points for each standard with the number of standards to be tested and the overall length of the test. Figure 12-5 could be a test map for a criterion-referenced reading test assessing the four reading standards identified above. The test map indicates that each reading standard will have at least 12 points. In addition, the map indicates that students must demonstrate their reading skills on two different types of text: narrative and informational. In this way, those who use the scores from the test can be more certain that students' scores for each standard are reliable (there are sufficient points for each standard) and that scores for the reading test as a whole are more valid (performance on the test is more likely to generalize to reading performance in the classroom and everyday life).

Once the test map is defined, test specifications are written. These are detailed rules for how the test will be put together. Test specifications for a reading test are likely to include the types of text to be used (e.g., informational, poetry, excerpts from short stories), whether the text is to be from published sources or written for the test itself, the length of each reading selection, the number of different selections in the test, the reading difficulty of selections, and how many items will be associated with each text. Once test specifications are completed, item specifications are created that provide very specific guidelines for writing items for each content standard and for each item type.

Testing the Test

Well-developed standardized tests go through several stages in their development. First, test items are written to the item specifications. Next, the items are reviewed (often by teacher committees but also by content experts from various professional fields) to ensure that (1) they make sense, (2) they are appropriate for the content standards, (3) they are grammatically straightforward and correct, (4) they have clear scoring rules that are appropriate for the content standard targeted, (5) they represent information that will be familiar to students at the given grade level, and (6) they don't misrepresent any ethnic, racial, or gender group.

Once items pass through these reviews, they are field tested with hundreds of students to see whether students understand what they are being asked to do and whether the items are of an appropriate level of *difficulty* for the grade level to be tested. For criterion-referenced tests, students who have been taught the knowledge and skills should do well on the items; therefore, criterion-referenced test developers look for items that measure the content standards for the particular grade level and that are not too difficult for students who are well taught. Norm-referenced test developers look for items that range in difficulty from very hard to very easy, with most items being moderately difficult. Although most items measure knowledge and skills appropriate for the particular grade level, some items will measure knowledge and skills that are well above grade level and some will measure knowledge and skills that are well below grade level. In this way, all students in a grade level can be ranked using the same test level.

If criterion-referenced and norm-referenced items function well, students who do well on the test as a whole (and thus know and can apply the tested knowledge and skills) should do well on the individual items and students who do poorly on the test (indicating a poor grasp of knowledge and skills) should do poorly on the items. The measure of how well an item differentiates between those who do well and those who do poorly on the test is called *discrimination*. In addition, for multiple-choice items, a *distractor analysis* is used to check that those who do well on the test as a whole are attracted to the right answer and those who do poorly on the test are attracted to the wrong answers. For short-answer and performance items, scoring rules are also checked to make certain that some examinees have earned each score point and that item performance shows clear differentiation between high performing and low performing students. Finally, items are also evaluated for statistical *bias* against gender or ethnic groups.

Test Scores

Once items have passed through these checks, they are organized into tests and administered to groups of real students. Each student receives a *raw score* (the number of points earned) and interpretive scores based on the purpose of the test. Criterion-referenced scores indicate whether students are learning the targeted content standards. Norm-referenced

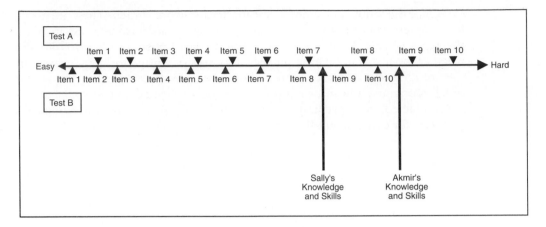

Figure 12–6
Comparisons of Students' Performance on Two Tests of Differing Difficulty

scores indicate how well students are doing compared with other students in the same grade level and at the same time of year.

One of the limitations of external tests is that the test users (teachers, school administrators, etc.) do not usually know much about the content on the test. Scores that tell how many points a student earned (*raw scores* or *number correct scores*) are not terribly useful. If the items on a test are fairly difficult (say only 50% of the students get each item right), a score of 30 out of 40 means something very different than if the items are very easy (say 90% of the students get each item right).

Figure 12-6 shows how two hypothetical students would perform on two different standardized tests with the same number of items but with items that differ in difficulty. The line with arrows at both ends represents a scale (measure) of item difficulty from easy to hard. The items are in order from the easiest to the hardest for each test. Each marker represents one item with a certain amount of difficulty. The easiest item on Test A is slightly harder than the easiest item on Test B. The hardest item on Test A is quite a bit harder than the hardest item on Test B.

Each student has the same level of knowledge and skills regardless of which test he or she takes. Based on her ability (level of knowledge and skills), Sally would probably get a score of 6 on the first test and a score of 8 on the second test. Based on his ability, Akmir would probably get a score of 8 on the first test and a score of 10 on the second test. Even though the students' actual knowledge and skills have not changed, the number of points they earned would be different depending on which test they took. In addition, if Sally got the second test and Akmir got the first test, they would earn the same raw score even though they actually have different levels of knowledge and skills. Imagine how large these kinds of differences would look on a test of 40 or 60 points.

Clearly, number of points earned on a large scale test cannot provide the information needed to make important decisions about students. Another important point about Figure 12-6 is that the space between items is not always consistent. For example, on Test A, the distances between items 8 and 9 and between items 9 and 10 are very different. This shows that the *increase in knowledge and skills* necessary to move from 8 to 9 points is *greater* than the *increase in knowledge and skills* necessary to move from 9 to 10 points. When standardized tests are created, these issues must be taken into account somehow. The process used to make raw scores meaningful is called *scaling*. Items are placed on a difficulty scale based on how difficult they are in comparison with each other. If all of the items in Test A and Test B were analyzed together and placed on the same scale before they were divided into two tests, Sally would get the same *scale score* regardless of which test she took; Akmir would get the same scale score regardless of which test he took. Scaling takes responses from test items and creates a score scale with equal intervals between the score points so that the scale scores can be used like centimeters or inches to measure students' level of knowledge and skill at a single point in time, as well as how much they have grown over time.

Although scale scores are more informative than raw scores, they, too, have their limits. Suppose you measured the height of one of your students and found that she was 48 inches tall. What do you know about this student? Only that she is 4 feet tall. Before you can make sense of her height, you need to know why you measured her. If you wanted to know whether she was developing normally, you would need information that allowed you to compare her height with the heights of other students who are the same age. If she was 10 years old, you would probably say that she was normal for her age. If she was 5 years old, you would probably think she was very tall for her age. Finally, if she was 13 years old, you would probably think that she was very short for her age and may not be developing normally. These are all examples of norm-referenced comparisons.

On the other hand, if you were taking your class to an amusement park, you might need to know whether all of your students were tall enough to be allowed on a certain roller coaster ride. In this case, students must reach an absolute height before they can go on the ride. This is a criterion-referenced comparison. In the next sections we describe how criterion-referenced and norm-referenced scale scores are interpreted.

CRITERION-REFERENCED SCORE INTERPRETATIONS

In Chapter 2, we discussed several different types of standards: curriculum (content) standards, proficiency or achievement standards, and opportunity to learn standards. Criterion-referenced score interpretation is based on the notion of *proficiency* (also called *mastery* or *competency*). Assuming that the content standards are the foundation of the test items, proficiency standards indicate how well students must do on the test to be considered proficient on the content standards. When students have tried their best, reports from well-developed criterion-referenced tests can provide clues about their accomplishments and their needs. However, follow-up with classroom assessments is vital to ensuring that standardized test scores are not given too much weight when making decisions about individual students. There are three typical criterion-referenced scores: *proficiency classifications, proficiency levels,* and *objective* or *standard scores*.

As mentioned earlier, scale scores require some sort of comparison in order to be interpreted. The comparison used for criterion-referenced tests is the proficiency standard or proficiency *cut-score*. Students who earn scale scores greater than or equal to the cut-score are considered proficient on the knowledge and skills tested. Those who score below the cut-score are considered not proficient. While this may seem like an arbitrary division, however, careful steps are taken to set proficiency standards for criterion-referenced tests. The two most common ways to set proficiency standards are student-centered and item-centered methods. These methods are used widely and are central to criterion-referenced score interpretation for standardized tests; therefore, we describe them here.

Setting Proficiency Standards Using Student-Centered Methods

There are two student-centered methods for setting proficiency standards: the *contrasting groups method* and the *borderline group method*. For both methods, teachers are identified who are familiar with the content standards and the test items. These teachers are given a list of their students and asked to identify those students they believe are *definitely proficient* on the content standards, those they believe are *definitely not proficient*, and those they believe are *borderline* students. Once the test has been scored, scores for these students are gathered.

For the borderline group method, the proficiency cut-score is the *mean* or *median* of the scores for the students who are judged, by their teachers, to be borderline. For the contrasting groups method, the range of scores for the definitely proficient and the definitely not proficient are compared. The point where the score ranges cross is used as the proficiency cut-score. For an alternate contrasting groups strategy, the means of the scores for the proficient and nonproficient groups are computed and the cut-score is the score halfway between these two means (i.e., the midpoint). Figure 12-7 shows how the cut-score is set based on the comparison of scores ranges, and Figure 12-8 shows the midpoint between the means for the two groups. In this example, the midpoint is slightly higher than the point where the two distributions intersect. This would not always be the case.

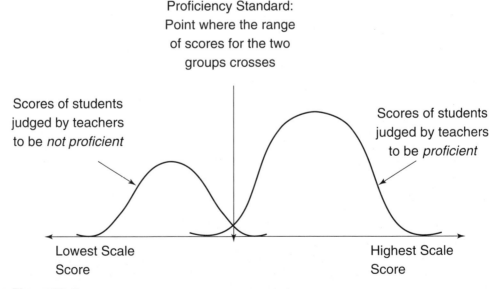

Figure 12–7
Contrasting Groups Version 1: Using Point of Intersection Between Range of Scores for Students Judged to be Proficient and Non-proficient

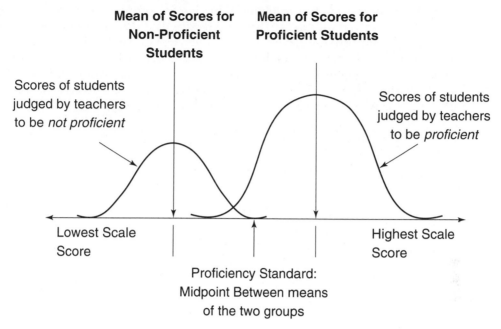

Figure 12–8
Contrasting Groups Version 2: Using Point Midpoint Between Mean Scores for Students Judged to be Proficient and Non-proficient

Setting Proficiency Standards Using Item-Centered Methods

Item-centered methods are based on professional judgment of teachers and other educators regarding the content that students should know and be able to do to be proficient. Two commonly used item-centered methods are the Angoff method and the bookmark method.

Angoff Method   The Angoff method was proposed by William Angoff (1971) and has been used for several decades. For this method, judges review the overall test (sometimes taking the test themselves). They then look at each item on the test and judge what percent of 100 minimally proficient students would get the item right. For example, if a judge considers an item to be very easy, she might say that 90% of the minimally proficient students should get the item right. If another judge considers the same item to be somewhat difficult, he might say that only 60% of the minimally proficient students would get the item right. For short-answer and performance items, the judges decide what percent of minimally proficient examinees would earn a perfect score on each item. In essence, these percents indicate the estimated *difficulty of the items* for minimally proficient students.

Once each judge has judged every item, an initial cut-score is computed for each judge. Because percents can easily be converted to decimal values, the decimal values are multiplied times the number of points possible for each item. These values are summed across items for each judge, resulting in the judge's proposed cut-score. Judges discuss their decisions at various stages. They may receive data that shows how *all* students (not just the minimally proficient) performed on each item or data to show how many students would pass the test with the resulting cut-scores. After each round of discussion and examination of data, judges can make new estimates of difficulty of each item for the minimally proficient student. At the end of the process, a final cut-score is obtained for each judge and the mean or median cut-score across judges is set as the proficiency standard.

Bookmark Method   For the bookmark method, the process begins much like the Angoff method. Judges review the items and take the test themselves. Next, judges are given an ordered booklet in which the items are ranked based on the difficulty of earning a particular score for the item. Multiple-choice items have only one difficulty—the difficulty of earning a score of one. Short-answer and performance items are included in the ordered booklet based on the difficulty of earning each score point. For example, a 4-point item would appear in the ordered booklet 4 times.

Judges work through the ordered booklet deciding whether minimally proficient students would be able to earn each successive item score. Judges place a bookmark after the last item they are sure about. This marks the cut-score for the judge. Once all judges have set their bookmarks, they compare their decisions and discuss the reasons for the decisions. Judges may go through several rounds of discussion and may examine data regarding difficulty of each item as well as the percent of students who would be considered proficient based on their cut-scores. After each round of discussion, judges may move their bookmarks. At the end of the process, each judge makes a final decision about the bookmark. The average cut-score across judges becomes the proficiency standard for the test.

Each of these four methods for setting proficiency standards is an accepted strategy and has been widely researched. At the same time, studies that have compared these different ways of setting proficiency standards show that each method results in a different proficiency standard (Buckendahl, Smith, Impara, & Plake, 2002; Chang, 1999; Livingston & Zieky, 1989). Hence, standard setting is a matter of judgment and the degree to which educators and the public trust proficiency standards depends on the confidence that they have in the process used and the qualifications of the judges.

Interpreting Scores

The first type of interpretation made based on criterion-referenced tests is that of *proficiency classification*. Once proficiency standards (cut-scores) are set for each subject area, students who take the tests are classified as proficient or not proficient based on whether their score meets or exceeds the proficiency standard.

In most states, and in the National Assessment of Educational Progress (NAEP), other cut-scores are set to account for differences among those who meet and don't meet standards. These are called *proficiency levels*. When students take tests with multiple proficiency levels, their scores are used to assign them to one of the categories. The lowest cut-score is used to distinguish between students who are making progress toward achieving the proficiency standard and those who are far below the standard. The highest cut-score is used to distinguish between students who have met the proficiency standard and those whose performance is well beyond the proficiency standard. For the NAEP, students may be classified as *below basic, basic, proficient,* or *advanced* based on their test performance.

Proficiency standards and proficiency levels are established for total test scores. However, educators often want to know whether students are achieving the individual standards within a subject area. Recall the reading test example given in Figure 12.5. There were four content standards assessed by the test and each one was measured in the context of narrative and informational text. To determine strengths and weaknesses in the educational programs in a school, district, or state, scores for individual standards may be more useful than total scores and proficiency classifications or proficiency levels. Therefore, objective or content standard scores are generally provided for criterion-referenced tests. These scores provide indications of whether students are achieving each of the individual standards measured by the test. For the reading test example given in Figure 12-5, objective scores could be reported in three ways. Scores could be given for students' proficiency in reading informational text versus narrative text. These scores would be useful if teachers wanted to know whether students had adequate instruction for reading both types of text. It would also be possible to give scores based on the individual reading standards: literal, inferential, analysis and interpretation, and critical thinking. In this case, the focus would be on students' strengths and weakness related to each of the reading skills, regardless of the type of text. Finally, scores could be reported for all eight categories presented in the test map. In this way, it would be possible to evaluate instruction and students' learning in terms of how well students apply the individual reading skills to different types of text.

Figure 12-9 shows Ken Jones's individual student report from the Grade 7 *Washington Assessment of Student Learning*—the criterion-referenced test used in Washington State. This report is divided into four sections. The upper section tells the name of the student, the teacher, the school, and the school district, as well as Ken's date of birth. The next section is a note to parents describing the purpose of the report. The third section presents Ken's performance on each of the subject area tests. In addition to the scale score for each test, Ken is classified as meeting or not meeting standard in each subject area. For Reading, Mathematics, and Science, the proficiency levels are simply called Level 1, Level 2, Level 3, and Level 4. The notes at the bottom of the page define these levels as above standard, meets standard, below standard, and well below standard. These levels roughly correspond to NAEP's categories of below basic, basic, proficient, and advanced. Level 3 is the proficiency standard for these three tests. Writing and Listening have only two levels: meets standard and does not meet standard. For all but the Writing test, students must earn a scale score of 400 or higher to meet standard. For the Writing test, students write two essays in response to writing prompts. They can earn 6 points for each of the essays for a total of 12 points. Students must earn a total score of 9 to meet the proficiency standard in Writing.

Ken's scores indicate that he has met standard in Reading, Listening and Writing, but not in Mathematics or Science. A shaded area on either side of the line that marks the cut-score is called a confidence band. The footnote on the score report indicates that scores within the band (whether above or below) are very close to the standard. The confidence band is created using the *standard error of measurement* at the cut-score. Box 12.1 explains standard error of measurement in more detail.

Washington Assessment of Student Learning
Individual Student Report
Grade 7
Spring 2002

Report for: Jones, Ken	Date of Birth: 12/14/89
Teacher: A. Johnson	School: ANYTOWN MIDDLE SCHOOL
	District: ANYTOWN PUBLIC SCHOOLS

Dear Parent:
Last spring, schools across Washington administered tests to measure students' progress toward the state's Essential Academic Learning Requirements in Reading, Writing, Mathematics and Listening. Students are expected to read with comprehension, write clearly and solve math problems as they answer multiple choice and short-answer questions, draw graphs, complete charts, write short essays and explain steps in problem solving. Information derived from these tests will help teachers plan for instruction and help schools evaluate programs. Your child's teachers have more information about the assessment program and your child's achievement.

Performance in Relation to the Standard: In Reading, Mathematics, and Listening, a scale score of 400 or higher is required to meet the standard. In Writing, a raw score of 9 or higher is required to meet the standard.

Content Area	Did Your Child Meet Standard?	Maximum Score Possible	Your Child's Score	100 150 200 250 300 350 400 450 500 550 600 650
Reading	Yes (Level 3)	460	408	
Listening*	Yes	482	421	
Mathematics	No (Level 2)	552	378	
Science	No (Level 2)	580	389	
				0 1 2 3 4 5 6 '7 8 9 10 11 12
Writing*	Yes	12	10	

Note: Scores within the gray band are very close to the standard.

Your Child's Performance Profile:
NOTE: The Listening test does not include sub-areas for a performance profile.

Your child's performance on this test in each of the following areas was **similar to** or **exceeded** the performance of students who met the standard:

Reading	Mathematics	Science	Writing
Literary Text	Mathematical Processes	Science Concepts	Content, Organization & Style
• Main ideas & details	• Mathematical Communication	• Properties & Characteristics	Conventions
• Analysis & Interpretation	• Making Connections	• Systems & Interactions	
Informational Text	Mathematical Concepts & Skills	Science Processes	
• Main Ideas & Details	• Measurement	• Designing Solutions to Problems	
• Analysis & Interpretation	• Geometric Sense		
	• Algebraic Sense		

Your child's performance on this test in each of the following areas was **below** the performance of students who met the standard.

Reading	Mathematics	Science	Writing
Literary Text	Mathematical Processes	Science Concepts	
• Critical Thinking	• Solves Problems & Reasons Logically	• Changes in Matter & Energy	
Informational Text	Mathematics Concepts & Skills	Science Processes	
• Critical Thinking	• Number Sense	• Inquiry	
	• Probability & Statistics		

Level 4: Above Standard	Level 2: Below Standard
Level 3: Meets Standard	Level 1: Well Below Standard

Exempted includes "PP" Previously Passed, IEP Exemption, ESL Exemption. NLE indicates No Longer Enrolled.

* Only two performance levels were established for Listening and Writing: Meets Standard and Does Not Meet Standard

Writing Key:
T1= Off Task Prompt 1 (Expository)   M1= Off Mode Prompt 1 (Expository)
T2= Off Task Prompt 2 (Narrative)   M2= Off Mode Prompt 2 (Narrative

Figure 12–9
Example of an Individual Student Report From the Washington Assessment of Student Learning

BOX 12.1: *Standard Error of Measurement*

Any measurement can have a certain amount of error. An individual student's score may be exactly the same as his ability; however, it is also possible that the score is not exactly correct. Across all students, some error is likely. Error can be caused by many things: carelessness, copying another's responses, fatigue, a fire drill during the test, etc. The *standard error of measurement* is a way of *estimating* the amount of error in test scores for a given test. The confidence band for the scores shown in Figure 12-9 is created by adding one standard error of measurement to the cut-score and subtracting one standard error of measurement from the cut-score. Suppose the standard error of measurement for the Reading test scores is 9. The confidence band for a scale score of 400 (the proficiency score) would be 400 ± 9 or 391 to 409.

The fourth section of the report gives Ken's performance on the content standards assessed by the test. The report on the content standards suggests that Ken has both strengths and weaknesses in most subject areas. To make sense of these scores, classroom teachers must be familiar with the standards as well as the types of items on the test. As can be seen, Ken has done well on most of the reading standards. His main weakness is critical thinking about text—both literary and informational. If classroom assessment information corroborates this report, Ken's language arts teacher can help him work on critical thinking about text. However, the teacher needs to know what "critical thinking about text" means for these content standards (e.g., identifying an author's message and purpose, evaluating author's use of devices such as metaphors or graphic aids).

In mathematics, Ken has performed as well or better than students who met the standard in mathematical communication, making mathematical connections, algebraic sense, geometric sense, and measurement. He performed lower than students who met the standard in problem solving and reasoning, number sense, and probability and statistics. Ken's mathematics teacher can look at his work and see if he is struggling with number concepts such as negative numbers, properties of number, place value, fractions, decimals, ratios, percent, and proportions. She can check to see whether Ken understands and can compute mean, median, and mode; whether he can determine simple probabilities; and whether he can create, read, and interpret graphs, tables, and charts. The mathematics teacher can also give Ken some open-ended problems to see whether Ken knows how to approach and solve problems.

As is evident, reports from criterion-referenced tests are merely starting places as you begin your work with students. You will have to delve deeper than standardized test scores, using classroom-based assessments that give more complete pictures of each student's knowledge and skills. In addition to high-quality instruction and classroom assessments, your success with students depends on becoming familiar with the content standards used in your state or district—making certain that you know what the standards mean. If you have a solid understanding of the content standards, you can teach to the standards rather than to the test. You can use the investigative tools available to you through good classroom assessments to examine your students' strengths and weaknesses in more detail. Then you can adapt instruction to make certain that all of your students are successful.

For example, Ken's mathematics teacher has to know the seventh-grade state standards for *number sense, probability,* and *statistics* in order to help Ken improve his performance in mathematics. She must also know what *problem solving and reasoning* means in a mathematical context. His language arts teacher must know the meaning of *critical thinking about text,* and also the kinds of narrative and informational text used on the test (e.g., stories, biographical sketches, autobiographical sketches, excerpts from textbooks, timelines, charts) so that she can help Ken learn how to do the critical thinking defined in the content standards. In sum, the effectiveness of criterion-referenced score interpretation, for individual students, your classroom, your school, or your district, depends on the depth of your knowledge of the standards. High-quality classroom assessments must take you beyond these scores to a deeper understanding of your students.

NORM-REFERENCED SCORE INTERPRETATION

The purpose of a norm-referenced test is very different from the purpose of a criterion-referenced test. Criterion-referenced tests provide information about what students know and are able to do, whereas norm-referenced tests provide information about how students' performances compare to the performances of their peers. Therefore, although the steps in test development are similar, the items selected for norm-referenced tests measure a wide range of content. This allows for a spread of scores, for clear differentiation between students, and for the measurement of all students in a grade level—even those who are far above average in a particular subject area.

Group administered norm-referenced tests (e.g., *Terra Nova, Stanford Achievement Test, Iowa Test of Basic Skills, Metropolitan Achievement Test*) have a different test form for each grade level. Hence, many of the items on a test are appropriate for the grade level—although there will be some items that are more appropriate for 1 to 2 years below grade level and other items that are more appropriate for 1, 2 or 3 years above grade level.

Recall that standardized tests require some sort of score scale in order to ensure constant difficulty and measure growth with consistent units of measurement. To make this possible, all test levels for norm-referenced tests are *calibrated* (mathematically linked) to one underlying scale from the easiest item on the first-grade test to the hardest item on the 12th grade test. This makes it possible to measure growth over time on the same "ruler." Norm-referenced tests are also timed tests. This means that students must complete all of the items on a given test in a fixed amount of time. Student scores can be compared more readily because all students are tested under the same testing conditions.

Individually administered norm-referenced tests (e.g., *Wechsler Individual Achievement Test, Woodcock Johnson Reading Test*) have only one test. Test administrators begin testing by selecting an item from a particular grade level and presenting it to the student. If the student responds correctly, the administrator presents a more difficult item. This continues until the student responds incorrectly to several items in a row. At that point the administrator either moves on to another test or ends the test session. If the student responds incorrectly to the first item, the test administrator moves backward in the test to items from a lower grade level and presents an easier item. If the student responds correctly, the session moves forward until the student can no longer respond correctly to items.

For some norm-referenced tests, enough is known about the score scale that scale scores provide sufficient information for decision-making. For example, most college students know that a score of 500 on the *SAT I: Reasoning Test* is considered average; 600 is above average, 400 is below average, and 800 is the highest possible score. In such cases, there is little need for *derived scores*. In other situations, such as norm-referenced achievement tests for kindergarten through 12th grade, the range of scale scores varies by grade level; therefore, derived scores are quite helpful. Derived scores are scores that are derived from notions of the normal curve. There are four derived scores commonly used in norm-referenced tests for prekindergarten through high school: percentile ranks, stanines, grade-equivalent scores, and age-equivalent scores.[6] These scores are derived from the performance of a nationally representative *norm group*. In what follows, we describe how norm groups are selected for and how derived scores are computed.[7]

Norms and Derived Scores

When a norm group is selected, all of the schools in the United States are classified in terms of region of the country (e.g., Northeast, Southeast, Midwest, Rocky Mountain, and West Coast), type of community (large metropolitan area, suburban, emerging suburb, small city, etc.), school size (large, medium, small), and socio-economic status (high, medium, low). A sample of schools is selected to represent the population of the United States as a whole. For example, the northeastern part of the United States has many large cities; therefore, the majority of students in the norm group who are from the northeast would be from large cities. In contrast, the Rocky Mountain states have a few large cities and many small towns and ranches. Therefore, the majority of students in the norm group who are from Rocky Mountain states would be from rural schools or schools in small towns.

Once a nationally representative sample of schools has been identified to participate in the norming study, students in the selected schools take a form of the norm-referenced test. The distributions of their scores are used to derive percentiles, stanines, and grade-equivalent scores. In what follows we describe each of these score types and how to interpret them.

Percentile Ranks The most commonly used norm-referenced score is the percentile rank.[8] The percentile rank indicates the percent of students in the norm group who earned a score lower than the score earned by a particular examinee. For example, suppose Ken Jones took *TerraNova* (CTB McGraw-Hill, 2002) in sixth-grade. Figure 12-10 shows his individual profile report. The first page of the report shows his performance on each of the tested objectives.

---

[6] Age-equivalent scores are provided with individually administered ability and achievement tests. Because the focus of this chapter is on group administered tests, age-equivalent scores will not be described here.

[7] The norming of tests such as the *SAT I: Reasoning Test* and the *Wechsler Intelligence Scale for Children* is done quite differently. If you are interested in the specifics for these tests, the best source is a technical report for the particular test.

[8] Although this discussion is focused on achievement tests for kindergarten through twelfth grade, percentiles are also the most popular derived scores for ability tests such as *Wechsler Intelligence Scale for Children* and the *SAT I: Reasoning Test*. Therefore, the information presented here also applies to these tests.

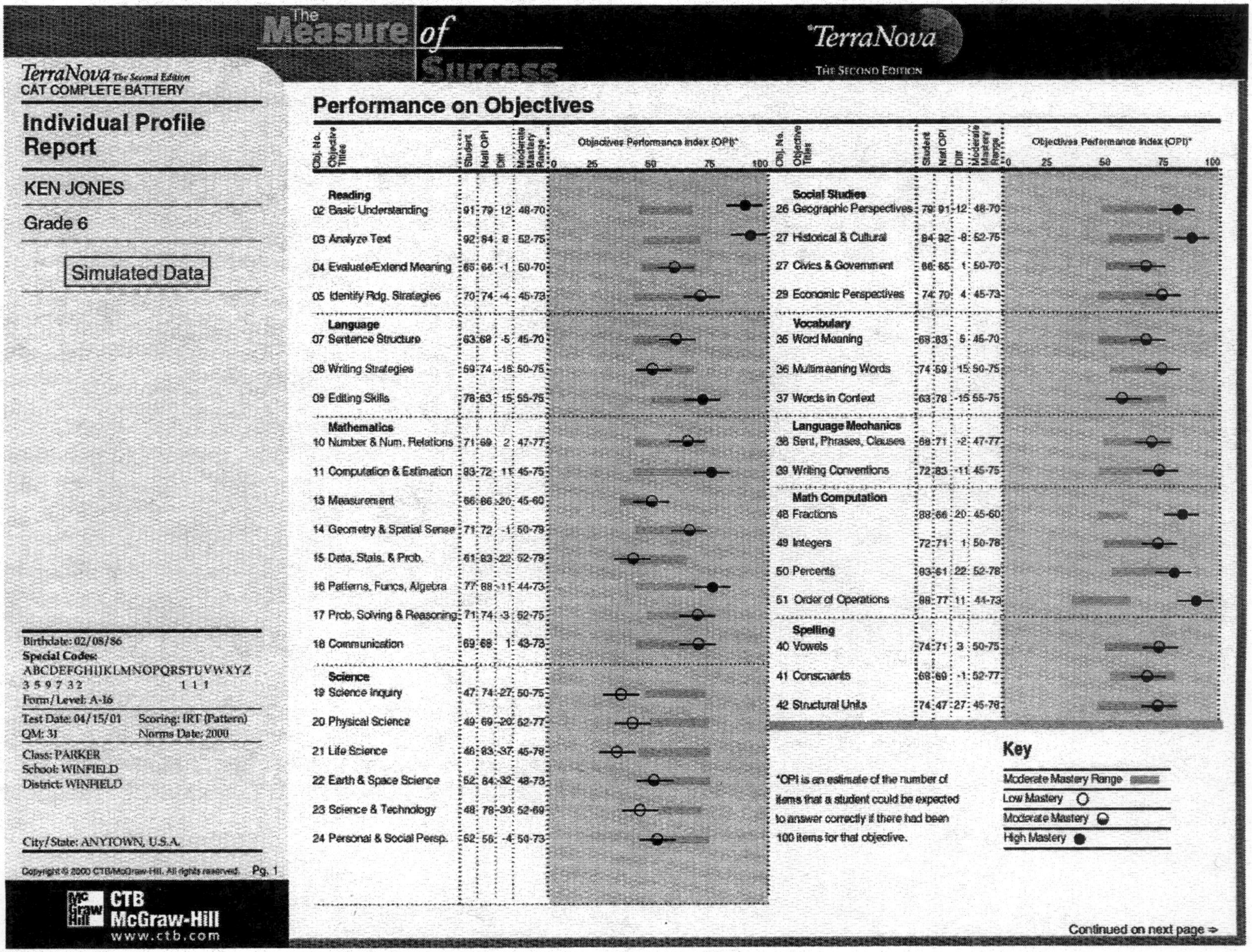

Figure 12–10
Ken Jones's *TerraNova* Individual Profile Report

Individual Profile Report

KEN JONES

Grade 6

Simulated Data

Norm-Referenced Scores

	Scale Score	Grade Equivalent	National Stanine	National Percentile	NP Range
Reading	677	8.8	6	65	55-75
Language	657	7.3	5	53	43-60
Mathematics	699	9.8	7	82	74-89
Total Score**	681	8.8	6	72	60-81
Science	671	7.4	5	55	45-66
Social Studies	669	7.7	5	58	48-68

**Total Score consists of Reading, Language, and Mathematics.

National Percentile Scale

National Stanine Scale

Skills and abilities the student demonstrates:

In Reading...
Students use context clues and structural analysis to determine word meaning. They recognize homonyms and antonyms in grade-level text. They identify important details, sequence, cause and effect, and lessons embedded in the text. They interpret characters' feelings and apply information to new situations. In written responses, they can express an opinion and support it.

In Language Arts...
Students identify irrelevant sentences in paragraphs and select the best place to insert new information. They recognize faulty sentence construction. They can combine simple sentences with conjunctions and use simple subordination of phrases/clauses. They identify reference sources. They recognize correct conventions for dates, closings, and place names in informal correspondence.

In Mathematics...
Students identify even and odd numbers; subtract whole numbers with regrouping; multiply and divide by one-digit numbers; identify simple fractions; measure with ruler to nearest inch; tell time to nearest fifteen minutes; recognize symmetry; subdivide shapes; complete bar graphs; extend numerical and geometric patterns; apply simple logical reasoning.

In Science...
Students are familiar with the life cycles of plants and animals. They can identify an example of a cold-blooded animal. They infer what once existed from fossil evidence. They recognize the term habitat. They understand the water cycle. They know science and society issues such as recycling and sources of pollution. They can sequence technological advances. They extrapolate data, devise a simple classification scheme, and determine the purpose of a simple experiment.

In Social Studies...
Students demonstrate skills in organizing information. They use time lines, product and global maps, and cardinal directions. They understand simple cause and effect relationships and historical documents. They sequence events, associate holidays with events, and classify natural resources. They compare life in different times and understand some economic concepts related to products, jobs, and the environment. They give some detail in written responses.

Skills and abilities the student can work toward to show academic growth:

In Reading...
Integrate the use of analogies to generalize an idea; identify paraphrases of concepts or ideas in text; indicate specific thought processes that lead to an answer; demonstrate understanding of an implied theme; assess intent of passage information; and provide justification for answers.

In Language Arts...
Understand logical development in paragraph structure; identify essential information from notes; recognize the effect of prepositional phrases on subject-verb agreement; find and correct errors when editing simple narratives; correct run-on and incomplete sentences; eliminate all errors when editing their own work.

In Mathematics...
Locate decimals on a number line; apply basic number theory; compute with decimals and fractions; measure to the nearest quarter-inch; read scale drawings; find areas; identify results of geometric transformations; construct and label bar graphs; find simple probabilities; find averages; use patterns in data to solve problems; use multiple strategies and concepts to solve unfamiliar problems; express mathematical ideas and explain the problem-solving process.

In Science...
Differentiate between instinctive and learned behavior; develop a working understanding of the structure of the Earth; create a better understanding of terms such as decomposers, fossil fuel, eclipse, and buoyancy; interpret more detailed graphs and tables; understand experimentation.

In Social Studies...
Synthesize information from sources such as maps and charts; create a better understanding of the democratic process, the basic principles our government was founded on, as well as roles and responsibilities of government and citizens; recognize patterns and similarities in different historical times; understand global and environmental issues; locate continents and major countries; summarize information from multiple sources in early American history; describe how geography affected the development of the colonial economy; thoroughly understand both sides of an issue.

For more information, refer to the Guide to the Individual Profile Report, or visit CTB's website, www.ctb.com.

Birthdate: 02/08/86
Special Codes:
ABCDEFGHIJKLMNOPQRSTUVWXYZ
3 5 9 7 3 2   1 1 1
Form/Level: A-16

Test Date: 04/15/01   Scoring: IRT (Pattern)
QM: 31   Norms Date: 2000

Class: PARKER
School: WINFIELD
District: WINFIELD

City/State: ANYTOWN, U.S.A.

CTB McGraw-Hill

Figure 12-10 *(continued)*

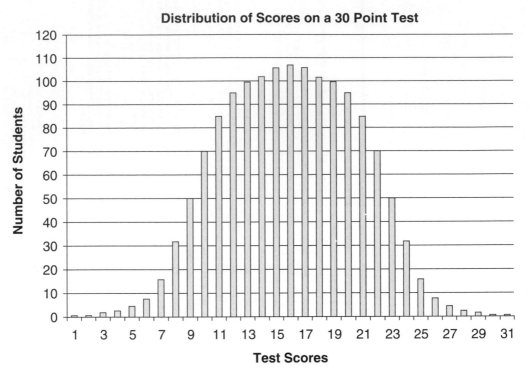

Figure 12–11
Distribution of Scores for a 30-Point Test

The second page shows his norm-referenced scores. There are scores for five tests given in the report. Ken's percentile rank for Reading is 65 and his percentile for Mathematics is 82. This means that Ken scored as well or better than 65% of the sixth-grade norm group in Reading and as well or better than 82% of the sixth-grade norm group in Mathematics.

Percentile ranks range from 1 to 99. The number system for percentiles is very similar to percent correct scores, therefore, the two types of scores are often erroneously used interchangeably. However, there may be absolutely *no relationship* between percentile ranks and percent correct scores on the test. If a test is very easy, and 30% of the students get a perfect score, the likely percentile rank for a perfect score will be 85. Similarly, if only one student in the norm group earned the highest score on a test and the highest score was 36 out of 40 points, then a score of 36 would result in a percentile rank of 99 even though the student only got 90% of the possible points. In fact, students who have learned what they should have learned at their grade level will have percentile ranks near 50. A percent score of 50% is generally considered to be failing work. Hence, when interpreting percentile ranks, it is very important to help parents understand that they are not the same as percent scores.

In a normal distribution, very few students will have high or low scores. Most students have scores that cluster near the mean. Figure 12-11 shows a stylized picture of a normal curve. The bars represent the number of students who earned each score on a 30-point test. For example, 50 students earned a score of 9 and 70 students earned a score of 11. As can be seen, there are very few students at the bottom or the top of the score scale. This presents problems in inter-

Table 12–1
Raw Scores and Percentile Ranks for Three Students

Student	Raw Score	Percentile Rank
Tom	2	1
Matt	10	11
Maria	12	22

pretation. Table 12–1 shows the raw scores and percentile ranks for three students who took the 30-point test. As can be seen, although the differences in percentile ranks between Tom and Matt and between Matt and Maria are nearly the same, Matt's raw score is 8 points higher than Tom's, whereas Maria's raw score is only 2 points higher than Matt's.

Stanines   Given the difficulties in interpretation of differences in percentile ranks, stanines were invented to provide a more understandable metric and to help prevent inappropriate interpretation of percentiles. The name *stanine* comes from the fact that stanines are standard scores that range from 1 to 9 with a mean of 5. Stanines result in clusters of percentile ranks that represent similar amounts of growth in learning. So, for example, a stanine of 1 represents percentile ranks of 1 through 4. A stanine of 2 represents percentile ranks of 5 through 10. A stanine of 3 represents percentile ranks of 11 through 22. A stanine of 4 represents percentile ranks of 23 through 40, and so forth.

By clustering percentiles into stanines, it is easier to interpret the percentile ranks. Generally stanines 1 through 3 are considered below average, stanines 4 through 6 are considered average, and stanines 7 through 9 are considered above average. By these conventions, percentiles of 1 through 22 are considered below average, percentiles 23 through 77 are considered average, and percentiles 78 through 99 are considered above average. A look at Ken Jones' stanines on page 2 of his *TerraNova* report shows that he has a stanine of 6 in Reading and a stanine of 7 in Mathematics. This suggests that he is average in Reading and above average in Mathematics.

Grade-Equivalent Scores   Grade-equivalent scores are probably the most misunderstood of the derived scores for norm-referenced tests. Grade-equivalent scores were created so that norm-referenced scores would be on a scale that made sense to parents and teachers—that of grade level in schooling. Recall that there are scale scores underlying all of the test levels on group-administered, norm-referenced tests. Once the multiple levels of a norm-referenced test series are administered to the norm group, it is possible to obtain the average scale score for the norm group at each time of year (fall and spring). With the average scale score for each grade level and time of year, grade-equivalent scores can easily be established. For example, for the *TerraNova* Reading test (CTB McGraw-Hill, 2002), the average scale score for sixth-graders in September is 658 and the average scale score in May is 661. The grade-equivalent corresponding to a scale score of 658 is 6.0 (beginning of sixth year) and the grade-equivalent score that corresponds to a scale score of 661 is 6.8 (sixth year, eighth month). In other words, the grade-equivalent score represents the typical performance of examinees at a given grade and month in school.

Because the score scale for group administered norm-referenced tests spans all test levels from first through 12th grade, no matter what test level a student takes, the scale score can be compared with that of the norm group to obtain a grade-equivalent score. A look at Ken Jones' *TerraNova* profile report shows that he has a grade-equivalent score of 8.8 in Reading and 9.8 in Mathematics.

There are limits to grade-equivalent scores. First, when norm-referenced tests are developed, sixth-graders don't take the eighth-grade test or the ninth-grade tests—nor do eighth- and ninth-graders take the sixth-grade test. The link between scale scores and grade-equivalent scores depends on the mathematics used to link all of the test levels. Therefore, although Ken's scale score for the Reading test is 677, he would not necessarily earn the same scale score if he took the eighth-grade test. The text on the eighth-grade reading test is more difficult and the items ask for more sophisticated thinking. Also note that, based on his stanine, he is performing within the average range in Reading. Therefore, although he may have earned the same scale score as students in the eighth month of eighth-grade, it appears that this level of performance is within the average range for sixth-graders.

The second problem with grade-equivalent scores is that very small changes in scale scores can result in large changes in grade-equivalent scores. For example, the highest scale scores that can be earned at the end of eighth-grade and the end of ninth-grade for the *TerraNova* Reading test are 676 and 680, respectively.

When explaining grade-equivalent scores to parents, it is important to use caution. In the case of Ken, it would be a more reasonable interpretation to tell his parents or guardians that his score represents what an eighth-grader in the eighth month of school would probably earn if he took the sixth-grade reading test. It would be unwise to move a student to a higher or lower grade level using grade-equivalent scores from a group-administered, norm-referenced test alone. Decisions about whether students should be moved to higher or lower grades in school should depend on a wide range of information, such as classroom assessment information, standardized test scores, teacher observations, interviews with parents, as well as other considerations.

Individually administered achievement tests (e.g., *Wechsler Individual Achievement Test* and *Woodcock Johnson Reading Test*) also provide grade-equivalent scores. However, these scores are based on students' responses to the same items as the children with whom they are being compared. For example, if Ken earned a grade-equivalent of 8.8 on the *Woodcock Johnson Reading Test,* he would have correctly responded to the same items as average eighth-graders in the eighth month of school.

COMPARISONS ACROSS DIFFERENT TYPES OF TESTS

Ken's performances on the two standardized tests are somewhat different. For example, he performed in the average range on the *TerraNova* Reading test and met standard on the state standards-based Reading test. In contrast, he performed above average on the *TerraNova* Mathematics test but did not meet standard on the state standards-based test. There are several possible reasons for these differences. First, standards-based tests are supposed to assess what students should know and be able to do in a given grade level; hence, they generally include only on-grade level items. Therefore, it would not be surprising if a student who was within the average range for a norm-referenced test met standard on a state standards-based test. Second, different tests measure similar content in different ways. Standardized, norm-referenced tests generally measure what can be assessed in multiple-choice format. Many state standards-based tests include short-answer items and performance items in order to assess knowledge and skills that cannot be measured in multiple-choice formats. Therefore, Ken may do quite well in mathematics when the items measure discrete mathematical knowledge and procedures but may have more difficulty justifying a solution, showing the steps in his work, creating graphs, or completing multistep tasks that are assessed on a different type of test.

Given the differences in tests, it is important to look closely at *what* is assessed by different tests and *how* the knowledge and skills are assessed. Different tests provide different types of information and can be used together to get a more complete picture of students.

RELIABILITY AND VALIDITY FOR STANDARDIZED TESTS

In Chapter 1, we introduced a framework for use in examining the reliability and validity of classroom-based assessments. Standardized testing specialists think differently about reliability and validity. They create tests that can be used with a wide range of students; tests that must provide a great deal of information in a short period of time. Although you will be able to access multiple sources of evidence to make reliable grading decisions, testing specialists must determine the reliability of scores when tests are administered once. Therefore, they must use other ways of evaluating reliability of scores. When you create your assessments, you have the time and resources to give students opportunities to complete authentic work. You can ensure that all of your goals and objectives are assessed in valid ways because you have time to assess all of the important knowledge and skills related to your subject area or discipline. In contrast, standardized tests must assess the full range of knowledge and skills quickly and efficiently. Therefore, testing specialists must use other ways of evaluating the validity of the scores coming from the assessments.

When standardized testing specialists gather evidence for reliability, they ask questions like, "If I gave this Reading test again, would the students get about the same scores?" They are also asking, "Do the students respond in about the same way to all of the items in the Reading test? If they do well on one reading item in the test, are they likely to do well on the other reading items; if they do poorly on one reading item in the test, are they likely to do poorly on all the reading items?" When test developers and testing specialists gather evidence for validity, they generally ask, "Does the test measure what it claims to measure?" Testing specialists ask these questions about each content area test. To find out whether the scores from a test are valid and reliable, testing specialists conduct many studies.

Reliability Studies for Standardized Tests

In Chapter 1, we introduced a framework for reliability of scores in classroom assessments that included sufficiency of information about students at the time of grading, clarity of directions and items to ensure that students can demonstrate what they know and are able to do, and teacher consistency in applying scoring rules across students and over time. Some of the ways of gathering evidence for the reliability of scores on standardized tests are similar to strategies used in the classroom, but there are some fairly significant differences.

Rater 2

	4	3	2	1
4	21%	2%		
3	3%	32%	2%	
2		1%	25%	2%
1			1%	11%

Rater 1 (label on left side)

Table 12–2
Example of Exact Interrater Agreement of 89%

For the standardized test developer, reliability is the degree to which students will earn the same score if they are scored by another scorer or if they take another test that is intended to measure exactly the same knowledge and skills. Test developers have four different ways of determining whether the scores on tests are reliable: interrater reliability, test-retest reliability, alternate forms reliability, and internal consistency. If the tests include short-answer or performance items, test developers must establish the consistency of scorers in applying the scoring rules to students' responses. This is called *interrater reliability*. For example, if students' written essays are scored on a 4-point rubric, the test developer will be concerned about whether two scorers give the same score to a student's written essay. Table 12-2 shows a hypothetical situation wherein 100 students are given scores on their written essays by two raters. Using this table, it is possible to examine interrater reliability by counting each time two raters give the same score. They have 100 opportunities to do so. In this example, the rubric has four levels. By adding the percent of times two raters gave exactly the same score, it is evident that 89% of the time two scorers gave these 100 students exactly the same score. This is a very good level of agreement and is most likely to happen when the scoring rules are clear and the raters have been well trained.

Test developers are also concerned with whether students will demonstrate the same performance on two tests that are intended to measure the same knowledge and skills in exactly the same way. There are two ways that this is studied. Test developers might give students a test, wait 2 to 3 weeks, and then give students exactly the same test. This is called *test-retest reliability*. Using this method, it is possible to find out how consistent students' scores are from the first to the second time they take the test. The main problem with test-retest reliability is that some of the students might recall the items, intentionally or unintentionally focus their learning on the tested content during the interim period, and then perform differently during the second testing time.

A substitution for test-retest reliability is to give students one test and then give them an alternate form of the same test. Most standardized tests have alternate forms. Students would take one form, say Form A, and then take a second form, say Form B. This is called *alternate forms reliability*. This method of estimating the reliability of scores eliminates the problem of familiarity with the content of the test (and learning focused on the tested content); however, it is an arduous task to sit for two standardized test batteries. Therefore, students might lose interest or scores might be affected by fatigue. In addition, no two tests can ever be exactly the same, so some unreliability is expected due to the differences in the content tested.

Another strategy used by test developers is to treat every item within a test as if it were a parallel test and look at students' performances to see if they are consistent across different items in the test. This is called *internal consistency reliability*. This eliminates the problem of fatigue and intervening learning; however, the strategy depends on use of items that are very similar to one another. If items within a test represent a wide range of skills or knowledge (as is common in most content area tests), then the items are not really measuring exactly the same thing. Therefore, internal consistency reliability estimates are generally lower than the true reliability of scores. As can be seen, methods for estimating the reliability of scores all have limitations. Regardless of the type of reliability evidence, reliability estimates are all reported as a decimal number that ranges from 0 to 1.0. The closer the number is to 1.0, the more the scores are considered reliable.

Although test developers report data regarding interrater reliability, test-retest, alternate forms, and internal consistency reliability, they rarely report detailed information related to Reliability Dimension 2—the clarity of items. However, test developers focus a great deal of time and money in making certain that the items on standardized tests are clearly worded and have correct answers or precise scoring rules—all of which contributes to the reliability of scores on the tests.

Validity Studies for Standardized Tests

There is some overlap between how measurement specialists conceive of validity and how validity applies to the classroom. One type of validity study conducted for standardized tests involves having educators look at the test items (and scoring rules for open-ended items if appropriate) and judge whether they look like they are measuring the content and skills they are supposed to measure. This is often called *content evidence for validity*. This is similar to Validity Dimension 1 for classroom assessments presented in Chapter 1. Another type of study provides information about how well scores from one test correlate with scores from other tests or assessment tools that are intended to measure the same knowledge and skills. This is called *construct evidence for validity*. In other words, do the scores from both tests suggest that the tests measure the same *construct?*[9] For example, a testing specialist might investigate whether, when students take two tests of reading (say the *Iowa Test of Basic Skills* Reading test and the *TerraNova* Reading test), their scores on the two tests correlate (relate in expected ways). If a new test is being developed, it is common practice to find out how well the scores from the new test correlate with an established test measuring the same construct. This is a statistical way to investigate Validity Dimension 2 for classroom assessments, described in Chapter 1.

---

[9] A *construct* is a hypothetical or theoretical definition for some phenomenon. Constructs are always undergoing redefinition as we learn more from research. For example, there are very different definitions for the construct 'reading'. One definition involves reading speed, accuracy, and expression (fluency). Another definition is comprehension of text. A third definition has to do with how students make sense of text through identification of important ideas and details, interpretations, personal response, and critical response.

Read the paragraph. Then do numbers 1 and 2.

First you check to be sure the fabric is straight. This is done by folding the fabric in half and checking to be sure the corners come together. If the fabric does not lay flat when you put the corners together, pull the "short corners" of the fabric until the fabric folds into even halves. Next you lay the pattern on the fabric in the ways shown in the pattern directions. Pin the pattern to the fabric, making sure that the pins do not cross the darkest line. Finally, you cut around the pattern on the dark lines.

1. Which of the following sentences would be the best **topic sentence** for the paragraph?
   A. Before you can sew a dress, you have to cut out the pieces of the dress.
   B. Sometimes the pattern won't fit exactly on the fabric as you've folded it.
   C. It is usually best to fold the fabric so that the edges of the fabric meet.

2. Which of the following sentences would be the best **concluding sentence** for the paragraph?
   A. Lay the big pattern pieces on the fabric first.
   B. Now you are ready to sew the pieces together.
   C. The dotted line shows where the seams will be.

Figure 12–12
Multiple-Choice Items Measuring Paragraph Writing

A third way that testing specialists examine the validity of scores is to see whether the scores from a test (say a multiple-choice test of writing skills; see Figure 12-12) correlate with students' written essays and stories. This is called *criterion-related evidence* for validity and is also similar to Validity Dimension 2 in classroom assessments. It is called criterion-related evidence because the performances of value written essays and stories are the criterion performances. Standardized test scores are more valid if they are good predictors of the valued performance. The reason that testing specialists have to correlate indirect assessments with more direct assessments of valued performances is that, in order for the students' scores to be dependable, there must be several performances of the criterion performance, and it is generally too expensive and too time consuming to have students do several real performances in a standardized testing context.

Other validity studies for standardized tests occur when the test items are administered during *item tryouts*. As mentioned earlier, during this stage of test development, the focus is on how well the items function. Several statistics are used to determine whether the items are valid. Item scores are correlated with total test scores to see whether students who perform well on the test also perform well on the items. This is an element of Validity Dimension 2. Items are also evaluated in terms of whether there are factors that affect scores other than the conceptual understanding and skills that are intended to be assessed. These studies are called *bias studies* or studies of *differential item functioning*. In essence, the point of these studies is to see whether individuals in particular groups have an unfair advantage or unfair disadvantage on items. If items function differently for different groups of students (e.g., the items are hard for males and easy for females or vice versa), they are said to have bias. When bias is found in items, steps are taken to eliminate them from the tests or to revise them so that they do not function differently for different groups. Studies of this type are part of Validity Dimension 4—that of considering whether variables other than conceptual understanding and skills (e.g., gender or ethnicity), that result in different responses to items for students with the same level of knowledge and skills.

Test developers conduct many other studies to examine the validity of test scores. Suppose a test developer plans to use a criterion-referenced test to identify those who do and do not meet standards and expects that meeting standards on the test is related to success in life beyond school. The test developer may conduct a study to determine whether the cut-score truly differentiates between students who are and are not successful in life beyond school. Suppose the researcher defines success in life beyond school as admission to and success in the first year of college or as obtaining a job and success in the first year of work. The researcher would then identify individuals who were successful and not successful in college or work and compare their success or lack of success with passing or not passing the criterion-referenced tests. This would indicate whether the cut-score is valid for the outcome that the test was intended to predict.

Another validity study for standardized tests would be to investigate whether test scores differentially influence college admissions for white students versus non-white students. Yet another might be to investigate whether reading or writing skills had an undue influence on students' performance on mathematics tests. As can be seen, many different studies could be conducted to gather evidence for the validity of scores on tests; however, all of these studies would fit within the basic validity framework provided in Chapter 1.

The two areas that present the most difficulty for test developers are Validity Dimension 3 (the connection between instruction and assessment) and Validity Dimension 5 (the consequences of test score interpretation and use). As discussed earlier, standardized tests represent an attempt to assess a "common" curriculum or state or district standards. As such, no standardized test can exactly fit with the instructional focus and methods used in every classroom. In addition, studies to examine the link between tested concepts and skills and classroom practices are difficult to conduct. Consequences of score interpretation and use are idiosyncratic to the particular situation, making the study of such consequences difficult. Therefore, test developers rarely conduct studies to examine consequences. Hence, it is the responsibility of test users to conduct consequential validity studies.

USING STANDARDIZED TEST SCORES EFFECTIVELY

Thus far, we have discussed the interpretations made based on standardized test performance. Terms such as basic, proficient, advanced, above average, average, and below average are all *inferences* made based on the scores from standardized norm-referenced and criterion-referenced tests. *Using* test scores to make decisions about students, instructional materials adoptions, curricula, or other decisions requires careful evaluation of the information available. Teachers and other educators must use caution when interpreting individual students' test scores.

Although test scores for a single year may not be very informative, by looking for patterns over time, you can obtain useful information about individual students. For example, Table 12-3 shows the norm-referenced test scores for two students: Tanya and Caleb. Tanya's family emigrated from the Ukraine. She transitioned from the English as a second language (ESL) classroom to the regular classroom in sixth grade. Since seventh grade, Tanya's Reading and Vocabulary scores have steadily increased each year. Between seventh and ninth grades, her percentile rank for Vocabulary increased from the 54th to the 83rd percentiles. In contrast, Tanya's scores for the Language subtests have remained low. In fact,

Table 12–3

TerraNova Score Profiles for Two Ninth-Grade Students: Across Tests and Over Time

Selected Students' TerraNova Scores—Norms from Spring 2000

Tanya

Scores	Reading	Vocab-ulary	Reading Composite	Language Usage	Language Mechanics	Language Composite	Concepts & Applications	Computation	Mathematics Composite	Science	Social Studies
Grade 7 Scale Score	689	671	680	635	656	646	729	680	705	731	703
Percentile	72	54	64	23	39	33	91	60	80	93	81
Stanine	6	5	6	4	4	4	8	6	7	8	7
Grade 8 Scale Score	706	688	697	654	654	654	762	686	724	731	714
Percentile	76	61	70	34	33	35	96	47	79	88	85
Stanine	6	6	6	4	4	4	9	5	7	7	7
Grade 9 Scale Score	712	716	714	657	652	655	774	696	740	746	726
Percentile	78	83	81	32	28	32	96	51	86	94	90
Stanine	7	7	7	4	4	4	9	5	7	8	8

Caleb

Scores	Reading	Vocab-ulary	Reading Composite	Language Usage	Language Mechanics	Language Composite	Concepts & Applications	Computation	Mathematics Composite	Science	Social Studies
Grade 7 Scale Score	781	746	764	697	716	707	704	699	702	781	686
Percentile	99	98	99	83	84	88	77	78	78	99	62
Stanine	9	9	9	7	7	7	6	7	7	9	6
Grade 8 Scale Score	751	786	769	717	699	708	707	718	713	722	689
Percentile	97	99	99	89	76	84	67	75	72	83	61
Stanine	9	9	9	7	6	6	6	6	6	7	6
Grade 9 Scale Score	798	750	774	747	704	726	706	727	717	749	699
Percentile	99	95	98	97	76	91	60	76	69	93	67
Stanine	9	8	9	9	6	8	6	6	6	8	6

her scores for Language Mechanics decreased between seventh and ninth grade. Her Reading and Vocabulary scores show that she is continuing to develop as an English reader but the Language Usage scores suggest that she needs focused writing instruction. Although her Computation skills are average, scores for Mathematics Concepts and Applications and Science are consistently above average. Finally, her scores for Social Studies show the same pattern of improvement as is shown for Reading and Vocabulary.

Caleb's scores also have some patterns. His Reading and Vocabulary scores are consistently very high. His Language Usage scores are steadily increasing while his Language Mechanics score remain fairly stable. These patterns suggest that his vocabulary knowledge and reading skills may be helping him develop language knowledge and skills; however, as with Tanya, the Language Mechanics skills show no changes in terms of the relative strength over time.

With the exception of Science, the rest of Caleb's scores are in the average range across content areas and years. His Science scores are consistently above average; however, they are not as strong as his Reading and Vocabulary scores. Based on these test scores, both Caleb and Tanya should be doing fairly well in school. The fact that their scores seem to have consistent patterns (as opposed to erratic results across subject areas and grades) suggests that these scores can be trusted as indicators of their knowledge and skills in these subject areas as measured by the test.

When looking at individuals, patterns of scores over time are most useful. When evaluating curriculum or instruction, standardized test scores can be examined across time or across grades at a single point in time. Table 12-4 presents Santa Clara Elementary School's average norm-referenced scores on eight subtests of the *Terra Nova* for three grade levels. As with the individual students' scores, there are very informative patterns across content areas and across grades. For example, the stanines for third-graders suggest that the students are about average in Reading, Vocabulary, Mathematics Concepts and Applications, and Computation. The stanines suggest that they are below average performance in Language Usage, Language Mechanics, Science, and Social Studies. Fourth-grade stanines suggest average performance on all tests except Science. However, the percentile rank for Social Studies (23rd percentile) is not really different from the 22nd percentile for third-graders. Fifth-grade stanines suggest that students are about average in Reading, Vocabulary, Language Usage, Language Mechanics and Computation. However, they are well below average in Mathematics Concepts and Applications, Science and Social Studies. Based on the profiles for each grade, it appears that social studies and science may be low priorities in grades three through five.

Looking across grades, students' performances in Reading and Vocabulary are about average across all three grade levels. Performances in Language and Language Mechanics are quite low for third-graders but are average for fourth- and fifth-graders. One possible explanation is that the school had focused curriculum on teaching language usage and language mechanics such that students develop stronger skills over time. The fact that the language mechanics scores are steadily higher at each grade level supports this hypothesis. An alternate explanation is that the students in the third grade were struggling with language usage and language mechanics. It may be that in 2002 there were several ELL students or students with low English skills in the class. The fact that both Language Usage and Language Mechanics are low for third-graders supports this hypothesis.

One trend over grade levels is of concern. Although computation remains steady, mathematics concepts and applications is decreasing with each grade level. This may suggest that

Table 12–4
Average *TerraNova* Scores for Santa Clara Elementary School: Spring 2002

Mean *TerraNova* Scores—Norms from Spring 2000

School: Santa Clara   **Grade: 3**   **Testing Date: April 2002**

Scores	Reading	Vocabulary	Language Usage	Language Mechanics	Mathematics Concepts & Applications	Computation	Science	Social Studies
Mean Scale Score	622	613	599	589	601	595	563	601
Percentile for the Mean Scale Score	40	41	22	19	41	59	10	22
Mean Stanine	4	5	3	3	5	5	2	3
Number Tested	74	74	74	72	72	74	74	74

Grade: 4

Scores	Reading	Vocabulary	Language Usage	Language Mechanics	Mathematics Concepts & Applications	Computation	Science	Social Studies
Mean Scale Score	643	646	646	643	609	626	606	620
Percentile for the Mean Scale Score	49	60	55	59	28	60	22	23
Mean Stanine	5	6	5	5	4	6	3	4
Number Tested	72	71	72	72	70	72	72	72

Grade: 5

Scores	Reading	Vocabulary	Language Usage	Language Mechanics	Mathematics Concepts & Applications	Computation	Science	Social Studies
Mean Scale Score	658	657	655	661	616	648	609	622
Percentile for the Mean Scale Score	51	58	50	64	22	59	14	20
Mean Stanine	5	5	5	6	3	5	3	3
Number Tested	43	87	87	87	86	86	87	86

the teachers are focused on teaching computational facts and algorithms without teaching the mathematical concepts that will help students understand mathematics as they continue in school.

USING STATE STANDARDIZED ACHIEVEMENT TESTS TO ASSESS STUDENTS WITH SPECIAL NEEDS

Many of the recommendations for accommodating students with special needs in the regular classroom apply to standardized tests. However, given that scores from standardized tests are used for program evaluation, school accountability, graduation, and other important decisions, the comparability of scores is often a major consideration. In this section, we discuss some of the appropriate ways to accommodate students with special needs as well as the effects of modifying the tests. However, first it is important to place standardized norm-referenced and criterion-referenced tests in a larger context.

Elementary and Secondary Education Act (No Child Left Behind)

In 2002, the United States Congress reauthorized the Elementary and Secondary Education Act, known variously as ESEA and "No Child Left Behind" (NCLB). Their goals were ambitious: to bring all students in the United States up to achievement standards in core subjects by 2014. No Child Left Behind means, literally, that all students can reach state standards, and implies that excluding certain groups from this requirement runs the risk of sanctioning unequal opportunities for those students to learn. The assumption is, not tested will lead to not taught. There is truth to that statement. Schools and districts have a history of excluding low-performing students—English language learners and students with disabilities—from state-mandated standardized testing programs. This has had the effect of artificially raising test scores for schools or districts, while reducing the pressure to teach low-performing students and lowering expectations for their learning (Haladyna, et al., 1991). There is also evidence that when stakes are high and students with disabilities are excluded from testing, schools and districts may over-identify students as disabled (Almond, Lehr, Thurlow, & Quenemoen, 2002).

With ESEA/NCLB, the achievement stakes for schools, districts, and states have increased sharply. However, participation by students with disabilities and students with LEP is mandated.[10] The federal law requires that 95% of all children enrolled in public schools are to be assessed every year and sets a target for 100% of those children to reach proficiency on state standards by 2014. Achievement is to be tested in reading/language arts and math beginning in 2002, with science to follow in 2007-08. In addition, at least one additional non-test criterion (e.g., graduation rate, unexcused absence rate, etc.) must be assessed. To understand the implications of this act for students with disabilities and English language learners, and their schools and districts, a bit more detail is required.

Under ESEA/NCLB, achievement is monitored separately for each minority group, for students receiving services under the Individuals with Disabilities Education Act of 1997 (IDEA) or Section 504 of the Rehabilitation Act of 1973, and for English language learners

[10] This was true prior to ESEA/NCLB: the Individuals with Disabilities Education Act (IDEA) of 1997 had a similar requirement. ESEA/NCLB gives this requirement teeth.

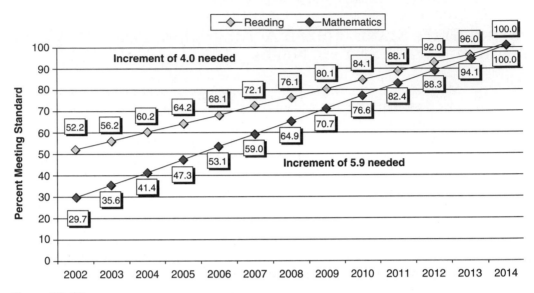

GRADE 4 STATE UNIFORM BAR
BASELINE CALCULATED USING 3-YEAR AVERAGE 20th PERCENTILE (2000–2002)

Figure 12–13
Expected Yearly Progress in Washington State Based on Rules Established by the 2002 Elementary and
Secondary Education Act (ESEA)

(students with limited English proficiency). If any of these subgroups or the group as a whole fails to make "adequate yearly progress" (AYP) for 2 years in a row in the same subject area, the school or district is placed in "improvement status," sometimes referred to as "failing." Schools or districts in improvement status must allow students to transfer to another, non-failing school, within or outside the district, and provide free transportation the first year and free tutoring the second year. Sanctions increase for each subsequent year that the school or district remains in improvement status. After 5 years in improvement status, the school or district must implement a plan to change their governance completely.

Each state develops a "state bar" that plots a line from pass rates in 2002-03 to the 100% pass rate required by 2014. The following example for the State of Washington shows how the baseline performance for adequate yearly progress is to be established.

In 2002-03, Washington State computed percentile ranks for all schools in the state, based on the percent passing in each subject (i.e., reading and mathematics). The *Washington Assessment of Student Learning* (WASL) was, in that year, administered at 4th, 7th, and 10th grades. The passing rate for the school falling at the 20th percentile was obtained for each of 3 years (2000, 2001,and 2002) and was then averaged to form the baseline passing rate. This was done for each tested level (elementary, middle, high school) and for each subject area. The state then plotted two lines (one for reading and one for mathematics) across years from the baseline to 100% in 2014. Figure 12-13 shows the results of these computations.

AYP requires that states calculate the difference between the baseline percentage of students meeting state standards in reading and in math and the 100% pass rate requirement, and divide that difference into 12 equal intervals. The intervals establish how much improvement is required each year to achieve adequate yearly progress. For example, in Figure 12-13, the baseline in 2002 for reading was 52.2%. The difference between 100% and 52.2% is 47.8%. Dividing that number by 12 gives an AYP increment of 4%. This means that in 2003, the pass rate target for all students, and for students in all of the targeted categories (special education, LEP, etc.), must be 56.2%. To meet AYP, 56.2% of the group of students with disabilities in each school and district in the state must pass the reading test in 2003, regardless of the actual pass rate for individual schools and districts in 2002.[11] ELL students must also meet this target. However, once students have mastered English well enough to move out of LEP status, they are no longer counted as LEP for the calculation of pass rates. In other words, students who are still identified as LEP status in any particular year must also achieve that year's percent passing rate. Paradoxically, this means that, once LEP students meet standards (are proficient in reading/language arts in the English language), they are no longer included in the LEP category and do not contribute to the percentage of LEP students meeting the reading/language arts standard. *If any single group* fails to meet AYP 2 years in a row in the same subject, the *entire* school or district fails and moves into improvement status.

At the time of this writing, there was concern among the states and testing professionals that these requirements would make it impossible for diverse schools or districts to avoid being designated as failing within a few years. Because of the consequences of being designated as failing, there was enormous pressure to raise test scores, especially among students with special needs.

If low pass rates are due to poor educational practices, and if pressure from the government results in improved practices (the intent of the law), ESEA/NCLB will have had a positive impact. To the extent that students' disabilities or English language proficiency make it impossible for all to meet state standards in reading, math, and science by 2014, this pressure could lead educators to find ways to raise test scores that have nothing to do with improved educational opportunities or increased achievement

Accommodating Students With Disabilities on State Tests

Clearly, students with special needs must be assessed in valid and reliable ways. Recall that testing accommodations for students with disabilities help to eliminate the effects of a disability that interferes with the students' ability to demonstrate what they know and can do in relation to the standards assessed. In contrast, modifications alter the standards being assessed. Providing a modification during testing invalidates the test score; hence, the score cannot then be combined with other students' scores for that test when figuring pass rates. Therefore ESEA/NCLB requires that non-standard administration of the state tests be limited to accommodations. Children for whom the test is *modified* are considered to have taken the test and failed. It is very important for teachers and other district personnel to be familiar with the changes that are considered "accommodations" and those that are considered

---

[11] There is one exception to this rule: If a category of students in a school or district reduces its failure rate by 10%, even if they do not meet the state standard for that year, *and* if they meet the standard on the additional indicator (e.g., graduation rate or unexcused absence rate), they are eligible for "Safe Harbor," and will be counted as having met AYP.

"modifications." At the time of this publication, each state will have developed its own guidelines, which will have been reviewed by the U.S. Department of Education for compliance. Your state is likely to have a Web site that lists the approved accommodations for the state test; check the Web site for your district, your state's department of education, or the office of the state superintendent; your teachers' union may also have information available. Your district's testing director will also have this information.

Who Decides Which Student Gets Which Accommodation?

For students served under IDEA, the IEP team is authorized to decide which students get which accommodations. Within state guidelines, ESEA requires accommodations to be the same as those specified by the IEP and provided during instruction. Accommodations for students with 504 plans are determined by the student's placement team and should already be specified in the plan and familiar to you as the student's teacher. When in doubt, contact the 504 coordinator for your school or district. The federal guidelines emphasize that accommodations should depend on individual student's specific disabilities, and should not be determined by a student's classification (e.g., learning disabled, autistic, hearing-impaired, etc.) A very small number of students with severe cognitive disabilities may be tested using an approved alternative assessment, which each state is required to develop. This number is generally to be no more than 1% of all students and should be restricted to students who cannot take the regular state assessment, even with accommodations. The law is specific: the only students with disabilities who are exempt from taking either the regular assessment with accommodations or the alternate assessment are those who are incarcerated as adults under state law. "The IEP or placement team determines *how* individual students participate in assessment programs, not *whether* they participate" (ESEA Non-regulatory Guidelines, March 10, 2003, p. 18, emphasis in the original).

Students With Limited English Proficiency

Students with LEP are those who have been tested using a test of English competence and have been found to be below a proficiency level on the test. All students with LEP must take the state assessment, regardless of English proficiency or time in the school or district. Upon enrollment, students with LEP are immediately eligible to be tested. For the first 3 years in which ELL students attend schools wherein English is used for instruction, ELL students who qualify for LEP status may take a version of the state assessment translated into their home language, if one is available. If no translated test is available, they may have the services of a translator to read the items in the home language. On a case-by-case basis, districts may make the case that a translated test would provide more valid results for no more than 2 years beyond the initial 3 years. At the end of the LEP time limit, students must be tested in English. In addition, states are required to assess all students with LEP annually on their English competence in reading, writing, listening, and speaking to determine whether they still qualify as having LEP.

For students taking the state assessment in English, some additional accommodations are allowed for students with LEP. These include providing audiotaped directions in the native language, extra time, small-group administration, flexible scheduling, simplified instructions, and the use of dictionaries. In addition, students may be allowed to respond in their native language or English using audiotape or may be provided with additional clarifying information (synonyms for unclear or idiomatic words and phrases.[12]) Although ELL students do not have IEPs, districts should inform schools and teachers as to which students qualify for which accommodations each year. At the time of this writing, each state will have developed guidelines for allowable accommodations. These guidelines should be available in the same locations as lists of accommodations for students with IEPs or 504 plans. State guidelines can also be useful sources of accommodations for students taking assessments you have developed for classroom use.

One final note about accommodations is necessary. For criterion-referenced reporting, accommodations that allow students to show what they know and are able to do should not affect score reports. If students need a translator for a mathematics test or need longer to complete a test, these accommodations simply remove roadblocks to students' ability to show proficiency. In contrast, any accommodations that alter the standardized administration procedures of norm-referenced tests invalidate the norms because part of the basis of comparison in the norm-referenced testing model is whether the students completed the test under the same conditions as the norm group. Therefore, if your state has elected to use a fixed percentile rank as the basis for setting proficiency cut-scores to meet ESEA/NCLB requirements, be sure to check with the testing administrators at the state or district level regarding how to report accommodations.

PREPARING STUDENTS TO TAKE STANDARDIZED TESTS

As we have discussed, the best way to prepare your students to take standardized tests is to familiarize yourself with the curriculum standards, teach students to meet these standards, and assess students' ability to apply the knowledge and skills you teach to *new* situations. For example, if you teach students a set of expository writing strategies in October as they write book reports and then ask them to apply the same writing strategies to a research report in November, their ability to use these skills in a new subject will give you valuable information about whether they can transfer what they have learned.

The following are a few more things you can do to help students prepare for testing week.

1. Throughout the year, make sure that students know that they are learning the knowledge and skills they need to do well in school, in life, and on standardized tests. One of the main sources of stress in students is the belief that standardized tests are scary, strange, but important events, and completely unlike anything they've seen before. If teachers are clearly worried about test performance, students are more likely to take this as evidence that teachers don't have confidence in their ability to do well.

2. A week or two before the test, introduce the item formats and give students some practice in responding to them. Talk about effective test-taking strategies (sometimes referred to as "test-wiseness" strategies). For example, if the test is timed, students should answer the ones they are sure of first, and then come back to work on the ones they skipped. Some teachers also teach their students relaxation strategies that can be used any time, but especially if they become anxious during the test.

---

[12] Idiomatic language should, to the extent possible, be removed from the state assessment for all students. Knowledge of American idioms is late-developing in most ELL students, and can get in the way of demonstrating competence in other skills.

Test preparation activity	Degree of ethicality
Training in test-wiseness skills	Ethical
Checking answer documents to make sure that each has been properly completed	Ethical
Increasing student motivation to perform well on the test through appeals to parents, students, and teachers	Ethical
Developing a curriculum based on the content of the test	Unethical
Preparing objectives based on items on the test and teaching accordingly	Unethical
Presenting items similar to those on the test	Unethical
Using *Scoring High* or other score-boosting activities*	Unethical
Dismissing low-achievement students on testing day to artificially boost test scores	Highly unethical
Presenting items verbatim from the test to be given	Highly unethical

*Ethical to the extent that the test publisher recommends it or to the extent that *all* schools, classes, and students being compared have the same service.

Figure 12–14
A Continuum of Test Preparation Activities.
Haladyna, Nolen, & Haas, 1991, Educational Researcher, 20(5), 2-7. Copyright 1991 by the American Educational Research Association, reproduced with permission of the publisher.

3. Make sure the students understand the appropriate way to mark their answer sheets or test booklets; this is especially important for machine-scored tests.

Haladyna and his colleagues (1991) provide a breakdown of test preparation strategies that have been observed or reported in schools preparing students to take standardized tests. They argue that, although there *are* ethical test preparation activities, other common activities are unethical because they prevent the test from making an accurate assessment of students' knowledge and skills. To the extent that some schools and districts use these strategies and others don't, Haladyna and colleagues argue that test scores become "polluted." For example, if one district uses test-preparation materials and teaches content from the test for several months prior to the test, and another district only familiarizes students with item formats the week before the test, scores from the two districts are not comparable. When high stakes are attached to test performance and districts are ranked by average test scores (as is the case in most states), such comparisons lead to inappropriate conclusions about the relative success of the two districts. Figure 12-14 shows continuum of test preparation activities developed by Haladyna and his colleagues (1991).

SUMMARY

In this chapter, we have provided information that may help you to adapt to the demands of external testing without sacrificing your ethical obligation to support students' learning and do no harm. As is evident from the brief history of standardized tests, the emphasis on standardized test scores has increased over time and is unlikely to diminish in the years to come. Therefore, it is important that you become a critical consumer of the information provided by these tests. Norm-referenced and criterion-referenced standardized tests are external to the classroom and, as such, can never completely fit with the instructional strategies and content focus in any one classroom. Still, scores from the tests can be useful as you plan instruction—as long as you look for patterns over time and/or across students and corroborate your findings with high-quality classroom-based assessments. School and district averages can help you identify strengths and weaknesses in curriculum and instruction. Patterns in individual students' scores over time can help you identify students' strengths and weaknesses. The trick to living with external tests is to take the time to understand how they are designed and what real work the test

items reflect. In all likelihood, that work will be some of the kinds of real work you want to teach students anyway. In many states, teachers are involved in the development and/or scoring of the items for standardized tests. Such involvement can be priceless in terms of helping you understand the underlying structure and design of the test. Therefore, if you are given an opportunity to become involved in your state's assessment system, it is a wise choice to participate.

Finally, most of the damage caused by standardized tests results from the interpretations and uses made rather than from the tests themselves. We hope that the information in this chapter will help you side-step some of the traps teachers fall into when dealing with accountability and standardized testing.

REFERENCES

Almond, P., Lehr, C., Thurlow, M., Quenomoen, R. F. (2002). *Participation in Large-Scale State Assessment and Accountability Systems*. In Large Scale Assessment Programs for all Students: Validity, Technical Adequacy, and Implementation. Gerald Tindal & Thomas M. Haladyna (Eds.). Mahwah, NJ: Lawrence Erlbaum Associates, 341–370.

Angoff, W. H. (1971). *The College Board Admissions Testing Program: A technical report on research and development activities relating to the Scholastic Aptitude Test and Achievement Tests*. New York: The College Board.

Apple, M. W. (1990). Is there a curriculum voice to reclaim? *Phi Delta Kappan, 71* (7), 526–530.

Bloom, B. S., Madaus, G. F., & Hasting, T. J. (1971). *Handbook on formative and summative evaluation of student learning*. New York: McGraw-Hill.

Buckendahl, C. W., Smith, R. W., Impara, J. C., & Plake, B. S. (2002). A comparison of Angoff and bookmark standard setting methods. *Journal of Educational Measurement, 39,* 253–263.

Chang, L. (1999). Judgmental item analysis of the Nedelsky and Angoff standard setting methods. *Applied Measurement in Education, 12,* 151–165.

Haladyna, T. M., Nolen, S. B., & Haas, N. S. (1991). Raising standardized achievement test scores and the origins of test score pollution. *Educational Researcher, 20* (5), 2–7.

Livingston, S. A., & Zieky, M. J. (1989). A comparative study of standard-setting methods. *Applied Measurement in Education, 2,* 121–141.

Lomax, R. G., West, M. M., Harmon, M. C., Viator, K. A., & Madaus, G. F. (1995). The impact of mandated standardized testing on minority students. *Journal of Negro Education, 64*(2), 171–185.

Madaus, G. F, & Clarke, M. C. (2001). The adverse impact of high stakes testing on minority students: Evidence from 100 years of test data. Unpublished research.

NCTM (1985). *Principles and Standards for School Mathematics*. Reston, VA: National Council of Teachers of Mathematics.

Nolen, S. B., Haladyna, T. M., & Haas, N. S. (1992). Uses and abuses of standardized test scores. *Educational Measurement: Issues & Practice, 11*(9–15).

Popham, J. W. (1993). The merits of measurement-driven instruction. *Phi Delta Kappan, 68*(9), 205–207.

Reardon, S. G. (1996). Eighth grade minimum competency testing and early high school dropout patterns. Unpublished research.

Shepard, L. A. (1989). Why we need better assessments. *Educational Leadership, 46*(7), 4–9.

Shepard, L. A. (1991a). Psychometricians' beliefs about learning. *Educational Researcher, 20* (7), 2–16.

Shepard, L. A. (1991b). Will national tests improve student learning? *Phi Delta Kappan, 73* (3), 232–238.

Smith, M. L. (1991). Meanings of test preparation. *American Educational Research Journal, 28*(3), 521–542.

Wiggins, G. (1989c). A true test: Toward a more authentic and equitable assessment. *Phi Delta Kappan, 70* (9), 703–713.

Appendix A

WEB SITES FOR NATIONAL CURRICULUM STANDARDS

Title of Standards	Web Site
Business Education Standards	http://www.nbea.org/marketfstand.html
Foreign Language Curriculum Standards	http://www.actfl.org/
National Curriculum Standards for Social Studies	http://www.ncss.org/standards/
National Economics Standards	http://www.ncee.net/ea/program.php?pid=19
National Geography Standards	http://www.nationalgeographic.com/resources/ngo/education/standards.html
National Health Education Standards	http://www.aahperd.org/aahe/pdf_files/standards.pdf
National History Standards	http://www.sscnet.ucla.edu/nchs/standards/
National Science Education Standards	http://www.nap.edu/books/0309053269/html/index.html
National Standards for Arts Education	http://artsedge.kennedy-center.org/professional_resources/standards/natstandards/
National Standards for Civics and Government	http://www.civiced.org/stds.html
National Standards for Physical Education	http://www.aahperd.org/naspe/publications-nationalstandards.html
National Standards for the English Language Arts	http://www.ncte.org/store
Principles and Standards for School Mathematics	http://www.nctm.org/standards/
Standards for English as a Second Language	http://www.tesol.org/pubs/catalog/assessment.html#714

Appendix B

WEB SITES FOR PROFESSIONAL ORGANIZATIONS

Professional Organizations	Membership	Web Site
American Alliance for Health, Physical Education, Recreation, and Dance	Teachers of Dance, Physical Education, and Health	http://www.aahperd.org/
American Association of Geographers	Geography and Social Studies Teachers	http://www.aag.org/
American Association of Physics Teachers	Physics Teachers	http://www.aapt.org/
American Council on the Teaching of Foreign Languages	Foreign Language Teachers	http://www.actfl.org/
American Speech-Language-Hearing Association	Teachers of Children with Speech, Language, and Hearing Disabilities	http://www.asha.org/
Association for Educational Communications and Technology	Teachers who use technology to improve teaching and learning	http://www.aect.org/
Center for Civic Education	Civics, Government, and Social Studies Teachers	http://www.civiced.org/index.html
Council for Exceptional Children	Teachers of Children with Disabilities	http://www.cec.sped.org/
International Reading Association	Reading Teachers	http://www.ira.org/
National Art Education Association	Arts Teachers	http://www.naea-reston.org/
National Association for Bilingual Education	Bilingual Educators	http://www.nabe.org/
National Association for Gifted Children	Gifted Educators	http://www.nagc.org/
National Association for Sport and Physical Education	Coaches and Teachers of Physical Education	http://www.aahperd.org/naspe/
National Association of Biology Teachers	Biology Teachers	http://www.nabt.org/

National Business Education Association	Business Teachers	http://www.nbea.org/
National Center for History in the Schools	History and Social Studies Teachers	http://www.sscnet.ucla.edu/nchs/
National Center on Educational Outcomes	Teachers of Students with Disabilities	http://education.umn.edu/nceo/
National Council for History Education	History and Social Studies Teachers	http://www.history.org/nche/
National Council for Teachers of English	Secondary Teachers of the Language Arts	http://www.ncte.org/homepage/
National Council for Teachers of Mathematics	Elementary and Secondary Mathematics Teachers	http://www.nctm.org/
National Council for the Social Studies	Teachers of the Social Studies	http://www.ncss.org/
National Council on Economics Education	Economics and Social Studies Teachers	http://www.ncee.net/ea/
National Science Teachers Association	Science Teachers	http://www.nsta.org/
North American Association for Environmental Education	Environmental Education, Social Studies and Science Teachers	http://www.naaee.org/
Teachers of English to Speakers of Other Languages (TESOL)	Teachers of English as a Second Language	http://www.tesol.org/

Name Index

Subject Index

State tests
accommodating students with
disabilities on, 407–408
in assessing students with
special needs, 405–409
Stem in multiple-choice
items, 192
Stereotype threat, effects of, on
motivation, 65
Student-centered methods,
setting proficiency standards
using, 384–385
Student engagement, feedback
in supporting, 112–113
Student goals, motivation
and, 51
Student-led conferences,
preparation for, 353–354
Students
effects of assessments on
conceptions of the
disciplines, 66–67
effects of classroom-based
assessments on, 51–67
informal assessment of
perceptions, using paper-
and-pencil or oral
assessment, 139–141
opportunities for
improvement and
relevance to, 64
preparing, to take
standardized tests,
409–410
professional discussions
about, 362–367
role of, in communicating
their learning, 346–348
using informal assessments
to teach and provide
feedback to, 145–149
using study guides to help, on
classroom tests, 169–174
Students with disabilities,
accommodating, on state
tests, 407–408
Students with individualized
education plans, 17
grading, 306–307
Students with special needs, 267
adaptations for, in classroom
testing, 177–179
assessment of, 15–17
grading, 305–307
performance items and,
256–257

state standardized
achievement tests for,
405–409
validity issues in using
traditional items to assess,
226–228
Student work
authenticity in, 71–73
method of evaluating, in
grading policy, 284, 287
Study guides, using, to help
students be successful on
classroom tests, 169–174
Subject areas, 29
Subjects
defined, 29
integrating performance-
based assessments across,
116–117
Sufficiency of evidence in
grading policy, 289–290
Summary grades, 262
feedback through, 282–283
Summative assessment, 47

T

Task analysis, 371
Task-involved classroom,
creating, 56–59
Task involvement, 51, 55–56
encouraging, for
performance items,
258–260
feedback and, 60–65
Teacher-made tests, 370
Teachers
control over student
achievement, in grading
policy, 289
effects of assessments of the
experiences of, 11–13
Teaching
learning objectives in guiding
day-to-day work of, 32
supporting autonomy in,
59–60
Teaching objectives, 34–35
Telephone calls, positive,
349–350
Telephone conferences, 355–356
Term grades, 358–361
TerraNova test, 390, 391,
395, 399
Tested knowledge, students'
retention of, 29

Test maps, 154–155
for a standardized test, 378,
380–381
Test-retest reliability, 398
Tests. See also Classroom tests
bias in, 2–3
high-stakes, 4
layouts of, 155–166
multiple choice, 191,
192–205, 372, 373
norm-referenced, 370,
371, 372
standards-based, 272, 370
state, 405–409
teacher-made, 370
true-false, 191, 218–220
Texas Assessment of Academic
Skills, 245
Timely feedback, 63–64
Traditional item development,
190–229
developing and evaluating
test items, 191–224
reliability issues for, 224–228
validity and reliability issues
for, 224–228
Traditional testing
accommodation for children
with special needs on,
177–178
modifications for children
with special needs,
178–179
True-false tests, 191, 218
rules for writing and
evaluating, 218–220
Trust as issue in assessment,
104–105

V

Validity
in classroom-based
assessment, 17–24,
175–176
in performance-based
assessment, 127–129,
255–256
for standardized tests,
399–401
for traditional test items,
224–228
Vision-impaired students,
accommodations for, in
traditional testing, 178

Visual arts, showcase portfolio
in, 311
Visual effects of feedback,
179, 182
Voicemail, 351

W

Washington Assessment of
Student Learning (WASE),
387, 406
Web sites, 350–351
for national curriculum
standards, 413
for professional
organizations, 414–415
Wechsler Individual
Achievement Test, 390, 395
Wechsler Intelligence Scale for
Children, 391n
Weighing the evidence in
grading policy, 287–292
We the People, 81
Woodcock Johnson Reading Test,
390, 395
Word choice in writing, scoring
rubric, 249
Work
importance of, in grading
policy, 287–288
interesting, 57–58
types of, in grading
policy, 284
Working folders, 311
Writer's voice, scoring rubric
for, 248
Writing
direct assessments of, 232,
243–248, 372, 373
exit performances in
informational, 80–81
scoring rubric for
conventions, 251

Y

Young children, participation in
parent-teacher conference,
346–347

Z

Z-scores, 264